LOST AND FOUND

LOST AND FOUND

STORIES FROM NEW YORK

EDITED BY THOMAS BELLER

MR. BELLER'S NEIGHBORHOOD

Printed in the United States of America

FIRST EDITION

Book design by Nick Stone
Front, back, and inside cover photographs by Nick Stone
Man and his dog logo by Elisha Cooper

ISBN-13: 978-0393331-91-2

Mr. Beller's Neighborhood Books
270 Lafayette Street
New York, NY 10012
www.mrbellersneighborhood.com

Distributed by W.W. Norton

09 10 11 12 13 14 15 11 10 9 8 7 6 5 4 3 2 01

CONTENTS

PART II

INTRODUCTION
BY THOMAS BELLER

1.

There are many people in America who are tired of hearing about
New York. Some of them even live in New York. This is, in some
ways, understandable. The city gets a lot of play. But which city?

This book attempts a true picture of New York City when
there are so many faux versions floating out there in the culture.
The viewpoint is not so much street level—there are many ele-
vations represented—but eye level, the city as seen by its citizens,
many of whom, by profession or inclination, are writers. The
question this book tries to answer is not why New York deserves
to be written about, but rather why life in New York produces so
much writing.

The essential ingredient is density. The density is the drug.
With so many people, the odds are better that some of them are
willing and able to tell stories, but even this statistical rationale
gets only half of it. New York is a city where most of the residents have no choice but to look at one another. It is, for the most
part, a pedestrian city. Except for a tiny sliver of people with their
own car and driver, it is a city where just about everyone uses
public transportation, and where everyone walks on the street.
It's nonstop theater in which the audience and the actors are one

and the same. And it takes so much effort to live here that people invariably have a kind of morbid curiosity about who else is making the effort. It is a city filled with preening show-offs, anxious that someone is looking at them and equally anxious that no one is looking at them. To put it less judgmentally, New York is a city of averted gazes, and its anonymous swirl creates a hunger for acknowledgment in even the most fulfilled souls. Such is the peculiar ecology that has provoked so much writing, including the myriad stories that make up this book.

2.

I once had the amazing good fortune of spending some time with Joseph Mitchell. It was during my brief stint as a staff writer at *The New Yorker*. One day I found myself hectoring a man on the phone who seemed befuddled at my request for information about what was once the baby-furniture district on the Lower East Side. It turned out I had forgotten to dial out, and had reached the office extension of Joseph Mitchell. It was the middle of summer. I had seen him in the hall wearing a summer suit and hat. Mortified, I appeared at his door in shorts and a cardigan to apologize. He invited me into his office and we became friends.

I mention this partly out of pride, but also because Joseph Mitchell is in a way the Dean of New York writers, someone who managed to convey a powerful sense of time past, of history lost, and yet did it in an eternal presence tense—Mitchell Time. He was never ambiguous about his role as a reporter, a journalist, and while the pronoun "I" often appeared in his writing, it was always used as a means to witness the takings and doings of someone else. With the exception of his last published piece, "Joe Gould's Secret," he never turned the focus on himself.

The pieces in *Lost and Found* are, for the most part, entirely different. Though many are concerned with what Vivian Gornick has called "the landscape of marginal encounters," most feature an "I" that is not merely a narrator, but a subject. Yet like

Mitchell and his colleague John McNulty, whose remarkably colorful sketches of life beneath the Third Avenue Elevated are in some way the platonic ideal of the urban sketch, there is an odd kind of dissociation often found here. Like Mitchell, many of these narrators are here but not here. Their writing is like Orwell's proverbial pane of glass: the reader peers through and watches the doings of others.

The stories in this book are completely autonomous from each other, but they are also pieces of a larger puzzle. Now and then, one lifts one's head on a crowded street, on the subway, in a restaurant, and thinks, *who are these people?* This book is an answer, even if inevitably partial and ongoing, to that question.

3.

There is a certain type of piece that I have always liked to write—a *feuilleton*, a vignette, an urban sketch, a slice-of-life set in the city. The life from which I am taking a slice is my own, but it's not really a personal essay. A personal essay is, usually, personal. In the urban sketch, the narrative voice is often impersonal. "I am a camera…" begins Christopher Isherwood's *Berlin Stories*, and there is some of that dispassionate sensibility in the pages that follow.

I've always felt a bit guilty about this kind of writing because there is something almost passive and myopic, or just microscopic, about it. All writing is an act of both memory and forgetting, but these urban vignettes make the city do all the work of contextualizing—I saw something, something happened to me, and here it is, unvarnished, spiced with a pinch of understanding in hindsight and then polished, over and over, until it takes on the same dream-like momentum with which it unfolded in real time. Unlike writing fiction or personal essays, I don't really have to invent a world. The world is the city, New York City in my case, where I was born and raised. For as long as I have been a writer I have often dipped into this almost diaristic mode, written a piece, and then tried and sell it to one of the many publications with the words "New York" somewhere in the title. The the available space for this kind of writing has been shrinking. A couple of my pieces in this book first appeared in *The New York Times* City section, where I was a frequent contributor for nearly a decade, and which has just been shut down.

In the winter of 2000 I had the idea of starting a Web site that took these sketches and put them on a map of the city. I called it Mr. Beller's Neighborhood, in homage to Mr. Rogers, of the children's television show, and Mr. Ross, founder of *The New Yorker*. As an afterthought, I put in a button that said "Tell Mr. Beller a Story." The stories came in.

4.

This is the second anthology of work that first appeared on Mr. Beller's Neighborhood. The first, *Before and After: Stories From New York*, was a double A-side that pivoted on the axis of the 9/11 attack. It came out in early 2002, and the number of stories published on the site in the seven years since approaches a thousand. It is a near certainty some of the stories that were left out should have been included. In making my selections, I didn't have any overt agendas other than reading interesting writing. In hindsight, though, I gravitated to pieces that touched on New York's subterranean flow of grace in both its positive and negative incarnations, a dissonance that is a gift from the city to its citizens, or at least its writers. Examples of that dissonant gift range from Saïd Sayrafiezadeh's fraught exchange with a prowar heckler, to Samantha V. Chang's relationship to the Korean women who perform her pedicures, and Sarah Miller-Davenport's adventure down the rabbit hole of New York's small claims court in search of retribution, justice, and a sum whose value ends up far outstripping its actual worth. Although some of these pieces are light-hearted, many of them redeem a cruel twist of fate through the act of writing about it.

For a while the question was whether to organize these pieces by neighborhood or by theme. While this was being mulled over

I was getting packets of galleys organized in no particular order. As I was reading through them I happened to attend a lecture that mentioned Charles Babbage, a once famous mathematician who is now mostly remembered for two things. One is a pithy note he sent to Alfred Lord Tennyson about the poet's line, "Every moment dies a man, Every moment one is born." Babbage wrote, "If this were true, the population of the world would be at a standstill. In truth, the rate of birth is slightly in excess of that of death. I would suggest [that the next version of your poem should read]: 'Every moment dies a man, Every moment one one-sixteenth is born.'"

Babbage's other claim to fame is inventing the first known prototype of a computer. He called it a "Difference Machine."

What struck me immediately was the irony of this—it's true the Internet has opened incredible possibilities for communication among people who would never otherwise meet, but if there's one thing computers and the Internet do efficiently it is group people together. It's a sameness machine. Everyone with a special enthusiasm for pet ferrets, or the Knicks, or vintage espresso machines, can find others of a like mind. That's fine if you are looking for someone with whom to discuss vintage espresso machines or politics, but few things exhaust the spark of life in human experience faster than holding one experience beside another one just like it.

Meanwhile, these galley packets each had a kind of music to them, a vibrancy that derived from their randomness. The city experience is one in which order and predictability are constantly interrupted by the unexpected and the irrational. You could say this whole book is a collection of those interruptions. And so we have these pieces assembled, essentially, by the roll of the dice.

5.

There is a great deal of diversity in voice, topic, and form among the pieces in this book. Some are elegiac snapshots of something or someone that has vanished, such as Gabriel Cohen's "Document," in which he narrates an imaginary documentary about the elderly siblings who are his Brooklyn landlords and housemates. Others narrate startlingly intimate scenes, such as Allan Goldstein's account of going to visit his mentally challenged brother to inform him of their mother's death, Courtney Coveney's description of an afternoon with her Uncle Ayman, who sells hot dogs, or Betsy Berne's navigating the city with an adopted child of another race, where attacks can come from all sides.

There are artful recollections of misguided romantic obsessions from the past by Rachel Cline and Charles D'Ambrosio, among others. Suhaey Rosario makes a kind of manic poetry out of walking to an obscure hideout with a friend, while Stacy Pershall recounts the more literal mania of bipolar disorder, and Michele Carlo crawls into her garden in the dead of night to hollow out an eggplant—I leave it to her to describe what goes into it.

There are dispatches from the front lines of various professions written with an intimacy that combines confession and polemic. JB McGeever offers dispatches from his post as a teacher at a public school that has been written off by the city, where students are treated like enemy combatants. Thomas Zeigler offers a series of startling portraits from his career as a fireman, including one that speaks to the moral and political corruption of Giuliani administration. The pseudononymous Mr. Murphy illuminates the backstairs doings of a doorman on Upper East Side. Peter Nolan Smith offers a view from behind a diamond dealer's glass counter on Forty-seventh Street. And as one might expect, a cab driver weighs in too.

6.

In many of these pieces, the city itself becomes a kind of dreamscape where the stars align and a curious kind of serendipity prevails. Patricia Bosworth gets a back stage glimpse of President Kennedy taking in *The Sweet Smell of Success* on Broadway, and then, in a mirror image of that evening, finds herself in the same spot watching her friend sing the same song, this time with tears streaming down his face. Christine Nieland is browsing in a toy store when she suddenly gets caught up in a morally ambiguous situation that leaves her feeling like an accomplice to racism. Matthew Roberts is sent on assignment to photograph a bank manager who had been handcuffed to a briefcase-bomb. All the bank manager wants is privacy, and yet Roberts' awareness of the reasonableness of this wish somehow propels him into attack mode and he feels a rabid need to confront the manager with the documenting force of his camera.

The idea that the act of writing is a way of getting control of a narrative seems particularly acute here, a desire to render the chaotic fabric of the city manageable by focusing on a single thread.

7.

Current events flicker at the margins of the pieces in this book, with two exceptions—the run up to the war in Iraq and its attendant protests, and the Republican National Convention, held in Madison Square Garden in 2004. Though 9/11 is mentioned in a couple of pieces, it remains for the most part off-stage.

After 9/11 we were maimed, grieving, afraid, totally freaked out, furious, and a bit numb. Or I was, at least. Just as there had been a certain directness in the attack, there was a directness in the city's collective expression of grief. By 2004 the feeling had become one of sputtering incredulity and outrage. There was a sense—by no means universal, but widely shared—that something was being stolen. Our grief had been manipulated. The story of 9/11 had been misused.

This outrage should be considered in the context of the boom years in New York that got underway in the eighties, accelerated rapidly in the nineties and accelerated even more in the aftermath of 9/11. New York has always been a place of violent change. I don't make any special claims for this era's displacements. Nevertheless, implicitly or explicitly—in the case of co-op owner James Braly, whose identity is wrapped up in an apartment he can no longer afford to keep, and Denise Campbell, who writes about being an African American woman gentrified out of one neighborhood and then another—one can feel the squeeze.

Density has always been one of New York's great offerings. Not mere density, not a constant crush, but the high-pressure, low-pressure transitions from one neighborhood to the next. Those contrasts were still there in 2000 and are still there today, but they are less pronounced. If density is the drug on which New Yorkers have come to depend, any fluctuation of its dose sends a tremor through the city.

8.

The great buildings, unlit, blunt like the phallus or sharp like the spear, guarded the city which never slept. Beneath them Rufus walked, one of the fallen—for the weight of the city was murderous—one of those that had been crushed on the day, which was every day, these towers fell.
—James Baldwin, *Another Country*

My first thought when I read this passage was of the Twin Towers. But Baldwin's novel was written in 1962. I realized then how much the very act of narration is connected to surviving the pressure of these buildings that, however figurative their fall in Baldwin's passage, can still weigh a ton. And thinking it over I detected a note of triumph in many of these pieces. It's not the triumph of victory but rather of survival. Of staking a claim and, in an odd way, of asserting ownership. It's as though the writer were putting a place mark in time—I was there, I could lift my head, and write down what was happened around me and in doing so, own that moment.

While assembling *Lost and Found*, I often fantasized about some future historian or archaeologist examining it. What would it tell them about the first decade of the twenty-first century in New York City? About the years after the dot com bubble burst, after the horrible spectacle of 9/11, when the city went into a frenzy of sorts, older buildings vanishing and replaced by sharp spears of glass. Whole neighborhoods metamorphosed like stop-motion movies of flowers going from tender shoot to full bloom in seconds. Perhaps it is in response to this rapidity of change that the pieces in this book, for all their variety of experience, share a desire to stop, or at least manage time—a wish to hold a moment up to the light and save it.

PART I

★ **MORTON ST. & HUDSON ST.**
WEST VILLAGE, MANHATTAN

THE LIGHTED WINDOW
BY CHARLES D'AMBROSIO

She arrived in the city ahead of me to work as an assistant to the producer of a movie, a pretty girl's job, a blonde's job, and soon, very soon, while I was still talking to her by phone from Seattle, making arrangements for my move to New York City, she began sleeping with the director. In the business, these girls are part of the spoils of a mass mobilization involved in making a movie. It seems stupid even saying so. It happens all the time, but a fierce self-loathing I confused with a sense of loyalty kept me from believing it would happen to me, even while it was happening to me. I was from the hinterlands and these dirty stories of people with no probity had previously amused me quite a bit—being insular and backwards didn't seem so bad, with all that corruption out there. I braved coming to New York anyway, a cuckold, and under pressure of the constant humiliation of it, I became achingly and excessively earnest, which eventually unfit me for life in the big city and just about everywhere else too.

I was so desperate for orientation that I persisted in the broken thing, the empty relationship, in whatever form it could take at that point. She eventually moved from the apartment she shared with her brother in Brooklyn and started living in a place on Morton Street that was really the former residence of a famous New York restauranteur. He still held the lease and I believe she was living in the partially furnished place for free. As a boy my best friend's dad was a bartender at a place called Mike's but until I lived in New York City I wasn't aware that somebody who owned a restaurant could become a celebrity. I learned. I also learned that in making a movie, in banging the director, in being in your twenties and beautiful, a person could ascend the social scale, could occupy interesting rungs on a ladder that seemed, within the provinciality of Manhattan, securely leaned against real life itself, and I saw her rising up and away, climbing toward that lighted window where it was all happening.

Morton Street is one of those lovely locations that can become, for a fresh-off-the-boat New Yorker, the repository of vague dreams. It seemed leafy and hopeful in some recollected way, a living memory, even though I grew up in a world where the really boss trees, the firs and cedars, are so deeply green they appear black and claustrophobic and horrifying to non-natives. Still, I liked the way the lamps—burning behind the new green leaves of spring—turned the light gold and gave it a filigree. I spent a lot of time looking into the leaded windows, at the bookshelves and the objets d'art, wondering idly who lived there, how they had managed to inhabit such calm lives. But this nostalgia that swept me up was for a memory not my own, for some New England scene of stability and love and a good far quainter than I'd ever known. It was a world I'd read about in first grade, in those primers where people raked and burned leaves in the fall, and I was hungry for it. I wanted quaint, I wanted stable.

But when you're a cuckold, you either become chaste or murderous. I would sometimes spend the night on Morton Street but there would be no sex. We'd sleep in bed together like a couple of beings with moral purpose. The place was only partially furnished, but its emptiness seemed stylish, impressively so for someone who came from a cluttered house, where the white tundra of carpeting in the living room was a luxury considered worth scrimping for. The bed on Morton Street sat jarringly in the middle of the living room, like a sacrificial altar. The floors around it were beautiful hardwood and shone like butter. Despair sent us separate ways, her to sleep and me to restive all-night vigils, awake, watching little things stir. A slip of paper, set free of its stack by the breeze from an open window, would sail across the waxed floor. The collar of a white blouse hung on the back of a chair seemed bold because it possessed its own shadow.

Eventually, the movie wrapped, the tent-show moved on, and she stopped her thing with the director. Losing that orbit, she lost the place on Morton Street, but soon there was another movie, another orbit. Where do you live? How'd you manage that? I remember those questions as key to my time in New York. Everyone does, I'm guessing. You want to put the package together; you want the place; you want what it implies; you want the cosmos in your corner. I wanted it in New York, but I wanted it before that too, earlier, in Paris, where she and I had gone to be young and romantic together. A week after I arrived she said she wanted to go to Geneva alone, but it turned out, in fact, that she went to Barcelona with a man she'd met before I showed up.

I don't know what's wrong with me.

Let me explode time:

Walking this afternoon: from the studio on Rue Dupin down to St. Germain and then back here by way of St. Sulpice. A cold day, crisp, silent, so the sounds themselves seemed brittle, apart, each one discrete and clear—so few of them: a car horn, some children in the square at St. Sulpice, and the water from the fountain there, brimming over the tiered rims to the wide basin at the bottom. No more: just these. Not the slosh of noises the rain brings, not the soft floating sounds of spring, not the dead still of winter. The fall. Sight had something of the same clarity and resolution as sound, the colors all hard and distinct, neatly, sharply shadowed, the shapes correct and acute—precise, cold, aloof, stately. So often in Paris there's that soft wash of mist, a thin gossamer blur between you and the world that blunts the lines and fuses the colors, and in general blends everything seen into a continuous shifting haze. Romantic. But today, everything seemed very much resolved into itself, alone into its nature.

There were only a few couples and some families out strolling, stopping now and then by storefront windows, discussing the displays, moving on in a desultory, maundering way. Unhurried, the shops being closed, and therefore more detached—not at all the breed of fevered consumers Saturday brings—the one or two slow clusters you might see on any block seemed incredibly, even abnormally, at ease for Paris. They, too, like the shapes and sounds around them, around us, were sunk deep into their own peculiar natures, alone in their special lives.

At the corner of Raspail and Sevres, in the direction of the park, to the west, where the street and the huddled toppling apartments open up and give way, the sun, low and voluptuously round, was setting and streaking the sky and the horizon a lush, yellow, pinkish color something like a grapefruit, skin and meat together. Everything now melting together, and I paused to watch, to summon a mood from the beautiful sky. Then I hurried around the corner quickly, up the stairs, and into this dead space.

It's fall now and I live on a mountainside overlooking the Flint Valley and the town of Philipsburg, far from New York. At night, it's so quiet I can hear men and women fighting in their homes. When the bars close, wrecked trucks rattle off in a brigade of drunks and then the silence returns, and after a minute or two I can see the stream of headlamps grope their way across the valley floor. Each light seeks out another light, a home miles distant, and from where I live I can watch them connect. I often feel enclosed and trapped in my house and grab a sleeping-bag and sleep outside, at the bottom of what seems like a huge black bowl. The stars are cold in their vast spaces, but rather than fear, I find comfort in their indifference. The lights in the valley are seamless with the stars in the sky and only slightly dimmer, and we are all here together, alone.

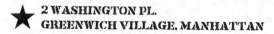

**2 WASHINGTON PL.
GREENWICH VILLAGE, MANHATTAN**

THE FRACAS
AT WASHINGTON
SQUARE PARK
BY SAM LIPSYTE

The comic Bill Hicks once said, famously, apropos of the first Gulf War: "I find myself in the unenviable position of being for the war—but against the troops."

Nobody that I've heard has come up with a similar corker this time around, a line which can sum up the personal confusion and official hypocrisy so succinctly.

There were some placards on Saturday in New York City that were charming in their way—"Just Another Dyke Minister Against the War"—but most of the declarations were pretty annoying. The guy in a smart leather jacket carrying a "Bush=Hitler" sign and talking feverishly into his cell phone seemed like easy fodder for some smug cartoonist, and tired puns on "Bush" and "Dick" abounded.

Walking down Broadway, it was nice to see a topless woman with very shapely breasts cheering us on in our march against the war. I know the hippies alienated the working class with their bourgeois individualism and sold out the revolution, but breasts are breasts.

Half a block away, a crowd had gathered around some old geezers in berets who'd unfurled a dark velvety banner. These were the remnants of the Lincoln Brigade, who'd fought Franco in Spain. They were doing interviews and basking in applause. I thought about what I'd read by Orwell and others about the Spanish Civil War, what a tangle of interests it was, how the Soviet Union betrayed the cause. But these guys had risked their lives to fight fascism without Bill O'Reilly or Ted Koppel rooting them on. I clapped heartily.

Someone tapped me on the shoulder around Twenty-eighth Street. It was a former writing student. We walked together in the sunshine and talked about the difficulty of "finding a voice." I looked around at all the signs, the protesters, the flag-wrapped mad dogs on the sidewalk spewing bile at us. Everyone had found a voice, it seemed, though it might not be their own.

Will you can it with your bourgeois individualist bullshit? I said to myself.

I feel bad for the poor kid from Texas who just wanted a college education and is now an easy target for a sniper or a bomb. I feel bad for the poor kid from Basra who's maybe dying of some preventable disease that won't be prevented without medicine and running water. I feel bad for the 99 percent of the world that is fucked by the other 1 percent. I feel bad for me. I don't understand the people who say that now that war has started you have to shut your trap. By that logic we'd still be in Vietnam. This is not a bar brawl whereby if your friend is an asshole and started the whole thing, you have to back him up.

I wonder about all those polls showing that most Americans support the war, too. Polls have always been skewed, and now we have the added bonus of Ashcroft-paranoia. Some stranger calls you up for your opinion, maybe you say what you think will most reduce your chance of being audited by the IRS next year.

We all got jammed up down at the Washington Square arch. It was a three-way stand-off with the media trucks, the cops, and the protesters. The cops kept urging us to disperse, first with megaphones, then with their bodies. Some of the protesters had formed a phalanx which the cops tried to split with a slowly moving van. The protesters wouldn't budge and the van backed up. There was some fracas; it was hard to see in the center of the crowd. People started chanting at the cops "Arrest Bush!" and "You Work For Us!"

The first sentiment I agreed with, but the second rankled. For one thing, the cops don't work for us; they are simply paid by us. When I was in a revolutionary socialist group in college, it was patiently explained to me that though the army, made up of poverty conscripts, could be won over by the revolution, the cops, who are maybe the closest thing the ruling class has to a Republican Guard, could not. I'm a little more confused about the world than I was back then, but I see the point. For another thing, there was something in that latter chant—"You Work for Us"—that reminded me of that story about Harvard kids screaming "That's all right, that's okay, you'll all work for us someday" at superior non-Ivy League sports teams.

The Fox News types have been berating antiwar activists, saying they are missing the complexity of the situation. That you can't simply be against war. They say it like it's being against air, which I guess it is to them. But the situation is complex. It's the Bush administration that has over-simplified, reducing the geopolitical scene to schoolyard logic. "I am bigger and I will take that ball now."

A man stood in the center of the antiwar throng with a prowar sign. He posed for the television cameras while protesters screamed at him and got up in his face. A woman shouted that he was probably CIA. The sign did look a little weird, as though trying very hard to look homemade. Others begged the crowd to let him have his say. Then someone ripped the sign out of his hand. The camera people backed off. They had their shot.

That guy with the leather jacket appeared again. He had a new "No Blood For Oil" sign, one of the mass-produced kind.

LOST AND FOUND

He was jacked up and he kept running off to tell others not to disperse, to come back to the group, that we had to stick together.

"Who's he?" a woman asked her friend.

"I don't know," said the friend. "I think he's the stick-together guy."

THE SINK
BY ELIZABETH MANUS

In the beginning, there was a brownstone with a crackled façade and a ground floor apartment for rent. I took the tour. Hardwood floors, a tiled fireplace, and a country kitchen. But the rooms didn't get much light. I wanted sunlight, the kind that slid from four windows into the diamond-bright bathroom, the kind that was missing from the window-free bedroom.

Then I took a closer look at the kitchen sink. It was a farm sink of sorts—very large, very white, and very old. In fact, it was wonderful; wide and deep enough to wash a large dog.

I could wash a dog!

Time for the moving boxes. As I taped and folded, I imagined washing dishes in the huge, white sink. I like washing dishes, but I'm fussy about sinks; I need elbow room. Now there would be elbow room to spare. No more splashing water onto the floor; no more stepping in splashes; no more dampened slippers.

I had, essentially, signed a lease on a white sink in Brooklyn.

Life proceeded as usual, until one night at a fancy party I spotted a tall man. He was bursting with some kind of frenetic energy and seemed lost. He was wearing sneakers. I had to talk to him. It turned out we had spoken once on the telephone, months before. He had sounded glum; now he was a sprung rhythm. I was all ears. Suddenly I had sprouted two new erogenous zones.

He did not live in the area. E-mails, telephone calls. Finally, an evening meal in Brooklyn.

He had abominable taste in clothing. He threw the newspaper all over the floor. He snapped beans using a knife and fork and a plate. Too often he did this whistle thing, a sort of "sheesh" without saying the word.

After dinner, he stood at the sink rinsing dishes. I watched from the doorway. Here was the man who would never bore. Here was a club I wanted to join. Instead of feeling hemmed in, monitored, pedestaled, or any other annoying emotional byproduct of being romantically involved, I felt comfortable. I felt curious.

I observed and waited. This was unusual for me, waiting. Generally I'm in motion—Hurry, or it may be too late. (Too late for what? Everything.)

Not anymore. Now, time was in step. Here was Nowdom, somewhere near talk show healing territory: I was okay, he was okay, our parents did the best they could, everything was going to be all right. I felt no inclination to kick the man out of my home, nor did I feel self-induced pressure to talk through silences or reach into my mental files for some bit of wit intended to charm and delight. My critical faculties had eloped to God-knows-where. Instead, a song from the 1970s musical *Pippin* floated into my mind, the one the woman sings about missing the man whose face was far from fine, who wasn't a hero, who didn't outshine the sun, and who wasn't a simple, good man. This man is like the man in the play, I told myself.

The point was that I knew my own heart for the first time in a long while (as the song might have said). And the other point was that he, instinctively knowing my feelings, would return them in kind. Then we would fly to Cuba for dinner, just like they do in *Guys and Dolls*.

Somehow, I was missing the larger points: that an overindulgent fantasy life could be ruining my chances for a normal relationship (whatever that was). Or that a woman in her early thirties was interested in shaping her life into a wanton stage. When my college English professor advised his students to "Make your life a work of art, kids," he probably did not mean it this way.

The dishes were done. To the bedroom, then. "It's a coffin," he said. I laughed. It was funny—he was funny.

In the middle of messing around, we stumbled into a stop-and-start conversation that halted with him saying something on the order of, "You mean bad sex!" I came up short. The phrase "bad sex" hadn't turned up in my spoken lexicon, and I didn't know what to say. I tried to say something. He also said he didn't think he could satisfy me sexually. I had no idea what that meant. (Years later, I might know.) He turned over. Did I kiss his back? It was a wall of a back. No kissing allowed. He had retired for the evening.

How could sex with him, somebody I liked so much, be bad? His harsh tone had risen so suddenly, I failed to point out that he was putting words in my mouth. Everything had been better when he was rinsing dishes at the sink.

Morning arrived. He had found the coffee bean grinder and was grinding. I listened from the coffin. Now it seemed he had stepped again into that song, only this time I was an audience member instead of the woman who loves the misfit. Maybe it was worse than that. Maybe I had been playing the role of the woman who loves the misfit. But I did adore him, as much as you can adore somebody you barely know. I was willing to take a chance. That was close enough.

"Milk?" I offered.

"Black," he said.

We drank our coffee. His socks were balled up on the kitchen table. He spread paper around again, and then it was time to catch his train. I goodbyed in my robe, and looked toward the dishes just long enough to decide to take a bike ride in Prospect Park.

LOST AND FOUND

Feels like a beginning, I thought as I pedaled. There was a beginning. Really, there was.

Things didn't work out.

The sink didn't work out, either. Beyond its perimeter lived an entire set of realities—shouting landlords, screaming children, leaky pipes, shoddy wiring—that could only be overlooked for so long. One evening, the sink didn't drain. There was gray water in it for almost three days. Eventually the plumber came.

Eventually I left Brooklyn.

OUT WITH THE OLD

BY FRAN GIUFFRE

"**I** probably should have done this ten years ago." This was
the theme that ran through my mind when I replayed the
decision to leave my profession and take up teaching at the age
of forty-nine. But then getting out of the garment business was
no easy feat. I felt like *The Godfather*'s Michael Corleone trying
to escape from the family business: "I keep trying to get out but
they keep pulling me back in." When I finally decided to make
the transition from manufacturing girls' dresses to teaching elementary education, it seemed logical in spite of the fact that it
meant going back to school for my Masters. I was accepted into
the NYC Teaching Fellows program where the cost of my degree
in education would be paid for, provided that I spent two years
teaching in one of the many "high need" public schools located
throughout New York City.

I was psyched. I liked the idea of the support system provided
by the Teaching Fellows program and knew that I would find
myself among a small percentage of other career-changers. I
needed to focus on this fact, as it had been close to thirty years
since my now-bunioned feet had walked through a college campus. I was assigned to Brooklyn College, which was fine with me

as my commute from my apartment in Prospect Heights was under thirty minutes.

But some things never change. It didn't take long for me to notice that I was still the type of student reluctant to bond with the other students. I was shy and hesitant to join the cliques that were quickly forming. My cohort members seemed to possess a sense of desperation, leading them to glom onto those with whom they felt the slightest rapport. Sure, it would be nice to develop camaraderie, but for me the need wasn't that urgent. Instead, the familiar feeling of being an outsider returned, even if it was self-inflicted, reminiscent of my earlier schooldays at the Yeshiva where my mixed background (Italian father, Jewish mother) differentiated me from the other students.

I decided to take an atypical approach outside my comfort zone, by making an effort to mingle. During a class break, I approached a young woman who mentioned in her "getting to know you" speech during the initial class that she had grown up in Park Slope. "So, you're a neighbor of mine," I said, trying my best to sound cheerful and friendly. "I live in Prospect Heights," I added.

"Oh, yeah, I grew up on Sixth Street," she said pleasantly.

"I lived on Third Street when I first moved to the Slope in 1981," I replied.

"That's a while ago," she said. "I wasn't born until 1982."

I desperately tried to keep my smile from forming into a grimace as I thought, "Now was that really necessary?" As far as I was concerned, the conversation was over. I wouldn't be able to concentrate on what she was saying anyway.

Most people I spoke to about my decision to start a new career were very supportive. Even my parents came up with positive and encouraging things to say, in spite of the fact that they were concerned about me riding the subway to neighborhoods like Brownsville and East New York. My father was raised in East New York during the 1930s and 1940s and although he had not been back to the area, he knew, as we had been trained in the lingo of the program, that they were neighborhoods facing "huge challenges."

Although the Fellows Program provided support in many areas, after the vigorous seven-week training, we were expected to find our own teaching positions for the upcoming school year. I sent out numerous résumés, but nothing panned out. Taking a proactive approach, I decided to visit some schools in the surrounding area to hand-deliver my résumé and perhaps even get to meet some of the principals in person.

I put on a nice pair of slacks, a short-sleeved sweater, and some sensible-but-stylish sandals, and set out on foot to an elementary school I had read about on Carroll Street between Third and Fourth Avenues. I opted to walk along Sixth Avenue, preferring this tree-lined and less hectic route. It was a beautiful summer afternoon and I was feeling grateful and happy, allowing myself to enjoy the moment, pushing aside the pressures of the job search and nerve-wracking thoughts of the vigorous school program that lay ahead.

I passed four construction workers who were refinishing the steps leading up to a brownstone. I was almost completely past them when one man said, "Oh man, you must have been really hot a few years ago."

I was mortified. It was fortunate that he couldn't see my expression of disbelief mixed with outrage at this left-handed compliment. I couldn't decide whether to say, "Thank you" or take the opportunity to display my agility (that was not completely gone) by swirling around and delivering a nice swift kick.

Not sure of how to respond and stymied by this sharp blow to my ego, I kept walking. But my blissful moment from only a few minutes earlier was gone. I was like a Thanksgiving Day Parade balloon with a bad leak. I wondered if I could ask him to clarify."Excuse me, but when you said I must have been hot a few years ago, did you mean like two years or more like twenty years?" Because after all, it made a difference. As I was fantasizing my reply, I heard his voice again, "Did you see her? She must have been about forty-two or forty-three. She looked damn good," he told his co-workers.

And although the damage had been done, being mistaken for a woman approximately six years younger did soften the blow. I was happy to take comfort wherever I could find it. As painful as it was to admit, this was my reality. Any compliments directed to me would now come with a disclaimer. I was a middle-aged woman in fairly good shape for her age. In spite of the way I pictured myself, I was no longer a woman in her twenties or thirties. No matter if I was embarking on a new profession, reinventing myself, starting on a path that perhaps I should have taken back when I was just out of college, I had to face the facts. In a few months, I would be turning fifty. I was back in school, about to go through the hell of first-year teaching and all the lessons I would learn, having chosen a profession that was not known for making anyone rich. Actually, I couldn't think of a place I'd rather be.

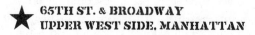

★ **65TH ST. & BROADWAY**
UPPER WEST SIDE, MANHATTAN

COCO ON THE FORTY-SEVENTH FLOOR

BY PAUL FELTEN

My girlfriend, Emily, recently got a job as personal assistant to a stockbroker who lives on the Upper West Side, on the forty-seventh floor of a building directly adjacent to Lincoln Center. The stockbroker goes to work at eight or so and often doesn't get home until eight or nine in the evening, at which point she eats and goes to bed. This routine is repeated until the weekend, when the woman and her daughter drive to the New Jersey countryside and relax like crazy until the inevitable Sunday evening. Emily starts her own workday by consulting a detailed list and spends the rest of it traveling to far-flung, expensive stores to find the desired items. She also cleans and cooks on the rare occasions when the family doesn't order out. She once spent an entire hour trying to understand the controls on the apartment's state-of-the-art oven. The woman returned home before Emily had figured it out, and Emily asked for some help. "We live in building with seventy employees," the stockbroker replied. "You can call one of them. I hired you because I work hard all day." Then she went to lie down until dinner was ready.

A substantial portion of Emily's work involves the woman's Shih Tzu dogs, which are expensive and fragile animals. Emily takes them to the groomer every two weeks, buys them gourmet baby food, and is generally required to keep an eye out for any of the myriad health problems that plague the purebred toy breed. The youngest, Kaluha, is cheerful and affectionate, unaware of her terrible breath. Coco is older, wizened and mean as hell. The first time I visit Emily at work, I lean down to pet the dog, trying to quiet the little bark that sounds like the laugh of an elderly woman who's smoked since her teens. Coco stops barking when my hand gets close, but her tiny black lips curl into a sneer.

"Don't," says Emily.

Coco makes a low sound like a cat purring, which slowly morphs into a full-fledged growl that any Mastiff would be proud of.

"Christ," I say. "What's the matter with her teeth?"

"The vet has to pull them sometimes." Emily lies down on the floor. "You have to be perfectly still," she explains.

The animal walks over and sniffs her head. Emily asks if I think she's walking funny. "I think it's her hip," she tells me, as Coco climbs onto her chest and eyes her suspiciously, like the Lilliputians with Gulliver. Coco lets herself be pat on the head a couple of times, but isn't really into it and climbs down after a few moments. She seems contrite, but as Emily begins to sit upright Coco once again sneers and growl-purrs and bares her infrequent teeth, finally limping to the water bowl only after we've ceased to give her our full attention.

The next time I visit Emily at work, she's rushing to clean the apartment before her boss gets home from a business trip. The dogs are doubly excited because I've brought a friend. After Coco barks at him for a while, she regards me with some trepidation but gives my hand a light lick when I put it down for her to smell. I find myself wanting Coco's approval. I think of her as an emissary for the stockbroker, a little representative whose own personality is a perfectly distilled version of her owner's manic shifts from genteel ferocity to condescending affection. But, I remind myself, I don't know this woman, apart from Emily's descriptions. I've only been acquainted with her apartment and her dogs.

I take my friend to the window. We stand and look out over the Hudson and on to New Jersey, then turn for a comprehensive view of Manhattan's Upper West Side. The city looks beautiful from here, especially this afternoon in the muddy winter sunlight. "Is this the tallest building in the area?" my friend asks, and while the answer is no, one could almost believe from this vantage point that he or she stands at the very top of New York. I turn around, a little dizzy.

Emily brings us some coffee and tells us that she finally figured out how to work the big TV. We all sit as she explains that the remote control to the television is so large and elaborate that it's unrecognizable as a television remote control, and so she never thought to pick it up and point it at the television. Then her eyes catch on something and she stops, mid-sentence. We look towards whatever's interrupted her.

It's Coco. She's in the middle of the living room rug, circling and sniffing a discolored, saliva-hardened teddy bear.

"Uh-oh," says Emily.

After a few more circles, Coco positions herself on top of the bear's head, shifts a little for comfort, and starts fucking it. Her eyes, which already protrude from her head to an alarming extent, bug out impossibly further as she scoots along the length of the bear, making low noises that sound vaguely human.

My friend starts laughing. "She's nervous," says Emily. "She wants to show us that she's dominant." Any authority Coco hopes to establish, however, is seriously undermined by the complete abandon with which she violates the defenseless toy. Coco may want to show us that she's the boss, but when in the throes of her inexplicable passion, clearly Coco is the one being dominated. She humps with a fervor born of terrible compulsion. We laugh and sip on our coffee while she thrusts and grunts, without any evident pleasure and certainly not with the hope of eventual release.

Emily stands up, a sign it's time for us to go. "I've got to finish cleaning," she explains. "I don't know when she's coming home." We head out the door, and I kiss her and tell her my greatest hope is that the stockbroker's in a good mood that evening and that she isn't reprimanded for no good reason. "Oh, whatever," says Emily. "I'm not sure she can help herself." Coco stands to one side, glaring—now she's angry we're not staying. I scratch her behind the ears, and we leave Emily to her view.

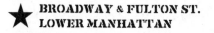

ABOUT A TOY

BY PAUL FELTEN

It was my first day and Beth, who worked in the cubicle across from mine, was talking on her cell phone about sex.

I was doing the kind of mindless work that provides a perfect cover for eavesdropping. I kept my eyes on the insurance forms I was stapling and got to know her a little.

It seemed like she'd been singing Sunday nights at the Village Underground. Her specialty was mid-century jazz standards like "Summertime," and "Love Doesn't Live Here Anymore." She told her listener, Stacy, that she had really knocked them dead last Sunday. "Applause like crazy, and then a standing ovation." She went on to describe some grade-school boy who'd also sung that night, with an alarmingly precocious display of erotic self-confidence. He wiggled his hips, he gyrated, he lowered his eyelids. I was trying to picture Morris Day at age nine when she segued into a description of the Underground's bouncer.

"Stacy," she said, and then again "Stacy," as though she were waiting for Stacy to sit down and concentrate. Her voice got a little lower.

"He was fine. He was so fine. Not too small, not too thick. Not too tall, but not a shorty. And the way he was talking to me…Girl, I had to go home and get my toy out."

There was a short pause, prudery on Stacy's part.

"You don't understand," said Beth. "I use the damn thing three times a week! Stacy. Stacy. Get one. How else you gonna scratch your itch?"

Here I looked over. I half expected her to pull the toy out and gesture with it, but she was doing the same thing with her hands that I was—stapling.

Stacy was still protesting. Beth was adamant.

"It's necessary!" she cried, slamming the stapler hard with one hand. "And you gotta get one like mine." Another pause. "The thing takes three batteries."

I pictured many things. Stacy, the perfect wallflower complement to Beth's self-gratifying extrovert. The agonizing process by which Stacy would approach the store that sold such a toy. I supposed it would be the female equivalent of a guy entering a peep show. Stacy emerging, hurrying home with the brown paper bag.

And, of course, I pictured the toy, which had now evolved in my imagination from a straightforward dildo to some life-sized ambidextrous pleasure robot. Three batteries! Three batteries to my one lousy member, which I now pictured as only powerful in its adverse effect on my ability to reason. I was mulling over the fate of man (if not human) kind when our supervisor appeared and snapped at Beth to get off the phone.

The cubicle, the object itself, has been much complained about. It is a soul-crushing staple of the modern workplace ridiculed (and made to seem insurmountable) by something like the Dilbert cartoons. It is an exposed, soft cage, a negative counterpart to the wood-lined offices where company executives wallow in privacy. The cubicle pretends to offer privacy while providing managers with the optimal geography for surveillance. It is very useful in this regard; it is easy to sneak up on someone in my office.

A lot of men sneak up on Beth. Some just pop in to say hello and then move on. Others linger and chat her up. One guy, who I've never officially met, creeps up behind her at least once a day and suddenly rubs her shoulders or puts his hands on her forearms and jiggles her upper body. It feels like the what-not-to-do part of a sexual harassment video, but Beth shakes him off with playful impatience. There might be a history there. He talks low into her ear as she tries to wave him away. I once heard her say, laughingly, that she'd tell her man if he kept it up.

Her man is named Brandon, and he is the source of daily consternation. They are planning a wedding, which isn't supposed to take place for another two years and about which the couple's families have some keen differences. She's never talked to me about Brandon, but she talks to the rest of my cubicle quadrant about him. Constantly. Beth is one of those self-dramatizing people for whom no crisis is private. Her indignation is always righteous.

Our one real conversation, though, charmed me. It happened after she belched. It was really loud. She smiled at me when I looked over.

"Sorry," she said. "My stomach is fucked up. Not too ladylike."

Now was a good time to repay her with some personal info of my own. "I live with a woman," I told her. "The whole idea of 'ladylike' went out the window a long time ago."

She liked this. "Tell my fiancée. I burp and he can't believe it. He looks around to blame it on someone else." A wider smile. "There's no such thing as ladylike."

The guy in the cubicle next to me, who spends his free time playing in a rock band, says that everyone with a permanent job in the joint is a former temp. Most of them came from my agency. There is an information-sharing policy between the insurance company and the temp place that puts our government intelligence to shame. I got a message on my cell phone one afternoon from Olga the temp supervisor. "They love the work you're doing," she said, "but I had a call from someone in HR today who saw you wearing sneakers. I know it's Friday, casual dress and all that, but sneakers aren't good. 86 the sneakers." I reacted to this like anyone would who's been tattled on. I vowed to wear sneakers for the rest of my borrowed time at this place. Fuck it, I'll wear sneakers on my hands.

Of course, I showed up the next Monday in my casual dress shoes, which stain my socks brown and hurt the balls of my feet. Soon, I think. Soon I will wear whatever shoes I want. This stupid sneaker indignity isn't even worth a footnote in the story of my brilliant forthcoming career. And I will glare hard at that HR stoolie the next time I see her. Human resources, my ass. Why couldn't she have just come over and said, "You know, sneakers aren't really appropriate here." A little respect, huh? What a way to treat a guest.

"Workplace casual." This phrase never describes an actual place of work. It is a dress code, pure and simple, seemingly conceived by multi-national conglomerates and Internet startups who have some sort of backdoor deal with the Gap. "You're at work but it's casual!" Making people feel at home at work by making work feel more like home.

But the code is less stringent than the dressier alternatives. For every unimaginative guy who daily trots out a blue shirt tucked into black slacks, every woman who seems to have stepped into the office out of an H&M catalogue, there are the employees who have interpreted "casual dress" as something that affords self-expression. There are the male dandies; there are middle-aged woman in unforgiving neon-green heels; and then there are those who express contempt for the workplace itself by pushing the code envelope to the point of slovenliness. You can do this without wearing sneakers, especially if you're a woman. The workplace is still a place where women are seen as inherently more elegant than men, and so their "casual dress" can be pretty damn casual.

Beth has spoken to this. A co-worker who was trying to rearrange the rumpled collar of her quasi-dress jacket got a reprimand. "What are you doing?" said Beth. "Who am I trying to impress? I'm at work."

There is a guy in the cubicle adjacent to Beth's who has interpreted the "casual workplace" mandate in conservative terms, but he makes up for it. His name is Elvis, and the following description comes with a disclaimer: I've never spoken to him, and I have the same limiting assumptions that the reader does when he or she hears about someone named Elvis who's not, you know, Elvis.

Elvis is a wolf. I say this with confidence because his body language is embarrassingly recognizable as my own when I've tried to snow some girl into premature intimacy. He's always leaning against something, with a hand in one pocket. He goes around in his pink polo shirt with a quarterback's swagger. I have only ever seen him loitering—leaning, flirting, listening to one of the office's few younger women with the kind of glassy-eyed look that passes for undivided attention.

But he doesn't do this with Beth. He poked his head over the cubicle once and made some crack about getting her work done. Beth showed him the palm of her hand and, without looking up, said "I'm not in the mood."

He fired out of sight like a punched-down jack-in-the-box.

Two days ago, Beth became a mentor. Her student is named Eve, another temp, and they've already developed a rapport. Eve is very young and Beth is enjoying the role of seasoned elder. Beth is much taller than Eve. She tends to put her arm around Eve's shoulders. Beth talks to Eve about Brandon. I only hear this in snatches now, because I've started listening to music for most of my workday. I've chosen the most aggressive CDs I own—a *Mission of Burma* compilation, the two-disc soundtrack to Godard's *Nouvelle Vague*. I will drown out the workplace chatter with the sounds of loud aging radicals who wear sneakers all day if they feel like it.

I take off the headphones to carry some files to the mailroom. Beth and Eve are consulting a calendar.

LOST AND FOUND

"See," says Beth. "The week after your cycle is OK. Then, you're safe. If you have sex after that, it's trouble. You've got to be careful."

Eve nods solemnly, like she's listening to a priest. They look at one another. Beth smiles and rubs Eve's shoulder, and then the supervisor creeps around the corner with some fresh bit of instruction.

A poem. I found it the same day I heard Beth's toy story, in the drawer of my cubicle. It was underneath a pile of staple boxes, miscellaneous unfinished work, and timesheets from the same temp agency that set me up with this gig. It was scrawled on the back of a spreadsheet where clerks document the daily number of insurance bills sent out to clients.

It was composed by whoever had the desk before me. I transcribe it below, without the author's permission:

Don't get mad at me 'cause my
[unreadable] got admission fees.
Don't hate me cause my shit is
insured.
Priceless, timeless, and forever fresh
Never knew nothing free
Especially one of the best.
Only given to a chosen few
No need to waste good—
I ain't got to show and prove
Only open to those that
acquire the finest
the sweetest.
Those who appreciate the finer
things in life.
Fuck the baddest bitch.
I'll leave that title for Irina
'Cause I'm positive that mine is meaner
forget hot.
You get in and feel the humidity.

So moist and hot I'll sweat out your
pubic hair.
Nevermind vacation.
Once visited you'll be
talking 'bout living there.

18 W. HOUSTON ST.
GREENWICH VILLAGE, MANHATTAN

AISLES OF NEW YORK

BY DAVID EVANIER

On one of my last days in L.A., where I'd lived for nine years, a producer I was speaking to on the phone was having difficulty reeling out a coherent sentence to me. "I'm sorry," she said, "I had a ninety-minute massage yesterday. Since then I've been unable to think clearly or speak."

I hadspent all my years in L.A. missing New York. On my first week back in Manhattan, my wife Dini and I sat two seats away from an elderly woman in the Angelika Cinema. We were about to watch *Sidewalks of New York*.

Before the movie started, the woman turned to me and said, "Would you tap me if I fall asleep?" I said I would.

During the course of the film, I must have glanced her way at least twenty times (perhaps five times at Dini), and felt a twinge of resentment that this stranger was taking my attention away from the film. In the darkness, her sideways, slanting posture made it difficult to determine if she were awake or not. To tap or not to tap? But I did tap her once. At the end of the film, I said goodnight and she thanked me and gave me a great smile.

Such a confession of vulnerability, the genuine eccentricity of it, an elderly person not afraid to reach out to be touched, not likely at the Sunset 5 next to Crunch. Nine years older now, I know we are all in this together.

A few days later I saw some girls on the subway. There were eight of them, beautiful Latina girls of eighteen or nineteen in bloom. They cascaded into the subway car like trilling birds. They were celebrating one of the girls' birthdays, and they rapped together and sang out in unison: "Girls! Girls! Girls! Girls!" But mostly I could not understand a word of what they said or sang; they were so noisy and they were laughing and chattering at once. Their smiles, their joy and energy was so infectious, they were so devoid of malice, that I grinned at them. They spotted a tired, wasted black man of thirty in the corner of the car and they called to him, "What shall we sing to you?" He looked at them; they seemed to have woken him up or he had wandered into a dream. He was shaking his head and grinning. "What do you like? We'll sing whatever you request. We like you." And they sang, "I think I want you baby. I think I want you too. I think I love you baby I think I love you too." And he bobbed his head, smiling, not quite believing it. Then he got into it.

When I got to my stop, I got up to leave. They called out to me, "You like us! We like you." I waved.

I remembered the start of my life, when blacks and Latinos bowed their heads on the subway. I thought of Lucy, the black maid who came to clean our apartment once a week in Queens. Lucy spoke in the slurred, whining, singsong cadence, the forced Aunt Jemima merriment of the Negro in those days, the half-voice that said, "I am of no consequence whatsoever." I remember Lucy entering the apartment and saying, "Tha's old Lucy, that's me right heah…hee hee." My mother kept a separate dish to feed her, so that our food would be kept pure. Lucy sat in a corner eating. Sometimes, during the week, my mother would forget which dish it was and have a fit.

All those first days of my return to Manhattan were freezing after sunny California, with snow and piercing wind and cold rain. Each day I walked across the shining necklace of the Brooklyn Bridge, the icy winds lashing against my face, wondering why I did not feel the cold. I was filled with an inner warmth that seemed to lift me, as if I were in a carriage in a bitter storm.

Like that woman in the theater, I was home.

★ 120 GREENWICH ST.
WEST VILLAGE, MANHATTAN

THE MODEL APARTMENT
BY ERICH EISENEGGER

We were from out of town. We had finished school, were about to get engaged, and we were moving to New York at the end of the summer. They showed us a "model apartment." They put the hard sell on us. They asked us for a deposit in the form of a money order (can't cancel 'em). Then they asked us to "put up with some minor inconveniences for a half a month" while they put the "finishing touches" on the building. This was four months before the move-in date.

We went back to Boston believing we had successfully found our first apartment. Then they called and pushed back the move-in date a month. Then they sent us the actual lease to sign—two months later. We were in California, on our engagement trip, but they needed the lease ASAP or we might lose the apartment.

Of course, the additional rider to the lease they asked us to sign did not say please endure minor inconveniences. It said that the "continued construction activities" may cause us to "not have immediate and/or full use and enjoyment of the apartment," including the use of air conditioning, elevator service, the supposed gym/health club and twenty-four hour doorman, and that we would "knowingly, willingly and voluntarily" agree that such construction activities "shall not constitute a violation of…any rights…enjoyed by the Tenant," because it was "understood that, but for" our agreement, "Owner would not have entered into this Lease with" us.

One week before the move-in date on October first, they took our two months' rent in advance in the form of a money order (can't cancel 'em) and then showed us our actual apartment for the first time. "They'll fix it up," they said, "before you move in."

We didn't check the hot water. We didn't check the heat. We didn't check the gas. "Fix it up?" They must have meant the disgusting state of the floors, the sawdust covering the counters, the lack of shelves in the cabinets, the dried paint in all the wrong places?

After all, the "model apartment" we saw was beautiful.

Couldn't have been that, since the apartment was in exactly the same shape when we moved in. Could they have meant the elevator service we finally received (albeit without a proper license)? The mailbox we finally got? The gym we finally had access to, whose costs were built into our "luxury rental?"

Couldn't have been that, since we received them only several months later. But not getting our mail and taking the stairs up and down to the fourth floor were the "minor inconveniences" we had agreed to when we gave the deposit.

By "fix it up," maybe they meant we would have a doorman? Yes we did—to guard the construction, not us. Sometimes the "doorman" would leave the building. Oh, but he was guarding the place, all right. He would padlock the front door shut with a chain and lock to which only he had a key. Sometimes he would put a wooden stake through the handles of the door while he went off to have a beer off-premises. It was almost charming, if he was there to let us in—sort of a quaint, pre-twentieth century feel to getting into your own building. Sort of like us needing to put a hard hat on to get through our lobby.

The problem was when he wasn't there. Like at 2 a.m. on a blistering night, and our doorman was passed out in a car across the street with the only key to the padlock. Or when the fire alarm went off because of smoke from the boiler in the basement. At least the fire department was able to get in.

By "fix it up" they must have meant getting heat? Couldn't have been, since we didn't get heat until mid-December, long after the City statutes demand heat for its citizens. But we agreed to be cold in that lease we signed months after giving them the deposit, remember?

Maybe they meant they would fix the gas? Couldn't have been, since we didn't get gas for the stove until the end of January. But we agreed not to be able to cook in that additional rider, remember? Maybe they meant we'd get hot water? Maybe. We actually had hot water on most days—except, of course, for the mornings when it seemed we most needed a hot shower. Like our first day of work. Like when it was fifteen degrees outside.

And even though they never returned our phone calls, they did try to communicate with us. Like we were on a deserted island. The only mail we received from them were new riders to sign stating that we agree never to sue if they knock off some money from a month's rent. We were confused, at first: Why give us a new rider when we had already explicitly agreed to be cold and hungry in the original lease? Why offer us a few bucks now when we already had agreed to be unable to have people visit us for months? Hey, we already agreed to put the tremendous strain on our engagement, this was a good test for our relationship! It might have even helped, since it was impossible to have my in-laws over for Thanksgiving.

There were some other correspondences. Like undated memos stuffed under our door announcing that heat or gas or the elevator would "soon" be in service. ("Soon" means something different in New York than I was used to.) Or the sudden, unexplained appearance of a space heater inside our apartment. Ah, yes, must have been to avoid liability under the city statutes. I guess it says somewhere in the statutes that if you feel heat in a small corner of your apartment at any given time, you're heated.

LOST AND FOUND

And then there was the gracious hot-plate they provided. How did they know ramen noodles were my favorite food? Getting a hot plate wasn't even in our lease!

I know, we should have moved, right? Try and break the lease and just move out, like some people did. Like our neighbors, the lawyers. Or the doctors down the hall. We would have sucked up the re-packing and moving everything ourselves since we couldn't afford movers again. And, after a couple of yoga classes, we probably could have psychologically gotten through almost immediately re-locating while trying to plan a wedding and managing our new jobs. We would have, that is, if we could have afforded to pay another realtor fee and put down another first and last month's deposit. We would have, if we had a place to go in New York or the surrounding area. Our family's house near Syracuce really offered too far of a commute. In the end, we put our faith in that all-important Lease, a document with more teeth than the United States Constitution, a document in which the City of New York allows us to waive every right imaginable.

All we wanted to do was move here.

TIME TO FLY

BY OPHIRA EISENBERG

"Leap and a net will appear." Right. You know what appeared the last time I leapt? MasterCard debt and an empty bottle of vodka. Don't get me wrong—vodka can really cushion a blow, but a net it is not.

I moved to New York City on a whim. Well, most people call it moving. I call it running away. I usually move after a bad breakup. Some people say, "Your troubles will follow you wherever you go." To those people I say, "Not if you move far enough!" But there will always be new problems. That's how the game works.

I was living in Toronto, working as stand-up comic. I had just shot my own half-hour special for the Canadian Comedy Channel. I was in love with a guy who was an emerging celebrity movie critic and I never had to pay to see a film again. I could hold my liquor. I was considered above average at karaoke. And I wanted to kill myself. The good life left me fifteen pounds heavier and constantly perusing self-help books. I felt insane and couldn't refuse a cupcake.

I started experimenting with anti-depressants. I tried drinking, not drinking, working out, not working out, spending time alone, surrounding myself with friends. The only thing that seemed to fill the void was a cocktail of my own invention called a Driftertini: it was a combination of chilled Grey Goose and talking about moving away from Toronto. But why would I do anything as stupid as that? C'mon, everything was finally going my way! My life was almost perfect. Then why am I tying a noose?

One autumn evening my boyfriend came over for dinner. He had been thinking about "us" and he thought we should go the next step and get a place together. I froze. Of course, that's exactly what I wanted, but instead of a tearful yes, "I'm moving to New York" fell out of my mouth. We stared at each other for a while in disbelief. Clearly my emotional brain had beaten down the logical side to the point where I was all id. And where do you go to bond with all the other ids? New York City.

My way of approaching a major change is through chaos. Here's what you do. Get a non-refundable plane ticket and then forget about it. Live in utter denial until the week before. Put the possessions you planned on selling for hundreds of dollars in a box on the street marked "FREE STUFF." It's so much easier to move in a state of panic.

I boarded a bus to the airport with a big blue knapsack full of high-heeled boots and hope. I saw my boyfriend cry for the first time as I pulled away and I felt like I was making the biggest mistake of my life. What was I thinking? I was alone, had no comedy connections in New York and only enough money to last me a couple of months at fifteen dollars-a-day. Really, who did that clichéd move-to-New-York-bags-in-hand thing anymore? I mean, I didn't know how to tap dance! But it was all too late. I was on a bus, then the plane, and then a cab to the East Village. My friend Tracy had offered to put me up in her East Village apartment for "as long as it takes." (Thus moving her into the "yes, I will help you move a dead body" category of friend.)

Tracy lived in a tiny basement apartment with no windows. It stunk of pee from the two mangy cats she had rescued off the streets of Spanish Harlem. I had to lose that fifteen pounds just to fit into the bathroom. The kitchen only had a microwave, mini-bar fridge and a coffee maker. Okay. Dinner parties were definitely out. I also found out that her boyfriend from South Carolina would be moving up and in next month.

The no-windows-lack-of-light-and-air thing started to really get to me. I would fall asleep at night in the bed that Tracy and I shared under a duvet of cat hair, and would wake up panicking. In the tomb, as I referred to it, it was impossible to know how much time had passed or whether it was day or night. I felt suffocated by the darkness. To soothe my anxiety, I developed a Jedi mind trick. I would imagine gusts of nourishing outside air flowing through the cracks in the brick walls, under the door and in-between the hinges, slowly drifting through room after room until it would get to my nose and mouth. God, I was a long way from my two-bedroom apartment in Toronto for $400 a month Canadian. But I still didn't want to go back.

Tracy's boyfriend showed up. I was moved from the bed to the couch. The boyfriend and I got along…not so well. Both vulnerable and New York City green, we competed for Tracy's attention. I kept finishing in a solid second place. I, in turn, rekindled an old friendship with Grey Goose.

Every morning preceded another late night at the bars hoping to down enough to pass out. One Tuesday morning, I was, as usual, harshly woken up to a huge fluorescent ceiling light switched on above me and the TV screaming in front of me. The sofa was the only place to sit other than on the bed, so I squished myself into the corner. They drank their coffee, talked to each other at full volume, and clattered around the space as if I were nothing more than a pile of dirty laundry. I squinted at them while fantasizing about their murder. My hair tickled the back of my neck. I kept brushing it away, but it continued to bother me. EVERYTHING WAS BOTHERING ME! Bleary-eyed and half-conscious, I gave my neck a good scratch when my hand met with a big crawling blob. I screamed and whipped it off my neck and across the room. A cockroach. No, not a cockroach, but the largest, meanest, scariest cockroach I had ever seen in my life.

It smirked at me in mid-air. I couldn't take it anymore. Tracy tried to comfort me while the boyfriend looked at me with a "serves you right" kind of look. Like it was my fault I moved to New York.

But maybe the flying roach was just the kick in the ass I needed. Maybe it was time for me to fly. As delusional as I was—trying to find a nice apartment in the West Village for five hundred dollars and getting up at open mics saying "What's up with orange toques, eh? After a two-four, ever wonder why there aren't there garburators in washrooms?"—I slowly found my way. I found a reasonable apartment share and then another and another, I found a place in the comedy scene and others of my kind. I even had a friendly drink with the boyfriend (but just one). So if "leap and a net will appear" means leap off the couch when you find a roach crawling on you and then decide it's time to get your shit together, then yes, I agree, the universe is magic.

LOVE AND MONEY AT SUN LIN GARDEN
BY TOM DIRIWACHTER

It's common practice for a bar or restaurant to save their first dollar and hang it on the wall. A sort of diploma from the school of capitalism. Some eager businesses even save their first dollar bill, five-dollar bill, ten-dollar bill, or twenty-dollar bill— the higher denominations like graduate degrees. There are establishments with a dozen or so bills on display, no doubt commemorating certain milestones, like finally turning a profit, a year in business, their first million. I've seen places that exhibit foreign currency, marks from Germany, lira from Italy, yen from Japan, even though they're not accepted inside these borders. But Sun Lin Garden takes this tradition to another level, the entire interior of the restaurant wallpapered with bills scribbled on by patrons in thick magic marker.

You don't need reservations at Sun Lin Garden. In fact, you don't really make plans to go there. It just kind of happens. The idea pops into your head. You're in the neighborhood. You get a craving. On this particular night, Karen and I had dinner at Acme, then drinks at Time Café before seeing Sonic Youth at the Knitting Factory. When we emerged from the club, the summer breeze seemed to carry the aroma like the wavy lines that lead to food in cartoons, and we followed it up Canal to China-town.

Turning off Mott, with its touristy restaurants, Bayard is a cramped side street, and the storefront isn't much bigger than a phone booth, with an oversize neon "69" glowing red and green in the window. That's how people refer to it: "69" Usually with a grin on their face. But it's cheap. And the food is great. Best of all, it's open twenty-four hours.

It's late and the dining room is empty except for the round table in back where the cooks eat family-style. A frail Chinese man in a tuxedo vest approaches, tells us in his broken English to sit anywhere. I seat myself, as Karen spins around like she just set foot in the chocolate room of Willy Wonka's factory. This is her first time. She's an actress from Chicago. We met when she audi-tioned for a one-act that I'd written, and was directing. I offered her the part on the spot. We've been dating for almost six months.

"Do you see this?" she asks.

"Pretty cool, huh," I respond.

As we open our menus, I tell her they have the best beef chow fon, and she says, "Let's get that." She says that she's in the mood for sweet and sour chicken, and I say, "That sounds good." Split-ting an egg roll, we share the ramekin of duck sauce, engaging in a dipping contest. The beef chow fon comes out next, and Karen takes charge and serves it, half of the greasy noodles land-ing on the table as we laugh drunkenly. By the time the sweet and sour chicken arrives, we're full and picking more than eat-ing.

Karen's eyes wander, looking over the notes on the near wall, and she starts reading aloud. "JULIAN LOVES ANNA." And "JEN AND ALBERT 4 EVER." And "BIG ANTHONY + JASMINE." And "ROTH FROM LONG ISLAND." And "TKE," conspicuous on a six-dollar block colored red so that the letters are outlined. Inevitably, she asks the question that every-one finally gets around to asking, "How much money do you think is here?" We make a game of counting the columns and multiplying them by the rows, for each wall. Then add everything up. The total we arrive at is $4,865. To allow for the random five and ten we make it an even five grand.

Three bucks of that is mine. Memorials to past relationships. "TOM+LAURA" is located two-thirds of the way up the main wall. Laura was my first love. The girl that broke my heart. I was still living on Staten Island at the time. She came from New Jersey. We were on one of our first dates, but I already knew she was the one. I'll never forget her, and I'll never relate to women in the same way.

There's also a "TOM AND LAURA," higher up on the same wall. Different Laura. Commonly referred to as "Laura Number Two." She and my mother once had a twenty-minute phone conversation wherein Mom thought she was talking to *the* Laura, and when she finally realized, made it worse by trying to explain. It was all a terrible coincidence. Or maybe I was trying to recapture the past. Either way, Laura Number Two and I only dated a short time. She never really stood a chance.

The third one, simply two names, "TOM" and "CHLOE," on the ceiling, is from the summer of '99. Chloe was a French girl with dreadlocks, like a Bo Derek for the millennium. A co-worker introduced us at a party, and she ended up living with me for the next two months, trading porno sex in exchange for room and board. There was no lease. She stole my Topps baseball card collection and never even said goodbye.

The words, "we should do one," interrupts my reverie, and I turn to see Karen smiling at me. Looking into her twinkling eyes, I can practically hear the people back home saying that with a smile like hers, she should be an actress. But I had vowed never to pledge another dollar.

"There's no more room," I say.

"On that wall," she says, pointing.

"I don't know if I have a single."

"I've got one."

"It's against the law to deface legal tender."

"What?"

LOST AND FOUND

"Someday they're gonna bust this place. And track all these people down."

"Don't you want to?"

We stare at each other, until I finally raise my hand for the waiter.

ART GARFUNKEL AND OTHER PROBLEMS OF THERAPY

BY MEGHAN DAUM

I t's 1993 and I have been in psychotherapy just over a year. The whole experience at this point boils down to the single image of a young private school girl sitting two seats down from me on the crosstown bus. She is accompanied by her Dominican nanny, who gazes absently out the bus window on to Ninety-sixth Street as it crosses Fifth Avenue, then Madison, then Park. The girl, perhaps eight or nine, has bypassed cuteness for something closer to what Linda McCartney looked like in the early 1970s or Ali McGraw looked like in *Love Story*.

Her hair is pulled back in a head band and she has huge eyes that somehow suggest she already knows a good deal of French. She wears a blue blazer and knee socks.

My therapist's office is on Eighty-third Street and Park Avenue and my appointments are at nine o'clock on Friday mornings. Before beginning therapy, I rarely rode the bus or visited the Upper East Side, and now that it's been a year of back-and-forth, a year of so many versions of this girl and her nanny, and so many mornings stepping around the maintenance men who hose down the sidewalks of Park Avenue, I am starting to see why so many people pay someone to listen to their problems. A resident of a cooperative building on Park Avenue in the Eighties probably shoulders a hefty maintenance fee in exchange for services that include a washing of the sidewalk every morning. This is a wonderful thing, particularly in the summer. It's wonderful not just to feel those cool water droplets whirling beneath the awning, but also to observe those squares of concrete going from unclean to clean. There must be a daily catharsis to living in one of these buildings, to step outside every morning and tip-toe over sheets of water and soap.

I went into therapy because the constant presence of a low-grade anxiety was making me a very irritating person. I was twenty-three. Before my first session, I'd been in a bad mood for three and a half months. It started suddenly one day when I walked out of a movie theater and passed a line of people waiting for the next show. I looked at their hair and at their scarves, which were wrapped perfectly around their necks and chins as if they were all professional scarf wrappers. I looked at the way their hair came springing out of their scarves, an effect I would never be able to produce, and thought about how terrible the movie had been and about how they had yet to experience the terribleness but that I already knew. I walked past that line and was in a bad mood for a solid three months. It was the longest sustained mood I'd ever experienced. I disliked all objects and individuals, especially those who walked too slowly down the street. For two weeks, the thought of getting on the subway to go to work made me choke back tears, so I took cabs. For two months, the only people I didn't despise were my roommates, my boyfriend, and the woman with whom I shared on office. She had recently entered therapy herself and, like me, was diagnosed with Generalized Anxiety Disorder, which is coded as 300.04 on most insurance claim forms.

My father, who has always disliked Simon and Garfunkel, has on several occasions equated people who engage in psychoanalysis with people who don't realize that Paul Simon's "American Tune" is in fact a derivation of *Mein G'müt ist mir verwirrt*, Hans Leo Hassler's 1601 composition, which was later popularized by Johann Sebastian Bach. One of my earliest memories involves watching Paul Simon on television in the mid- 1970s and hearing my father say "He is just lame." My father holds a doctorate in music and is now a composer and arranger of commercial jingles. When I was growing up, his musical sensibility was a totalitarian regime. There were, and probably are, only about fifty songs in the world that my father approves of—they manage to simultaneously be wide in scope and slim in picking. One of my father's favorite songs is "Just Once" by James Ingram. He is also a fan of Sergei Prokofiev's ballet *Romeo and Juliet* and when I was a kid once called the police in order to shut up the neighbors' barking dogs so that he could finish listening to the end of the fifth act, to which he was following along in the score.

It took me over twenty years to revise my opinions according to my own musical tastes. When I was about twenty-one, driving home to New York from Boston, I remember listening to Paul Simon while merging on to the West Side Highway from the Saw Mill Parkway and seeing the buildings on Riverside Drive enter my line of vision. I remember the bumpy, messed-up texture of the road and seeing all the beat-up, New York City cars closing in around us and thinking, with the kind of revelation particular to twenty-one-year-olds, that, just like Paul Simon sings in "American Tune," I really didn't "know a soul who's not been battered." Then I decided that Simon and Garfunkel could be a good thing.

For many, the principal image of Simon and Garfunkel—particularly for those of my generation who experience *The Sound of Silence* and *Bookends* as relics of a seemingly momentous but ultimately perhaps rather facile period of history—is that of Central Park in 1981. This was when Art Garfunkel made a sheepish yet valiant appearance next to his far more talented and celebrated partner and mustered the courage to sing his only known composition, "A Heart In New York," in front of more than 500,000 people, who used the occasion to visit any of the hundreds of Port-O-Johns provided by the Parks Department. Another salient aspect of Art Garfunkel's performance, as any listener of the *Concert in the Park* album will know, is his unfailing knack for saying the stupidest possible thing at the worst possible time.

As Paul Simon begins strumming the initial chords of "American Tune," Garfunkel, like a stoned college freshman with a girl in his room, says "I'm so in the mood," with a voice so self-conscious you wonder if he spoke the words into a tape recorder three hundred times in an effort to sound "dreamy." Then he starts up in unison with Simon, singing those lyrics about being mistaken and confused. At this point, the listening experience is a matter of putting out of mind the issue of the song being stolen from *Mein G'müt ist mir verwirrt*. Then they reach the line about the Statue of Liberty sailing away to sea, and I remember that I actually do like the song.

I've heard that for years now Art Garfunkel has been walking across the United States. He does this in increments, walking perhaps ten or fifteen miles at a time, and then getting back in his limousine and returning to wherever he was before. I often wonder about the precise details of his treks. Does he walk along main roads or hike through mountains? Does he bring a canteen of water? A stereo headset? I would imagine that he wears a pair of top-of-the-line walking shoes, which makes me wonder, why he hasn't become the spokesman for a line of athletic gear? I also wonder what Art Garfunkel's chauffeur does in the space of time between seeing Art off and picking him up at the finishing point. Usually I picture the chauffeur leading against the hood of the car and smoking a cigarette, the Rocky Mountains exploding all around him. Other sources have told me that Art Garfunkel takes an airplane to his walking spot and sets out from there. I wonder if he flies on a commercial airline and, if so, how he gets to his destination from the airport. Does he save up frequent flyer miles specifically for this purpose? I have a hard time imagining this is true, even though several popular magazines have confirmed it. Still, Art Garfunkel seems more likely to be puttering around Southern California in a not entirely new, not entirely top-of-the-line European car. He seems more likely to be stopped at a light than moving in the traffic flow. And it's precisely these burdens, precisely this "everyman" quality that gives us all such a fright. He's our national nightmare, the guy who didn't become a superstar, the guy left at the altar. He's the guy who millions of Americans see on TV every once in awhile and say "He is just lame."

My guess is that Art Garfunkel is in therapy and that these issues come up all the time. Of course, there is the chance that he forgoes psychoanalysis altogether. That his walks, the kind my mother might prescribe, prove more cathartic than fifty minutes staring at some Degas or Monet lithograph in a shrink's office and rehashing his childhood in Forest Hills, Queens.

But he does seem like a therapy kind of guy, and how could he not discuss his feelings about being left behind on a national scale? I feel sad when I think about "A Heart In New York," the only song he wrote that anyone has ever heard. I feel even sadder when I think about the way Art Garfunkel introduces the song on the *Concert in Central Park* album. He says "This is the only song in the show that is not a Paul Simon tune." It's not the wrenching nature of his being upstaged that gets me but his use of the word "tune." This usage is presumptuous and cheesy. He's assuming a kind of collective, earthy rapport with the audience that, because of the crowd's sheer size and because it is 1981, is inherently false and therefore totally impossible. It's as if he thinks that using the word tune will momentarily revive his supposedly formerly cool persona. He thinks it will cause everyone to shed their snobbery, to get back to the days of being just folks playing folk music and singing the tunes that make everyone feel like they're okay and Art's okay and the Pan Am building still says "Pan Am" on the top and there's still even a chance that Art will have a solo career.

I brought this up with my therapist and she was curious as to why Art Garfunkel's career presented such a source of anxiety for me. I said I didn't know, I had started thinking about Simon and Garfunkel as I was riding the bus through the park and it made me feel depressed and anxious. I said I hated to think about how a normal person with an above average voice could be turned into a national joke just because of his proximity to a genius. Then I corrected myself. I said, "thought by many to be a genius." I didn't feel comfortable deifying Paul Simon considering my father's feelings about him. I started to tell my therapist about my how my father once said that Paul Simon's marrying "that Princess Leia actress" wasn't going to kid anyone into thinking he wasn't the shortest celebrity in the country. This is what I started to say, but we ran out of time.

As I walked home from that session, I thought about my father and the fact that the only Simon and Garfunkel song that he can name is "Me and Julio Down By the Schoolyard." He pronounces Julio with a hard "J." Whenever I try to think of my father as a kid in a schoolyard, the only image I come up with is one of the few ever described to me, which involves him standing in line in a Midwestern parking lot waiting to receive a polio vaccination. Other than a specific recollection of drinking a glass of milk at his mother's kitchen table, that is practically the only incident my father claims to remember from his childhood. It's a good thing he'd string himself up by his incisors before setting foot in a therapist's office. He'd have nothing to say. I wish the same were true for Art Garfunkel.

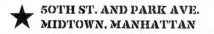

MANHATTAN SEX CLUBS: THEY HAVE THEIR UPS AND DOWNS

BY DAPHNE

The sex club looked more like a cheesy New Jersey nightclub than a happening orgy fest. There were balloons on the ceiling and people dancing to seventies music. Most of the people were not very attractive. The women were bleached blondes with frizzy hair, a bit dumpy or had fake boobs. The men had beer guts and receding hairlines.

I guess I had thought that the couples would be as attractive as they had been at other places. However, some of those places were "takeout," meaning you meet and go elsewhere for sex. Here the pickings were slim. My boyfriend and I were among the better-looking. For many people, looks aren't that important anyway. For me, looks and brains are extremely necessary

There are many different sorts of sex clubs. It's sort of like choosing a restaurant—it depends on what you like to eat. There are sex clubs that are held in apartments that are intimate, and then there are ones that are at the same place, week after week, that are more like regular clubs.

LOST AND FOUND

I had been to a few private parties in the city hosted by a nice couple I had found through mutual friends. They interviewed me over e-mail and I sent them pictures and answered basic questions. They were selective to a point, but personality and cash spoke volumes.

Their parties were very intimate. Held at townhouses and apartments, they were always beautiful places full of character and warmth, lots of beds, clean and exciting. As with all parties, no alcohol was served, but you could bring your own and a bartender provides the mixers. Condoms, mints, wipes were all provided to tidy up.

There were beds in each room and couples having sex everywhere in all sorts of positions with all sorts of couplings. The interesting thing is that the men were more tame in the apartment parties than at the clubs. They didn't try to pick me up because they knew at the end of the night, they were getting lucky. They let the women do the work.

Then are other places that have been around forever that used to be great but that are now mediocre at best. Back in the day, my friends went to a club and saw an older couple: a woman was being double penetrated by two brothers. Her husband was looking into her eyes and holding her hand. They said they had never been so turned on in their lives. These days, I wouldn't walk in there without my shoes, let alone without my clothes.

Then there's the club where a former boyfriend, along with six other men, was asked by a famous model to drop his pants, "You," she said to my boyfriend, "Come with me," and off he went. I guess she liked what she saw.

Some people are into S&M, but I don't want a guy to lick my boots. Once, when I was at a club, someone tried. I really tried to be polite but it wasn't going to get me off. Rather, it made me want to throw up, because I am a little OCD and all I could think about is where my boots had been. I do like a light whipping, but that's a private thing. Another story.

The cheezy sex club was in a nice neighborhood. I am sure the people outside had little idea of the goings-on inside. I kept telling myself: "The club is clean, it's full of people wanting to have fun. The balloons and tackiness are just a little out of the ordinary." I watched couples dancing while eying each other.

After a few minutes, people stripped out of their clothes and retreated to the back rooms and onto beds. They paired off into groups, started having sex. Very clinical. I got the feeling some of them did this every weekend.

Being a voyeur and anthropology major, I had a really good time even though I wasn't attracted to anyone and didn't participate with anyone but my boyfriend. The difficulty was keeping the women's paws off me—that was definitely a challenge. There are rules at places like this but they are lax. Still, I loved watching, it didn't matter how attractive the people were. What was a turnoff, however, was listening to the women in one of the rooms, chatting in their heavy Long Island brogue about getting pedicures, and the fungus that had ensued from one such pedicure, in between giving blowjobs and being fucked. Talk about losing my sex drive! I felt like I was in a surreal dissociative alternative reality. Something as pleasurable as sex in conjunction with nail fungus really blew my mind.

When we were leaving, a couple in the elevator tried talking to us. I pretended not to hear. After all, we had just been in a sex club.

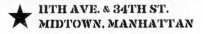

UNCLE AYMAN'S HOT DOG STAND

BY COURTNEY COVENEY

My Uncle Ayman is out of Lemon Snapple. I fish through the drink compartment, a deep bin on the far left of the hot dog cart, and settle for a Diet.

"Please. Courtney. Take whatever you want."

He always says my name like it's a sentence all its own.

He's selling hot dogs, lukewarm pretzels, iced teas, and sodas on Thirty-fourth street, on the West Side, near the Javits Center. It's not his usual spot, but there's an Auto Show and he was hoping for a busy day.

"Business is not so good today," he says. "These people, they're not hungry."

I watch the auto-show-goers from my comfortable station, leaning against Ayman's green SUV, which is parked on the street behind his hot dog cart. Some approach the cart, and many are looking for a Lemon Snapple. Ayman, frustrated, makes a phone call and yells in Arabic at someone whom I can only assume is his supplier.

He works quickly; his fast hands grab at tongs, napkins, cans, and bills. He stores cash above the drinks, in a compartment sealed by a sliding metal door which he slams in his fervor. Singles go in a low cardboard box, easily accessible for change, I figure. Larger bills he puts below the box. I soon realize that no item on his cart has a fixed price.

"You see, it's one-fifty for him," Ayman says, gesturing toward a Jersey Dad, who is enjoying a hot dog with sauerkraut, "but not for everybody. Sometimes two dollars, sometimes seventy-five cents. Depends how they look."

I've always suspected as much, but I don't tell him so. Instead I glance up and down Thirty-fourth Street, counting the brightly colored umbrellas. There are five other hot dog carts on this block. I'm sure the Jersey Dad could have saved fifty cents, had he really tried.

I hear a loud call for a Peach Snapple from the street, and Ayman runs, drink in hand, to a man in a black Chevy Blazer. The Blazer peels off and Ayman returns with a dollar and some change, though he had previously quoted the price at two dollars.

There's a table full of pink, blue, and purple sunglasses to our left, and I tell Ayman I want to take a look. He helps a customer, a burly man who asked for a "beef frank," while I examine the table.

"Something you want?" Ayman calls to me. He reaches into his pocket for a roll of bills. I assure him that the sunglasses aren't the right sort, that I don't want anything, and then return to the cart.

Three kids about my age, two boys and a girl, gather in front of the cart, talking quietly at first.

"How much for your drinks?"

"Which drink?" Ayman asks them.

"Drinks. Drinks. Your drinks," they say, making drinking motions, as if he hadn't understood.

"I have different drinks. All different prices."

The girl speaks up.

"Are you giving me attitude because I asked for a drink?"

"No, no. I have different drinks. There's not one price for a drink."

The boys say, "A soda. A soda."

Ayman replies, "Soda? One dollar."

The girl continues, "You know, I'm doing you a favor by giving you my dollar. This is my money that I'm giving you. I'm doing you a favor. And you give me attitude?"

"Oh, shut the fuck up," I say quietly. She doesn't hear me, and I'm relieved. Their fight continues until the boys decide to walk away.

"Is this your dollar, ma'am, sir?" Ayman shouts after them, and then tears the dollar to shreds. He tosses the pieces into the air and they land on the sidewalk, in puddles, under the car's tires, and on top of other trash. He's silent for a few minutes, raging, smoking a Marlboro Light. He sees me scribbling, looking at the fallen bits of dollar.

"Courtney. Don't write this."

"But it's wonderful," I say.

"Keep it for yourself. Nobody needs to know this. It's bad!" He pauses.

"You know," he continues tentatively, "she thinks she's doing me a big favor. With this one dollar. I get two tickets a day! Two hundred fifty, three hundred dollar each! And she thinks this is 'big favor.' It's no big favor. Look."

He takes out his wallet and pulls out a pink ticket.

"Every day?" I ask.

"Every day we fight with cops. Last night I came home, I had no…" he gestures to his throat, "from yelling at cops. But I know, they just do their job."

He turns away for a second, frustrated.

"This is hard job. When I was at home, Egypt, I was not hard like this. I was soft, like nice, I never had fights. New York is hard place. Not like Egypt."

He looks up, startled, and runs out into the street at a white van. He says a few words to the driver, and then returns.

"You can go to the city in Egypt and say hello to people. Not here in New York. I work the same corner for three years, same people. Some nice, but some don't say good morning."

He crosses his arms and imitates the people who don't say "good morning."

"How much is a hot dog, man?" A short, older man in a security uniform asks.

"One dollar," Ayman responds. To me he says, "He works here, at Javits, so for him, one dollar."

I nod.

A tall man comes up to the left side of the cart and sets down a case of Lemon Snapple. Ayman says a few words to him in Arabic.

"My niece," he says in English, and the other man shakes my hand. He leaves, but returns shortly with a few boxes of pretzels. Pretzels come packaged like new shirts, unsalted, in blue and white boxes marked "New York Pretzel." Ayman rolls each one in salt and stores them in a compartment on the right side of the cart that reads "Hot Pretzels."

I watch a young man across the sidewalk smoke a cigarette, pace, and make calls on his cell. He's been there for about fifteen minutes. He calls at Ayman and gestures with his head.

"Yo."

Ayman doesn't hear him.

"Yo, *papi*. How much for a hot dog?"

"One dollar."

"A dollar?"

"You want to pay more?"

"Make me one."

He walks away.

"What does he want on it?" Ayman asks me.

I shrug my shoulders. He returns after a few minutes and says that he wants onions on his hot dog. Ayman makes it speedily and the young man eats it in three bites.

Behind him is a family, an old father and his three sons, all in Ralph Lauren, all of whom want "everything" on their hot dogs. For them, hot dogs are two dollars apiece.

"It's an okay day," Ayman says after they leave. Business is picking up. He leans into his green SUV and turns up the Arabic music on the radio. When he turns around again, he has another customer. He serves the man quickly, saying a few words in Spanish.

"*Cebollas?*"

"*Si.*"

"All of the Spanish men, they all think I'm Spanish. Everyone thinks I'm Spanish. Especially when I have…" he traces the outline of a beard around his chin.

The young man from across the sidewalk returns. He thrusts a dollar at Ayman.

"Make me another one, *papi*. They're good today."

"I speak a little Spanish," he says to me.

"Me too," I reply.

"One more, *papi*, one more."

He hands Ayman another dollar. Ayman hands him another hot dog. The young man catches sight of something in the road and runs off.

"I speak French too," he says, "I studied. In school. English was worst for me. My dad, he had someone come teach me at home, two times a week. My teacher ask me, 'why don't you want to speak English?' I say, 'It's not my language.'"

A small boy asks for a Gatorade, for which Ayman asks two dollars.

"Two dollars for a Gatorade? Man!"

"You want to pay more?"

"Hell no, man, that's too much money already!" He continues to speak, but I don't hear him. I'm busy watching the young man from across the sidewalk. He's come back for more.

"Hey, *papi*! I'm gonna give you two more dollars. I want two more hot dogs, but not now, okay? I'll tell you when I want them. Okay? I'll be back."

"Yo! Man!" The small boy yells at a friend, "This guy's charging two bucks for a Gatorade!"

Ayman sighs, "See? Some people nice."

"Make me another one, *papi*! I got five, right? If I get another five, I get one free, that's how it works!"

"See, he's nice."

"Man, check it out, two dollars for a Gatorade!"

Ayman sighs again, "See, that one, he just likes to talk. Some people, they just have to talk."

WAGNER IN THE PARK

BY JEROME ERIC COPULSKY

The dark woman hated me because I listened to Wagner without guilt or regret. She said that she could never understand how I could enjoy the work of such a fierce anti-Semite. I told her that was not a problem; I had learned to separate the music from the composer, and, besides, Wagner pretty much hated everybody. She said that was untrue, that one could not dissociate art from the artist, that Wagner's music would always be tainted with his Nazi affections, that I was a poor Jew for listening to his so-called operas, and that she considered this a character flaw, and a serious one at that. I told her that Wagner wasn't a Nazi, he couldn't be, actually, as he died many years before the founding of the National Socialist party, but might have been had the Nazis been around. And yes, I was a poor Jew, but that had nothing to do with Wagner, and we should leave him out of it.

I did not understand my infatuation with her. We had been working together at a dusty second-hand bookshop on the edge of ruin where I was slumming until I could find more lucrative employment. I felt better about myself that I was working, even if it was only a few days a week, and for just slightly above the minimum wage. The bookstore itself was a strange and frustrating place, resembling, I came to believe, a prison for the over-educated. There was something poetically just, I thought, about these PhD candidates working the cash register or reshelving wayward books, not being able to stop and sit and read them, something quite sinister about this class of torment. We had to entertain ourselves in covert ways, with in-jokes and by making fun of our customers' philistine tastes. On occasion, a crazy man who we called "the mayor" would burst in through the front door carrying an old wooden tennis racket and shout, "Revolution!" raise his racket-wielding fist in the air, and babble well-worn verses of Marx and Lenin. Every day we all looked forward to his entrance, though he would inevitably be escorted out of the store by the manager, who, unlike her employees, failed to see the humor in the situation.

The first time I saw her, I had forgotten my glasses and could only detect the outline of her figure. She had thick dark hair that spread over her shoulders, big, dark eyes, and she always wore dark clothes. Her complexion was poor, and when I stood close, I noticed that she had black hairs on her fingers and the beginnings of a faint mustache sprouting at the corners of her mouth. Normally, I would find that such features would disturb me and dampen any desires, but there was something about the dark woman, so that they did not arrest her appeal, but in fact served to deepen it, in a way that I considered, at the time, as having some kind of occult significance. I tried to comprehend my desire for her. I suspected, after thinking it over a bit, that it was because she never smiled. I imagine that this revealed a melancholy disposition that at the time I found irresistibly seductive.

It took me weeks before I worked up the courage to chat with her, and when I did, I found her to be aloof and ironical. She had been employed there for many months though she informed me she was on the verge of quitting. I beat her to it, having grown desperately bored and deciding that my paltry wage was akin to exploitation. Perhaps influenced by the mayor, I became a half-revolutionary myself, and tried to incite an insurrection among my co-workers, scribbling the outlines of a future manifesto next to the arcane philosophical and literary graffiti that spread across the wall of the bathroom stall, but I have notoriously bad handwriting. My arguments in favor of higher wages and medical benefits went unheeded, though I thought I had the last laugh when the store was at last pushed out of business by the Barnes & Noble megastore that opened up a block away. As it turned out, I did endure a pang of nostalgia and regret over this, and began to see, in the inexorable gentrification of the Upper West Side, the error of my ways.

On my last day at work, she came over to me and said she'd be sorry to see me go. She had not spoken to me for the first few weeks and she said she didn't like to get to know people until she knew if they'd be around. I asked her if she was being ironic. She said she didn't understand the question. "My apartment's rent-controlled," I told her. "I'm not going anywhere."

"That's not what I meant," she replied.

We made plans to spend a day together the following week.

I sensed in her deep crooked eyes, in the way she turned her silver rings around her fingers when we spoke, a sort of shy interest. During one of the conversations I forced upon her, we discovered that our ancestors came from the same city in the Ukraine, and I wondered if she was perhaps a distant cousin of mine, and if my implausible attraction to her was rooted in the magnetism of common blood. I kept these theories secret, not wanting to lose the upper hand, which I had thought I had gained, despite the fact that she gave no concrete indication that she desired me except for her occasional sarcastic comment while we should have been dutifully at work. I spent many nights picturing her naked, my hands caught in her thick hair, my tongue running along the hairs on her body. I imagined that a dim light would make her oily face shine radiantly, perhaps mystically, and I wondered if her uncanny beauty would be altered under certain conditions—of light, water, gravity—if it was something that was hidden and only visible through a special lens, only pronounced by a certain rare ink. I saw her face casting off light; I saw her shimmering naked and wet, her hair dripping over her slight shoulders, the tiny droplets clinging desperately to her olive skin as they rolled down her body; I saw her above me with sealed eyes, moaning softly with evident pleasure. I was impressed by the specificity of these visions, and easily fell asleep.

The day we agreed to meet was disappointingly cloudy and unseasonably cold, as if the fledgling spring had reconsidered and turned back. I was early and she was late. Across the river, I could see through the haze the grayness of New Jersey. She wore black, as usual, said hi without gesture, and sat beside me against the low stone wall of the park, glancing at the book in my hands.

"Céline," she said, pushing her hands deep into her coat pockets. "You're so cool."

"Stolen," I lied. "My final revenge against those degenerate capitalist exploiters."

She didn't seem to be listening and muttered something like "such the hipster," and tossed her mane over her shoulder with the backs of both her hands, and then dug them back into her pockets.

"Not really," I said, stuffing Céline into my backpack, silently pleased that she considered me hip. "I'm interested in his use of ellipsis. You know," I added, "dot dot dot."

"Uh huh," she responded, a note of sarcasm in her voice.

Who could tell if she was kidding? For all I knew, she was the hipster, in her black frock and silver rings. She said that she wanted to be a writer, but hadn't written anything yet (or wouldn't tell me if she had—I was unclear on this); it was she who drank her coffee black and with several packets of unrefined sugar (ever nursing a cup at work); she who borrowed (stole?) torn copies of tracts long out-of-print by French philosophers and symbolist poets. Her parents were divorced, she hated her father, and she pointed to a house across the street and said that a colony of Buddhists lived there. She would never look you in the eye, her face forever pitched at an awkward angle. She never smiled.

I ached for her.

I needed a plan, that much was clear. She was not inexperienced, and it was obvious that poetic allusions and Shakespearean sonnets committed to memory were not going to impress her. I sensed that a forward or audacious approach might backfire with the dark woman, as she seemed to be suspicious by nature and not at all forgiving. Still, she had consented to spending some time with me, and that could be taken as an indication of favor, of the possibility of amorous intent. The ultimate destination was my apartment, where I had a bottle of Chilean cabernet I had heard about and an unopened box of condoms hidden in the back of a drawer by the bed. But I couldn't venture an outright move. I decided to play it safe, to be subtle, seemingly disinterested, though allowing, here and there, the occasional double entendre and flirtatious glance. Such a tactic, I believed, would let passion build up on her side. The pressure would build, and I would be ready for her certain advances. All I had to do was be patient and wait.

Of course, it should have been a tip-off that she said to meet her in a park, rather than, say, in a café or a bar, as I would have expected. The lack of furniture and open surroundings made me nervous, and for a moment I wished that I smoked. There was the wall I was leaning on and the obvious allure of nature in the city, but these were to my overanxious mind only mildly satisfactory alternatives. Moreover, this setting had too many diversions: haughty pigeons and squirrels, passersby, children, people walking dogs, changes in weather. A closed, quiet space would be much more suitable for the kind of thing I had in mind. I concluded that this was an examination, and I was being judged on how I dealt with the inopportune situation.

I had hoped that I wouldn't have to deal with any of this pre-coital nonsense, that we would meet here at the appointed time and could then, after exchanging a few pleasantries and stating our disappointment about the weather, just withdraw to my apartment, so to speak. But clearly, I was not the one in charge. This was her turf, and she knew it well. There was nothing to do but take her up on the challenge.

She had grown up in the neighborhood and continued to point out particular buildings on the street that overlooked us and told me what influence they had over her childhood. I wasn't surprised when she told me it was unhappy, and I nodded sympathetically and told her that mine was unhappy too. She said that she used to come to this park when she was growing up, to take refuge from her parents' frequent fights, repeated that her parents were divorced, her father was a schmuck, her mom was crazy, and her stepmother was a bitch. She did a lot of drugs in high school and went to college in Oregon, where she became a vegan for a while, and then gave it up for plain old vegetarianism, shacked up with some guy named Ulandt for three years until, she said, rather cryptically to my ears, they "could do so no longer." They still loved each other, but it just couldn't work out. With serious eyes, I said that was sad, and moved a bit closer and asked her why not. She just turned away and said she didn't want to talk about that.

A group of children were playing in a small playground nearby, their mothers looking on, and she mentioned she didn't understand children. I thought this might have been an effect of her unhappy childhood, and replied that I didn't understand them much either. "If I ever have kids," I said. "I don't want to have them until they're thirty and they're rich." "I love this," she then said, pointing to a tree stump with a series of gargoyle-like faces carved into it. I agreed that it was pretty interesting.

She asked me what I intended to do, now that I had left the bookstore, and I said that I wasn't really sure but I supposed I could always go back to waiting tables, and by the way, I hoped that I, too, would get some work done on my Gesamtkunstwerk (but, to maintain some measure of mystery, I added, "that is another story altogether"), and hopefully, find a better-paying, more interesting job (though I suspected that I'd soon be pulling espressos in one of the yuppie coffee shops that were springing up throughout the neighborhood). In the few days since I quit, I had done little, however, spending my days taking long, aimless walks, and laying in bed, thinking about her. I did not think it would be prudent to tell her this. So I said that I had been reading and visiting museums and listening to music and she asked me what I liked, and so I ran off a litany of famous and obscure artists and bands, a list that I had compiled precisely to answer the question of what kind of music I liked, which every woman I went out with seemed to ask, and added, almost as an afterthought, Wagner.

"Wagner?" she asked.

"Richard Wagner. The composer," I replied. "Of operas, music dramas."

"I don't believe you," she said.

"Really. It's true. I developed a fondness for him when I was an undergraduate romantic. I turned off the lights and listened to opera while fading on over-the-counter cold remedies and weeping sometimes," I confessed. "It was a very good year."

"That's sick," she said, and I thought she was joking.

"Well, yes," I replied, "that accounts for the drugs."

"That's not what I meant."

I figured that she thought that I was lying, faking my interest, perhaps as a way to impress. "I admit it was a bit pretentious," I told her. "But, such things are bound to happen when you're off for four years in some terribly expensive liberal arts college. As you well know."

"Know what?

"I mean, okay, fine, it's pretentious and overbearing, but I liked it and I still do."

"Don't you know that he was an anti-Semite?" she asked.

"Yeah," I said. "So?"

"So?" she repeated. Her eyes narrowed and I could sense that she was sizing me up. "Doesn't that bother you?"

"Not if I don't worry about it," I said.

"I don't understand you," she continued. "You sit around and read Céline, you listen to Wagner. Who do you think you are?"

"Is this an ontological question?" I asked.

"What about your ancestors?" she demanded.

"My ancestors?" I said. "What about them?"

"How do you think they would feel?"

"I don't know. I never knew them."

"Funny," she retorted.

"It's true. Besides," I added, "they're dead."

"That's not the point," the dark woman said.

"What is the point?" I asked. I just wanted her to shut up with her disputation and get her back to my apartment where I could show her the mark of my ancestors. I looked at her straight on as she spoke, to signal sympathy, sincerity, and romantic feelings.

"The point is," she began, now appearing a bit upset, "that you...you are...that by your behavior you are betraying your people."

"My people."

"Yes."

"What people?"

"The Jews."

"I am betraying the Jews?"

"Yes," she said.

"I don't see what the Jews have to do with this."

"Everything," she said. "You are betraying your heritage."

"How so?"

"Because you listen to Wagner."

"Because of Wagner I am betraying the Jews."

"Yes."

"Oy vey," I said.

A bird sang nearby, and in the distance I could hear the barks of dogs.

"You know," she said. "Hitler loved Wagner."

"Hitler loved children and dogs," I replied, pointing over to the playground. "Should we ban them too?"

She proceeded then to inform me of my moral flaw, how I was corrupting myself by means of this Wagnerian immersion, that in doing so, I was siding with the enemy and being forgetful of history and so on, and I said, come on, that's silly, and she said, no, it's not, and that I was a bad Jew, and I agreed and said yes, that may be so but it is my life, after all, and if I want to be a bad Jew it is my business and besides many Jews before me liked Wagner. Gustav Mahler and Leonard Bernstein came to mind, as did James Levine and Daniel Barenboim, and the guy who conducted the premiere of Parsifal at Bayreuth was a Jew as well. In fact, Wagner himself handpicked him for the gig, though he did ask him to convert. I added that I was sure I could come up with a more extensive list given some time to research the issue, there being an entire tradition of Jewish Wagnerites, and there were even those that wanted to perform Wagner in Israel nowadays, which would mean that if merely listening to Wagner made one a bad Jew, well then these guys had a lot to answer for.

She was unimpressed.

"Look," I said. "I really don't think my listening to Wagner has all the cosmic significance you suggest. That he was a bit of an asshole does not mean that we should ban his music or burn his CDs. I mean, most great artists were kind of jerks, right? So why don't we get some coffee. Or better, some wine? I think I can use a drink right now." There was that bottle of wine waiting for us in my room, after all, and, despite its perils, her anger was somehow inciting. I had not considered her in such a state in my previous meditations, and was now sorry and a bit surprised that I hadn't, for was not beauty heightened at times of anger? Yes, I thought, I've located the magic spot, her Achilles' heel. Her hatred belies her desire. I thought of Isolde and the love-potion. I knew, though, that this park was not the optimum locale for a scuffle, and was about to suggest that we retire to my apartment when she preempted me: "Well," she said, staring at her watch, which she wore on a leather cord around her neck. "I've got to get to work."

"You work today?"

"I'm filling in for someone."

"Who?" I asked. She looked at me cruelly with her crooked black eyes, and I knew it was best not to press the issue. "I'm just curious, that's all."

"A new guy. I forgot his name."

We began to walk back towards the street. I knew if there was time for my move it was now and, though a bit worried that she might actually be serious about the Wagner thing, which would be a shame, really, as I had had this fantasy about slowly screwing to the gorgeous "Liebestod" in *Tristan und Isolde*, bodies struggling, intertwining to the swelling, undulating, anticipating yet unresolving powerful waves of music, culminating in an orgasm of sound, yet, thinking that our argument was really flirtation in another mode, and her anger really magnetic, only barely masking her desire, I touched the small of her back with my left hand, which, admittedly, isn't the more subtle move, and as I did, she stiffened, turned to glare at me with hostile black eyes, and said, "What are you doing?"

"Nothing," I said, quickly removing my hand.

As we walked out of the park, as if in revenge, I tried to whistle the prelude to *Tristan*, for I had always found it exquisitely, painfully beautiful, an expression of the most profound longing and desire, and I thought that a hint of the melody might make her reconsider or would gently taunt her, but there was no note to which I could grab hold, and I ended up sounding a bit foolish.

She left me at the intersection saying "I'll see you" without looking back and strolled off, hands in pockets, southbound down Riverside Drive.

I stood there for a moment, watching her figure fade into the darkening afternoon, in suspension, like the famous *Tristan* chord. After a few moments, when she was no longer visible, I turned, tossed my backpack over my shoulder, and headed back into the park.

As I walked back along the path, I noticed a crowd of people gathered about where the children were playing. One of kids was sobbing while the others looked on with cold faces, not unlike those carved into the tree trunk. I walked on, in no hurry to get back to my room, now that I was alone and without chance of amorous adventure. I decided to continue through the park, amid the intermittent birdsong and the banter of dogs, thinking by chance I might run into a pretty girl who would strike up a conversation with me and would be more inclined to listen to Wagner.

I strolled along among the squirrels that stared warily at me and then turned to run up a tree. It seemed exorbitantly silly that a mere mention of a controversial nineteenth century composer of operas would destroy any chance of an intimate encounter. A squirrel turned and, part way up the trunk, peered down and studied me with his black, distrustful eyes.

"Well, what do you think of that?" I asked him. He watched me with black eyes, not so different in color, I reflected, than those of the dark woman. I walked a bit closer to the tree and the creature did not move but continued to stare down at me with reproach.

"Is that a good reason to cut short a love affair?" I inquired. "Don't you think that she should at least give it a listen? Who is she to give me a hard time because of my taste in classical music, this woman who reads the novels of Dostoevsky, not exactly a goody-goody liberal nice guy when it came to Jews, and lived with a guy named Ulandt? What kind of name is "Ulandt" anyway? Do you think for a minute he was of the Levantine persuasion? And what the hell does she mean that they "loved each other but could do so no longer?" So who is the greater criminal then? Me, who listens to Wagner, and not the operas al the way through, mind you (I'm not one of those crazy devoted Wagnerites, after all, and who has the time for that anyway?), but the good parts, particularly that sublime prelude from *Tristan*, which is probably one of the most beautiful pieces of music ever written, by gentile or Jew? Or her, self-proclaimed defender of the Jewish race, a woman who gallivants with good Prince fucking Ulandt of Sweden? I at least make no grand claims.

"I…" I told the squirrel, still watching intently, "I am at least somewhat honest."

The squirrel continued to gaze at me, mocking me with unflinching eyes. I kicked the base of the tree so it would scurry up the tree and go away.

He did not move.

"Fuck you," I said.

I returned home pissed-off and wounded by the notion that I was rejected because of an odd affinity toward romantic opera, wondering if I should call her or if she would call me. I did not listen to Wagner when I was cozy in my apartment nor could I get back into reading the book I had carried faithfully all afternoon. I did have my pride to consider. Fuck it, I thought. What am I thinking? She isn't even that pretty. Nevertheless, after drinking half the bottle of cabernet, I resolved to stop in at the bookstore in a few days, ostensibly to pick up my final paycheck. When I did, she greeted me coolly.

"Are you angry at me?" I asked.

"No," she said, and turned away to deal with a customer.

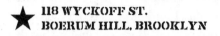

DOCUMENT

BY GABRIEL COHEN

I should have made a film about my landlords. A documentary. A document. It would have started in darkness. You would have heard an odd *skrik...skrik...skrik*. Fade in on the inside of a window; zoom close to peer down into a backyard. A man pushes a hand mower across a tiny lawn. Words appear:

Brooklyn. Early 1990s.

The man hitches up his pants, draws the mower back for another push. Frankie: He's old and stocky, with unruly white hair; a cowlick sticks up. He wears cracked shoes, paint-stained chinos, an age-thinned beige shirt.

The yard lies at the center of a block of brick row houses in Boerum Hill; it's separated from the neighbors' gardens by a chain-link fence. Over one side drapes a trail of impossibly bright roses, a shock of magenta in this world of summer green. A picnic table at the far end sits next to a fig tree, its broad leaves rounded like patterns for a fat person's glove. Wind sifts down through the trees in the center of the court; in the corner, an orange swing-chair creaks.

LOST AND FOUND

Sparrows chirp aggressive single notes—Brooklyn birds are too tough to sing.

Beyond the block, a distant swirl of traffic, voices, sirens. Every now and then a plane slowly tears the sky overhead, La Guardia Airport-bound. Some of the neighboring yards are carefully tended, with fancy gardens. In Frankie's, a few weeds spray up and the flowers, stubborn perennials, seem random, but the place is neat. A tabletop made out of the door of an old stove sits on a curlicued wrought iron base he found on the street. When it comes to lawn furniture, Frankie improvises. Three pots of basil perch on a slab of marble, which rests on two porcelain toilet tanks.

Over his head, up in the house, a face peeps out of a window, recedes.

Finished with the lawn, Frankie walks down the foot-wide concrete path sunk around the grass and pushes the mower into a shed at the back of the house. The walls are a patchwork of old boards, tar paper, and rusted metal. Inside, light filters through dusty windows onto rakes, clay pots, the hulls of dead wasps. Frankie travels through a basement hallway, past the open door of his workshop, where neat rows of coffee cans hold nuts, washers, bolts; his tools hang from time-stained sheets of pegboard.

He mounts the stairs in the dim light. At the top, he reaches down and tugs a string slung below the banister, clicking off the 40-watt bulb below. The ground floor hallway is also dim, illuminated only by a little daylight that struggles through the front door's narrow panels of frosted glass. The potted plant is plastic; Astroturf carpets the floor. Behind the mail slot sits a tray, also Astroturfed, like a tiny lawn. Under the solemn gaze of a little statue of the Miraculous Infant Jesus of Prague, Frankie continues on up the stairs.

On the second floor, he pushes a door open. Inside, his sister Rose bends down to pull something from an old oven. The stove is massive and streamlined, like the front end of a DeSoto. Rose reaches a hand back to support the base of her spine, turns, holds up an angel cake. She smiles a crinkly big-toothed smile, and her dentures shift, click. Her hair is white as sugar.

"Siddown," she says. "Have a piece a' cake." Her voice is deep, husky, kind.

She reaches up into a cabinet over the sink, lifts down a plate webbed with faint cracks over an enameled picture of Niagara Falls. From a shelf below the window, covered with the same delicately flowered beige paper as the walls, she pulls down a box of Lipton's tea. Next to it a stack of grocery coupons sits in a Tupperware container.

Rose crosses the cracked linoleum floor, which slopes toward the center of the room, and fills a teapot at the sink.

Frankie reaches into the refrigerator and pulls out a cold can of Pabst Blue Ribbon.

Rose shakes her head, puts the tea back in its place, and returns to a pot on the back of the stove. Every Wednesday she makes her macaroni and basil soup. She gets the basil from the garden, fresh.

The room is ripe with smells: herbs and garlic simmering in the pot; figs ripening in a bowl; the sour essence of old bodies in summer heat.

"Hey, Vincent," Frankie calls. "Cake's ready."

His brother shuffles out of the doorway; it was his face peering out of the window before. Vincent's slack smile reveals only a couple remaining teeth. His hands lift nervously from his belt to touch the buttons of his blue-and-green Madras shirt, which hangs open over an ancient undershirt. He peers shyly through heavy, black-rimmed glasses and runs a hand over his slick gray hair; in back it's faded sea-water green.

The brothers and sister sit in their usual chairs as they eat cake from their usual plates. They've lived in this house for seven decades. Frankie rules the yard and basement, Rose the kitchen, but the front parlor is Vincent's domain. That's where he sits in a spavined armchair by the window and watches life pass in the street outside.

Over the years it ebbs and it flows.

Now some of the brick houses across the way have been sand-blasted and resurfaced, the iron railings lining the stoops given a fresh coat of shiny black paint. In front, bundles of swanky catalogs are bound in twine and set out at the curbs; new tenants push blue-eyed babies in massive strollers. But Vincent knows the street will never be completely fancied up, not with the public housing project looming around the corner; from the window he can see its towers glowing in the dusk like a honeycomb, squares of yellow and orange and red.

He sits in his chair. He has seen the stock market rise before, and seen it fall. Some day soon he won't be surprised to see the swanky catalogs disappear and the iron railings return to rust.

At night, he peers out from behind the curtains as two men meet outside the gate in front of the house, under streetlight filtering down through summer leaves. One offers money and the other palms something into his hand. They go their separate ways.

At midnight, couples conduct bitter traveling marital spats all down the street; Jeeps with tinted windows swing by broadcasting angry chants. Later still, the pop! pop-pop! of gunfire in the projects punctures Vincent's sleep. In the morning, when he goes down to sweep the sidewalk, he finds tiny brightly colored pieces of plastic. He doesn't recognize them, the stoppers of crack vials.

An ice cream truck endlessly repeats the same bars of the Maple Leaf Rag.

On holidays, a relative from Staten Island drops by. The stories flow like the shots of Seagrams 7. Frankie and Vincent talk about their early childhood in a Little Italy tenement, about the years they took a bus to Jersey every morning to work in a tool-and-die plant. Rose had a job outside the house, too, in a bakery out beyond Prospect Park.

"Oh, yeah." She grins shyly. "I had ta' get up at three in the mornin' ta take the bus up there. I used ta' work on the donut line. I got the job because of my brother-in-law Francis, he worked in the office. His wife was the supervisor, but we didn't get along. She wanted Francis ta fire me, but he wouldn't do it on account 'a my husband bein' his brother and all, so she was always lookin' ta make my job harder. Sometimes she used ta speed up the line, so I could hardly keep up, but I never said nothin'. Wouldn't give her the satisfaction."

She tells how she quit the job after twenty-seven years, one year shy of her pension, because the neighborhood was changing. One time a drunk accosted her outside the bakery, and her mother was afraid for her to take the bus anymore. She tells how her husband broke his back at his factory and how she supported them, how he finally had to go into the hospital for good, how she would visit him until he passed away.

Her brothers never married.

Vincent goes off to the parlor and comes back with a photo album. He sets it on the kitchen table and flips through the pages, stopping at a picture of him and Frankie in soldier's uniforms, the time they met up in Paris. He was on his way to Normandy after the invasion, and Frankie was on leave from being an orderly in an English field hospital for amputees. With an arm around each other, they smile at the camera, two Brooklyn boys.

In Manhattan, they've never gone above Times Square.

Vincent turns to a series of snapshots he took when his infantry unit liberated the concentration camp at Sachsenhausen. In one, he stands next to a pile of emaciated corpses. I've seen such images on TV before, but there's been a distance to them— they almost looked like cords of wood. With two of my landlords in the foreground, they look like human beings.

Vincent disappears into the back again and pulls out a prized possession. He opens a browning copy of *Life* magazine to a picture of a cobblestoned Paris square filled with people. They grin up at the photographer perched atop a light pole, hundreds of them, holding up copies of The Stars and Stripes with the banner headline "Victory Over Japan."

"Look," Vincent says. He extends a bony finger towards a face in the center of the crowd. It's his own face, solemnly gazing back at him across an ocean and nearly fifty years of time.

Just after sunrise, Rose and Frankie step out onto the sidewalk for their monthly trip to Atlantic City. (Vincent never travels; he stays behind, holding down the fort). Brother and sister trek up the street and around the corner, where they wait for the senior citizens' special bus.

Later in the morning, they stroll down the Jersey boardwalk as gulls swoop overhead, cawing into the wind. Frankie holds Rose's elbow and she clutches her purse against the shore breeze. Later still, her broad, shy face fills with wonder as a small avalanche of quarters clatters into the tray of her slot machine. But she and her brother are not really here for the gambling—they spend most of their day out in the salty air. On the way home, Frankie's tousled head droops forward in sleep as the bus rolls past the bizarre industrial moonscape sprouting alongside the Jersey Turnpike, stalky refinery towers winking red through the haze of dusk.

After they're safe at home, a car alarm whoops out in the street in front of the house. Just before midnight, bottles clink as they're dropped into recycling bins. The next day, the important clang of the front gate announces the mailman; church bells ring in noon. Another day; another year.

I never made the film.

One night, Rose turned away from the stove complaining of a pain in her chest. Her brothers continued their pinochle game at the kitchen table while she trudged off into her bedroom, lay down on her neatly made bed, and died.

Four years later, Vincent went to the doctor to check out a pain in his stomach. The x-rays showed it was riddled with cancer. Vincent was gone within a week.

"We lost Vincent," his brother informed me, out of the blue.

"Where was he the last time you saw him?" I wanted to ask, until I realized what he meant.

One week after September 11, 2001, Frankie had a stroke and lay on his kitchen floor for hours until I found him. He survived, but was quite infirm. He had to go out to the Midwest to live with relatives, had to leave his beloved Brooklyn house. He eats store-bought soup out there now, and he's getting very old, fading into the unrecorded history of the world.

A CAB DRIVER PREPARES

BY ANDY CHRISTIE

One morning, a week before the 2004 Republican National Convention, I took a cab to my studio in the Film Center Building on Forty-fifth and Ninth Avenue. My cabdriver was wearing a natty chauffeur's uniform, cap and all. Once we got going, he smiled at me in the rearview mirror and said, "I guess you're wondering why I'm all dressed up." He was wrong. I wasn't wondering anything. I just assumed he was a typical New Yorker: a little nutty. But I didn't want to hurt his feelings, or cause him to snap, so I said, "Yeah, I was curious about that." And he launched into a well-rehearsed soliloquy.

"When I lost my corporate driver's job last year, I traded in a black car for a yellow one, but I didn't see any reason to stop providing professional, courteous, *positive* service to my clients. Think of me as an icon on your computer desktop. A "POSITIVITY" icon. If you're feeling down, just double-click on me."

Then he passed a homemade computer-generated greeting card through the bulletproof divider. It said, *"Thank You..."* in fancy script on the front above a bucolic scene of swans on a lake.

LOST AND FOUND

The message continued inside: "...*for being a valued client! I have appreciated serving you. Paul J.—Your POSITIVE Cabby.*" And despite my usual cynicism, the guy actually brightened my morning. I imagined him sitting in front of his computer late at night, trying to decide between decorating his card with swans or butterflies. And the thought made the world look a little better. I smiled and thanked him for the card. He gave me a dapper tip of the hat in the mirror, and drove for a few blocks in silence. When we reached a congested intersection near Port Authority, he leaned on the horn and said, "Once the convention gets here next week, this traffic's gonna be a fucking *nightmare*."

And I was back in a familiar world.

FOREIGN TONGUES AND NATIVE TOENAILS

BY SAMANTHA V. CHANG

Pretty much every woman in New York City gets her nails done And why not? There are at least six or seven per two-block radius, give or take; it's a cheap and standard luxury here, courtesy of lots of supply, lots of demand.

They all are pretty much the same: seven to ten mostly Asian women sitting in an assembly line; bent over sudsy feet and chipped fingernails, toiling together in unison: not unlike ants in an ant farm. Many of them have varying degrees of red, burgundy and orange highlighted hair, and you hear that slipper-on-bare-floor scuffle. Calves are slapped in varying shades of pallor and depth, form and transparency, knuckles are popped into place while their owners' eyes gaze into unthoughtful space, fixated upon misspelled advertisements on cramped walls. Upon entry, the chorus greets you: "Pick-uh-culla! Pick-uh-culla!" as the hum of efficiency drones within this well-oiled machine. Gossip and chatter ensues among the manicurists, often in Korean or Chinese, with a sidelong glance here and there at a strange or difficult customer, or at the odd-woman-out Chinese among Korean staff, or vice-versa.

But, then there is me, and I am neither strange nor difficult. "Spa pedicure today?"

How much?

"Fitty dolla."

I politely shake my head no. "Okay, next time, you do." The nail-shop chatter builds momentum as I sit on my foot-bath throne; I get a couple of sidelong glances and the "Lalalala-oh" or "Num-ni-ya-ya." As I flip through the pages of US Weekly, I scan my brain with its many thoughts of bemused paranoia, "Yeah, so what? I am cheap: I never get the spa pedicure. The twenty dollar manicure/pedicure combo suits me just fine…the bottoms of my feet are filthy, but that's what wearing flip-flops in a damp subway station will do for you…I wish she'd stop tsk-ing at my leg stubble! She should try shaving her legs on a regular basis with two kids and a pig-pen husband!" Alas, none of these things are chatter-worthy.

The fact is that I am Korean, but really, a fake one. Being adopted at the wee age of four months, with a Midwestern Ger-man-Catholic mom, I speak no Korean, except for "Hello," "How are you," "Thank you," and "fart,"—the little I retained in a pamphlet ("fart" was learned from a twelve-year-old) on a chance journey to Seoul.

Twelve years later, the pamphlet-learning is a bit rusty, and I can count to ten in German: I am neither immersed (nor embraced) in either Nature's or Nurture's worlds. I must say, I do feel some relief if the manicurists are Chinese, as then I am not expected to converse in my "native" tongue, and we all leave well enough alone. But even that has a caveat: the adoption agency speculated my birth father may have been Chinese, but that's a different story and all too vague to even talk about.

Most of the time, I just happen to pick those darn Korean nail shops, and when I perform the uncouth non-reaction to their friendly inquiries and banter (all in Korean, of course), I get the whole quizzical-pity routine. In resigned embarrassment, I slump further in my seat and disappear into the latest tabloid disaster.

Sometimes I am not let off so easily and become the victim of some friendly interrogation: "Lalalalalala-oh?" Huh? "Lalalalalala-oh!" I don't understand. "You Korean, yes?" Yes? "Lalalalala-oh?" "I'm sorry…" I am a nice shade of pink now and a few curious eyes look up from the tabloid pages: Is she rude? Is she stupid? "Ahhh, you no uh-speak-eh Kah-lee-en." Then she has an epiphany and triumphantly exclaims even louder: "You born here!" This offers her and all of the others a suitable excuse for my Eastern cultural ineptitude: I'm an ignorant, Americanized brat of privilege. But, no such luck. I was born in Seoul. I came here at four months of age: at this point, my answers become so low and quiet, they are almost inaudible. Hers however, boom in annunciation and contrast to my discomfort: a not-so-funny comedy of errors. "Where your parent at—they in Korea?" Uh, yeah…I think so… She misses the subtlety of the last part: "When you go visit them?" My feeble attempts to be polite enough to answer her inquiries, while retaining a sense of anonymity are failing miserably…I went to Seoul about thirteen years ago.

"You see your parent thirteen year ago!" Scowls and gasps ripple down the line. I hear low1decibel gossip rumbling. Sweat beads are on my nose now. My relaxation is melting in the foot tub along with my heel calluses.

Here comes the climax and the end, as I hiss through gritted teeth: "I. Am. Adopted."

By now, the entire salon knows about me and my angst about being a "banana"—a Chinese friend summed the phrase up to me one night over cocktails: I'm "yellow on the outside, white on the inside." My pedicurist pityingly pats my leg and just smiles a curious little smile. I am irritated and slightly angry now and cannot enjoy the calf massage. Why don't they ask the hard-ass black woman with the size eleven feet next to me if she speaks African, and then chastise her if she does not? Why doesn't the blond girl with the iPod and yoga mat get the third degree about her childhood, socioeconomic condition and parental relationship? For them and everyone else (including Koreans who speak Korean and Chinese who speak Chinese), a pedicure is simply, a pedicure. There is minimal conversation, minimal interest. For me, perhaps it's their opportunity for a first-hand view into a more-American-than-Asian American's life: accent-free and void of cultural resonance and richness; having the audacity and inward guilt of having "your own people" massage your tired and dirty, roughened feet.

I can't help but notice the running trend within Asian culture of willingly abandoning one's own: blond Pamela Anderson-esque girls in Tokyo, ghetto-fabulous Filipino rapper girls with "booty." These are two extreme examples of Asians not really into being Asians, and fascinating parodies of popular culture. I am the polarity of this: longing for that ability to communicate and identify with who I am.

The latex exam gloves snap off. I guess these days, you can never be too careful. She helps me down from my foot-bath throne and carries my shoes and handbag to the manicure table. No more questions now, we are in our own comfortable worlds of real Asian/fake Asian, manicurist/customer.

I come armed and prepared for these encounters. I work the coy and enigmatic "I speak a little bit." Then, I quickly slump into my seat and dive into the magazine, giving un-averted attention to nonsense, while hiding my sheepish little smile…it works brilliantly for me. The chatter and laughter usually stops. (Yeah, yeah…good idea: let them think I am antisocial, as opposed to ignorant.) The leg pat comes only when it is supposed to, when the lotion gets slathered on my legs, right before the polish. There is no illicit gossip and commentary: "What if she understands us?"

This parachute has holes in it, as the Asian affinity thing often extracts intimate and public details about if I am married, who is my hubby and what does he do, how tall is he and what is his race; how are our finances, do we have any children; why am I so thin, issues of my background and its voids are always a factor in the equation. Nonetheless, in the end, the strategy is sound enough.

The plain truth is that you don't have to maneuver the mechanics of language to understand universal logic. The rude woman yelling into her cell phone, smudging her nails carelessly only to have them repainted twice, while holding up the five-person wait when there are not enough chairs and outdated magazines to go around doesn't require an interpreter. It's understood in all of our minds:

"Move along, crazy bitch…"

And so do we all.

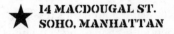

14 MACDOUGAL ST.
SOHO, MANHATTAN

LE GAMIN

BY ANDREA BRUNHOLZL

As almost everyone knows, a little family of French bistros lies scattered over the lower half of Manhattan, as if arranged by the single pass of a great pepper mill. Named Le Gamin (save one Le Deux Gamin), each is a neighborhood place, a paradox of quiet and noisy, sunny and dark, boring and piqued, where woody rosemary stems turn your plate of crepes into a miniature Provençal landscape and your drained café au lait reveals *le gamin* himself at the bottom.

People say their histories are written on the body. Most New Yorkers would revise that to include the menus, salt shakers, and chairs of their favorite restaurants. A whole mini-life of my own occurred at the Le Gamin on MacDougal Street, which has sadly since moved to Houston. MacDougal was quieter, and there was only room for two tables on the sidewalk, which made it a bit like winning the lottery when you got one, which I did on my first try. It was a charmed time, the beginning of a short-lived affair with a man six years younger who spoke French and sulkily wished I did too. It was our first meeting during the day. Lunch. I ordered the ratatouille crepe, and he had one with eggs and cheese, but what I remember is that he remarked that I'd made the better choice, and not playfully. His last girlfriend was Belgian, and he was still suffering even after two years, though he hid it from me well at first, holding my hand continuously through lunch, then pushing me (playfully this time) into the crooks of buildings so we could make out on his way back to work. It was a sweet and sexy time, but he still thought the world was his *moule*, while I had already learned that it's no use prying the closed ones open. In fact, they make you very sick.

After that ended, I would go alone to the MacDougal Le Gamin to write and drink coffee, or even for breakfast before work, and I would scan the French posters and plaques on the walls, squinting to read the specials, written on a small blackboard in a nearly illegible European hand. You could find these things at The Mall of America, but the items in Le Gamin are original. They had a life in France, then immigrated. The bathroom was papered with labels from French wine and a few discreet scribbles, mostly the names of tourists and the year. But the really irreplaceable thing about that location was that the front windows had been shop windows, so an odd, revolving collection of French memorabilia sat staring out at the sidewalk, a ceramic bunny, a small sled, sometimes an interesting shoe.

When I started a real relationship with P., a man closer to my age, this Le Gamin became our place. I can still feel the heat through the back of the chair, after having frozen ourselves walking into the wind down Prince and side-stepping our way through the tightly knit tables to the gloriously free one next to the radiator, which hissed and sputtered through our entire conversation. He always drank tea, and it would come in the same au lait bowl, the steeping wand slowly turning the steaming water green or brown or blue-black when the tea was blackberry. Because the MacDougal spot didn't have a liquor license, people, Europeans mostly, would bring in bottles of wine and compulsively share it, if only because your table was within inches of theirs. I soon discovered the apple tatin, which comes with crème fraîche, a combination as warm and slippery as sex. P. wasn't much of a sweet tooth, so I would eat the whole thing before we pushed off again into the icy night, leaving only a pool of buttery liquid and a sprig of mint on the plate.

In summer, it got hot and our Le Gamin had no air conditioning, or else it was always broken, but we went anyway, and sweltered, and had salad niçoise because of the cold eggs and icy haricot vert, trying to finish the slightly crispy squares of tuna before the daubs of mayonnaise melted completely. When we won a spot on the sidewalk, the table was small enough for me to easily lean over to kiss P. or cup his cheek in my hand. This table also allowed us to stay on the look out for Patti Smith, who lived catty-corner and was frequently on the stoop, and listen to snippets of French or Italian or Long Island spoken by patrons leaving the place. We could quietly admire his BMW motorcycle, too, hopped up on its kickstand across the street, the headlight ignoring us, the entire vehicle sleek and shield-less for summer riding. When I still had room, even in the heat, I ate the warm apple tatin, and he had more tea.

Sometimes we fought, but that was mostly when we sat indoors, and mostly in winter, when my job would get to me and the fact that despite the years passing, he lived on the Upper West Side and I lived in Brooklyn. I cried there more than once about things in my life that weren't happening, between us and in general, but even then I felt grateful that I could always count on the salmon crepe with basil, and the crème fraîche, and his face across from me at the table.

P. and I went to Le Gamin on MacDougal almost weekly for years, but then it closed and moved to Houston. It was one of those strange coincidences. Our relationship was closing, too, and though we did go the one on Houston a few times, this period of time and the two of us became history.

My next Le Gamin relationship, like the first, was relatively short and ill-fated. The new one and I and his darling little boy went to Le Gamin on Houston one hot day in August, and I fed the little one eggs and bits of croissant and took him to the bathroom to change his pants, which he'd wet because he was in training. Afterwards, the new one walked ahead of us down

Houston, then when we caught up, he spoke to me sharply about not keeping a tight enough grip on the toddler's hand. As I stood there deciding it was not worth defending myself, I noticed we were at the corner of MacDougal Street. I looked down it briefly, scanned the sidewalk for Patti Smith, and realized there was no choice but to move on.

SWIMMING WOMEN
BY ANDREA BRUNHOLZL

I first came to Williamsburg in 1992, to visit a painter friend's studio. He would travel there every day from the Upper West Side, a long but worthwhile trip because the studio space was so cheap. Back then, the crowd of people that got off with us at the Bedford Avenue L stop disappeared quickly and mysteriously, and we walked down empty streets with nothing but shreds of paper blowing around. The industrial buildings and strings of attached houses we passed all seemed oblivious to the Manhattan skyline across the river, as if it were a foreign place not even worth visiting, which is exactly what most people thought about Williamsburg back then.

In 1998, I found myself emerging from the same subway stop to sidewalks thronged with twentysomethings wearing clothes my hip Aunt Jackie from Ireland wore in 1975. Some even wore long pigtails, like hers, and there was lots of suede everywhere. I was only thirty-three, but in that scene I suddenly felt old and matronly, especially since I'd only recently cut my long, straight hair into something too neat and tidy. The haircut had been one of those preliminary, obvious-to-everyone-but-you signs of a much larger transition: my marriage was breaking up, had broken up really, though I wasn't ready to face it. I was simply looking for a sublet to spend some time away, on my own.

I took a sublet in Williamsburg. Before long, I had set up a little life for myself, with a new routine that included a morning swim at the Metropolitan pool—just across the street from the loft I was sharing with a roommate on North Third (the same street I'd first walked down in 1992). Swimming was a way to stave off the sadness that would eventually envelope me every day, as the reminders of my married life accumulated, springing up from mundane things, moving me to tears.

On a day off from work, a Tuesday, I went to swim a bit later than usual. At first the pool was as crowded as ever, but near 10:00 a.m. all the thrashing, ready-to-race-you men suddenly cleared out. It seemed too good to be true, so I asked the lifeguard if I needed to get out, too. He was hanging up some thick, living-room drapes on a long rod to obscure the front windows looking out onto the lobby.

"No, you're a girl," he said. "You can stay."

I was a little startled when the Hasidic women started coming in, their shaved heads in puffy, old-fashioned shower caps, their bodies draped in flowered housedresses with long sleeves, the kind that snap or button down the front, with two patch pockets at the thigh. Their only traditional pool accessory that I could see were flip-flops, which they lined up carefully along the tiled wall.

As they came into the pool, one by one, using the ladders at either side of the shallow end, their swimming dresses ballooned up to the surface and floated there for several seconds before the water soaked the fabric and dragged it back down. I couldn't help but think of women drowning themselves in their housecoats, too depressed that day to even get dressed. But soon it was clear how happy these women were to be together, laughing and gossiping as if they'd saved up their stories all week.

More and more women kept coming, and I realized that there was going to be very little swimming going on. I imagined that this was their hour away from duties and children and prayers, when they could all sit in a huge bath together and talk freely. Even their bodies were as free as they could be: No wigs, no stockings. Now I understood the curtains. Men were not allowed to see them this way.

I don't know if it was their hairlessness or their playfulness together, but they exuded innocence, which was probably the desired effect of the shaving and the covering up. They didn't look anything like the contained, competent Hasidic women I would see on the subway, pushing their well-behaved toddlers in strollers and wearing shiny, chestnut-colored wigs, mid-calf skirts, and well-made shoes.

I swam slowly toward the shallow end, keeping my head up because the pool was now thick with bodies, and I didn't want to run into anyone. The women made room for me to pass. That was as much acknowledgement as they gave me. I didn't take offense at being ignored, but I felt an excitement about the potential to bridge that distance. It would only take a smile, even a look. But there was none.

In the shower, I took off my suit to soap up as usual. Because they moved much more slowly, only the older women were left in the locker room. Their energy was different from the younger women, more natural and relaxed. A heavy woman in a terrycloth turban fastened with a brooch yelled "Ooooo, Kalt!" when her bare feet hit the cold shower floor, then she looked around and giggled good-naturedly at herself, her eyes including mine as they traveled from face to face.

I couldn't help but watch these older women as I shampooed my hair, then realized that I was being watched, too, by a small and wizened old woman who dressed like the others but wore a more modern rubber swim cap, the snap strap undone and dangling to her shoulder. She had bright eyes, sharp like a professor's, and when I smiled at her, her gaze wandered over my body, and she let out a delighted grunt before turning away. I couldn't tell whether her look had been mildly sexual, or if it was merely her own brief celebration of a woman's body, unconfined. It didn't matter what it was, because it had left me happy. I dried off and got dressed, feeling for the first time that I wasn't a foreigner in Williamsburg anymore.

BROOKTI & ME:
A STORY OF ADOPTION
BY BETSY BERNE

Brookti came from Ethiopia eight months ago when she was around two. Initially I'd tried to adopt domestically, but it turns out that adopting in the United States as a single mother, aside from being a twenty-first century version of some kind of slave trade, (i.e. black/interracial children are "a third of the price" of Hispanic children), and assuming you're not a celebrity or loaded, is a slow and ludicrous nightmare.

So when I came across an article about adoption programs in Ethiopia, I thought, why not? Not because I knew much about Ethiopia or Africa, although I had taken my only liberal arts class while at art school on the history of Africa and had recently read a lot about the genocide in Rwanda. Friends who'd been to Africa had traveled to enclaves of wealthy white American and European quasi-hippies in Kenya and had seemed most disturbed by the extinction of the animals by the nasty poachers. I cringed when they raved about how beautiful the "people" were in the same breath as how beautiful the countryside was.

It wasn't the idea of "exotic" Ethiopia and its "exotic" people that caught my attention. It was common sense. Here was a country with plenty of orphans who needed parents. So I called Americans for African Adoptions, Inc. in Indianapolis (which turned out to be an excellent agency run by a superhuman woman Cheryl Carter-Shotts) and that is how I found Brookti.

I chose Brookti from a list of available children because she was delivered to the orphanage on my birthday. She was described as "tiny, eighteen to twenty-four months, hepatitis B positive, able to stand for a few seconds." After I'd claimed her, it turned out she was no longer hepatitis B positive, but that she still wasn't walking and they were worried she never would, although there was no specific diagnosis. (It also turned out nothing was known of her origins except that she'd been found in Adwa, the city where the Ethiopians—citizens of one of the two countries in Africa never colonized by Europeans—beat back the Italians for the final time. This means that Brookti is a member of the Tigrays, the original ruling tribe, no surprise there.)

Six agonizing months of waiting and pictures and videos followed, and in May 2003, tiny Brookti arrived at Newark Airport and tottered into my arms with a huge smile and huge red sneakers. (The huge smile was a fake-out; she was sobbing bitterly moments later in the car). Eight months later, she is seven inches taller and has twenty-four pairs of shoes (at press time) in which to show off her particular "don't mess with me" strut, and in ways I will subsequently demonstrate, in which to reduce little blond white boys to tears.

It was not an instantaneous process, neither Brookti's learning to strut nor Brookti's inadvertent habit of reducing little blond white boys to tears. It was a gradual process. As was the attachment process between Brookti and myself (some of which I have blocked out, such as Brookti's initial distrust/distaste of me, which manifested itself in a mute, pissed off Brookti or a loud, wailing pissed off Brookti or a generally going-nuts pissed off Brookti.) It is well documented that the attachment process is a dicey affair when a child is adopted as a toddler, especially one who has not had a stable background, i.e. been shuttled around to various orphanages, etc. Brookti was (and still is) highly unusual (and highly intelligent, of course). By the end of one month she had become my third leg, although not necessarily an obedient one In fact, she was a goddamn stubborn mule third leg—bossy, and some would say, aggressive.

Which brings us to another gradual process: my growing distaste for white people, females in particular (which could very well be part of a growing distaste for modern mothers in general). And that other gradual process: black females distrust/distaste of me…as well as the eventual championship of the women (mostly the babysitters) I've had a chance to win over—yet another gradual process in the bizarre world of race and class relationships/warfare.

EPISODE 1

I realized I was starting to hate white people (females in particular) when one prissy member of the race (of which I too am a member, in this case a Jew) yelled at my two-year-old daughter Brookti (who is black, in this case a genuine African direct from the old country) for pointing her finger at said white person's little boy, who had begun crying (the kid was clearly a pussy), and telling my daughter it was "impolite to point."

I realized it again when the two of us were trapped at a birthday party in an indoor playground, sitting on the sidelines with the babysitters—Brookti's people (who were rapidly becoming mine)—after Brookti had returned from a scuffle with yet another blond little boy in tears and another blonde mother glaring at the offender. Brookti is inordinately gregarious, some might say bossy, some might even say rather aggressive (as mentioned earlier). But my feeling is that two-years-old is two-years-old. It takes one to know one.

I realized my distaste was not abating after the fiftieth time a grinning Caucasian had saluted Brookti with "Hey girl (or girl-friend)'" usually accompanied by a hearty "Give me five!" Perhaps all two-year-olds are greeted with a grinning "Hey girl (or girlfriend)!" and a hearty "Give me five!" Perhaps I am becoming as paranoid as a black person, but I don't think so, at least not according to my source, Amowei, Brookti's morning babysitter.

The first time I realized that some black women were not so terribly fond of us either was during an innocent visit to Buy Buy Baby (a plastic paradise of "gear" for sucker parents). Brookti had a high decibel breakdown in the line to pay which required repeated exits and re-entries from the line and not one of the cashiers (black) would make an exception for the crazy white woman who had committed the sin of perpetrating a misbehaving black child on the American public (a misbehaving black child in public is unheard of). No, they looked at us disdainfully, if they deigned to look at all. Needless to say, the white people would not allow us back in line either. Finally, a kindly Puerto Rican took pity and waited on us.

Now the Asians: they really hate us…

EPISODE 2

I expected freaky racial—and class—"episodes," which are inevitably intertwined, when Brookti touched down. I knew the most common ones to expect and assumed I'd easily brush them off. What I didn't expect was how intricate the race/class hierarchies are, (I did expect the level of hostility on both sides), how fiercely protective I would be of Brookti (I knew I would be fierce, but not vitriolic), or how insanely defensive, or how ridiculously paranoid I would become. Actually, I probably knew all of the above, but when these "episodes" happen to you it's a different feeling altogether.

The first indications that it's a comically cruel world out there in upper middle class parentland became quickly apparent in gymnastics class. As everyone knows, New York City parents schedule two-year-old children for an inordinate amount of activities, which I, in pre-parent days, scoffed at, thinking, can't they just let the children entertain themselves? Three weeks of entertaining Brookti, primarily at the park, I was entertaining thoughts of homicide (against who I was undecided). This wasn't because I didn't enjoy Brookti's company—or the company of the lovely man who ran the park, Brookti's first and best friend, or his ten-year-old son, Brookti's first crush—but because I did not enjoy the company of the (mostly, but not all) prissy, humorless, judgmental parents who at the first sign of a toddler scuffle or theft will dive in and cause fullscale warfare. The more sensible babysitters, of course, do no such thing; they sit back and wait until necessary, i.e. when fisticuffs occur. And, as intimated earlier, Brookti initiated many a scuffle and commited many a theft after her early mute period wore off.

Instead of committing homicide (against who I had finally decided: the next smarmy parent who lectured a wailing two year old, specifically my two year old, on sharing), I enrolled Brookti in a "gymnastics" class called Bouncing Babies or Trouncing Toddlers or something like that. I could hardly wait, and arrived at our first class all go-team-go, attempting to buddy-up with my fellow students (that is, parents/caretakers who are mandatory participants in all scheduled toddler activities, shows you how high the desperation factor is), hauling Brookti, who was still tottering but tottering valiantly, along with me. No luck with the buddying-up tactics, which included conspiratorial giggles, eye-rolls, and generally making an utter fool out of myself—nor with trying to force Brookti's peers to buddy up with her, which involved more foolishness.

Among the races represented were two Asian parent/daughter teams, a black babysitter with one of the dime-a-dozen little blond boys, and a parent/caretaker /little boy team, both of indeterminate race. The teacher was a determinedly bright and cheerful gal with an ominous, steely look in her eye whose welcome to Brookti was not nearly as effusive as it should have been. However, I was willing to give her the benefit of the doubt—for Brookti's sake.

Oh yes, Brookti. Who had arrived pissed off that I'd rushed her out of the house too quickly after her nap and who refused to take off her shoes as instructed. (She has had a severe shoe attachment from day one, not exactly discouraged by her mother). That was a big no-no. I had to wrench them off her feet which only made her more pissed off as we bounded onto the mats (a wailing Brookti, needless to say, was nowhere near bounding). I looked to my fellow mothers/caretakers for sympathy but they remained stony-faced, particularly the older black babysitter clutching her precious charge close to her breast like he was a Kennedy, glaring at Brookti as though she was going to infect Blondie.

Our next no no occurred as the various teams gathered in a circle to do our "stretching." (Show me a toddler who needs to stretch and I'll show you someone over forty without back pain.) Since I was wearing a sundress in the hundred degree heat, I couldn't stretch without the possibility of being arrested for public indecency (by the parental police force not the other one; again my fellow comrades were not having any sympathy) and Brookti couldn't begin to follow the rapid movements. Barely anyone could follow, since the teacher was moving as rapidly as Amtrak on a good day. Again, I looked around eagerly for some conspiratorial smirks or something. The black babysitter avoided my goofy grin assiduously, cheering on Blondie, who, wouldn't you know it, was the only child able to follow the teacher (and as quickly became clear, was the teacher's pet). The Asians were too busy trying to pry their children's recalcitrant limbs apart. The indeterminate caretaker or parent was too busy running after her child who wanted no part of the circle, which to me seemed promising, as far as potential friendship for either Brookti or me, since Brookti was trying her best to get the hell out of there too.

When the teacher asked me if I was Brookti's mother during the third class, I wanted to reply who the fuck else do you think would go through this charade? (Another thought running through my mind: I'm paying thirty-five dollars a class for this benign neglect/abuse?) Neither did it help that Brookti started each class so indignant that she had to take her shoes off, or that trying to tumble or walk on a balance beam at ninety miles per hour when when she was bemoaning her forsaken red shoes was the last thing on her mind. On the brighter side, I had learned my lesson and begun dressing like a good mommy should. I was also ready for an oxygen tank from trying to tail Brookti to each station, trying to force her through. However, I was still giving it my all. No one else crawled through the goddamn tube in order to get her balking child through.

As for friendship, still no acknowledgement from the Asians, who were moving grimly from station to station, and certainly none from the black babysitter who had eyes only for her beloved—who I had targeted for my first murder victim the day she would not help Brookti onto some idiotic apparatus, refusing to give even an encouraging smile, even when Brookti collapsed and fell. (I couldn't get there fast enough because I was too busy seething at the teacher, who I now actively despised, for not giving Brookti extra help, muttering "thirty-five dollars" under my breath like whatever the opposite of a mantra is). Meanwhile Blondie/Teachers Pet was getting wet kisses and hugs from not only his keeper, but the the aforementioned despicable teacher who I now referred to as Little Miss Hitler. (I think Amowei and I had one of our first bonding moments after I relayed the black babysitter story to her; she was as defensive as me, muttering, "She's just old school.") However, we'd made great strides with the indeterminate pair since the little boy was almost as bored and uncooperative as Brookti and the parent/caretaker was despairing/giggling along with me.

By the fourth class everyone except Brookti was moving from station to station at a relatively reasonable clip. It also seemed to me the indeterminate pair were trying to disassociate themselves from us...okay, maybe I was being a little oversensitive. And maybe I was asking too much, but couldn't Little Miss Hitler give Brookti a little extra attention? Just a little? By the fifth class, after we'd successfully engaged in the usual battle to wrench her shoes off, Brookti refused to venture on to the mats entirely, leading to another battle forty-five excrutiating minutes later when she refused to put them back on, which to my mind was two extra very unnecessary battles I was paying for, mind you, in an average battle-strewn day.

The next class, I said fuck the thirty-five dollars and we didn't attend. And when we arrived (guiltily) for the class after that, there was a new group of teams in place. The semester was over and we were sent home.

EPISODE 3: THREE YEARS ON

I've been reading a lot recently about our new "post-racial" world where we have "transcended race," where a black man is running for president and white people are actually voting for him. I'm wondering if we have transcended race so successfully, why are we reading so much about it's impact on the presidential contest? The black man in question, who also happens to be white, hasn't played the race card.

Judging from my own experience, we have not transcended race. I am white, my five-year-old daughter Brookti is black. It's frowned upon to live vicariously through your child, and rightly so, but when it comes to their skin color, it's impossible not to. Pre-Brookti, I felt fairly anonymous walking down the street in New York City. Now, walking together, people stare at us (or glare), essentially making non-verbal assumptions—or they make verbal assumptions (in other words, inappropriate comments).

When I first adopted Brookti, being new at the game, I would often lose my temper. Perhaps my outrage was due to the loss of an unconscious Caucasian sense of entitlement, in this case, the right to walk down the street obliviously. Back then I thought, "When I get more accustomed to this, I will learn to turn the other cheek." Nearly four years later, the amount of daily scrutiny we receive still causes me to lose it on occasion.

Like Senator Obama, my daughter is not African American, as they say, but African and American. Unlike Senator Obama, she is not "mixed race" (at least, not any more "mixed race" than anyone else in the modern DNA-obsessed world). I am frequently asked, "Is she mixed?" by strangers. Sometimes I am not even asked. Instead I am told.

I was told in no uncertain terms about six months ago when we were walking to pre-school. Brookti, who has loved wigs since her first Halloween, was sporting a blond ponytail wig. Suddenly there was a loud, furious voice from behind us: "That child should not be wearing a blond wig! She is half-black and you are denying her blackness!"

Instantly blind with disproportionate rage, I replied (illogically): "How do you know she's half-black?"

The woman repeated, "She is half-black. You are denying her heritage!"

I was about to retort: "She's blacker than you motherfucker, she's from the goddamn motherland!"—which might have ended the confrontation right then and there.

I refrained, however, and the ludicrous back and forth continued (with intermittent cursing from me, I confess), showing no sign of subsiding, until I said, "Get away from us!" at which the woman shouted: "What are you going to do about it?"

Visions of former junior high battles dancing in my head, I was about to regress to an oldie but goodie, "Meet you after school—reserve your spot in the graveyard!" Instead, I picked up Brookti, who was absolutely terrified and screaming bloody murder, and turned my back to shield her. Somehow we reached the end of the block, and for whatever reason, the woman takes off. I was practically in tears myself, holding a sobbing Brookti, when another woman who witnessed the scene comes over to console us, assuring us how nasty and unfair the woman had been.

For the "post-racial" record, both women were African American or African and American or, for all I know, they're mixed. For all I know, I'm mixed! Who knows and who cares!

Obviously, my own childish behavior, sinking to this low level na-na-na-na-na exchange, instead of just ignoring the woman, cannot be excused. I can only offer these irrational reasons. Number one, the goddamn blond wig had been a gift from a well meaning white friend living in the aforementioned "post-racial," dare I say, "fairy tale" world, which leads me to number two.

LOST AND FOUND

Don't think I hadn't anticipated this kind of incident occurring, leading to a long bitter battle with Brookti that very morning, pleading with her not to wear the wig. It was a battle wielded against my better moral judgment, because why shouldn't she wear a yellow wig (it could as easily have been pink, purple or red) since she, at five, has no idea of the political implications of blonde wigs and even if she were fifteen, why couldn't she wear a blonde wig? Furthermore, the word "'blonde" had not entered her somewhat limited vocabulary, unlike most American five-year-olds, who'd been here since birth.

Number two: after three years, I was so sick of hearing about the condition of Brookti's hair. It only served to create hair "issues" where there were none. I speak from experience as a dark, frizzy-haired Semite—although I know, I know, it's not the same. I'm aware of the complicated political and personal relationship black women have with their hair. Just as I'm aware of white people's moronic attitudes towards their hair, Brookti must have her hair touched or fondled by white people a hundred times a day. But here's the thing: my skin may be white but my fine motor skills are still perfectly adequate. I too have the ability to comb or brush all kinds of hair. I can buy hair products that detangle, that moisturize, that keep the frizz at bay. Take my word for it, attending to Brookti's hair was really not my most pressing problem, especially in her early days when her language delay and low muscle tone were far more pressing. And wigs are part of her goddamn heritage, because in Africa, many women wear wigs! As do many West Indian women and black American women in this country.

And most importantly, number three: how dare this woman attack me when she has no idea who I am or who Brookti is or what our relationship is and more egregiously, how dare she terrorize an innocent child?

Six months later, Brookti still talks about the "mean woman." She still asks me "why she was so mean" and is still hesitant about walking on that particular block. And I'm still telling the story to anyone who will listen. Most people do not want to listen.

They are quick to change the subject, which leads me to the conclusion that it's not really "cool" to talk about everyday racism here in New York City—not like it's cool to go to a benefit for Darfur or discourse on AIDS in Africa.

Recently, Brookti and I were on the way to school when a woman stopped us and said, "What a pretty skirt!" We smiled back, exchanged a little small talk, but the woman showed no signs of leaving. This is not unusual since Brookti and I have a million daily conversations on the run with people who I don't know, or if I do know, I don't remember half the time. I have become fairly adept at faking it. But when she said, "You don't remember me, do you?" I conceded defeat. She explained that she was the woman who'd witnessed the blonde wig incident . I thanked her again and she told us that her daughter who was Indian (East or West or American Indian I have no idea) had always loved long wigs when she was little.

Brookti had became petrified again. After the woman left, I proceeded to talk her down. I reminded her this was the "nice woman" and it was okay, that we'd never see the "meanie" again, and if by chance we did, we'd ignore her or call the police. After dropping Brookti off, I had to laugh at myself. In my oft-repeated story and in my mind's eye, I had the "nice woman" firmly planted in the "black people" camp. But this time she'd looked pretty damn white. If I hadn't become so hyper-conscious of race and color and hadn't been scrutinizing her for other ethnic blood coursing through her veins, I probably would have pegged her as white long ago. Did I make her black so that the story would have a happy ending? Or had race consciousness, or paranoia, or whatever you want to call it, caused me to completely lose my marbles?

Quite possibly the latter.

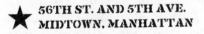

**56TH ST. AND 5TH AVE.
MIDTOWN, MANHATTAN**

WAITING ON MY AGENT

BY JILL BAUERLE

On a Friday night not too long ago, I approached a new deuce in my section, a couple. The woman seemed familiar; I pegged her as a publishing type. I don't know why I decided this, except that I wait on a lot of publishing types and they are different from other business people. She seemed intelligent and fashionable, someone who could reference both Dostoevsky and *Sex and the City* in the same phrase. I thought that perhaps she was someone I had waited on before. I brought drinks and conducted the usual menu FAQ, describing the skate wing and what Basque-style means in reference to the veal tongue. Meanwhile, a bass drum thudded in my ears. I recognized the woman's sultry voice. I was waiting on my agent.

I'm not the first nor will I be the last writer to wait tables. More illustrious authors in this category include Tennessee Williams, Michael Cunningham, who tended bar before he penned *The Hours*, and Cynthia Huntington, who was once told by her boss that she was the "best-educated barkeep in New York." While I don't aspire to become a "lifer" in the restaurant business, restaurant work has provided me with a flexible schedule and lucrative means to support myself while I work on a novel.

The last time my agent and I had met face to face had been four years ago at a restaurant near her office on the Upper West Side. She had just offered to represent my first novel. The next logical step, it seemed, was that my novel would sell—a work that had been four years in the making. No such luck. Now it was almost one full novel later and we were meeting in a restaurant again. Only this time I was wearing a designer uniform and a little leather pouch-belt full of pens, wine key, paper, and mints, and I was selling her on the poached salmon tartar.

It was 8 p.m. My section was slammed. In the back of the house, co-workers noticed the dazed expression on my face and asked, "Everything okay?"

"I think the woman at table seven is my agent," I told my friend Erica.

"What's her name? I'll check the reservation." Erica ran upstairs to the maître d'. A minute later she passed me in the crowded aisle as I balanced a tray of spent cocktails. She leaned against my shoulder and spoke into my ear.

"It's her."

"Fucking great," I murmured.

"Do you want me to take it?" she said. Erica, a Columbia graduate, understood the humiliation of serving an acquaintance. Her bane was that former classmates always sat in her section, usually out to dinner with their parents. Whenever this happened, we swapped tables. Being a servant, however high-paid, requires a delicate balance of pride and anonymity.

Just a week before, my agent and I had exchanged e-mails. She was planning to attend a reading series that I curated. Surely, when we met again, she would remember me from the restaurant and wonder why I hadn't introduced myself. Each time I approached her table I tried to forget my discomfort while she, not totally unaware that something was up, seemed to study my

face for clues. I decided to wait until the end of the meal, prefer-
ably when she was on her way to the door, to say something.

My biggest challenge was executing the rest of table seven's
dinner, and those of the tables around it, without disaster. Dou-
ble-checking my work, I saw that I had indeed mis-ordered table
seven's entrees. A trip to the kitchen to correct my mistake helped
me focus. Pots and plates clattered. The chef called out the tickets that kept rolling out of the printer. I realized that this was just
another night, one that I would get through. Soon I would be on
the F train heading back to Brooklyn, reading my *New Yorker*,
and recovering from eight hours of accumulated adrenaline in
my bloodstream.

After dessert, as my agent was walking towards the ladies
room, I stopped her beside a wine bucket. I had been holding
back for two hours now. What if I said something stupid? I reintroduced myself, starting with, "This is kind of awkward,
but—"

She smiled. Yes, she recognized me. What were the odds? We
stared at each other in disbelief, exhilarated by coincidence. She
was flushed from her meal.

"You know, after you came to the table the first time I told my
husband that I knew you were a writer."

Her husband's response had been, "Fiction or non?" but she
said she'd known the answer to that. I swaggered. I leaned into
the outside edges of my shoes. My hand gripped my leather
pouch-belt as if it were a holster.

"In fact," she said, "I told him that you might be one of my
clients. But I wasn't sure. You look different from the last time I
saw you."

She looked glamorous. Her hair was a bit longer. She was
wearing a low-cut dress. I told her that she looked great.

She was clasping her handbag daintily in front of her with
both hands, staring at my shoes. She too seemed embarrassed and
at a loss for words. Embarrassed to be waited on by someone she
knew in a professional context. And possibly embarrassed for
me.

"How long have you worked here?" she asked in a non-judgmental tone.

"A little over a year."

"It's a nice restaurant," she affirmed. "Our meal was great. Service was great too!"

I wanted to crawl away. Shit! Why wasn't it my night off? What was I doing?

"I was looking for a day job," I explained, my heart beating faster. She stepped a little closer, to hear me over the din, and I backed away.

"This is the best way for me to get writing done. And go to colonies. They let me take leave here."

"Nothing wrong with that," she said. I became aware of her blinking and I felt myself also blinking excessively. Her thoughts came across loud and clear. Who was this client? A loser with a waiting job? Can she pull it together? When is she going to finish her goddamn novel?

I wanted to plead. I'm not a loser! Sorry that the first novel didn't go off, but the next one is coming along! Thank you for your patience and for believing in me!

My agent was everything a writer could hope for. I'd known this before. Smart, cosmopolitan, successful, and genuine. A winning combination. We often communicated in baseball metaphors. I was glad to have her on my team. The first novel had struck out, but she wanted me to rally with book two.

But seeing her again this way made me sad about what might have been. There was a time when I desperately needed her to sell my book. My self-esteem hinged on a sale, and she was the one to make it happen. How many agents had I queried before her? She alone had liked my work enough to take it on. When it became clear that my novel was a tougher sell than she'd thought, she urged me to move forward with the next project.

I suddenly felt badly that I'd cut her off on the way to the loo. Maybe I should let her go. But she didn't excuse herself. I took this as a good sign. She wasn't so uncomfortable that she had to escape. She told me that she and her husband were celebrating their tenth anniversary.

"Hey, you don't want to go to Bread Loaf this summer, do you?" she asked, referring to the writer's conference with a caste system more rigid than a Soviet gulag. "I just got the nomination forms." Now it was my turn to lean towards her.

"The only way I can apply is as a waiter." I shrugged.

"I guess not!" she laughed.

Now I wanted to cry. Why didn't I give the table to Erica? If she'd been sat even two tables away in the aspiring rock star's section, I might not have even noticed her. But I had chosen not to be anonymous this one time. Having an agent was my "at least" these days as I plodded along in anonymity. Tonight I was more than just a waiter to one person in the room. Two, counting her husband.

She was waiting for my manuscript. I was waiting tables. Her job was to encourage. Mine was to produce and seek support. Obviously business was good for her. Even her skin glowed with success.

My eyes darted to table twenty-four. The needy four-top of Westchester retirees were finishing up entrees that they had waited too long for, and would be raising their hands for dessert menus soon. At seven, my agent's husband waited patiently. The room was busy and I couldn't count on co-workers watching my back. We had about twenty seconds left, tops.

"How's the novel?" she asked strategically. I could tell she'd been saving this question.

"Good," I said. "It's coming along." I didn't want to go into detail, but I was making progress.

"Good. I can't wait to see it!" She was earnest. My spirits buoyed. Could it be that we still had a chance, that she was still the one? I wanted to go home that night and finish my book.

My Westchester people were goose-necking. Time was up. As my agent and I said good-bye, she leaned over and hugged me. I felt a huge relief. She went to the ladies room. I disappeared into the crowd of diners, anonymous again, thank God.

INSIDE THE TENENBAUM HOUSE

BY ADAM BAER

Just east of Amsterdam Avenue, in a section of Harlem called Hamilton Heights, I went a little too far with my latest filmic obsession. I had spent my first week in a new and barren uptown apartment with the DVD of Wes Anderson's *The Royal Tenenbaums*. Holed up with my TV and books, I sang along with the quirky soundtrack songs (Nico, The Clash, Paul Simon) and listened carefully to the director's commentary, amazed at his penchant for detail. I gelled with his cast of endearingly gloomy has-beens, characters who just didn't feel comfortable outside the house—and family—they called home.

I couldn't help myself. The film's unfailing weirdness, melancholic narrative fog, and tales of co-dependence were good companions for someone who'd just quit his first post-college job and moved back to his childhood city only to find himself feeling dislocated in a foreign section of it—someone who just felt a little off.

Which is why I wasn't surprised when, out of Saturday morning boredom, I found myself driving downtown from my new neighborhood. I began to think maybe I could find the Tenenbaum house; the actual home used in the film.

I then remembered Anderson said the place was somewhere in Harlem. And here I was—on Broadway with a view of the Hudson to my right and blocks of tree-lined streets to my left. I remembered that City College was somewhere around here. Maybe some nice brownstones were in the vicinity. The rooftop views of the river definitely came left from the position of my old hood ornament. And the streets were flat and green, not like the slopes west of Broadway. It had to be east.

"Between here and here!" I said with karate-chop hand gestures to my friend Lina, who looked suddenly frightened of my passion.

I then made a left into the City College area and met my Manhattan real estate oasis: one gorgeous stone home after the other, replete with Gothic architectural embellishments, gardens, and a feeling of solidity that made similar houses on the Upper West Side seem like garden sheds. From the look of it on film, the Tenenbaum house was a home I could live in, attractive narrative symbolism and kitsch factor aside. The conical turrets, circular rooms, dark red blocks, and black-iron gate gave it the majesty of a fortress. Here was a place that could protect you.

The only problem, I figured, was that I'd likely never find it. There had to be thousands of these houses in Manhattan. What really were the chances I'd make a random turn onto the right block?

Rolling down the street at no more than five miles an hour, I pointed to a building.

"That's it," I told Lina.

Look at the short half-block behind it. Picture the trees bare, the street empty. Ben Stiller tapping his chin as he peers down from a third-floor window. Owen Wilson crashing into the front gate in a vintage convertible. Luke letting his falcon free from the elaborately tiled roof. Hackman hiding behind the huge built-in staircase, ready to inspire his grandkids with a throwback line: "I'm not talkin' about...dance lessons. I'm talkin' about…puttin' a brick through the other guy's windshield; I'm talkin' about…taking it out and choppin' it up."

We parked and walked toward the house. I noticed the windows outlined in blue tape, that the doors were new but designed to look antique. The front yard had been gutted of foliage. On the side of the house sat a few planks of wood and a construction hat. And affixed to the windows were documents stating that the city had allowed a two-family conversion following a renovation.

I walked up the stoop and peeked through the mail slot to find a familiar wood-paneled foyer.

"Put your hand in there and see if you can unlock the door," I told Lina.

She gave me an odd look—since when was I this dictatorial?—but bent down and slid her hand through the metal all the same.

"There's something blocking the lock," she said.

We descended to the sidewalk in defeat.

Then I saw a woman with a laundry bag exiting the building next door.

"Did someone shoot a movie in this house a year or two ago?" I asked her.

"Yeah," she said. "Something with Gwyneth Paltrow. I heard it was supposed to be funny."

Some thirty minutes later, after a layover in a home built by Alexander Hamilton, now a museum, Lina and I returned to the Tenenbaum house, still determined to find our way in. To essentially climb into a movie.

Waiting was smart: A man with a beeper and work gloves was now carrying in wood and construction materials.

He opened the door after a few knocks. He didn't look surprised. Lina followed my spur-of-the-moment script and mumbled something about an interest in real estate, feigning surprise, as if we were at the wrong house.

"Wait," I said, speaking my pre-arranged lines, "is this *the* house that Wes Anderson—"

"Yeah," said the man, scrunching up his eyes with doubt but still managing to appear friendly.

"Are you renovating it?" I asked.

"Yeah, I own it."

"Oh," I said, feeling a little silly.

"Are you looking for an apartment?" he asked.

"Are you renting one?"

"We're splitting the place up into a two-family. But there's one rental unit in the back with a separate entrance."

The man showed me the rental, where Richie, the suicidal Luke Wilson character, entered through a back window after checking himself out of the hospital. I asked the man if we could tour the house, maybe even peek upstairs. He acquiesced. We followed him and walked about the foyer. We saw the phone-booth where Angelica Huston spoke Italian, the living room where Gwyneth and Luke listened to the Stones in a tent, the closet full of board games where Stiller hid Hackman's stuffed javelina and Dalmatian mice ran free. It was all there, despite the new flooring.

"How'd your house end up in the movie?" I asked.

"One day I came home and there was a note from Wes in my mailbox," he said. "Simple as that."

"You only dealt with him?"

"Yeah. Very nice, very down-to-earth guy. Paid in cash."

"People love the movie in part because of all the cool things he did to your house," I said. "He's pretty interested in the details."

"Yeah, but it wasn't that hard undoing it all. Disney paid for it. Decent job, they did."

My inner groupie was on fire.

"So are you really interested in the apartment?" he said, clearly intimating he knew the real reason I had invaded his living room.

"Well, I just moved into a new place not long ago, but I've always wanted to live somewhere like this."

"That's how me and my wife felt when we first saw it," the man said as he took down my name and number. "There's something about it. It just sort of feels the way a home should."

We shared a smile. Then I looked around the house again and realized that it was just that: a house belonging to someone else.

My new home was waiting for me fifty blocks north. It was empty, in an unknown neighborhood. But maybe that just meant it was ready to be a character in my life, for me to fill it with the people and memories that make me who I am.

Lina looked at me sympathetically, and the credits rolled.

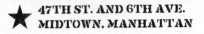 **47TH ST. AND 6TH AVE.**
MIDTOWN, MANHATTAN

THE DIAMOND-CUTTER'S DAUGHTER
BY HADARA BAR-NADAV

The mysteries of Forty-seventh Street—men in oily black suits and beards the color of tar, swollen red noses and black eyes lined in soot, wiry eyebrows, faces half-hidden by coarse pepper-black hair, *tallit* dragging from the sweaty hems of their coats. Men with secrets. In their pockets, translucent wax paper folded and folded again like some ancient origami. Papers passed hand to hand in secret, passed to and from my father in his pressed khaki pants and button-down shirts opened at the collar. Over six feet tall, he seemed like a giant to me. An Israeli man with black curly hair who spoke seven languages and could turn an ordinary nub of stone into a diamond.

He was the prized diamond-cutter, the one every man on the street knew by name: Moty—Mordecai to the American customers with their hard, angular mouths who could not pronounce the *o* with its soft underbelly of *w* and *u*.

I thought he was in the CIA, the KGB, the Mossad. How else could I explain the glass rooms and monitors, the hushed men whispering to hushed men, my father writing in Hebrew, in Arabic, in secret codes and numbers I couldn't understand? And there were the papers, the square paper pockets that seemed to hold light itself. Could I cut off a piece of my hair or pull out a tooth? Could I pull out my bones, iron my skin flat as a shirt, and slip inside the paper folds? I was invisible to the men on the street, to the merchants, to my father himself.

In Jaffa, we walked the pockmarked streets, the bright white stone of the city making us squint. A city of reflections. As we walked by the docks, the city seemed to flash its teeth, daring the water and the sun. My father cried out when he saw the sign, a flier stapled to a pylon that announced the fisherman was dead. *Nadav, Nadav,* my father cried, muttering the name into his hands. Our last name belonged to the fisherman who had fed my father, who gave him chicken, salt, and bread, and watched over him when he was twelve and had run away. Homeless. My father's father had already run off to Canada with another woman, abandoning his wife, two daughters, and a son. And that son never stopped wandering—Paris, Brussels, Lisbon, Marrakech, Cairo, Kinshasa, and Englewood Cliffs, New Jersey. A stranger wherever he went.

By the time I was twelve, he had contracted Lyme disease. A sick father. A father with an enlarged heart, a father with electrical impulses eating through his skin, a father with schizophrenia and dementia. A father who had suffered four strokes. A blind father. A paralyzed father who I will visit this summer in a nursing home in Tel Aviv. There was a father there once. And a father before him.

I remember a large, rectangular fish tank filled with sapphire chips sculpted into the shape of a wave. And coming home from school one afternoon and parked in our driveway were two Citroens—one gold and one a sparkling green, each for one of my brothers—and two Jeeps for my mother and sister. Yes, the land of plenty. Of empty. A five-bedroom, colonial-style house in New Jersey with elaborately landscaped bushes and trees, an Olympic-sized pool, and a father who was never home. My father who only seemed to belong to Forty-seventh Street.

He would disappear for months or years at a time, and then there was no money, no cars, no food. My mother and I hiding on the kitchen floor when bill collectors came. My mother sending me off to friends' houses so I could eat. My mother's affection for Valium and staying in bed for days. Once overdosing and collapsing in the front hall, where EMTs pumped her chest until she coughed and vomited, alive again. She had her secrets, too, and pockets full of Tic Tacs and pills. She was a first-generation Holocaust survivor. That was supposed to explain everything.

What I remember about Forty-seventh Street was being buzzed in. The maze of glass hallways and rooms I had to pass through in order to get to my father. One glass chamber after another while a monitor, placed in each chamber, stared down at me like a silt-covered eyeball in which I could see myself, nervous and disfigured, stretched impossibly wide and bloated at the middle. Panicked and beginning to hold my breath, I would arrive at my father's office and watch him lean over his record players, those metal disks on which he set a diamond suspended by a metal arm in order to shave away part of its face, surface, facet, sheen, grace.

He surprised me once at my friend Jara's house; I hadn't seen him in six weeks. He pulled a black film canister out of his pocket, popped open the top, and poured a wide arc of gold dust and diamonds across a glass tabletop in the living room. He told us that gold and diamonds often are found together. We believed him.

I noticed the scars spread across his hands, several waxy pink holes drilled into the skin. He claimed the scars were from the acid he used to clean stones before he cut them. *Like peroxide on a wound*. I listened for the sizzling, the bubbling, and wondered if he had been tortured by secret service spies, if that could explain why he left and would leave again.

THE DIAMOND-CUTTER'S DAUGHTER

Forty-seventh Street ignored me. I was a child, and a girl at that. The diamond-cutter's daughter. I traced my name in the black carbon soot that covered every surface in my father's office while men came and left. I played with the digital scale that could measure my breath, blowing out hard while red numbers registered my presence, my absence.

Occasionally my father and I went to other offices in other buildings. We passed through familiar glass cages until we arrived at another soot-covered office. Sometimes it seemed like we were inside a diamond ourselves—a tilted world made of glass. My father would send me off to a corner with a legal pad, some pens, and a Snickers bar. And I would watch him, always his quick hands, folding, unfolding, and refolding those paper squares. I'd watch as he put the magnifier loop in his eye, a hallucinatory light on his face, as he hovered over something I couldn't see, something remarkably precious and small nested inside the paper crease, a diamond like a prayer inside.

**FLUSHING AVE. AND BOGART ST.
BUSHWICK, BROOKLYN**

FLUSHWICK
BY TONY ANTONIADIS

There's a small pocket in Brooklyn east of Williamsburg, west of Bushwick, known by its residents as Flushwick. In this small pocket, mattress fires attract drum circles. Catalpa trees burst from the shattered windshields of bulldozers. Pedigrees with silk bandanas growl behind fences crowned with razor wire. It's hard to get a fix on this neighborhood. Trust no one or trust fund? There's a perpetual buzz that the neighborhood is on the verge of exploding, but I don't know if they mean this in the good way. I'm not even sure who they are. I've lived here for three years, and I've had a tough time describing it to folks who aren't curious enough to visit to help me figure it out.

Late one night I was climbing out of the subway, taking the steps two at a time. It was one in the morning and I was getting my second wind. There was only one other man on the street, about a block ahead of me, and he seemed to be headed in the same direction I was: Flushing Avenue. He periodically turned around while walking forward through the snow, presumably to take inventory of the scene behind him.

I was wearing my first winter coat in seven years. It was a bulky black parka named after an Antarctic research camp. It had six horizontal chest pockets and detachable fur trim. I looked like a hip-hop soldier whenever I wore it, but the coat was so warm that it effectively eliminated winter. I was also wearing a pair of form-fitting Express jeans a girlfriend had bought for me shortly after we began dating. And in those fem jeans I walked towards this strange man who, as I got closer, seemed to have a look on his face that said *I am hungry tonight.*

I'm not a bad person, I told myself as the gap closed.

He turned right on Flushing Avenue. That was my route home too, so I followed him. I also did this because of a New Year's resolution I'd made to "just live my life." This meant allowing myself to sneeze on the bus if I had to, to say goodbye to a beautiful woman on the elevator as I got off at the floor of my office, where I would gather boxes of textiles and bring them down to Thirty-fourth Street on a hand truck loud enough to make lifelong New Yorkers cringe. It meant taking the route I was supposed to take to get home, and not walking blocks out of my way to avoid a potential encounter.

Separated by a block, we walked past the benchmarks of any neighborhood on the verge of exploding: a pallet jack store, an extinct laundromat, a beauty salon that had the hours of a speakeasy. We breezed past hills of construction sand and slunk around Rottweilers bike-chained to forklifts. He walked past a gigantic condom that I stopped and hunched over to examine. It seemed to be filled with bourbon and cilantro. I felt my chest tighten as the man turned around to watch me. I could see his breath.

The way he moved, the way he would stop and go in frenetic bursts, how he braced himself against the wind by getting low— he transformed in my mind from a man to a man-sized rodent, pensive but committed, one who'd pulled himself out of the sewers and thrown on a leather jacket and feigned human citizenship by walking among men. "Be counted, young rodent," I wanted to say, to share in and affirm this decision.

He sneered and turned down Bogart Street. I stood up and moved away from the condom and followed, plunging my boots in his footsteps. When I turned the corner I saw him standing there, waiting for me, outside the empty parking lot of the Boar's Head distribution center. He stood under a flag with a boar on it. It whipped in the wind.

"I'm mugging you now," he said.

My head grew light.

"I've been waiting for this," I said.

"I'm serious," he said. "Give me the money in your pockets, chump."

He sized me up. "You have like seven of them, dude. Pockets."

Silence.

"Dude," he said.

I couldn't read him, but I inched closer. I wondered if he was one of the men who'd moved into my neighborhood, presumably from some suburb or township that produced malcontents who fetishized ruin. He was wearing a leather jacket, jeans, canvas shoes, and had a beard. There was alcohol on his breath and his cheeks were bright red, and I wondered if he had broken capillaries like me.

I patted down my pockets and shrugged. "Sorry, looks like you're out of luck. I'm broke."

"You're lying," he said. He stepped back and gave me a once-over, from puffy parka to skinny jeans. "You totally occupy a different socioeconomic class than me, you fuck."

"Looks can be deceiving," I told him.

He got closer to me until we were crotch to crotch. "Well, if you don't have any money, give me anything else you have of value, a cell phone, an iPod, anything I can sell." His teeth clattered like castanets. I'd remembered being that cold for quite some time. But now, in my beautiful, seam-sealed cold-weather parka, all I could do was feign sympathy.

"Is this for crack?" I asked. I'd meant to say it meaningfully, but it came out as more of a weird fey chirp. I followed that up with my notorious medicine laugh. That's when things started to get awkward.

Into the echo of my laugh: "Dude, I am going to kill you!"

I looked around. The streets were empty.

"Wait a minute," I said. I did have something.

I pulled from my pocket a copy of *The Shipping News,* by Annie Proulx. I crouched and extended my arm far out from my body, handing him the book as if it were a loaded gun.

He snatched at the book and scanned the cover. A smile beamed across his face.

"Annie Proo," he said, eyes warm, pressing the book to his chest.

"That's all I've got," I said as he laughed. There was a long pause. Then he said: "She's a great fucking conservationist. My dad worked with her when we lived in Wyoming."

He handed the book back to me and we fell into stride. He asked, "Have you read *The Accordion Crimes?* That book demolished me. Different generations. This accordion. These murders," he said.

Then: "I'm still going to have to bludgeon you."

"Ah, go ahead," I said. "This novel is making my eyes cross and my mouth pucker. You'd be putting me out of my misery."

"That's a good one," he said, laughing. I laughed, too.

"It's a good one," he said, "because it's true."

We walked together toward Varet Street, the street where I lived, talking about our jobs, how long we'd lived in the neighborhood, and what it was exactly we were trying to do.

We shook hands and exchanged names at my door. It was a firm handshake. I raced up the steps, four flights to the top of a half-renovated factory, and after getting into my room, I paced. I could not stop pacing. It was the last time I saw him. I must have walked ten miles of unfinished space, rife with potential, until I fell asleep on my floor.

THE GATES, IN CONTEXT

BY MINDY ALOFF

Central Park exists because of two writers who cared about the well-being of New York City, including all its people: the poet William Cullen "Thanatopsis" Bryant, who proposed his idea for the park when he was still studying at Yale and also editing a periodical called the *Evening Post*, and the landscaper and editor of *The Horticulturalist*, Andrew Jackson Downing, who developed plans for the park in tandem with a partner, Calvert Vaux, and who might well have been the park's chief designer, had he not died in a steamboat accident in 1852, at the age of thirty-seven or thirty-eight. (Apparently, it was the democratically minded Downing, in particular, who wanted the park to benefit New Yorkers from all classes.)

During the decade prior to the Civil War, Bryant, and Downing saw that the poverty-stricken throngs in the notorious section of the Five Points in Lower Manhattan had nowhere to walk or let off steam, and the two of them wrote a series of newspaper stories calling for a park or preserve that might serve as such a cooling-off place (which, the City officials realized, would help to defuse potential riots). At the time the decision was made to construct the mammoth park (843 acres), land in Manhattan north of what is now Forty-Second Street was primarily devoted to farming and some estates and country houses. One area—where the park now is—was a kind of wilderness of squatters and their wild pigs. The land was swamp, mostly, and undesirable for country houses. It was also studded with monumental rocks, the detritus left over from glacial movement during the Ice Age. Eventually, more dynamite would be used to blast away or reshape those rocks than would be detonated at the Battle of Gettysburg. By 1858, portions of the park were opened to the public, including an area for ice skaters.

Frederick Law Olmsted, a visionary city planner—the embodiments of whose ideas for public spaces, realized in cities across America, can still be visited today—was put in charge of a competition to design Central Park. He also contributed a design of his own to the competition, and he won it. His partner was Calvert Vaux, a native of France who, unlike Olmsted, was actually a trained architect. And yet, in the service of this extraordinary public project, Vaux agreed to serve as Olmsted's assistant, despite Vaux's bruised feelings at what he felt was a demotion. Eventually, Vaux's position on the project was upgraded to that of partner. These two men, so different in temperament and background, and their team of engineers and craftsmen, created from the rock-strewn swamp what is, for many New Yorkers, the greatest single art work on the island of Manhattan. Apart from the sky and the air, everything about Central Park, even the terrain as it has undergone considerable changes in the past century-and-a-half, is the result of decisions made by human beings. The contour of the land. The position, size, and shape of the rocks. The trees, every one of which has been planted, including the forest growth in the Harlem Meer, the lovely little wood at the park's northeastern tip, in which one can walk by a stream and fish without seeing any evidence whatsoever of the surrounding city. The points of perspective, in which one rounds a corner and "just happens" to see a charming confluence of greensward, trees, and, perhaps, a wooden structure. All of these were the result of planning—the point of which was to make a pedestrian forget that they had been planned. The size of the project, and its impact on the city, bespeak the planners' heroic belief in themselves, of course; however, the intellectual and philosophical principles that governed their actions also bespeak a staggering humility.

Central Park has, as focal points of its overall plan, outstanding formal elements, most notably the Mall—an *allée* lined on either side with elms, the quintessential tree of America's small towns. Their towering boughs gently bend toward the center, suggesting the long nave of a cathedral. Below the elms on each side are benches arranged to form a straight line the length of the Mall, so that, when one walks the length of it, the eye is entertained by the contrast of the softly shaped "tree" roof and the rigorously geometric "pews." This grand statement concerning the sanctity of the union between Art and Nature in America leads to what is considered to be Vaux's greatest single contribution to Central Park: the sweeping Bethesda Terrace, whose sandstone balustrades have been intricately carved with figures and shapes derived from Nature—some of the iconography stretching back to the Middle Ages—and from nineteenth century human endeavor. With the exception of one small section, no two of the dozens of sculptural or friezelike carvings are identical. Those on the west side of the Terrace are concerned with themes of autumn and winter; those on the west side with spring and summer. From the Terrace, one looks on a spacious vista north, a kind of miniature version of the eighteenth-century's ideal of the Sublime. Almost directly below the Terrace, accessible by a commanding set of stairs and then a brief, preparatory walk through a womb-like passage under the barrel vault of a bridge, is a spectacular, tiered fountain, overseen by the figure of an angel in the form of a striding woman, wings outspread. (This fountain was featured in the movie of *Angels in America*.)

When I last saw the fountain, one recent, frosty day while *The Gates* was up, a tightly packed crowd of giggling adolescents were crowded around the base, posing for a group photograph. As with many of the park's most formal places, the people in the picture were incongruously vivid and high-spirited against the meticulously composed setting, designed for such pastimes as meditation by the poor on the aesthetic and social possibilities that earned wealth could bring them. Indeed, as I stood on the Terrace with my companions—Janice, my friend from California; her nineteen-year-old daughter Mimi (who had never been to New York before); and Michelle Nevius, a wonderful tour guide (www.walknyc.com) whom Janice had engaged for the park trip that day and who provided a wealth of information about New York, some of which I've reproduced in this story—the subject of our conversation was the fact that it took decades for the people of Five Points to be able actually to reach the park as a matter of course on their Sundays off. Originally, one was not permitted to bring carts or even wheelbarrows into Central Park, or to picnic on its lawns, or to play ball anywhere in its environs. Until the development of affordable streetcars the length of Manhattan, to travel the miles that separated Central Park from Five Points would have been an odyssey, and much of it would have been accomplished by walking—in the case of a young family with several children and no umbrella strollers, an almost unendurable idea.

My companions and I tried to imagine being parents who lived in a five- or six- or seven-floor walk-up, crushed into a small, dark apartment with one or two other families. The father—and, in many cases, the mother, too—would have worked twelve-hour days, Monday through Saturday, in a factory or sweatshop, well before the existence of OSHA to regulate conditions of ventilation and safety, sometimes leaving their children in the care of family or neighbors, or taking them to work, or leaving them home entirely on their own. Perhaps on Friday or Saturday night, one or both parents would have tried to shake off the effects of the work week by getting drunk—one of the few ways to unwind, when one didn't have much money, in a world without television, radio, or telephones. And then, on Sundays, they were supposed to dress in their best clothes and trudge from the southern end of Manhattan to Fifty-Ninth Street, so that they could perambulate for four, or five more miles, their little children in tow, in order to concentrate their thoughts on higher morals and values one might possess, if one were a resident of a townhouse? And then trudge back the miles to their tenement? As much as I mourn the loss of so much of nineteenth and early twentieth century New York—the theaters; the small, idiosyncratic shops; the midtown sky; the last vestiges of chivalry and decorum; and, most especially, Stanford White's Penn Station, which, as a small child with my parents, I'd gaze at drop-jawed on our visits from Philadelphia to shop at Best & Co. or attend a Broadway musical or the New York City Ballet— I'm very glad to be living in our own moment.

In one of its more ephemeral dimensions, this moment includes *The Gates*—the cheerful and very charming installation over twenty-three miles of Central Park's walkways, conceived by the Bulgarian-born artist Christo, who, assisted by his wife, Jeanne-Claude, a native of France, directed the laborious, twenty-six-year process of permissions and realization—that will occupy Central Park for two weeks, then be dismantled and completely recycled, leaving behind no evidence whatsoever that it had ever been. I'm going to presume that readers of *Mr. Beller's Neighborhood* know what *The Gates* consists of, since magazines and newspapers—*The New York Times*, in particular—have flooded the zone with stories about those 7,500 meticulously placed, painstakingly engineered tangerine-colored post-and-lintel frames, each one bearing a curtain of tightly-loomed vinyl fabric, with a six-stitch grid pattern that gives the curtain texture and helps its sunny color to sparkle and to appear variously translucent or solid, according to changes of light and gusts of wind. Below each curtain are some seven feet of clear space for people to walk through.

We didn't see very many birds in our two-hour walk (Central Park attracts some two hundred species of birds, as it is under a major flyway), and Janice, who is especially interested in fauna of all kinds, asked Michelle about that. Michelle answered that the Audubon Society had objected strenuously to the project, although she didn't know if Christo and Jeanne-Claude had been able to satisfy the society's objections. However, an amateur birder and bird watercolorist, who, on the park's Eastern border, had set up a telescope for the public, focused on the nest of New York's celeb red-tailed hawks, Pale Male and Lola, said that it was his understanding that *The Gates* wasn't harmful to birds; they just were lying low until the masses of pedestrians had dispersed. We looked in his telescope and clearly saw that the hawks had, in fact, returned to rebuild at the top of the Fifth Avenue co-op that had destroyed the nest. At least, we saw the nest; Pale Male and Lola, the birder suggested, were out foraging for lunch. We also saw some extraordinary carved faces under the cornice of the limestone building—faces that were so far removed from the street that only Pale Male and Lola would have been able to regard them with the naked eye. Imagine carving faces into the part of a building that hardly anyone would ever see. It's like the little embroidered designs that Barbara Karinska would incorporate into tutus for the ballerinas of Balanchine's ballets—designs that would only be seen by the dancer. Benign secrets in the shadows: in our fishbowl world, the very concept seems as exotic, and as costly, as beveled glass.

Christo and Jeanne-Claude, themselves, raised the twenty-one million to make, install, maintain, and remove the installation, primarily through sales of Christo's art work on paper, and all proceeds from books, T-shirts, coffee mugs, and other souvenirs go to charitable organizations. Their positioning of the gates minutely respects the park's design, as well: for example, none of them line the formal areas, like the Mall or the Terrace or the fountains, and, along the walkways, the series break to make way for large tree branches. When Christo and Jeanne-Claude's art intersect with that of Olmsted and Vaux, Christo and Jeanne-Claude always give their predecessors right of way. Nor is there any corporate advertising of any sort on the banners. (Think of the possibilities: all those curtains, layered in perspective, look like Windows, and with the title, *The Gates*—despite its inspiration in an Olmsted idea for the park that was never embodied—it wouldn't take much to turn the whole thing into a celebration of Microsoft.) Instead, it is a selfless gift to the city of New York, as well as to the artists' obsessions; and that fact, along with the festive nature of the work, helps to account for the tremendous enthusiasm it has inspired in New Yorkers, as well as in people who have traveled to see it from across the United States and elsewhere in the world.

"I want to see The Gates," my daughter, a college student in Boston, said on the phone, and, on a visit home, she at first allotted a half hour or so for the excursion. Seeing them, though, in the narrow sense of the word "seeing," isn't, for me, anyway, an aesthetic experience. The structures are awkward, and although the fabric has nuance, the repetitive design doesn't provide a lot of the simplicity and authority I associate with art at its best. Also, just to look at the installation doesn't seem to be the point exactly, the way seeing Christo and Jeanne-Claude's wrapped islands or wrapped Reichstag is. In this case, even aerial photographs won't give one the intended experience, in which one's own changing perceptions as one proceeds along the park's pathways are crucial elements: time and reflection are factored into the work's identity. As insistent as those tangerine-saffron constructions are against the subdued greys and browns of Central Park's winterscape, the look of them, alone, isn't the reason to go to the park while the work is there. What one is meant to see—and to feel— is the park as one moves through it. The park and its continually surprising people. Indeed, when my daughter did finally get to *The Gates* with her dad, they ran into the ultimate Gates-coordinated visitors: a group of Buddhist monks. Way to go, saffron!

Orange is also the color of safety vests, and another thing that makes this project a success is that it feels secure. Christo and Jeanne-Claude hired a little army of people to patrol the extent of the installation; their jobs are mostly turning over wind-ruffled curtains with long sticks that have tennis balls on the ends, answering questions, and giving out swatches of the curtain fabric, of which one million were made for visitors. However, their very presence is something of a deterrent to muggers and mis-chief-makers, as, once, the park attendants who would pick up leaves with poking sticks were in many of the city's public parks. (The patrollers can also swipe off graffiti.) As I write, the instal-lation still has a few days before it is taken down, and my heart is in my mouth that those days will pass peacefully, without acci-dent or mayhem. As I articulate this anxiety that something might go wrong with this project—a marvelous social event and kamikaze marketing tool for the beloved park, regardless of its optical vulgarity—I feel my own age, even though I realize that the park is apparently its own police precinct, and, according to Michelle Nevius, fewer crimes now take place there year-round than almost anywhere else in the city. Still, the park has been the site of some spectacular crime, and not all of it is violent. After Michelle's tour, I'll never again be able to pass by Tavern in the Green without remembering that it was once a sheep barn, whose sheep were released to graze on what is called Sheep's Meadow—a kind of county-fair exhibit to attract people to the park that occasioned Olmsted's resignation. Or that the sheep barn was turned into a family-type restaurant (an antecedent to Tavern on the Green) during the 1930s, in order to replace an elegant casino on the other side of the park that New York's mayor wanted destroyed because it was attracting riffraff—even though, in destroying the structure, the City was also demolish-ing what had originally been Olmsted and Vaux's charming pavilion, built for ladies to take tea and refreshment. It is not only the people who hate our way of life who seek to bring down New York: New York, itself, has swung the wrecking ball against its own legacy numerous times, and, on occasion, with glee.

The afternoon before my walk through the park with Janice, Mimi, and Michelle, I met another friend there to saunter through some of *The Gates*: the retired film editor Mimi Arsham, a native New Yorker who has lived in the city for much of her life. We walked the west side, mostly, and stopped to rest on one of the benches facing the exquisite little Bethesda fountain. (Note to self: Who was this ubiquitous Bethesda? Must look up.) Mimi, who is thirty years my senior, is also in much better physical shape than I am, and she wasn't so excited at sitting down for a while, but she acknowledged the enchantment of seeing how different the color of the curtains looked momentarily in the sinking light or when the wind barreled through them, and how curious were some of the color-coordinated passersby. The only instance of orange or saffron we didn't see was Washington Irving's pumpkin. At one point, a lovely, fluffy dog, some kind of shepherd, trotted along the path. "I wonder if the dog feels anything from this," Mimi ruminated, then she added in a self-critique, "That's ridiculous. Of course he couldn't." As if on cue, the dog stopped, lay on its back, and began to squirm in what looked to me like a classic example of euphoria. "He must have fleas," said Mimi. Of course, I was born and grew up in Philadelphia, so I wouldn't have known that.

FRANKENSTEIN'S TEARS
BY KATE ANGUS

During my first year of teaching, I became used to crying in public. Not subtle sniffles that I could have, with a considerately discreet audience, played off as a common cold or allergy attack (the watery eyes, the reddened nose, nostrils like cavernous mines), but sheer go-for-the-gusto wailing, sobs shaking my body like I was caught in some Santeria possession-dance. I didn't cry because of my job; if anything, the students gave me a reason to drag myself out of bed each morning. Though my personal life was a barren wasteland, my heart some desolate Siberian tundra, as I told my long-suffering roommate over cigarettes and cheap wine on the roof each night high above Second Avenue's clamor, at least my students needed me. The blond violist in Florida might not want me in his bed or on the other end of the phone any longer, but there were fifty bright-eyed parochial school sophomores and seniors who needed me (me!) to teach them about Christopher Marlowe's influence on Shakespeare and how John Donne simply and admirably alchemized his passion for sex into devotion to God. No, teaching was not the catalyst for my tears. I loved my students passionately. In fact, at a particularly low point right after my breakup (I believe it was shortly

after the conversation in which he told me that I was most definitely "not awesome" and visiting me again in New York was
less of a draw than sleeping on the secondhand leather couch his
friend Johnny Cowboy had recently given him), I made a list of
what I still enjoyed in life. I came up with five things: gangster
rap, coffee, Wellbutrin, sleeping, and my sophomore-year journal entries. My roommate disqualified number four by saying
what I really meant was that I enjoyed being unconscious, which
was tantamount to saying that I wanted to be dead, but I still
think she failed to appreciate the voluptuous pleasure of waking
up from a dream of some Paris cafe, noticing the red lines of the
alarm clock blinking 3 a.m. and rolling over to return to one
more glass of red wine, the gray rush of the Seine, and another
soft murmur in the ear of "*je t'aime*" from some devoted Rim-
baud look-alike.

But to return to the weeping. My students only made me cry
twice. The first time was when Erica gave me a poem. It was
about a teacher who didn't realize how much her students loved
her, even if the guy she thought she would marry was a jerk.
(Catholic school girls, you are all wise beyond your years.) The
second time I wept was during the latter half of *Frankenstein*,
when the monster tells Victor that everyone else has a friend, a
mate. The monster, who never asked to be made, who is misshapen and afraid, is eternally lonely, wandering the wilderness
in the dark and the rain, forever unloved. I cried then too, though
I told my class I was deeply moved by Mary Shelley's brilliant
use of allegory. I think they bought it, as they rolled their eyes
and sighed.

Although I did not cry at the school, I wept everywhere else:
on the subway, in the streets. I cried in the cramped aisles of
Commodities Health Food store on Eleventh Street and First
Avenue where we used to buy kale and free-range eggs, in
Dempsey's Bar on Second Avenue and Third where we played
darts to win rounds of drinks from each other or, as the evenings
progressed, promises of pleasures to come. I cried in St. Mark's
Bookshop, in the poetry section, endlessly re-reading Rilke's "be

forever ahead of all partings / like the winter that has just gone by / for among these winters, there is one so endlessly winter / that only by wintering through it will your heart survive." I cried at Franks where Marah told me, over wine and gnocchi, that my heart would die soon enough and then I'd be free. At Decibel where three lychee martinis allowed me to let Ezra kiss me, knowing my lost violist was twining around his new lover in Helsinki already. I cried in Times Square, in a cab at midnight on New Year's Eve, already late to another party where he would not walk through the door.

My therapist said it was good for me to get it out of my system. My friends said I had to let it run its course. My roommate, a budding art therapist, asked me to paint while I wept and wailed. She brought my pathetic pastels to her class to discuss, turning homefront irritation into a useful case study. People on the subway, at the stores, and on the streets, simply averted their eyes and let me pass, my gaunt body the Flying Dutchman's ship, a cursed framework, my coat flying behind me like a ragged sail, the devil of grief and loneliness riding shotgun on my shoulder, steering them away.

One person, one stranger, said something to me once. I was walking back to my apartment, tipsy from a few drinks slugged down at a friend's show. I was weeping, of course, the streets almost deserted. Cabs sweeping back, slow and intermittent, and the street lights casting their sickly glow. A man huddled in a doorway called out to me, "Hey, do you have a light?"

It was late at night. I had matches in my pocket and a crumpled cigarette that I'd bummed from Julie for the walk home even though I'd already quit smoking and for good that time. I sat down next to him. I can't even tell you what he looked like really, since the wine from the club was singing in my veins, and I was sailor-drunk once I sat down, the street lurching back and forth in front of me like waves. I lit my cigarette, passed the matches to him, stretched my legs out in front of me and watched the lights shine on my cheap leather boots. There was a long silence, nothing but the soft sounds of our inhaling.

"You seem sad." His voice was thick, blurred by the cigarette, rough as the cracked fingernails on the hand he placed on my knee.

"Don't touch me." I didn't move. I was just, suddenly, too tired. I didn't really want anything at that moment. Not to wake up at dawn cradled in the arms of my lost lover, not my friend who'd hugged me and sent me lonesome out the door of the club, and certainly not a stranger's hand trying to inch up my leg in a doorway, no one around on the street.

He took his hand away. "Why are you crying?"

"Bad breakup."

"Aren't they all?"

And, yes, of course they are. Probably even the violist feels bad about me sometimes, secretive and guilty like I do about the friends I've stopped calling, the boys in high school and college that I kissed a few times and left, all of the promises of the body that I never managed to keep.

"Well, shit," he said, after a long pause. "You need to stop crying. It's a waste of tears. You know he's not worth it. You're beautiful and you're out in the middle of the night, all alone, talking to strangers. No one's worth that."

"I know." And weirdly, I did know, suddenly, just like that. It was late at night, and I was alone, sliding down the wall into the shadows of doorways, letting strange men tell me things while I shivered in the early spring air, drunk enough to be almost stupid. This wasn't me. I've never been like this. And the man I thought I loved who would barely take a bus to see me was auditioning in Finland, crossing oceans to be with someone else. There was no doubt in my mind. This wasn't worth it. It was a waste of tears.

I looked at the man. He could have been any East Village hipster, a little older than me, white-boy dreadlocks spilling over his forehead, the cigarette a long tube of ash dangling from his lips. He could be sitting next to me at Mud tomorrow morning and I wouldn't recognize him. He could live in my building or date one of my friends.

"You're right," I said. "Thanks." I started to get up.

"No problem." He reached out his hand and touched my face. It wasn't a come-on, I don't think, not like before. Just an acknowledgment that something slightly weird had happened here, that we'd made some kind of connection, even if it wasn't the kind he might have been looking for. His hand rested lightly for a moment on my face, cupping my jawbone. "You're beautiful," he said, "Don't fuck it up."

I didn't say anything, and I didn't look back as I wobbled down the last few blocks to my home. He's wrong that I'm beautiful—I'm average at best—and I will fuck it up, probably many more times before I end up with the right person, if he even exists, but I don't cry over people who leave anymore unless it's in movies. I read quietly on the subway, or I stare into space. I listen to my iPod. I grade my students' papers. I occasionally talk to strangers. My eyes stay dry.

THE FIRE SPINNER
BY ABIGAIL FRANKFURT

Our protagonist, Skunk, in action: Dan, a.k.a Skunk, and his girlfriend Erin pick me up on the corner of Broadway and 116th Street on a freezing winter day. Skunk briefly reminisces about his days at Columbia. After a few years of "getting stoned and sitting on the couch" he dropped out and found his calling.

Skunk aspires to be a circus freak. And his way to the big top will be on the tails of Manhattan's new subculture of fire spinning. The Greek philosopher Heraclitus, circa 470 B.C., declared fire to be the highest good. The flame incorporates the two essential forces of reality: creation and destruction. I believe Skunk would agree. By way of Phish concerts and raves, fire spinning has segued into the Manhattan underground. Meeting on rooftops, waterfronts, vacant lots, and desolate spots in Central Park there are at least thirty spinners in New York, of which Skunk is one.

We board Erin's car and head to East Seventy-second Street. From the front seat, Skunk tells me the intricacies of fire spinning. First the chain—a homemade series of links that vary in length, and at the end of each is a folded mass of Kevlar attached by twisted wire hangers. The Kevlar serves as the wick or *poi*.

Poi translates to "balls" in New Zealand, the country from which fire spinning was born. The Maori used the ancient ritual to keep their women agile.

Skunk built his first set of chains on Memorial Day of this past year and has already acquired above-average skills. He interrupts the mini-lecture to ask Erin a question: "I wonder if I'll have the balls to try out my new move tonight?"

Speaking of balls, I ask Skunk what exactly is the attraction of spinning flaming Kevlar. "At first," he replies, "it was the fear, you feel like your nuts are in your throat. It's the adrenaline rush and it's a really good way to work out. It's also intensely spiritual. All you hear is the rush of the whirling flames and your concentration is diverted from day-to-day worries. You just focus on not getting burned."

Skunk was drawn to fire spinning after watching "Joe Mamma" perform at some MTV *Oddville*–like event. Joe Mamma has been spinning fire for four years, "And is, like, a fire spinning god," says Skunk.

Erin pulls the car up to a curb on Fifth Avenue and we head into the park via Seventy-second Street. A voice calls from the dark, "Skunk?"

"Splinter is that you?" The two men shake hands with one another and psych each other into a "polar spin session."

Under the Navy Terrace, adjacent to the Bethesda Fountain, Skunk asks Splinter, "Whatcha got for juice?" Splinter whips out a jug of kerosene and the boys saturate their wicks with its stench. A towel is soaked in water, "fire safety" in case anything should get out of hand. "It's best to wear cotton, polyester is bad." Skunk tells me. He continues, "It's pretty rare that anyone catches on fire. I've been on fire briefly."

Splinter is ready to spin. His wicks are lit and he begins twirling. I hear Skunk exclaim, suddenly, "Are you on fire?"

At that point one of Splinter's wicks comes flying off and Skunk rushes it with a wet towel. "Fire safety," says Skunk.

Next it's Skunk's turn to twirl. He lights his wicks and starts dancing hip-hop style while spinning his chains throughout the

Terrace. Like a Dallas Cowboy cheerleader tossing her baton, Skunk has his chains whipping over his head, behind his back, under his legs, windmilling them so quickly the links become invisible and it's just Skunk in a T-shirt in twenty-two degree weather, dancing with two balls of burning Kevlar.

He tries two new moves—both wicks hit his legs but he doesn't catch fire. He keeps on spinning for nearly ten minutes until his wicks burn out. The sight is utterly majestic, medieval even, and though we are all freezing and reeking of kerosene it was worth watching. In between my compliments and commentary Skunk warns me, "We're a bit more flammable than the average person now." He also explains to me his deep consideration of developing fire-breathing skills. What I want to know is the long-term plan: what is fire spinning's final destination? "One of these days," Skunk begins, "I'm gonna make some cards and really start networking."

At the edge of the park Splinter departs and the three of us head for Erin's car. Ironically, we are boxed in by a Hess truck pumping gasoline into the underground of Manhattan. Erin, Skunk, and I find a diner in which to bide our time. While piling french fries into his face, Skunk says he and Erin are toying with the idea of organizing their own circus troupe and taking it on the road. "I wouldn't mind joining the circus, for at least a year. Hanging around clowns all day can be scary but very rewarding." At this point I can hold back no longer and tell Skunk that he is, indeed, a freak. Skunk rejects this by telling me, "Fire spinning is going to be a huge thing in a couple of years, everyone's gonna be doin' it, and at that point," he adds, with a tone of melancholy, "I probably won't be able to join the circus."

"So, Skunk," I ask. "Do you believe this to be your calling?"

"Well, there's only one thing in the world that I do as well as spinning," Skunk responds stoically, "and that's ping-pong. The ping-pong thing, I don't think I'm gonna pursue that. I think I'm too old for it."

LITTLE DEVIL

BY ROBERTA ALLEN

After work on Tuesdays, my mother comes home to the apartment in the Ansonia Hotel where we live with my grandmother and takes me to acting class. The year is 1952. I hate acting class even worse than I hate second grade. My mother says I will learn how to speak with "charm and grace." But she doesn't fool me. I know why she sends me there. She wants me to stop talking out of the side of my mouth like my father. Talking out of the side of my mouth makes me feel like my father. I can be my father when I talk like him. I can be strong and tough. I can have him with me all the time, not just on Saturday night at C & L Restaurant, or on Sunday afternoons, or on nights when he stops by Nana's apartment—which is across the hall from the room he rented after my parents separated—to say goodnight.

In acting class, I don't say a word. I don't look at anyone. For an hour, while I stand under a spotlight in front of a heavy black curtain beside other kids, mostly older, who, unlike me, really want to act, I keep my head down, stare at the wooden floor of the stage, and pretend to be invisible. The kids stifle giggles when the teacher asks me to read a line in a play, or repeat a line exactly the way he has said it.

When he calls on me, I get the same feeling I had in the auditorium at P.S. 87 the day all the kids in second grade were sitting in assigned seats and the teacher at the podium pointed to me out of two hundred pupils. She was checking to see if we were in the right seats. I was sitting in the center. All eyes were on me. "What's your name?" she said.

In a whisper, I said, "Roberta Allen."

"What?" the teacher said. "Speak up!"

"Roberta Allen," I mumbled.

"Louder!" she said. "I can't hear you!"

"Roberta Allen!" I said, my anger beginning to show.

"I still can't hear you!"

"ROBERTA ALLEN!" I finally screamed, my voice powered by rage.

One day I decide I've had enough of acting class. I am standing in the noisy school yard with Diane Pine, a girl in my class, waiting for the bell. My mouth set, my arms folded across my seven-year-old chest, I say to her, "I'm not going to acting class! My mommy can't make me! I'm gonna run away!"

"You are?" Diane Pine's blue eyes open wide.

"I'm gonna make greeting cards and sell them on the street!"

"You are?" Diane Pine says.

With Diane Pine as my accomplice, I run away after school on Tuesday, the day of my next acting class. I have everything I need. A drawing tablet. Blue ballpoint pens my father gave me for drawing. Pencils. Crayons I stole from the supply cabinet. At night, after I sell greeting cards and pay Diane Pine for leftovers from dinner, I am going to sleep under her bed so her mother and father won't find me.

Diane Pine lives on Seventy-fourth Street between Columbus Avenue and Central Park West in a basement apartment in a brownstone. In order to get there, we have to walk down a dangerous side street. We pass drunks, low-lifes, women in short, tight skirts. They stand around, talking loudly on the stoops of decaying tenements. I watch them out of the corner of my eye. This is an adventure! I tell myself. But when we cross Columbus

Avenue on our way towards Central Park West, we are back in ordinary life.

"Remember," Diane Pine says, "you have to be very quiet."

We creep down the stone stairs to her apartment. Diane Pine unlocks the door. To our left is the living room. The blinds are drawn. The only light comes from the TV. The sound is turned down real low. Her mother, The Burnt Log, lies on the sofa, dozing under a blanket. Diane Pine told me she does that every day. The Burnt Log fell asleep one night with a lit cigarette and burned most of her body and part of her face. We tiptoe past her, over the living room carpet, to reach Diane Pine's room in back, but suddenly the floor creaks and wakes up The Burnt Log. She opens one eye, then the other. The fire has not damaged her sight. Or her hearing.

"What are you doing, Diane?" she says, lifting herself, painfully it seems, onto her skeletal elbows, and looking me up and down. "Who's this?"

"Roberta," Diane Pine says. "She's in my class."

"What is Roberta doing here?"

Diane Pine is quiet. She shuffles her feet.

"What's going on?" The Burnt Log says. To look at her, you wouldn't think she had that much of a voice.

Diane Pine sighs. "Roberta ran away. I said she could sleep under my bed at night. She's gonna make greeting cards and sell them on the street."

"She's what?" The Burnt Log is silent for a moment. "She can't stay here! Diane, give me the phone!"

Diane Pine looks at me, helplessly, while she obeys her mother.

"What's your last name Roberta?"

"Allen," I say, in a whisper.

"Where do you live?"

"The Ansonia."

"Does your mother know what you're doing?"

I shake my head no.

"She must be worried sick! Diane, you better not try anything like this!"

"No, Mommy." she says.

I feel sort of bad for Diane Pine, but not nearly as bad as I feel for myself. The Burnt Log calls my mother.

When my mother arrives, she puts on her "nice act" for The Burnt Log. As soon as we are out the door, however, she wears her gargoyle face and drags me up the stairs to the street. Shaking me like a dirty rag, she shouts, "Little devil! You humiliated me in front of that woman!"

But she never makes me go to acting class again.

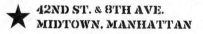

**42ND ST. & 8TH AVE.
MIDTOWN, MANHATTAN**

THE DAY THE WAR STARTED

BY GERALD HOWARD

At about quarter to five this past Thursday, I got into a cab at Fifty-sixth and Broadway; my destination was the Port Authority and the Short Line Bus to my home in Orange County. It was a rainy, miserable day, and I was damned glad to get the cab. My driver was relievedly Haitian—one checks these days.

As we drove down Broadway, we saw ahead of us a huge phalanx of police vehicles almost two blocks long, every one of them with their emergency lights flashing in an alarming fashion. My first reaction was, naturally, worry. What now? My second was annoyance—there are too many official vehicles on the road these days with their lights flashing self-importantly. But their slow, almost stately progress down Broadway counter-indicated any real disaster, and my feelings settled into the familiar groove of commuter pique at obstacle and delay.

Broadway looked to be impossible, so the driver turned left at Fiftieth Street and then right onto Seventh Avenue. But within two blocks we hit terminal gridlock. There was a big hubbub ahead of some sort, complete with television trucks with their satellite dishes and police vehicles alight. So I paid the cab driver and got out to hoof it.

At Forty-seventh Street the cause of the blockage became clear: a rush-hour antiwar protest march in Times Square. Police were everywhere and protesters were chanting the familiar mantra "No blood for oil." At that moment of recognition a strong surge of anger shot through me that was both simple and complex. The simple component was: How dare these people get between me and the 5:26 bus? The complicated part broke down like this:

1. A tactical beef: How could they think that a protest action snarling traffic at the city's busiest crossroads just as tens of thousands of people were heading home could generate anything but counterproductive resentment?

2. An atavistic and surprising spasm of wartime disgust for their silly rote mottoes and reflexive anti-Americanism. These feelings combusted in my brain, and I just caught myself before yelling some sneering imprecation at them in native New Yorker fashion.

At that moment, there came back to me a gut-based memory of 1970. On May 11th, antiwar activists marched down Wall Street to protest the Vietnam War. An American flag was burnt, whereupon an assault column of inflamed construction workers from the World Trade Center site arrived to inflict serious physical violence on the marchers. The police were less than proactive, let's say, and the construction workers were cheered on enthusiastically by the spectators, almost all of them downtown office workers.

That's where my parents worked, my father at the Chase Manhattan Building, my mother for Standard Brands, and while they were not among the cheering, they certainly approved of the actions. I know this because they so informed me that night in our Brooklyn apartment, to my utter dismay. As my mother said, and I can quote her precisely: "We went through World War Two, Gerry, and we respect our flag and our country."

Jesus, World War Two, the trump card in every political argument!

And there were plenty. You can imagine the subsequent conversation, which realized every cliché of generation-gap misapprehension but was no less bitter for its formulaic nature.

And here I was, thirty-five years later, about to berate a new generation of antiwar protestors, marching against another American…well, another American what? Imperial misadventure? Act of preemptive self-defense? Whatever it is, my animus against the marchers was discomfiting in the extreme, creating a spasm of self-questioning. Had I somehow managed (baby boomer horror!) to turn into my parents? Maybe so. I mean, I hate the way we have entered this war and I have nothing but distaste for, and suspicion of, the people who have led us into it. I hate what war does to this country: the awful admixture of moistness and macho that news commentators adopt, the smug insider way that the annoyingly endless string of retired general "news consultants" intone "shock and awe"; the mindless, tasteless triumphalism.

But the war itself[1] and the people fighting it for us, I don't hate.

In this mood, I walked south to Father Duffy Square, when I heard my name being called. It was a fellow named Ken, son of a noted avant-garde publisher, a fixture at various downtownish and bleeding-edge literary events where I sometimes find myself in my guise as an older publishing guy. I said hello, and then, with a confident smile and demonic timing, he asked me, "Want to join the march?" Whipsawed!

But it was never even close.

I shook my head and said, "Ahh, no thanks." Then I made my way to the bus station in the rain.

---

1. Man, did I get that wrong. (2009)

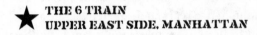

LOCAL STOPS

BY WILLIE PERDOMO

This dude I know from Wagner—Lucky—boards the train and as soon as he sees me he starts talking about open cases, offers, pleas, and deals and I look for something that can hold the weight and there's Emily Dickinson, a poem in transit, talking about planks and experience—twice.

Coffee cup lids have coughing fits and a blind man with two good legs says that I could be him one day. Jane runs into Dick all surprised and shit like, wow, when did you move up here?

On Ninety-sixth Street a heart-broken voice yells, "Damn, why don't you fucking say excuse me!"

José from Lenox Hill Hospital (it says José on his shirt) rushes for a seat and taps out a happy hour blues with his Daily News.

I almost transfer for the R at Fifty-ninth Street when a walking confectionary almost went to hell with a sweet tooth for stepping on Lucky who had just finished saying that he was looking for an excuse to lose it. Instead, Lucky has a grill contest with a *blanco*'s steel toe eyes all the way to Grand Central.

Two nickels miss and hit the Section Eight Gospel Trio at Union Square. That's the thing, though, with these trains…they promise good skin, better memory, and right after the conductor's static announcement confuses you, the quietest person in the car stands up, right in front you, and starts talking about Heaven, who going, who staying, and just when the train pulls into Brooklyn Bridge, Lucky tells me that he already decided—if the judge offers him a two-to-four, he's gonna take it.

THE LIQUOR STORE
BY SAKI KNAFO

When I was sixteen, I got a summer job at the liquor store in my neighborhood, Windsor Terrace, a sleepy Irish-American enclave in Brooklyn. I worked as a stock boy, counting the bottles on the shelves and moving boxes around in a dank cellar. The manager, Mac, spent most of his time on a stool behind the counter, gazing at the sports pages. Mac was a tall man with a big belly and skinny legs. He spoke sparingly. Sometimes one of the neighborhood outcasts would shuffle past the storefront window and Mac would grunt and mutter some sardonic comment. He had nicknames for everyone. There was "Sylvester," like the cat, for a middle-aged man who lived at a residence for the mentally retarded and made loud "meowing" sounds as he walked down the block. There was "Mr. Clean," a gaunt Vietnam vet who dressed in gray, filthy rags. And there was "Sweat."

Sweat was about forty years old, a wiry black man with sharp cheekbones and bloodshot eyes. His forehead glistened, and he wore a white undershirt stained yellow under the armpits. He drank Wild Irish Rose in great quantities. It was a fortified wine, meaning the wine was spiked with liquor. It came in a screw-top flask bottle, like cheap whiskey. For one-fifty per bottle (then the cost of a subway token) it was the cheapest product in stock. It was also the most popular, and Sweat, a connoisseur of the stuff, was the store's best customer.

Sweat came into the store about three or four times a day, and each time Mac would make a big production, pinching his nose or waving a hand in front of his face. Sweat didn't seem to mind. He would head straight to the refrigerator where the "Irish" was kept, grab a bottle, and clap some change on the counter. I suppose that the advantage of buying wine in small quantities throughout the day was that he could conceal the pocket-sized bottles in a brown bag and drink on the street without fear of getting caught.

One morning, while Mac was ringing up his purchase, Sweat made the mistake of starting a conversation with him. "You guys are all right," he said. "Murphy's down the street raised the price to two bucks, but you still got it at one-fifty, same as it's been for years."

Mac shot Sweat a withering look.

When I came to work the next day, the price of Wild Irish Rose had gone up to two dollars. And yet Sweat remained the store's most faithful customer. I couldn't help wondering whether he enjoyed Mac's abuse.

That summer, I played guitar in a rock band. We played a few shows around the city, and I earnestly hoped that we would become famous, mainly because I needed a girlfriend. All the other band members had girlfriends. Sometimes they called out of practice to attend to "relationship issues," which meant I was left with the responsibilities of goading people into practicing, sending out demo tapes, setting up shows, and making sure everyone showed up on time.

About halfway through the summer, just after the Fourth of July rush, Sweat stopped showing up at the store. I wondered what had happened to him: Had he fallen ill? Had he finally switched loyalties? I expected Mac to say something, to find a way to ridicule his absence. Instead, in the long and listless afternoons leading up to Labor Day, Mac began to talk about his life. It wasn't any great outpouring of emotion, just a few terse anecdotes here and there, but the difference was noticeable. For one reason or another (probably boredom), he was opening up.

One of the things he told me was that he was in a band that played every Wednesday at a bar in Brooklyn. He played guitar, as I did, and it turned out that we liked some of the same bands. I was surprised to discover that we had something in common. My rock-star aspirations, however, were mine alone. Mac never said anything about wanting to be famous. He seemed to accept his career for what it was, which I couldn't quite grasp: If you couldn't be famous, why bother playing at all?

I might have started to like Mac, but during the second half of the summer he got involved with a woman who began spending a lot of time at the store, a small, attractive woman with a pixie-style haircut and, curiously, an English accent. Whenever she came around I would shut myself in the basement, where, for lack of anything else to do, I'd leaf through old *Wine Connossieur* magazines. When I ran out of magazines, I read the labels on every bottle, and then the names carved into the ceiling beams—Dave and Dan and Pete and Frank—generations of stock-boys who had spent their summers counting and shelving bottles and collecting a wage from Mac and moving on.

Those were sluggish weeks, and I passed the time by writing hit songs in my head and fantasizing about how popular I'd be once our band got that lucky break. But the break never came. At the end of August, our lead singer left for college, and suddenly I was no longer a guy in a band. One morning, pricing bottles of cheap rosé wine in the store window, I tried to think of what I was, and all I could think of were things I wasn't. I wasn't anyone's boyfriend and had no immediate prospects of becoming one. I wasn't a man—my voice had barely changed—but I wasn't a boy. After all, I had spent my summer vacation working. I was a stock boy in a liquor store, and that was all. On my next trip to the basement I carved my name in the ceiling beam, next to Dave and Pete and Dan.

That evening, while walking home after work, I stopped across the street from the traffic circle, where the neighborhood outcasts spent their days sitting around on benches, amid a cluster of trees. Sweat wasn't there, but a few other drinkers milled about, leaning against a granite war monument, the axis on which their world seemed to pivot. Two women tussled over a paper bag, hurling epithets. They were old and angry and broken-down and strange. The road around them yawned like a chasm.

One day, just before school started, I got together with Jonas, the guitar player in my late band, and his girlfriend, Valerie. As we sat on our backpacks in the middle of a muddy field in Prospect Park, Valerie produced a pint of scotch and untwisted the cap. She said she had pilfered it from her parents' liquor cabinet. She had been siphoning their liquor for years and had developed a taste for it. She handed me the bottle.

I took a furtive sip. "A superior blend," I said, trying out some the jargon I had picked up from *Wine Connoisseur*. She nodded appreciatively. "That size bottle costs about six-fifty," I added.

I'd tasted alcohol before but always in moderation, and I'd certainly never had any hard stuff. I'd always been afraid of getting drunk and embarrassing myself. Now I was curious. I took a gulp, and another. I was drunk. Jonas and Valerie finished the bottle and soon we were clambering up a mound of dirt next to a baseball diamond, pushing each other into the dirt and laughing. I tried to wrestle with Valerie. Jonas tackled me. We threw our arms around one another's shoulders and promised to start a new band that would be better than our old one because it would have a horn section. It would launch us to super-stardom. I shoved Jonas playfully. He laughed and shoved me back roughly. "You fuckin' sellout!" I shouted. I tried to trap him in a headlock. "What are you doing?" he said. Was I trying to hurt him? If so, I wasn't doing a very good job. I gave up.

A while later I trudged home across the field. I thought about Valerie. She wore dark eyeliner and a dog collar. She drank whiskey. If I were her boyfriend everything would be great, even with the lack of a band and the crappy job. I imagined her running across the field to be with me. It was so easy to imagine, I thought there might even be a chance it would happen. And yet I knew my hopefulness was in some way a result of being drunk.

By September, Mac's lawyer-girlfriend had stopped hanging around the store and Mac had gone back to his old ways, reading the sports pages, making snarky remarks about passersby. Then, a week before school started, I told Mac I was going to quit. He instructed me to wait until after Labor Day. I couldn't bring myself to refuse him, so I decided to allow myself a unit of merchandise as compensation. No one would notice its absence. Only I had a complete knowledge of the inventory.

But there was one hitch. Mac might suspect me if all of a sudden I showed up to the store with a backpack on. That meant I would have to choose a flask-shaped bottle, so that I could tape it to my leg (it was still too warm to wear a jacket).

Alone in the cellar, I surveyed the shelves for the right type of bottle. The best stuff didn't come in flasks, but there were plenty of decent liquors that did, including at least one brand of scotch. But as I plotted my crime I thought about the store's owner, a nice older man who worked the cash register on occasion, and I decided against taking anything too expensive. That evening, after saying goodbye to Mac, I walked out the door with stiff legs, a thumping heart, and a bottle of "Irish."

I drank the wine alone in my room with the door closed, listening to a melancholy rock song. I played the same song over and over. Then I ambled out of my house into the dusk.

I walked up the street with no particular destination until I found myself standing opposite the traffic circle. Cars spun around the spot of green like horses on a carousel, their headlights streaking red and yellow and white. Through this swirl of color I looked for Sweat. He wasn't there. I crossed the street and sat on a bench in the middle of the circle. I watched the cars, letting my eyes go out of focus.

I slumped on the bench and let a shameful sense of self-pity wash over me. I contemplated my future: I would never become a rock star. I would never get a girlfriend. I took a swig of fortified wine and rolled it around in my mouth. How warm and delicious to be lonely.

PART II

CONFESSIONS OF AN ACCIDENTAL VOYEUR

BY MICKEY Z.

I was sitting in the front seat of Frank's Cadillac Seville when he pulled out of the parking space and whipped into a U-turn without looking. We saw the approaching headlights too late…and yeah, we got hit.

In those pre-seat belt law days, my left hand reached out to the glove compartment to brace myself and I hurt my wrist a bit. It hasn't been the same since.

Two young guys were in the car that hit us. Frank knew he was in the wrong, and handled the situation coolly until one of the kids said, "You can't make a U-turn here."

"Hey," Frank yelled at him, "I don't need a fuckin' traffic cop right now."

This shut the kids up fast.

We ended up walking home. As we approached the bridge over the Grand Central Parkway, we heard loud moans. In a parked car, some guy was on top of his girl in the front seat with the windows wide open.

Her legs were sticking straight up and we could see his hairy ass humping away.

That unexpected sight got me thinking about something I saw when I was working for Thrifty Rent-a-Car. I had been on my way back fromdropping off customers at the airport, crossing over the Grand Central Parkway on a small two-lane trestle. Cars were lined up on one side going north; cars lined up next to them going south, all waiting for the light to change.

As I sat there in the maroon station wagon that passed for Thrifty's customer shuttle, I glanced over at the car to my left and was taken aback when there wasn't anyone in the driver's seat.

Sitting with his head lying back against the passenger side headrest was a skinny black guy in his forties He looked uncomfortable, his face displaying something approaching pain. I did a double take just as the driver reappeared.

She was an overweight Latina, pretty with long hair, and she immediately busted me gawking. Her eyes twinkled as she watched me register that she had just given the skinny black guy a blowjob while waiting for the light to change

Her face flushed from her efforts, she laughed out loud, and to my everlasting astonishment, opened her mouth to show me that her passenger had indeed achieved orgasm.

"Yeah, I got it all," she said as she wiped her chin. The skinny black guy smiled the way only a man in that situation can smile. The light turned green and they were gone.

The car behind me honked loudly.

Early one summer morning as I was walking to the gym, I had an all-time great accidental voyeur moment. I heard a cry of passion, the unmistakable sound of a female in the throes of pre-orgasmic pleasure. I looked around and zeroed in on a first floor window, and peered in to see a moaning Asian woman, maybe twenty-four, with dyed pink hair. She was riding atop an unseen sex partner.

The streets were Sunday-morning empty. Confident I was alone, I lingered to watch. Ms. Pink was naked with her back to the window at a slight angle, enough to see some of her profile and her full breasts bouncing up and down. Her body glistened with a light film of perspiration, the sun streamed in through the blinds to create shiny stripes across her torso.

The image stayed with me.

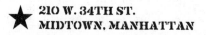

★ 210 W. 34TH ST.
MIDTOWN, MANHATTAN

DISSENT IS A MARATHON, NOT A SPRINT

BY MICKEY Z.

The revered pugilist/philosopher Iron Mike Tyson once mused: "Everyone has a plan until they get hit." And get hit everyone will. Case in point: many of the Anybody-But-Bush (ABB) protesters who took to the streets of the Big Apple during the Republican National Convention in August 2004. I don't just mean blows suffered at the hands of an over-eager policeman—I'm talking about the slings and arrows of activism as a life choice.

At the time, I wrote an article that questioned the strategy of only protesting the Republicans when the Democrats are barely distinguishable. I asked: "Where was the planned-for-months-in-advance outrage in Boston last month? The Hitler mustaches? The warnings about fascism? The cataloging of candidate crimes?" I also pondered the efficacy of "anti-authority types submitting to New York's demands for polite opposition restricted to a pre-determined venue." I summed up, calling this the "Michael Moore era of dissent" and declared I would skip town during the RNC. (I did spend two days at my in-laws' house on

Long Island but was back home in Astoria for at least half the convention.)

The result of my stance was a predictable mélange of misinterpretation by design, overreaction, and personal attack. Most interesting was the righteousness. Individuals much younger than I essentially branded me a traitor and scoffed at my absence. My commitment and activist "credentials" were being seriously questioned. Fine. I've heard much worse and my skin is NYC-thick.

Although I'm aware how sincere and dedicated many of the demonstrators were, I kept hearing a line from The Clash over and over in my head: "I believe in this and it's been tested by research: He who fucks nuns will later join the church."

Even in the face of urgent issues, dissent is a marathon, not a sprint. Activism is not about hating one man or even one party…it is holistic.

Twenty-somethings making clever Dick and Bush jokes may cultivate a more nuanced understanding of the "system" but sadly, many will lose faith and focus, many will embrace compromise and denial.

What do my youthful critics know of my choices and sacrifices? Sure, I'm not digging ditches in Myanmar and I have no desire to overstate my meager hardships, but how many of those who paraded through Manhattan for a few hours on a Sunday will stay the course, evolve, and maintain an open mind over the next few decades, when, as Tyson warns, they get hit? How many will stick to the plan?

Reality: Carrying a sign when you're twenty-one rarely translates to remaining steadfast into your forties…and beyond.

CHEMICAL FIRE

BY JASMINE DREAME WAGNER

The building that Morgan described was a monolith of brick with a flat, black hole blasted out of the side. Standing at the edge of the entrance, he peered inside and swore that he saw someone moving. He shivered and stumbled to the curb, then quickly retraced his footsteps back up First Avenue, skirting the fringe of industrial Sunset Park, passing broken factory windows and the rusty metal loops of barbed-wire fences. The sky was navy in the weak pre-dawn light.

Six months later, Morgan was still talking about the warehouse. It was the weekend before Christmas; Morgan and I were sitting in his apartment in Bay Ridge, drinking Jack Daniels and wasting the daylight. The walls glowed blue with the light of the muted television screen.

"Come see it," he said. "You'll be impressed." I set my drink on the windowsill and ran my finger along the dimpled wood. Heat bubbled up from the radiator, causing the paint to pocket. I cracked the window.

"You don't want to go alone?" I said.

Morgan paused. He was a solitary wanderer and an even more solitary drunk. Morgan didn't drink for confidence or for social stamina, he drank because his limbs demanded it. Whiskey loosened him like hot water on packed ice. It caused his joints to pop and crack.

"No," he said, shaking his head. Morgan's fingers began to sort bottle caps on the table.

It wasn't a long walk down to the water but it was cold. A chill whipped down First Avenue like a frozen slice of a hurricane. My hands turned red in the wind. We found the building just as Morgan had left it: hole blasted out of the side, crumbling bricks, graffiti that read "ENTRANCE TO HELL, DANGER, DO NOT ENTER" in thick, red swirls. We squeezed our way through the entrance, taking care not to trip over the piles of tires, smashed ceramics, and metal scraps that spilled from the gut of the building onto the sidewalk.

Once we were inside, the brightness of the air took us by surprise. The sun was setting, painting a slate of deep powder blue above us where a ceiling should have been. In the center of the room, a looming tower of corroded steel caused the floor to bend. We followed a path through the trash and saw that the tower was actually a pile of abandoned cars that had been smashed and set aflame. We moved as close as we could without causing the ground to collapse. The floorboards buckled beneath my feet; plastic bags snaked around my ankles but I didn't stop to tear them away. Morgan pointed to the places where the steel had melted with the paint and chemicals, then dripped like candle wax, burning through the floor.

"A chemical fire," he said. "Whatever it was, the flames were hot enough to weld the cars together." I looked backwards, towards the jagged entrance. Someone had driven through the wall in order to drag the wreckage inside and burn it. The tower was powdered with ashes and dust. I couldn't understand why the fire hadn't spread, why the rest of the building hadn't burned to the ground.

Morgan lit a cigarette, smoked half of it, and put it out on the floor. An aura of emptiness and stale anger hung in the air, twisting with the hooks that dangled from the ceiling, swinging in the wind.

"The basement," Morgan said. "I want to find the basement."

We toed our way around the cars and headed into the rear of the warehouse. The floor sagged, creaking in places where it had caved in and had been patched with slats of plywood. The garbage was becoming sordidly domestic: broken records, ripped books, spent needles. A pile of trash blocked our way to the back wall, an area where the floor had collapsed at the foot of an iron staircase. A gaping black hole opened like a set of jaws. Morgan began to part the trash with his hands.

"Don't," I said. I grabbed his shoulder. Morgan froze. There was something finely-tuned and immediate about his body, as though his muscles were composed of tightly-wound copper springs. He looked at me without looking, like an animal about to disobey, then threw the plastic crate he'd been holding back into our path. I took a deep breath. The air stank of gasoline and decaying meat.

"We can try that one," I said, pointing to another rusted staircase, one whose bottom stairs had collapsed and fallen to pieces in a rusted heap on the floor. The stairwell rose almost forty feet into the air, connecting the ground floor to a small, precarious balcony and a doorway that glowed black in the waning light. Morgan hesitated, then nodded quietly. I grasped the banister and began to climb, testing my weight on the edge of each step before I trusted it with my entire weight. I felt Morgan's breath on the back of my neck. He jerked the rail nervously, then stepped around me and sprinted up the stairs, disappearing into the doorway.

At the top of the stairwell I paused, surveying the ground below. I squinted my eyes and listened, hearing nothing but the rustling of plastic bags in the wind and the clanging of chains and levers.

"It's safe," I heard Morgan call. I hesitated, then stepped around the corner and into a small room. The walls were covered in brightly covered designs, tags layered over other tags, some done artfully, others in violent slashes of paint. Another hole in the wall led to a crawl space between buildings. The room was almost empty, save for a pile of rusted tin cans and a spotty, stained mattress that lay askew like a limber body.

"Come look at this." I tip-toed to the top of the next staircase, following Morgan's voice onto the third tier of the building. The stairwell let out onto an expanse of exposed concrete, boxed off like a chessboard. Square holes opened up in the floor in order to let the chains of the meat hooks through. Metal beams hung above us like the rib cage of a decaying whale. Morgan waved for me to walk over to where he was standing, and when I did, the floor opened up in a sea of shattered glass that twinkled blue and silver in the dying light.

"It's like being in a movie," he whispered. I nodded. In the shadows, Morgan's shoulders took on a soft, molded contour. He buried his face in his scarf, then reached into his jacket pocket and pulled out his flask. We stood side by side, passing the flask back and forth between us, watching our breath condense, waiting for the sun to sink below the horizon. When it did, the warehouse sank into a cave-like darkness. I could hardly distinguish the holes in the floor from the floor itself.

When Morgan turned to leave, I followed. We walked home in silence, side by side. We followed the BQE, stumbling along Third Avenue underneath the trembling metal rails of the freeway. The wind whipped around us, freezing the puddles on the sidewalk into slick plates of glass. Morgan turned up the collar of his pea coat and pulled his hat over his ears. As we got closer to Bay Ridge, the streetlights coated us in a tangerine glaze. Morgan's cheekbones were glossy. After a second glance, I realized he was crying. We took a left on Seventy-third and headed home, cautiously, stopping at each crosswalk to wait for the changing of the lights.

THE SUPER WITH THE TOY FACE

BY ENNIS SMITH

They called him the neighborhood watchdog. He was the ancient, antic super of 515 Edgecombe Avenue, an immense, pre-war slab of yellowed bricks and mortar at the corner of 158th Street. His complexion, shaded always by a bibbed cap, was so pale it resembled a whitewashed wall. Forever dressed in a soiled white T-shirt and painter's pants, he was tiny, built as if he might blow away, but his Cagney-esque air assured you he was no pushover.

His most entertaining feature was his voice. When he spoke in that croaking drawl that reeked of age, whiskey, and cigarettes, he sounded like a pirate set loose in Harlem. That rasp annoyed me on mornings when I was late for the train. Whether I was running or merely walking fast, he'd scrunch up his small toy face, and in that bark on its way to a cough I'd hear, "Ennis, slow down, you'll kill yourself one day." In winter, if my coat was open or I was without a hat, you could be sure he'd let me have it: "Young man, you'd better put something on your head." Always he'd fling the words like someone who'd been deprived of his morning coffee; always I'd toss him a shrug and a stupid grin as I hurried past, piqued at the man's paternal presumption—as if knowing my name gave him the right. I didn't know his.

Most mornings, my craggy super sat across the street in Highbridge Park. Often he was with this massive guy whose head belonged on the face of a nickel. He and the Indian made a strange pair, but when I saw them together I was grateful: so focused were they on each other that my passing went unnoticed. By evening he'd be back by the gate at his building's rear, alone— I assumed the small alley beyond, piled with stacks of lumber and rows of garbage cans, led to his apartment—ready to scold my morning lateness with some variation on "I see you slowed down." Sometimes he'd drop his admonishments, cornering me instead with neighborhood gossip: who got evicted, who got arrested, who had a fire, or who had a fight.

He was a fixture on my street, like the woman who minded the stoop of the building across from his, or the man who went in and out of her apartment, the one who smoked and pitched bootleg DVDs to every passerby. I didn't know their names either, but I'd say hello. Occasionally the woman on the stoop would tell me how nice I looked as I headed for work, or a night out with friends; once, the smoking man confided he'd been in prison and asked for money. My response was a too smiley "No, sorry," walking a hair faster in case he didn't like my answer.

The super's arrival dovetailed with an unexpected shift in our Harlem Heights landscape. Around 1997, 515 Edgecombe went co-op, something I discovered when the then-super—a decrepit black man, from whose tentacled mustache dribbled bits of crust—accosted me like someone looking to unload hot goods before the feds arrived. After I demurred, he never spoke to me again, which kind of hurt my feelings. How to explain that I was in no position to purchase a doorknocker, let alone property? Back then I was an actor on a low budget with no assets. My office gig just covered rent, food, Con Ed, phone, cable, and the essential tools of my trade: headshots, acting classes, voice lessons and the maintenance of my one good suit. It wasn't just that I'd become adept at the art of living below my means—I was a trans-planted Midwesterner mired in the belief that one bought a house, not an apartment.

Poverty, and an appreciation for old things, slowed me down one night outside 515 Edgecombe Avenue. The garbage was out, and as someone whose apartment comprised a fair amount of street finds, my heart leapt at the possibilities. Out of the heap of busted chairs, bundled paper, dusty lumber, and garbage bags, two items got my attention: a cement pedestal and an iron grate, its Art Deco curves dotted with minor bits of rust.

Examining the pedestal, I heard a voice over my shoulder. "What cha' gonna do with that?" The super ambled up, his blue eyes accusing as he pushed his round specs off the tip of his nose.

Nosy and proprietary—I should humor him for fear he'd claim ownership and try to weasel a few bucks. "I could put a plant on top of the pedestal," I mused, noting the caked mud at its base and a squiggle of graffiti down one side.

He saw the markings too. "Damn kids, I swear they muck up everything."

"That grate—did it come from one of those windows?"

He flipped it over. "Nah, it's been in the basement. They're clearing it out so people can store stuff down there. You used to see 'em everywhere, but people want those new gates…"

"Fire gates," I said. "I had to buy one of those when I first moved to New York."

"Yeah, well, guess you need to get out if something happens." We both laughed at his dark jab. "Nobody likes this stuff any-more. New, new, new, that's all I hear from these folks here—and the crap they buy still isn't worth a good goddamn."

I picked up the grate; it was awkward but manageable. "I'm gonna take it."

"You want this too?" He ran a cracked dry hand over the pedestal. "It's heavy as hell."

"Jesus," I gasped as I lifted an edge. It must have been the base for a birdbath or a water fountain. Getting it across the street would be one thing, but up five flights? Still, I wanted it. "Let me go change and drop this off, I'll be right back."

When I returned, the super was sitting on his stoop, smoking. I tilted the solid cylinder and began to roll it down the street, stopping every few yards to catch my breath. On it went, my Sisyphean slog caught in the super's gaze, until I finally made it to my front door. As I pulled the pedestal up my stoop I heard a croak from down the block: "Careful, don't hurt your back."

At the beginning of the twenty-first century, the notion that buildings on our stretch of Edgecombe might convert to co-ops seemed absurd. The mere sight of our streets would have given the most desperate buyer pause. Though it overlooked the Harlem River and Yankee Stadium, the avenue was a function-ing dump for anyone looking to abandon shopping carts, unwanted dogs, and especially stolen cars—shredded tires, smat-terings of fenders and transmissions competed with the refuse left by motorists who assumed we wouldn't mind the mess.

The noise was a challenge. Nevermind the occasional blood-curdling screams, lover's spats, or the bass woof of someone's stereo. Buses rumbled up and down the block—standing on a particular spot in my living room they'd deliver a jolt every time the wheels rolled across the uneven streets. They set off car alarms, a jangled dissonance melding with the roving SUVs and revelers who hurled empty liquor bottles against the sycamore trees. You could chart the seasons by these glass showers: summer nights increased the likelihood a jarring crash would shatter my middle-of-the-night peace.

Crack addicts lurched along the avenue like demented pup-pets. They'd buy their dope on the cross streets between Broadway and Amsterdam, then beeline over the hill to Edge-combe. None of the neighborhood's residents could forget the sight of men and women anyone might peg as homeless, if not for their jerky physicality and their speedy gait. Back then the papers shrieked the rise of random drug-induced stabbings, so when-ever I'd pass one of these frantics on the street I imagined he or she could turn killer in an instant. There I'd be, the victim of some crack-addled derangement.

About a year after the craggy super boldly croaked "good morning" for the first time, I woke to the grinding whirr of trucks and cranes. Five floors below green-clad men were on a mission of auto exhumation, pulling car doors and engines, pieces of fenders, trunk hoods, sometimes even whole automobiles, up over the cliffs through the thick brush of Highbridge Park. This went on all week, until the salvage resembled a sprawling metal sculpture done in shades of battered reds, scratchy blues, and rusty yellows.

The junk got whisked away. Sternum-high black iron fences went up on the park side; aluminum barrier strips appeared along the curb, a highway accessory out of place on a tree-lined city block. Green trucks emblazoned with the words "NYC Parks Department" became fixtures on our streets, followed by foot brigades of trash gatherers, mostly black and Hispanic women in smocks, the "welfare-to-work" crowd created by the Giuliani Administration. No matter the weather, they'd be out on the avenue, stabbing bits of trash by rote with long wooden spears.

The addicts who'd dodged Edgecombe's swerving traffic to reach the park began to thin out, possibly fearing a Disneyland invasion similar to the one that robbed Forty-second Street of whatever character it once possessed. But not before they left their mark. For years I'd watched those poor fools scurry in and out of the park's tangle of trees and grass, pacing the streets as if searching for remnants of life before the word "crack" invaded their consciousness. Over time their wanderings etched a narrow trail. Someone—the parks department perhaps—carved their path into a formal walkway that set off the jutting Manhattan schist in ways that were positively Olmsteadian.

The familiar voice leapt out of the dark back alley: "You guys wanna buy an apartment?"

Jonathan and I were headed home. We'd lived together for two years, our courtship begun during what would be my last major performing gig. My own gentrification began shortly after; I'd decided to finish the undergrad degree I'd abandoned more than twenty years before. I found I couldn't get enough higher learning—the night the super called us over, I was on the verge of finishing my first year of grad school, a debt-laden situation that made his proposition sound hilarious. Only later did his implied presumption land: of course he knew we were a couple. He knew everything.

"It's goin' cheap, I tell ya. The tenant got sick and had to move down South with his people." More background spilled out: the renter was one of the last holdouts, and in a few years, all of 515 would be co-opted. The super was giving us an inside track on the place.

"Sorry—right now it's not in the budget." I didn't even want to hear the price, for fear it'd be in the ballpark of my tuition costs.

The super spat back. "How much you pay for rent?"

Why not just ask how much we made. "We've got a two bed-room. It's still in the eight hundreds." I couldn't believe I told him.

"You been there a while, huh?" The cool blue eyes turned curious, more consideration than stare.

"Since 1983. It's only the second New York place I've lived in."

That impressed him. "Don't give it up. These greedy bastards are asking too much. If I had your deal, I wouldn't move either."

I could tell J was ready to go, but I wanted to know more. "Are there a lot of renters left here?

He cleared his throat, and I thought, God, don't spit. He didn't. "About ten. They got a lot of 'em out for nonpayment; some of 'em were Section 8. One of the long-timers died last year. But they're not messin' with the renters who are keepin' up every month. Makes you wonder what people gonna do who can't afford to buy. Around the corner, those buildings went co-op too.

Piece of shit, those buildings, but people are buyin'. I tell you, money's flyin' roun' this neighborhood like rain."

In late June I was clearing the dead blossoms from my fire escape garden. Across 158th Street, the super was snatching up tattered sale circulars left by one of the area supermarkets. I'd noticed the folks streaming in and out of his building were of a different class—a snootier crowd less inclined to say hello, or tolerate the quips of an old man who earned his living changing lightbulbs or picking up trash. For them, I wondered if 515 Edgecombe was a dress rehearsal, a way station before a brownstone or the suburbs, or if their interest in the neighborhood was genuine. If anyone knew the truth, it was the tiny wisp of a man who'd stopped his cleaning to chat with a woman waiting for the M2 limited.

But the new immigrants were easy to spot. Young strivers dressed in suits, or armed with iPods and a mod confidence that screamed Williamsburg, USA sprang out of the usual sea of dark complexions along the avenue, at the supermarket and on the subway platforms at 155th Street. Designer dogs and their owners took daily promenades on a strip that now gave semblances of other, better-groomed Manhattan burbs. I'd ponder these obvious signposts of gentrification as I calculated their rents, and the odds of whether such changes meant that tastemakers would now perceive my neighborhood as cool and hip.

I doubt the newbies were barely noticed by seekers of the neighborhood's original flavor. On weekends, busloads of foreigners besieged the historic Jumel Mansion for their dose of the way we were circa late 1700s. As part of the package, they also visited a few prominent Baptist churches—not for the gothic architecture, but to see the natives at prayer. Holy flashbulbs: the *Times* reported various pastor's complaints of noisy, disruptive crowds that made them feel like sideshow attractions, but that did nothing to stem the flow of Anglo Europeans anxious for a glimpse (and a photograph) of pagan worshippers caught in the rapture of the Holy Ghost.

LOST AND FOUND

The August morning I breezed past the shrine of flowers and prayer candles at 515 Edgecombe's back gate, I was late again. That evening a light shower coated me with drizzle as I headed home. Approaching 515, I saw how the day's heat had withered the bouquets, how the rain had extinguished the candles fragile flames. I stopped to read a typewritten placard sheathed in plastic. The shrine was for the super. The placard referred to him as Shag, and announced an upcoming service somewhere in Jersey. It also gave his real name: William.

A man's voice tapped my shoulder. "Man, was that Shaggy?"

The corner streetlight shone on pockmarked caramel skin and deep circles under filmy brown eyes. He was in his thirties, wiry, a hair taller than the deceased. I paused, annoyed by the stranger's easy use of a nickname I'd only just learned.

"Yeah, the super." I couldn't call him Shag so casually, didn't feel I had the right to call him anything. I wondered how the stranger knew him—casually? As a tenant, or was he like me, another neighborhood resident unwillingly shanghaied by a familiar manner, by cool blue eyes? For the first time it dawned that others welcomed Shag's peculiar familiarity. This man knew his name, and I wondered how often they'd stopped to chat, to hash over things that bond men easily, like sports or politics, subjects the super discussed freely with the Indian perhaps, but ones in which I had no special knowledge.

I hadn't seen the Indian in a while.

We stood there, two black men mourning the absence of an old white guy under a crying sky. Behind us the M2 bus rumbled as the evening traffic keened across the wet asphalt. Other commuters—some solitary, some trailed by kids with backpacks babbling tales of school or daycare—passed, but none stopped. From the sky over Yankee Stadium came the crack of thunder; the rain thickened. Such storms meant that by morning, broken branches would litter the avenue, a guarantee I'd be woken prematurely by a brigade of Parks Department trucks.

My new friend shook his head. "Man, that's a shame. He was a damn nice guy…damn shame. That cat got around, he used to be everywhere."

And now Shag was nowhere; there was nothing left of him here except the memory of his toy face and that disgruntled rasp. I found out later from a friend who lived in the building that Shag had died of a heart attack. One of the tenants looked out of her window to see him face down on the walk beyond his back gate, as if he'd jumped.

A TROLL MUSEUM CURATED BY AN ELF

BY MARK YARM

I t would be accurate to describe Jen Miller's five-foot-three frame as pixyish, were it not for her very strong self-identification with another sort of sprite. Miller, a twenty-nine-year-old Lower East Side performance artist, would love to wake up one morning to find she'd become an elf. Barring that unlikely miracle, she'll have to settle for wearing her prosthetic elf ears, which she does nearly every day.

The Reverend Jen, as she's known in downtown circles, also has a thing for another woodland creature: the troll. More specifically, she loves troll dolls—the fuzzy-haired, saucer-eyed plastic figures that became hippy good luck totems in the 1960s—so much so that she's converted the front room of her Orchard Street tenement apartment into the Lower East Side Troll Museum. The institution, the only one in the U.S. celebrating troll dolls, has been open for a year and a half.

A Maryland native and School of Visual Arts graduate, Miller has declared herself the "Patron Saint of the Uncool." She has founded a rule-free religion called "Hal," which celebrates all that is not cool, and has been self-ordained by the Universal Life Church, a mail-order ministry.

Among Miller's multitude of other, uniformly colorful accomplishments is her book, *Sex Symbol for the Insane*, a handmade volume of essays and letters; co-founding the Dance Liberation Front, an organization protesting the city's cabaret laws; hawking "magically worn panties at human prices" at her site, elfpanties.com; and hosting the Reverend Jen's Anti-Slam, an open-mic night held every Wednesday at the Collective Unconscious performance space. Between all those activities, she supports herself working temp jobs. One Christmas, she played one of Santa's little helpers at Bloomingdale's. She was hired despite telling the employer that she was a real elf.

The small, light-blue room that constitutes the Troll Museum is crammed with trolls and related paraphernalia, as well as the curator's paintings, including several self-portraits (with elf ears, naturally). There's a chart explaining the subtle differences between Norfin, Russ, Ace Toys, and "black market" trolls; a television and VCR for viewing troll-themed videos (including the 1986 horror movie *Troll*, featuring Sonny Bono); and a gift shop complete with T-shirts and trinkets. Admission is free, though donations are encouraged.

Miller estimates that she has two hundred and fifty troll dolls. Among the museum's highlights are the pregnant troll (a visitor favorite) and what Miller calls the "Mona Lisa of This Louvre," a two-headed troll, reverently encased in Plexiglas. Unlike many collectors, Miller says she is not particularly interested in the monetary value of her collection. "I'm not a troll snob," says Miller, who even speaks in cheery elfin tones.

Miller insists that the museum, thought up while having a beer with a friend in 1999, is not ironic. She does, however, indulge in a whimsical brand of satire, leveled against what she sees as the pretentiousness of the mainstream art world. One target is the 2000 Armani exhibit at the Guggenheim. The Troll Museum features its own Armani show, where the "designer" outfits are made of felt.

"I saw the people who were at the museum—all those ladies in fur coats on the audio tour—and they were taking the fashion so seriously," she recalls. "There's this idea in America that when you go to a museum you have to be very serious and quiet. And I hated that. I'm just trying to bring back fun to museum-going."

Despite her genuine love of trolls, Miller admits to some ulterior motives in opening her apartment to the public. "The Troll Museum is a good ruse for getting art dealers to come: 'Oh, would you like to see my paintings?'" she explains. "It's also a way to get cute guys here."

One male lured to the museum was underground filmmaker Nick Zedd, who became Miller's boyfriend. It's curious that Zedd, who founded the bleak, taboo-shattering Cinema of Transgression movement in the mid-1980s, would visit a place as benignly kooky as the Troll Museum in the first place. The director of *They Eat Scum* and *Geek Maggot Bingo* explains that while reading about the museum on the Web, he felt a strong attraction to Miller. "I'm drawn to my opposite," Zedd says. "She seems to epitomize goodness, and she's very popular and charming, whereas people have referred to me as a dark cloud."

(Zedd has since directed Miller in *Lord of the Cock Rings*, a bawdy Tolkien parody; *Thus Spake Zarathustra*, based on the first chapter of the Nietzsche book of the same name; and *Elf Panties: The Movie*, in which Miller models underwear in the Troll Museum.)

Zedd theorizes that when his girlfriend writes about trolls and their charms, she is writing about herself and her own allure and that Miller's guided tour of the museum tells the story of her life. There's the artist's first troll, an orange-haired Norfin (now stuffed with loose change) that she got when she was twelve. And there's the poor troll that had its hair chopped off by Miller's sister's boyfriend, the captain of the football team, as she looked on, aghast.

Miller can't fully explain her fascination with the dolls, except to say that she's always been attracted to cute, yet slightly disturbing things. "When somebody collects art or fine china, people don't ask why they collect it. That's just accepted," she says, paraphrasing author Pat Peterson's book *Collector's Guide to Trolls*. Miller adds, "Something about trolls struck a chord, and that's all I know. I try not to analyze my obsessions too much."

HILDA STILL LIVES HERE

BY KATE WALTER

I was waiting for the elevator on my floor when I saw a sign on the bulletin board that an elderly painter was going into a nursing home and her work was in the basement, free to residents.

I live in Westbeth Artists Housing in the far West Village; the note was from the management office, and it said something about keeping Hilda's spirit in the building.

Since I needed something for a big vacant wall, I raced downstairs and rummaged through about forty paintings that were stacked up in rows on the walls near the boiler room where the janitors hang out and sneak smokes.

I selected two large, mellow, impressionistic works, four by five feet, one vertical, one horizontal. They looked like companion pieces from the same blue/gray/green series. I lugged one upstairs and then went back for the other. When I got them resettled, I was surprised to notice one was painted in 1981, the other in 1985.

Hanging side by side in my living room, the paintings make my four hundred square foot loft seem bigger by drawing attention to its high ceilings. And I liked the idea of keeping this woman's artistic energy in our complex. I had never met Hilda, but she was now part of my home. Her art is the first thing I see upon waking from my convertible couch.

The canvases ripple: grass waves and clouds shimmer upon the water. The shades of blue are calming, meditative. To me, the paintings recall Monet. Several viewers have observed, "look like lily ponds, without the lilies."

Several months after I hung them, a resident yenta who must be near eighty rang my door bell about the tenant council election. I invited her in and she gushed over the two paintings. When I explained how I got them, she became teary. She had known Hilda and told me she was now institutionalized with Alzheimer's.

"Oh, Kate, I am so happy you have her paintings," my neighbor said, while giving me a perfumed hug. "She is still with us."

Now I started to wonder, what did it say about me that I was attracted to work created by someone who had lost her faculties? And I wanted to know more about Hilda. I started playing detective and was directed to Mark, her next door neighbor of twenty years, a portly, middle-aged gay man who works in theater. I'd heard Mark was upset when Hilda was removed from the building, so I expected to hear stories about a sweet old lady.

"She was not a nice person," Mark said as we sat on my couch and chatted over tea, staring at her gorgeous paintings. "She was nasty and antagonistic and acted superior to others. For years, she wasn't nice to me, until she got older and needed help. We got friendly about ten years ago. She was alone and so was I."

Hilda was eighty-seven when she left Westbeth Artists Housing in 2001. Her walking and vision had been impaired for fifteen years, her mind in the last five. Mark felt it was wrong to put her away, but other neighbors disagreed. Hilda had been active in the gallery in the building and left behind about a hundred paintings No one from her family wanted them. When she had better sight, Hilda did representational work.

According to Mark, she'd been "in la-la land" since at least 1997, when Hilda was eighty-two, and he greeted her on the street and she didn't recognize him. She later told a mutual friend that a stranger had talked to her. Around this time, Mark asked Hilda for the number of her uncle who visited and brought food for Passover and Rosh Hashanah.

As her illness progressed, Hilda started knocking on Mark's door several times a day asking for food—yogurt, oranges, cookies—but she mixed up the food names. Soon Hilda was wandering the seventh floor, going door to door, ringing bells, asking for yogurt. "She seemed to think the front desk was like a deli counter," Mark said, "and she was always asking the guards to get her food, like they were store clerks."

Suddenly I knew who Hilda was! "Did she have gray bangs and big black glasses?" Yes, that was her! I recalled a day last year when this older woman got off the elevator and marched up to the front desk and insisted the security guard get a light bulb for her apartment. I thought she was gone. I remembered another time two years ago when I was posting a flyer and I spoke to her about the event, and she was shockingly nasty. It was probably the disease speaking, but her venom was scary.

Mark and another neighbor, Adrienne, offered to grocery shop, but Hilda was stubborn. She insisted upon going to D'Agostino's herself, but when she got there she forgot what she needed. She told Mark money was no problem but he had no idea about her income. Neighbors brought her food and got her into Meals on Wheels, but she resisted the delivery guy. The building social worker arranged for home care, but she threw the attendant out. She let two cooked chickens rot in the fridge while she wandered around he hallway begging for peach yogurt. Near the end, everyone on that floor was talking.

"She could not admit she needed help," Mark said. "I took her aside and told her 'Hilda, you need help or they will put you away.'"

"She was like a six-year-old in an old lady's body," said Adrienne, an abstract painter. "I'd hug her because no one else touched her." The uncle gave Adrienne money to buy inexpensive clothes on Fourteenth Street. because Hilda—once immaculate—had stopped doing laundry.

The night the police came with a psych unit, (after Hilda was reportedly walking around exposing her breasts) she went away quietly to St. Vincent's for testing.

Two weeks later, Mark and Adrienne visited her hospital room. Hilda told them she liked her new home; Mark said she looked happy. She did not recall their names, but chatted about neighbors from twenty years ago. Hilda now lives in the Hebrew Home for the Aged in Riverdale, where two of her paintings hang in her room.

From what I learned, Hilda had no husband, no kids, no significant other, no relationship. She used to read *The New York Times* over the phone to a blind painter every day. She did not spend much money. She walked around the Village and visited SoHo galleries. During her normal life, she painted regularly, her easel overlooking Washington Street. Years ago, she sold a painting to someone famous. Early in her career, she lived in Paris and sold her work to private collectors. Hilda studied at the American Art School and the Art Students League and showed in New York galleries in the sixties and seventies.

By all accounts, she was belligerent, feisty, aloof. Family tragedy shaped her personality. Hilda grew up in Brighton Beach. When she was a young woman, her brother became paralyzed from an accident and then committed suicide. After this, her mother lost her mind and was institutionalized. "She had a lot of anger from that," said Mark. I wonder if she was ever happy.

Hilda moved to Westbeth in 1976, when she would have been sixty-two. I try to imagine her younger, in Paris in the 1930s or 1940s. I pictured her as a lesbian hanging out with Gertrude and Alice. How I would love to have been a part of that scene! I asked, but Mark said he had no clue about Hilda's sexual orientation. I imagine her easel set up along the Seine and her brush strokes capturing its ripples and reflections. Maybe that experience is in my paintings.

The lone caring relative said Hilda had alienated everyone over the years. Her version was that "They're no good. They never liked me because I was different."

Perhaps we are kindred spirits in some way. I certainly can relate to feeling different and alienated from my family. Like Hilda, I've turned people off with my anger. But I'm from the therapy generation and spent years working out family issues. As I sit on my couch, chilling out, looking at Hilda's paintings in my studio, I wonder how someone so angry could paint so serenely. Maybe it was her release.

DOWNTOWN DYKE IN A MIDTOWN SPORTS BAR

BY KATE WALTER

We were three gay women surrounded by a ring of testosterone in an Irish pub in Midtown. The Rangers were on TV playing the Sabres in the semifinals taking place down the street in Madison Square Garden. Grown men sat at the bar in team jackets and hats and cheered the on-screen action. Maybe they couldn't get tickets. What was I doing there?

Whenever my New Jersey friends Crissie and Marie came into the city we landed in some place this downtown dyke would normally avoid—the Molly Wee Pub on a Sunday night, with a crowd of rowdy sports guys and a cute female bartender with a brogue.

My friends had tickets to a Van Morrison concert in the Garden and invited me to meet them for an early meal in the Theater District. After dinner at Zen Palate, we walked down Eighth Avenue towards the Garden and they suggested we grab a drink before the show. I'd recently been dumped by my long-term partner, so I was glad to hang out with them.

In the weird nether land between Chelsea and Hell's Kitchen, the selections were limited and the Molly Wee Pub looked more inviting than the Blarney Stone. It wasn't until we sat at the wainscoted bar and ordered draft beers that I realized we were the only women in the place unaccompanied by men. Several females were seated at the tables behind us but they were all with dates.

"Go, go, go!" the bulky guy sitting next to me started screaming as the clock ran down on the screen. He was pumping his fist in the air. "Oh, no!"

"Overtime," said Marie, a recently retired gym teacher who still reffed high school soccer and basketball games. The score was one to one.

By now, the whole place was hysterical with excitement and everyone rushed the bar to order more drinks. I could not recall the last time I'd been in a crowd like this. Maybe decades ago when I was still straight and in college?

I was an arts queer who was not into competitive sports, although I played on Bonnie & Clyde's basketball team when I moved here thirty years ago. The league was a great way to meet women. I mostly warmed the bench, but one night I got into the game (we were way ahead) and scored a long jumper from the right. The team captain slapped me five.

Today, my idea of exercise is taking yoga classes and bike riding in the park. If I want a Corona, I go to the Cubby Hole, a cozy women's bar in the West Village with kitschy decorations dangling from the ceiling and a smattering of gay men. So I was out of my comfort zone sitting in the Molly Wee Pub with two Jersey friends.

"Kate, you should see the look on your face," said Crissie, who was an old flame of mine. We'd met in 1979 and had an affair when we were both high school English teachers. We'd lost contact but reconnected a few years ago when I bumped into her on my corner. Crissie and her partner were visiting Marie's cousin, a dog walker I knew from the block. We caught up after that chance meeting, which we deemed synchronicity.

"I can't take all this male energy," I replied. "It's too much. Makes me glad I'm gay."

When the game resumed, everyone except us was fixed on the screen. A few more minutes passed as my friends tried to tell me about their upcoming trip to Europe and their side junket on an all-women cruise, but it was hard to hear with all the shouting. Then I heard roars from the captive audience.

"Double overtime," said Marie as she ordered another Guinness.

Now the room was insane with tension. Even I peeked at the TV a bit. "Let's go, Rangers," the place was chanting. "Rangers, let's go."

We tried to resume our conversation, but it was nearly impossible, so we gave up and watched. Crissie ordered an Irish whiskey and offered me a sip. Groups of men pressed us against the bar trying to be as close as possible to the televised action.

"Yes, yes, yes!" some guy screamed right into my ear, pissing me off. I looked up. The Rangers had the puck. Some player got off a great shot and scored. It was two to one. At that point, the patrons in the Molly Wee Pub went nuts, yelling and hugging and high-fiving each other. I wondered if straight men liked sports because it gave them permission to be physical with each other.

Just when I thought the craziness was over and the place would calm down, a parade of guys wearing Rangers shirts and caps arrived fresh from the Garden, stomping into the room like conquering heroes. They revved up the crowd, yelling "Let's go, Rangers" and everyone except us joined the jubilant chorus.

I felt like I had walked into a frat party and I was twenty years old again. I was stunned that middle-aged men got this wild over team sports. I knew this happened, but to be in the midst of it was bizarre. My intellectual father had been an analytical baseball fan who read the box scores at breakfast. My brother and nephew were into surfing and fishing. I had stepped into a macho world I did not understand. Was this what heterosexual women had to deal with on a regular basis?

In fairness to their insanity, I later read a sports column that described the winning play—a fifty-three foot hard drive scored in double overtime—as "one of the great hockey moments in the Garden." It was also the longest Rangers game in thirty-six years.

"That was some game," Marie said to the new arrivals who sidled up to the bar squeezing between us to order. "Must have been exciting inside."

"Unbelievable," said the fan who smiled at us and soon he and my friend were chatting about the incredible winning shot.

As I walked downtown, I thought, *this* is what's great about New York: three lesbians stumble into a sports bar during a heated playoff game and everyone skates through. I was the one who'd been judgmental about male sports fanatics. My suburban friends seemed more relaxed, maybe because they're used to sharing a golf course with straight men. My Village lifestyle is hipper, but can also be insular.

The next Sunday I was home working at my computer when I heard my yuppie neighbors cheering from their terrace on West Twelfth Street. I looked up and saw several couples watching a hockey game on the big screen TV inside their apartment. The Rangers were back on the ice. I got up and turned on my set to check the score.

FILING AWAY

BY KATE WALTER

I felt a little nostalgic as my W2 slips started arriving in the mail. For the first time in two decades, I did not receive the form letter from Sheldon, my long term accountant.

His annual reminder always opened with an awkward phrase: "Winter is here and with it the knowledge that April 15 will soon be here." That stilted sentence always made me smile. He was good with numbers, not words. I was just the opposite

He died last spring right after my taxes were done. This winter I was desperately seeking a replacement. I first met Shelly twenty years ago in the East Village. He did the books for the printer who had a business in the storefront of my building. The shop was a gossipy hang-out where the mailman delivered our packages; the place reeked of cigarettes.

In the early eighties, I had a disastrous experience with a street corner tax moron who urged me to deduct all expenses for a trip to the Caribbean because I'd sold a travel article about it. I was just starting to freelance seriously and didn't realize this would send up red flags. I was audited that year and had to pay hundreds more dollars. I vowed to find someone who knew what he was doing. That's when my partner and I became Sheldon's clients.

We could not have been more different. He was a religious Jew living with his wife in Brooklyn and we were a lesbian couple living on St. Mark's Place. We had to remember not to call him on Saturday.

After the printer downstairs retired, we no longer saw Sheldon in person. Although I hadn't actually seen the man in years, I felt a strong connection. This man I called Shelly was privy to personal details about my life. He knew I was in psychotherapy for over ten years, and he knew when I stopped. ("That's good but now you need another big deduction," he said.)

Shelly knew the publications I wrote for and how much money (or how little) I made. He even put a positve spin on the a small fortune in dental work I'd spent several years in a row. Most importantly, he knew when I moved to another apartment and my lover stayed put.

"How's your friend?" he asked that spring. "Everything okay?"

"She's fine. We see each other all the time," I said.

Looking back, I think maybe he worried if I could survive in Manhattan on my own, or maybe he cared about my relationship. Or maybe both. When I told him I'd landed a studio in subsidized housing after years on a waiting list, he seemed relieved.

Shelly's rates were very reasonable, so I knew I'd have trouble finding someone comparable. This crisis reminded me of when my long term dentist retired to Florida unexpectedly. He knew my teeth were bad; Shelly knew my financial situation was bad. Both knew better than to lecture me. They accepted me as I was and worked wonders with what I brought them. How would I find a new CPA?

As usual, my partner, Slim, was not as anxious about this dire situation. She always did her taxes at the last minute.

"You can't do that this year," I said. "We don't have anyone lined up." She accused me of being nervous and neurotic. I lashed back, "I'm not the extension queen, like you." Slim remembered that someone else had signed her forms last April. Were mine the last papers Shelly inked? Did an assistant finish those jobs left behind? Recouping this name—John—was like finding a life line. For once, filing late had saved the day.

We both called John in Brooklyn. He said Sheldon taught him everything he knew about taxes; he worked for him five years. John was familiar with our names, recalled our forms. And he'd do our taxes—for the same rate. So now we have the master's apprentice—it's kinda like Shelly is still doing my taxes, punching that old calculator in the sky.

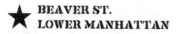

BEAVER ST.
LOWER MANHATTAN

PLAYERS
BY JENNIFER SEARS

The young musician met the older musician after a concert. It was on the fourth floor of a building just south of Wall Street, a part of the city that turns into a ghost town on weekend nights. The concert space was run by an organization dedicated solely to the arts, and therefore was unheated despite the brutal January cold snap. Audience members had kept their coats on as they sat for hours on frigid metal chairs. Band members kept blowing on their hands. The young musician wore a poncho made of alpaca fur, which kept him warm and gave him freedom to move his arms as he played. The older musician had simply gotten a bit drunk.

He approached the younger musician after the concert to compliment the way he played. Tall and imposing in a puffy down jacket, the older musician kept one hand warm in his coat pocket, and with the other, used his plastic beverage cup to emphasize his remarks. After they were introduced, the young musician realized who the older man was. His cousin had studied with him.

"George?" The older musician considered the cousin's name. Then he said loudly, "Oh, yes, George. George is very depressed. He never should have married that woman."

The small crowd around us laughed.

The young musician agreed about the woman. Then he tried again, "He's a good musician, though. Don't you think?"

The older musician shrugged. "He was good. But he didn't listen to me. I told him, 'Don't marry that woman.'"

It was late. The concert had gone on too long for an experimental thing. Beneath the high white walls and exposed support beams, the scene had taken on that surreal big sky feeling that often happens in arty warehouse settings, all of us milling about in a performance piece no one was directing. Practically speaking, there were drums and chairs to put away; the remains of a makeshift cash bar spread across a folding table needed clearing. Trash was piled high against the inactive furnace. To avoid working, people started line dancing to the recorded music. I was getting a ride with the young musician and hoped he'd gather his belongings together and finish speaking with his remaining admirers before I was assigned a task. He'd already packed his instrument in its battered silver case. The thick chain that substituted for a handle that had broken off years ago and was wrapped around his wrist.

When we were finally walking out, the older musician caught the young musician's attention again. He couldn't leave the subject of cousin George alone. George who had fallen in love. George, who had actually gone off and married a woman. "I'm telling you," the older musician began again, "it never works." Men standing close by laughed in commiseration. Soon, the musicians from the evening were all there, with the exception of the drummer who was preoccupied in a corner with his wife pulling sleepy children from warm down sleeping bags.

Laughter erupted from the men who began to form a huddle around the older musician. They looked up to him and expected him to make bold declarations.

"Listen to me," the older musician said. He stared intently at the younger musician.

"I'm married to my music," the young musician promised him.

But the old musician wasn't satisfied. Drawing the men closer together, he spoke quietly.

As I stood outside the circle and leaned against a folding chair, a jittery, dark-haired girl touched my arm. She wanted me to introduce her to the young musician. She said she was interested in him for professional reasons.

"I've lived in his country," she said, excitedly. She was beautiful. And young. She loved how he played in the concert. "Incredible," she said. I nodded. He was.

When she saw that I wasn't going to provide her with an introduction, she tried to go at it alone. I watched the girl inch around the outside of their circle, trying unsuccessfully to get their attention. Backs turned, all of the men kept laughing as the older musician rumbled on about that impossible mix of loyalties: music and women.

Finally, the young musician and I made our way down to the street and toward his enormous silver pickup truck that matched his old instrument case. Wind cut through the tall buildings on Beaver Street where he'd parked. He slid the chain off his wrist and carefully secured the case behind the driver's seat as I opened the door on the passenger side and climbed inside. He turned the heater on at full force and we sat enjoying the first bit of warmth we'd felt that night. We stared out at Bowling Green Park. Locked for the night behind iron gates, the old-fashioned lamps made the snow glisten on the trees and park benches arranged neatly in a circle.

It could have been romantic sitting there, looking out, but it wasn't.

Though he rarely listens to music when he gives me rides home from gigs in his truck, it's all we ever talk about: composers, style, other musicians and dancers we know, jobs. We've had arguments about the conflicting values (in his mind) between entertainment and religion. That night, as we made our way toward the eclectic bustle of the Lower East Side, we discussed the private downfall of his cousin George who'd wound up in jail, music-less, entangled in a strange mess for the love of a woman.

"Terrible," the young musician said, shaking his head. "Now he can't play at all."

We circled around Houston and Orchard looking for a parking spot near Bereket, the all-night Turkish café. He asked me how well I knew the older musician. I told him I had a couple of great recordings. He built his own instruments. I'd met him a few times and always liked talking to him.

"But," the young musician hesitated. "Isn't he a womanizer or something?"

"A womanizer?" It was a word I'd only heard my father use. I wasn't even sure what it meant. "I don't think so," I said.

"He told me he never sleeps with a woman more than three times."

"That was the advice he was giving all of you?" I laughed.

"Did he hit on you?" the young musician asked.

"No," I said, though the older musician had put his arm around the back of my chair for a song. Maybe two. I hadn't moved away, not even when he leaned in toward me with that sarcastic grin on his face. "He just wanted to see what I would do," I said.

"You know what?" the young musician began. "He just hasn't met the right girl yet."

"Come on!" I said. "He's a musician. He meets plenty of girls."

"But he hasn't met the right one," the young musician explained. I was silent, uncomfortable. His optimism and sincerity often baffled me. I was never sure which one of us was naive.

"You know," he kept going. "He hasn't met the girl who makes him dizzy."

"Dizzy?" I said. "You get dizzy?"

"Sure," he said and pulled into the perfect parking spot that had just magically opened up in front of the Cairo Café. He leapt out of his truck and grabbed his silver instrument case, the chain wrapped around his wrist. Newly aware of the utter lack of dizziness in my life, I opened my door and stepped knee-deep into a crusty snowbank pushed up onto the sidewalk.

Inside Bereket, one of the guys behind the counter recognized the young musician standing in line with his instrument case. He shouted to the others in Turkish. To the dismay of the other midnight meat-eaters, the men behind the counter abandoned their prep stations and the enormous rack of grilled meat. They crowded behind the register, talking at once, excited to see the young musician. They wanted to know where he'd most recently performed in Turkey. They begged him to take out his instrument, but he refused. He'd been playing all night, he explained. He was hungry. One of the men behind the register started singing. The guys all joined in, singing a few phrases from a song the musician knew.

When they got to working on our order, he told me about a time he'd come late at night with another musician, a guitar player, and two belly dancers, and they'd opened their cases and started playing Turkish music between the tables. That's why the guys always remembered him.

"We were right there," he said, pointing to a small, littered table in the corner of the unassuming seating area.

As they had played, passersby from Delancey Street came in and started dancing. The guys behind the counter danced too, in their white hats and red aprons. They kept playing and singing and the belly dancers had to dance on the tables because the room was so crowded.

"Everyone was so into it," the musician said. Though he'd played for crowds of thousands around the world and in upscale concert halls, he'd never described playing with such enthusiasm as that impromptu moment after hours on Houston Street.

"Who were the girls?" I asked, thinking I might recognize my colleagues.

"What girls?" he said, absentmindedly, remembering only the music. Not the women.

"The dancers," I said. "On the tables."

He shrugged. "What a night," he said again.

Carrying his instrument case and the bag filled with our sandwiches and the complimentary desserts the guys from Bereket had thrown in especially for him, we stopped in front of the Cairo Café. The sliding glass doors were shut tight against the cold, but we heard live music, drums, and finger cymbals. The scent of apple tobacco exhaled from the shisha pipes drifted onto the sidewalk. We tried to see who was playing, but all we could make out inside the room lit with Christmas tree lights were the diners cramped inside the narrow restaurant. Beneath an artist's rendition of neon bright pyramids and a sorrowful Tut, friends shared pipes. Lovers huddled together. The music was tucked in the background as regular people concentrated on each other.

"I'm starving," the young musician reminded me.

At my nearby apartment, we listened to one of the older musician's recordings. I ate my sandwich in silence, and when I got bored, started in on the remains of his. The young musician was busy listening. He only spoke when he wanted me to repeat a track we both liked, a quiet piece that began with an oud solo. Pensively, the older musician's fingers pulled at the strings. It was as if he was there and we were all listening, each one of us dedicated. Each one of us alone.

★ **4910 14TH AVE,**
BOROUGH PARK, BROOKLYN

OASIS

BY JOSEPH E. SCALIA

The summer of 1952 I was ten, and the center of my universe was Brooklyn. The Dodgers were still Brooklyn's team and Ebbets Field was where they played baseball, not a housing project. Everyone hated the Yankees, even Tony Costa, who was the only Giants fan on Fifty-seventh Street.

In early July, the end of school was still so close that the pinch of freedom felt as unnatural as the stiff pair of dungarees my mother bought for me, and September was far enough away that the terror of Labor Day wasn't even a thought. Back then, summer seemed an endless coil of days filled with stoopball, hit-the-penny, and marathon stickball games that broke for supper and continued later in the dusk under the streetlights. A person's worth was measured by a "spaldeen" hit two sewers, and the only shoot-outs were water pistol fights under the hot sun in the vacant lot, or marbles "played for keeps" in the narrow grassless strips of dirt along the curb. Afternoons, Bernie the Ice Cream Man pedaled his ice cream cart and tantalized us with the tinkling bells we heard from blocks away, causing us to quit our street games and call up the alleyways, "Hey Ma, throw down money for ice cream!"

LOST AND FOUND

In the cooler evenings, it was ring-a-leveo or hide-and-seek and manhunt, hiding in the bushes of Mr. Lotito's house, until the old man rushed down from his front porch to chase us with a spray of water from his garden hose. Nights, the older boys and girls paired off in the vacant lot to lie down in the weeds among the crickets and mark the passage of the stars between kisses and gropes in the darkness.

"Jo-seph," my mother's voice called my name like a lilting melody, "time to take a bath!" After, I would fall asleep to the thrum of summer, the murmur of crickets and cicadas mingled with quiet conversations that carried into my bedroom from the stoops, as another long summer day came to an end. All was as it should be then, in that world of comforting sameness where nothing ever changed.

That was why I was so surprised that early afternoon when two colored women walked onto the block. "Colored" was the term we used then, before "Negro" or "black" or "African American." I had often heard my mother say, referring to an actress, or some woman she might have seen on the downtown bus, "She's very pretty, for a colored girl." Of course, I was aware of the other word from the rhyme we recited whenever we'd choose up sides for a game: "—and if he hollers let him go." But to me it was just word, devoid of emotion or power, another name for those strange people I knew only from the *Tarzan* movies I'd seen at the Loews 46th Street Theater. In my brief life I had never seen a real colored person, except of course for Jackie Robinson, who once waved to me at Ebbets Field before a game. Back then my entire world was Catholic and Italian, with the possible exception of Henry Hernandez, who was only half-Italian. His father was from Puerto Rico, but his mother was Sicilian. My world was entirely white.

With their light summer-floral dresses trailing in the warm July breeze, the two women were a stark contrast in that white world, as they stepped carefully, eyes lowered, heads down, holding firmly to each other for support. Their dark skin glistened with perspiration from the July afternoon's record heat, and their bent-forward exertions to negotiate the uphill walk toward Thirteenth Avenue.

From the safety of the shadows where I was hidden from their view, I marked their slow progress up the street until they stopped on the sidewalk directly in front of my house. As they stood there for a long moment looking up at the screen door, I was able to study both women without being seen. One had her gray hair pulled in a tight bun under her white straw hat, and the other, who looked younger, though I couldn't really tell, wore wire glasses like my grandmother's. The gray-haired woman struggled up the steep cement steps and rang the doorbell. Then she hurried back to the sidewalk and re-joined her companion.

When my mother appeared behind the closed screen door she didn't try to conceal the look of surprise on her face. "What do you want?" she asked curtly, with that tone of suspicion I knew so well.

"Excuse me, Missus," the woman said with a slow accent. "But I was telling my friend here that I use to clean this house some years back. For the Parkers."

"Not this house," my mother said quickly, about to shut the door on them. "You're mistaken."

"But," the woman persisted, "I did, Missus," she said, fixing my mother with a glance, and then she turned again toward her friend whose disbelieving eyes rolled up behind her glasses. "I started back in forty-eight," she said, nodding to re-enforce her recollection. "That's right, Missus. I clean for Mr. Parker and his wife." And there was a note of pleading in her voice. "You must remember, Missus? I work here three days a week for years."

My mother paused, looked at the woman, and then nodded her head. "Uh, yes," she said. "The Parkers. Yes, I remember now." Her answer surprised me. We had lived in that house on Fifty-seventh Street all my life and my mother was the only one who ever cleaned anything.

"I told you I work here," the gray-haired woman said with satisfaction to her friend. "Didn't I tell you?" She turned to face my mother. "How is Mr. Parker?"

"Oh," my mother replied, and her voice took on a different tone, "Mr. Parker died in December of 1950."

The woman shook her head. "That's a shame," she said and touched her fingers to her lips. She seemed genuinely concerned. "And Mrs. Parker? How is she?"

"Oh," my mother said again without hesitation, "she died too." And then added, "Last year. Got sick right after Mr. Parker passed away."

"Oh, that's too bad," the woman said, shaking her head. "They's nice folks, the Parkers. Always treat me kind. Not like some of them other white people. No disrespect, Missus. Always make me lunch when I clean for them. And give me things to take back home. Clothes and toys for the grandchildren." Her eyes were wet. "That's too bad," she said again. She wiped her face with a gray handkerchief from her pocketbook and blew her nose, making a sound that startled me. "Now I don't mean to be no trouble, Missus," she said after she composed herself, "but do you think my friend and me might have a glass of water? If it wouldn't be no bother, I mean? It sure is hot today."

"Water?" My mother balked at the request, as though the woman had asked to borrow money.

"Sure is hot today," the woman said again. "And we'd sure be grateful. But if it's too much trouble, we don't want to be no bother to you, Missus."

"Yes," my mother said finally, "it is hot today. You wait there." She deliberately locked the screen door. "I'll go get some water for both of you."

In a moment she returned holding two sweating, green depression glasses filled with the cold water we kept in the refrigerator. My mother opened the door and handed down the glasses to the women.

"Thank you, Missus," the gray-haired woman said when she finished her drink. "And bless you."

They put the empty glasses on the steps. Then the two women turned and continued up the street.

"See," the older woman said with great satisfaction to her friend, "I told you I work in that house."

When they were gone, my mother went outside and picked up the empty glasses from the steps. I watched her from my hiding place in the shadows as she carried them to the side of the house. She opened the garbage can where she dropped both glasses inside. Then she climbed the steps and went back in to finish her housework.

Nearly fifty years have passed since then, but I never forgot the incident. Neither did I ever tell my mother that I saw it all. I'm sure she wouldn't remember if I had. Today the whole world is different. My mother is almost ninety-six, and although the years have taken their toll, she is still healthy and alert. She lives on her own in that same house where I grew up. I visit every Sunday to check on her and to bring her groceries. In winter I shovel the snow. In summer we sit together on the porch and watch the Mets on her little portable television, a Christmas gift from me.

"They lost again last night," she says with disgust. "In the ninth." A momentary passion ignites the spark in her old eyes, and I nod in sympathy. "They couldn't buy a hit. They play like a bunch of sandlotters. A pack of bums," she continues, and I wonder if she is thinking about another team and another time.

My mother has a companion, a woman in her sixties, who comes to fix my mother's meals and to keep her company. Her name is Lotti, and she is from the West Indies. At first it was just a job, but over the years the two women have become friends. They eat together and play cards. Lotti never seems to mind, or even notice, when my mother cheats. They tell jokes, and they complain about life, alternating family stories.

"She's a beautiful girl," my mother whispers to me, as Lotti returns to the porch with the lunch she made for all of us. "Beauti-ful."

"Momma talking about me again?" Lotti says with mock indignation. The cadence in her voice is musical. "I know she always talk about me when me back is turned," she says, and then turns and winks at me. "She think there's something wrong with me hearing. That I don't hear too good, but I do." She hands over the tray of sandwiches and a pitcher of cold, fresh-made lemonade she hand squeezed.

"Lotti, I just told my son that you are a beautiful girl," my mother repeats, and she reaches out to touch Lotti's dark hand.

"She don't think I know all the bad things she say, especially after I have to get tough with her. Momma is a very stubborn woman sometimes." Lotti lays out the three glasses filled with ice and places a sandwich cut in triangles on my mother's plate. "Now what stories you been telling this boy about Lotti?"

"I would never say anything bad about you, Lotti," my mother says, and she touches Lotti again. They are a contrast of white on black. "I love you."

Lotti covers her face and shakes her head with genuine embarrassment. "Oh, Frances, how you do make me blush. Is my face red?" And she throws back her head in a hearty, openmouthed laugh that shows her gold crowns. "But you just be quiet now, Frances, and eat that sandwich I made," she scolds her, wagging a crooked finger at my mother. "Sometimes," Lotti turns to me, "Momma talks so much she gives me a headache!" But I can see that both of them are pleased. "Now you hush and eat your lunch, Frances."

It surprises me that my mother doesn't answer back. She just picks up her sandwich like a dutiful child, but waits for Lotti to sit before she takes a small bite.

Pouring a tall glass of the lemonade for each of us, Lotti says, "Have yourself a cold drink. Let's all of us have a drink before we dry up in this hot air and blow away." And then she adds, "Sure is hot today."

And I smile at her words.

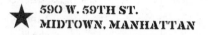

**590 W. 59TH ST.
MIDTOWN, MANHATTAN**

THE SHAVE
BY JOSEPH SCALIA

My father was a man of few words. Not because he was the strong silent type, but rather because in the twenty-three years that we spent together, it was my mother who did most of the talking. He had few opinions, my father, which he mostly kept to himself, and besides, my life was too full of other things to be remotely interested in, or have the time to listen to, the ones he expressed openly.

Because he was so soft-spoken it was easy for me to dismiss him. I remember that Sunday morning, November 24, 1963, when all of America was still reeling from what Lee Harvey Oswald had done to our president. "Mark my words," my father said with tears in his eyes, "someone will kill that man."

"Don't be ridiculous," I answered sharply in my private grief, so appalled at my father's simplicity and lack of sophistication. "This is America, not some banana dictatorship." But within the hour we both watched in shock, along with the rest of the country, as Jack Ruby turned my father's foolish words into prophecy on live TV. He never said "I told you so," and I never acknowledged that he was right.

LOST AND FOUND

For me, 1964 was a year of endings and new beginnings. In June I graduated college, and began my first teaching job in a local junior high school that September. In December, I married Ginny, my childhood sweetheart, the girl next-door, and moved out of the only house I ever knew as home, into an apartment. Though it was a time of great excitement, it was also a time of great difficult for my parents. My father, unable to work, had been home for the months leading up to the wedding, recovering from yet another operation, the third in as many years. The first two had been to repair a detached retina in his eye, the last, more serious, to remove a "blockage in his intestine," the doctor told my mother. After each procedure his barbershop had to be closed, and there was little income, except for what my mother earned operating a sewing machine and what I was able to contribute from my part-time job after school.

In the middle of it all, I was in too much of a hurry, running off to meet friends, making social plans, preparing lessons for my classes, getting ready for the wedding and the big move, so I hardly realized the seriousness of his situation, or the rapid passage of time. When I did take the opportunity to notice, the signs of depression were there, cut deep in the lines on my father's face. But he didn't complain. He didn't say much. Yet whenever I looked, I saw it in his eyes from all those long days he had spent sitting on the couch in his bathrobe watching TV, or counting the loose change in his pockets with his glasses pushed up on his forehead. He had begun his search for old coins to replace the collection of Indian head pennies he'd sold a year before to help pay some of the hospital bills.

On the weeks leading up to the big day, when my father felt strong enough, he helped me paint and wallpaper the new apartment. And there were some days when he had tried to open up the barbershop. "It made me feel useful and productive," he said. Over the long months the shop had been closed, many of his customers found other barbers, and his small clientele had grown even smaller. But it didn't matter that there were no customers, because by mid-afternoon he was too tired to stand and he had to close the shop and return home to rest.

When the morning of December 19th finally arrived, it was difficult for me to believe that in a matter of hours I would be a married man. Following the reception, Ginny and I would fly off on our honeymoon and the official beginning of Christmas vacation. For the two of us, it was a time of firsts—first time in an airplane, first Christmas away from the family, and first home in an apartment that wasn't the only home I knew. When I returned with my new wife, it would be to a new life.

"Come on," my father said to me early that clear, crisp Saturday morning. "I have something I want to do at the shop."

"What?" I asked, in my anxiety to get dressed, to be on my way.

"It won't take long. You won't miss the wedding, I promise. Come on."

We walked together the three blocks from the house to his shop. When I was a little boy, walking with my father had been difficult, trying to keep up with his long strides, taking two steps to his every one. It took my breath away. But now he was the one out of breath, the one who had trouble keeping up, and I had to slow my pace for him to stay with me.

When we arrived he paused on the steps until he was able to breathe. He waved to Lou Gould, the dry cleaner, whose store was next to the barbershop. Lou looked surprised to see my father so early on a Saturday, to see him there at all. He nodded and waved from behind the foggy window at the two of us, as my father fit his key into the door lock. The electric barber pole outside the shop was still. On better days, the red and white stripes spiraled up from early morning when he arrived until quitting time.

"The pole is an ancient symbol," he had told me when I was little. "It says to everyone who passes, 'The barber is in.' But even more than that, the pole dates back to a time when barbers didn't just cut hair," my father said with great pride. "Barbers were like doctors. Better than doctors. They were the surgeons. And the red on the pole is for blood." It was something I always remembered.

Inside the shop was dark and it smelled of the Jeris Hair Tonic and the lilac talcum powder that lined the shelves in front of the two leather-covered barber chairs. One chair he used to give haircuts, the second was never used. Business was never good enough to support even a part-time second barber. It was where my father sat to work on crossword puzzles, or where he took short naps between customers. Many times as a kid, on my walks to the schoolyard or the candy store, I would see my father asleep, reclining in the chair with his feet up and his arms tucked behind his head.

On the wall behind the chair my father erected a photo tribute to all the neighborhood boys who had served in the military from World War II, Korea, and after. A young and smiling Tony Petti looked out from Germany where he was wounded back in 1945. Andy Bundy, who everyone called "Bunny," and Don DeCanio were both in their smart Air Force uniforms from somewhere far away. Louie Yodice, who married my cousin Loretta, squatted among a bunch of sailors in dress- blues. Even Gene, who would later become my brother-in-law, dressed in army drab and holding an M-1, smiled from a town in Korea where he guarded POWs. There were others too, faces I didn't recognize. The most recent were color pictures from Viet Nam, guys my own age in jungle camouflage trying to look fierce. All the photographs with their names printed below them lined the wall.

On the mirror in front of the chair, displayed for everyone to see, were the family pictures—my sister Beverly's high school graduation, me in my college cap and gown, my sister in her wedding dress with her husband Gene, returned safe from Korea, and the smiling pictures of my father's grandchildren, Lisa and Richard. I took it in, seeing all and noticing nothing. To me, little had really changed in the years that he had worked in the shop.

"Sit in the chair," my father said, dusting off the seat with a clean towel from the folded pile that he always kept handy on the shelf. He pumped up the chair with the lever and he tilted me back gently in the seat.

My father was the only barber I had ever known, the only person to cut my hair. When I was little, sitting on the booster board that he kept for children, I screamed and was terrified of the electric sound of his clippers. When I was older, a protestor, I resisted getting even a trim, until my hair was so long that my mother threatened to cut it when I was asleep. But always, I remember the coolness of the hair tonic that he rubbed into my scalp, the softness of the sable brush he used to dust lilac talc on the back of my neck when he was finished.

"It's your wedding day," my father started awkwardly, "and I wanted to do something special for you today. I want to give you a shave." He turned on the warmer and dropped in a fresh, new towel. In a minute, his hands pressed the towel over my face, and it was startlingly hot and soothing at the same time. In the silence there in the shop I thought about how many thousands of times in the course of his lifetime my father had done this very same thing for his customers. I closed my eyes.

"You know," he said softly, "I guess there are a lot of things we should have talked about before. And things we need to talk about now."

I opened my eyes and watched him walk to the new electric soap machine to warm the shaving cream. He had bought it just before he got sick and hardly had the opportunity to use it. He hesitated there for a second, and instead he took his own shaving cup from the top shelf where he kept it. He ran the water hot in the sink until it sent up clouds of steam. Then he wet the soft bristles of the shaving brush with the hot water and dipped it into the cup. Expertly, his hands whipped the scented bar of soap into a thick lather before he carefully set the cup aside and removed the towel from my face. Then I felt my father's soft, smooth hands touch me, something he rarely ever did, even when I was a child. Slowly and lovingly, he lightly caressed my skin with his fingers. In another moment I felt the soft shaving brush spread the thick, warm soap along the line of my jaw and over my cheeks. I pursed my lips as he lathered above my mouth. I watched as he selected a straight razor from those that he kept on the shelf, passing over two of them until he found just the right one. He pulled the leather strap that hung down from the side of the chair and began slowly and methodically stropping the delicate edge of the blade until it sparkled, catching and reflecting the overhead fluorescent light.

It was then that the tiny bell on the back of the door tinkled as a man stepped into the shop. "Joe," the man said, pleased to see that he had found my father there, "you're open!"

"Not today, Mr. Parker," my father answered. "It's my son's wedding day," he said with unmistakable pride, and turned to me on the chair, "and I just opened the shop for a little while so I could give him a real good shave."

Mr. Parker smiled and nodded. "Congratulations, young man," he said to me. To my father he said, "And good luck to you, Joe. Please open up soon. All of your customers miss you." He smiled. "I really need a haircut, and I won't go to anybody but you. Congratulations!" he called again as he closed the door.

My father went back to the task of shaving. He used his razor deftly, cleaning off all traces of my beard along with the soap.

"It's very late, I know, but not too late." He paused. "I guess I should ask," he said and hesitated again. "Do you have any questions? I mean, is there anything you want to know, before you get married?"

I looked into the mirror and smiled into his reflected face, amused by his embarrassment and touched by it as well. "No," I said after a long second. "I think I'll be all right." And then I added for his benefit, "Is there anything that you want to know?"

My father looked back at me across time and space and a smile crinkled his eyes in the corners. I hadn't seen him smile in a long time. He wiped my face clean with a towel and cooled my skin with a splash of Pinaud Lilac Vegetal, my favorite. Although I really didn't need it, he powdered the back of my neck with talc and that soft sable brush he knew I loved so much. And then he closed up the shop and together we walked slowly back to the house in silence.

I was twenty-two.

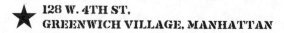

THE SWORDSMAN
BY SAID SHIRAZI

There used to be this guy who came to the park in a business suit and a thin black tie with his straw hair slicked back and wet-looking, to make the case against Darwin's theory of evolution. He had a clutch of professional-quality charts, which he set up on an easel behind him to help illustrate his points while he was speaking. His whole style was a corporate version of sincerity, like a fifties ad man.

The students and occasional professors walking by would mostly mock and jeer at him; he wasn't worth the trouble to refute anymore, not here, at least. Whatever Christian souls might have been passing had no stake in such controversies. By trying to be intellectually respectable he had lost them as well, falling, as the saying goes, between two stools.

I would watch his efforts from a distance, curious but not wanting to be drawn into argument. His cornflower blue eyes had a buried panic in them, like the modern world was too much for him, like he felt compelled by his very fear to come to the heart of downtown, to fight against its mindless, swirling madness, to have his say against error, to save. He was in the park for two years before vanishing.

LOST AND FOUND

Another guy I saw a few times was this shirtless, retarded-looking white dude in loose green sweatpants missing the drawstring, who sang his heart out over tapes of old soul classics. He had black plastic glasses held together by tape and a likeably ugly face like Stephen King. People stopped to laugh at him but soon began to enjoy his performance. He really had the moves down, all that old gut-bucket showmanship of pointing accusingly at the sky, going up on your toes to wail a high note and then dropping to your knees to plead with your baby not to leave.

That was the first time I had ever heard "I Can't Get Next To You." His repertoire was all agony: "Standing In The Shadows of Love" and "Bernadette," the tragic Temptations and Four Tops stuff you don't hear much on the radio. He looked like he lived at home with a TV-dead maiden aunt and had never had a date, but he was feeling it. Those songs were probably his best friends. Maybe his heart had been broken or maybe no one had ever bothered and that was what was killing him, or maybe he felt just fine.

The police walked him out and took his batteries—radio-playing is illegal in the park—and I followed after to make sure they weren't rough on him. I saw him one other time a few weeks later and they shut him down again, to the boos of a fair-sized crowd. My girlfriend was moving up that winter and I hoped he'd come back in the spring so she could see him too, but as far as I know he never returned.

Some days nice weather is as annoying as a fire drill; it requires you to evacuate the premises but gives you no particular place to be. After much circling around I always seem to touch down at the park. For one thing, it's about the only place you can sit. I don't like to read outdoors, there's too much to see, but it's good to have a book with you to reassure people you can still hear the small silent voice of reason rising up invisibly from the pages.

It shows how little power the police really have that just walking from one end of the park to the other, three or four guys will try to sell you pot. One dealer used to call me Mr. Book-Man whenever he saw me, which always cracked me up, but most of the time the offers felt like insults.

In the southwest corner, guys are waiting to hustle chess and in the northwest sometimes there's speed-Scrabble. These games are like an emblem of city life: Here we do it fast and we do it with anybody, and money has to change hands. This is what happens to childhood games here, they all grow furtive and professional.

I suspect our lunatics are sent to us on a rotating basis, like missionaries. The new one is a Latin gentleman with a wooden sword who wears a dirty grayish-brown trenchcoat hanging off his shoulders like a cape. Waving the sword about him, he delivers a long speech asking for work in the movies. You want to tell him he's in the wrong place, that even shows set in New York come from LA, but you're afraid to wake him from his enchantment.

Some air of olden grandeur clings to his person despite its recent shabbiness. He seeks fame and glory like the musketeers of yore, but on the screen, the only place it exists now, maybe the only place it can ever exist. He wants to live full-time in the world of human dreams, with the moon for a nightlight and his feet propped up on a pillowy silver cloud. He is looking for the secret door to that large and brighter world, oddly by asking after it on the street in broad daylight.

Where's he from? Somewhere. What'd he do before this? Something else. The truth is questions are rude. I don't ask because I don't care enough to be genuinely friendly and I don't really like to play with people anymore either. I confirm a secret pact of silence, not with a look even but by not looking very long, by more or less minding my own business and moving on.

The creationist, the soul-singer, the swordsman: I don't collect crazies but it does cheer me up sometimes to see them. If they can get through the endless plate of days set before us then maybe Mr. Book-Man will too, and with no drug stronger than fresh air and a few of the more common household illusions. That people still read, that our better feelings will always matter, and that there are some things only a stranger can hope to understand.

SCAFFOLDING

BY SAID SHIRAZI

Lately when I go for a walk, I make a vow not to walk under any scaffolding, in protest of there being so much of it these days. Two minutes later I realize I'm walking under scaffolding.

One day I stopped and looked at the scaffolding around the NYU tower at East Eighth Street and Mercer, and realized it had no purpose. It wasn't even next to the building, but instead twenty feet away around the edge of the plaza. If there were any reason at all for it to be there, it could only have something to do with security, as some kind of camouflaged fence. Soon after I concluded it was secretly not temporary, it vanished.

I started to look more closely at things and realized that the chain-link fence around the arch at Washington Square was not protecting any kind of renovation. There were no workers, no tools lying around, no project underway; it was simply there. My best guess is it was installed to prevent graffiti, that its pseudo-utilitarian ugliness was considered preferable to allowing human insult to the social order. Recently I noticed they took it down for commencement weekend and put it back up again when the parents were gone.

In April, they put scaffolding up outside my apartment building. It's like the building is in fourth grade and had to get braces; it won't be smiling anymore this year. Men perch out there hammering in a lax and sporadic fashion, the work going pretty slow when it goes at all. I sit at my desk imagining them as a flock of heartbroken woodpeckers come to roost, or Bunyanesque infants grown bored with their pickax rattles. Sometimes the knocks seem plaintive, like the moans of zombies calling a town's remaining survivors out to join them in the penultimate scene of a horror flick. Sometimes the hammering falls into a groove and almost begins to mean something, to speak like drums—but I can't answer, can't even stick my head out to see because they've stapled heavy sheets of plastic over the windows, leaving me sealed in like a funky Tut.

No one knows when it will come down; they seem to find it comicthat I should ask. I watched them assemble it from my window, my last view of the world not the outlaw's gallows but a marvel of modern efficiency built from specially-made blue tubes resembling designer pasta, X-shaped crossbars that snap into position in seconds, and a platform of ordinary two-by-fours nailed firmly in place. It was done in half a day and then no one showed up for a week. You take so much on faith in the city.

Life was good growing up in the suburbs, before you knew that's where you were. You had a discreet and obedient little thermostat instead of a madly clanging radiator, thick shag pile to roll around on instead of clackety cold polished wood, and a nice garage to pull into. You were expected to parallel park exactly once in your lifetime, on your driving test. At twilight, the fireflies lit up like unstrung yellow Christmas bulbs and the crickets chirped their vespers of senseless lust and glee, and a carpet of glory rose up from the lawns until you felt you were wading through it.

There was always scaffolding around at college but no one minded, since you were usually moving in a matter of months. Freshman week, we drank fruit punch mixed with grain alcohol and climbed around on it like we were playing a giant Donkey Kong game. Junior year, my girlfriend ate mushrooms and sat out on it in a state of trippy wonder until campus security came and gently talked her down. My last summer, I even got a cushy job guarding it, with a hard hat and folding chair and thick novels by Melville, Joyce, and Pynchon which seemed themselves pointless feats of engineering, intricate sponges to sop up the flood of superfluous time.

It took me months to get used to the street noise here. People pour out of the bars wildly and triumphantly oblivious to my need for rest, just as I and my friends once poured out of the bars in someone else's neighborhood. Prostitutes fight over the corner in voices as loud as opera divas, their indifference to the hour more shocking than their profession: sure, they're shameless, but do they have any idea how late it is? Sometimes the city bus stops at the intersection and just waits there a full minute or two to get back on schedule, with a row of backed-up cars behind it, each honking angrily at the one ahead. I hear car alarms and jackhammers more often than "thank you" or "you're welcome."

I guess I stay here for the conversation, but it dies out a little more every year until you start to understand why they keep the jukebox turned up so loud in bars. Old friends get wary or just worn out; our lives either converge to such a degree they're hardly worth discussing or diverge beyond all relation. Still you stay for friends you never see, the way you came for museums you never visit.

I tried to look at all the renovation in my neighborhood as a glad indicator of prosperity, but it didn't help. I'm tired of this place, tired of streets that are torn up every time you turn around for no reason while a trash can someone had to drag out to warn of a pothole will be sitting in the middle of the street for a week, tired of cones and vests of safety orange and the urgent warning beeps of trucks backing up, tired of plywood tunnel detours and signs that say pardon our dust. I don't want to live in this city anymore, where the very walls perish around you only to be reborn in the agony of time. I want to live in a city that's done.

THE BARBER SHOPS ON AMSTERDAM

BY RACHEL SHERMAN

Inside Miguel's Barbershop on 942 Amsterdam Avenue, Spanish-speaking men sit in barber chairs facing the mirror. It is a sunny Friday in the early afternoon and the shop is busy.

I ask a guy named Anthony, who is sitting in the back, about Miguel's.

"This is a guy's place," he tells me. The barber working on his hair with an electric razor is giving him a fade-to-low trim.

"It's family-oriented," Anthony says, "so you have a lot of guys who grew up with each other. They knew each other in the Dominican Republic. Men come by and tell little stories. That's how we are in our culture."

It certainly is a guy's place. There are no women inside the shop. There are Yankees posters on the walls and Yankees caps on some of the men who have just come to chat.

Miguel's Barbershop has been open for three years.

The owner, Miguel, came to the United States four years ago from a place called Nagua in the Dominican Republic. Miguel was a barber in the Dominican Republic, and once here he started working in the barbershops on Amsterdam. He was able to acquire enough customers and funds so that he and his brother could open Miguel's Barbershop, their own place.

"You can come here and not waste a lot of time," Anthony tells me. "You can get any kind of style you want.

"They have competition from the guys across the street from 107-108th, but I think this is the best one - you got more room. Over there it's always packed."

I cross the street to the competition--Santana's Barbershop on 965 Amsterdam. Santana Solis, the owner, came to the United States in 1966. He is also from the Dominican Republic and does not speak much English.

Santana's has been open for thirty-four years, and through a translator, Mr. Solis points across the street to two other stores he owns. He says that he moved his barbershop from the other side of the street five years ago.

Mr. Solis has a large brown cat that sits in the sun on one of the chairs. I pet the cat and take pictures of the men. Santana's is as busy as Miguel's. When asked, all the customers are happy with their haircuts. There are no other women here, just like Miguel's. I pet the cat again and talk to it.

"You want it?" one man with an accent asks me. "Take it."

"It is a boy or a girl cat?" I ask.

"I don't speak English," the man tells me, smiling.

I cross the street again and enter Barberia Barbershop at 980 Amsterdam. A boy gets his hair cut by the barber, Gilberto.

Gilberto has worked here for seven years, and he looks like an actor in a Fellini film. The boy getting his hair cut is at the age where he should shave his moustache but hasn't yet.

The man in the chair tells me this is a very old establishment. It is quiet inside and I wonder if after I leave, Gilberto will give the boy his first shave.

I have always wanted to go in Las Divinas, the hairdresser at 994 Amsterdam. The big window has a pair of colorful scissors crossing each other, and through it you can see the gold-colored mirrors inside.

There are no customers yet, so Nelly, Clarisa, and Wendy, the women that work here, do each other's hair. The women are from the Dominican Republic as well. Wendy, who speaks some English, tells me she is getting extensions. I watch as Nelly glues a piece of black hair onto the back of Wendy's scalp. The extensions will last for three weeks and cost seventy-five dollars.

The three women talk in Spanish while I take pictures. A homeless man runs in and sits in the back of the store where the blow dryers are.

"No pictures! No pictures!" he says when he sees me, putting his hands in front of his face.

I tell him that I will not take his picture, but he runs out of the store anyway.

"He's crazy," Wendy says. "He comes in here to get warm."

Melvin and Pat's is a unisex salon at 998 Amsterdam. It is not as big as Santana's or Miguel's, but it is packed with people and mirrors on both sides of the wall, so that it seems bigger.

Melvin and Pat's has been open for three years. The clientele today is almost all young men, although the barbers tell me the salon is for both sexes. It is cramped, and some of the men snicker while I ask questions, although I am not sure why.

"Theres a woman back there," one of the barbers tells me.

I go to the back where a woman sits watching television. She does not want me to take her picture.

I backtrack to 926 Amsterdam to a place with a sign outside that says Leo's Barbershop. It is a small store with one barber named Tulio, who is known in the area as Leo. Leo tells me he has been open for only two months. He has worked in the neighborhood in various barbershops on Amsterdam since he came here from the Dominican Republic eight years ago. He saved money while he worked so he could open his own place.

"Business goes slow at first, but it's starting to pick up," he tells me.

When the man who is getting his hair cut leaves, the place is quiet except for the television, turned to the Spanish channel, like in all the shops I have been to.

LOST AND FOUND

Leo speaks more English than many of the other barbers. He gives me his card and his e-mail. I wish him luck and pass two more barbershops on the way home.

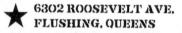

**6302 ROOSEVELT AVE.
FLUSHING, QUEENS**

STRAIGHT TALK
ON HAIR VILLAGE

BY RACHEL SHERMAN

To get my hair the way I always wanted it, which was straight and easy and flat on my head, I had to go to Queens.

The hair had been a problem: I remember when my college boyfriend told me—after six months in Spain—that when I ran to him at the airport, the happiest girlfriend in the world, all he could see was my hair. Eight years later and I still see me running: a body with hair for a face.

So, Queens. I had only been there twice: once to go to an anti-Semitic beer garden where I avoided being harassed like some of my friends had been, even though I still had Jewish hair, and once to eat Indian food. It was not so far, but it felt far, going on the train that went out from underground.

Hair Village is small. Neon lights and a room as big as my studio, filled with girls getting their hair straightened and the women who straighten them.

Later, I would see that everyone left Hair Village beautiful. I went there because it was cheap.

I had learned about Hair Village from an Eastern Bloc bartender in a Mexican restaurant after a few Cadillac margaritas. I asked her for more free olives and told her I liked her hair.

"It's fake," she said.

Then she told me about Hair Village.

No one who does Japanese hair-straightening at Hair Village is Japanese.

You can't have highlights if you want your hair straightened.

You can't touch your hair, or even put it behind your ears, for three days afterwards.

You can't wash your hair for three days either.

You should probably wear a shower cap when you are near water. Just in case.

When you get to Hair Village, first you go to a Korean woman. She is the boss, and everyone directs you to her. She tells you to wash your hair and then blow-dry it. Completely dry.

There are seven processes:

1. Wash hair. Dry.

2. Chemicals for up to two hours, depending on hair.

3. Wash hair and dry again.

4. Some other chemical where they put this thing that goes all the way around your neck that looks like one of those throw-up catchers in hospitals, only super-sized.

5. Wash and dry.

6. Have woman take an hour to use a tiny iron to straighten each part of your hair in tiny sections. She blows on your head so it is not too hot.

7. Watch as she cuts your hair and makes you the new you who is a better you and does not have to worry anymore about big hair.

I am told that in the morning there is a line out the door. I am too late for the line, which is good. A mother who sits next to

me tells me that she needs to get the process again. Hers is growing out, but it is her daughter's first time.

Her daughter is in high school and has long dark hair. I ask
her questions, and she tells me she is interested in psychology.
She is only in tenth grade, but I ask her about colleges. She tells
me Cornell. Her mother checks beneath her shower cap.

While waiting for my hair to cook, I watch a little girl, about
four or five, lie on the dirty floor and cry for her mother. Her
mother is there, getting the process, but the little girl is having a
hard time. I wonder about the ventilation in the place, since there
does not seem to be much, and the air smells of chemical upon
chemical, burnt hair, and something I can't define.

The little girl's mother threatens she will leave her with her
father, which suddenly seems like the worst thing this little girl
has heard. She cries and whines and is tired. Her mother has been
there for hours.

While my hair is wrapped up in plastic and there is a string
of cotton "protecting" the skin near my hair, I start to fall asleep.
I set my watch for the time I get to stop waiting. I doze/jerk
myself awake/doze.

Another girl has strawberry blond hair and is with her
mother. They look like they are from the suburbs. The mother
gives the girl a hard time about the cost of the process, and about
having friends over that night in their basement. There will be
boys and the mother does not want them. She carries a fancy
purse and her hair is dyed blonde and she has those driving shoes
on which always mean something other than that she has a car.

The girl just wants to get her hair done. It is big like mine.
There is a lot of room for talking and bonding in this place, but
I am watching the girls in the mirror watch themselves as they
transform, easily, surprisingly, wonderfully, and finally into the
girl they had dreamed themselves for so long.

The big hair they have left behind is the kind that frizzes in
the rain, needs blow drying each morning, makes the shadow of
your head a triangle. It is the kind of hair that makes you tie it up
and tie it down, twist it into ringlets while it's wet, use any prod-

uct that says "de-frizz," and constantly touch it to check its height and width.

With new hair, there is a possibility you will look Japanese from behind. You will wake up and shower and leave your hair down. You will go into stores, to parties, to best friends houses who will stand so close in front of you and touch your hair. They will stand so close it will feel like they are going to kiss you, they are so happy, telling you that it is the best thing you ever did. You will hope that at least once, you have done something just as good, or better.

When you walk out from Hair Village, straight-haired and new, you will go up in rank from from one to ten: those numbers the boys give girls. Some of you will even go up two points.

When I leave, it is five hours later, and dusk. The air feels good outside in Queens, although I don't know if I will come back. Except for a re-touch, when my old hair grows in. For now, I don't worry. I am straightened. My hair waves behind me, and I leave for the train.

THE DUKE OF ROCK

BY PETER NOLAN SMITH

Tompkins Square Park had basketball courts. Full-court games were played close to Avenue B. Half-court was against the fences of the asphalt baseball field on Avenue A. Players were fifty-percent neighborhood and fifty-percent from the rest of the city. The quality of the competition was not up to West Fourth Street or 125th Street standards, but a total stranger could walk onto the court and claim "next" without a beef.

My apartment was on East Tenth Street. My dead sneakers hung on the streetlights at the intersection of Tenth and A. My offense was an embarrassment. Only my defense kept me in the games.

"Stop the big guy," my teammates told me.

No one had more fouls than me.

My clumsy hands deflected drives to the basket. My squat body blocked the path to the rim. Players would swear at me and I'd apologize. There were never any fights and the East Village was tough. The Rock was around the corner. Two of my teammates came from that drug den. Carmelo lived on the second floor. Duke was on the third. Crack was their business. They smoked "blunts" for fun. Carmelo shot three-pointers and drove to the basket behind my picks. Duke needed no help. At six-foot-two, he was a pit bull under the boards.

No one is supposed to use their product. Carmelo stayed clean, but the pressure on Duke was too much. He had two girl-friends. They both had kids. The cops were after him and so were the other dealers on the block between B and C.

Those rivals played ball too.

Tompkins Square Park was a truce zone. No guns. No knives. No fights.

It couldn't last forever and one afternoon in August 1991, Duke, Carmelo, and I had the run of the court. Carmelo's shoot-ing was unstoppable, I got all the rebounds, and Duke tapped the ball into the hoop from the paint. We beat a squad from Harlem. 15-6. I had one point.

"Who's next?" Duke spun with a smile on his face. We were invincible.

"We got it." The speaker was six-foot-one. A scar ran down his cheek. Biz lived across the street from the Rock. His gang was at war with Duke's posse.

"This just b-ball, right?" Carmelo dribbled the ball looking at Biz's two other players. They were his boys.

"Just basketball." Biz hadn't taken his eyes off Duke.

"Our out." I waved for the ball at the top of the key. Soon as it touched my hands, I sent it back to Duke under the basket.

"One nothing." To Duke this was more than a game.

"That's the way we're gonna play." Biz and his team settled into defense.

"That's the way." Duke tossed the ball out to me. "Check."

Every basket from that point on was a battle. My opponent outweighed me by twenty pounds and had a few inches height advantage. If he had just shot the ball we would have been los-ing fast, but he wanted to stuff the ball in the hole.

"No one stuffs on my boy," Duke declared from the baseline.

"I'm gonna." My opponent knocked me off the wall and started for the rim.

I grabbed his jersey and declared, "Foul."

"You can't call fouls for me." He was in my face.

"Sorry." I backed away. "Your ball."

Biz and Duke were sumo-wrestling for position. Biz backed up, dribbling the ball.

"Man, you like butting into me so much, why don't we make a date?"

It sounded like a joke. It wasn't a joke. Biz dropped the ball to take a swing. Duke blocked it with his left forearm and laced a straight right into Biz's face. He went down and Duke grabbed a bottle from the trash. He smashed it on the fallen player's head. It was a deadly weapon now.

Biz's boys were standing with hands at their side. This wasn't their fight.

I grabbed Duke's arm. Carmelo grabbed the other.

"Don't ever stop me." Duke shook us off. He had a reputation to uphold. "I'm getting my gun, Biz."

Duke stormed off the court. Biz disappeared into the park. A little war started over this fight. I didn't see Duke in the neighborhood after that day and the police soon closed down the Rock for business. Everyone was happy about that.

A few years later, I was in the Bronx with Jim Rockford. We were on the job checking out KFCs for the parent company. I was standing on Jerome Avenue and I saw Duke walking across the street. I called out his name. He checked the sidewalk with his heels lifted to run, until he saw my face.

"What you doing up here?" he asked with a little girl in tow.

"Working KFC." I handed him five of the chicken bags from the back of our late-model sedan.

"For a second I thought you were the cops."

"The ride is a little square." At least it was a Crown Victoria. "Why you never come around the park no more?"

"My ghosts have brothers." He touched his girl's hair. "I was a little crazy back then. Probably a little crazy now. But I got me a real job now too. You see Carmelo. You tell 'em that. But don't tell no one else."

"No, I won't."

He stepped away and vanished into the crowd of early evening shoppers. Carmelo was glad to hear he was alive. Everyone thought he was dead and we both agreed it was better that way.

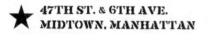

47TH ST. & 6TH AVE.
MIDTOWN, MANHATTAN

FOREVER EVERYDAY

BY PETER NOLAN SMITH

I work at a ground floor diamond exchange on Forty-seventh Street between Fifth and Sixth Avenues. This block is the diamond capital of the world, and so diamonds are about as rare as lightbulbs on West Forty-Seventh Street. They come in all shapes, all sizes. The dealers and brokers on the street profess that their stones are no different from those sold at Tiffany's and Harry Winston's, but anyone with the smallest amount of gemological acumen could look at the diamonds on offer and pick out the gems from the dreck. Fortunately for people in my business, most buyers don't have any gemological acumen.

This edge over the public does not mean that the experts are beyond being fooled by the unknown.

Several years back, an Australian couple were shopping around a ruby inherited from a dearly departed relative's estate. The ruby was a little off-red and most dealers passed on purchasing the gem or lowballed the price much lower than the Aussie couple were expecting for their family heirloom. Finally, an Indian color-stone merchant from Jodphur offered them $9,000 for the three-carat ruby.

They produced ID, signed the police report to assure the gem had not been stolen, were paid, and went on their merry way to spend the money in New York. Maybe they were too happy and the Rajahstani dealer had second thoughts on the ruby. Something was off with the color and he sold the "ruby" to a Mumbai dealer.

"How much you want?" asked the dealer. His family had been in the ruby trade for centuries. He was certain this stone was special, but pretended it was just another "ruby."

"I paid ten thousand, give me twelve."

"I like it, but not for twelve. I more love it for ten-fifty."

The Rajahstani surrendered the stone for the agreed price, content to have earned fifteen hundred dollars in less than an hour, but the Bombay dealer also had misgivings about the ruby and took it up to the Gemological Institute, the nation's most esteemed appraiser of diamonds and semi-precious stones.

A day or two went by and the GIA report came back to declare that the ruby is indeed not a ruby. The Bombay dealer was devastated, until he was told that the stone in question was a red diamond and worth nine million.

The next day, the Bombay dealer was back at work. When asked, "Why haven't you retired?" he answered, "That was only one sale, maybe I'll get lucky again."

On Forty-seventh Street you never know when.

Rough diamonds are mined from volcanic vents in Africa. Two tons of earth to retrieve one carat. These rough stones are separated into parcels for the London sight-holders who have the diamonds cut in Antwerp, Israel, or India. The finished products are divvied out to various diamond brokers and then brought over to New York. Over eighty-percent of the diamonds sold in the United States pass through Forty-seventh Street, making the block between Fifth and Sixth Avenues a crossroads of the world for jewelry. Sapphires and rubies from the Orient are transported here from Hong Kong and Thailand, while Israelis brave the dangers of Colombia for precious emeralds. Having handled jewelry for over ten years, I sometimes act as if I were dealing with chopped liver at a deli counter. We are, however, occasionally blessed with something to get excited about, an opportunity to deal with truly valuable gems.

Several years back, my boss and good friend, Richie Boy, was introduced to a big player from the West Coast. A CEO of several companies, this man had expressed interest in purchasing a Christmas gift for his mistress, a Palm Beach blonde who was married to another millionaire.

His call was for a very rare ruby. It had to be over five carats, a natural from Burma, internally perfect, and the color of the blood bleeding from a pigeon's nose. The vein, not the artery. In his own way he was a bit of a poet.

Richie Boy phoned several dealers and within a day found a ruby answering the CEO's specifications. It wasn't cheap. The dealer flatly told us "$875,000 and I don't want to hear any bitching about the price."

The dealer brought the stone down. It was not big, but the color was a sublime blood-red hue, and clean to the point of flawlessness. Richie Boy asked me, "What do you think?"

"It doesn't look like a house in the Hamptons with a beach view."

"Beach houses in the Hamptons cost more than a million." Richie Boy had already added on his profit to the stone.

"What do I know? I'm from Maine." A cottage on my lake cost $100,000, but there were no millionaires on Watchic Lake.

"Maine, Montauk. Same thing." Richie Boy decided to bring two diamond necklaces for back-up. He then called the client. The CEO was interested in the ruby, but wanted us to meet him at the St. Regis Hotel. His room was on the tenth floor.

Richie Boy's father, being from the old school, immediately announced that we were being set up for a robbery. Neither of us disagreed, since we would be carrying over a million dollars in jewelry into a hotel room to meet people we didn't really know.

His father wanted to kabosh the entire deal.

"No way." Richie Boy loaded his 9mm and pointed at me. "Plus, I got my bodyguard."

"I'm good to go." I stuck a single buckshot shell into a snakebite pipe.

Richie Boy stuck the jewelry inside his suit coat and his father swore we were crazy. He was right, but we were insured for the full value of the merchandise. Neither of us had medical coverage. The ruby was worth more than our lives, and I put my hand on the snakebite pipe in my jacket pocket.

"Taxi or walk?" Richie Boy shifted his 9mm to the side.

"Walk. You can get trapped in a car."

We walked over to the St. Regis Hotel, half-expecting to be shot in the head. Every passerby was a potential thief, even the cop directing traffic on Park Avenue. We arrived at the hotel without incident. Two businessmen tried to get on the elevator with us. Richie Boy and I glared a warning for them to take the next car up.

Richie Boy and I proceeded down the corridor like we were being set up: hands on our guns. His father's old school caution had inspired a shared paranoia. When we reached the customer's door, we rang the bell. A woman laughed and several seconds later the door opened. The blonde in the doorway wasn't wearing any clothes. Her boyfriend was lounging on the couch in a bathrobe.

"Lady, could you move away from the door," I asked in a low voice.

The man frowned, "Who are you?"

Richie played it right and took the two diamond necklaces from his jacket. "He's the protection for these."

He draped the diamonds on the woman's bare neck and she went to the man's side. Even though they weren't dressed, I still didn't trust them, but by the end of an hour Richie Boy had sold one of the necklaces. We took a cashier's check for more money than either of us could earn in several years, but Richie Boy wasn't happy, because he hadn't sold the ruby.

"There was no way you were going to sell that stone," I said.

"And why not?"

"Because no man, and I don't care how rich he is, will buy a million dollar gift for another man's wife," I said.

"Don't be so negative," he said. "You never know."

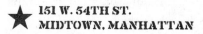

151 W. 54TH ST.
MIDTOWN, MANHATTAN

VICE PRESIDENT
OF PROCUREMENT

BY MATTHEW ROBERTS

The anti-terrorism "Command Center Cars" parked curb-side in front of the Rihga Royal hotel, black SUVs with satellite dishes on their roofs, were supposed to be on exhibit for the public to view and admire, but when I approached there was no one there to take ownership or lend a generous tongue. A bell-boy indicated there was someone inside the first car. I couldn't see; the windows were tinted so I approached and knocked on the glass. The rear right door swung open approximately ten inches; I maneuvered around to peer inside. A man in a suit came partially in to view. He was fat and red, with a mustache, a red tie, and sunglasses.

Yes, he was wearing sunglasses *inside* his tinted command car.

He did not exit the car; he exuded suspiciousness. I could see that he didn't have much room in there. He was surrounded by banks of monitors and servers. Half-hidden, he waited for me to explain myself. I told him my particulars, held out my camera and asked if there was anything he could recommend I photo-graph.

Stony silence. He remained wedged and unmoving. He told me that perhaps I should first have a look at the bigger conference inside on the fifty-fourth floor. I told him I'd do that, and maybe stop back afterward for a tour. I felt like I'd interrupted a significant bowel movement. Like a hermit crab, he shrank back out of view and quietly closed the door.

Three steps inside the lobby, I was approached unexpectedly from the left flank by a man in plain clothes who was clearly something else. He had an earpiece. "Can I help you?"

There it was, my least favorite question, asked in that clipped, authoritative tone that always means one thing: *I will not help you.*

I told him of my intentions to go up to the fifty-fourth floor and he said immediately, "That's a private function. You can't go up there."

I stared at him blankly for a two count. "The guys in the command car told me that I should go right on up. They said it's fine."

"You can try, but they won't let you in."

Turned out he was wrong.

At the fifty-fourth floor, I exited the elevator and approached a table where two dark-haired, attractive women sat stiff and straight. They appeared mildly alarmed at my presence; the camera didn't help. But I talked fast and unflinchingly until one of them stood up and said, "I'll get Jennifer."

The room all around was full of men in suits. They were milling stiffly. They ignored me and I stood to one side, arms folded, affecting the air of someone who is very calm and pleased with the current progress of the day. An explanatory poster by the elevator read "L3 Communications. Ticker Symbol LLL." Below that was a description:

"L-3 Communications is a prime contractor in Command, Control, and Communications, Intelligence, Surveillance, and Reconnaissance (C^3ISR), Government Services, Aircraft Modernization, and Maintenance (AM&M) and has the broadest base of Specialized Products in the industry. L-3 is also a major provider of homeland defense products and services for a variety of emerging markets."

Jennifer was tall, attractive, sandy blonde, and powerful. She may have been thirty-two. She scanned my face and her eyes were like a vacuum of shrewd discerning. Had I been illegitimate, she would have detected my doubt immediately. I told her the truth, that I'd been sent on a recon mission, to find at least one compelling photograph of high tech gadgetry for tomorrow's *Daily News*. She seemed to take to that idea. It was a glorious thing to come out on the other side of her keen scrutiny with approval.

We went first to the "Wescam MX-15."

This high-powered surveillance camera, designed to be mounted on the belly of an aircraft, was suspended like a large, metallic, larval cocoon near a window that faced west. Its encased telephoto lens was, at that moment, zoomed in on a helicopter flying far beyond the reach of the human eye, somewhere over New Jersey. The helicopter appeared on a thirty-inch monitor and filled the frame.

"That news chopper's about seven miles out," said the salesman proudly.

We discussed focal lengths. I expressed amazement and the salesman found his stride, barraging me with data and statistics.

The image of the helicopter on the monitor appeared to waver slightly. Heat and air pollution kept it from appearing crisp. To demonstrate the tremendous range of the equipment, he spun the camera 180 degrees using a handheld remote, and pointed it in to the room. There we all were in a wide-angle frame.

"Ya wanna see something scary" asked the salesman in a disconcerting undertone. He flicked a switch and now we were all visible in infrared. This, he explained, was for night vision. The camera was reading our heat. "Bunch of monsters," he said, and it was true. When people talked, you could see the movement of blood in their necks and faces. A close-up on my face revealed a spidery galaxy of hot capillaries radiating out of one cheek. I was frightened to look upon myself.

The cocoon camera was captivating, but it didn't lend itself to a photograph. Too much backlight. Too many reflections.

A man and a woman behind me were standing over one of those dummies that lifeguards used to learn CPR. This dummy could blink and had operative internal organs. The two salespeople connected to "Stan the Dummy" were good sports and pretended to be resuscitating Stan for my benefit. They wore doctors' outfits and one had a stethoscope.

I took a few shots, then conferred with Jennifer, who had an idea. "There are some guys on the far end shooting guns," she said, leaning in a little to whisper.

"Really? That sounds excellent." I was fully tantalized by her new confidential tone.

"I believe they're laser-guided," she said and she looked at me.

Jesus. Perhaps I only imagined it—or wanted to—here was a brief glimpse of deceit.

We walked over to the handgun range.

Executives in suits, surrounded by other executives, were shooting handguns at digitized targets on screens. There were two kinds of targets: traditional circular or human. One shooter was a "Vice President of Procurement." He was clearly excited. He was gunning-down bad guys and taking a body count. No one was hooting or waving their hats. This was a fairly controlled, senior NRA type crowd. But the good ol' boy feel was there.

With a flourish, one executive attached to "the system," pulled a previously unseen semiautomatic rifle out from under a tablecloth to stifled sounds of surprise and approval. That was fun for a while, but the gun's report wasn't satisfying enough, so the rifle guy warned everyone in his immediate vicinity and put blanks into the rifle. Then he fired off about fifteen rounds in rapid succession, spent shells arcing away as though desperate to flee his proximity. He grinned as he fired. Others on the far end of the wide room looked over, fearful and delighted at the sound of what appeared to be real gunfire.

Jennifer was at my side again. She indicated another man who was watching. "That man over there is John Shalikashvili. He used to be the Chairman of the Joint Chiefs of Staff under Clinton."

He was short, shorter than I. His face was so reddened by rosacea, I wondered what it would look like through the infrared lens. He spoke with an accent. I asked him if it would be all right if I took some shots of him firing one of the handguns and to my amazement, he said "Yes."

On a good day there are moments like these, when you know that this is the shot, that you have actually found, begged, hunted, or simply asked for it and it has appeared. My heart was trembling. I was silently, deliriously excited as John Shalikashvili and I simultaneously steadied our respective weapons, took aim, and fired.

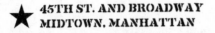

**45TH ST. AND BROADWAY
MIDTOWN, MANHATTAN**

SHOOTING FITTY

BY MATTHEW ROBERTS

Different day, same shit, old mac, new clip. Thirty two hollow tips, gloves, no rubber grip…

The reporter and I stand quietly in the underground garage. We don't want to look like we're interested in shooting anyone, in any sense of that word.

Two minutes earlier the reporter received a call in the deli across the street. His desk told him that the rapper known as 50 Cent had just finished taping upstairs.

"He's coming down, but they said he has to wash his hands…something about making a cast in cement," says the reporter.

I wonder how far the tentacles of our organization extend that we are getting eyewitness information from the MTV studios upstairs.

"I did that once when I was four," I say. "Made a cast of my hands in clay. My dad still has it."

Three women and two men are standing in the hallway with us; they're waiting for their cars to be brought up. Everyone is quiet with exhaustion. It's Friday evening, after all. It's been another long, grim winter fist of a workweek and everyone just wants to get home.

Our heart rates are up, possibly going faster than anyone else's in the garage. We know that soon, 50 Cent will step out of that elevator and we will have to get decisive.

What happens in the next three minutes may become a measure by which I am judged, certainly by the reporter, possibly by myself.

I tell myself that I will try to get between "Fitty" and his SUV and fire off—at the very least—one clear shot without taking a hollow tip to the back of the skull.

I can hear the testimony now: "I thought he had a gun…it was small, black. He was concealing it for Chrissakes…I had no clue it was a camera."

Earlier in the week, 50 Cent, an erstwhile crack dealer from Queens, kicked this guy named The Game (also a former crack dealer) out of his posse for lack of loyalty. The Game is now pursuing his own musical interests and thereby competing with 50 Cent. Shots were recently exchanged between the two artists' gangs outside Hot 97, a New York City radio station that specializes in creating opportunities for this kind of controversy. One of 50 Cent's guys was literally "capped in the ass."

Whether you think the "Rap Wars" are publicity events to boost record sales, or if you think these are bona fide hate crimes, it's all theoretical at this point. The fact is there's been gunplay, and I am standing in a hallway waiting to ambush a man who has scars from past shootings.

The army of goons in the parking lot are testament to the possibilities.

It starts happening. The giant by the elevator commands us all to clear the hallway. We do what we're told. We all slowly file outside and stand around in a mercifully tight group. The reporter goes to one side of the double doors. I go to the other. There's a little bit of a crowd outside. The black SUV backs up between the Buick and the doors. Moments of intense expectancy. The three women want to see who's coming out, and the Buick owner on the other side is on to me.

She's whispering to a friend and looking right at me with a conspiratorial smile. "Watch that guy," she's saying. The reporter and I make intensely brief eye contact. The big gears are stirring.

It's no longer easy to act casual, and some of the goons are starting to notice my furtiveness. Some cops only watch your eyes.

"If you're with the press," one cops shouts, "show your badges and leave the garage."

There's no way. I'm rooted.

There's a little bit of doubt in his command. I can tell he's not sure if I'm the potential press agent or if someone else in the group is. He's looking around.

Partially concealed by an innocent bystander, I swivel my camera in front of me and quickly check the settings. There's no point getting this far, then suffering a technical miscalculation.

A black man in a fur coat, sunglasses, and a hat comes whisking down the corridor, through the double doors which are held open. In less than two seconds, he takes the three steps to the door of the SUV and disappears inside. I do my level best. I raise my camera and lunge sideways and over the top of the woman in front of me. Immediately two sets of policemen's hands are lifted to block my shot.

I'm not happy. I've missed it. No amount of lip service is going to overcome the brutal actuality of this thwarted outcome. I waited. I tried my best on a Friday evening when I could have gone home to the warmth I know.

I'm standing off to the side, looking down and checking the blurry state of my digital failure, and someone quite close says, "Hey."

I look up and there is 50 Cent, four feet away, the real deal. He's looking right at me. His hand is outstretched to shake.

I can't tell you how uplifting this is. Perhaps I need greater perspective but I am, at that moment, elated.

The first guy into the SUV was a decoy. The real deal has a true and palpable animal charisma. He wears a yellow Yankees hat, slightly cocked and has on a yellow-hued fur coat.

I shoot him. I think he thinks I'm a fan. He steps back and poses, I take another shot of him.

He says something, I can't remember what, something like, "Here we go." Then he drapes both his arms around two of the cops who moments earlier had been trying to block my shot. All three smile.

I thank him. I'm deliriously happy at this unexpected act of generosity.

Fitty's boys all look pissed off, like they're angry he stopped to talk with a white boy fan, but hey, that's why they're not Fitty.

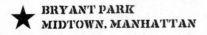

★ BRYANT PARK
MIDTOWN, MANHATTAN

FASHION WEEK FRUSTRATION
BY MATTHEW ROBERTS

At the southwest corner of "The Big Tent" in Bryant Park, a snaking, huddled mass of photographers gathers in the cold, waiting for access to the warm, partitioned press cell within. Fashion Week has arrived once again and we, the rabble of visual collection, are worming towards the issuance of glossy laminated press passes without which we can achieve nothing for the next seven days.

While waiting in this line, I am reacquainted with the photographic pool that specializes in Fashion Week. I can say with authority that at least sixty percent of all photographers are mean-spirited, egotistical thugs (significantly better percentages than those of lawyers and politicians). "Cocksuckers" is a sometimes apt description. But among the cadre of photographers who attend this event every year, there are individuals who set new standards of untrustworthiness. Looking at this idle group of slouching predators I wonder: who here has already been through the witness protection program? Then I remember what this week will involve.

There will be a lot of territorial pissing and positioning for a tiny piece of real estate on a press riser the size of my kitchen. There will be hours of utter boredom and waiting while watching near-maddening displays of petty vanity from all points of the compass. There will be whinging. There will be frayed nerves. There may even be another airborne chair incident (unable to take it any longer, a photographer named Dino once heaved a chair at another photographer's head at the end of a show). Invariably, there will be a photographer who is losing his or her struggle with obesity—a man with a name like "Dooshko"—who will arrive ten minutes before a show and attempt to insert himself directly in front of me.

And throughout, there will be the celebrity/paparazzi melee; pariah dogs falling all over themselves to photograph Katie Couric or Nicole Ritchie, possibly together. And for what?

RACIST NOTE

It's always the Italians. Three are cutting the line. They're ahead of me now. I tell them they're going to have to go to the end of the line, and one of them looks me in the eye and tells me in broken, lilting English that his friends were already here an hour ago, but went away to get lunch and he was just saving their spot. I tell him I was here two hours ago and didn't see them. There's further abject explaining with pacifying hand gestures. I'm not buying it. There's a stare down which I think I win.

But they still don't move.

THE TYRANNY OF THE LIST

Nowhere in America are there more ineffectual PR flunkies walking around with lists on clipboards than at Fashion Week. To get in, you're supposed to be on a list, to go backstage, check the list. While waiting for the show to begin, people will approach you, ask for your identity, and then add you to new mysterious lists. In this way the list-Nazis of Fashion Week are taking a cue from the growth industry of national security.

Lists—and requisite telecommunication headsets— are the new talismen of control.

Then I see it: the very first list. It's in the hands of a Junior Varsity unassertive PR floozie with heels. She is veering aimlessly through the crowd, a queen bee drunk on royal jelly. She is empowered by her clipboarded list. Like mindless drones, the photographers keep stepping out of line, swarming around her, trying to see if they are on this list.

During all of Fashion Week 2005, I wasn't on a single list. My office either neglected to put me on any, or the flak routinely bobbled the ball. Ultimately, this didn't matter. The list is just a ruse, an oar for steering. If you show up with the correct laminated press pass ready to photograph the show, it doesn't matter if you've made the list or bear a terrible resemblance to a former member of Aerosmith. You are wanted inside.

SERGE'S RUDE BUDDY

There shouldn't be fashion shows held in the lobby of the Algonquin Hotel. Three blocks north of Bryant Park, the Algonquin is a satellite venue for shows, sometimes avant-garde, that want to vamp it up in front of velvet curtains and elaborate tea settings. The problem is, there isn't enough space. The photo area is sadistically small and the models at the "HollyWould" show on the first Friday night did not have enough room to stretch out. They were also moving too quickly.

Frustrated by the speed of the models, some of the photographers start shouting at them to slow down. The median age of the models appears to be seventeen, and they don't understand what is being shouted at them. All they appear to pick up on is the anger. They advance even more quickly but with unhappy scowls. The photographers become more abusive. It's like witnessing the evolution of a doomed marriage in time lapse. In twenty seconds everything's gone to shit. I'm having a hard time believing what I'm hearing from the photographers. Unrepeatable oaths.

A cell phone rings. It is answered, behind me, by a photographer with a French accent.

"What are you doing calling me now, Serge? I am shooting a show!" Pause. "What do you want?"

After the show, I turn and have a good look at Serge's buddy. He is older, probably forty-six. He has long gray hair pulled back in a ponytail. I've seen him before. I watch him pack his gear and feel overwhelmed by rage and helplessness. I seriously consider hitting him or just poking him relentlessly with my monopod until I can formulate a verbal bullet to kill him with.

I take his photograph instead.

THE STARBUCKS TROLLER

I walk down the street to the nearest Starbucks. It's at Forty-first Street and Broadway. I throw my stuff down and begin the process of downloading, editing, captioning, and sending my photographs to the office. There's a game I play, more of a neurotic compulsion, where I try to see how rapidly I can accomplish all the tasks required of the transmitting process and still get a cup of coffee.

A young, pretty, dark-haired woman behind me asks in foreign English, "How much does it cost to get a shoot?"

I tell her it depends. I ask her if she wants to be a model.

No, she is just curious. She thinks "the people who run the models" might be untrustworthy. I look into her face and she stares back at me intensely. I invite her over to my table and she sits down opposite me. The speed routine crumbles. Magda is her name. She's from Poland on a visitor's visa. She's been in the United States for two weeks, and is looking for work as an au pair. The mere mention of that job title: I instantly ache to take her into the bathroom and show her my favorite yoga position.

She's magnificent. I'm married. I also have this thing called a job to attend to.

Magda makes me guess her age. I say twenty-one. She says I'm right; I decide she's nineteen. She performs this little trick where she peeks at a well-worn fortune from a fortune cookie, then tries to hide it. I say what does your fortune say. She hands it over. It says, "A friendly chat may lead to romance."

I ask her to tell me a secret.

She thinks about it for a little while, then she releases it, in a whisper in my ear: "I believe in angels."

THE BENJAMIN CHO SHOW

The trick is to get to the site of a show early so you can pick your spot. I get to the Benjamin Cho show about two hours early.

This show is happening inside the ABC carpet showroom on Broadway near Nineteenth Street. Soporific, dark-skinned Indian men are slowly moving carpets around on dollies. Models and makeup people are everywhere; the models all appear to be on muscle relaxants and have voluminous hair.

A half hour before the show is supposed to start, someone comes up behind me and starts yanking on the milk crate I'm sitting on.

"Can I have this? If you'll just get up, I'll take this."

I'm talking to a *New York Times* photographer to my left, but stop mid-sentence to turn and face this new effrontery. A man with white hair, pale skin, and slightly recessed eyes, has descended in to my field of view. I see from the credential hanging around his neck that he's from *Vogue* . His name's Eric. He's probably forty.

"Are you actually thinking you might take this seat right out from under me?" I ask, incredulous.

"Well yeah, someone left that crate laying around and I want it."

I explain to him that I bought this milk crate at Staples and brought it here for the exact purpose of sitting on it, and if he thinks he's going to take it…I raise and cock my left fist.

I'm the kind of person who wants to see a fistfight break out during Fashion Week, but I'm not generally interested in taking part in one. I don't like being punched for one thing, especially in the nose, and I'm not a particularly gifted brawler. None the less, I am now fully prepared to unleash a combination of punches on the face of this great white whale before me.

He backs off a little and chuckles insanely—to signify that he's only kidding.

My desire to hurt him fades. He appears to be suffering from something, an illness of rage and social dementia and it has twisted him inside.

For the next hour, I listen to him give genuinely funny commentary about the people passing by our perch. "I know," he says at one point. "But this is my year. It's the Chinese year of the Cock."

The photographers are tiring, the models too are starting to trip in their heels.

And Salman Rushdie may not get out much, but his wife with the thundering scar on her right arm appears to be everywhere.

VANITAS, VANITATUM, ALL IS VANITY

I felt as though I achieved a state of Zen during the Derek Lam show. Every model who approached down a two-hundred-foot runway stared me down, right into my glass. Out of twenty-five models, I was twenty-five for twenty-five. EVERY SINGLE ONE. As they approached, I felt as though I was the only one in the room and they wanted to give me some…Lam. There must have been twenty still photographers behind me. With the music booming, I went in to a keen and pleasurable state, a trance of visual hunger satiation.

For a tiny, fleeting moment, I know the genius of vanity.

I mull over the strong, nuclear bond that exists between model (shoot me) and photographer (show me)—there is hatred in both sets of wanting.

I paced myself and I drank it in, digitally. And when it was over, I fled out the nearest available exit with everyone else, not looking to left or right, feeling dirty for having been party to so much desire.

BUCKET BOY

BY MATTHEW ROBERTS

1201 University Avenue in the Bronx is no place to live. The front door, lockless and crooked on its hinges, wouldn't bar entry to dogs, rapists, or to us, the media. Austin Fenner, a reporter and a friend of mine, arrived there before me. We began patrolling the building together, staying away from the bucket boy's apartment on the ground floor for now. Austin, businesslike and sympathetic, always went to the source first, but what he'd encountered in there earlier I could only guess at from the low, subdued pitch of his voice as he told me, "They're not ready."

I wouldn't want to go in there without him.

Intrigued neighbors milled around the lobby. They wanted to talk; they wanted to show us the terrible condition of their apartments. One rasping woman with asthma and diabetes told us she had lost her babysitting license because her apartment was considered a health risk by the city. She eagerly led us inside. The place smelled fungal and sweet. Her floors buckled. Light fixtures hung on wires from the ceiling as though they'd been pulled and twisted in a fit of rage. Jagged holes in the ceiling had never been patched over. Plaster bulged where leaking water pipes lay behind the walls. A chubby boy played quietly by himself on an ancient carpet in the former babysitter's living room. He was dreaming with a toy helicopter. Last night's bright snowfall covered an empty park in a window behind him. You had to squint to see him.

The stout Spanish superintendent arrived. He looked like he'd been spackling. He claimed to speak very little English. One of the neighbors, a hanger-on, translated for Austin. The super had been hired by the management company three weeks ago. He knew little about plumbing, and had spent his short time there trying, unenviably, to patch over the major difficulties with the building.

He ended the interview by separating from us and knocking on the dreaded door. It cracked open and a woman we would later learn was the grandmother spoke to him in Spanish. Stacked metal bowls were passed out to him. He took them and the door closed for a second, then opened again, and a dark-skinned man in a dirty blue parka coat stepped quickly out. We didn't know he was the father. I didn't get a good look at him as he and the super moved purposefully together toward the service exit.

We watched them from a grated window as they hugged the building and walked with the bowls down a basement staircase and disappeared.

Outside of the family's apartment, a small shrine of candles, toys, and flowers had been set up by the door. Large pieces of paper had been taped to the wall. On them, people left short messages to the dead boy.

Ten minutes later, the father, Juan, shuffled quickly back through the lobby. Austin intercepted him. There was a brief conversation and then Austin asked simply, "Can we come inside?" Juan capitulated. Two enormous holes gaped in the ceiling at opposite ends of the kitchen. Through the holes I could see piping hung wrapped in black plumber's tape. The pipes were wet, and after all that had happened, continued to leak. Someone upstairs must have turned the water on. The velocity of the leak increased as we stood there.

Juan was softspoken and had a pronounced overbite which caused him to slur his speech slightly. I guessed he was twenty-five. He told us in slow, broken English: "The super sat me down, and he said, 'Look, I'm telling you this because you're my friend. The landlord came to the building on Sunday night and he wouldn't come in to inspect the repairs. He was here to collect the rent from an apartment upstairs and didn't want to come in.'"

The landlord had been variously described by neighbors as "a Jew," "a rich guy from Brooklyn," and "the guy in the hat." His name was A. Gross. His management company only offered a PO Box in Brooklyn as an address. One neighbor swore he drove a black SUV with tinted windows.

In the hallway, camera crews from the TV stations, both English and Spanish, were arriving with their anchors. You can always tell the anchor by their makeup and their myopia. One young Spanish anchor had that crazed look about him. He seemed to be feeling an unwholesome pressure in his forehead. He needed a story.

Rhodesia, the overweight mother, made her way out and sat by the shrine beside her door. She spoke occasionally on her cell phone. An aunt and a grandmother came by, left, returned. I overheard the grandmother, who was forty-eight, speaking Spanish in the kitchen. I knew what she was saying by the vitriol in her voice. Someone was to blame.

No one but the grandmother was outraged. No one was crying. It was all slow and sad and soft. I wondered how had the child been allowed to wander off into that watery kitchen? Hadn't someone been watching him? These questions were never asked. How could you ask them? The family was in dire circumstances and already had two other children.

Juan curled up in a fetal position on a bed in another room with a false wall. He spoke softly on a phone. His mother and the angry grandmother sat on the bed next to him. Reporters and cameramen had the run of the place now. They were everywhere. One reporter, an impetuous young man from *The New York Times*, rifled through a few drawers. Then one of the family members, I think an aunt with blue colored contacts, announced: "Juan wants you all to leave now." She meant it, if Juan didn't.

We left with bags and cameras and notepads. One man stayed behind. He was short, Spanish, and unimposing. He was wearing a sharp gray suit, an undertaker.

Outside, Austin wanted to show me something. On a trash heap in front of the building there was a five gallon grouting bucket exactly like the one the boy had supposedly ended up at the bottom of. On the side of the bucket, in Spanish and English, there was a printed warning over an image of a child climbing into the bucket.

The boy who drowned was named Malik.

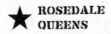 **ROSEDALE
QUEENS**

THE BOILERMAKERS
BY MATTHEW ROBERTS

They were boilermakers. They were blue-collar union guys in the Local No. 5 in Queens, and they'd made a ton of cash by daytrading on the market. These guys had done it all legally and legitimately, sort of, doing the same after-market trading that Putnam Securities and other mutual funds are now under investigation for, and parleying their 401(k) plans in to a collective two million dollar gain. I was driving to Queens to photograph their group and I was prepared to shake some weathered, strong hands and congratulate them. A story about blue-collar guys making good is such a rarity in the news these days, almost as rare as stories about the homeless. So I was looking forward to this. Hell, I'd ask these guys for a stock tip.

When I got out there a reporter named Ruth was sitting in her blue Volvo station wagon, trying to stay warm.

"The secretary in there is such an idiot," she said. "None of them will come out and talk."

I rang the bell four or five times and even flashed a prolonged smile and my press tags at the surveillance camera, to no avail.

They didn't seem to understand that I was a brother and that I had come in good will. Twenty minutes passed and during that time I got to know some workers from the concrete factory next door. One guy was named Rob.

Rob was clearly insane or else extremely excited by my camera. Like a child, he kept asking that I take his picture. At one point he imitated the bionic man.

The boilermakers were supposed to be coming out of a meeting at 4 o'clock.

At ten to four, Rob drove by in a forklift at top speed. He shouted to us: "Watch your back!"

We turned and sure enough, two men came down the stairs and exited the Local No. 5 building. We were only three steps away. One guy in sunglasses looked a little like Nick Nolte. "I want you to get off the property," he said in a low and menacing voice. "Do you hear me? I want you off the property."

The property he was referring to was the sidewalk. Ruth, a little tentatively, asked him a question about the daytrading successes.

"The SEC is investigating their company. As long as the SEC is investigating, there is nothing to talk about." He was already at his green Buick and opening the door to get in.

The mesmor principle (personal terminology for when the photographer is too fascinated by what he is seeing to take a picture) had set in on me. I had yet to raise my camera, but didn't like the way this was going.

"But you made so much money," I blurted. "We think it's laudable."

"You wasted your fuckin' time coming out here, aright? You wasted your fuckin' time."

He was in his car now and was set to drive away. He had established himself as an asshole, so I took two giant steps backwards and raised my 70-200 lens to take an identifying picture. Instantly, before I could shoot, he leaped out of the car and lunged towards me.

There are only a few things I can do well in this world. Running fast is one of them. I bolted from the spot and raced around a car.

"Jesus Christ, buddy." I said as I stopped and turned to face him.

"Don't Jesus Christ me," he said. He looked like a man who was capable of unspeakable heights of rage, and that was something I could respect.

A dark streak moved in our periphery. The boilermaker, in his haste to kick my teeth in, had forgotten to put his car in park. Rob, the crazy concrete worker, leaped in the moving car and stopped the green Buick a few feet short of hitting one of the concrete company's flat-bed trucks. The boilermaker returned to his car and grunted some thanks to Rob. He turned to shout at me one last time and that was when I got my only good shot of him at the edge of the sunlight.

As he drove away I photographed his license plate number. Ruth called it in and had the desk run it. The car was registered to the union. No ID on the driver. I didn't notice it, but apparently the guy circled around and eyed us for a while from a backstreet. Lord knows what he was thinking about—crushing my head in with a tire iron perhaps.

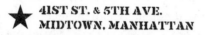
THE BEHEADING
OF A BANK MANAGER

BY MATTHEW ROBERTS

When I was assigned to photograph the bank manager,
something inside me gave a decisive nod. The bank manager was someone I could hate. The bank manager was someone
I could hunt.

Even though he had suffered this horrible experience the day
before, I looked at the photographs of him flailing on the ground,
attached to what he thought was a bomb, and I thought, "This
fat, helpless man…must be photographed again."

I didn't have a scrap of sympathy for him. In fact, looking at
him in the pictures from the previous day—porcine and pros-
trate—I worked myself in to quite a state of loathing for the man,
which would help to get the job done.

The day before, I'd been working a shift for the *Daily News*.
This meant that from 11 a.m. to 6:30 p.m. I had to be ready to go.

I'd wandered over to Rockefeller Center with my bag of
equipment to take in an exhibition celebrating one hundred years
of air and space travel. I was just pushing away from the acrobats

when my two-way pager started to chirp. My blood pressure spiked immediately.

Charlie at the desk told me: "Kid, there's some kinda bomb scare going on at Fortieth Street and Fifth Avenue."

I ran the ten blocks south through the lunchtime crowds. There's a primordial art to crowd running; children and the aged are the most likely to veer unexpectedly. As I ran, part of me mulled over the topic of health insurance and my lack thereof.

They were already starting to block off the streets. The cops were putting up the red tape and though several of them barked angrily at me, I stood my ground for a while and tried to discern what was happening. The street up ahead was empty save for a loose sprawl of cops standing immobile, looking around. They looked nervous. A large special ops truck was straddling Fifth at Forty-first Street.

"If you want to blow up, then you'll stay right there," a cop mused loudly.

I shot cops and pedestrians. The pedestrians were relatively calm— just another bomb scare in Manhattan.

A young German man named Felix appeared at my side and said, "I got ze best pictures of ze whole thing." He'd been in an internet café four stores up and across the street when things had started to happen. I asked him what he had, and he said, "Every-thing."

He seemed confident so I called in to the desk and told them that I was going to look at his film. He'd shot the scene with a tiny camera and I asked if it zoomed. "Yah, zoom's Good." He said. He asked me how much the *Daily News* would pay him for the film, because he and his girlfriend Joanna wanted to get a flight to Miami, and when I told him roughly one-fifty to two hundred dollars, he said that wasn't enough. He was an emergency medical technician back in Berlin and he said that in Germany you get paid two hundred to five hundred Euros.

"Have you done this before?" I asked him.

"No, this is the first time."

The *Daily News* will pay you two hundred dollars at the most."

He said maybe he should go to the *New York Times,* and I said, maybe he should.

We took his Advantix film to Duane Reade. I paid for the processing and when I came back an hour later and looked at it, I was amazed at Dabin's prescience (Dabin, a co-worker who answered the phone at the desk that afternoon, had casually guessed the outcome).

The shots were taken so wide angle, you couldn't tell what was happening. In one shot a speck in the bottom left corner was a bomb expert crouching over a bomb. It could have been a dog or a manhole cover, it was so difficult to discern. So much for the right place at the right time.

The next morning, Charlie said, "Go look at the *Post.*"

Front page. Someone named Paul Salazar had taken the most extraordinary photographs of the bank manager on the ground attached to a brief case.

I can say this for whoever Paul Salazar is: either he didn't know the risk he was taking or he's a courageous photographer.

This is how the story was reported in the *New York Post* and the *Daily News*: A well-dressed bank robber (he'd overdone it a bit in a tuxedo and bow tie) had gone in to the bank with two Louis Vuitton bags claiming that he had a large amount of cash and would like to open an account. When the bank manager went to shake his hand, the robber slapped a cuff to the bank manager's wrist, thereby attaching the bank manager to a brief-case which he then claimed contained a bomb. He made a point of opening the briefcase to expose a network of wires and what appeared to be sticks of dynamite.

He told the bank manager that he too was wired with explosives and directed the surprised banker to take him to the vault. The banker gave a "secret signal" to set off the loud alarm. The robber fled the scene and was later captured, huddled in a bush, near the library. Meanwhile, the bank manager, burst out into the daylight and screamed to the police who had just arrived, "It's a bomb! I've only got thirty seconds!"

According to the *Post*, police threw him some universal hand cuff keys—no heroics there—and the bank manager, quite on his own, released himself and squirmed away from a briefcase filled with dormant wires and painted drumsticks.

So here I was the next afternoon, outside this same bank, an HSBC branch, hunting the manager. Amazingly, he'd shown up for work. You'd have thought the experience might have changed him irrevocably, perhaps causing him to seek a spiritual life in the woods upstate, to wander like Siddartha, or at the very least to take the day off.

My colleague, Andrew from the *Daily News* was there. He covered the front. Robert was also there from the *Post*. He and I were covering the same side and rear exits.

As I waited at the corner of Thirty-ninth and Fifth, looking back and forth from the eastern exit to the southern, I chanted to myself: "Fat bank manager won't get away. I will bang him this very day."

A PR lady from the bank approached warily and asked Robert and I what news organizations we were from. We told her. She tried to remain calm and professional, but it was clear that our presence taxed her poise.

"I am trying to assist in our employees right's to privacy," she said.

Robert, who might be Brazilian and definitely looks the part of a paparazzo, with long hair and three-day shadow, tried the persistence bluff. "Even if we don't get him today, we will come out here day after day until we do, so he might as well come out now and get it over with".

"He hasn't done anything wrong. In fact, he's sort of a hero," I lied.

She disappeared, calculating PR ratios.

A little after 5 p.m., a Lincoln Town Car with tinted windows pulled up and backed in to a loading bay on the southern side of the building. Robert and I knew this was the banker's ride when they closed the hydraulic gate to conceal the car. We made rapid, imperceptible adjustments to our gear. I set my focus to three feet and cranked up my flash.

Two female reporters, who realized they wouldn't be getting a quote, watched us with morbid curiosity as though they were about to witness a beheading. We stood to one side of the loading dock and waited. The gate started to open. Three beefy security men stepped out. Then the car started to roll out behind them. The bank manager was in the back of the car.

Robert and I broadsided the Lincoln. We pressed our cameras up against the side-back windows to reduce reflections and flashed hard strobic spikes, inward, repeatedly. Robert was straddling the car, one leg up on the hood, as it turned and made its way out on to Thirty-ninth Street. The driver gassed it and sped down the block. Robert fell away.

This was where I figured I had an advantage over Robert. I sprinted after them.

I got lucky. They were stopped by a red light at Sixth Avenue. I ran up to the car and shot through the tinted glass. Again, the bank manager was holding his hands up in front of his face to protect his identity. This infuriated me. The man had lived through a bomb scare and now he was scared of being photographed? I cursed him as though he were a murderer. I scrambled around the car taking photographs from any angle that might work. I considered yanking his door open and blasting him that way but no stylebook would have recommended it. The driver got involved and thrust his hand towards the back to assist in the masking of his client.

Finally, with a squeal of tires, the car pulled away. I went back and looked for Robert but he was gone. One of the reporters who had watched the whole thing said, "Robert jumped in his car and chased after them. Can you believe that?"

I was impressed. Robert had taken it to another level. I imagined him following that town car all the way to Western New

Jersey and terrorizing the subject as he shuffled, exhausted, towards his front door.

After all that excitement, I chimped through my frames to discover that I had only one photograph of the bank manager and it was blurry. The tinted windows had made it impossible to avoid obscuring reflections. I was livid. Then the shame crept in.

I imagined what I must have looked like chasing down that car. Specifically, I imagined a girl I'd known in college witnessing the whole thing from a car directly behind the banker's. "Is that Matthew Roberts?" she might have wondered, aghast. "What kind of monster has he become…"

The next day, worried that Robert had made his shot, I went down to the nearest deli and scoured the papers over a fifty-cent coffee. I was relieved to discover that neither of our papers ran a new shot.

And the *New York Times*, for the second straight day, made no mention of the failed bank robbery.

THE MAN IN THE WINDOW
BY V. L. HARTMANN

I noticed him during the first week of living in my new apartment in Spanish Harlem. I was staring down from my sparsely furnished fourth floor two-bedroom. He sat in a window on the south side of the block, just to the west of Kelly's Flat Fix. He faced Third Avenue, his elbow hanging out the window as if he were driving along in a car somewhere out in the country.

The man in the window was a thin man, Hispanic, balding; he looked to be in his sixties. I sipped my coffee and watched him smoke a cigarette and pull another from his pack as he watched Kelly's men fix a flat tire on a Buick. A Puerto Rican woman dragging a cart of laundry waved to him as she passed, and he gave her a nod.

I had just moved uptown because I wanted a year without distractions. In Spanish Harlem, I thought there would be few on the street level. The nearest Starbucks was thirteen blocks away. In my new neighborhood, there would be no window-shopping and no compulsive coffee-buying. There was hardly a reason to leave the apartment, and that was exactly what I wanted—to bore my material impulses until they atrophied. I needed a year to do work without interruption, no friends stopping by; just a two-bedroom, two-bath, newly renovated and vermin-free place with a boyfriend who cooked dinner every night.

Every morning after the boyfriend left for work, I'd set myself up at the desk by the window in the living room. I didn't like the second bedroom that was my study—there was something off about the light in it. I stored my clothes and books in it like it was a big $500-a-month walk-in closet. I drank my coffee and sat with my new kitten and watched the street below. I followed the people; the kitten kept track of the pigeons.

The man in the window had white shirts and brown shirts, or maybe just two—one of each color that he alternated—and an old tan leather jacket that made me think of Patagonia, of cattle ranching. He smoked approximately three packs of Marlboros a day. At first I thought he couldn't walk and that was why he sat there all day, but once I saw him get up and disappear into his apartment and return a minute later. He seemed perfectly agile, almost athletic.

Sometimes people brought him things. Once he handed something to one of Kelly's Flat Fix guys, maybe Kelly himself, who then went to the mid-block bodega, El Chile, and returned a few minutes later with a small paper bag and what appeared to be change. Another day a woman handed him something and he handed her something which she put in her purse, and then they chatted for fifteen minutes, smoking cigarettes, words punctuated with nods and long silences. On sunny afternoons, when the sun glared down on his side of the block, he closed his window and pulled down the shade until the sun set. There was a small wooden cross ornament that hung from the window latch. In the evening, he pulled up the blinds and opened the window and people stopped by on their way home from work.

When I told others about the man, they said he must be a bookie. They said off-track betting, but the man was never on the phone. There was no computer in sight. He never read the *Daily Racing Form*. All he had in front of him was the window. Some people suggested he was a drug dealer, but he was too old, and the only people he talked to were middle-age-family types.

Teenagers walked by and never seemed to acknowledge his presence.

"Maybe he's a poet," I said one evening, staring out the window.

"Old men sit in windows all over this city," the boyfriend said, staring down a manuscript he brought home from his publishing job. "Did you write anything good today?"

I decided to think that the man in the window was an exiled poet even though I never saw him writing or reading anything, not even a newspaper. He had escaped the military dictatorship in Argentina and when the country recovered, people had forgotten him and he'd been waiting to be invited back ever since. Or maybe, since the neighborhood was mostly Caribbean, he was Dominican. Perhaps he had known Trujillo and they'd had a terrible falling out. I searched for his face in a pictoral history of Spanish Harlem that a friend gave me, but I found no trace of him. Some country has forgotten their poet, I thought. The man is famous and no one remembered. "I'll tell them who you are," I said aloud one day, standing at my window looking down at him as he lit another cigarette. Then I tried to remember the last time I left the apartment.

I was waiting for a great story to unfold down on the street. After a few months, the cast of characters grew at the little commercial strip across the way. The owner of La Fonda Boricua paced outside his restaurant, smoking in the late morning. He wore steel-toed cowboy boots, beige Armani suits, and a very expensive ten-gallon that seemed precariously perched on his small head. Some days he wore bling, other days, bolo ties. I called him the Restauranteur. He normally chatted with the West African man who ran a hole-in-the-wall junk shop that sold sunglasses and fake leather purses a few times a day. But the Restauranteur and the man in the window never talked. Though at times I thought I caught them glaring at each other. I was waiting for a showdown, pen poised above paper, ready to write it all down.

LOST AND FOUND

One day, I was in my study, which I had finally set up, when I heard the most unnatural yelling. I ran to the window thinking this was it. This is when the man would finally do something. Maybe he'll get up and leave his apartment; maybe he'll confront the Restauranteur! I had imagined how their feud began: how the Restauranteur had taken everything the man had—a bet gone wrong—and started La Fonda, the most successful restaurant in Spanish Harlem. I peeked out the window, hiding from view.

The sidewalk was empty except for the man who was standing, leaning half his body out his window. He was squawking, yelling from deep in his throat as if it was the first time in years that he'd spoken. I couldn't make sense of the sounds he made, aside from that he was very angry. He carried on for five minutes and I kept my eye on the dark door of La Fonda, waiting for the Restauranteur to emerge. The West African man sat in his folding chair calmly, as if he didn't hear the yelling.

A man from Kelly's Flat Fix came out, stuffing a greasy rag into his back pocket and raising his arms, palms upward in a questioning gesture as he walked to the man's window. He grabbed some bills the man held out and walked next door to El Chile. A minute later he returned and tossed the man a pack of Marlboros. The man in the window had been out of cigarettes, and that was all.

MOLE PERSON

BY KURT RADEMACHER

On my way down the steps to the subway, I was stuck behind a man with a cane. I missed the D train. In my head I said, "Curses," then clarified out loud, "ot you," to the guy with the cane. He had enough problems.

I didn't think the next train would be long though, because it wasn't late and it was a weekday. I was heading home early because I was out of money.

I could see four tracks from where I was standing; trains came on the three others out of spite. The tunnel of the D uptown lit up, so I gave myself the obsessive-compulsive pat-down of someone who subconsciously believes his wallet could go missing at any second, then I stowed my book in my knapsack. The train wasn't slowing, though. I noticed that it wasn't lettered, and when it came closer, that it was altogether different from the usual passenger trains. It looked how I imagined trains when I was a child: a barred, muzzle-like grill, two front windows glowing yellow like raccoon eyes. The conductor even wore overalls and a denim cap.

The engine barreled by and I noticed that rather than pulling cars, it was tugging along two-foot-deep wagons, beds sparsely strewn with rubble: rocks and dirt. The first wagon was almost past and my thought was, "I could definitely make it," by which

I meant, I could jump over the wall and into the wagon. I checked my wallet again as if I was really going to do it, jump onto a moving train and go wherever it took me.

I don't know where I thought it would go. I'd become accustomed to thinking of the subway tunnels as hallways, totally enclosed somethings that demarcated inside from outside, just like houses did. But that there were real trains (as opposed to the domesticated passenger versions) driving the tracks implied that somewhere there was something undeveloped, somewhere that progress had yet to reach.

I imagined this train was coming from somewhere deeper than the passenger trains could go, that someone was digging into the planet and this machine went there to cart the earth away. For some reason I imagined these digging people as mole men, or I guess mole people, since the city probably wouldn't discriminate.

The next thing that occurred to me should have been, "there is no reason to do this," or "it is very likely that you'll end up bouncing off the side of that train, because you are not very athletic," or "if you jump, your wallet will come out of your pocket, and some crazy hobo will be drawn to it as if by instinct and charge a $1200 baby stroller on your credit card: you should check your back pocket again." But instead, I was already thinking about the awesome story I'd have to tell my friends about how I jumped onto a moving train. I'd land on the flatbed of an open wagon car and roll three times (like a guy in a movie who jumps out of a speeding car), before popping up unscathed to ride like a superhero through the dark bowels of New York.

I wanted a train story that beat my friend's train story, which he could bring up in nearly any context and leave knowing that his was the best, even now, five years after it happened.

My friend was an undergraduate at the time and it was the night before his twenty-first birthday, which meant he drank at his apartment until midnight, then went to a bar to buy his first legal drinks. He repeated this final step, or people repeated it for him, until he couldn't do it anymore. Then his friends carried him to a car and took him back to his apartment, so that he could vomit or drink or both.

Train tracks ran fifty yards behind his building. Stumbling around outside, he noticed that a train was stopped there. Because birthdays in our twenties glow romantically in the subconscious, we're more willing to act boldly and inquisitively, so my friend decided to do some exploring. He staggered through the weeds to the halted train. Once he got there he didn't see any reason not to climb on, so that's what he did. He stood triumphantly atop a freight car, and the train started to move.

It occurred to my friend that freight trains might not stop too often, that he could end up in Kentucky before he had a chance to carefully climb off. But he was quite drunk and it'd taken him a fair amount of time to think of this, so the train was moving thirty miles an hour before he jumped.

Knowing he'd been out celebrating his birthday, I never would have called him so early the next morning, but it was September 11th and I'd just watched the second plane hit on television, and I was stunned and not really thinking.

"I don't know what just happened," I said to him.

"I know, I can't believe this," he said.

But we were talking about two different things, me about this awful thing on television and him about the torn tendons in his left ankle.

I wasn't thinking of his ankle when I was standing there on the subway platform, just about the wind rushing by him when he stood atop that freight car and about how I'd feel when the wind was rushing by me in the tunnels. The third open wagon passed and I bent my knees, coiling for the leap. The fourth car was not an open wagon, though. It was enclosed, seven feet tall. If I'd jumped, I would have slammed into a steel wall, which would not have made a very good story at all, if I'd survived it. The story would have gone as follows: "I got hit by a train last night." Then they'd ask me how, and I'd shrug, and if they would press, I'd let my mouth hang open like I had some mental infirmity, which would be the answer to their question.

The train pulled away, disappearing into the D tunnel, and I told myself that I'd never really considered jumping, that I was neither suicidally reckless nor particularly dim—that I was just a rational man with a wandering mind.

I pawed the back of my pants to make sure my wallet was still there.

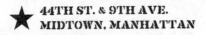

**44TH ST. & 9TH AVE.
MIDTOWN, MANHATTAN**

LICK US

BY KURT RADEMACHER

It's thirty-one degrees on the third Saturday in February. I'm ignoring everyone on Ninth Avenue. I am not a native and my ability to ignore is still a blunt instrument, numbing when engaged. Walking down the street feels a bit like being led by a string out of a dark tunnel into the bright lights of the world, while I only notice the texture of the string.

I am Gordon Gecko, and the sidewalk is my free market. I slide past a woman piloting a scuffed stroller and scurry by an elderly couple ambling along the curb. I cut like popular music between a father and his teenage daughter and overtake a Japanese girl and her urinating Labrador. A work crew jackhammers at the street's surface, taxis honk, pedestrians chatter on cell phones and at each other, but I am unseeing, unhearing locomotion, a machine built specifically for trips between apartment and barber shop. I can neither be stopped nor delayed. By the time I'm traversing Forty-fourth Street against the impotent red hand of the crosswalk signal, I'm challenging records for pedestrian efficiency.

Ahead is the first real challenge of the five-block course, a confused bottleneck of tourists and errand-doers. People press against the storefronts to edge past the blockage: a middle-aged woman gesticulating in the middle of the sidewalk as if she is directing a jet into its terminal. She wears heels and a burgundy dress and clanging gold bracelets and delivers an individual, taut direction to each passerby, as if a general pronouncement of her nonsense is too informal for the occasion. She is alarmed by my relentless advance, but she gives me the same admonition she gives everyone else: "Lick us," she proffers in her Italian accent, waving once toward the street. Like a priest handing out communion wafers, she believes her offering should suffice to redeem me, and she ignores me completely after she hands it over.

She turns toward the storefront to address emerging shoppers. "Lick us," she says, this time with an apologetic shrug of her shoulders, as if she's embarrassed to have to be telling everyone this. I see my chance to slip by. While others hug the store windows or cross the street altogether, I slip in behind her with a spry twist of my hips. For a brief moment we fit snuggly together, like dancers.

I plant my right foot on the sidewalk and it flies skyward, dragging the rest of me with it. I watch my feet up in the air; just off the tip of my left shoe, a jet heads south toward JFK. I hear the warning once more, but interpret correctly this time: "Slick ice," she says.

I lead with my elbow, plowing into the single square of ice about which we are all being warned. I lie back for a moment and consider staying here for however long it takes to meaningfully reassess my place in the world. Before I can reach any conclusions beyond the realization that I'm very likely to be dead soon, the warning woman's head hovers over me like a passing cloud.

"I said—"

"I know," I say. "Thank you."

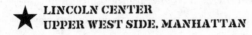

MADAME BUTTERFLY GOES DOWN

BY THOMAS PRYOR

Saturday night, I ate smelly cheese, cashews, black bean dip, spooned Hellmann's, and three Coronas for dinner. I had over-bought crap for company. It was causing me stomach problems, but I had to finish the stuff.

Sunday morning, I met an editor on Cathedral Parkway who took too much money to tell me too little about my work. I left her apartment feeling down.

Driving east, I saw a woman trip in the middle of Manhattan Avenue. She hit her head. I parked along side her, forcing traffic around the scene. Her face was pressed to the asphalt. It was hard to see her injuries. Someone called an ambulance. After a few minutes, she turned her head towards me. She was bleeding from two cuts, one on her nose and one on her lip, but otherwise looked okay. Her name was Grace, an Asian lady in her sixties, curly gray hair and weak English. I knew her name because the guy helping me help her was her neighbor in the tall building across the street. Once Grace got her bearings, me and the other fellow walked her into her lobby. After she sat down, she tried to force an envelope into my hands.

"Take this, take this."

"I don't want it."

"Take this, take this."

The other guy said take it, so I took it. On the sidewalk, I opened it and found a single ticket for *Madame Butterfly* at Lincoln Center, Row A in the second ring. Performance started at one-thirty. It was twelve thirty-five.

My life-long opera experience was limited to Alfalfa's *Barber of Seville,* Elmer Fudd's *Siegfried,* and Bugs Bunny's *Brunhilde.* Despite this handicap, my interest was high because the "Un bel di, vedremo" aria was my Mom's favorite music. Coming home from school, if I heard this sorrowful melody coming through my front door, I knew Mom was having a special afternoon. She'd have a look on her face that nothing else ever put there.

I parked the car on East Eighty-second Street, dropped my stuff off and hailed a cab at one o'clock. The Greek parade cut off cross-town traffic through Central Park. We ended up going down to Fifty-Third Street, to go west, and back up Eighth to get to Broadway and Sixty-Third Street. I made it on the button.

Walking through Lincoln Center's plaza, I felt a breeze on my crotch through the hole in my dungarees. I remembered Mom pulling me back into our Yorkville apartment when I tried to sneak out of the house in a torn shirt. She'd be so proud.

Entering the theater's second ring, sitting in my first row seat at the end of the aisle, I floated back to the late sixties when I regularly scored a single ticket for a New York Giants football game at old Yankee Stadium. Being at the opera was strange and familiar at the same time.

Despite my best efforts, Act One had me on the ropes—the dark space, the sweet music and a comfy chair conspired. I couldn't stay awake. I was having these mini-dreams involving Sigourney Weaver, loose clothing and me. I didn't want to stay awake. I only needed to hear Mom's aria in the second act. Unfortunately, the lady next to me was an armrest hog. She was eating and swigging soda with a friend, and felt that half my air space was sovereign for her meat hook. Every time Sigourney went to lick my ear, my neighbor's elbow took my arm out from under itself with a judo move.

At one point, my glasses flew off as my chin bounced off the wood armrest. In the distance, I heard B.F. Pinkerton romancing Cio Cio San in Italian, my ancestors' tongue. I didn't understand a word. Recovering my specs, I plotted revenge.

Gathering all the gas in my intestinal tract, I secured it in a single room right above my exit passage. I held it still, built pressure and blocked it. Saturday night's meal was the perfect storm. When I fatigued my sphincter muscle, I lifted my right cheek and let her blow. The strength of the release lifted the rest of my ass off my seat. Using my arms, I arched right to ensure my aim was true. The invisible cloud sucked the oxygen out of the air. I got a quick look at the woman's face, her bushy eyebrows were waving and she was barely conscious, then I ran out to the lobby.

After the intermission, my neighbor switched seats with her friend. I had no further armrest issue. The cold air during the break woke me up and I was all there, listening to the beautiful soprano sing "*Un bel di, vedremo*" gorgeously. I cried and thought of Mom.

During the second intermission, I scouted one of the information tables in the lobby. There was a brochure for a free Big Band concert the following week. An attractive volunteer leaned into me.

"Do you like Big Band music?"

"I adore it," I answered.

"You're kind of young to be into it."

"I have all my dad's reel-to-reel tapes, Dorseys, Miller, James, Shaw, and a lot more. We fought over music, but ended up liking a lot of the same stuff."

"Oh, that's wonderful. My late husband loved the Big Bands. I have one hundred and fifty albums that he played all the time," she said.

"You're very lucky. I love vinyl."

"I don't listen to them anymore. I have most of the stuff on CD and that's fine for me."

"Give them to your kids."

"They don't listen and don't want them. Would you like them?"

"That'd be great, but please think about it before giving them away."

"No, no, I've thought about it, and they're clutter to me. I'd feel much better if someone was enjoying them." Edith smiled.

She and I exchanged personal information and kept talking until the chimes went off signaling the start of the third act.

As I walked back to ring two, I thought about my day. I thought about Grace and her cut face. I thought about Mom humming along to *Madame Butterfly*. I thought about fights with Dad over Sinatra's best song. I figured my day at the opera would give any O. Henry character a run for their money.

I'm picking up the records next week.

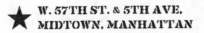

HERE I AM IN BERGDORF GOODMAN

BY SARAH MILLER-DAVENPORT

Here I am in Bergdorf Goodman, and not for the first time, holding up the left half of a pair of $900 boots with the kind of delicacy usually reserved for fine antiques and newborn babies. It's an exercise in frustration, a form of self-inflicted torture. I barely have $900 in the bank, let alone the kind of expendable income that allows for such a frivolous purchase. Plus, I tell myself as I place the boot back on the display case, spending that kind of money on shoes is wrong. People are dying. And I haven't even made my annual contribution to public radio.

It is a beautiful boot, though—Marc Jacobs, in black pebble leather with pinstriped suede trim and a small heel—and for a moment I wonder what it would feel like to go into credit card debt for the sake of fashion. I glance around at the well-heeled women in the shoe department and try to conjure up a feeling of righteousness to ward off the sense of shame that kicked in as soon as I passed through the revolving door downstairs. Shame over being trespasser, a class-tourist in a rich person's department store. Shame over caring what rich people thought of me. And shame at what my mother would think about the whole episode.

When I was growing up in New York City, my mother never took me into stores like Bergdorf's. We went shopping for shoes and nice dresses to wear to synagogue on the Lower East Side. That was where Jews went for shoes and nice dresses, even as late as the 1980s, even though the store was next door to an empty lot piled with bricks and dirty needles.

The rest of my clothes came from Conway, the discount stores in Herald Square, or maybe even Macy's, if they were having a sale. My mother would go shopping on her lunch break and come home with bag loads of outfits for me to try on at home, returning what I didn't want the next day. I would model them for her in the living room and agonize over the prospect of offending the manufacturers of the items I had rejected. I must have known, through the fog of child-logic, that my feelings of guilt were completely misplaced, that what I was really afraid of was hurting my mother. That is how I ended up with a pair of pleated acid-washed jeans in the style of A. C. Slater from *Saved by the Bell*, worn once and then stuffed into the back of my closet.

A common refrain in my family, at least one spoken by me and my father, was "We're not going to the poorhouse!" This was usually met with indignation by my mother, who would snap back, "You don't understand how little we live on. You don't pay the bills!" And both my dad and I would have to let it go since she was right—certainly about the bill-paying part.

Still, I was resentful and felt downright deprived when in the fifth grade she refused me a pair of metallic spandex leggings that were deemed too expensive. As a consolation prize, I got some ribbed pseudo-leggings from Conway that were barely tight enough to fit into my slouch socks. (The socks were not quite right either.)

I should say here that we lived in a comfortable prewar apartment on the Upper West Side of Manhattan. I grew up in relative privilege. We had a car, a dog, and went on the occasional family vacation. I went to private school, which was paid for by my grandmother. But money was always tight, and spending it was fraught with anxiety.

LOST AND FOUND

The department stores on the east side—Saks, Bendel's, Bergdorf's, even Bloomingdale's—were off-limits. They were the bastions of the rich and insouciant, with snooty salespeople and spoiled customers, easier to scorn than to risk their rejection. My parents, liberal stalwarts in a time of Reagan-era excess, wore their fashion cluelessness like a badge of honor. They rooted for the downfall of junk-bond king Michael Milken and cheered when Barneys was tarred by charges of racial discrimination.

My mother liked to tell me I had expensive taste, and not without a hint of admonition. The daughter of a rabbi, her wardrobe as a teenager consisted of hand-me-downs from her father's congregants. When owning a cashmere sweater was all the rage in 1950s Baltimore, she had to wait until some other girl got tired of hers. My mother didn't have many stories about growing up, but this was one of them. Somehow, I sensed that the sweater trauma was somehow connected to the other iconic story of her childhood, in which my mother spent most daylight hours after-school alone, in the public library.

My father had not known such want as a teenager. His disdain for fashionable clothes was less an embrace of frugality than it was a rejection of his WASP upbringing. One summer during high school, his parents had sent him to a tailor for a custom-made suit to wear to all the Louisville debutante parties and he came back with a jacket and pants made of mattress ticking. He dismissed my material longings with the casualness of someone who had never coveted a cashmere sweater.

In the ninth grade, when I transferred to a fancy private school on the Upper East Side, my own fashion sense went a little haywire. Realizing there was no way I could keep up with my wealthier peers, I turned to buying all my clothes at the Salvation Army. I thought I had special skills when it came to spotting the best T-shirts—soft and worn, with some sort of ironic slogan or nonsensical text on the front—from among the rows of musty closet detritus. This, to my mother, was more economical and thus better than shopping retail, even though I went through most of high school wearing a hot-pink ski jacket as an overcoat.

That all changed once I had my own place in New York and a small, but independently earned, sum of money in my bank account. Shopping in New York is like a drug: the more money you spend, the more you want to spend. And once you pass your limit of what is an appropriate price for, say, a perfect black cotton top or a really, really great pair of flip flops, it is hard to go back. Instead, I justify any extravagances with the argument that for people like me, with no innate style, expensive clothes make us look better.

This doesn't mean that I won't immediately call my mother to confess when I spend too much money on a pair of shoes and then refuse to tell her how much they cost. When she asks me, with an innocence that verges on poignant, "Were they more than seventy-five dollars?" I realize that if she knew just how much more, she might think less of me.

This is a woman whose own mother, two generations out of the shtetl, washed and reused tin foil—and not because she was an environmentalist. I am pretty certain my mother, who has lived in New York for four decades, has never seen the inside of Bergdorf's, the ultimate gatekeeper of the upper caste lifestyle. Bergdorf's radiates posh. It has soft, flattering lighting and etched mirrors in the escalator shafts. It lacks the crushing din of manic shoppers looking for the sale rack. Even the shopping bags— lavender with indigo text in deco font and a graphic of figures who look like they're on their way to a Jay Gatsby party—are a paradigm of high-class understatement. And although many of the customers are teenagers and women in their twenties wearing oversized sunglasses and skinny jeans, the whiff of old money in Bergdorf's is pungent.

Walking through the ground floor, past rows of jewels that cost as much as a car, I can't help but feel that being here is a small act of betrayal. This is a place where it is acceptable, in fact encouraged, to spend $900 on a pair of boots. Not that I ever have spent $900 on a pair of boots. But I plan to someday. Then I will call my mom.

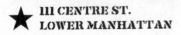
SMALL CLAIMS IS
A WAR OF ATTRITION

BY SARAH MILLER-DAVENPORT

It is a cool, dry August evening and I am in a windowless room at 111 Centre Street. I leave New York, the city of my birth, in less than a week. Yet, through a series of escalating events, I choose to be here, stubbornly clinging to the dream of winning back a minor sum of money with the help of the New York City justice system.

This is my sixth visit to the small-claims court building and I am beginning to feel like a regular. There are the friendly cops downstairs who scan my purse for weapons and ask if I know where I'm going, always more cheerful than I ever am—because yes, by this point I know all too well where I am headed. Once I get upstairs, I can tune out while the clerk reads the script about the rules of the courtroom, as I've nearly got it memorized. And after much trial and error, I now know the quickest route to my new favorite Chinese restaurant on East Broadway, which serves delicate little dumplings that are my reward for spending several hours on a hard courtroom bench.

Small-claims is the ugly stepchild of the Manhattan court system. The main room, besides the lack of windows, is shabby and overcrowded. It smells like stale body odor. The fluorescent lighting makes even the healthiest people look like they are recovering from a nasty case of food poisoning. Since damages are limited to five-thousand dollars, the demographic tends to lean toward the mid- to low-income and the paranoid. Almost no one dresses up—not even the judges, who by the end of the day cannot help but look rumpled.

Small-claims court has neither glamour nor grandeur of purpose. This is where people come to complain about a botched kitchen renovation or auto body damage from a routine fender bender. But if you look up from your book long enough to eavesdrop on the other cases, a narrative begins to emerge. Between the lines of testimony are stories of broken friendships and lives eked out on the margins—of life in a city that defies you to stay here in spite of its everyday injustices.

One night I listened, rapt, as a woman tearfully told the judge one of those New York horror stories involving a shady roommate service, a surprise eviction, and an inconvenient cat. Occasionally, the drone of the air conditioning is punctuated by moments of excitement when, for example, a witness who cannot contain himself speaks out of turn and the judge has to reprimand him—just like it happens on television.

Sometimes it feels as if the city itself is on display in the rawest form. Drama, banality, joy, pathos—it's all there. Or maybe I have just spent too much time here.

The first time I appeared in court, way back in March, I was fresh-faced and hopeful, like a rookie defense attorney on my first big case. There was no way, I thought, that any honest judge could possibly side with my opponent, the venal management company that was trying to deprive me of my $1100 security deposit. File folder in hand, I wore a blazer and freshly-pressed trousers, only to discover that the dress code was more along the lines of "No Shirt, No Shoes, No Service," and that justice can be elusive in the face of bureaucracy. It can take several court appearances to actually see a judge, and even if you win, it is up to you to retrieve your money. Now I am like that young attorney's older, hard-drinking coworker, embittered and world-weary from years of disappointment. Cynicism is my new best friend.

My lawsuit, which began as an intimidation tactic to get my deposit back, has devolved into a war of attrition, or more accurately, a game of chicken. One of the last times I was here, the woman representing the management company, whom I had mistakenly dismissed as an amateur, outsmarted me. We had finally sat down for a trial when she announced to the judge that she had only just now realized that all along I should have been suing the landlord, which was technically, if not practically, a separate entity. The judge looked at me sympathetically, told me that this was a common stalling technique used to wear people down, and gave me another date and time to add a new party to the suit.

Later that evening, my mother—who, bless her, has faithfully come as my witness to each appearance—became emotional over dim sum: "These people," she said, referring to the management company, despair creeping into her voice, "are capable of anything." She shook her head at her dumplings. "*Anything*!" This is what small-claims court does to you—it saps you of your innocence even as it fills you with righteous indignation.

This being New York, however, there are people who treat small-claims court as an opportunity. On one of my visits to 111 Centre Street, I got asked out on a date by a man using that tired line, "Don't I know you from somewhere?" I considered it for a moment, if only because it would make a great story—You may not believe this, I'd tell people, we actually met at small-claims court—but the guy creeped me out and I decided that no story is worth ending up with a potential stalker. I made up a lie, told him I couldn't give him my number, and watched my back all the way to the subway.

As I wait for my name to be called on what I hope will be my last court date, I begin to long for Chicago, where I have lived for most of the last year and where I will soon return after spending the summer in New York. In Chicago you can find an apartment in an afternoon, no brokers or roommate services needed. Public transit workers smile at you when you pay your fare. And it even has a great, hulking skyline that from certain angles almost rivals the view from the Brooklyn promenade.

Chicagoans like to put on their most jaded smirk and tell you that the reason their city runs more efficiently is because of all the corruption. Restaurants may have to bribe someone at City Hall for a liquor license, but the streets are cleaner. Going to the DMV is like visiting a warm, chatty aunt. And though I've never been, I have a feeling you wouldn't have to show up to Chicago small-claims court more than three times to get a resolution. Life there is, well, easier.

But easy is boring; there is no thrill in ease. A few months after my last court appearance, when I finally get back my security deposit, I feel a rush of joy all out of proportion to the amount printed on the check.

I know I have earned every dollar.

GOOD NEWS AND REVELATIONS

BY DEBBIE NATHAN

Mara from upstairs, who lives off flute lessons in her dining room and touch-and-go pit-orchestra gigs on Broadway, knocked on my door and everyone's door, begging us to start a tenants' union. We each had a reason. I was terrified of the dawn in July when half the sixth floor burned and everyone was out on the street in bathrobes. The landlords said the tenant forgot a candle. The tenant said he turned on his computer and a fuse box malfunctioned. The electrical system in the whole building was fucked, he said, a time bomb for future disaster. A few days later, Manny was standing by his SUV, blasting Celia Cruz from the tape deck, steeping the block in mambo. I asked him in Spanish who he believed, since he was the super and should know. Manny took the tenant's side, partly because he liked me, partly because he didn't like the landlords, and partly because of something bigger. The sum of his reasons scared me so much that I went to Columbia Hardware and paid too much for a three-story rope ladder with window prongs.

The building sucks, but who can be picky? The young lawyer in Park Slope who'd offered us a sublet bailed at the last minute without telling us. These days in New York, the rent increase for new tenants is so fat that landlords advise people like the young lawyer, "Why bother subletting? Just break the lease." We'd already loaded our things and our kids into a van in Texas. Now we were facing homelessness. Then some luck: a friend got a job out of town and bequeathed us his place in Morningside Heights. The landlords were an ultra-Orthodox Jewish family named something like Kleiner with a realty office on Fifth Avenue in Midtown. I learned later that they're notorious slumlords, which you see from our place. It hasn't had a paint job in forty years and the old jobs are thirty layers thick. Daily, the dog's bowl disgorges drowned roaches. The living room parquet is bald with splinters. We arrived in June. In July there was the fire.

The time I asked Manny about it, his wife put her hands on her hips. "*No hables con ella,*" she muttered. She didn't want him dissing his employers to a tenant.

But Manny had a conscience. A new one, Mara said. "He used to be a big pothead, and mean," she told me after our first tenants' union meeting. "When he was smoking he was a space case, just useless as a super. Even when he wasn't high he mostly refused to fix anything unless you left lots of notes in the basement and threatened to withhold rent. Dealing with him was one big snarling match. He changed a couple of years ago. All of a sudden. I heard he had a born-again experience. He got a lot nicer about fixing things. Though he sure hasn't helped me lately."

The first time I saw Manny with a Bible was after we'd talked about religion once and he went off about Jews. That was just after we moved in. He was by the SUV. It was a pretty morning in June and already we had problems. A hole had opened in the bathroom floor; you could see the downstairs neighbor peeing. "Old Mr. Kleiner," Manny said. "He's dead now, but he was very *judío,* always wore that thing on his head and the black coat. Always came around to take care of things himself. He would have had me fix your floor right away. But very greedy, like all *judíos.* They all get rich from the greed. Mr. Kleiner died and his daughter is also very *judía* but never comes around here and things are going to the dogs with her new generation of bigger Jewish greed." I made the obvious points. I'm Jewish and I'm not rich. Lots of Jews aren't rich.

I've heard socialism is big in the Dominican Republic, where Manny was from, so I mentioned that socialism was led by Jews, maybe started by Jews, and socialism sure isn't for the rich and greedy. Furthermore, women in realty offices on Fifth Avenue who wear ugly wigs and ignore holes in tenants' floors: this is not my brand of *judío* and mine is just as popular. I tried not to be pissed off.

A people's lawyer came from the West Harlem Tenants Council—idealistic, not so young anymore, hair cut like Carl Sandburg, last year's clothes. We held the meeting in the vestibule, leaning on the mailboxes. Some people talked about the fire and about how the electrical system hadn't been worked on since 1907. A guy in frayed cords who went to Manhattan School of Music a long time ago spoke. The guy's instrument was trumpet: you could tell he never left home because all day you heard his playing through the walls. He mentioned that every time he turned on his living room light switch, his hand got a big jolt. "Shit," another tenant said, "the same thing happens to me!" We voted Mara president.

But Mara did not want to talk about fire. "My shower," she said, "is covered with creeping black mildew. Mildew with red stripes, and the stripes appear to be eating into the tile. The tile has become more and more virulent in the past month, and I'm convinced the mildew is making me sick. Last week after I took a shower, I felt anxious. All day afterward I had trouble breathing. The doctor said yes, it's possible I have a problem with mildew. Shana Kleiner won't let Manny do anything. She says mildew is harmless and I should just get Ajax. I want to know if everyone else has mildew in their apartment, and if you're getting sick. We need to organize around this!"

People looked blank. Mara turned and saw Manny standing at the front doors. "Out, Manny!" she said. "You're just spying for the Kleiners!"

"I am not espying," said Manny. "I am *preocupado*."

"Out!" said Mara. "You got born again and you got nicer. But what did you do for my mildew?"

"Manny, how come you were at the meeting?" I asked next day. "Were you spying for the Kleiners?"

"No way," he said. "I am worried for the tenant, very worried. This is mildew we're talking about! I've been reading the Bible.

Mildew is an abomination. A curse according to the most fundamental laws, along with the commandments against sodomy and pork. And so, even though the Kleiners are greedy, as *judíos* I cannot understand why they won't let me make the repairs. Why do they ignore this sacrilege?"

"What are you talking about?" I asked. That's when I saw his Bible for the first time. It was a Spanish version of the Good News edition, leather-bound, fat, with satin ribbons streaming like froufrou from a baby girl's hair. Good News was published in the 1970s. Its vocabulary is modern, and effortless to understand. "I shall not want" in King James' twenty-third psalm becomes "I have everything I need" in Good News. "Why do the heathen rage?" turns into "Why do the nations plan rebellion?"

Good News, Leviticus, chapter fourteen does have much to say about mildew. If the Lord sends mildew into a house, you are obligated to immediately tell a priest. The priest is ordered to scrape the interior walls, then leave the city to dispose of the contaminated plaster. All who have been in the house must wash their clothes. Everything is to be ritually purified. And so on and so forth for twenty verses or more.

When I checked my King James, the word mildew was missing. In its place was "plague." I couldn't imagine what kind of plague would destroy plaster. Could this be merely symbolic? I asked Manny if Leviticus chapter fourteen might really be about, say, leprosy. Or just plain evil.

"Who ever heard of leprosy eating bathroom walls?" Manny said curtly. "Or evil, for that matter? The Bible is talking about mildew. I'm a super. I know. I'd like to pull the old tile out, treat the subsurface with a good fungicide, then caulk everything over. But the Kleiners say no."

"Why get worked up over mildew?" I said. "If you want drama, go all the way to the end of the Bible and try the Book of Revelation. Fire mixed with blood. A third of the earth burning. Stars falling to earth, endless smoke from an abyss, sulphur."

He wasn't interested. "I spent my life hearing the Bible from priests. One of these days I'll do the New Testament. But now that I've found life in the Lamb, I must start from scratch. No more priests, no more Catholics. My wife hates that I've left the Church.

Hates it! But the Templo Evangélico has it right. First I will do the Old Testament. On my own. I'll read with my eyes and think with my own mind. After that, maybe I'll get to Revelation."

By September, Manny had made it to Deuteronomy and the tenants' union had fallen apart because Mara was only interested in her shower, whereas everyone else wanted to focus on electrical. On the morning of the eleventh, I was in Queens and my kids were below Fourteenth Street, where they attended school, as always, in high-rises, and on this day saw people jumping from towers. By midafternoon we had all made it home on foot and the next day I ordered my daughter to stop cowering in the apartment and go outside. I went first and saw Manny on the stoop, with the *Good News* open to Revelation. He was weeping and you could smell the air from Lower Manhattan. "I'm not ready for this," he said. "I wanted to finish the *judío* Bible first."

A few days later he had a fatal stroke.

The wake was at Funeraria Ortiz on 190th Street. The little plastic cards with his name, date of birth, and date of death also had saints, which I think he would have disliked, but that was the family's choice. The Kleiners did not show up—it was Friday night, they couldn't drive on shabbos, and they certainly didn't live close enough to walk. Their absence felt like a stain; after all, this was the death of their super, who tended their building for twenty-five years. Mara came and shifted from foot to foot like she wanted to say say something redeeming but felt too embarrassed. Her silence also left a taint. And I was sullen. Muslims, *judíos*, Catholics, *evangelicos*: there was too much religion around just then, and if I thought about it straight, it would have felt scary. So I thought crooked about mold, which just seemed like a dirty joke on Manny.

Only his wife came clean. "Manolo! Manolo!" she wailed, speaking his name in the old way. Clinging to the bier with her left hand, she wrung with the right, scrubbing the air with her grief.

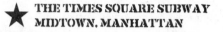

THE MESTIZAS

BY DEBBIE NATHAN

On a Saturday afternoon, in the half-gloom of the subway station at Times Square, while W and N and R trains were barreling through, two girls stood on either side of the platform, each guarded by a patrolman.

They were just *mestizas*, the kind who were raised in their own big cities and nowadays are all over this one: those moon cheeks on high cheekbones, lax black hair, proper gold earrings, and mild, careful eyes. Each had on jeans and a femmie tee with pastel ribbon at the neckline and big writing on the chest about nothing. The jeans and shirts were so polyester that if a set had been bought with a twenty, the cashier would still give back change. Snug clothes, and the girls' breasts were high, though one had a stomach that comes after babies. Each stood by a big and intricate arrangement of cardboard, a table-like thing draped in a big square of faux silk and quickly collapsible. A set-up like this is made for instant disassembly and permanent abandonment with no regrets after a lightning escape. The sides of the "silk" can be grabbed on a second's notice and bunched at the top, making a sack that's easy to run with.

But when I got there, the tables were still up and the cloth still laid with goods. There were "amber" necklaces—chunks of tiger-striped, see-through acrylic—strung on slim, fake suede thongs. Bracelets of tiny, razzle-dazzle glass rosettes that aren't really glass. Plastic turquoise and plastic coral on plastic brass: a big, cheap joke to some, yet perfect for the bare arms and summer collar bones of the low-paid young females of New York, their skin every smooth shade of coffee-truck coffee with varying cream. The baubles were still arranged just so on the "silk," supine and perfect like women on sheets.

Shoppers were still looking and asking for prices.

"Sorry ladies," the cops said. "Store's closed."

The *mestizas* were street vendors without licenses. In the whole city just a few hundred permits exist, compared to thousands of sellers who need them. These vendors were two of the criminal thousands, so today they were being fined and their wares were being seized. "Put your stuff out of sight," one cop said in English, pantomiming to make himself clear. Each vendor took a long overhang of "silk" from the front of her table and folded it backward. Now the jewelry was covered.

One officer was baby-faced, with hair and eyes too dark for his skin, like a black Irish. The other man, who was bigger, was simply black. Neither was much older than the shoppers or the vendors. With their navy, box-like jackets and their guns, they looked way too serious for the job at hand. They stood by the tables writing $50 citations.

The vendors stood, too, with their backs to the trains and rats. Their torsos were stock-still and their heads cast down, but their eyes were all over the place. I saw they wanted to use their hands, but one couldn't. She belonged to the black-Irish cop, who was efficient and stern. While writing the ticket he hardly looked at the paper. Instead, he monitored his *mestiza* constantly and unconsciously, like a driver who knows to check mirrors.

The African American cop was different. His eyes were doing a wistful, even philosophical dance around the vendor with the postpartum stomach. Slowly, head down, he wrote a few lines on the citation. He rotated toward the opposite train track, which removed her from his line of vision, and wrote a little more. Then he turned, slowly again, but still excusing her from his sight.

She too, was slow, but also fast. Each time her cop looked

away, she crept a hand under the "silk," stealthily extracted a bracelet or necklace, and slipped it in the left back pocket of her jeans. When the left pocket was full she switched to the right. By the time the cop finished the ticket, her jeans looked like a child's story about squirrels storing acorns for winter.

Which isn't to say she saved everything. Far from it.

It's unsettling, seeing a loving display of women's jewels— even the paste kind—swept up by ham fists, then crammed and crushed in a plastic evidence bag. Like expensive gold chain, even plate knots so it never unknots. The leaden tangle inside the bag molded it to the black Irish cop's palm the way a firm feather pillow molds to a head, or the bodies of babies settle on mothers. The black-Irish cop squeezed air from the bag. He twisted the top and locked it with a sawtooth tie. The bag was transparent ,though, and by now the jewels somehow resembled those tour-ing Never-Again displays of toothbrushes and eyeglasses from the German camps. "What's going to happen to it all?" I asked the cop. He was already walking away and didn't slow down.

Free again, the *mestizas* stared dully at their citations, then folded their cardboard tables.

"We didn't see them coming this time," one said.

"*¿Por qué venden aquí donde hay tanta vigilancia?*" I asked. "Why sell here where there's so much security?"

"When it comes to police, the Times Square subway is the most dangerous place in the city," she said. "But it's also the best for sales."

"*¿Cuánto valió lo que acaban de perder? Dos cientos?*" "How much did you just lose? Two hundred dollars worth?"

"*Más.*" She gave the same philosophical look that I'd seen in the eyes of her cop.

I spotted them a month later in the same place—the *mestizas*, that is. Customers were still everywhere, oohing and ahhing, shelling out bills in small denominations. There was still the cardboard, the dazzle, the goods with their names in quotes.

The cops weren't around, and I hurried on since I was in a rush. I'd just bought some "amber," a piece with an "ant" in it. I'd paid a buck for it from a vendor on Canal Street. I'd sped off then, not wanting to witness what the real price might be.

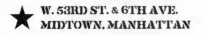

A DAY WITH THE
DELEGATES FROM TEXAS

BY DEBBIE NATHAN

I'm a long-time Texan currently living in New York City. I recently spent some time in the company of the Lone Star delegation when they came to New York for the Republican National Convention. Most were esconced at the New York Hilton on Fifty-third Street and Sixth Avenue—"Avvnoo of the Amuricas," as the delegates pronounced it.

Today is "compassionate conservatism" day at the RNC, when delegates from every state are urged to visit soup kitchens and other nonprofits that comprise unfettered capitalism's mop-up detail, to show how caring and faith-based charities and thousand-points-of-light Republicans can be. The Texans are heading out from the Hilton, over to the Passaic River to pick up trash.

But first, a speaker says, everyone should check to see if they've used up the complimentary sixty-minute calling cards they got in their RNC goodie bags, courtesy of Verizon, or the complimentary bus and subway passes provided by the city. If they are still good, the delegates are instructed, "Give them to

April and she'll give them to the Salvation Army to help those who are less fortunate and can really use them."

The mass, high-pitched "Oooooooh!" and applause that follows is exactly like what happens when a yellow duckie receiving blanket is unwrapped at a baby shower. I consider telling April that sixty-minute cards last far less than an hour when you're homeless and lack a cell or residential phone—when you use a Verizon pay phone in New York, a calling card gets docked fifteen minutes even before you get a dial tone. But I keep quiet.

Oh, that troublesome nanosecond when English speakers grope unconsciously for the proper word! Most buy time with "uh" or "um" or "you know." (College students and professors—particularly those plugged into the deconstructionist and social constructionist disciplines—often use "sort of.") Then there's the Texas delegation.

At a sumptious breakfast in their honor, sponsored by Halliburton, a man giving the invocation demonstrates the Christian fundamentalist, GOP version of "um."

It is "just."

As in, "Lord, we just pray for the police officers. And we just thank you for the great country we live in. We lift up the New York Police Department, and we just thank you for their leaders. In Jesus's name. Amen."

Out on the street after breakfast, not far from the Hilton, across the street from the horse-drawn carriages and a park so gorgeous that it might be that non grata nationality for Republicans: French.

On the side with all the luxe hotels there's a chilling absence of people except for cops, cops, cops, and more cops and pedestrians in male and female power suits, their big RNC credentials hanging on grosgrain like royal dog tags.

Well, there are a few others. For instance, the two fellows shaking their fingers at a credentialed couple of a certain age—she with still slim ankles, silver hair, and expensive reading glasses on a chain, he just as tasteful and patrician. "Go back south where you came from, fucking Republicans," shouts one of the men. "Goddamn hicks," adds the other in a voice dripping venom.

The RNCers look stricken, perhaps not so much by the verbiage as by the demographic of their hecklers. No smelly, raggedy kid anarchists: both are pushing forty and wear Dockers' pants and nice sport coats. Both have good, recent, blond haircuts. If not patrician, certainly tasteful enough. The social equality of their fury is breathtaking, and the Republicans choke as they scurry to a carriage.

That evening there is a gigantic party for the Texans at a ballroom on Thirty-fourth and Ninth Avenue.

Two days earlier, when I was walking on Broadway and Ninety-fifth Street, someone stopped to admire my "NYC to RNC: Drop dead" button and confessed to managing the catering company that agreed to work this gala. "My employees are FURIOUS!" complained the manager. "Some of the chefs are joking about poisoning the food. We were asked to serve—get this—PIGS IN BLANKETS! Well sure, we know how to make pigs in blankets; we use kosher hot dogs. The chefs want to wear T-shirts under their uniforms that have something anti-Bush on them."

The T-shirts remained hidden and the food was not poisoned.

Inside the Hilton, a button seller has set up shop on the plush, quiet carpet of the mezzanine hallway. There's the usual inventory: "Bush and Cheney" and "W for President."

But I'm drawn to the girl material. One button says simply, "Woman Republican," bordered all in sweet, art deco flowers that look just like those femmie courageous posters that hang in the waiting rooms of…abortion clinics. "All my men are cowboys," says another button, with a picture of the president in a ten-gallon. And then there is: "I only sleep with Republicans."

My absolute fave shows a red, white, and blue elephant straddling a donkey, fucking it. "Keep Bush on Top," it says, "Hey,"

I say to no one in particular, "Here's the sex area!" No one seems to think that's cute—a couple of Texan women wince and turn away.

Sotto voce, the vendor delivers a lecture about how he's a button-history expert, and the elephant / donkey sex motif is almost a hundred years old in United States political iconography (first attested during a Teddy Roosevelt campaign, he intones). I want to buy that button but do not wish to donate three dollars to the Republicans. "Do you sell at Democratic conventions, too?" I ask.

"Uh, yeah," he says, still confidential-like.

"Do you do protest buttons?"

"Uh, yup." Even quieter.

Turns out he's just a button guy from Kalamazoo, Michigantrying to make a living. I plunk down the three dollars and pocket my RNC bestiality souvenir.

WHAT MEAN "YO"?

BY DEBBIE NATHAN

When I first working as ESL teacher twenty year ago, I was a little nervous. In that time I am more young than now, and when I turn around to writing at blackboard, I am think the students looking at my ass. But that a long time ago. Now my ass, she is nothing for look.

Today I am teach in Bronx, my students from the Republic Dominicana, from Mexico, and from others Latino America nation, many in this country too many years but they still speaking too less English and that English, it is just like this. Three hour a day three day a week, it student English have it own sabor it will get inside a teacher head and duration there even after class is finish. Immigrant English living in the teacher mind, even if teacher is no want.

My student, they are too intelligent even student they got no too much education in they country. José from Guatemala by example. In he country he was farmer, now butcher at Hunts Point, working here fourteen year. He have only little bit of opportunities for study English, but he know all words of Gettysburg Address. Also read maybe all books in English, every one, on construccion the Brooklyn Bridge. He was only person

286

from his town to immigrate. José, he have cassette player he play music from *Rocky* too many times, he say because when he first come to USA in 1988, walking through Mexico, crossing to LA over hot desert, cold mountains, *Rocky* is still popular music in he old country and now he in new country, want to remember that especial time of challenge and hopes for surpassing in the life. In New York he marry once but only for green card. Loved her too much anyway, but she no loving him. He not married now, living by heself. He getting up 2:30 a.m. to go to work, work overtime because boss say he have to, no extra pay. If he say no, he be fired. Lonesome he say, and his back hurting. Bad neighborhood, the boys outside in summer with marijuana, it coming smell through the window. He cannot sleep! Still, he no have plans return his country. Very difficult, life here but still better than Guatemala.

I ask José, he have problem cutting up animal? No, he say, because in Guatemala on farm he kill the pigs and others similar. The pigs screaming, the baby goat screaming this was hard, he thinking many things. But here at job in New York, he just playing *Rocky* on headphones while he cut the meat, and anyway already dead. Already dead, José tell me. And I am not exact know who he meaning dead—pig, goat, or he?

Vicente is from Ecuador, he worrying, too, very much about correct language. "Teacher," he say, "what is mean 'Yo'? Is okay to use or is bad, angry talk? And it's black people talk only?" I tell it is okay, not angry, is not just black people, either, but also white. Vicente is not believing. "Teacher," he say, "I want to talk like a University but all day at work on train on bus, I hearing only street English. People saying yo. Maybe they going to fight. And a man on TV say, 'The couple was making out.' Teacher you say 'make out' mean only kissing and hug but I know the TV mean real sex, so teacher please don't tell class other thing because it sound ugly if I use wrong. Maybe I offend someone maybe I no get better job."

Vicente back when in he country he have a small business: computers. Now he working night shift in one box factory in

Brooklyn. "Teacher," Vicente say, "I try on the subway talk to American women and they no talking to me. Teacher, what is? They afraid? This is racism? Or what?"

"Teacher," Vicente say, "I am be frank with you: I no like the United States so much. I have friends in France. I thought United States is going to be like France. It is not. Teacher: We see Enron. Martha Stewart. United States policy to Iraq. Starvation the kids. Being bully in all place, dishonesto to the people. Nine Eleven—of certain manner, I believe the United States is deserve it. I only being frank with you teacher."

I no say nothing to Vicente about Martha Stewart and Nine Eleven, just listen him. But I worried about what he say about TV talk, this "make out" thing. At home after class I ask my daughter. She a student at Cooper Union, never go to Bronx but very young, still having good ass, knowing how the English sound in street and others places. "You ever hearing one person or any peoples say 'make out' when they meaning not just kiss, hug—but real sex?" I ask. She say yes, she do hear. She laugh at me say "Mommy, you're too old. You don't know slang anymore. It's not what it was twenty years ago. When it comes to teaching ESL you're over the hill!"

I am don't believe her. I am published writer too many year. Often I watch the TV. I reading. I am pay too much attention to our cultura. How it's possible I do not knowing all of English? I lie in bed sleep not good. I wonder if students noticing not my ass but other thing about my age. Thing like I not knowing some English they need. I toss turning all night.

On bus next day a man say, "yo." He is young, black man. Say to other black man. I listen I get nervous. His "yo," it is friendly or unfriendly? I no can tell but keep think about Vicente. He say "yo'" is black people talk and is angry. I feeling I want to get off bus. I go to class. Vicente he have new haircut, new glasses. "Very fashion, teacher," he say. "Fashionable," I say, smile. But no say nothing about "yo." I come home miss another sleep.

I decide write one letter to William Safire on *New York Times Magazine,* ask him who exactly say "yo" in these days and why they saying. Does mean yo "Hello?" It friendly thing? Unfriendly? Hip Hop? Only black?

I am tell students I writing important *New York Times* person with Vicente question. I wait too many days then same letter back in my mailbox—I not put enough stamp, thirty-four cent but price change to thirty-seven cent. My daughter laughing again, "Mommy," she say, "Didn't you read the papers about how it was going up three cents? You're the one who needs the English lessons!"

I read letter again see words misspelled, not one but two. Maybe good it come back, I think, and plan to fix, mail next week.

Not so important, though, because before I have free time, Vicente disappear from class. "Where is Vicente?" I ask others student. No one heard from he, but soon I reading about INS raid at box factory in Brooklyn. This article not in *New York Times*, this article in *Daily News*. *Daily News* no have articles about right language wrong language. But maybe have the news about Vicente.

Well I hoping he safe wherever he is. Hoping he not very angry. Hoping he no hate my English. Wanting he understand "yo." Wonder he think teacher ass.

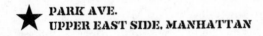
THE DOORMAN'S DOUBLE LIFE

BY MR. MURPHY

"It's nice today," says 15B as he enters the elevator, taking off his gloves and Dartmouth Alumni Association baseball hat. "Maybe a little chilly."

"Yeah, it's nice," I agree. I close the elevator door behind him.

"Forty now, but they say forty-five later on."

"Great."

We've reached his floor, but the retired cardiologist won't get out until he's given me the complete five-day forecast. Can't he see me squirming? Doesn't he recognize the look of agonized boredom on my face? He must. He is intentionally torturing me. Finally, someone rings for the elevator, providing me with an excuse to cut the old guy off. He lets me escape, but promises to keep me abreast of any breaking news from the National Weather Service.

I am always polite and forbearing with the tenants, especially the old timers, but today I let 15B ramble on even longer than usual. I'm not proud of it, but there has been an undeniable change in my attitude and behavior lately. I'm not the only one. When I came into work today, Jimmy was sitting on the couch reading *The National Enquirer*. The elevator rang, but rather than finish the article as is his custom, he jumped off the couch and ran into the elevator to answer the call. Dry cleaning that would languish in the package room for a week in May or June is now promptly delivered to the tenants as they enter the building. The super, who usually grunts at the tenants, is suddenly friendlier than a politician at a fundraiser.

As any doorman, porter, or elevator operator in the city can tell you, Christmas is coming. Yes, we are in holiday mode. The payoff for a year's worth of abject servility is almost within reach, and we are working ourselves into a sycophantic frenzy. We fawn over their children and pets, we laugh at their stale jokes, and we humbly beg forgiveness if we've kept them waiting for more than ten seconds.

I wish I could say I was above this seasonal obsequiousness, but damn it, I want a new computer. So last night, I cravenly accepted 1C's insincere apology as I mopped up after her Pekinese. I wanted to kick the incontinent rodent across the lobby, but Gateway isn't giving those laptops away.

Although I am counting on the tenants' Yuletide sense of *noblesse oblige*, this in no way changes what I know to be the fundamental truth of tenant-staff relations: THEY HATE US. Sure, things are cordial and even friendly on the surface, but if you doubt their enmity I suggest you take a look at the uniforms— nay, costumes—they parade the doormen around in. The sartorial manifestation of their animus can be seen in the ungodly brown-and-green polyester suits with bright yellow piping, the ridiculous looking hats and bow ties and gloves. And, worst of all, the item that most emphatically expresses their contempt, the epaulets. Epaulets! What reason can they have to dress the help in the accoutrements of warriors, except to mock us? I can hear them snickering, "Hey, Admiral Nelson. Throw my clubs in the Beemer for me. I tee off at Winged Foot in an hour."

Oh, they can laugh at us, but it doesn't hide their fear. And make no mistake, despite the fact that it is we who depend on them for our livelihood, it is they who fear us. For we know their secrets, we see them stripped of their armor. We know who had a hooker in his apartment while his wife was away at the summer house. We know which teenager didn't spend the summer at a camp in Vermont, as his parents told the neighbors, but at drug rehab in Minnesota.

The lies and pretensions they pass off to the rest of the world are to us laughably transparent. You can go to all the Urdu film festivals and Jackson Pollack exhibits you like, 8C. I see you in the gym watching TV, going up and down on the StairMaster, but never taking your eyes off *Access Hollywood* or *Entertainment Tonight.*

Prior to coming to work here, my only exposure to the denizens of the Upper East Side was in Woody Allen movies, so I expected to hear lots of witty repartee and recondite references to August Strindberg and Bauhaus architecture. Imagine my disappointment when I discovered that *People* magazine subscribers outnumber *The New York Review of Books* subscribers four to one. And the conversation is as laden with references to their status-obsessed consumerism as any you'd hear in an inner-city high school. The only difference is the brand names of choice are not Fubu, Phat Farm, or Tommy Hilfiger. They are Mercedes, Bridgehampton, and Yale.

"Hey, Carlos. Where we going?" I ask the deliveryman from the diner.

"7D, amigo."

I call the tenant from the elevator phone and bring Carlos up. When we get there, 7D doesn't have the money ready, so we are both kept waiting. When the tenant finally returns, he says he wants thirty-five cents back, leaving fifty cents for the tip. Carlos only has quarters, but the Goldman Sachs investment banker isn't going to let this Ecuadorean con-artist beat him out of ten cents. While 7D goes off in search of the exact change, the elevator rings angrily. I can't answer the calls because I am forbidden from leaving the delivery man alone, lest he steals someone's doormat.

After the transaction is complete, we return to the lobby. When I open the elevator door, I am greeted by five scowling faces. I should tell them to save their nasty looks for 7D, but I've been here long enough to know nothing is ever a tenant's fault. One of the people impatiently awaiting my arrival is the new pro-prietress of the penthouse. She is in a foul mood, not only because I've kept her waiting, but because, as I hear her rant at Johann, her personal trainer, her bastard of an ex husband has had the gall to send her the bill from the stable that houses Junior's horses.

Mercifully, when I get back to the lobby, Vince has returned from his break. I gladly hand the passenger car over to him and return to the solitude of the service car to resume picking up the garbage. This is my favorite time of the day. It's the final hour of my shift, the boss has gone into hiding until tomorrow morning, and the tenants are now Vince's problem. As well as being the most relaxing part of the day, it is also the most instructive. It is in the trash where the most interesting revelations about the lives of the tenants are discovered. In a typical day I might learn that 3C thinks she's pregnant, 2D is trying the latest cure for baldness, and the kid in 8A failed his geometry test. But not all the artifacts I unearth are so easy to interpret. Often, I have to utilize what I know about the tenants in order to make sense of their garbage. For example, almost every day I collect five or six crushed Coors Light cans from the metal recycling bins on the sixth floor. I've never seen who puts them there, but I'd be willing to bet all my Christmas money that it's Mr. 6E taking out his frustrations on something less ferocious than his shrew of a wife.

I finish the garbage and return to the lobby to give it a final mopping before going home. Vince is sitting on the couch look-ing more forlorn than usual. "She just went out," he said. "She not wearing any underpants." The number of women in the building wearing panties fluctuates daily in inverse proportion to the number of hours Vince stayed up the night before watching pornographic videos. The woman he's talking about is 9E, the trophy-wife-in-waiting. She's been fired from three jobs since coming to New York, but her parents back in Texas still support her in the hope that someday soon her beauty will persuade some middle-aged mutual fund manager to abandon his wife and children and relieve Mr. and Mrs. 9E of their daughter's colossal credit card debts.

"I no have chance," Vince continues glumly. "Maybe I show her the checkbook." Whenever a tenant angers Vince, he threatens to show them his bankbook. It should go without saying that he makes the threat to me, not the tenant. He works two full-time jobs and lives with his brother, so he doesn't pay rent. Except for an occasional trip to a strip club, he never spends a dime, and has amassed quite an impressive nest egg for an unskilled laborer. "They think they something 'cause they have money. I have two hundred thousand dollars!" he screams at me. "What the fuck! They see this shitty suit and they think we nothing."

Vince has just hit on the other reason why they dress us like buffoons: emasculation. Working in proximity to the wives and daughters of Manhattan's elite, we must be as sexually unthreatening as possible—the eunuchs that guard the harem. If Vince were the best-looking man in the city, the women would still only see this sad, polyester-clad castrato.

I go downstairs to the locker room to change. When I get in the elevator with Vince a few minutes later, he is more morose than ever. "I go home, I see in the bars everybody holding hands, kissing. That's why sometimes I get pissed off. This is not a life. This is not a life." I know what he means, but I'm not exactly moved to tears by his lament. I've heard him say it a thousand times, and what's worse is I've said it at least as many times myself. The day wouldn't be complete without at least one chorus of: "we're poor, we're stupid, we're ugly, women hate us, and we're stuck in these shitty jobs until the day we die." Of course, we always conclude that we have no one to blame but ourselves.

As I leave the building for the night, I look into the lobby of the building across the street. My grandmother was a nanny in that building. It was her first job in America. Sixty-five years and two generations later, I've managed to move the family place of business about twenty-five yards to the north. The doorman in that building is talking to a boy about ten years old. He seems to be studying a pack of the boy's baseball cards. It is my habit to spy

on the doormen of all the buildings I pass on my way to the subway. By the time I get off work, their evening rush is over. Some
read the *Post*, others step out on the sidewalk for a smoke and to
watch the lady pedestrians passing by. They sometimes look
bored, but they never look as miserable (Vince's self-pity is catching) as I feel. Am I a snob? Do I think I'm too good for my job?

Yes.

I am here less than an hour before I slice my finger with a box
cutter while breaking down some boxes 8B left in the hallway—
her weekly fix from the Home Shopping Network. I should
probably put a bandage on it, but the boss is bellowing for me to
polish the brass in the boiler room. He says it looks like it hasn't
been cleaned in months. In fact, I haven't ever cleaned the brass
in the boiler room. It's news to me that there is anything brass
down there. Anyway, I get a rag and the polish and go to work on
the two brass doorknobs that the boss has suddenly decided must
be positively luminous in order for the building to survive another
day. I'm rubbing one of the doorknobs vigorously when some of
the polish gets into my open wound. It feels like I've been given
an injection of napalm. I cry out in pain, but get no sympathy from
the boss. "I know, it hurts for you to do a little honest work once
in a while," he says. I run up the stairs to wash it out. The service
car is ringing furiously. I ignore the elevator until after I've
cleaned out the cut. I say a quick prayer that I don't die of blood
poisoning and answer the call.

Mrs. 18A is shrieking at me before I get the elevator door open.
The woman is so frantic I assume there must be an emergency, a
flood or a gas leak. But the situation is even worse than I feared—
her dog has pulled a glue mousetrap out from under the oven.
Miraculously, the trap did not get stuck on the dog, but it is now
lying sticky side down on the linoleum tile. She's screaming at me
to get it up. It's ruining her beautiful new floor. I try to peel it off,
but it might as well be painted on the tile for all I can move it. I
pull harder and a small piece of the cardboard trap comes off in
my hand. I throw it in the garbage before giving the trap one final

yank. "Don't pull too hard," commands Mrs. 18A. "I don't want you to pull off—"

Rip! Too late. The mousetrap and the tile are now both in my hand. From her agonized expression and banshee's howl you'd swear I ripped out her pancreas along with the tile. I am cursed for my incompetence. She threatens to have me fired, sued, arrested, and killed.

Although I am blameless in this case, (then again, maybe I'm not; I suppose if I had held down the tile with my left hand while pulling with my right, the tile wouldn't have come loose) she is right. I am the worst porter this building has ever had. That's not to say I don't work hard or that I'm unreliable. I'm never late for work and I haven't missed a day in the two-and-a-half years I've been here. I'm also still young enough, despite my ever expanding girth, to be an effective beast of burden. But any task that requires an iota of intelligence or manual dexterity is beyond me. For example, on Sunday the old lady in 4C asked me to change the battery in her smoke alarm. I tried at least ten times, but could not get the new battery to fit into the slot. She looked at me with disgust. "Get down from there," she snapped. "Let me try." I got down off the chair and helped her get her arthritic, osteoporosis-ridden old bones onto it. Within five seconds I heard the battery click into place. She beamed triumphantly atop her pedestal, look-ing down on me with scorn and pity. I should've kicked the chair out from under her. She wouldn't look so goddamned smug with a broken hip. To add to my humiliation, she wanted to pay me for my trouble. I said I didn't want the money because I hadn't done anything. "For trying," she said, forcing two crumpled sin-gles into my hand.

Having said that, I'm the last person who should be throwing stones, the absolute helplessness of the tenants is pathetic. True, I have to ask my brother or father to come to my apartment to hang a set of blinds or fix a bookshelf. And despite countless hours of instruction, I still can't change a tire. My helplessness is born of a singular stupidity, but the tenants: they wear their infant-like dependence as a badge of privilege. They remind me of something I read years ago in the *Guiness Book of World Records*. In it there was a picture of an Indian guy with the world's longest fingernails. His nails were so long (I don't remember the exact length) that they spiraled inward like the horns of a ram. The book said that long fingernails were a status symbol in the highest caste of Indian society. The incapicitatingly long nails were a way of saying that he could afford to have someone perform even the smallest tasks for him. So it is with the tenants. Unlike me, they could probably learn to program their VCRs or change their own lightbulbs, but then the neighbors might get the impression, not that they're self-sufficient, but that they can't afford to have someone do it for them.

I make it to six thirty without destroying any more apartments and relieve Vince for his break. As he goes out, Mr. 3B and Mrs. 10A enter the building followed by one of the dry-cleaning delivery guys who is carrying what looks like the entire men's department of Bergdorf's on his back.

"I know that can't all be for me," I say.

"Sorry, my friend." He doesn't look too sorry, unloading his cargo piece by piece: 12B, 7C, 18A, 5E. The two tenants in the elevator are waiting for me, so I don't have time to put the clothes in the package room. I take them to their respective floors, operating the elevator with my right hand and carrying about twenty-five pounds of dry cleaning in my left. The metal hangers are biting into my hand and it takes all of my willpower not to drop the clothes until after 10A gets out of the elevator. As soon as I close the door behind her, I lay the clothes neatly on the floor. When I get back to the lobby, I pick up the dry cleaning before I open the door because I know there are people waiting for me. This goes on for about twenty minutes before I finally get a chance to put the clothes away. I'm hanging the clothes in the package room when the elevator rings again. I hurry back to answer the call. Mrs. 14E and her friend Mindy are waiting in the elevator. 14E is carrying her infant daughter. "Watch this," she says to Mindy. She holds her left hand in front of the baby's face. The child is mesmerized by the reflected light shining off two obscenely large diamond rings her mother is wearing. "She could stare at them all day."

"Like mother, like daughter," says Mindy. "Can you even bend your finger with those on?"

"Nope," 14E proudly replies, demonstrating her inability to move her ring finger.

Like the Indian guy with the long fingernails, this woman is determined to cripple herself with conspicuous consumption.

A few minutes later, Mr. 14E and 7A arrive home from work. Now, here is an interesting study in contrasts. On the one hand, you've got 14E, the husband of the woman with half of South Africa's Gross National Product on her left hand. He is a securities trader, a paragon of predatory, high-pressure, Darwinian capitalism. The man is buying and selling with tens of millions of other people's money at stake every day. Not surprisingly, he is a wreck. When I see him returning from work (which isn't often, since he usually doesn't get home until after I've left) he looks like a shell-shocked veteran home from the front. He stands outside the building trying to get every last bit of nicotine from his cigarette because he knows he has to get all the way through the lobby, up fourteen flights in the elevator, and down the hall to his apartment before he can get another hit of nicotine.

On the other hand, you've got 7A, an accountant for an insurance company. True to the image of his profession, he appears to be a quiet, even timid man. He is not the bundle of nerves that his fellow passenger is, but his discontent is just as obvious. It can be seen in the blankness of his expression, in the slow, mechanical, marching-to-the-grave rhythm of his gait. Despite his appearance as one of the living dead, 7A is, in fact, quite the wild man. He rides a Harley, has climbed all the major peaks in North America and Europe, and is an avid skydiver. So, which of these two men would be a better role model for me: the man with a job so stressful that he will probably be dead of a heart attack within a year or the man with a job so soul-suckingly stultifying that he is doing everything possible to get himself killed?

PART III

FRESH MEADOWS
REVISITED

BY MIKE WALLACE

In 1949 I arrived, aged seven, at the threshold of P.S. 26 in Fresh Meadows, Queens, and saw there, graven in the imposing door frame above, the words: Rufus King Public School.

Who, I wondered, was Rufus King?

It was quite likely my first historical query, though I wouldn't have been able to conceptualize what I was experiencing in that way. The question did not, however, keep me awake nights, and since (as I dimly recall) no one else knew or cared in the slightest, I let slip this first opportunity for plunging into historical research and thought no more about Rufus King, whoever he was.

Indeed, it was not until I got to graduate school that I actually got around to looking Rufus King up. His story turned out to be rather fascinating, and not because of all the official things he did: Signer of the Constitution, presidential candidate, and so forth. King arrived in New York City shortly after the Revolution, from Massachusetts (on whose behalf he had signed), wedded Mary Alsop, daughter of a rich New York City merchant, and thanks to excellent connections to Alexander

Hamilton and other Federalists, got himself appointed by the State Legislature (as was then the fashion) to the United States Senate. There was a good bit of harrumphing at this carpetbagging presumption, but King argued that "the novelty of my inhabitancy could be no objection," and in a city then rapidly filling up with immigrants from near and far, his assessment proved correct.

But King is interesting for weightier reasons. He was resistant to Irish immigration, particularly of Irish rebel republicans, who he was convinced would bloc votes on behalf of that raving republican (worse, democratic) demagogue Thomas Jefferson. And King was in a position to do something about it. He'd been plucked from the Senate by President John Adams and made minister to England in 1796, from which perch he persuaded the Adams administration to bar Thomas Addis Emmet and other Irish "Jacobins" on the grounds that "their Principles and Habits would be pernicious to the Order and Industry of our People." It was only after 1800, when, in realization of King and Hamilton's worst fears, Jefferson ascended to the Presidency, that rebels like Emmet (and worse, Tom Paine!) made their way to New York City and into local politics. This boded ill for Rufus King, who bragged of winning the "cordial and distinguished Hatred" of the burgeoning numbers of Irish, and who now, in election after election, found his efforts at winning the office stymied by, indeed, bloc voting by Irishmen enraged at the "British collaborator." Nor did King endear himself to the the overwhelmingly white electorate by his equally ardent opposition to slavery, both in New York itself, and in the country at large. He comforted himself by getting reappointed to both his former offices, in the Senate and the Court of St. James, and by retreating to the countryside—purchasing in 1805 a small farmhouse at present day Jamaica (not far from Fresh Meadows) that he proceeded to renovate into a stately country manor. There the gentleman farmer and local patrician bred prize cattle, and a family that for several succeeding generations served as the county's political leadership (his son rose to the Governorship).

Fresh Meadows, the first postwar project built in Queens, was a self-contained 170-acre development of row houses, low- and high-rise apartment buildings, spacious greens, a movie theater, schools (including Rufus King), and its very own shopping center (anchored by a Bloomingdale's branch, with novel front porches where postwar mothers could push their babyboomer-stuffed prams, one of which contained my sister, born in '49).

All this I took for granted: it was my childhood universe. What puzzled me was that just in back of our apartment, on the very eastern fringe of the great complex, separated from us by a chain link fence, sat a farm. A small farm, but a farm. I distinctly remember being nonplused, but fascinated by it, staring through the fence at the rows of verdant vegetables. The strangeness of the contrast was no doubt enhanced by the fact that although the farm sold fresh tomatoes, corn, peppers and eggplant, my thoroughly modern mother was suspicious of things unwrapped and uncanned, so we got our goods from the supermarket; and never visited the place, which made it seem as mysterious as a haunted house.

At age eight or nine, I wasn't quite up to struggling with juxtaposition of city and country, or more precisely with the fact that our model suburb-in-the-city was cheek-by-jowl with what was, and, more amazingly, is still the last working farm in Queens County. I was puzzled, but not quite capable of grasping that, once again, I was being presented with a historical problem worthy of investigation, nor did anyone at P.S. 26 try to set the community into some larger historical context.

Had either they or I done some rooting about in the past, we would soon enough have found out that our two adjacent terrains—residential development and working farm—had both once been but a small part of the marshlands and meadows stretching out east and south from Flushing Bay, a terrain which prompted the Dutch settlers to call it Vlissingen, after a town in Holland whose name means "salt meadow valley." That settlement at Flushing (as subsequent British settlers soon renamed it) expanded slowly through the eighteenth century. Farmers moved outward into an area known as Black Stump, a name seemingly derived from rows of blackened stumps used to separate large farmsteads, or perhaps from the fact that during the Revolution, occupying Brits cut down vast numbers of trees for fuel (and spite).

In colonial days, only two roads led out of these meadows: Black Stump Road, which ran northeast to Bayside, and Fresh Meadow Lane, which headed south toward Jamaica, where lay one of the new farmhouses, built between 1733 and 1755, which Rufus King would acquire in 1805. The area remained under cultivation through the nineteenth century, and the late 1800s found the eastern part of Black Stump occupied by the one-hundred-acre Voorhis Farm, at Seventy-third Avenue and 193rd Street. In the early 1900s, it was sold to Adam Klein, and it is his grandson, John Klein, who today works the little one acre farm patch that remains.

Adjacent to Adam Klein's farm sat the Black Stump School— taken over for a time by the Black Stump Hook, Ladder & Bucket Company, as a base from which to fight farm fire—which became my P.S. 26, when the Board of Education purchased a chunk of land from the Klein family to provide for the children of Fresh Meadows. Just to the west of Klein's farm, at the intersection of Fresh Meadow Lane and Nassau Boulevard, lay another Black Stump farmstead whose potential one Benjamin C. Ribman recognized in 1921. He purchased the site, and in 1923 opened the Fresh Meadows Country Club, whose golf course became the setting for the National and Professional Golf Association Opens.

In 1946, the 141-acre club was sold to the New York Life Insurance Company for one million dollars for a residential development, which opened in 1949 in time for our arrival. The development was intended to ease the postwar housing crisis by providing affordable apartments for lower middle class families, particularly veterans. Inaccessible by subway, it was perched alongside Union Turnpike, which Robert Moses-led WPA construction crews had widened in the thirties, to the dismay of the

Klein farmers, and what would become the Long Island Expressway (whose construction I witnessed with zero sense of its larger
implications: no Marshall Berman, I).

I had no clue that Fresh Meadows was in fact part of a larger
battle over the nature of appropriate housing for the postwar city,
nor that Lewis Mumford (of whom I of course knew nothing)
had hailed my home as a counterweight to what he called
Stuyvesant Town "gigantism," nor that Mumford had praised
Fresh Meadows as the closest thing yet to his ideal of a horizontal garden city, in his words "perhaps the most positive and
exhilarating example of large-scale community planning in this
country." I was growing up in Utopia!

I was in no position to grasp something that Mumford had
missed, the one way in which Fresh Meadows was deeply and
unfortunately quite like Stuyvesant Town—both were virtually
all white. In our case, not as result of the quite explicit exclu-
sionary rules that made Stuyvesant Town one of first
battlegrounds of the what was already, in my childhood, the burgeoning civil rights movement in New York City.

My sense of where Fresh Meadows fits in the larger metropolitan scheme of things did not improve later in life. Once I left
the area in 1953, heading out to Valley Stream as part of the great
postwar suburban trek, I quite lost track of what was going on
there. Indeed it was only recently that I did some quick historical rooting about on the internet and learned that the
development had been bought in 1972 by Harry Helmsley for
fifty-three million dollars, that the development had begun to
change demographically, at first slowly, then in the eighties with
dramatic speed, boosted by a successful anti-discrimination suit
brought by the NAACP Legal Defense Fund in 1983, and that
African Americans, Hispanics, and Asians now make up forty
percent of the population.

I was well aware that the third great wave of immigration
had transformed many Queens communities around Flushing
into dazzling multinational venues, but I hadn't realized that the
1990 census reported that among the languages spoken by sig-

nificant percentages of the Fresh Meadows population were—
in addition to English—Spanish, Chinese, Italian, Korean,
Greek, Indic, French, French Creole, German, Tagalog, Polish,
Russian, South Slavic, Yiddish, Portuguese, Hungarian, and
Japanese.

Mr. Helmsley, it seems, was not a popular landlord, and
when ownership passed to the John D. and Catherine T.
MacArthur Foundation, "We all cheered," recalled a Mrs. Kle-
infeld. But they in turn recently sold off the development to
two separate real estate investment operations—the Witkoff
Group of Manhattan, and Federated Realty Investment Trust,
with Lehman Brothers financing the transaction. Just last year,
I learned in my quickie historical investigation, Fresh Meadows was rife with rumors that John Klein had sold his property,
was closing the farm stand, and joining the rest of the family,
which had long since decamped to a spacious farm in River-
head. Not only would they miss his produce, but the area was
zoned R-4 and could be developed for high rise apartments. As
recently as the spring of 2000, Klein stated that the farm stand
in his front yard would reopen on July 10th, and would sell
fresh fruits and vegetables throughout the summer, with cider
and honey to follow in the fall.

There's one last piece of the puzzle that in fact I came to
know something about in a quite roundabout way, and only in
the last ten years or so. During the 1950s, not only did I not have
the faintest idea who Rufus King was, I hadn't the slightest idea
that his house still stood, quite nearby, on Jamaica Avenue and
150th Street, nor that it was in perilous condition. The house had
passed from heir to heir until 1896, and in 1898 was deeded to
the city. In 1900 it was turned over to the King Manor Association, a group of civic minded club women out to "foster
patriotism and good citizenship."

In the early twentieth century, however, Jamaica began to
change from a comfortable white community mixed with
descendants of former slaves, with an economy built around agri-

cultural wholesalers, white collar firms, town hall, and a substantial shopping strip. Rapid transit transformed the area into a
prosperous suburb, replete with department stores, movie theaters and, on the other side of the tracks, a growing black
minority.

After the Second World War, the black population accelerated rapidly. In the 1950s and 60s, whites scurried to the suburbs,
transferring their custom from old downtown stores to immense
new shopping malls. Their exodus further darkened the area's
complexion (by 1980, three-quarters of Jamaica would be African
American) and sapped its economic base. At the Manor, a dwin-
dling corps of increasingly elderly white ladies struggled to keep
the house open on a one afternoon per week basis. Frightened
by social change and a growing crime rate, they refused to unlock
the door for any but the clearly non-threatening. Would-be black
or Hispanic visitors—apart from school groups—were primary
threats.

Relations between the community and its genteel enclave
degenerated rapidly. Drug users and pushers took over its park,
the police occupied it for surveillance operations, and vandals
scarred its exterior. By the eighties, battered and decrepit, it was
all but abandoned. I became aware of this state of affairs only
when, with the building at the point of extinction, Jamaica business and civic leaders stepped in. Intent on revitalizing the
downtown area, and aware of the value of an historic anchor,
they got the borough and city to ante up several million dollars
for an extensive physical renovation and a new professional staff,
who consulted both my wife, Hope Cooke, and I on how to interpret the manor's story, and reknit the building into its current
community.

Why, you may ask, am I regaling you with trivia about farmsteads and forgotten statesmen? Partly to make clear that
whatever latent dispositions toward historical research might
have been stirred up in me, they remained thoroughly quiescent,
and indeed I quite clearly managed to survive to adulthood

knowing none of this. I didn't need to know that when I bicycled along Utopia Parkway, Fresh Meadows's far western boundary, I was traversing the only remaining sign (literally) of the defunct 1905 Utopia Land Company, which had planned to build a cooperative town there for Jews from the Lower East Side. Or that the white overpasses on the eastern frontier along Francis Lewis (another Signer) Boulevard were part of the former Vanderbilt Motor Parkway, built in 1906 as an automobile racetrack, and later a toll road, the prototype of expressways to come. Nor does anyone in Manhattan need to know that Canal Street once drained the old polluted Fresh Water Pond into the Hudson (and, indeed, that conduit is still there beneath the surface of things).

You don't need to know—you can get there from here if you know where Canal Street is—but you'll be at least slightly the poorer for being deaf to the song the streets signs are singing to you, the stories they carry of the sites, sounds, functions, realities of the ground beneath your feet. And I've found as a teacher that alerting people to the multiple temporal realities within which they move can be illuminating, exciting, adding depth and dimension to the way one experiences the city.

Historical analysis is a powerful critical tool, a way to get beneath the surface of things, to get a handle on the way things work, to inoculate oneself against glib and facile characterizations of the contemporary order. To some extent, this goes against the American grain. Americans in general, and New Yorkers in particular, have long been far less interested in the past than in the future. Already in the early ninteenth century some worried about this. "Overturn, overturn, overturn! is the maxim of New York," declared former Mayor Hone in 1845. "The very bones of our ancestors are not permitted to lie quiet a quarter of a century, and one generation of men seem studious to remove all relics of those who precede them." Putnam's 1853 series "New York Daguerreotyped" fretted that the businesses spreading "with such astounding rapidity over the whole lower part of the city" were "prostrating and utterly obliterating every thing that is old and venerable, and leaving not a single land-mark, in token of the former position of the dwelling-places of our ancestors." The result, said *Harper's Monthly* in 1856, was that "New York is notoriously the largest and least loved of any of our great cities. Why should it be loved as a city? It is never the same city for a dozen years together. A man born in New York forty years ago finds nothing, absolutely nothing, of the New York he knew."

One consequence of this has been a certain contempt for history. It seems dead and done with. History is a repository of names and dates students memorize, regurgitate, and forget. Or it's a listing of prior achievements which, like those in *The Guinness Book of Records*, are certain to be soon surpassed. What's the most cutting way to dismiss someone? We say: "He's history." We prefer the present. We want to "be here now." Or to focus on the future, and make today "the first day of the rest of our lives."

This impatience with the past has its attractive qualities. It has fostered innovation (Joseph Schumpeter hailed capitalism's capacity for "creative destruction"). It gave Americans an exhilarating feeling of freedom, a sense they were exempt from the crushing weight of history under which Europeans seemed buried. Yet ultimately this feeling was, and is, illusory. It's not, in fact, possible to step outside of time. A culture that adheres to such fantasies promotes an ahistorical temper, obscures the ways the past continues to shape the present, and leaves people marooned in the now, adrift on the temporal surface of things.

In fact, the world we've inherited has an immense momentum; actions taken in the past have bequeathed us the mix of constraints and possibilities within which we act today; the stage onto which each generation walks has already been set, key characters introduced, major plots set in motion; and while the next act has not been written, it's likely to follow on, in undetermined ways, from the previous action. This is not to say that history repeats itself. Time is not a carousel on which we might, next time round, snatch the brass ring by being better prepared. Rather the past flows powerfully through the present, and charting historical currents can enhance our ability to navigate them.

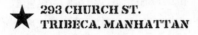

WANDALLAH

BY BETH SCHWARTZAPFEL

Mohammad B. Miah is a small man. He stands about five feet tall with his red and white and black leather high-top sneakers on. He lives in Astoria, Queens, and he wants to know whether I work for the city. He motions in the direction of City Hall.

"You have a job?" he asks.

"I'm a writer," I say waving my notebook, which is green and skinny and has spiral binding on top.

"You work for the city?" he asks.

"No, for a newspaper," I answer, waving my notebook again. His English is not great, and I think "freelance" will be too hard to explain.

Every morning, Mohammad spends two dollars to ride the subway to 293 Church Street, a garage-like space tucked between two fancy restaurants in a bustling corner of Tribeca. It's more like a not-place than a place. Mohammad calls it a *gar-iz*. It is run by a bristling man named John who has a grey mustache and a heavy Eastern European accent. For six months, Mohammed came to the *gar-iz* every morning to pick up a silver cart, which he would wheel from there to the base of the Brooklyn Bridge, and sell hotdogs. On a good day, he made about sixty dollars profit. On a slow day, forty dollars.

Mohammad has a vendor's license, which he keeps in a dirty plastic sheath in his otherwise empty brown leather wallet. The license cost him sixty dollars, plus fifty-six for a required two-day class which taught him that he must wear plastic gloves to handle food, and offered guidance as to how to dress appropriately. The rent on the cart is approximately six hundred dollars per month. It varies, though. "If I am making good business," he says, "rent go up."

A vendor's license allows you to sell food on the street, but a permit is necessary to own your own cart. One day, he showed up at the garage to find that the cart he was renting was no longer available. Permits expire every seven months, so Mohammad speculates that the cart owner's permit ran out, or that someone else laid claim to the cart. In any case, he says, pointing to a blue and yellow Sabrett umbrella on the other side of the approach to the bridge, "Maybe he have permit. I have no permit."

So now he arrives at 293 Church Street each morning with two blue coolers and an old silver hand truck. "Water! Cold things!" he says to a group of tourists walking by. "One dollar!" It comes out sounding like, "Wada! Coldings! Wandallah!"

He pays the managers of the *gar-iz* about thirty dollars to fill up the coolers with water, soda, Gatorade, and ice. Then he wheels the hand truck down Church Street, weaving in and out of parked cars and traffic. The wheels on the truck squeak as he walks. The two coolers are stacked on top of each other, and the lid on the top cooler doesn't fit quite right. Handfuls of ice cubes fall onto his feet and hit the pavement. His small frame moves quickly and, struggling to keep up, I keep an eye on his blue and gray and yellow baseball cap, which is made from parachute material and Velcros in the back. He is a compact little rectangle, with a tan fleece top and blue polyester pants.

He makes a left onto Chambers Street, passes a fruit vendor and a hotdog cart, passes Ralph's Discount City, and tells me we're going to the Blooklyn Biliz.

"The Blooklyn Biliz. You know the Blooklyn Biliz?"

I think he's saying "Brooklyn Village," so I shake my head no.

"I show you."

The sky is looking gray, and despite the temperature, which is only in the mid-fifties, the haze and the humidity make the air feel hot and sticky.

"Maybe coming rain today," he says, "people no buy cold things." Mohammad looks up at the gathering cloud cover. "It's hard making people like water."

Mohammad picks a spot at the foot of the Bridge where there is a brass symbol of a walking person inlaid into the sidewalk, with matching arrows inlaid on either side, in each direction. The on-ramp for cars hugs the left side of the walkway, and the off-ramp hugs the right. Clumps of tourists walk by, holding cameras and guidebooks. Joggers and bikers pass too, sweaty and fast. The Blooklyn Biliz looks dishwater gray on this cloudy day. Its usual majesty is dwarfed by all the taillights and the buildings, which from this angle, seem at least as tall, if not taller. Even the buildings on the Brooklyn side of the bridge seem tall enough to jostle for the skyline's attention.

"I set here," says Mohammad. "People come across. They tired. They buy water." He lays the two coolers side-by-side, takes their lids off, reaches into the ice, and pulls the bottles of Gatorade—which, at two dollars, are his most expensive item—to the top of the chilly pile.

"Wada! Coldings! Wandallah!" he calls to a passing blonde family.

"No thank you," says one woman.

"Okay," says Mohammad, "have a nice day."

His voice is slightly nasal, and he speaks quickly and confidently, as though he is not aware of the fact that he is often hard to understand. He has dark brown deep-set eyes and a square-shaped dark brown beard with a few gray hairs. Mohammad came to this country from his native Bangladesh when he was thirty-four years old. The lawlessness and random violence in his country had been wearing him down. "My country too much crazy people," he says. "People gun. You have money, they take it." He had been trying to get a visa through the lottery program since 1990. He hit the jackpot in 1998. "This country very nice. I like this country," he says. "Here, you have one thousand dollars in your pocket, nobody takes it."

After an hour here at the base of the Brooklyn Bridge, Mohammad has made four dollars.

"Gatorade, Miss?" he asks a passing woman. It sounds like "Gatorid." "Want Gatorid? That's good."

Mohammad wonders if it's too cold for people to want soda. "I looking for another job now," he says. "Outside work, vendor, too headache." Rain, cold, people's whims—his living is too uncertain. "People buy water, I have money. People don't buy water, I don't have money." When he wants to go to the bathroom, he must cart his coolers to a nearby bench and ask some people sitting there to watch them while he runs to Starbucks.

He lives in a two-bedroom basement apartment which costs eight-hundred dollars. I ask him if he lives alone.

"No, not a loan," he says. "Rent. Monthly rent."

He lives with a friend, another Bangladeshi. His wife is still in Bangladesh. He wants to bring her here, but it's too expensive. "How come you no make America for me?" he says she asks him. "I say 'No, maybe later.'" When he goes to City Hall to try to get her a visa, they always ask about money, always money. "City say 'how much you make money?' If you have money, city give you visa."

He interrupts himself. "Yes sir, wada?" He continues. "If you have no money, city says, 'how can your wife eat?'"

The Urban Justice Center recently released a report about street vendors in lower Manhattan. They interviewed one hundred vendors in five languages, and they found among them a median yearly income of $7,500. I cannot imagine Mohammad making even that much at this rate. "The typical vendor," wrote *The New York Times* in an article about the report, "is a married immigrant man who is the sole provider for his family and has no health insurance." That's Mohammad. "Only twenty percent of the vendors reported English as their first language," the *Times* went on to say. "Forty percent said they were uncomfortable speaking it."

Mohammad is Muslim. He belongs to the Alamin Mosque on Thirty-sixth Avenue in Long Island City. He prays five times a day. He might not get a chance to pray five times today, though. He looks at his watch. He sometimes goes to a mosque near here, if he can get away while he's working. "You watch?" He gestures at his coolers.

"Sure," I say. "I'll watch."

"Really? No problem?" he asks. "You watch, I go?"

I nod. "No problem."

"You watch, I go." He's happy. I watch his little blue and gray and yellow hat bob through the crowd towards the Assata Islamic Center, a mile north on Allen Street.

A sign above my head reads AREA UNDER NYPD VIDEO SURVEILLANCE. I watch the twin yellow lights flash at the off-ramp. I try to look busy by writing in my notebook. I wait. I am white, in my late twenties, dressed nicely. Some people do double-takes, looking at the coolers, then me, the coolers, then me. Apparently, I am an unexpected street vendor. I try to act casual. A red double-decker Gray Line bus drives by, people spilling off the roof with their cameras. The yellow lights flash. I look at the Bridge. More than two dozen people died during its construction, most of them immigrants from Ireland, Scotland, and Germany. One tourist in an orange Red Hot Chili Peppers T-shirt passes, doubles back, asks for a beer. When I tell him it's only water, soda, and Gatorade, he leaves. While Mohammad is gone, I sell two sodas and one water. It's been about two hours, and Mohammad's total is now seven dollars.

He returns in about twenty minutes. He smiles at me when I hand him the crumpled dollar bills. "Oh," he says. "You sell?"

Mohammad has four children. The oldest is seventeen, the youngest—he has to count forwards on his hand from 1997—is nine. They live in Queens, too, with their mother, his first wife. She's Bangladeshi but they met here. She divorced him a few years back when she fell in love with another man. After that, Mohammad went back to Bangladesh "to make another marriage." It sounds like he says *mat-iz*. He gives his first wife money for their children.

"Wada?" He pauses to ask a passerby. "Cold dlink?"

"No thank you."

"Okay, bye."

He turns to me. "You *matiz*?"

I'm wearing a wedding ring. I am, for all intents and purposes, married, although my partnership is not valid in forty-six states and until 1993, was flatly illegal in fourteen. For simplicity's sake, I shake my head. No. It's not a lie, not exactly.

"No?" he asks. "What happen?"

I shrug silently. He leaves it alone.

Mohammad says he has tried to get a job in a restaurant, but he can't because of his beard. The weather is getting cold, and he knows he won't be able to sell cold drinks for much longer. So he has decided to try to get a job with the City. His options are limited because he can't read or write much English. But he wouldn't mind working with trash. "I make cleaning job," he says, "Okay. No problem. Garbage okay. I like this." He looks appraisingly towards City Hall.

"Wada?" he asks the next person, and the next. "Wandallah."

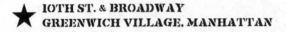
ME AND MY CANE
BY CANDY SCHULMAN

"**W**hat happened to your *knee*?"
Not since my pregnancy have so many people elevated
a distended part of my body to public discourse. My neoprene
knee-stabilizer invited countless questions and unsolicited advice
from friends and strangers in Greenwich Village, where I live, on
the 6 train, and in the physical therapist's office in Union
Square—where I shared stories about doctors and joint recovery
with patients my parents' age.

Here's the short version of my knee injury: I'd planned to
spend two weeks' vacation in a bucolic rural setting four hundred miles from the city. After an hour of tennis, my knee
mysteriously became swollen beyond recognition, and I ended
up trading my sun visor for the dark basement X-ray units from
the local hospital. Limping my way through vacation, I paused
every few hours to ice my grotesquely engorged right knee.

I suffered through everyone's knee stories, including assorted
cures: from reflexology to Reiki. We had all become our parents,
talking unabashedly about our aching joints—not over bridge
games, but while pairing blush wines with hummus and
Mediterranean olives. Of course, I also endured everyone's rota-

tor cuff, lumbar, cervical, and feet tribulations—including my husband's reiteration of his year-long struggle with plantar fasciitis. By the time we reached dessert, we were talking orthotics.

So began my search for a doctor in today's labyrinth of managed care restrictions and pre-certification numbers, slick doctor websites and blogs on knee treatment disasters. Years ago, when I ruptured a disc in a dance class, I could choose any doctor I wanted. I didn't like the arrogant young surgeon who immediately pronounced I'd need surgery. I spent thirty days in traction as a conservative approach before capitulating to the surgeon's scalpel. I was cured immediately; he had that I-told-you-so look my mother used to use; soon after, he became famous for saving a celebrity's back after a car crash. "That's my surgeon!" I'd brag, pointing to him on TV.

Just as everyone has a knee story, everyone has a much hated or greatly admired knee doctor. I made two lists, researching only the ones with "love" after their recommendations. Then, narrowing down possibilities based on medical school qualifications and residency training. I was trying to find a doctor match the way some of my friends searched for soul mates on the web. One had impressive credentials, but he was as young as my back surgeon had been—and I had grown much older. Could I entrust my knee with someone who hadn't even been born when President Kennedy was getting back injections?

My first blind doctor date was a basketball player on the West Side. There had only been a "head shot" on this former dribbler's website, but I shouldn't have been so surprised at how tall he was. College team photos hung on his office wall next to his residency in orthopedic training.

"You ever been scoped?" he asked.

"No," I said. At least I didn't think so.

In five minutes he said, "We're looking at arthroscopic surgery." And on the white paper used to cover the exam table, he created an original rendering of my alleged torn cartilage, illustrating which part he would cut away. My back surgeon had also drawn pictures of my ruptured disc. Perhaps medical school ended their art careers.

"We do it on Friday, you're back at work on Monday," said the basketball player artiste, handing me a referral for an MRI.

More research to find an open MRI on my insurance plan and a second opinion doctor. My knee injury was now my career. I spent sleepless nights poring over KneeHipPain.com.

The basketball player called me at 8 a.m. "Surgery," said he. "This is what you want to hear. I can repair it. I'll put Novocain into your knee. It's like going to the dentist."

I needed a Valium just to *schedule* a dental appointment.

"The tissue is not functioning and cannot repair itself," he insisted. "You have a big tear in the medial meniscus."

"How big?"

"Big. We do it on Friday, you're back at work on Monday."

The second opinion: a handsome child doctor told me arthritis was my real problem, and we needed to treat that. "You may not be a candidate for surgery," he said, adding with a smile, "If I operated on everyone who walked in here with a torn cartilage, I could retire in three years." He explained that my knee was swollen because it "wasn't happy," and he drained it with a needle, insisting on showing me the vials of yellow fluid. "Fifty cc's!" he said enthusiastically. "Ten times normal."

I visited six doctors, was told to put orthotics in my shoes, change my sneakers, get 'scoped, strengthen my quads, stretch my hamstrings, switch to clay tennis courts, give up tennis, swim but avoid the butterfly, get a steroid injection, take glucosomine and ibuprofen, massage my muscles with arnica, ice my knee, use heat on my knee, elevate my knee, wear a knee sleeve, not wear a knee sleeve, avoid stairs, avoid doctors. And of course, I kept bumping into other knee sufferers, like the colleague in the dressing room of Banana Republic, once crippled with knee pain, who ignored five of New York's top orthopedic surgeons, went for rigorous P.T., and was absolutely fine. "But what do you think of this dress?" she inquired, before sending it to the tailor to shorten it just above her knee.

I went home and did what any confused, aching joint patient should do: opened a bottle of wine and made sure to elevate my knee by my third glass…and contemplate acupuncture.

I was born in this city and always assumed I'd grow old here. Little did I know I'd experience a preview of what it's like to be a frail New Yorker after my arthroscopic surgery, when I had to navigate these fast-paced streets with a swollen knee, a limp, and a cane. My injury and surgery had transformed me from a speed walker racing to work into a woman patiently waiting for the bus driver to lower the entrance steps, only to feel on display to the impatient travelers behind me as I slowly ascended.

What a rush I'd always been in before! Running for traffic lights, dashing for the express train, lest I have to wait another three minutes, sprinting to the ticket holders' line so I could secure an aisle seat in the movies.

Now I hobbled. Everyone on these dense Manhattan side-walks left me behind in the dust, soot, and bus fumes. I got bumped and pushed, jostled and nearly swept off my one good leg, with mumbled "sorries" or more often no apologies at all. Despite the stereotype, New Yorkers are not rude or uncaring; they're just in such a rush, unable to slow down, and don't notice the tortoises slogging behind. I missed countless lights, and while I waited for the traffic to whiz by and the light to turn green, I wondered: What was I losing with all these missed seconds and minutes?

Actually, I began to see new things: the tops of buildings and their unique architectural details, nannies escorting well-groomed children to school, bicycle riders (with and without helmets), flowers painted on taxis, different styles of gardens in front of concrete buildings, and many older city residents with shopping carts, walkers, hunched shoulders, and canes just like mine.

In spite of my former fast-paced city gait, I (almost) always stopped and helped seniors across the street. "Are you all right now?" I'd inquire, and they'd nod yes, even though I worried that they were too frail to navigate these dangerous streets...vulnerable and alone.

Now I planned my day around my disability. Avoided rush hour subways, feared to walk through throngs of shoppers in Soho on a sunny weekend afternoon, went to restaurants at the unhip hour of 6 p.m. It was an odd dichotomy: I felt as if everyone were staring at me, and at the same time I was invisible—except to the injured and the elderly. We shared park benches and waited for lights to turn green and sometimes even struck up conversations about total joint replacements.

When I threw my cane away and even started jogging to make the light once in awhile, I reminded myself to slow down—life didn't have to be this fast. There would always be another light, another train, another lingering citizen who was my companion in waiting. I'd take a deep breath and ask if she needed assistance in crossing the street, and when a fragile hand extended my way, I took it with a keen understanding, and we both walked slowly across the street while the cars edgily waited to zoom past us.

THE ENCHANTED
JURY SUMMONS

BY LAREN STOVER

I had gotten a summons for jury duty. Or should I say, yet
another one. I was afraid of those tall, gloomy, impersonal
Wall Street area buildings full of people in somber look-alike
suits. Jury duty was some sort of gulag. Stripped of rights. Where
was the joie de vivre? What about poetic justice? Besides, I was-
n't feeling any great affection for Manhattan; it was the
late-eighties and the city was acting like a jerk, showing its true
colors. It was snobbish—too conscious of fashion, even if I did
write about it; crooked—I'd been pickpocketed on an escalator;
smoky—clubs, restaurants…even my office puffed away. And
the men were all lousy—I'd dated a morose lighting-designer
who had tombstone-shaped rocks lined up against all the walls of
his (poorly-lit) apartment and a baby he'd neglected to mention;
a Swiss textile guru with a villa in Bergamot and a live-in girlfriend he'd neglected to mention; and a single, charmingly
dirt-poor Columbia student who had anger-control problems he
neglected to mention, until he punched a hole in my door.

I worked at a start-up magazine with crazy hours and I was
trying to establish myself as journalist. I was writing for a living,

321

finally. I interviewed celebrities and wrote deconstructive (yes, fashion) essays. *Me* help out this nasty old city? *Me* help empower the people? I had my own life to sort out. Unless jury duty was going to be potential material for the next *In Cold Blood*, forget it. I attempted my third deferral. "Look weird. Wear blue lipstick," advised photographer Henny Garfunkel in her slow-motion voice. Henny always sounded like she'd taken some kind of drug that slowed you down to a luxurious, unhurried speed and never sped back up to normal. I'd met Henny through my home-town comrade, John Waters. She'd done film stills and taken a picture of him with a two-headed calf that we'd published with my article on bad taste. Henny had an eye for curious things that other people missed or shunned; her photographs cast a spell, evoking both gasps and smiles. She was original in every way. She had at least fifteen ear piercings and a nose ring before it was trendy and wore deep-red lipstick painted in a dramatic Morticia Addams arch. Her hair was buzzed close on the sides and the top stood straight up like Nefertiti's headpiece. She'd worn blue lipstick and got off jury duty.

I had normal hair and no blue lipstick. But I did have blue eye shadow, and taking my cue from the expert, I globbed it on my lips. I got in that line and when I presented my summons to the lady at the table and said I needed a postponement, she took one look at me and stamped MUST SERVE in angry red letters.

I've since served here and there, dressed up for the occasion and even tried to be chosen, though I refuse to answer invasive questions in front of strangers—e.g. What do you do? Where do you live? Do you have any family members who are convicted felons? Of course, I have a family member who is a convicted triple-felon, and his crimes aren't even sensational enough to exploit and FYI, prison hasn't helped rehabilitate him in the least—and I wish they'd reveal astrological signs. (Aries/Taurus cusp, very psycho.) I'd pondered, why the whole ordeal is so unpleasant? Why is the region tilting toward Wall Street so uptight, oppressive and depressing? Why can't they make jury duty more…charming?

Felons are exempt, but movie stars, lawyers, and doctors aren't anymore. Robert De Niro has served. So has Harvey Keitel and former mayor Rudolph Giuliani. Even weirdos have to show up now. So when I got a summons last year I deferred by phone and punched in my ideal serving time, March. My sense of patriotic duty blossomed, I openly admit, after September 11th. But I was ignored. Never heard back. Until last week. A summons arrived declaring I'd postponed twice and been absent the third time. Not so! I never got the March summons. But I would be away on the September date they had randomly chosen. Would they believe me? What paperwork did I need as proof? Our ferry ticket was in my husband's name, better get a wedding certificate. What if they made me cancel our vacation? I ran through all the worst scenarios and then determined to go in with a smile and a bounce in my step.

So yesterday, dismissing Henny's advice (I hadn't seen her in over fifteen years, where was that blithe spirit?) and wearing a neutral lipstick called "Brave" and my most beautiful earrings— large, dangling clip-ons, the ones I'd worn on my wedding day—I took a cab to Sixty Centre Street. I was sure those earrings would set off the metal detector, and they did, but the friendly, smiling sentinels waved me right in. What's going on? I wondered, when did these people become so trusting and adorable? I asked for room 139 and was told, "Walk toward the light." Gliding through the palatial atrium, I gazed upon bronze zodiac figures embedded in the floor that made me feel as though I might be in a cultured European city or Nostradamus's castle. The sun was in Virgo, sign of service, healing and anal attention to detail. Was that beautiful floor always there or was I finally noticing it? I imagined trumpets sounding the arrival of a guest or royalty, and fairly floated toward a light at the end of a hall.

I got to the room with the light. There was a sign saying "If you need to blah blah…you've come to the right place." You felt like you'd won a prize.

I told my story to a woman behind a desk. She was actually smiling. "Take a seat." I was the only "customer." I thought they might make me wait forever, but within sixty seconds my name was called. I followed the direction of the voice and sat at a desk. There were Xeroxed photos of *Naked Lunch* author William Burroughs on the side of his cubicle. More Burroughs behind the computer.

Thank heavens; I got someone with a rich, intellectual life. Thank heavens I got the Bohemian. (Never mind that this guy's hero had shot his wife.) He had a thick head of dark wavy hair, and he was easy on the eyes. I was explaining that I'd never been absent, my paperwork proof of vacation in hand, when I noticed a book on his desk, a writer's guide. "Are you a writer?" He paused, espresso-brown eyes too dark to see the revealing pupil of emotion…he seemed to be considering the question as though I'd asked him if he had a disease.

"Why, yes I am," he admitted, grimly.

"Do you ever write about this place?"

He looked around the room. "Nothing ever happens here."

"What do you write?"

The next thing you know, Prince Charming and I were exchanging contact information, talking about writers from Burroughs to Kerouac. I gushed, "I'd love to read your work!"

He was reluctant but I insisted. "Do you want a novel synopsis?" he asked.

"No," I said. "I'd rather read a short story."

Am I crazy? I began to think. He might be an Aquarius, but what if his work is terrible? He's unpublished. Everyone's writing a book. People give me amateurish, awful things to read all the time. What if I hate it and he's the punitive type? What if he sends me a summons every month?! I'd been candid with him, telling him a confidential truth about my unpredictable timetable for the next twelve months.

I was relieved to see an understated, fabulous title on his manuscript. *Black Car Service*. He seemed a man misplaced, like Melville or Kafka, with a job that in no way exploited his ambition or talent. I didn't want to leave. Over the years I had metamorphosed out of fashion and into literature. Hardly anyone I know in the fashion business talks about books unless, of course, it's *The Devil Wears Prada* or a biography of an overdosed star whose "look" is being rediscovered. I bet if I posed the question, "Do you like Anne Sexton?" most of them would ask if she designed clothing or sex toys. I stood up to leave. At the front desk in this otherwise client-free room, I saw the back of a woman with a familiar, languid voice. She turned around. The red lipstick made its siren-call clear across the room. Henny Garfunkel! It felt like a cocktail party!

I introduced Henny to the misplaced, Burroughs-obsessed writer, and they shook hands. Where was the champagne?

As we walked out into the August light, Henny, off to the Toronto Film Festival, asked me if I was serving.

"Oh that. I'm off for a year!" Yes, like a genie, the writer granted me my undeclared, secret wish.

In the cab on my way back to the office I began reading *Black Car Service*. The words sparkled on the page, a spine-chilling, supernatural tale that started like this...

"The sky had been an insane pink that only occurred with any regularity in the fall."

Bram Stoker meets William Burroughs meets Mickey Spillane. I couldn't put it down. Ignored e-mails and phone calls and finished it at my desk. At six or so, I called him and told him he was brilliant. (Like most undiscovered writers, he was at a bar.)

He was wrong about nothing happening there. I fell back in love with the city.

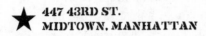

**447 43RD ST.
MIDTOWN, MANHATTAN**

DEAD RAT WALKING

BY JEAN STRONG

I electrocuted a rat early this morning. It was approximately 2:20 a.m. There were no eyewitnesses. I heard the electrical noise. It was a sustained bug-zapping sound that went on for a good thirty seconds. I knew immediately what was happening when I was startled awake. I just listened, victorious, with a great feeling that my vigilante justice had been served.

This is what happened:

My first sighting was around 1 a.m. on Labor Day, in the bathroom. I saw its pink fleshy tail flip around the corner when I turned from washing my hands. But had I really seen it? I wasn't positive when I thought of it later on in the day.

I saw it again early Tuesday morning as I turned on the light in the bedroom after hearing a clawing along the floorboards. Yep, it was a rat, Goddamn it. I was really pissed. I had gone a whole year in my new apartment without a problem.

You see, I had had an incident, a whole semi-private war really, with a rat in my old studio apartment in Brooklyn. The evildoer had morphed its body into a pancake and squeezed its way through the *front door*. I saw it with my own eyes. I threw a shoe at it. It jumped vertically, five inches in the air. It was agile, dexterous, and crafty. I fought that mammal for weeks to no avail. I used the sticky stuff, mouse traps, poison, etc. Then one day I found it decomposing on the studio floor. I think it had just starved to death. The stench of a decomposing rat is the worst smell you will ever smell. Even in death, I felt it had won.

There was no way I would lose again. I resolved to kill this new intruder as quickly and efficiently as possible.

After work, I went to the hardware store on Forty-third Street and Ninth Avenue, conveniently located next to the Cheese Market. They carry everything. The skinny, pony-tailed clerk who is always there was helpful as usual, and pointed me towards the regular pest control bullshit. I turned to him and said, in the most conspiratorial man-to-man tone I could muster (being a woman), "You know, I don't really want to deal with this small, hokey stuff. Do you have anything, you know, professional? Something…in the back?"

He got excited and quickly went and retrieved this big, rectangular, battery-operated execution device. OK, he didn't go in the back, which I think would have been much more dramatic, but he reached underneath the front counter and got it. I would have also preferred if it had been handmade, had sharp little mechanical knives, and looked like the jaws of death, but that wasn't the case, either. It was in a nice colorful box, but it was substantial.

Suddenly, other guys started collecting around the box. There was a palpable excitement in the hardware store.

"This thing will work—guaranteed," the clerk with the ponytail said confidently.

Another guy added, "Yeah, I'm a superintendent of that building over on Forty-fifth Street. You know, the real fancy one? Well, the truth is, I'm killing rats all day long there with these things. If any of the tenants complain, I just stick one of these in their apartment." I swear he had a gleam in his eye. Satisfaction.

"It takes four AA batteries, not included, and as an added bonus, I will give you surefire bait." An older, more serious looking hardware clerk behind the counter had taken over the sale.

He reached deep into the shelves behind him, found a smaller container, and brought out what looked like a sausage, but with birdseed in it. The guys around me grunted with approval. I didn't ask what it was. I don't know why I didn't, but no one offered up any information, either.

"Rats cannot say no to this stuff. Period."

He cut off a chunk of the sausage-like stuff, put it in a baggie, and handed it to me.

I paid sixty-five dollars and change for this contraption and the batteries. With the guys giving me words of enthusiastic support and cheers, I left the store. "Go get 'em."

Back out in the perfect August day, I thought, "This better fucking work."

I am a killer. An executioner. I am the Rambo of rats. It's hard to sustain this sort of homicidal resolve walking by the well-intentioned theater advertising *The Vagina Monologues*. When will that show ever close? But I retained my deadly resolve. I would win.

I hurried back to my fourth floor walk-up and immediately opened up my purchase.

Most of the housing was bright blue industrial-strength plastic, but its back room was all shiny steel. You could see the square plate where the rat would stand to trip the switch. I thought of Errol Morris's documentary *Dr. Death*. I thought of that electric chair.

I installed the batteries.

There were huge yellow warning stickers on the sides of the housing, which said, pretty much, "Don't stick your dumbass hand into the device, especially when it's on."

I didn't put it anywhere in the kitchen. Too obvious. I decided to put it in the bedroom closet. That's where the chase had ended the previous night. I left the door cracked open a couple inches.

Again, I believed subtlety was needed. I have no idea why. I was literally going by my killer instincts. I was not playing around.

Then I waited. But see, it didn't happen until all the lights were off, in the dead of night, when executions always happen, during the rat's regular hours. I couldn't believe the rat had fallen for it.

I didn't immediately go look at the corpse. I didn't want to catch a death rattle or let him get one last surprise swipe at me like in a horror movie.

Instead, I went back to sleep. In the morning, I took a peek, first thing. It was dead, all right. Dead and about three inches long with a three-inch tail. The light on the top of the blue plastic rectangle was flashing red. Alert! Alert! I turned it off, picked it up, and dumped the contents in the trash. It was actually anticlimactic. The rat looked small and harmless lying dead on top of last night's spaghetti.

One of the guys at the hardware store had told me that once I electrocuted "one of them" with the box, all the other rats would find out about it and steer clear of my apartment. So I suppose I'm known in these parts now. If you're a rat and you live in Hell's Kitchen, you know I'm a rat killin' motherfucker and you better steer clear of me.

GANGLAND IN GREENPOINT

BY COLIN P. DELANEY

K*rea-Krac!*
Thick, guttural laugher floats up from the street into our bedroom.

Krea-Krac! Krea-Krac!

I grope the nightstand for my glasses. The bedside clock tells me it's just past midnight.

Krea-Krac! Krea-Krac! Krea-Krac!

When I was a boy and it was time for bed, my father had a favorite ritual. He would stand up, a lumbering giant swaying over my brother and me, and slowly unbuckle his belt. With mock ferocity and deep-throated growling, he would fold the strap in half and crack the leather.

Krea-Krac!

My brother and I would scream with laughter and sprint upstairs, the snapping of the belt chasing us into bed and under the covers.

Krea-Krac! Krea-Krac!

Dream-drunk as I am, I can't help but wonder if my father is standing outside my window, snapping his belt as if I'm a seven-year-old again.

"What is that?" Anne says, rolling over and pushing herself over on my shoulder.

"I think it's my dad."

"What?" Her voice is full of sleep and mounting irritation.

"It's nothing. Go to sleep."

Krea-Krac! Krea-Krac! Krea-Krac!

"That's nothing?" she says, mounting over me. She pads over to the window.

"It's nothing," I repeat, curling up in her body-warmed section of the bed. "It's nothing."

The snapping repeats three more times. More laughter, this time punctured by a man's sharp retort in that most melodious of all languages, Polish. Not knowing any, however—even after five years of living in Greenpoint—isn't an impediment to understanding what was just said (drunken slurs are universal). It must be a fight, I think, a spill-over from the bar on the corner. Every month or so, there's always some sound and fury on the street, a preamble that either dissolves into a free round for the injured parties or (more likely) a black-and-white shows up.

"Colin."

Anne's voice is urgent and stripped of sleep.

"Colin, they're belt-whipping him."

I throw off the covers and cross the room to where Anne is standing, her usage of the collective pronoun making me slightly queasy. Greenpoint is hardly a hot-zone of violence, better known for three things: pierogis, fifty-dollar Social Security cards, and pierogis.

"Look," she says, pointing. "Look."

Across the street is a man—a man? A boy. Probably around fourteen, wearing a red and white jersey and splayed up against the back of a parked car, like a suspect on a late-night airing of *Cops*. He's surrounded by a group of other boys, a little under a dozen, all equally young and, from the looks of their staggering and swaying, all equally drunk, stoned, hopped-up, etc.

The kid up against the car is getting cracked on the ass with a belt by one of the other boys. There's cheering and hooting and chanting of what are probably numbers in Polish.

"What the fuck?" says Anne.

"I don't know. Maybe it's a, uh, I dunno…maybe…I dunno."

The belt is getting passed around now, like a brown-bagged Smirnoff, until everyone gets a shot. In between cracks of the belt, the boy grabs his ass and hops around, trying his best not to whimper or cry. One of the bigger kids shoves him roughly up against the car where he takes up his former position as another member of the group eagerly winds up for his turn.

"Is it—" Anne starts.

"I don't know. A gang initiation?"

"A gang initiation?" Incredulous.

"Sure. Think Herbert Asbury, but PG-rated. *The Gangs of Greenpoint.*"

"And that's how they bring in new members? By spanking them? That's pretty lame."

"Sure," I say.

"I mean—that's really lame."

I really hate to call it a gang. Even three stories up and across the street, I can tell that more than half of them still have baby fat. Let's call it a gaggle. The gaggle seems to be wrapping up the initiation with a rousing chorus (in English, oddly enough) of "You're a man, now," from each of the boys. The newly-made "man," one hand clenched tight to his rear, is making the rounds, hugging each new "brother," looking elated that he's passed the test.

There's more hooting, more cheering, more embracing, and the boys start peeling off, exchanging convoluted handshakes and high-fives with the new member, who is leaning heavily on the largest of the boys, still clutching at his soon-to-be-swollen ass, or as the Poles say, his *dupa*.

THE POLE GREASERS
BY VESTAL McINTYRE

I stepped into the crowded subway car and a little girl sitting next to the door yelled something at me.

"Hey Mister!"

I shot her a look that said: "I don't know if I'm going to pay attention to you, but at least let me claim my standing spot and my pole before I decide." But then my hand met the pole at the same instant I heard her words: "...there's Vaseline on the poles."

The palm of my hand was covered with the slick, greasy stuff, and I had to steady myself with nothing to hold onto as the train lurched into motion. The little girl laughed, and I blushed but didn't resent her for her laugh. She had earned it, I supposed, unlike all those others who were smiling into their newspapers. I tried to laugh, too, as I rummaged through my backpack.

The girl's parents, sitting beside her, were oblivious, conversing animatedly in another language—Hindi, Bangla, or something.

There were no tissues in my backpack, so I had to tear a college-ruled page out of my notebook and use it to hold the pole. I looked around and saw that all the poles and hanging straps were greased, and the riders had come up with their own methods of dealing with it: some had cleaned off a little area to hold onto; others, like me, were using tissues or handkerchiefs as shields; still others clung to the tops of seats or braced themselves against doors to avoid the tainted surfaces altogether.

I had gotten on at Delancey and would change at West Fourth—three stops. I decided it would be much more interesting to watch what happened than to take out the book I was reading.

Second Avenue is never a busy stop; only two people got on. A businessman entered the same door I had and was successfully warned by the little girl. He gripped the top of a seat and thanked her. She beamed. This must be the best subway ride of her life, I thought. No squirming in her seat as her parents talked on and on about grown-up stuff—now she had her little job. I imagined her to be independent in that only child way, a girl you can imagine leaving home at eight rather than eighteen and doing just fine.

The other new passenger, an old man in a fedora, was less lucky than the businessman. He entered farther down in the car, and the murmured warnings offered him were too little, too late. He took out a handkerchief, cleaned his hand, then carefully started cleaning the entire pole.

Among the seated people, the warning-murmurers watched in guilty amusement, while the majority—the hard-faced advertisement-gazers and book-readers—tried to pretend nothing was happening. The only ones who laughed aloud were the little girl near me and three Asian high school girls who sat together at the end of the car. These three were observing as intently as I was, speaking in low tones, erupting occasionally into loud laughter. I wondered if they were the pole-greasers. I began to write a story about them in my mind. They were a three-member club, who had been pulling pranks since middle school. It had started with the obvious: short-sheeting and greasing toilet seats at Korean Baptist summer camp. Then, gradually, their pranks became more sophisticated—greasing bus stop benches or elevator buttons and hiding to watch the results. They were becoming artists of social disturbance and observation, and Vaseline was their medium of choice—completely harmless, yet spectacularly annoying.

As we pulled into Broadway-Lafayette I quickly planned my own approach. I didn't trust my voice like the little girl trusted hers; I could not call out. Instead, I staked out a little area of which I was steward and prepared to give gentle warnings.

Several people got off, then only one person came into my area—a stylish young black woman in expensive jeans who didn't notice the little girl yelling, "Hey! Hey, Lady!"

Keeping hold of my pole, I leaned her way and quickly said, "Be careful." She shot me a hostile look, preparing to be preached to or hit on. "There's Vaseline on all the poles." She didn't thank me, but returned to lean against the door, which had just closed.

Success.

In the time it took to warn her, though, a man about my own age had grabbed my pole. Now he was squatting down, searching his backpack, just as I had. Another man seated nearby, who clearly had not warned him, offered him a tissue.

The businessman who had been warned by the little girl at Second Avenue had become a warning-murmurer. The old man, on the other hand, had fully cleaned his pole, and other passengers were now hanging off it, trying to figure out what all the fuss was about. Further down the car, a white woman in her mid-twenties was in a real mess. She had not grabbed the pole at a distance but put her arm around it and leaned her body against it in order to better hold her magazine. Now she was looking down in dismay at her vintage-shop, fall-color argyle sweater. "Dry clean only," I silently commiserated.

Another woman near her—short, Puerto Rican, perhaps— was huffing angrily and muttering to herself as she cleaned her hand. She was of the age, late-fifties, that I expect Latina women to have accents, but I was proved wrong at the next stop—my stop, West Fourth—when the doors opened. "People entering the train," she said loudly and clearly. "Do not grab the poles! They are all greased up and messy!"

LOST AND FOUND

"School teacher," I thought appreciatively as I exited the train, squeezing past those first people who might hear her warning, then the people behind who would not. I looked into the face of one commuter after another. They were exhausted and impatient, and expected nothing different from their last thousand subway rides.

THE GOOD, THE BAD, THE UGLY

BY JOSH LEFKOWITZ

At the risk of sounding terribly cliché, I was mugged in New York. It was July 2005. I was a block away from home when two gentlemen—black, wearing backward hats—pushed me up against the wall, took the phone out of my hand and asked if they could make a phone call. I said I was on the phone with my girl-friend, but maybe when I was done they could use it, so long as it was to someone within the United States or Canada, because my phone plan didn't extend to international calls. Then one of them asked if he could borrow two dollars. Two dollars didn't seem like that big of a deal, so I said okay, and took my wallet out of my pocket.

I was removing two singles from the money clip when the first gentleman changed his mind and said instead of two he wanted twenty, no wait, all of it. He grabbed at my wallet and I hung on for a moment, my instincts in high gear, and struggled in vain to remember what to do in emergency situations:

Stop, Drop, and Roll. Not applicable.

Hide under the desks and wait for the all-clear signal. Also not applicable.

Find the nearest adult. None in sight.

They didn't have a blade or a gun, or at least none that I saw, and I didn't trust my self-defense training. The last karate class I took was in fourth grade. I was actually asked not to return after I begged the instructors to teach us how to "wax on" and "wax off." Having only made it to orange belt, thirteen years ago, I decided this was not a fight I could win. So I let go of my wallet and the mugger took the money out and gave me back the rest, cards, license, and all. I thought this to be a most gentlemanly exchange until they began walking off with my phone.

"Wait," I said, "Can I please have my phone?"

"You ain't calling the cops, buddy," the second man said, and they continued walking off with it.

"Please!" I shouted, warm streams beginning to pour down my cheeks as the shock of what just happened began to take hold. "I really need that phone! I have to call Condé Nast tomorrow! I'm going to try and get an internship at *The New Yorker*, and I can't do that without my phone!" And then, long after they were out of earshot, I added, "If my parents call, please tell them that I was mugged but that I'm all right." More tears.

I arrive home, and my roommates are in a stoned daze. Pot smoke hangs in the room like many jackets on a single coat rack.

"You guys, I was totally just mugged," I say.

"Whoa, man," my male roommate says, "Whoa."

"Are you alright?" my female roommate asks.

"Yeah," I say, "but I'm pretty pissed and also scared."

"Whoa," my male roommate adds.

I call 911. Now the anger inside is rising to a tumultuous pitch. I haven't been this mad since they took *The Cosby Show* off the air.

"Nine-one-one, what's the emergency?"

"The emergency," I yell, "is that I was just fucking mugged!"

"Well whatchoo shouting at me for? I didn't do it!" the operator replies.

"I know," I say, "I'm just a little upset right now…"

"Well calm down!"

"Okay," I say, then add, "Sorry for yelling."

Four cops arrive. They are, all of them, the living embodiment of an NYPD stereotype. These broad characters enter the scene and if I wasn't so mad and freaked out I would have giggled with glee.

"So you say you were jumped?"

"Yes sir."

"Where?"

"Sixth between B and C."

"Did they hurt you?"

"No."

"So you weren't really jumped, you were mugged, then."

"Um, okay, I guess I was mugged then. Fine."

"Uh-huh. So how come it smells like a party in here?"

"My roommates were getting high."

"Uh-huh. And these muggers, did they take your weed?"

"I didn't have any. I don't smoke anymore cause it makes me paranoid."

"Sure you don't," lead cop says snidely.

"Sam," the second cop says to the leader, "this pot smoke is giving me the munchies."

"So where you from," the third cop asks, "Idaho?"

"Michigan."

"Same difference. So what brought you here?"

I'm so tired of having to answer that question, of verbally stumbling as I try to define what I'm trying to do, sort-of-an-actor that-doesn't-act-because-now-he-writes-these-kind-of-story-things, that I simply reply, "I guess I just wanted to get mugged."

"Well," the third cop says, "Mission accomplished."

The female cop, Irish Catholic all the way, pipes up: "This is a nice place you got. How much is your rent?"

"Twenty-seven hundred for the three of us."

"Twenty-seven hundred! Get outta town! That's so much money! I pay nine-fifty and I got my own place and it's bigger than this."

"Where is it?" I ask.

"Brooklyn," she says, "And I ain't never been mugged, neither."

Don't they teach these cops sensitivity training, I wonder?

With nowhere else to turn, my male roommate and I go for drinks at a dive bar. A natural storyteller, I'm telling everyone about my nighttime encounter.

"That sucks," the bartender says.

"Would you like a shot?" a customer asks me.

"Pardon me," a gentlemen with an orange shotgun in his hand says, "I couldn't help overhearing your tale of woe. I'm playing this video game right here where you pump this shotgun and shoot deer. I just wanted to offer my next turn, because I thought it might help you feel better if you shoot some deer."

"Thank you, sir," I reply. "That's very kind of you. And I will take you up on your offer. I would like to shoot some deer. I would like that very much indeed."

Walking home. We pass two black gentlemen. My body clenches. Am I going to turn into a full-blown racist because of this?

Maybe I should just go back home. Back home to the plains, to the suburbs, where everyone looks like me and nothing ever happens. Who's going to mug you in Michigan? The cows? No, not the cows. They haven't learned the value of money yet, foolish cows, standing in the grass, chewing their cud, the cows, without a cow-care in the world. Maybe I should be a cow.

I lie in bed and make up a story. That the muggers see me pass by and the first one says to the other, "Isn't that autobiographical writer Josh Lefkowitz?!"

"He writes about what happens to him," the second one reports.

"Let's mug him," the first one says. "That way, he'll have something about which to write."

The Good: I am alive, unhurt.

The Bad: I'm out $150 of hard-earned, wine-pouring money.

The Ugly: I can actually feel my plush Midwestern heart hardening into a cold, dense stone.

GOOD VIBRATIONS
BY STACY PERSHALL

I do okay for a while. I'm good, I go to therapy, I make the bi-monthly trek to my psychiatrist for drugs. I ride the Q train from Brooklyn to Central Park West, a trip that takes over an hour, and Dr. Howard meets me at the door. He has unnaturally dark hair that smacks of the Hair Club for Men, Canadian diplomas hang all over his walls, and that preternaturally calm voice that must come from some kind of requisite speech class for shrinks. I like him just fine, but I also like to sleep, and therein lies the problem. He always wants me there by 10 a.m, which is like 5 a.m. for people like me. My therapist, Lynn, whose office is a five-minute walk from my apartment, lectures me weekly about the importance of keeping appointments and reminds me that Dr. Howard is under no obligation to keep seeing my oft-suicidal ass. She makes it sound as if he's doing me a favor, doling out scripts for the drugs that make me fat and sleepy, but do tend to keep me out of the hospital. Yeah, yeah, I say, preventive care. Sleep, eat, exercise, Depakote, lather, rinse, repeat. If only it were that simple.

Take today, for instance. I haven't left the apartment in a good seventy-two hours, which means I also missed an appointment with Dr. Howard and am out of drugs. I decide to test my ability to go out by making a trip to the deli for toilet paper and cat food. If I can do this, I tell myself, if I can just go to the corner and buy these, maybe I can manage the longer trip to the pharmacy, where they can call Dr. Howard to authorize refills. I summon all my courage, race to the corner in my platform flip-flops, and manage to fall into a pregnant woman on a cell phone who stops suddenly in the doorway. I twist my ankle and stumble, managing to knock down the three-year-old who stands lolling beside her.

She yells, but not directly at me: rather, she gives a blow-by-blow of my actions to the person on the other end of the line. "GodDAMN," she hollers. "Fucking bitch just tripped me. Fucking cunt wasn't looking where she was motherfucking going."

"I'm sorry," I say, "I didn't mean to." A crowd of snickering teenage boys turn away from the counter to stare at me huddled on the floor.

"And she knocked down a goddamn baby, too," shouts the woman.

"I'm sorry," I say, "I'm honestly trying to apologize to you." I manage to at least stand up, to attempt to salvage something of my dignity, to brush off my ass, but the day is ruined—nay, the week. Because when I'm off my meds, I believe that I am subhuman and hated by God and everybody, and am sure that I have been punished for leaving the house, and everybody around me can see that I'm just a dog, and I don't deserve to purchase things in stores like actual people.

In case anyone was wondering, this would be a fine example of the bipolar brain off drugs. I would like to pause for a moment to ask that if you are sitting in the room with a bipolar person at this moment, you pause to peg them in the head with their lithium and tell them you did it out of love, as a gentle reminder.

So I go to see Lynn, the setting Brooklyn sun harsh and blinding and punishing, and I think how much I hate the fucking sun. Lynn's office is connected to her apartment, and I am met by her two yapping, flatulent schnauzers who always sit in on our sessions, whether I want them to or not. Today they annoy me more than usual. I try to ignore them as they jump onto the couch, gnawing on mangled rawhide chews, and I tell Lynn I've run out of drugs and that I'm too scared to call Dr. Howard because I missed my last appointment. She is, to say the least, not amused.

"Look, Stacy," she says, "at some point you have to take responsibility for getting your medication when you need it."

"I know," I whimper. "I know, but I'm afraid he's mad at me and I can't deal with going all the way to the Upper West Side to be lectured about keeping my appointments. I just can't. It's not worth it."

"Worth it? What did you think was going to happen if you quit taking your drugs?" she asks. "You're a smart woman. You've been on and off medication for almost ten years now. You know what happens when you stop."

There is, of course, no arguing with that. I huddle between her farting dogs, hugging my knees to my chest, trying to fathom actually getting on the subway and riding into Manhattan and switching trains and bumping into people and such. There is no way I can accomplish that. Three days ago, maybe. A week ago, sure. But not today. Today I am too far gone, in heavy withdrawal from the SSRIs. The woozy Celexa-head has taken over, and I am a helpless infant, dizzy and nauseous and weak.

Lynn sighs. "Okay, look. You can go to the emergency room at Kings County Hospital and get your prescriptions written there. It's not the most pleasant place. You'll see a lot of indigent people, especially at night. You'll wait a long time. But it's a ten-minute taxi ride, and you can go there right now and get your meds."

I nod. I'll do anything at this point, even though taking any action, no matter how small, seems overwhelming. Lynn gives me directions and tells me to hail a cab immediately and go straight there; on second thought, she's going to walk me down the stairs and hail one for me. When we get to the bottom, she touches my arm.

"You know that as soon as you take your drugs it's going to be better," she says. "Just go get them and call me tomorrow to let me know how you're doing."

I nod. My head buzzes.

I ride to the hospital in the taxi with one hand over my ear to steady my head, to stop the pinballs banging around in my skull. When we arrive at Kings County Hospital, I see that it is a drab, functional, sixties-style building—gray, like they all are. There's a broken chain-link fence around the parking lot with razor wire dangling off of it. I trudge inside, trying to stoke the urban guerilla inside me. Yay, I tell myself, I'm using public health care. There is actually a sign on the side of the building for the psychiatric emergency room. Beyond that are three sets of doors and a metal detector. I take a deep breath and go in.

The bored-looking guard asks for my purse, and I give him my overloaded messenger bag. He takes out everything; all the crumpled ATM receipts and candy wrappers and the three heavy books, which he flips through before setting them aside. Then he finds my nail clippers.

"Can't have these," he says. Not "let me hold these for you until you come out," or "safety regulations require me to hang onto your nail clippers while you're in the hospital." Just "can't have these."

I am so close to losing it that I want to lunge at him and strangle him for being a rude, callous bastard, but I remind myself that that might not be in my best interest. Still, in my unmedicated state, those three words are all it takes to rocket me from depression to Incredible Hulk-level anger. Here is a man who sees people in pain every day, people whose brains are exploding, and he doesn't give a fuck about extending anything like basic human courtesy. Just shuffle the crazies on through and take away their possessions while you're at it. Smug fucking bastard.

"Fine," I say, imagining my T-shirt bursting open so I can smack the shit out of him with my daunting green pecs.

He waves me through the metal detector. I do not beep. He never looks up at me. Even later, when I am hungry and ask to walk back through the metal detector to the vending machine ten feet away, he gives me only a cursory glance as he tells me nope, can't.

The waiting room is surprisingly empty. The only other people there are a young African American couple, probably still teenagers. The boy sits with his legs wide apart, elbows on his knees, hands clasped together, staring at the floor. Beside him, wrapped in a baby's blanket, the girl eats twenty-five-cent nacho cheese tortilla chips. She wears house slippers. Her eyes are almost closed.

I watch them, pretending to read the first book I pull out of my bag, which happens to be *The Good Vibrations Guide to the G-Spot*. There is something wrong with this girl's eyes. Her long eyelashes curl tight against her lids, and she peers out from beneath them with her chin slightly lifted. I realize that she has to have her head at this angle to see. She cannot open her eyes all the way.

We pass the hours together without speaking. Every now and then the boy reaches over and strokes the girl's shoulder beneath the blanket. He cuddles her like a treasured puppy, whispering to her and occasionally making her smile. She finishes her chips and he wipes the thin layer of orange dust from her mouth. The fluorescent lights flicker.

When the doctor comes out to get them, as expected, he doesn't see how beautiful they are. I stare at the dirty tile floor while he stares at the girl. He grabs her chin, lifts her face, and demands of her boyfriend, "What's wrong with her eyes?"

I want to kill him. I want to scream and cry and stomp my feet and shout, "WHY AREN'T YOU TALKING TO HER? Just because she can't see doesn't mean she can't hear and talk and think and feel. It doesn't give you the right to put your hands on her face without asking!" But I remain as mute as she and scuff my shoe hard, leaving black marks on the floor.

"They're always like that," says her boyfriend. "It's a birth defect."

"Ptosis," says the doctor gruffly. The boy does not respond.

"So she's having hallucinations?"

"Yes sir," says the boy calmly, just as he might if asked if she had a cold. I imagine that he is used to his angel's visions, that she hovers over their bed and sings to him at night, seeing things through her hazy fringe of lashes. She tells him stories of what floats by. He learns from her of mermaids in the trees.

"Is she taking her meds?"

"Yes sir," says the boy, producing a bottle of pills from his pocket. "But I don't think she's taking enough anymore."

The doctor nods.

And they sweep her away, her blanket wings flowing, and she leaves an orange pixie dust trail behind her.

I do not see her again but I know that she leaves with prescriptions, as do I, three hours later. I walk out exhausted and starving but thankful, cramming a Snickers in my mouth as I rub my recovered nail clippers like prayer beads.

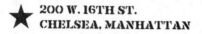

**200 W. 16TH ST.
CHELSEA, MANHATTAN**

THE MAYOR

BY ANNA McDONALD

A guy on my street, let's call him Eddie, is probably thirty-eight, only two or three inches shorter than Wilt Chamberlain, with a pirate's crook nose and a Russian infantry-man's sinewy muscles. He doesn't seem to mind the smell of trash. I know this because he's my trash man. He used to live somewhere far beneath my building (in the alley, I believe) and now he lives in it, on the first floor, where a whole community of sketchy people come and go, and where, if you stop too long to check your mail, you might eavesdrop on a "fuck you" or two between the clanking of saucepans.

Eddie also sweeps the stoop, greets the visitors, buzzes-in delivery guys, and holds the door for women. He is the mayor of our block. I mean this in a libertarian sense. If every tenant in the West 200s on Fifteenth Street had to identify the one person they made eye contact with most in any given month, it would be Eddie. When I go to work in the morning, he's there; when the unemployed insurance salesman across the street steps out to check his P.O. box or pick up wired cash from his mother in Lansing, he's there; when the smoking hyena ad-sales girls who live below me go out for the evening, he's there. I officially inaugurated Eddie myself in 2002, a few weeks after I moved in, when I noticed that I didn't have to separate cardboard from plastic in the recycling bag—Eddie would do it for me, with the sort of alacrity that only inspires those who truly enjoy their occupations. It is a specific "I enjoy service" face. He is not thinking, "You are a shithead" under his breath.

Over the years, Eddie has teamed up with various lieutenant mayors, but none of them have lasted even a half-term. Some of them were too cracked out; others too lazy. The only first lady was a midday snoozer with a penchant for Swiss Cake Rolls and caterwauling at rival congressmen around the block. Her committees convened during trash pick-up hours, which left her other half constantly in the lurch.

Recently, he acquired a really lusterless but functional lacquer folding chair from the mid-century. He wears a bomber in the winter lined with fuzzy shearling, with a pair of gamekeeper tweeds. He wears a pair of original Nike Air Dunk hi-tops, and his shorts in the summer are mesh—short mesh, like the Lakers in 1969.

Trash days are Mondays and Thursdays, and on the off days, he sells books and socks around the corner on Eighth Avenue. The likelihood of him reading this essay is nil, but he has been known to pawn off back issues of *Artforum* to unwitting midwestern Chelsea boys on their way to or from the Eighth Avenue New York Sports Club. When my girlfriends nominate their ugly crushes—Jeff Goldblum, Bill Murray, Peter Gallagher, it comes my turn and I don't have one. And then I realize when Eddie walks out of the alley in the middle of the day in a kind of disoriented pleasure-wooze with a big sucker kiss—a hickey the size of the dial on an industrial washing machine, but a little less circular—that I am jealous. Eddie is my ugly crush. And not only that—to me, he is not ugly.

My boyfriend, only a Jerry West to Eddie's Wilt Chamberlain, said he once saw Eddie hand off a dime bag to a murky street skulker in the middle of the night, just outside my apartment. Then he deduced that the clanking pots and pans might be a kitchen for cooking methamphetamine, about which all I know is this: because of it, there is a growing demand for dentists in Kansas.

I'm moving out next month, and I've thought about calling the cops, or the management company, or the super about the drug stuff. But there are bigger problems (like the woman who feeds the birds and rats with Grape Nuts), and anyway, I know he's in cahoots with the super—he has tammanyed almost anyone who might get in the way of his platform.

Truth is though—he's too damn cute.

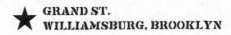

GEORGE ISN'T HOMELESS

BY MELISSA DUNN

"Hi George," I said with a wave as I rushed toward the subway. George, who was sitting in his low-to-the-ground folding chair at his usual post in front of the liquor store, sat up with a jolt, as if I had touched him, giving him a shock of static electricity, and said with some outrage, "How do you know my name?" Despite his fierceness, he seemed truly frightened. I tried to be reassuring. "George, you told me your name, don't you remember?"

"I did?" he said, giving me the squint eye.

"Yes, George, you did," I assured him again. He calmed down, settled back into his chair. But he gave me a look that let me know he would be keeping his eye on me. Maybe he had forgotten to take his meds—if he even took meds. I was sad to see George was having a bad day, and that my attempt at a friendly greeting had fueled some paranoid torment.

I have known George since I moved to the neighborhood—Williamsburg—in 1998. He is out on the street most days, sitting in his folding chair—sometimes in front of the liquor store on Lorimer Street and sometimes in front of the Optimo convenience store just over on Grand. When I first moved to the neighborhood, it was an outpost just off the second L stop. Grand Street, where I still live, was and to some extent still is a sort of a line in the sand between the Italian neighborhood—replete with Madonna statues, aging wise guys and aluminum siding—and the Puerto Rican neighborhood south of Grand—where the building facades are brick and people sit out on the sidewalk playing cards or listening to music on hot days. Though the neighborhood has become more fluid, and the demographics have been gentrified by a rash of new condos, ten years ago this line was very strictly observed—the Italians stayed on their side and the Puerto Ricans on theirs, with the exception of occasional skirmishes. George was a border-dweller, occupying a post on the margins of two worlds. But he didn't belong to either, being neither Italian nor Puerto Rican, but African-American and somewhat out of place here. I had no idea why George chose to bivouac on this particular corner. It wasn't clear what connected him to this neighborhood, other than occupation of a patch of sidewalk, or how historical or deep that connection might be.

I assumed George was homeless; I never saw him on the street at night, but I had no idea where he slept. He wore casual clothes—jeans, T-shirts or flannel shirts, but was mostly put together and never looked dirty. Occasionally, some small detail would be off, like he wouldn't be wearing socks. He projected a persona that was alternately large and formidable or small and vulnerable, and his scale seemed largely a function of his mental state on any given day. He was a tall man, over six-foot, and appeared bear-like when he wore a puffy winter jacket, which he sometimes did regardless of the weather. Other days, wearing a thin T-shirt and jeans that were too big for him, he looked frail and old. I had no idea how old he was, but I suspected older than he looked, maybe in his sixties—and I worried about him when it was cold or snowing. But he would disappear when the weather was bad, so I assumed he went to a shelter somewhere.

I have passed George on the street several times a day, most days, for the last decade. Wearing his signature knit cap or bandana, he sits in his chair, watches, listens to the radio, sips from a tiny bottle of vodka, and occasionally chats up or calls out to passersby. I am always happy to see him. Often he's laughing out loud at something or looking as if he's about to laugh, but not in a crazy way; he just seems to see the humor in things, especially the constant tide of Brooklynites that flows across his corner en route to and from the subway. Sometimes he will hold out his hand expectantly, rub his fingers together, and say in a languorous drawl that is more south than north: "Gotta little something for me today, baby?" His tone, which often makes his pitches irresistible, is never desperate or pleading, but more cajoling and teasing, and somehow promising that giving him money will likely be the most fun I have all day. Sometimes I hand over some change or a dollar bill, and sometimes I say, "Sorry George, not today"—to which he replies casually, disinterestedly, and with no hard feelings, "Okay baby, maybe next time." Mostly, he doesn't ask for money. Sometimes he will just greet me, "How you doin', Baby?" Or to my boyfriend, a tall man, whom George always seems especially excited to see, he might call out, "Hey there, Big Guy!" or "Chief!"—followed by a series of cackles that indicate he gets a lot of pleasure out of using these made-up names. And sometimes he just stares off into space in a sort of catatonic stupor, seemingly unaware of anything around him, but intently focused on something troubling in the distance.

Once I saw George chase a teenage boy down Lorimer Street with a two-by-four. I admired something in this action, but I am not sure what exactly. Maybe it was his exhilaration, his absolute domination of his corner, his unwillingness to yield any ground to business owners, cops, hipsters, or smart aleck kids. I had never seen George move so fast—or move at all. It inspired a sense of awe. I wasn't afraid for the boy; I knew George wouldn't hurt him (or I was pretty sure). But it did give George a dimension of menace or at least unpredictability. He was a warm, gentle man, but not always himself. I tell all this to my boyfriend, who says that it was he who saw George give chase with a two-by-four. I am startled by the profoundly mysterious mechanisms through which I made the story my own and the way it had so thoroughly, so insidiously, invaded my own memory of George.

In some way, the borrowed story speaks of the way I distance myself from George. As much affection as I have for him, as much as seeing him makes me happy and reassures me that he is okay, and his absences make me anxious, I have some apprehension that conversations with him might be destabilizing for me and I keep some distance. George conjures people for me. My mother was an alcoholic and had spent some time living on the street; being a small child living with my grandparents, I never saw her during this period. I also connect George to mentally unstable people I have known, especially a close college friend who had suffered a schizophrenic break. He once made me a sandwich from dandelions he picked in vacant lots, that I ate with some trepidation. He would confide in me about the voices he heard and his secret fears, because, he said, I was like him— we were both underdogs. I liked talking to Rick—he was smart and funny, and his insights often struck me as piercingly true— but afterwards I often experienced a sort off-kilter feeling that would stay with me for hours in which all the angles of reality didn't quite seem to line up. It was scary because I felt how remarkably permeable that boundary is between sanity and insanity.

I have had very few conversations with George over the last ten years, maybe a half dozen, but all memorable. I learned he had once been a security guard, and I tried to imagine him putting on a uniform every day and going to work. I pictured him chasing people around with two-by-fours. I wondered later if maybe he had worked in the neighborhood, if that was his connection; but I never asked him. In what was probably the longest conversation I ever had with him, just before the election in 2004, I was leaving Optimo with the Sunday paper under my arm. I think George responded to an image or a headline on the front page and we started talking. He expressed great enthusiasm for his candidate, George Bush. We talked about Iraq and George's belief that Bush was going to straighten some shit out over there and get all those terrorists. I asked him what he thought Bush would ever do for him—a poor, disabled black man living on the streets of Brooklyn. He told me he liked Bush's style, liked his instincts and his decisiveness—and that he didn't trust Kerry, who struck him as shifty. I couldn't hide my exasperation, which made George laugh. He liked that he had gotten a rise out of me. For months after the election was over he good-naturedly teased me about this, saying things like "How about that George Bush!" and laughing to himself when I passed.

For all his many moments of disconnection, George had a vice-like memory when his mind would seize upon a certain detail. Once George asked me for money and I told him that I had a jar of change at home that I would give him. He got very animated and wanted to know exactly how much change might be in the jar. I told him maybe four or five dollars. He wanted to know—was it mostly quarters, dimes, nickels, pennies? He wanted to know everything I could tell him about the jar, any details that might make it more tangible. I kept forgetting to bring George the jar, and he would remind me every time I saw him. Weeks went by. Once I remembered, but George wasn't there. It was too much change to lug around with me all day. Though George was generally very casual about money, he would demand to know each time I saw him when I was going to bring him this change. Finally, having failed George yet again, I asked him if he would accept a five-dollar bill instead. He mulled this over, seeming to take a moment to calculate which was the better deal—the change or the bill—but Abraham Lincoln settled the matter for him.

Once George asked me for money on a day I was feeling particularly broke, and I told him no. Because he asks so rarely, I felt I owed him an explanation. I said, "George, I am really sorry, but you know, I am a student and money is a bit tight for me these days."

He was sympathetic and seemed to feel bad that he had asked me for money. "Look, Baby, don't worry about it," he said. "I shouldn't even be asking you for money. Look." He pulled out a disability card from his wallet. "I'm doing alright," he said. "I get a disability check from the government every month." I was surprised. All these years I had known him—five or six at this point—I had assumed he had no resources. He continued, "I live with my sister; she takes care of me."

"Where does your sister live?" I asked.

"In Manhattan," he said. I was relieved to know that someone loved George and took care of him—if it was it true. Another revelation: George took the subway from Manhattan to Brooklyn most every day to come and sit on this corner as if it was a job or a mission. What brought him here every day to the corner of Lorimer and Grand Streets? I didn't ask; George kept talking. Lowering his voice to a conspiratorial whisper and leaning in closer, he said, "I got something for you." He told me that he had a special talent, that he could see lottery numbers in his mind. He said that he had seen one today—and that this number was for me. He opened his wallet and handed me a small scrap of paper on which he had neatly written a number. Giving me this number seemed to make George really happy. I took it but didn't buy a lottery ticket. I carried George's gift in my wallet for months. It made me feel lucky.

Several days after I finished writing this, George disappeared from his corner; I haven't seen him since. The liquor store—caught up in the final paroxysm of Williamsburg's building boom before the financial crisis left a trail of half-finished structures in its wake—was undergoing a gut renovation and an addition of several stories. Maybe George had been asked to leave, or maybe all the construction made the corner less hospitable. I had the uncanny feeling that writing this story had somehow disturbed whatever fragile connection we may have had—that the writing, through some supernatural effect, had initiated George's disappearance. Maybe it was easier to think it was something I had done than to accept loss as part of the risk of engagement. But I still look for him, thinking maybe when the construction ends, George will return. Or maybe he has found a new corner.

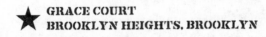

INTERSECTIONS ON A DEAD END STREET

BY ELIZABETH GROVE

In 1971, the man who ran me over with his car moved to Brooklyn Heights.

My family had moved there earlier—in 1966—and so I spent my first birthday, and the next seventeen, on Grace Court. My father, Brooklyn born and raised, had decided, not unreasonably, that a one-bedroom on West Tenth Street was cramped for three. My mother, Boston born and raised, declared that the trail would lead no further than Brooklyn Heights. She still has a kind of lioness pride that she spared me and my brother an upbringing in Flatbush or Sheepshead Bay.

And Grace Court was a beautiful block, with Promenade views without the pedestrian foot traffic. And the building where we lived—then rent-controlled, now co-op—was big and rambling and in disrepair. There was the super, Mr. Nader, his three daughters, and his German Shepherd, Lobo, who spent much of his time sticking his head out of Mr. Nader's first floor window and barking at anything that came near him. Grace Court was a dead-end street, now a cul-de-sac, and was perfect for stickball, with first base roughly demarcated by Mr. Nader's window. This was fine as long as you were under four feet tall. If you were any taller, you risked being scalped or decapitated by Lobo.

Lobo died terribly, poisoned by something concealed in raw hamburger meat, and everyone believed that Sarita had done it. Sarita was British, but not really particularly from anywhere. She read tarot cards, and was certainly capable of poisoning Lobo. Years later, she attacked a friend of my mother's who had befriended her for a time, and years after that a friend of my brother's got a peek into her apartment and reported she was running a dog mill.

There was also Mary R. who used to pass out in the lobby, and who was saved from certain Mr. Goodbar fate by her conversion to Sufism. In the basement laundry room, I would watch as she unfurled yards and yards of white cloth from the dryer. I could remember her in the hallways with her business suits, her cigarette and her highball glass, and then, one day, there was all this whiteness.

And there was Mrs. Sours, who always wore purple wool. Adults always seem indistinguishably old to children, but Mrs. Sours really was about a hundred years old. She had gnarled hands, chin hair, and unusually sparkly eyes. We called her, not inventively, "The Witch." Once, when my father was in the elevator with her, a cockroach crawled out from her purple sleeve. Mrs. Sours died in her apartment during the heat wave of 1977 and no one noticed for a while.

Mrs. Thacker was the doorwoman and was from Kentucky. Her son had been the super before Mr. Nader, but young Thacker had left and Mrs. Thacker had stayed. I don't know if she was an official employee of the building—very little was official in those days—or if she just liked to sit in the lobby, but she was there every evening. The front door of the building would be propped open and Mrs. Thacker would sit. What she was preventing or welcoming is unclear since she was grossly overweight and hobbled by diabetes. Most likely everyone would have been much safer if the door had been locked and Mrs. Thacker had been in her apartment. Still, she was there to tell us not to run

357

through the lobby, and to bear witness, and to chat with passersby in speech that would be of interest to linguists; Mrs. Thacker pronounced the past tense of regular verbs as their own syllable, as in, "Sarita attack-ked Vivian…"

Which is all just to say that when the man who ran me over with his car moved to Grace Court, he fit right in.

In 1971, air conditioning was a luxury. So were push button phones, and there were no such things as answering machines or VCRs. And so it was not exactly a mark of abject poverty in 1971, on a hot summer day, to anticipate the opening of the fire hydrant, though it was as illegal as it is today. But Mr. Nader had a wrench, and he had the special cap that made the hydrant sprinkle rather than dribble or push you back like a rioter. And sometime in the early afternoon I heard the sound of water on pavement.

I had a one-piece bathing suit in pink. When the bathing suit was wet, if you ran your hand over it one way it turned a sleek and shiny icy pink with tones of metallic gray in it. If you ran your hand over it the other way, it became a rough deep rose, spiky like freshly turned earth. It was transfixing. Perhaps too transfixing for street play, even on a cul-de-sac.

I appeared in the living room in it and my mother looked dubious—she hated hot weather and I had never been allowed to play in the hydrant unattended. I could hear the shrieks of joy from the other kids on the block, the uneven sound of the water being held back by the older boys and then released with renewed vigor. I could tell I was in for grave disappointment unless something radically new and unexpected happened. And I don't know what it was, but it happened, and I was allowed to go downstairs after being told to be careful.

The water was cold. Everyone was either in the spray or on the sidelines, baking up before another pass. The jets were forceful but not overwhelming and on the edges the mist was fine, producing rainbows when viewed from certain angles.

I remember the deliciousness of running through the arcing water over and over again, the rough feel of cooled-down wet asphalt. I remember my last run, the dim realization that no one else was in the water with me; that in fact they were all on the sidewalk; that in fact they were all looking at me with a mixture of concern and pity; that in fact, they were all yelling various things at me.

Like, "Hey!"

Like, "Watch out!"

Like, "Car!"

And I remember seeing, at the last moment, the blue Volkswagon Beetle, right before it hit me, right before I slid up the triangular surface of the Beetle's hood and almost up to the windshield and then back down to the ground.

The next thing I knew, I was on the sidewalk across the street from my building, bleeding, worrying the nap on my bathing suit—smooth, icy gray! rough, spiky rose!—and repeating, idiotically and futilely, it seemed even to me at six, "Don't tell my mother!"

My mother appeared shortly after that.

As for the man who ran me over, he drove us to the hospital. He was in his mid-twenties and had just moved into the building; this had been one of his first drives down the block as a resident. He talked a lot, and it would be reasonable to assume it was because he was nervous, but the following thirty years proved he was always nervous and he always talked a lot.

As for me, I was more or less okay. Banged up. I had a bad bruise on my right leg, the one that had led the hip-check of the Beetle. The blood had come entirely from biting my own tongue. By evening I was recuperating on the couch, the TV rolled out from my parents' bedroom, as it was on these convalescent occasions, which would expand to include, before the year was up, a tonsillectomy, a broken arm, and chicken pox.

Then the man came into the apartment with a stuffed animal, a maroon owl with white wing and breast accents. "Now don't go getting hit by cars to get presents," he said to me, before moving into the dining room to present the next and more important element of his apology: a small baggie of pot for my parents.

While they torched up at the table and got to know one another, I watched the TV, named the owl—not inventively—Hooter, and listened to the rise and fall of their conversation over the familiar acrid smell that constituted Happy Hour at Grace Court in 1971.

In the late seventies, the man who ran me over with his car wanted to be a rock star. He played at Max's Kansas City, a place I had discovered with older friends. We would go to see The Speedies and my mother and her friends would go to see the man. Or, they went once. Because, apparently, the man was not a very talented musician. But we wound up with his 45, the cover shot a photo of his wife's foot in a furry high-heeled mule on the octagonal black and white bathroom tile of Grace Court. I spent some time staring at it, trying to reconcile the leg in the bathroom with the man's wife, who I saw mostly in sweatpants and who wore glasses and was a little bit bent over.

Then the man converted to orthodox Judaism, adopted two daughters from Korea, single-handedly destroyed a New Year's party of my mother's with an a capella version of "Proud Mary," and told us one day a long story about how a goldfish in his apartment had died, but he had brought it back to life.

My friends began to refer to that day in 1971 as the day I hit the car.

I went to college and lived away from Grace Court for ten years. The building went co-op and couples with no children moved in and there were no more stickball or volleyball games in the circle at the end of the block. The absence made me remember the sheer numbers of us—girls playing jacks in the front of the building, older boys trying out their hockey skates, younger boys playing handball. "Outside" was simply a destination, a place to be. The Good Humor man came every night of the summer, invariably during dinner, and the year of the bicentennial the street was packed with all of us—old and young. And Mr. Nader guarded the building and its prime rooftop view of the tall ships with, it was rumored, a gun; Lobo kept a little patch of sidewalk open in front of his window.

When I'd grown and moved away, it was always interesting to see who I ran into when I came back. And I usually ran into the man who ran me over. He was always out on the street, talking, smoking, hanging out. It was difficult to talk to him because, while he expressed great interest in anyone's doings, he did most of the talking, got most of the details wrong, and there was little opportunity to correct him. In 1999 I was living back at Grace Court for a few months and wound up leaving for work the same time as him every morning. I tried to walk slowly; I walked the long way to the subway, avoiding him.

And then one night, a few years later in the fall, I went over to my mother's for dinner and there was the man, sitting outside the building.

"Welcome home, Lizzie!" he said. His eyes sparkled. He looked thrilled to see me.

"Hey," I said. "How are you?"

"That's what I do," he said, "I sit here and I welcome everybody home. Welcome home! Where are you living these days?"

"Just on Henry Street," I said.

He'd let me go, he said, so my mother could have me over, he was sure she was waiting eagerly. Since I went over about once a week for dinner, I wasn't as confident as he was about her enthusiasm, but I went upstairs.

"What's wrong with Michael?" I asked. "He welcomed me home. It was creepy, it was like 'The Sentinel' where the suicide guards the gates of Hell."

"He's in very bad shape," my mother said. "But he has very good meds. He's in a great mood. It's terrible."

Then in the winter, I went over again, and he greeted me once more: "Ellen!" he said. "Welcome home!"

"I'm Lizz," I said.

"I meant Lizz," he said. "I know who you are. I meant you were going to see Ellen."

"Why are you standing so far away?" he said. "Come closer."

I'd been standing in front of the door, but I walked over to where he was sitting by the shrubbery.

"Where are you living these days? Tribeca?"

"No," I said. "Just on Henry Street."

"One of the kids from the building is living in Tribeca," he said. "So I thought maybe that was you."

"No," I said.

"It's cold," I said.

"I'll let you go," he said. "Go and see your mother."

I wasn't going to see my mother; I was feeding her cat while she was away. But like so much of life among neighbors, the details, the distinctions somehow aren't important, or important enough. Perhaps we all only ever get a few of them right.

I fed the cat and stared out the kitchen window into the courtyard, a vantage from which I'd often looked, tossing water balloons and, later, cigarette butts. Sometime in the early eighties, a sign had been posted in the lobby requesting the cessation of chicken bone tossing into the courtyard, but that hadn't been me—I was already gone.

The kitchen was quiet, the apartment was quiet, the street was quiet—everyone on their way to somewhere else. Which is exactly where we'd always been heading all along, despite the way time can warp at a moment of impact, or suspend itself in the daily living of life behind so many identical doors, fooling you, for a time, into thinking that all the trajectories are the same.

SEX AND THE GOP

BY REBECCA SCHIFF

I was sitting in the pen when Pinchas walked by.

"Pinchas!" I howled. "Pinchas!"

I ducked under the police barricade and gave Pinchas a big, showy hug. Maybe the two FBI guys questioning the guy with the "Pfizer Lies" sign see that I'm nice now, I thought. Maybe they like me.

Even protesting the Republican National Convention, I wanted to be liked. My sign said "Fuck You" but I couldn't master a facial expression to go with it. Instead, I made meaningful eye contact with the cops, hoping they'd see a daughter or a sister in my gaze. Some would smile until they read what I was holding.

My roommate and I had markered the epithet onto a giant piece of butcher paper on the floor of our kitchen in Brooklyn. We downloaded a copy of the RNC schedule and held up the message to Republican delegates as they went to fundraising events. This meant waiting outside Midtown steakhouses, often with righteous, issue-oriented leftists who objected to our sign.

In between events, I kept sneaking into bookstores to read *He's Just Not That Into You,* a book about how to tell that your boyfriend doesn't like you. I didn't have a boyfriend, which was why I had decided to sit in solidarity with the Pfizer guy in the first place. The two FBI agents were asking him questions you might ask on a first date: So, where are you from? What college do you go to? Why do you think Pfizer lies? I'd sat down next to him so the agents would know somebody was watching the exchange in case they disappeared him. When the protestor mentioned that he was majoring in dance at Hampshire, I lost interest.

Instead, I disappeared myself from the pen as lamely as I'd entered it, with a boy as the reason. Apparently I was willing to drop the whole "witnessing injustice" thing as soon as I spotted Pinchas.

"Sorry, I can't talk right now, I'm on the phone with my sister in Israel," Pinchas mouthed, pulling out of my hug.

Pinchas was a former co-worker, a twenty-two-year-old married Orthodox Jew, but we'd had some office banter back in the day. He was cute, Pinchas, even if he wore ill-fitting suits and had a cell phone permanently attached to his ear. (Why do religious Jews love the cell phones? It's tribal, I think.)

"Oh, okay. I'm in a protest."

But he was already scurrying down Fifty-third Street, tefillin flapping.

I felt a pinch of rejection and turned back to the Feds for validation. They seemed to have forgotten who I was, or that I'd ever been inside the pen. The beauty of being a New Yorker protesting the RNC was that if you just rolled up your sign and acted the part of a New Yorker rather than the part of a protester, the cops and delegates would treat you like a harmless civilian. My roommate and I got close to the entrance of important events by just walking along, chatting about boys who weren't that into us. Then, when we saw a laminated pass hanging down the front of a suit, or someone in a patriotic hat, we'd switch into guerilla mode, unrolling the "Fuck You" and smiling.

The movement was revolutionary.

But I didn't want to be a revolutionary. I wanted Pinchas to like me. I wanted the cops to like me. I wanted the other protesters to like me and stop telling me my sign was "doing more harm than good." What did they know? At least my sign had a clear message.

It was also the most fun sign to hold, during the brief stretches when I let go of the idea of being liked. Soon, my roommate and I could spot a conventioneer from a block away—tiny flag pin on lapel, outdated fluff in hairstyle. Fuck you, fuck you, fuck you. The sign started ripping from all the tugging and unfurling. It got soft. My roommate rolled it up like a yoga mat and kept it in her backpack while we rode subways up and down Manhattan, following the Republican money trail.

We switched tactics in crowds. The butcher paper was too big, too unwieldy. We grabbed free CNN ping-pong paddles from a press table and defaced the backs of them with what we now considered our slogan. When a Republican walked by us, we would reach into our bags and quickly flip them the paddles, the "Fuck," then the "You." Right in the face.

The night of Bush's acceptance speech, we decided to take the big "Fuck You" closer to Madison Square Garden. We were strolling down Eighth Avenue when we spotted a herd of young delegates. They were beef-fed, fraternity-flushed, a bloated, jacketed mass floating down the sidewalk. We unrolled and waited for their response.

"You want me to fuck you?" jeered one blond.

"IF I GOT PREGNANT BY YOU, I'D ABORT IT," screamed my roommate. I was quiet. We walked on, but I kept wondering, what would have happened if I'd asked him to skip the convention and come to Brooklyn. Would the blond have blown off George W. Bush to get blown by me?

But even if he had said "You're the prettiest faux-anarchist I've ever seen," and left his GOP keg buddies behind, I still would have had my doubts, my insecurities. And who really would have been validated by our coitus? Weren't my roommate and I already validating the delegates by making a sign especially for them? Why was I engaging with Republicans at all, even to tell them to fuck off? Trying to get Bush to stop the war or to get Republicans to change their policies was like trying to get an inattentive boyfriend to start treating you better. "Fuck You" was a step in the right direction, but it still insisted "I want you to know how I feel. I care."

Of all the ways that the delegates had responded to the sign—indignation, sexual aggression, weird Christian sympathy—the most disconcerting reaction was glee. Young Republicans laughed and nudged each other and took our picture We had given them the New York they had expected, the New York of "fuhgeddaboudit," of "New York Fuckin' City," a slogan off a shitty T-shirt. We were playing to the tourists, and it was time to go back to Brooklyn, alone.

GOONS OF NEW YORK
BY JEAN PAUL CATIVIELA

Midway through the film *The Warriors*, a lesbian gang called the Lizzies lures a detachment of Warriors back to their party pad, treacherously plying them with music, dancing, and the promise of good loving. Waylaying the Warriors just as Circe waylaid Odysseus and his crew, these jaunty lesbians proceed to transform the street-tough Warrior boys into randy and helpless Sweathogs. That's when the girl gang springs its cunning trap. "The chicks are packed! The chicks are packed!" cries one Warrior as the Lizzies break out their guns and shoot up the place.

Evoking Homer may seem a bit grandiose for a cult film about oddball street gangs. But *The Warriors* is spiced with such literary pretensions, and its surprisingly diverse sources include a socially-conscious novel of the mid-sixties and an epic adventure of the ancient Greek writer Xenophon. Such underlying bookishness is all the more surprising given the overall, and unrelenting, hokiness of the film on its surface.

Each of the teenage street gangs in *The Warriors* is outfitted with a campy theme and a uniform. The gang called the "Baseball Furies" wear Marilyn Manson makeup and dress in full pinstriped baseball uniforms. "The Punks" wear *Deliverance* overalls and scoot around on roller-disco skates. The Warriors themselves wear shiny buckskin vests and Indian bead necklaces. Among the other gangs rounding out the cast: an all-mimes gang, an all-orphans gang, and another gang that can only be described as The Scott Baios.

A rally to unite all these gangs turns to chaos when someone assassinates the vaguely revolutionary leader, Cyrus. The assassination touches off a gang war and launches the film's premise: the Warriors are wrongly accused of the killing and must therefore march through enemy turf all the way from Van Cortlandt Park back home to Coney Island. Along the way, the not so scary Warriors must contend with such not very gritty realities as fighting the aforementioned overdressed rival gangs and puzzling out the MTA's subway maps. In other business, Deborah van Valkenburgh—later Sarah Rush on TV's *Too Close For Comfort*—plays a Puerto Rican whore who falls for the head Warrior and delivers a stirring apologia for the life of the hooker as an antidote to growing old.

In the foreword to Herbert Ashbury's book *The Gangs of New York*, Jorge Luis Borges described New York gang life as possessing "all the confusion and cruelty of barbarian cosmologies." The gangs in *The Warriors*, in contrast, are fanciful creatures, more native to the two-dimensional realities of comic books than fodder for a bloody Scorsese film.

Nevertheless, *The Warriors* is not just another cult film destined to be ridiculed on VH1 snarkfests (though it has, of course, been ridiculed on VH1 snarkfests). As one of the top films of 1979, grossing about $17 million, *The Warriors* was a commercial success and was taken quite seriously. Some saw art in it. Pauline Kael, without apparent irony, called the film "mesmerizing."

Walter Hill, the film's director, was also taken seriously. And for good reason. He had already made his excellent getaway-driver-as-cowboy film *The Driver,* and later directed the A-list blockbuster *48 Hours.* In 1980, film critic Robert F. Moss even included Hill in his somewhat shrill denunciation of movie violence in a *Saturday Review* article called "The Brutalists: Making Movies Mean and Ugly." Moss groups Hill with fellow "brutalist" offenders Martin Scorsese, Brian DePalma, and Paul Schrader, accusing them of defining "the urban scene as little more than the sum total of its most extreme forms of decadence." He singles out *The Warriors* for its decadent "brutality," scolding Hill because his "imagination is most fully energized by action sequences." Significantly, audiences at the time did not laugh off the violence in the film, if only because of gang attacks associated with a number of screenings in Los Angeles and New York.

Sol Yurick's book *The Warriors* appeared in 1965, the product of several years of difficult work gathering source material. As an employee of the Department of Welfare in New York City, Yurick had already worked with impoverished families whose children were in street gangs. He interviewed gang members and later spied on gang hangouts from inside a rented panel truck. And in his attempt "to construct a true reflection of the real world in which [his] literary gangs would move," he went as far as walking through the subway tunnel between 96th Street and 110th Street.

Yurick called the movie version of his novel "trashy." A more charitable view would simply describe the film as less authentic. The novel *The Warriors* is far more graphically brutal than Hill's film. Yurick's gang, the Coney Island Dominators, commits a random murder and a gang rape, and attempts to rape a drunk nurse in Riverside Park. Though not by any means a great novel, Yurick's work offers a social commentary and labors to present its subject with authenticity. Gangs like the "Borinquen Blazers" populate Yurick's novel, gangs more firmly rooted to their racial and economic status. Where Walter Hill's racially intermixed Warriors are led by a telegenic white guy, all of Yurick's Dominators are black or hispanic teenagers whose violence is often racially loaded. In the novel, when the character Ismael addresses the massive gang rally, on the Fourth of July no less, he frames his quasi-Marxist argument in terms of race and power: "Now we're all brothers, I don't care what you say. They make us think we're all different so we rumble in colored gangs, white gangs, Puerto Rican gangs, Polish gangs, Irish gangs, Italian gangs, Mau-Mau gangs, and Nazi gangs."

It was Yurick who borrowed the plot for *The Warriors* from Xenophon's *Anabasis*, a history written over two thousand years ago. The *Anabasis* chronicles how Cyrus the Younger, under the false pretext of a police action, leads a mercenary army of ten thousand Greeks deep into Mesopotamia—modern-day Iraq—with the purpose of unseating the Persian king in Babylon. When someone assassinates Cyrus (a javelin in the eye), the stranded Greek warriors must fight their way back to Greece. Xenophon himself leads the Greeks on their bloody retreat.

Beyond presenting an uncanny parallel to our nation's war in Iraq, the *Anabasis* presumably reflects the kind of "barbarian cosmology" Borges compared to New York gang life. The Greeks march north from Cunaxa toward the Black Sea, fighting through a brutal gauntlet of Kurdish and other barbarian tribes. The reality of barbarians dancing with severed Greek heads is only part of the "cruelty and confusion" that assails the Greeks on their trek up country. When the mercenaries attack one barbarian fortification, the natives rain stones down on them—when the supply of stones is exhausted, the native women throw their babies, and when they run out of babies, the women throw themselves. The men follow, leaving behind only "oxen and asses and sheep."

It may be tempting to view these comparatively more "brutalistic" acts as further evidence of a "trashy" lack of authenticity in Walter Hill's film. After all, how did the bloodier, grittier works of Sol Yurick and Xenophon lead to packed chicks and bellicose mimes?

But Hill would seem to have a point. His gangs may organize themselves into absurd, comic categories, but violence inspired by the absurd and the imaginary is in no way precluded from becoming lethal. One perhaps needs look no further than Los Pitufos, the Mexican gang based on *The Smurfs*. Indeed, as Borges reminds us, early New York was overrun with cutthroat gangs with vividly cartoonish names like the Daybreak Boys, the Plug Uglies, and the Swamp Angels. Many of these gangs wore thematic uniforms, as did the Plug Uglies, whose bowler hats and long shirttails might have provoked laughter if it were not for the huge bludgeons and pistols they carried. Of course none of this makes *The Warriors* any less of a giddy masquerade of violence, or less of a snark magnet for that matter. But it may help us to reflect upon our own ever more cartoonish tribalisms, and how they are colliding in the real world.

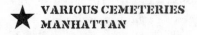
THE UNDISTURBED
BY JEAN PAUL CATIVIELA

During the nineteenth century, the accelerating sprawl of New York City forced the relocation of almost all of Manhattan's dead. From 1846 to 1851, nearly twenty thousand bodies were moved off the island, and by the Civil War most of the cemeteries in Manhattan were gone—moved to large, park-like cemeteries like Cypress Hills and Green-Wood.

Of the handful of cemeteries that remained—and still remain—in Manhattan, three belong to the Spanish and Portuguese Synagogue of Shearith Israel. In odd and somewhat obscure corners of Manhattan, these three cemeteries bear the marks of the city's intense urban growth. They are small, shabby, and hardly noticeable, but their centuries-long survival in New York City is both impressive and provocative.

The Sephardic founders of the Shearith Israel congregation were a sort of Mayflower group in American Jewish history. In 1654, twenty-three refugees from the Portuguese Inquisition arrived from Brazil, becoming the first permanent Jewish settlers in North America. Now known simply as "the twenty-three," the refugees fought off the peg leg Peter Stuyvesant's anti-

Semitic efforts to expel them, and went on to found some of the most prominent Jewish-American families.

The congregation of Shearith Israel built their first cemetery almost one hundred years before the American Revolution, in an area that is now just south of Chatham Square on St. James Place. Extending from the lower Bowery almost to the East River, it was one of the largest burial grounds in Manhattan, large enough to be fortified with artillery during the Revolution and for British troops to use as a parade ground.

But in the 1830s, the City of New York nibbled, then chomped at the First Cemetery's edges, finally pressuring the congregation to move the cemetery completely. Shearith Israel did sell a large unused portion of the grounds, and eventually moved many of the bodies uptown. However, the congregation refused to move the entire cemetery and succeeded in keeping a quarter-acre lot intact.

Today, the First Cemetery is a small trapezoid stuffed behind an apartment building in a neighborhood of drab government towers. It stands an incongruous five feet higher than the sidewalk beneath it, the result of the city leveling a hill to extend a nearby street. It is nothing like the picturesque verdure of the Trinity Church graveyard near Wall Street, where the graves of Alexander Hamilton and Robert Fulton preen side by side for tourists.

Nevertheless, there is a certain dignity to the First Cemetery. In fact, a first encounter with any of the Shearith Israel cemeteries can be one of those rare and improbable moments when you feel you've discovered something no one else knows about in Manhattan. As one of a pair of nice, pear-shaped women put it recently, as she stretched on her tiptoes to see into the First Cemetery, "You could walk down this street a thousand times and never see it. But see how nice it is?"

Shearith Israel's Second Cemetery at Sixth Avenue and Eleventh Street was also once several acres large. Many Jewish victims of the yellow fever outbreak of 1822 were originally buried there, but in 1830 the construction of Eleventh Street hacked off all but the tiny triangular patch of twenty-odd graves that remains today. The tombstones inside lean flush against the wall in a crowded line that suggests they no longer mark individual graves.

It is remarkable that the Second Cemetery survived in any form. Besides the threat of the city's expanding grid, yellow fever cemeteries were the target of public hysteria. Greedy real estate developers and other agitators inflamed public fears of toxic outgases from decaying corpses. The hysteria accelerated the removal of bodies from Manhattan, while other yellow fever burial sites were converted into public parks or were simply left unmarked. Somewhere between ten thousand and twenty-two thousand are still interred in the hidden potter's field underneath Washington Square Park.

"The city just paved over a lot of the other cemeteries," explained the leader of a recent walking tour for the Tall Club of New York City (literally a club for tall New Yorkers). "There are all sorts of stories of Con Ed accidentally digging up unmarked graves in the seventies. The bodies were still wrapped in their yellow shrouds." As he spoke, the rapt members of the Tall Club tour, as perhaps only they could, were peering over the Second Cemetery's wall, absorbing the anonymous and pleasantly overgrown red brick enclosure within.

The Third Cemetery, at West Twenty-first Street and Sixth Avenue, is about an acre in size, and some of its graves contain bodies originally buried in the First and Second cemeteries. James Thurber wrote about it for *The New Yorker* in 1928, reporting a department store's bizarre plan "to arch a building over the cemetery" that would supposedly leave it "undisturbed." Had it not been rejected, however, the plan would have reduced the Third Cemetery to something like a dark crawl space.

Today the Third Cemetery is anything but undisturbed by department stores. Tall retail buildings box the cemetery into its cramped lot, while large air vents behind the Scuba Network outgas hot air onto the cemetery's array of foundering tombstones.

Worse yet, in June of 2006 several dozen headstones were damaged by falling debris from the "luxury apartments" under construction next-door.

Like the other two Shearith Israel cemeteries, the Third Cemetery has somehow kept up its trick of endurance for several centuries now, accumulating its share of disfigurement in the process. And, again like the others, the Third Cemetery possesses an appeal that goes beyond its impairments and dilapidation.

"It's such a nice place," says Frank, an elderly man who lives under the scaffolding outside the offending luxury apartments. "You used to be able to go in there. The trees are beautiful, and they have little flowers in the spring."

Frank speaks with a proprietary tone that borders on defensive, as if he wants to make sure no one judges the Third Cemetery by its rundown appearance.

"There's a man who takes care of the place. He was in there earlier trying to get things cleaned up."

He points out the plywood sidewalk set off by yellow caution tape running along the edge of the cemetery.

"You can see they're going to do some work in there. I don't know what they're doing, but they're fixing it up a little."

★ **MADISON AVE. BETWEEN 78TH & 79TH STS.
UPPER EAST SIDE, MANHATTAN**

THE TOUCH ARTIST
BY JILL SAND D'ANGELO

It took me a while to realize that Kenny was missing. I had been out of town for the holidays, visiting family in California. After almost a week without seeing him since my return, I began to grow concerned.

I live on the Upper East Side in an area that used to be, in the sixties and seventies, a thriving art community, but is now home to sedate families and their privileged children. Kenny fit in about as well as I did, which is to say not at all. Kenny was African American, over fifty years old, with a slight build and a neat, unremarkable wardrobe. Kenny was our neighborhood beggar.

When I first moved to the area with my boyfriend, apartments were cheap. We previewed endless prospects all over New York City but much to the surprise of our bohemian friends, we settled on the Upper East Side.

"Imagine being able to go to the Metropolitan Museum whenever we want," said my boyfriend, a sculptor. I had some hesitation about the reputedly staid locals, but was eventually won over by the idea of taking leisurely strolls in Central Park after a long day at the typewriter. The reputation of the area as "boring," "conservative," "dead" (this was how our Brooklyn pals put it), would not deter me.

I first met Kenny on Madison Avenue. He was standing with a paper cup in hand, soliciting donations. Of average height, Kenny's defining feature was his easy, gap-toothed smile. I'd seen him regularly during my first few weeks in the neighborhood as I rushed past, carrying cleaning supplies or groceries or hardware or whatever we needed to finish moving in. The first time he asked me for money, I handed him an apple from my shopping bag and dashed off. "Thank you," he called out, "God bless you, Miss."

One day, shortly after my boyfriend and I had settled in, I stopped to chat with Kenny. I told him that I'd recently moved to the neighborhood and that—I put it nicely—he shouldn't ask me for money because I would save it up for his birthday. Wouldn't it be better to get a windfall once a year rather than being nickle-and-dimed on a regular basis? He looked wary of my proposition. I asked when his birthday was.

"November twelfth."

"Good. I won't forget."

"Sure you will."

"No I won't; mine is just a few days earlier."

Kenny was our only neighborhood beggar, with seemingly exclusive rights to the territory spanning from Seventy-second Street to Eighty-sixth Street along Madison Avenue. It was hard to believe that even one beggar managed to survive in this well-patrolled precinct, where, according to government surveys, ninety-nine percent of the sidewalks and one hundred percent of the playgrounds were acceptably clean, (according to government surveys) where there were few or no murders, and where less than three percent of the city's major felonies occurred. The nearby deli owner, with whom I'd become friendly despite his weak espressos, said Kenny had a talent for evading the local beat cops. On many occasions I'd seen the deli owner chatting with Kenny on the street, only to invite him inside to sit at the counter and enjoy something cool on a warm day, or the other way around.

It took Kenny a while to remember not to ask me for money. But eventually he overcame the habit. When time allowed, we'd chat. We talked about the neighborhood, the weather, current events. Whenever I had groceries in hand, I'd share something with him—some fruit, a cookie, a bagel, a package of nuts, whatever. He always thanked me the same way: "God bless you, Miss." That's what he called me—"Miss"—as we never exchanged names. At first, the idea of exchanging names felt inappropriate since I was little more than a passing stranger, then before long, our friendship had progressed beyond the point when introductions seemed necessary. I had even begun talking to him about my writing.

I started to search for a word other than "beggar," since the longer I knew Kenny, the less the term fit. To me, a beggar signified someone scruffy and undisciplined, yet there were many times when Kenny was already at work when I got my morning coffee and still plying his trade when I went out for my evening walk. In fact, it began to occur to me that he kept more diligent hours than I did.

Asker: too politically correct. *Hobo*: hobos rode train cars and had patches on their pants. *Vagabond*: same thing as hobos, but with knapsacks and without trains. *Lazzaroni*: this word was derived from the beggars of Naples, who used the Hospital of St. Lazarus as their refuge, and while it wasn't an unlikable term, I couldn't picture Kenny in Italy. *Pauper*: too old-fashioned. *Street person*: too bureaucratic. *Panhandler*: sounded like a synonym for "dishwasher." *Sponge*: same thing. *Mendicant*: not only were mendicants usually connected with religious sects, there was something too medicinal-sounding about the name. *Indigent*: with its associative whiff of "indignation," it wouldn't do at all. Then, finally, I came across *Touch Artist*. Something about this term felt right; derived from the expression "putting the touch" on someone, it seemed to fit, and from then on, this was how I thought of Kenny.

I began to wonder about the circumstances that had landed him on the street. Or was he really on the street? Did the fact that he was consistently clean-shaven hint at some kind of home base? Where did he sleep at night? Did he have parents? Siblings? Or a family of his own? In my mind I rehearsed different phrasings of these questions, hoping to find a means of inquiry that didn't appear either prying or condescending. Yet every time I bumped into him, something held me back. What if he were truly homeless? Would that somehow oblige me to provide for him beyond my shared groceries and chitchat? How would my boyfriend feel if I invited Kenny for a home-cooked meal? And because Kenny was a man and I'm a woman, would he read something into the invitation?

It was at 1014 Madison Avenue that I first learned of Kenny's artistic interests. In the middle of a conversation about the blushing leaves of Central Park, Kenny pointed to a stretch of sidewalk about seventy feet long, a black-and-light design (there is no such thing as white on the streets of New York), of an entirely different substance than concrete, and asked if I knew anything about it. The abstract lines caught the light of the afternoon sun, and perhaps for the first time I noticed the sidewalk's beauty. The high-contrast design—like a runway of giant commas, dashes, and hyphens—created a complex background for the autumn's sharp shadows.

When I confessed my ignorance, Kenny explained that the sidewalk had been commissioned by local galleries in 1970. The work was by Alexander Calder, who had generously donated it to the neighborhood—"and look here, you can see his initials," he said. Sure enough, near the curb was "CA" with the number "70" below. I'd walked by it on a daily basis yet had never really noticed. Kenny told me that the terrazzo itself wasn't meant to be permanent—it had been replaced three times that he knew of—but it was the zinc framework corralling the terrazzo that was important, what he called "the essence of the piece." I found it remarkable: not only had I been treading on a great piece of public art without realizing it, but Kenny was surprisingly erudite. "Didn't you know I was an artist?" he asked, his esses soft-ened by his incomplete set of teeth. "I have drawings in lots of these places," he said, sweeping his hand up and down Madison Avenue in a gesture that resembled a land-owner's prideful claim. And although this appeared to be an ideal moment to ask Kenny about his background, I found myself handing him the protein bar that I'd put in my purse specifically with him in mind.

"Here," I said laughing uncomfortably as I turned to go, "it's for you."

Kenny smiled. "God bless you, Miss."

On the morning of November 12th, I entered the William Greenberg bakery on Madison Avenue and bought a bag of cookies. I'd purposely not mentioned anything to Kenny about his upcoming birthday in order to surprise him. Inside the bag I hid two twenty-dollar bills. When I left the store, I was certain that I was about to commit the most magnanimous gesture on the planet Earth...yet as I walked south on Madison Avenue, I found my mood wilting: Kenny was nowhere to be found. What if I didn't bump into him today? This sometimes happened; recently there had several two-or three-day stretches when he wasn't around. What would he think if I failed to keep my word? That I was a heartless woman, no different from the types that my Brooklyn friends initially warned me about?

But there he was, on the east side of the street, soliciting dona-tions, paper cup in hand.

I approached him and gave him the bag. "Here you go," I said with rehearsed nonchalance intended to heighten his surprise.

Kenny put the bag into his satchel without glancing inside. He thanked me a bit less heartfully than usual—"God bless you, Miss"—then turned to the next passerby.

I didn't want to make an ass of myself by announcing my magnanimity, so I walked on, figuring he'd eventually discover the gift.

Two days later, Kenny rushed up to me like a puppy. The first serious rainstorm of autumn had recently passed, and awnings were still dripping. More than anything, he said, it was just so nice that someone remembered his birthday, and he turned to hide the emotion that was beginning to overtake his expression. I saw him wipe his dark eyes with their enviably thick lashes. He cleared his throat and asked if I'd be around later, then changed his mind.

"I want you to see my latest drawings," he said, digging into his satchel and finding his composure. He took out a stack of thick white paper and shuffled through a selection of line drawings as if they were a deck of cards. "You pick your favorite."

This was how I learned his full name—from his signature.

I chose a portrait of an African woman that I knew my brother in California would like, two views of a voluptuous beauty with bird in hand. While naïve, the work was rendered with a graceful touch, and I recognized the increasing dimensionality of the term *touch artist*.

And my brother did love it, just as he loved the subsequent drawings Kenny gave me, some of which I shared, some of which I kept for myself. At first, At first, Kenny gave them in response to his birthday presents, but then one year he beat me at my own game and surprised me by remembering my birthday. A few days later, on November 12th, I put a card inside the bag of birthday cookies—a signed card. I told myself that if Kenny called me by my first name the next time he saw me, it was the signal to finally ask about his background.

The following day, I chatted with him a bit longer than usual, trying to provide ample opportunity for him to speak my name. I even quoted a friend talking to me, thinking that if I said my name aloud, it would pave the way for him to follow. We talked about the crazy old woman who lived a few doors down— a retired socialite who could be seen at the crack of dawn wearing all her finery as if going to a cocktail party. I told him I was thinking of compiling a book of interviews with neighborhood characters. "Maybe," I said cautiously, "I could even interview you."

Kenny ran his hand over his close-cropped hair. "Aw, you don't need to do that." He smiled broadly. "You already know me."

I laughed uncomfortably, as I'm prone to do, and handed him a sandwich from my grocery bag. "I guess you're right about that."

As I walked away, I heard him call out, "God bless you, Miss."

It was after a trip to see my brother that I realized Kenny hadn't been around for a while. When I mentioned his name at the neighborhood bookstore, the store's owner came downstairs and took me aside. He explained that Kenny had died. His demise had been rapid. One of the bookstore's employees had visited him in the hospital every day.

I was stunned. I wanted to ask a lot of questions. What happened to Kenny's drawings? Who paid the hospital bill? Did any family members surface at the end? But, like Kenny the day he first presented me with a drawing, I was too overcome with emotion to continue. But unlike Kenny, my composure wasn't quickly regained. I walked home by way of the Calder sidewalk, contemplating the permanence of the zinc framework as compared to the ephemeral terrazzo. I had hoped to find something comforting in the metaphor, but came up empty-handed.

The neighborhood wasn't the same without Kenny. By now I'd become friendly not only with the local shopkeepers but also with my neighbors, eliminating any remaining prejudices against the staid locals. Even with this fuller sense of the neighborhood, Kenny's absence left a gap. My grocery bags were heavier and I experienced a strange sense of anonymity now that he was gone. It's funny how one person had given me such a feeling of belonging. Had I done the same for him?

I didn't bring up Kenny's name after he died. Months later, I went to a bookstore to purchase a literary magazine. When the bookstore's owner was ringing up my purchase, I asked if the drawing on the wall was one of Kenny's. I knew it was. I hadn't planned on saying anything; the words just came out. "Yes, it is," said the owner, then he went on to tell me about Kenny's funeral—how the mortuary on the corner had underwritten the whole affair, and that the entire neighborhood had attended. It really was something, he added, and an anonymous person had donated the flowers, and people told stories afterwards about their experiences with Kenny, and the funeral director had hung the walls with Kenny's artwork.

I took the literary magazine home and put it on my desk. It contained my first published short story. An innocuous little book, from a distance like so many others. I walked to the far corner where I'd hung one of Kenny's drawings. It was of a man standing on a city street. Certainly I was proud of my smidgeon of literary success, but threatening to usurp this pride was another pride: my staid little neighborhood had given Kenny a fitting farewell. I pictured the coffee shop owner, the Madison Avenue doormen, the vendors, store employees, friends and neighbors—even the crazy socialite dressed for imagined cocktail parties at dawn—all gathered in the chapel, all paying their last respects to Kenny, the Touch Artist.

I returned to my desk, picked up the magazine, and looked inside.

AFTER DARK

BY MICHELE CARLO

"Nothing good ever happens after 2 a.m." That's what my mother told me when I tried to get my curfew extended. I was twenty and thought I had made the right choice by choosing to stay home and go to the School of Visual Arts instead of trying for the Art Center in California. I could get Latin home cooking any time I wanted and still have my laundry done. I could do my homework on the subway and have more time to go out dancing. I didn't think my laziness would have its price, and that the price would be my freedom.

"But Mom," I said. "I'm in college now, I'm an adult." Now my mom was the Jackie O. of East 103rd Street. She spoke in a well-modulated stage whisper with no Spanish accent whatsoever, but when she was pissed off, she sounded just like Rosie Perez. "*Claro? Adulto? Como* you are *un adulto* you will live in your own house. *Pero*, as long as you live under my roof you will be home by 2 a.m!"

So for the next five years I obeyed her. I came home drunk. I came home tripping. Once I even came home without my underwear. But by God, I was home by 2 a.m.

And then, a miracle happened. I graduated, and within one week landed a job and moved in with my college boyfriend. Finally, I was an adult and could live the life I wanted. Unfortunately, soon after, my boyfriend decided to live the life he wanted, and threw me out. And instead of going back home to a 2 a.m. curfew, I proved I was truly an adult by getting an apartment by myself. Oh, excuse me, did I call it an apartment? Ever see the film *This Property Is Condemned*? Well, I lived there. The ceilings dripped, every outlet sparked like a Tesla coil, and there was a hole under the kitchen sink large enough for a German Shepherd to crawl through. All this for just five-hundred and fifty dollars a month. But it did have a backyard that could have made a pretty nice garden—if it was cleaned up. I was sure it would only take a week. Two months later, I had dug up a half-century of fossilized pets, (I kept some of the more interesting bones), a three-foot pile of rusted nails, and five dollars in Indian head nickels. And every time I cut myself on yet another beer bottle forged before my parents were born, I saw it as one more manifestation of my rotten, miserable life. And then, just when I thought things couldn't get any worse, I lost my job. My new job. The job where I hadn't yet worked long enough to qualify for unemployment.

I had two thousand dollars in my savings account, enough for three months rent and about $66.66 a month for everything else, including my two new kittens. Then, one morning, I looked out the window at the clean, tilled garden. When I looked at it before, I had pictured a soothing floral oasis for my tortured soul. Now I looked at it and saw dinner.

The next morning I went straight to the Brooklyn Central Library and took out every book I could find on organic gardening (the Internet, sadly, was still a couple of years away). In the afternoon, I went to the Caton Avenue stables and pushed home a creaking shopping cart of Key Food shopping bags overflowing with horse manure. Before the week was out, I had planted my miniature farm with plum and beefsteak tomatoes, green beans, zucchini, eggplant, and thirty-six stalks of Silver Queen white corn. This was all under the watchful eyes of my next-door neighbors, a family of indeterminate Eastern European origin, consisting of a fat mother with an eyepatch, an even fatter, drunken husband, and their skinny teenage son who liked to sunbathe in his rotting, yellowed underwear. They all had something to say while I planted garlic, scallions, marigolds and Nasturtium in between each row.

"*Vy* you is *plantink* flower *mit* food?" my neighbor said to me in her indeterminate Eastern European accent. "You are knowing nothing of garden. All plant *vill* be die. You *vill* see, ugly girl." I thought I knew what I was doing. According to the organic gardening books, planting the spices and flowers would guard my vegetables against mold, infestation, and rot. But, unfortunately, not against theft.

By the middle of August, my garden was like a Henri Rousseau painting bursting with life and color. My neighbor's: a soggy heap of mold and rot. "*Vat* you do my plants, ugly girl?" my neighbor said as she shook her fat fist at me. What could I tell her? That all the bugs and germs that were repelled from my garden were feasting on hers? Besides, I had other things to worry about, I was now living off the bottom of a ten pound bag of rice and the first veggie to be ripe, a fat purple eggplant, was still a couple of days away.

Have you ever been hungry? Really hungry? The kind that wakes you up at night and keeps you on edge all day? I knew I was always just a phone call away from my parents, but I was stubborn. I intentionally had moved as far away from them as I could (while still being in the same city) and I was determined to be *un adulto* and deal with this on my own.

That morning, I went into my garden and my perfect eggplant was gone. The next day, the next eggplant was gone. Then, a zucchini. Then half my tomatoes. I couldn't understand. And then one morning, a message in the dirt: a fat bare footprint next to the chain link fence, and on the other side, a stepladder. How could I have been so stupid? I looked into my neighbor's yard and she hurled smoke at me. "*Vy* your plant *livit* and mines is dic. Not correct, ugly girl," and she put out her unfiltered cigarette with her fat bare foot.

I had never been so furious in my life. I wanted to climb that fence, break off her fat fingers and her fat foot, and stick them into the fat hole where her right eye used to be. But I knew if I as much as touched her, I would be the one to go to jail. I went into my apartment and cried and screamed until I collapsed onto the floor. I was a total and complete failure as an adult and would now have to call home and beg to come back. As I resigned myself to a lifetime of 2 a.m. curfews, Boris, my skinny little Russian Blue kitten who I had caught eating a waterbug the night before, went into the litter box and took the worst-smelling cat crap I've ever smelled in my life. And through the miasma, the hunger, and the tears, came an idea.

I went into the backyard at 2 a.m. It was cool and peaceful under a fingernail moon. I waited until all the lights on the block went dark, and I crept into the garden. I compared the last two eggplants; only the plumpest, ripest one would do. Lying on my back, I took out my sharpest X-Acto knife and slowly, carefully, sawed a circular plug out of the bottom of the eggplant and hollowed it out, all the time comparing it to the circumference of the cat turd in the baggie at my side. The sky began to grow light. I was sweating. I saw a light go on in my neighbor's kitchen, slipped the turd up into the eggplant and replaced the plug as I heard their screen door open. I crawled back into my apartment just in time.

Later that day, I saw my neighbors on their front stoop. They wouldn't look at me. "How is garden?" I asked. They banged into their house and locked the door. I thought I was going to break in half laughing, because what I was dying to know was, how/when did they find out about the booby, or should I say "poopy" trap? Did it slide out into her hand as she picked it? Or did it liquefy inside as she steamed it for her family whole? I would never know.

What I did know was that nothing ever disappeared from my garden that summer or any other summer for the five years I lived there. Funny thing is, now, for some reason, there's one vegetable I just don't have a taste for anymore.

So nothing good ever happens after 2 a.m?

**★ 1441 METROPOLITIAN AVE.
PARKCHESTER, THE BRONX**

KILL WHITEY DAY

BY MICHELE CARLO

I was standing in the basement of Macy's Parkchester in the Bronx, in a line of what seemed like a thousand teenagers smoking both cigarettes and weed, chanting and cheering and waiting for Ticketmaster to open. Adult shoppers were nonexistent and salespeople had abandoned their posts either in foreknowledge or in fear, except the lone Ticketmaster employee at the window way beyond where I could see. All around me were kids I knew, but I acknowledged no one. I was on a mission.

It was a little past ten o'clock on a weekday morning. You might be thinking that we all should have been in school. Yes, we should have, and maybe some of us would have, except for one thing: Led Zeppelin was coming to Madison Square Garden and tickets were about to go on sale. In those primitive analog days before cable TV, cell phones, and the Internet, you listened to your favorite FM radio station day and night, non-stop, waiting for the DJ to announce the day and time concert tickets would go on sale. And then you lined up at the nearest Ticketmaster and you waited. If it was a weekday, fuck school. Who in their right mind would go to school when for seven dollars and fifty cents, you could see Kashmir.

I didn't get a ticket that morning. Not because they had sold-out, but because I didn't have enough money. Even the blue nosebleed seats were now five dollars and fifty cents—a whole dollar more than the year before—and I wasn't the only one who was disappointed. Some of the kids were so disappointed they started tearing up the sales floor, tagging walls, throwing mannequins around, and cursing. I was having none of that. I had spent a half hour in Central Booking for vandalism once and wasn't eager to repeat the experience. So at ten-thirty, I left Macy's with my five crumpled one-dollar bills, and walked back to school, figuring the day wasn't a total loss, as I had only missed three periods. I got to school a little past eleven, and right away saw something was up. For one thing, there was a phalanx of cop cars around Westchester Square train station. For another, I heard the yelling all the way down the hill. And then I remembered.

Today was Kill Whitey Day.

I know that in some alternate universe, one's high school days are a halcyon, carefree time, with fond, gauzy memories of homecoming days, pep rallies, and proms. But at my high school, Herbert H. Lehman High (fondly referred to in those days as Lehman State Prison), the pivotal events we had to look forward to each spring were Kill Whitey Day and Kill Black & Puerto Rican Day.

It's said that gangs are cyclical in NYC. There were gangs in the 1950s. There are gangs now. And in the mid- and late-1970s, teenage New York was a city divided and ruled from Parkchester out to Morris Park and up to Throgs Neck by the white gangs The Bronx Aliens and Bronx Ministers. Their black and Latino counterparts, The Savage Skulls, Savage Nomads, Mongol Brothers, and the biker gang The Ching-A-Lings claimed everywhere south of Soundview Avenue, and west, past Yankee Stadium and Fordham Road, all the way to the Harlem River. Every spring, every high school would have their week or so when they would be at war. And as in any war, any unfortunate civilians who found themselves behind the front lines would just have to get by as best they could.

The messed-up thing about it was, you knew exactly when it was all going to go down. The information crossed gang, racial, and ethnic lines and flashed through your entire school faster than group text messaging locks down a campus today. You *knew* when your Kill Day was going to be. And not going to school that day was not an option. Because everyone would know you had punked out and your own neighborhood would make you a pariah for being a faggot, a pussy, for not having enough heart to risk getting a major beatdown with everyone else.

Lehman High School, being in a mostly Italian neighborhood, was Bronx Ministers territory. But by some fate of late sixties decentralization, half the student population was white, the other, black or Latino. So Lehman was a school doubly "blessed" as it observed both Kill Days. Kill Black & Puerto Rican Day had been the week before, and luckily I had escaped unscathed. Not so the year before, when two Italian boys stabbed me in the shoulder with a stiletto. Not because they specifically hated *me*, but because a couple of Savage Skulls had whipped them with a car antenna. And since they weren't motivated (brave/stupid) enough to go down to the Bronx River Projects to exact revenge, the next best thing was to attack me. They both actually apologized to me later and hoped I understood it wasn't personal. I still have the scar.

Since not going into school was not an option, I went around the back way, where I knew (and security amazingly didn't) a door was always propped open. Fourth period was about to begin and something told me not to try to sneak a cigarette before entering the relative safety of health class. But I was nervous, so I took the chance. I peeked into the girls' bathroom and seeing no one, ducked into the last stall and immediately assumed the smoker's position: crouched on the toilet seat so someone bending down to check the stalls wouldn't see my feet, constantly waving my right arm back and forth so the curling smoke wouldn't give me away, either. A few minutes later, the New-port Light just wasn't doing it for me, but I decided to have one more drag. Famous last words.

I was about to flush the cigarette when the door opened and four black girls came in. I knew they were black because of their names. Keishas and Tawandas were in utero or just being born. Girls my age were the last of a generation who were still named after jewels and desirable attributes: Crystal, Ruby, Precious, and Unity. Delicate flowers who stashed razor blades in their afros and carried rolls of pennies balled up in their bandanas. I knew who they were because of their reputation. They were finely-tuned, Black Pride lionesses who hunted their prey with particular savagery: what they caught, they would not release. And I knew that if they caught me, I was a goner. Because none of them would stop to ask a light-skinned, freckle-faced redhead where her family was born before they beat the hell out of her.

"Dag, Ruby, you see that blond bitch face when we knocked her toof out?"

"Yeah, but shoo, my hand cut up. Precious, watch the door. Oh shit, you smell something? Who in here?"

I had neglected to do the one thing that could have saved me, which was to douse the cigarette and keep still. There wasn't a thing I could do except wait as the four of them opened the stalls one by one until they found me. It was pointless to fight back. One, definitely. Two, maybe. But there were four of them. And it would have been suicide to try to tell them they were making a mistake. The year before, an olive-skinned Irish girl named Ellen something-or-other had tried to say she was half-Puerto Rican and she ended up being held down and raped with an umbrella. That was not going to happen to me.

They pulled me off the toilet and threw me on the floor. I rolled into a ball and tried to protect my face as they punched, kicked, and penny-rolled me. How long? Too long. And then, the door opened.

"Yo, Nan-cee, we got another white girl, you want some?"

I looked up through one swollen, tear-and-Afro sheen-clouded eye and saw Nancy Ortiz walk in. Nancy, who really was half-Puerto Rican and half-Irish, was one of those anomalies in our little world, a blessed creature who moved seamlessly between the races, befriending everyone, beat up by none. She came over to look at me.

"Dag, man, that girl ain't white, she's Puerto Rican."

"What?"

"She's Puerto Rican. That's Shell, I know her from home-room. She's from St. Peter's, but she's Puerto Rican. She just looks white."

The punches stopped. A razor blade whizzed by my left cheek and clattered onto the tiles.

The one called Unity said, "She's Puerto Rican?" and prodded me with her Pro-Ked.

"I axed you, you Puerto Rican?"

I spit out a trail of blood and snot and croaked out the only thing I could think of. "Si."

"See, I told you. Stoopid!" And Nancy, having secured her eternal place in heaven, left the bathroom.

Four pairs of eyes saw me as a person for the first time. "Oh man! We sorry." "Oh man, we sorry." "Shoo! Why didn't she say something?" "Why didn't you say nothing?" "Come on, help that girl up." That was Unity, their leader talking. And Crystal, Ruby, and Precious picked me up off the floor, patted my hair, and tried to rearrange my clothes. "Get some water, clean her up," Unity commanded. The girls ran to the sink, wet their bandanas and daubed at my face. I took Ruby's pink bandana and walked to the mirror to clean myself. She didn't protest.

"This ain't right," Unity said. "We sorry, Shell. We didn't know. Why didn't you say nothing? You're not gonna tell, right? We gonna make it up to you. C'mon. Give her your weed."

Crystal, Precious, and Ruby all looked down at their sneakers.

"I said, give her your weed," yelled Unity. "Give it up!"

And one by one, the girls reached into their afros and their tube socks and pulled out crooked joints rolled in banana, chocolate, and strawberry E-Z Wider. Mutely, with averted eyes, they handed them to me. "We sorry," Crystal mumbled. "Yeah, man, we sorry," Ruby said. But not Precious. She had been standing on the other side of the bathroom and was now trying to sidle her way toward the door. But she couldn't get away from Unity's watchful eye. Unity's fist shot out: Biff! And punched the side of Precious' head so hard her afro pick flew into the sink, clattering in front of me. "I said, give her your weed, bitch!" Precious's hand trembled as she dug around her bra and finally handed me a crumpled, sweat-stained, half-full nickel bag.

"Look, we sorry, it was a mistake, right?" Unity said. "You're not gonna tell right? I mean, like we did you a solid and all. Come on, let's go kick some real white ass." And just like that, they left. I stood there for a moment and totally accepted what had happened as just the way things were. I still couldn't quite believe my luck in escaping with just a cut lip and black eye. And then I looked at what was balled up in my clenched fist—and I did believe it. I walked right out of school and over to Zappa's Corner where I sold all the pot, then ran back to Macy's, getting there just before Ticketmaster closed at four o'clock.

The day wasn't a total waste after all. I was going to see Kashmir.

ROOM WITH A VIEW

BY STACIA J. N. DECKER

Matt worked on the forty-third floor of a building one block from Grand Central. When people came to visit, we took them up to the forty-sixth floor conference room and let them look out the windows at the rooftop gardens and into other office windows and down Park Avenue, stretching away below in orderly blocks. Paint lines on the pavement, clusters of green along the medians, traffic massing and criss-crossing—it all looked neat and clean from that height, and you could see all the bus numbers painted on their roofs, all part of a system. At night, the city was a pattern of lightbulbs. The traffic signals would change color and the cars would stop and start for a mile, all champagne-yellow headlamps one way, red taillights the other.

The conference room was on the corner, half-walled with windows on two sides. We would silently move from one bank to another, raising the blinds and pressing our foreheads to the glass, and then cross the hall to a larger conference room and start again, pointing out to our guests where buildings were, or where they used to be.

The view was proof that Matt's father had been wrong when he asked him what he would do when he had to move back to

Kansas, broke, because he couldn't find a job in New York. Proof that Matt had not just gotten a job, but a real job, even if he had dropped out of college. Matt had interviewed for the position in a smaller version of these conference rooms, standing at the windows and looking at the view from the forty-second floor as he answered the lawyer in Philadelphia, whose disembodied voice came out of the speakerphone in the middle of the conference room table. The law firm hired Matt after that interview to run reports on the world's largest sex-discrimination class action suit. And sometimes, after ten or twelve or sixteen-hour days, Matt would slip into a conference room and look out at the view.

The building was entirely covered in black glass panels, with its street number prominently displayed above the revolving doors of its lobby. The building's owners had taken the number for the building's name—it was in the elevators and woven into the carpets, and appeared on the security guards' blazers. The building's official entrance was off Fortieth Street, and the building sat back, facing the corner of Fortieth and Park at an angle, with a triangular granite plaza before it, a fountain to the side. When the cow sculptures had come to the city, they had put one in front of Matt's building—a heifer in pink gingham.

Rumor had it that the makers of *The Devil's Advocate*, the movie with Al Pacino and Keanu Reeves, had planned to use the building and its conference rooms, but the deal had fallen through. *Seinfeld* did use the façade to stand in for one of George's workplaces. And I had recognized the plaza and lobby behind women photographed for a fashion magazine's on-the-street poll. Indeed, the first thing we had done after Matt found out he'd gotten the job was take pictures of him on that plaza, tilting the camera up to catch as much of the building as possible. We had to cross Park to get a better shot. It was spring, and the planters along the avenue were full of daffodils. We sent a picture of Matt leaning against a planter, the daffodils beside him and the black glass building behind him, home to his parents. Everything looked neat and clean, and Matt looked happy and successful already—proof that we hadn't been wrong to get married all of a sudden and move to New York. Proof that it wasn't all rats in the subway and us cashing in Matt's 401(k) to pay the rent.

As much as its skyline has been photographed, New York is a city fetishistically shown from above, by both the media and artists. ("Amazing how much we've been able to pack onto this island!") In November 2001, in the fit of a transplanted New Yorker, Matt ordered the entire seven-DVD series of Ric Burns's *New York* from Channel 13, clutching his credit card as he paced in front of the television on Thanksgiving Day. In every segment, the city is shown from above, by map and by camera. Often these shots look contemporary—the familiar patterns of lightbulbs at night—no matter what time period the segment features. This is the way we see New York. This is the way we get a handle on it. It is impossible to see for any distance down on the streets. We need to get on top to get perspective, to lose perspective, to feel in control, to feel awed, to feel free as the camera flies over the tip of the Chrystler Building.

Moving to the city, it seemed as though most of New York's great sights consisted of just that—the ability to see—whether it was the view from the Empire State Building, the Statue of Liberty's crown, or the World Trade Center's observation deck, which my friends from home, visiting in the spring of 2001, decided to skip when they found out it had an admission fee. I never went back to see it myself. After all, we had the view from Matt's office for free. And it didn't matter that his own office had no windows, or that our first-floor apartment had no view at all, beyond a stone wall and parts of old refrigerators, or that we would never be able to afford the apartments that were expensive because of their views. We had our own New York view—proof that we had made it.

MONTHLY NUT

BY JAMES BRALY

I am sitting at my desk in my co-op one day on the Upper West Side of Manhattan, going over my monthly expenses: co-op mortgage; co-op maintenance; co-op insurance; four other kinds of insurance—health, for four people (I've got a stay-at-home wife and two kids), life, in case I die on them, disability, in case I collapse, and car, in case I abandon them; along with the home phone, office phone, cell phone, wife's phone, credit card, wife's card, and on and on. Three inches of sedimentary expenses, that have accumulated layer by inexorable layer. And when I do the math: one month of income minus one month of expenses, I get minus-one-month of income. Twice as much as I earned, turning the black numbers on my computer's financial software red. Leading me to transfer enough savings over to my checking account to balance it and turn the red numbers back to black. Which leaves me, at my current fixed rate of spending, with about three more months of savings to go before both accounts are red. Financial ruin. A conclusion that leads me, as it did the last time I reached this conclusion—last month—to hyperventilate. I can't go on living like this. I can't afford to be me.

The problem is, I can't afford not to. I *am* my lifestyle, most importantly, most expensively, co-op on Central Park West; movie stars, moguls, and me.

I didn't grow up wanting to be a co-op. I was raised by my mom to believe I could be anything in life—as long as it paid well. So I thought I'd be the President of the United States. Or an NFL quarterback. Or a rock star. Then when I got to college, a Nobel Prize-winning writer—who I read somewhere get a prize of $500,000. I'd been writing lots of papers at the time, and this seemed like a logical career path.

So when I graduated, I rented a little apartment with my girlfriend on the Upper West Side and started writing marketing speeches for pharmaceutical executives selling drugs for things like seasonal allergies, and then a few years later, as drugs got more sophisticated and I moved up the speechwriting food chain, erectile dysfunction and schizophrenia—to subsidize writing Nobel Prize-winning stories at night about, well, nothing—because I was too tired to write about anything else. And too venal. Stories about nothing didn't pay like speeches on erectile dysfunction and schizophrenia. Okay, so I was losing my drive and my mind and my priorities, but I had bills to pay, and they were getting bigger all the time.

Every Sunday night, on long-distance life planning chats, my mom advised me "Dreams are important. But renting is for nothings."

So I struggled and saved and bought a one-bedroom co-op in a fancy building on Central Park West. I wanted to be a something.

When my mom visited, she proclaimed, "This is something. But isn't it a little small, honey?"

I said, "Space is money, mom."

She said, "I see no reason why a bright boy like you can't double your income every year."

This sounded like an excellent financial plan to me, so to get a jump on my future of infinitely-doubling wealth, I got straight to work doubling my monthly nut. I bought the studio next door to my one-bedroom, then combined the two spaces and renovated everything. Then subtracted my wife's salary when she stopped working to have a baby. Then added the baby, and then added another. Then sent the first one to private school (though, like most three-year-olds, he was illiterate). Until I found that I had stopped even trying to write stories in order to write speeches to write checks in a co-op where I worked, ate, slept, and on occasion, asked myself: *Who are you?*

The answer was, the co-op. In the same building as Keanu Reeves. Neo is my neighbor. And I am his. For another ninety days—at which point eviction proceedings will begin for nonpayment of maintenance.

Which is why I'm sitting at my desk, hyperventilating.

So I get up and walk to the lobby to get some air and get my mail, which today includes a letter marked "Personal" and addressed to "Resident" from a neighborhood real estate broker; when you are your co-op, brokers are your friends. I open the letter, and it begins, "Dear Resident: Do you know what you're worth?" going on to describe how the rise in real estate values has quite possibly made me worth more than I realize—a value that she, my friendly neighborhood real estate broker, would be glad to determine with a no-cost appraisal of my apartment.

That Sunday, as I'm reading the *New York Times* real estate ads—comparing my worth to everybody else's on the Upper West Side—I see an ad for our apartment. The broker had come over, talked to my wife, and listed it without ever asking us: a bold ploy to win our business that evidently is successful with the bold residents moving in to fancy buildings like mine.

Another reason I want to sell my apartment: I loathe my fellow residents.

Another reason I want to stay: to make them see how loathsome they are!

Where I come from, the whole point of being alive is to win—money and arguments, the more dysfunctional the better. For example, last Christmas, my next door neighbor—a forty-two-year-old female dot-com tycoon—submitted a formal complaint against me for "storing personal property in a public space." Exhibit A, a time-stamped digital photograph of my Christmas tree leaning against my front door, while I filled the Christmas tree stand in my living room with water. Now, some people might ignore such a complaint, or knock on the neighbor's door and offer her eggnog. I decided that the proper response was to run for the board of directors of the co-op, on a platform of exposing neighbors like the dot-com tycoon as loathsome—even if everyone moving into the building is just like her, and I have neither the time nor the interest to serve on the board of directors, and if I sell my apartment, I won't even be here.

So I'm sitting in my home, reading the ad in the *Times* and seeing my co-op—my self—for sale, for the first time, daydreaming: what would it feel like to let go…and be someone else? To care about things other than winning arguments and contests for money and approval that make me hyperventilate?

I call up another real estate broker: a low-key guy who is aggressively anti-aggressive and who tells my wife and me that he hates people like the dot-com tycoon next-door more than we do; he understands us as customers completely. And he comes over with a photographer, and the next Sunday our apartment is for sale again, with pictures.

A few weeks later, sitting on my desk is a signed contract of sale from a would-be buyer, waiting only for me to countersign and send it back. It's my birthday. So I take the day off and mull it over—staring out the window at a view that I may never again be able to afford and that I can't afford now—unless, once and for all, I abandon any hope of doing work that I care about, and commit the rest of my life to trying to double my income. Like I was raised to do.

That night, my wife throws me a little birthday party with a few friends on the roof deck of our building. It looks out over Central Park and Fifth Avenue and Midtown, so just standing there makes you feel like a movie star. Across the street, you can see a terrace filled with pink bougainvillea—a terrace that used to belong to my friend Ted, who sold it so he could do more in life than simply work to live there. It's a beautiful summer night, so everyone lines up at the edge of the roof to watch the sunset.

My friend Andy jokes, "What *do* you do for a living?" not knowing that I bought my co-op at the bottom of the market, and that I'm about to declare personal bankruptcy. Why spoil the party?

My friend John says, "This place is incredible." Which feels like he's saying, "You are incredible."

I say, "I'm thinking of selling it, and living some place cheaper." Then I tell my friend Ted, who's staring at his old bougainvillea, "Please say you're happier now than when you were living *there*, above your means."

"Absolutely," says Ted. "When I don't think about that terrace."

A few hours later, for the first time in memory—which is usually squeezed blank by the crushing weight of my overhead— I have a dream. I'm sitting on the face of a dark volcano—about halfway up, which is where I live in my building—holding on to a ledge, frozen in terror, trying to slide down without falling. Pebbles are rolling out from under my shoes and into the molten abyss.

Suddenly, from behind, it's Puff Daddy: white track suit, mirrored sunglasses, diamonds, and gold. He was up at Keanu's place. "This the way down?" says Puff. I say, "Yes." And off he goes—like a mountain goat in bling; this is his territory. Then I see a cave in the side of the volcano with a young boy in it, who is also afraid to move. I say, "I can help you," lying—I need help myself. Then bougainvillea-Ted appears and says, "There's an easy way down…over here." And he takes one boy's hand and I take the other, and the three of us start walking to Lincoln, the president I wanted to be growing up, who was shot for taking the road less traveled, before giving his name to a street in Brooklyn where my wife and I have been looking at affordable rentals filled with people my mom might call nothings, which in my dream feels like something much, much closer to home.

**2225 EDSALL AVE,
MARBLE HILL, THE BRONX**

ON THE TRAIN TRACKS IN MARBLE HILL A.K.A. MANONX, NEW YORK CITY—THE CIRCUMSIZED NORTH END OF MANHHHAAATAAAN

BY SUHAEY ROSARIO

That morning, I got up in the afternoon. My friend Micki came from 204th and Post Avenue, from her man's crib, complaining about his small penis saying, "My baby brother's got a bigger dick than his!"

I had to get up and shower, leaving her in my room, and I took the loofah with me because I scrub the dead skin off my body every Saturday. My father says that as a Puerto Rican he only showers once a week, on Saturday, so that's when I scrub; my arms, back, neck, between my breasts, and above my torso. I head into the bathroom head down, rolling and bobbing. She does not smoke one of her Newports, afraid of getting hit with a lecture; afraid the plan might crash and burn.

LOST AND FOUND

When I come out, I feel that weirdness of being half-naked. My closet is full of clothing that I am not allowed to wear, and I really can't remember what it's doing there, except that I have a sister and she has a job on Riverdale Avenue. I open the closet door to unwrap my body, and dress behind it as if it were a screen protecting Micki and me from each other, because we spend so much time together that I am uptight.

I get into my drawers, top, bottom, and kicks, and put a rubber band in my hair. We get outside and Micki does not light a cigarette. With "stupid" written across my forehead, I decide to go to her crib from my crib. We go through C-ROCK, which is like dope for delinquents. All the thugs around Marble Hill and Inwood have climbed it, and jumped off its erection. Diving into the river across the street from my flat has killed a few, but how many more birds or people has the Metro North taken? Obviously not nearly enough if you believe in learning the hard way: with a beating.

Watching our backs, we cross the street and take a quarter block uphill, then down the steps and walk past all the commercials. At the end, getting ready to jump off the platform, onto the rocks of the tracks—it makes my adrenaline rush and I feel quickly that I am "double-zero 35771105am" and not a wise ass, like my eee-con teacher says at City-As-School.

Micki and I will probably smoke a blunt of that cancer-curing marijuana in a White Owl cigar skin, maybe a Dutch Master. The coast is clear except for the people attending gym at John F. Kennedy High School outside on their football field.

We don't see the authorities and keep moving, first quickly, then just strolling. Finally we arrive at the place behind the sky blue letter C—framed in white and large for all to see, representing Columbia University. Here is a nice safe place where we settle down, a place you cannot hear the train ah-coming and everything is peaceful.

SMALLS,
OR THE PLACE WHERE
ALL THE LADDERS START

BY MAURA KELLY

If you asked me to choose a single event to mark the beginning of my long love affair with the city, it would be my first night at Smalls—the tiny West Village speakeasy where the jam sessions kept going past dawn, where some of the musicians lived in the back rooms when they had no place else to go, and where the city's jazz kids developed into giants.

It was 1999 and I was living in DC—doing some writing for *The Washington Post*, working at at a coffee shop in Dupont Circle—when I took a trip to Manhattan to spend a long weekend with a guy I'd just met.

James was his name—a scrawny architect, a friend of a friend. He lived in a studio on West Tenth, just down the street from Three Lives Bookstore. We'd sit on his fire escape to smoke, wear each other's jeans, and sleep together in his bed under an old map of the city, with calligraphic letters and fraying edges. He took me to all his favorite spots in his neighborhood. Of those, Smalls was best.

LOST AND FOUND

As we approached the club late that baptismal Friday night, a guy was sitting off to the side of an otherwise unremarkable door. He had the slow, wise eyes of a lizard and a head so bald it seemed hair had never dared grow there. Other than a crocheted hippie beret, his clothes were unremarkable. He appeared to be both older than me—I was young enough that everyone did—and somehow ageless. In his lap, a well-worn book was open like a hymnal, and he would glance at it occasionally, although he seemed less concerned with reading it than with watching the streets, waiting for someone to arrive.

But who? Godot? The Man?

Us, as it turned out. Or customers, at least. He was the Charon for that underworld, collecting the entrance fee. He was Smalls' owner, Mitch.

I was already tipsy by then, thanks not only to wine but also to the boy with good cheekbones by my side and the spell of New York. So when I saw that Mitch had a collection by Yeats, I interpreted it as one more omen that I was finally where I belonged. I couldn't help saying playfully: "Are we about to go down into the foul rag and bone shop of the heart?"

Mitch came right back with: "Isn't that where you have to begin? Where all the ladders start?" It was a quote from the poem I'd alluded to, "The Circus Animals' Desertion."

Mitch was an eccentric who seemed to plant a riddle in every sentence. And by uttering that Yeatsian shibboleth, I'd joined his game before he'd even invited me in.

After James and I descended, we pushed through a velvet curtain to a small, smoky room. It was packed with people listening to the slew of musicians crowded onto a wooden stage: saxophonists and saxophones of every size, a couple of trumpeters, a pianist, a bassist, a drummer, even a man pulling a slide trombone. They played underneath a sepia-toned photograph of a beaming young man, outfitted in culottes and argyle socks pulled up to his knees, his arms resting on his folded legs, who seemed to be guarding the place, god-like, a crucifix over an altar. But he hadn't died for anyone's sins—not Louis Armstrong.

In that shrine to jazz, the other pictures covering the walls were of Billie Holiday, Charlie Parker, Miles Davis, Nina Simone, Sidney Bechet. There were wooden icons of men blowing horns. There was the burning of a certain pungent holy weed by a few devotees in a far corner. There was the congregation in their seats, bobbing and swaying like they were swooning or praying.

We seemed to have been transported back in time. I couldn't believe a place like that existed outside of the past or my dreams. It was exactly where I'd wanted to be every other night in my life that I'd gone out—full of beautiful music and odd characters, where a new improvisational drama was always being performed—but I had never seen anything like it before.

Hours later, near dawn, full of pale ale and heavy jazz, James and I made our way out. We found Mitch at the bottom of the stairwell this time and gushed about what a time we'd had, before sauntering back to the apartment across Seventh Avenue. The sky was just starting to ripen into the gold of morning, and the only other people around were the dog-walkers and the grocery-delivery men. They seemed like extras on the scene. At that moment, I could have sworn that New York belonged entirely to James and me.

After that, I couldn't hold myself back from the Big Apple any longer. Despite my fears, despite my poverty, despite my insignificance, I was hopeful. I moved to New York a month later, certain that it would become—as it has—the only place where I've truly felt at home, even though I've lived in five different cities, four states, and two continents. James hadn't promised me anything, and he wasn't a big consideration as I made my decision, athough of course I'd imagined some kind of future with him in which we'd become regulars at Smalls, eat dinner at Chumley's once a week, and walk around those cobblestone streets like Dylan and his girl on the *Freewheelin'* cover.

When our fling ended after I'd been in town about four weeks, I didn't handle it very graciously. We'd spent a long, chilly, surreal day in Coney Island, drinking beers out of paper cups from Nathan's Famous hot dogs as we huddled on boardwalk benches, watching the waves roll in and the drunks stumble by. On our way back to the subway, we stared through a chain-link fence at old men with small brushes who were painting a roller-coaster black as opera music blasted from their boom box. Later that night, we tried to kiss in my loft-bed but we couldn't shake the cold and couldn't find the rhythm. Finally, James rolled onto his back and told me that he didn't know what was wrong with him, but he'd lost interest.

"Maybe you're gay!" I shouted, though I knew that wasn't true. Looking back, I realize that at least part of the problem was that I wouldn't have sex with him; I was still waiting, absurdly, to feel true love.

When he said he was going to leave, I furiously kicked a hole in the sheetrock wall near his head. That scared the hell out of both of us. He scrambled down my bed ladder and out the door. And after he left, in a fit of temporary madness, I decided that shoving off to Smalls would be the best way to cheer myself up. Nevermind that it was already early morning by then.

Mitch, who was standing at the back of the main room watching the performers when I arrived, wasn't surprised to see me. I'd become a fixture by then, laying the ground work before I'd even moved to town by scribbling out a poem by Philip Levine called "I Remember Clifford"—about the first time Levine heard his favorite trumpet player—on the back of the postcard which I sent to Mitch, care of Smalls. (Levine once said: "The poem is concerned with the sudden generosity of the world, the unexplainable giving that occurs in the midst of deprivation, for I discovered...Clifford deep in the misery of one of the hardest years of my life.")

Mitch greeted me with some kind of gnomic pronouncement, to which I responded with a comment that was incomprehensible, even to me. Then I hurried over to a free seat and promptly burst into tears. Embarrassed, I ducked into the broom closet, hoping to hide out until I could get my act together, praying that the darkness had covered my tracks.

No such luck. After swinging open the door, Mitch tried to tug me to my feet while I sagged stubbornly like a rag doll. "I can't let you be miserable all by yourself in there," he said.

"Sure you can!" I retorted. "That's the whole point!"

"You have to come out and be with people." He kept jostling my shoulder, and finally I understood he wasn't going to leave me alone until I cooperated. I stood up, hiding my face in my hands, and let him steer me to a seat at the bar. "My friend Richard is going to look out for you," Mitch said. "Right Richard?" Someone murmured yes, and then Mitch went on: "Cry all you want to him. He's a nice guy. I've got to go work the door."

When this Richard threw an arm around me, I buried myself in his chest without even looking to see if he was toothless or dis-figured or three-headed. Only after he'd been consoling me through one long song, only after I'd worked through enough of my hysteria to realize that the way he was rubbing my back felt very good, only then did I finally pull my head out of his armpit and took a good look at him.

It was frightening, how pretty he was. Shoulder-length black hair curled behind his ears, framing a handsome olive-skinned face with huge dark eyes and full rose-petal lips. Somehow, I managed to gather my courage and smile back at him. And then I started hiccuping. As if to quell my spasms, Richard pulled me into him again, but that only made me quiver more. I realized that if he tried to make out with me right there at Smalls, in front of Mitch and all the other guys I'd gotten to know, I'd be pow-erless to resist. So I pulled away and said, "Listen. I live really close, just over on West Eleventh between Greenwich and Wash-ington." (Miraculously, I was paying only $400 a month to share a friend's aunt's apartment.) "You should come sleep over. But all I want is for you to hold me. Then leave in the morning and we never see each other again. No sex, no strings, no nothing. Just one night of holding. Capiche?" Where was I coming up with my lines? I felt like I was playing the heroine in some   B-grade romantic comedy.

But Richard went along with it. "That sounds nice," he said. "And it's probably best, since I do want to spend the night with you but I have a girlfriend."

The girlfriend was away for the next few months, as it turned out. So that afternoon, after we made a late breakfast, we exchanged numbers, and for the next couple months, we had an innocent little affair. We'd stand on corners, kissing, like the happy couple in a breath mint commercial. We'd bring our own wine to a cheap Italian place, Tanti Baci, across the street from Smalls, and have dinner there. We'd often run out of things to say, but when we did, we'd just stroll around those cobblestone streets, swinging our hands while Richard whistled like a bird. He didn't have much of a brain, Richard, but he did have a sweet heart. For both those reasons, it was easy to drift apart once his girlfriend returned. My feelings for Smalls were much more complicated, though, so I stuck with the place much longer, often ending up there in the wee hours, alone, looking for trouble or solace, often finding both.

Two years of hard drinking and minor drug use passed. One night, I hid out at Smalls after bumming a ride across town with a crazy Russian limo driver, so he wouldn't be able to find me once he'd finished his duties. We'd snorted blow in the front seat, off his clipboard, and then he had to drop me off so he could pick up his paying clients, but he'd either promised or threatened to come back for me afterwards. On a few other occasions, I got so drunk that Mitch walked me to my door. (He never tried anything, and after a time or two, I realized he wasn't going to.) It was around that time that I started blacking out. I can only remember a few parts of the night when I escaped from the club without Mitch noticing, only to stumble into a bar a few blocks away. I ordered a glass of wine and didn't learn until it was down the hatch that they didn't take plastic. I had no cash. The owner, who observed me pleading with the barmaid, told me not to worry—and then took me back to his place so we could inhale a bag full of powder. What I remember is waking up naked in his bed with a black velvet comforter over me. He was on the couch, still fast asleep. I snuck out, tiptoeing across the black-and-white checkerboard of the parquet floor in the lobby, and when I stepped into the gray day, I had no idea where I was.

I'm not sure if it was luck or some kind of talent for picking particularly benevolent coke fiends, but it still amazes me that I never got into serious trouble. And yet some phone had been ringing with a wake-up call for a long time before I finally came to one morning, only to find myself on my futon, in a state of dishabille, with a stranger who was peeling open a condom.

"What are you doing?" I said. "And who are you?"

Then I recognized him: He led the big band that got top billing at Smalls. I kicked him out, and once I recovered from my hangover—about a week later—I realized the time had come to say goodbye to my wilding.

I swore off drinking and drugs. I quit smoking. I decided Smalls had to go, too. As much as I would miss it, that period of my life needed to end.

Though I never explained any of this to Mitch, I assumed he understood; I assumed he saw a lot of people come and go; I assumed he knew that he and Smalls would always have a place in my heart—and I hoped that he would have one in his for me.

But he was less and less friendly whenever I'd stopped by on my way home to say hello, so eventually I started taking a different route.

Two years had passed when I heard the news from some old Smalls friends: the joint was closing! The next weekend would be its last.

I went by early that Saturday night. No one was at the door so I walked down and grabbed a seat just as the music was starting. My buddy Ari was on bass, playing with some other guys

I'd hung out with a few times at his place. After they finished their first set, Ari came over and we were chatting when Mitch walked up to collect the cover charge from me.

"Ten bucks," he said, without acknowledging that he knew me.

"Come on, Mitch," Ari said. "She's free. She's my guest tonight."

"What?" Mitch said. "This girl is your guest? This girl who knows about Smalls and still never comes?" Without another word, he turned on his heel and walked away.

A few minutes later, the second set began, and I settled in, letting the tinkling of the piano, the swish of the brush over the cymbals and the chatter of ice cubes against glass soften the sharp edges of my mind.

Around midnight, feeling sated and sober and strange, I walked out, leaving a crowd of the faithful behind to see it through to the very end. After squeezing up the steps, which were crowded with people hoping to get in—Smalls had become something of a phenomenon by then—I spotted Mitch at the top, off to the side, observing the line that was stretching around the corner.

Stopping in front of him, I said, "Good night. And thank you for all this."

He glanced at me, then looked at all the waiting faces. "I feel like I'm at my funeral," he said to no one in particular.

I was trying to figure out the right response when someone else came over to ask Mitch what was happening. He turned his back on me to explain. And realizing we'd said our farewell a long time ago, I slipped off into the night.

GEE THE KIDS NEED CLOTHES

BY CHRISTINE CALIFRA-SCHIFF

My mother was a talented seamstress, so for the earlier part of my childhood, most of my clothes were homemade. She loved embroidering tiny flowers and animals on dress pockets, basting collars and hand-sewing French hems. This was the early-seventies and downtown parents had two choices in kids' clothing: they could shop for the cheap polyester found along Fourteenth Street, or take the subway uptown to Macy's, B. Altman's, or Bloomingdale's, and spend what seemed like a fortune on high-quality clothing. A good friend of my father's gave me an impractical article of clothing from B. Altman's every Christmas, and I remember the joy of getting to go exchange it for something exquisite and equally impractical. Foremost in my memory is returning a very lacy set of pajamas for an orange go-go dress when I was in second grade. But aside from these occasional jaunts uptown, my mother couldn't afford to shop for my sister and me in any of these stores with the living my father made as a sculptor, wood carver, and carpenter.

Then our next-door neighbor, a mother of two boys, one of whom went on to form the Beastie Boys (no, we never played together) opened a little shop on West Tenth Street called Gee the Kids Need Clothes. Most of the merchandise was second-hand, refurbished with cool patches that said things like "Keep On Truckin" and "Peace," as well as swatches of calico and velvet. I am sure my first pair of real Levi's came from that store, as about the only things my mother didn't make herself were jeans, socks, underwear, and the occasional red polo shirt. I remember the interior of the shop was painted a bright yellow, and there was probably a mural or at least stencils of some sort decorating the walls. It had that happy, sunny, kid-friendly feel, and how I loved going in to try on clothes.

Best of all was the official Gee the Kids Need Clothes T-shirt, with an outline of a little boy from the back, in a Paddington style hat. The name of the shop arched around the child who I had always assumed was a little girl—I'm now convinced it was a boy—and the words Greenwich Village sat below his feet. I had two of them—one in royal blue with white writing and the other in yellow with orange writing. My mother still has one put away in a box labeled "Chris's Favorites." I don't remember how long the shop survived during the tumultuous seventies. It doesn't seem like it was very long. I know the family moved out of their house and there was talk of a divorce. I remember my mother being sad the shop was closing.

There were no Gap Kids and Old Navy back then. There were barely any chain stores at all in Greenwich Village. I was well into elementary school before the first McDonald's opened near the West Fourth Street basketball courts.

I can tell you of at least four drugstores with soda fountains whose owners sold you a bottle of Coke syrup when you had the stomach flu. They have since been replaced at least three times over. Families that owned townhouses then hadn't paid a million dollars for them. Most had paid less than a hundred thousand. I don't know how a family like mine could ever live in New York City now, let alone the Village. And I know for a sure a shop like Gee the Kids Need Clothes could never open in the West Village these days.

But I'm a mother myself now, and my sewing machine sits idle in the basement. I bought it secondhand when I was in college with the best intentions, but the needle just moved too fast and I feared my fingers would end up attached to something other than my hand. I suppose a good amount of my mother's hard work was based on our need at the time. And I'll admit that I have no problem shopping at Gap Kids and Gymboree. But I also know when the stomach flu strikes, I'd be hard-pressed to find a bottle of Coke syrup in this town.

THE SCREAM
BY ELIZABETH FRANKENBERGER

It had been a shitty summer. I left one miserable job for another, better one that paid me a lot less. To save money, I moved from a one-bedroom apartment to a studio across the hall. The dead bolt on the new door was tricky, and so it slammed on my hand one day, leaving me with a broken middle finger.

"You were lucky," the surgeon had said before shooting Novocaine into my palm. "You'll have your nail back by the spring."

My other bad break wasn't as easy to mend, though the left-over Vicodin proved helpful. He was never mine and never would be. To make up for this fact, I spent an exorbitant amount of money on massages and pedicures and perfume and high-thread-count sheets—anything, I resolved, to slough and soften the sharp edges of my pain. Yes, I felt sorry for myself, even sorrier for my friends. They listened, and consoled, and made me promise that I wouldn't see him, or sleep with him again; of course they knew I would, and did anyway.

That summer, like most New Yorkers, I read *The Lovely Bones* and dreaded the anniversary of the 11th. And then it was over: the 2,801 names had been named, the 1/9 train would stop

416

at South Ferry, and he would ask for her hand in marriage. She would accept it, and I would accept that too. There was nothing left to cry about. It was time to heal, to move the fuck on. I threw away my dirty flip-flops and forged full-speed ahead towards fall.

I celebrated the change in season by buying a new alarm clock, a Sony Psyc. With its bright blue exterior and huge neon numbers, it was just what I needed to psyche myself out of bed each morning, early, and put me back on a writing schedule. I bought it on Monday, September 23rd, the first official day of the equinox. On Tuesday morning I woke up to music—late, since it was classical. Wednesday was better, a symphony of beeps, but I never made it to the computer. Thursday, ditto, as it was dark and rainy and I was still bleary-eyed from the Civil War series on PBS. And then Friday, I was awakened by something altogether different: a skull-shattering shriek from a woman outside.

The time was 5:30 a.m., fifteen minutes before I was set to get up. The sobs came out in successive spurts, like sneezes. Outside, I could see an ambulance at the corner of Third Street and Eighth Avenue, a few dog-walkers huddled beneath their umbrellas. Two police cars angled the end of my block. A siren roared—a fire engine had arrived—and then my real alarm sounded. I turned it off, turned the dial to now-more-than-ever 1010 WINS, and listened for the radio report of the incident. But I didn't hear a thing. Guiltily, I closed my eyes and tried for one last hour of sleep.

But thoughts of Third Street wouldn't let me rest. Who was this woman? What did she lose? I pulled up the window shade and watched as, one by one, each emergency vehicle left the scene. But for the rain, the streets were silent. I stared at the empty block, blindly, until I caught my own reflection in the window. Suddenly it dawned on me: I had lost something on Third Street, too.

It was our first night together. We parked his car there, right across the street from my building, both of us full knowing that he would come inside. Everything seemed so easy back then: he was a journalist on the road, his girlfriend lived in another city, and he was set to leave town the very next day. We didn't need to make any promises, or confessions. What was there to say, really? With him there, with me, in my bed in my one-bedroom apartment, time stood generously still. Unfortunately, the same could not be said for his car, which got towed right outside my window, right before our eyes. Reality is hard to bear in broad daylight, so we caved back into bed. We laughed, we wept, and then he was gone.

And then it was September 27th. I had a new job, a new alarm clock, and a new perspective, even if the only thing I could see when I walked outside that morning was that fateful parking space—which, on a dark winter night the year before, looked miles away from being a busstop. Instead of heading straight to the subway, I crossed over to Third Street to pay my respects to a woman whose identity was locked behind brownstone doors. Which one was hers? Would she be there now? There was no evidence of a crime—no yellow police tape, no chalk drawings, no WANTED: DEAD OR ALIVE.

I had come to associate a New York tragedy with candles and cards and flowers on the pavement, none of which I could find. All I knew was that another woman's heart had been broken, no doubt worse than my own had been, and there was not a thing I could do. I pointed my feet in the direction of the F train and fell into the familiar, jagged rhythm of the new day ahead.

★ 4 DENNETT PL.
CARROLL GARDENS, BROOKLYN

OFF-LEASH: HEAVEN IN BROOKLYN
BY MICHELE BOWMAN

We had already lived in New York for a year when we discovered the park. A year since my husband and I moved from New Jersey to Carroll Gardens in Brooklyn, a year since the the loss of a family member to brain cancer. That the family member was a dog—my best friend and companion of almost ten years—didn't matter. Or maybe it mattered entirely, but the fact was that Oso died two weeks after we moved to New York, and I had been holding a poisonous grudge against the city for the whole time I'd lived here.

None of us dealt well with the loss of Oso, including our other dog, Doxy, an agile Shepherd of dubious lineage who was also having to adjust to city life: no yard, as she enjoyed back in Jersey; alone all day, as we had taken "real" jobs in the city to support our new lifestyle renting in Brownstone Brooklyn; and suddenly, no big brother to protect her. She acted out on our walks, snarling at other dogs, and when she was off-leash, she cowered and drooled in the corner of our crappy neighborhood dog park by the Brooklyn-Queens Expressway.

Doxy and I were both at the end of our ropes, when our friends who lived in Park Slope mentioned the off-leash hours at Prospect Park. They had recently adopted a high-energy terrier mix who needed a lot of running, so they were in the park almost every morning. "You have to come," my friend gushed. "It's dogs—everywhere." Dogs running…that rang a heavy bell in my memory, of days back in North Carolina when Oso was a puppy, a wild, fiery-red puppy that I raised to run the parks and trails with his friends. The Chow in him made training him to come back to me a challenge, but his Golden Retriever genes evened that out with age.

I hesitated: Doxy hadn't been enjoying the dog parks in Brooklyn, and she was a runner, but of a different ilk—the kind that didn't always come back. What would our wild child do, unmoored? We decided to risk it. She loved our friends' dog, so hopefully she'd want to stay with the pack.

It was a cool spring Sunday morning the first time we went out. Doxy ran to her friend like she hadn't seen him in weeks, and they immediately began doing the most beautiful thing, something I had not seen in a long time, nor quite understood the importance of missing: running.

Dogs running free is a thing of such simplicity, such innocence, that those watching can't help but feel their joy. Especially in a place like this, where sidewalk life has such strict rules, and good leash behavior is prized above all. Here, they get to be free; they get to be dogs. Forming and easily breaking packs, sniffing new friends, chasing old ones, meeting new people, barreling into the lake at the "dog beach," these dogs must be as happy as it's possible for a creature to be. I was running in my heart with Doxy, aware for the first time of how wonderful a place this was, how lucky we were to live in New York, in a place where dogs can do this every morning.

Off-leash hours at Prospect Park kept me in Brooklyn. They opened a little door in my heart for the city. If it could be that cruel to one of my dogs, but good to another, it couldn't be all bad. And then I remembered: this was another circle closing. Oso and Doxy had both been to this place, long before, but not with us.

One weekend, years ago, we'd gone out of town and a friend who lived in Brooklyn kept the dogs. He took them to Prospect Park. But only Oso got to run; our friend knew he'd come back, but he wasn't sure about Doxy. She was confined to the leash and had to watch Oso run into the lake and come out spraying water all over a group of children who laughed and ran. Oso laughed and ran, too. He was here, and now that his little sister was tasting the same city freedom, the whole family was back together, for a moment, settled in Brooklyn at last.

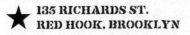

★ 135 RICHARDS ST.
RED HOOK, BROOKLYN

COUNTDOWN
IN RED HOOK

BY PATRICK J. SAUER

On a day of contradiction in February 2004, my wife Kim and I test drove a mini-SUV through a few of the less heralded 'hoods. The sun was brilliant, cutting through the brutal cold and lighting up the harbor with an intense glare off the snow and the ice floes, a simultaneously bone-chilling and body-warming type of day. It was one those winter New York afternoons, with empty streets offering the chance to get out and tool around the quieter edges of the city, to take in the upscale rehabbing of the down-and-out waterfront made famous by the dearly departed Hubert Selby, Jr., in *Last Exit to Brooklyn*.

It was the kind of lazy day where wandering around leads to an old trolley under a tarp with a sign noting Ebbets Field as the final destination, a collection of black-and-white photos of the shells of long-departed industries, a backseat mash session, a drive through heretofore unseen places like Ozone Park and Ridgewood, a best-in-show pastrami sandwich at Abraham's deli, and even a visit from two of New York's Finest, wondering why anyone would park in an empty Red Hook lot and watch the sun fade away into the freezing winter air.

It was the kind of day where we hoped to see things in our hometown that we had never seen before.

We were slowly traversing Red Hook blocks, going so far as to place an impromptu call to a realtor with fleeting thoughts of getting more space, when we passed this sign, posted in front of a nondescript house on a deserted block. At first glance, the sign struck me as goof, a working class version of the old midtown "national deficit" or "death by handgun" billboards with their continually updated electronic display of data. I was never able to look up at the handgun ticker without wondering where in the United States the poor soul lived who just bought it whenever the tally added another unlucky statistic, but those billboards wanted you to pause for the cause, to take a quick second to realize how much money we are wasting or how violent our society is. They were guilt-inducing public service announcements, but they weren't connected to anything other than some organizations desire to sell you a message.

This sign is different. To somebody, this sign means something. Quite possibly, this sign means everything.

"2 YEARS 134 DAYS SINCE 9-11-01 WHERE IS OSAMA BIN LADEN?"

Upon first seeing it, Kim and I stared at the sign in silence, rereading it in our heads and then aloud. We quickly tried to calculate the days passed, but without the benefit of a calculator, calendar, or pencil and paper, we decided to take the author's word for it. We knew for sure it was damn close, but there were more important issues than the exact number of days.

Why would somebody mark the lost time on a flimsy piece of cardboard? Who owns this vigil? Has it really been that long already? What do they want to say? Is the sign for them? Is it for us? Who updates if they go on vacation? When was this thing erected? Why not hang it somewhere people might see it? Where the fuck is Osama Bin Laden?

My journalistic instincts told me to get this person's story. Start off by finding out if they literally rise each morning—no matter how cold, humid, rainy, or snowy—walk out the front door of their house, and change the number of days, and once every September, the number of years. I stared at the sign, mesmerized by its frightening power, contemplating whether I should knock and extract the truth behind the sign. I toyed with the idea, but I decided against asking questions because they might be answered. I don't want to know the person behind the sign and I suspect they don't want us to know them either, because there is nothing but the question. There are no flags, no memorials, no political fliers, no pictures of the dead, no military insignias, no peace signs, nothing. There is only a cold, hard fact and its questionable aftermath. The sign is the message, the message is the sign.

It could easily have been left over from an anti-war protest as it could from a pro-war rally. It could be the ironic prodding of a yippee prankster or it could be the mournful longing of a bereaved family member. The sign could be a call to action, a cry for help, a plea to recognize futility, an admonishment to stay focused, or maybe it's just a clear-eyed query that needs a response.

For a couple of months, I thought about making a return trip, but I decided not to go back and see if it is indeed updated daily. I never returned to speak to the creators of the sign. For reasons I can't grasp, I find it comforting to believe that every morning someone in Red Hook wakes up and updates the sign hanging in their yard for their own private motives, and I don't need to know why. I'm afraid the rest of the story will change what I saw. What I saw was the sign of the times.

And as of tomorrow morning, it will read:

"2 YEARS 242 DAYS SINCE 9-11-01 WHERE IS OSAMA BIN LADEN?"

★ **10519 METROPOLITIAN AVE.**
FLATBUSH, BROOKLYN

JAM MASTER JAY: HIS SOUNDS WILL STAY

BY PATRICK J. SAUER

I would like to believe that I went out to Queens to leave the "My Adidas" sweatshirt in tribute to Jam Master Jay, but I'd be lying.

I've long gotten a superiority chuckle watching "mourners" on television who bring hand-painted signs, ninety-nine cent store teddy bears, daily newspapers with sixty-four-point headlines announcing the celebrity death, and acres of chrysanthemums, roses and white lilies to lay on a sidewalk somewhere in the vicinity of where the deceased lived.

When did public vigils with pine-scented candles and stuffed unicorns become mandatory? Does that crying woman think Lady Di cares that she painted a sign with angels on it? She is, after all, dead. Right? If I was related to someone famous, would I feel better knowing an anonymous stranger sent his or her love via a Mylar balloon?

Though I would mock them, at least those folks brought gifts they intended to leave behind in honor of the person who meant something to them. I, on the other hand, carried my fifteen-year-old, red-white-and-black "My Adidas" Run-D.M.C. sweatshirt to Jamaica, Queens, in order to take pictures of it among the leather hats, gold chains, unlaced three-black-stripe shell-tops, *Raising Hell* album covers, posters, prayers, notes, flowers, turntables, mourners, gawkers, and fans. And then take it back home.

The fact is that I am simply not prepared to part with it.

My Aunt Judy sent me the sweatshirt as a birthday gift from a shop in Philadelphia, when I was a high school junior in Billings, Montana. It was, and still is, the coolest item of clothing I have ever owned. It passed the ultimate test: no other kid in town had one.

I would venture to guess that most kids from Hollis during the depressing inner-city Reagan days would have been surprised to know that my circle—white kids from cattle country—couldn't get enough of rap music. Bad rap, good rap, political rap, sex rap, angry rap, loopy rap—as long as black folks were on the mic (and yes, that includes the Beasties), we listened. More than any of the others though, Run-D.M.C. blazed the trail.

In the 1980s, Billings was as white as it got, yet cassettes were worn out while rhyming along with "Calvin Klein's no friend of mine/don't want nobody's name on my behind," and "You told the Cavity Creeps to watch out for Crest." We whiteys knew the cuts long before the rap-rock hybrid made Run-D.M.C. MTV-safe.

What was it about rap? I guess it was the other. The black other. There were no blacks in my high school, and near as I recall, only a handful of black kids in town. Radio pop, Motown classics and heavy metal were in the mix (country was the only genre we disdained), but in my stereo, the Kings from Queens ruled. I loved it and imagined that outside of po-dunk Billings, we all loved it and each other. I was honest-to-God shocked when I got to a Midwestern Jesuit college and found upper-class white kids casually and bitterly throwing around the word "nigger."

I knew that things were darker and crueler than Run-D.M.C. made it sound. But the sound that Jam Master Jay pioneered was already imprinted on my brain as pure humanistic joy. Not that Run-D.M.C. ignored social questions; it's just that they sounded like three guys who ate the apple, enjoyed life on their terms and made it happen their way. The verbal dexterity, the leather suits, the fedoras, the gold chains, the video with Larry "Bud" Melman, and the wizard of the crossfade driving the engine with the wax and the scratch and the scratchy wax—in my head, it all added up to some raucous party that I might not have been personally invited to, but that they wouldn't care if I crashed.

I wore the sweatshirt out. The shiny Run-D.M.C. lettering on the back had long wilted away and the white cloth material ceased to be white years ago. It's stained, frayed, shapeless and smells like an item that's been in a closet for over a decade. I've saved other mementos from my adolescence, but they're all boxed up, kept mainly for bookkeeping's sake. That sweatshirt, however, has traveled with me to college, to the Bronx where I lived and worked as a volunteer for a year, to grad school in Snoop country, back to Gotham, and a few other spots in between.

I hadn't worn it in years, but I always knew it was at the ready should I get the opportunity to see the Big Beat Blaster, the Reverend, and the Goggled One. I decided to break it out for a Beastie Boys 9/11 benefit show in October of 2001. Although it was a minor battle trying to pull it over my no-longer-teenaged midsection, it was a hoot to have it on again. Fun to wear, but I'd forgotten that the "My Adidas" throwback had a New York City skyline across the front prominently displaying the Twin Towers. The Beasties promised special guests, but to my chagrin there was no Together Forever tour reunion and Run-D.M.C. didn't make an appearance.

On the way to Queens last week, I stopped and bought *Run-D.M.C.'s Greatest Hits*. I put it in the Walkman for the ride to the F-train's last stop, which dropped me nowhere near Merrick Avenue. I asked a black guy walking down the street if he could help me out, and learned that I would have to take not one, but two buses. He was getting on the same bus and offered to steer me in the right direction. He introduced himself as Eryq and we talked throughout the half-hour tour of Farmers Boulevard. He asked if I was a reporter. I said no, I was a "writer for myself." I didn't want him to think I was a news guy and not a fan. I wanted him to think I was a guy who would travel deep into an outer borough to pay respects to his hip-hop hero. I showed Eryq the raggedy-ass sweatshirt and explained how it just seemed right to take it to the Jam Master Jay memorial. He didn't ask why. He knew.

It unfurled from my backpack and the first thing he said was, "It's even got the Twin Towers." He told me about having seen Run-D.M.C. at Fresh Fest years back. There was a stabbing, he said, so the band stopped while order was restored and Jay made up a rhyme on the spot rousing the crowd to act responsibly. Eryq told me he was a musician from Long Island and said that he's a huge Eddie Van Halen fan; he went so far as to add white tape to his red Stratocaster. He told me how he took a lot of shit in his neighborhood for his Guitar God worship. I told him I grew up in Montana knowing only whites, but rap was king. At the end of the line, we exchanged information, two fans of both a murdered rapper and Diver Down.

In Jam Master Jay's honor, I'd like to say their music bridges racial gaps and batters musical assumptions, or at least it did on one bus ride through the neighborhood where it had all started. The sweatshirt was a conversation piece, even if the conversation only reinforced the broad power of popular music and the hyperawareness New Yorkers have of the missing World Trade Center. Still, talking to someone like Eryq was what the music had been all about for me growing up in Billings. Someday I'd live in New York City and have black friends and we'd listen to Run-D.M.C., just like back home, and I'd be a man of the world and it would be cool. Silly teenage fantasy? Sure, but for that ride, it felt like what I had envisioned life in New York City to be like long before I ever set foot here.

I took my sweatshirt out at the memorial and posed it for a few photographs. Nobody seemed to mind and one guy stopped to note he had the same one back in the day. A mother told her young son how Run-D.M.C. had started it all, and more than one passerby said "it doesn't make sense," or asked, "who could do this?" It was bitter cold, so the crowd was minimal and few lingered. I stayed long enough to snap some pics, smile at the collection of worn-out sneakers and sign a poster monitored by a guy with a Sharpie. A mixture of guilt and nostalgia hit me for a few seconds and I considered tying "My Adidas" to the chain-link fence. But then it passed. I couldn't do it.

The sweatshirt may be an old, shabby relic that I might've donned ironically before it became another reminder of 9/11, another reminder of a childish vision of a utopian community where blacks and whites partied together in Gotham with Run-D.M.C. as the backbeat, and now, another reminder of the brutal murder of their musical backbone, Jam Master Jay, father of three.

The ugly reminders are woven into the fabric, but to me, the sweatshirt is still listening to "King of Rock" while drinking cheap beer up on the Rims with my buddies. It's imagining that someday I'd find a way to let Run-D.M.C. know that, to me, they were *it*. And that, yes, "music ain't nothing but a people's jam / Run-D.M.C. rockin' without a band." All I can say is that I'm going to keep that sweatshirt in my closet. Every now and then, I'll take it down, put it on, crank up "Peter Piper," and bob my head in agreement with the two men who knew him best: "His name is Jay / to hear him play / will make you say / 'God damn that DJ made my day.'"

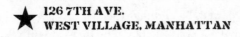

126 7TH AVE.
WEST VILLAGE, MANHATTAN

THE GOD OF HIGH SCHOOL

BY RACHEL CLINE

I wish I didn't think of Eli every single time I walk down lower Seventh Avenue, but I do. His parents' West Village brownstone was a shrine to me in high school insofar as Eli himself was a god. When passing it back then, I craned my neck at the upstairs window and said whatever magic words I believed would make him mine.

The last time I saw Eli was around 1984 or 5, late on a weeknight on a crowded uptown 1 train. I had become aware of someone sobbing at the other end of the car—insane and homeless people often boarded at Franklin Street; maybe there was a shelter nearby. Who else would sob like that, alone on the subway? I would rather have been boiled in oil than subject myself to the cruel stares of subway riders when feeling such despair.

After Christopher Street, the car was empty enough to sneak a peek at the hopeless soul, but I hesitated. I remembered that kind of weeping from childhood: it allows no sidelong glance; it drives comfort away. Then, as the car cleared out at Fourteenth Street, I realized the weeper was also getting off, and I was emboldened to stare. Through the grimy window, I scanned the scrum of people who'd just left my car. I was looking for someone ruined, disfigured, foreign, strange. But as the train pulled forward, I found myself looking, instead, at the face of the boy I had loved, ceaselessly and unrequitedly, for the longest four years of my life. It was Eli, his cheeks stained and mouth contorted. My train pulled into the tunnel.

That was the last time I saw Eli, but not the last time we spoke. For that, I have to go back to 1980. It was my first summer home in New York after four years of college. No surprise that it was dismally hot outside or that my college friends all seemed to be living in roachy, appalling tenements in the vicinity of Avenue A. I can remember picking my way among the crushed crack vials, dressed in shorts and tank tops and other clothes far too flimsy for the city as I had known it as a child, and as I came to understand it again, later. But that summer I was bulletproof, flaunting my youth and my skin on the streets of lower Manhattan.

My god our lives were repulsive, in retrospect. Stef worked till three every morning and lived next door to a storefront that sold headstones. On the avenues, junkies tried to sell artifacts that seemed incredibly personal, arrayed on stained blankets; things like chipped coffee cups and pre-owned brassieres. One of Christina's roommates was a convicted rapist and another was a girl-runaway from Virginia. But beers at the Polish bars were well under a dollar and no one, yet, knew about AIDS.

In the early months of that summer, I somehow got invited to a party at Eli's house, that very brownstone, which seemed like the perfect opportunity to exact my revenge. You see, Eli had scarred me in high school. He had teased me, and nuzzled me, and after trying to kiss me on the back stairs, had observed to a crowd of our classmates that I was "a freaking amateur." (I'd gone rigid and fled his embrace, I was so sure I would fail at whatever it was that people did in the dark, with their eyes closed.) I set out for that party flanked by my mesmerizingly hip girlfriends and, wearing lipstick and as little clothing as possible, planned to reveal myself decisively as the mysterious and petal-strewn *road not taken*.

Stef and Christina had balked at first at the idea of a party at someone's parents' house (we were still young enough that that seemed socially untenable), but I promised them it was "cool" and the house, with its interior balcony, strange overgrowth of plants, and menagerie of dogs, cats, and one (caged) monkey, would not disappoint. Even better, our friend Josh coincidentally turned up, along with his army of bad boys from Washington Square. So there was loud music and rowdy boys and drink and drugs and animals and plants and room to move. We started slam dancing and eventually broke a fair amount of glass.

And somewhere along the way, I wound up reclining against the back wall of Eli's boyhood bed and telling him the sloppy drunken truth about my four years of adolescent lovesickness. I told him how, in my journal every night, I'd charted the temperature of our interactions in a code known only to me. Pluses and minuses and arrow-pierced hearts spelled out the extent to which I had experienced eye contact, been smiled at, exchanged wiseasseries, or remained rapt yet unseen. I confessed I'd been the very definition of an amateur: in love with the idea of carnality but entirely ignorant of its practice. And I told him that this was no longer the case.

And so, at the party, Eli and I made out, at last. I think he even took off my shirt. I managed to overlook that the woman sulking in the loft above us was his actual girlfriend. I was just closing an old account. He would return to her in the morning.

Eventually, I had to excuse myself to pee. I waved briefly at my pals, before ducking into the bathroom and then, as I sat myself down on the toilet, the door jiggled and I opened it, expecting to admit Stef but getting Eli. I realized he was very drunk. Okay, I thought, I'm cool. Then he tried to sit on my lap and kiss me some more as I sat on the toilet with my pants around my ankles. Some wrestling ensued. Despite my physical and verbal insistence, Eli wouldn't leave the bathroom. In fact, he wound up peeing in the sink and showering me with refracted urine, which was ultimately more than even my still-teenaged heart could excuse.

So I rounded up the girls and whoever else was ready and we returned to our roach-motel apartments, laughing and full of fight. My friends were too drunk to know how humiliated I felt, and how disappointed. And though I thought of him often, that was the last time I spoke to Eli; that night he pissed on me, when I was looking my best.

I know many people have painful crushes in high school. I can only say, mine was worse. Twenty years later, I still thought about him once a week—just for a flash, as long as it takes to hear a sound or smell a smell. Particularly a smell like patchouli oil, for example, or a sound like the opening chords of Hendrix playing "Little Wing." In my mind, I can still hear the peculiarly falling Midwestern inflection he gave to the expression "My God," when we were fifteen—it was my father's voice, only hipper. To this day, I could draw his hands for you as readily as I could point out the color of that T-shirt only he could wear. It showed his collarbones, which were pronounced like my own.

We met in the library in the first week of high school (he was reading *Catch-22* and I was hiding). We liked each other, we got along, but I was as afraid of Eli then as I would have been of a grown man with body hair and an ex-wife. By the end of tenth grade, it seemed to me that all my girlfriends had diaphragms and I had never even "made out." And in the way of teenagers, I fervently believed this revealed a deep personal flaw. On my sixteenth birthday, I was waiting for a commuter bus in the Port Authority bus terminal, and a scruffy runaway with a guitar struck up a conversation with me. I told him what day it was, and he responded, "And never been kissed?" Having somehow missed the song lyric, I believed my inexperience was so transparent that this dimwit could see it on me like the mark of Cain.

So, Eli stayed a fantasy and that fantasy occupied my thoughts for the better part of twelve hundred nights. Even accounting for the odd visitor from another school, home-from-college older brother, newly discovered rock or movie star, I'd not go beneath a thousand on that estimate. When I look back, I see my loneliness and my secret virginity and I want to cry for all the wasted longing.

I remembered the content of those fantasies with startling clarity. I also remembered the encounters on which they were based. At least, that was what I believed until I was reunited with my journals from high school, about twenty-five years later, after a cross-country move. Appalled at the sheer mass of my recorded self-loathing, and suspecting that most of the five or so volumes contained nothing but hapless mooning over Eli, I almost put them back into storage, unread. They bugged me, though, and eventually I compromised by making myself a deal. I would open one and only one book, at random.

The section I read described a forgotten event: a school trip taken in tenth grade. We were supposed to go skiing but there was no snow and so we spent the rainy weekend at someone's parents' farmhouse, upstate. There were about thirty of us cooped up there, smoking pot, playing "Killer" and "Spit," and feeling as though we were in a Noel Coward play. The phys ed teacher, who resembled Charles Manson without the tattoo, supervised. A silent boy named Chris had a crush on me and pursued it by repeatedly offering me peppermint Life Savers. I avidly befriended Eli's younger sister, who had just arrived at school that fall.

As Saturday afternoon got soggier and avoiding Chris stopped seeming like fun, I went inside to read by the fire. Shortly, Eli appeared nearby and asked me to come upstairs with him, perhaps to smoke more pot. I needed no excuse, I went, and found myself almost immediately halfway underneath him on a bunk bed. It was nothing less than the moment I had been waiting for. Instead of kissing back, however, or even just succumbing, belle-like, I sat up and said, "Hold on a minute." At least this is what I wrote down in my journal.

Eli tried to arouse my sympathy—he said how much he liked to make love and how long it had been since he'd done so, but I held back, wanting to be told that I alone was lovely. Then he asked me to tell him "about the men in my life." As it had previously at the bus station, the terrible transparency of my innocence humiliated me.

"You really want to know?" I asked him and he nodded. I drew a big goose egg in the air, which he looked at uncomprehendingly and then, at last, understood.

"Don't worry about it," he said, "you'll teach a few men a thing or two before you're done."

And then we sat on the bed and talked about normal stuff—the lasagna we were having for dinner, and an argument I'd had with the gym teacher about the credibility of Leon Russell's version of "Youngblood." Later, back at school, my old pattern of distant suffering continued as before, while I erased all memory of the pass I'd passed up so decisively.

When I encountered this passage in my old notebook I was astounded. How could I have forgotten that I had rejected Eli, and that he'd comforted me? The entire character of my adolescence, which I had always described as lost, helpless, boy-wracked, and inconsolable, was a myth. Eli had valued me and I had prevailed.

Though the last time I saw Eli was the night I heard him weeping on the subway, that was not the last I heard of him. From one friend or another I learned that he was married, still living in New York, and was writing a novel. These sounded like good things. Then, one afternoon in Los Angeles, I ran into his older sister at a party. Amanda was married to a wealthy producer, lived in the country somewhere, had two beautiful children, horses, dogs. I'd recognized her instantly, though. And it didn't take me long to get down to my real interest and ask her how her brother was. Even after the golden shower, and especially after the subway *cri de coeur*, I still carried the flame. "Well," she said, "he's dying of AIDS."

435

LOST AND FOUND

I don't know if I began to cry right away. Probably not, it was a party. Time and again I tried to write Eli a letter, but found that I knew both too little and too much. The story Amanda told was that he had gotten a tainted blood transfusion. Naturally this was possible, but seemed the least likely source of transmission for the young satyr I had known. But why worry at causes? I guess because the fact, and its implications, were too unbearable.

Another five years have passed. I no longer know the people who knew Amanda and I don't hear much news about friends from high school. For all I know, Eli is dead. For all I know, he's alive and well. For all I know, his sister only meant he'd tested positive. I never sent the letters I tried to write.

As I've said, I loved Eli. Not the way you love family, or even pets. Not the way you love lovers, either. Another way, that never gets much credit or does much good. There's no plausible context in which to say goodbye to him, except on paper alone in my room: Goodbye Eli, you beautiful adolescent, wasted teenager, friend, example, thorn. I don't know what you leave behind. I can't offer you comfort or even sympathy but I do remember you, all the time. I hope that you aren't dead and I hope that you aren't alone, but most of all I hope that you remember me.

★ 2ND ST. & AVENUE B
EAST VILLAGE, MANHATTAN

SAVE THE ROBOTS
BY JANE RATCLIFFE

Early 1980s: Alphabet City. Segments are airing on national
TV about drugs, guns, general life-threatening disorder.
Still, it's where the artists live. Coax a cab east and try your luck.

On Avenue B, half-windowed buildings. Puerto Rican mafia
guys lurking. Streetlights, but they do little more than rattle and
buzz. Rats. You carefully watch your footsteps to avoid another
one-beneath-as-one-scuttles-atop scenario. Maybe one of the dis-
carded syringes will trip up the fucker before you do. The Gas
Station is on your left as you and yours tumble out of the cab,
which pulls off before you fully close the door. Kind of pretty in
its charred, regal manifestation. The usual gathering of performance artists, drug addicts, and experimental bands (as in
experimenting at being a band, as in GG Allin). Halos seem to
float above them. You swear you can smell the gasoline wafting
across the incessant breeze, but your date reminds you it's been
forever since the joint burnt or exploded or was just abandoned
and the drug addict artists took over. Shit. No electricity. No heat.
Around the corner on Second, Lucky Seven, a hopping heroin
den. More images of rats skewered on myriad needles. Doubtful.
You watch your feet.

Then: the door. Formidable. Gray. You seem to be alone on the street. How did that happen? A sound. Another. Closer? You've got to knock. There's a postcard-sized peephole that slides open, and two rather naughty eyes eye you. You try to look cool, which could mean a number of things depending on the doorman. Mostly, it means seedy enough to add that *je ne sais quoi*, but capable of paying for the illegal, overpriced, limited-option drinks. The peephole slides shut. Clang! You're fucked.

On other nights, perhaps, though, you're not. Perhaps you're selected by the six-foot-something bald guy in the mini skirt and high heels who works the door. He's a doll if he knows you. A sweetheart. A gem. If he doesn't, he's finicky, sassy and at times, downright mean. Of course, he's on drugs. Aren't you all? Cocaine is the prima donna at this affair. Most of the junkies prowling about aren't interested in what Save the Robots has to offer, though there's always an exception. Speed is the second place drug of choice. Good luck with the john. Most nights, Joey Ramone is developing his crack habit in its wet tomb.

So: you get through the door, through the gate, past Dean, the doorman. Then, the hall. Long, like shoelace licorice, skinny in the same way. Then a narrow (and not necessarily trustworthy) set of stairs. You're cooking now. You can smell the sawdust that awaits you on the floor below. The faux-Japanese restaurant decor, though perhaps it's hard to state as much with any authority. Dark. There's a couple of fold-out tables covered in white paper. Maybe they're bare. Does it matter? It's after 2 a.m. All the legal clubs are shut. You saunter over. Order a Budweiser or an orange and vodka. Ten dollars either way. Bud comes out of a plastic cooler. Top flips up. Then, flips down. *Pfft*. Early enough it's cold; as the morning unfolds, the ice melts. Brewskis become lukewarm. Orange juice, warm or otherwise, tastes like Kool-Aid. Bartender asks if you're from around here. You start hankering for spiked kids' drinks.

There's a lot of folks down here. And you wonder what they're all on about. What they're doing here. But you already know. Sally Randall. Rudolph. Diane Brill. John Sex. Terry Toy. Heterosexual. Homosexual. Bisexual. Transvestite. Yeah, those are hot. They draw the most glee. Big hair on the "girls." A lot of updos. Mermaid dresses. Lots of makeup all around in colors that twinkle and glow. A man in slip-on stilettos lets you borrow his lipstick. It's Dean, the doorman, and he's locked the door for a quick spin on the dance floor—not that quick, you notice, as he pirouettes and stomps and slithers, crammed in tight against others doing the same. The guys, the straight ones, still sport a few mohawks. Some are growing it long, hair trailing behind them like rainbows. Dean is bald, you notice, watching him go, the only one. Jesus, he's pale. Never sees much daylight. Who here does?

They all live in this neighbourhood, you discover. When the epic clubs—Area, Dancetaria, and so on—close at 2 a.m., the clubbies, those ebullient few who make the clubs *clubs* traipse over. Fuck the cabs, most of them walk. No money, and plus, they have a nice buzz from drinking free at marquee clubs, sweetened in by owners looking for the authentic goods—and the city looks beautiful at night. Plus again, who are they going to be afraid of? Okay, the mafia thing can get shaky, but mostly not.

Dean had opened his own club, he tells you, when you get to know him. Around the corner, just months before Robots opened. He'd named it Uncle Bud's Amway. After his Uncle Bud. And his Uncle Bud's employer. He refused everybody entry, perched on his high-backed chair behind the velvet rope, glittering beneath the murky stars in sequined skirts and iridescent tops. The lines grew verbose. Soon enough, the mob guys wanted in. Hence Dean's current employment where someone else tends to the tricky bits. Denis Provost and his wife Alexandria to be precise, the proprietors. Alexandria's father worked designing robots or parts of robots. Hence the name of the club. Or so the bartender tells you.

You've just purchased drink number two. Your date's ahead of you, number four, five, six? And he's mingling. You wonder how many of these people have made it into those segments on television.

One night, your date tells you how the cops busted the joint. The thing was, they'd just busted the after-hours hole a few streets over and confiscated everybody's crack. He smirks as he says "confiscated." Then they did all the shit themselves so by the time they got here they were all fucked up. They busted the place up royal. Holes in the walls. Handcuffing and shit. Took everyone down to jail and locked them in the same cell with the people from the other club. They fucking partied all night and were let go in the afternoon. You try to imagine your fellow revelers, heads bent over rolled up bills, released into the sun. Not likely.

And then? Well, they couldn't do shit to the club. I mean, they'd fucked up the bust. You search the spray-painted walls for cop-punched holes. There's so much smoke around you, it's how you imagine the eye of a hurricane. You think of Dean's eyes sizing you up the first time you came and you're glad you made it in the second.

There's music playing, of course. Dance, mostly, loud. Your feet vibrate. Your tendons too. And so on. Everybody's dancing. Thumping, pounding, whirling. Except Joey. He's still hogging the john. John Hall is in charge. He's spinning hip hop as well. You wonder what hip hop is and notice a bunch of black guys hanging around looking mischievous.

Later, when you're a regular and the door opens before you knock and Dean kisses you and slips you candies and the bartender sometimes doesn't charge you and Joey lets you use the toilet (sometimes) and you know all the songs John is spinning (except for a few, and when you ask what they are, he'll answer you), Alexandria and Denis open the upstairs. It's a lounge. They've acquired a couple of couches and chairs from somewhere. The street? They've embellished them: more spray paint. You can sit there for hours and think about all the folks on the outside who didn't get in. And you know, if you think about it, that their hearts are breaking. That somehow, Save the Robots is, inexplicably, The Promised Land. And Dean, teetering prettily in heels, holds your salvation in his large, overly-white hands. Though maybe that's pushing it.

It's after legal club time and there's nowhere to go. And now there's here. And everyone who's anyone, in those terms, has agreed that here is It. And Dean: eying. Later, around sevenish, the mawkish crowd moves northward, landing themselves at Pyramid. Reeks like old, old beer and smokes. Wired on coke and speed it's all talk, no listening. Then late afternoon sleep. Do they sleep? Or a job? Doubtful. Unless, of course, it's at one of the clubs.

Eventually Save the Robots gets sold to some out-of-towners. Out-of-countryers. Turns out, it's famous around the world. Punks and hardcore kids and goths and speed bands and the nascent hip-hoppers and old school dance-heads and the new school techno-heads and so on. Check it out. Bridge and tunnel, now, as well. And you start to make some inner-housekeeping changes of your own.

Flash forward: 2002. The same streets, same sense of cool urging about, but a new generation. And a whole lot of gentrification. Guernica, a trendy restaurant on hallowed Robots ground, serving up, well, what the fuck, no Kool-Aid here. The Gas Station, decimated. Brought down to honor a Kings Pharmacy and flights of yuppies. Lucky Seven, an Italian haunt. Good food. Visiting movie stars taste the fares: Julia Roberts, Benjamin Bratt. Separate dates.

Windows now, lots of them. Streetlights. Parents wouldn't let them live here without. Rents you couldn't make if you worked a dozen club jobs. Not true, not true. But where are the clubs these days? Still, it's hell over here. Carcasses of times barely recalled. You walk around a bit, check out the kids in their false-punk getups and mighty heels, know they are convinced they're the edge just as you were once convinced, stealing some other generation's way. But that was back before it took more than one beer, albeit Guinness, to give you a hangover.

Now: you put in a call to Dean, the doorman, to reminisce. Voice message response, "I'll tell you what I remember." Longish pause. "You know." Which you take to be code for "the drugs."

Wind still blows, northeast mostly. The Towers proved that. Alone? Hah, these days. Not likely. Then, maybe you are. And it smells like gasoline. Don't embellish. But it smells the same, like back in the day, somehow. And you pass Il Bagatto, hang a louie on B, pass Kings, there she is: Guernica. And you try, this quiet Sunday morning, to recollect. But you can't. They tore the fucking door down.

CHICO'S LOISAIDA
BY DAVID GERLACH

I find myself taking the same route along Tenth Street between Avenues A and B, day after day. I keep passing the spray-painted image of Tony's tightly clipped mustache and smooth fade. The mural is beginning to show its age—but Tony's dark eyes still stare out intently. His pupils appear guarded, perhaps harboring the memory of the violent episode in 1993 that brought about his untimely demise. Tony lives on after death thanks to a guy whose name is written in the corner of the mural: "Chico." If you look closely, that tag actually pops up on corner after corner throughout the neighborhood. Look for his name and you get a brightly colored guide to the history of the changing Loisaida—Spanglish for the Lower East Side. Chico's own story, however, is much harder to see.

People say Chico never wears a mask when he works. And the story goes that the noxious Krylon fumes have made him insane. No one can remember a time when the neighborhood wasn't one big gallery of his work. He used to do his own thing; hitting abandoned buildings with colorful motifs. Got arrested a few times. His first mural—long gone—was a jab at then President Reagan: a tank driving toward the words "World War III."

Then local businesses offered to pay him $100. Then more to spray paint walls near their stores. It's strange to see his rendition of larger-than-life cutesy pets on one corner and the sounds and sights of the barrio on the next. But someone was footing the bill. Chico was making ends meet. He was getting known. Families and dealers came knocking to put up memorials to the dead.

At Twelfth and A, a cartoonish cucaracha holds court with a fiendish rat to promote a local pest control service. Just after September 11th, 2001, Chico painted a simple, lasting memorial on Avenue A, just south of Fourteenth Street. Flowers and candles showed up within minutes. For a few years it aged peacefully, unblemished, part of the neighborhood fabric. Now a billboard is slapped on top of it. A lot of Chico's murals have slowly disappeared; mainly it seems because of easy advertising paydays and new building owners having different concepts of what constitutes art—and history.

According to those in the neighborhood, Chico's been at it since the early 1980s, maybe even before that, tagging the old redbird subway cars after sneaking into locked rail yards. Grew up in the projects on Avenue D, the Jacob Riis Houses. Wanted a job so badly after he dropped out of high school that he would tag "Chico" on the building manager's door—the name his mom used when he was little because he looked like old man Chico back in Puerto Rico. Each time his name was painted over. And then he would tag it again. One evening the police showed up at his door. Word on the street had it that Antonio Garcia was the perpetrator. They saw Chico's canvasses stacked against the wall next to cans of spray paint. He pleaded that he was an artist and simply wanted a job. He wanted to beautify and speak to his neighborhood. Fight back against the graffiti. Next thing he knew, Chico was getting paid to color the drab high-rise buildings of Jacob Riis.

It seems remarkable how difficult it is to find a man whose name is everywhere within the area bounded by Avenues A and D, from Houston to Fourteenth Streets. Someone mentioned a bar he frequents after work. A few more inquiries and ensuing directives to other bars and it seems pretty clear that the man enjoys a drink. Walking into a tiny joint on C, a small, spray-painted bust protrudes from a canvas with "Chico" scrawled tightly in its corner. The bartender hasn't seen Chico in a while. No one has seen him, actually.

Seems he disappears on occasion. Heard he was over in Germany doing murals in restaurants. Or was it Japan this time? They love his stuff over there.

The slick-haired bar manager saunters over in a pair of black pleated pants. Two henchmen with indecipherable foreign accents cackle next to him. They speak about Chico with simultaneous fondness for his art and disgust for his antics. They clench and unclench their enormous fists as they talk. A head pops out from behind two turntables. A skinny, pale guy practically trips over himself as he busts out a laptop. He throws a greasy bang behind his ear and begins a slideshow of the mural that Chico recently painted in his apartment. It's a subway car bursting through a brick wall. One of those old redbird varieties.

Over on Avenue D, an explosion of bright faces and words flicker from the walls, the drab browns replaced. Even in the snow, with bike frames rusting along a sagging chain link fence, it feels like summer thanks to a huge mural of the weekly farmers mercado.

Houston marks the end of the line, and the gateway to other parts of the city. High above the street, the recently departed Celia Cruz smiles broadly from a mural that went up right after she died. A guy cruises past and notes that before Celia the canvas contained the Pope, his hands held out with Saddam Hussein on one side and George Bush on the other. Legend has it, the FBI told Chico to take the mural down. Facing the heat, he proceeded to paint over the politicos and left the Pope. Here and there, a few poseurs have left weak tags on Chico's art. But for the most part, his work is left untouched. This is Chico's Loisaida. But he is nowhere to be found. And he seems to like it that way.

★ **BERRY ST. & BROADWAY**
WILLIAMSBURG, BROOKLYN

THE DINER
BY MADISON SMARTT BELL

The Diner in Williamsburg is a twenty-first century institution now, I guess—you can get arugula there! And the rest of their food is good, too. It's pleasant at their sidewalk tables if the weather's fine, though you have to watch your step if you don't want to trip over two dozen artists.

Me and the the artist Jean de la Fontaine went there last fall to drink a beer and recruit two strangers to match some images with text for an art book in progress, entitled *Rien à Voire*, that involves three sequences of images paired with texts that have nothing to do with each other. I paired one sequence, Jean another, and we wanted a third to be done by monkeys, but it was easier to make it happen with Williamsburg artists hanging out at The Diner. I had to use my Firm Resolution not to bore these beautiful strangers to death with first-settler stories of back in the day.

In the late 1970s, it was a very different Williamsburg. I lived in a second-floor apartment overlooking The Diner from across Broadway. I owned an indestructible '69 Dodge Dart which usually slept quietly, unmolested, somewhere in New Jersey. Once in a while (rarely, trepidatiously) I did park that car in my Williamsburg nabe, where the local thieves were so very dexterous that they managed to use an inch of play in the chain that locked my hood to walk the battery all the way over the engine block and drop it out on the other side. From this experience, I learned to take the battery up to the apartment whenever I left the car—a bit of trouble, but it did make for a surer start on cold mornings.

The Diner was open then—under previous management, with no arugula or anything like it—you could get fried eggs and hash browns there, and strikingly lousy coffee. It was cheap! No customers though. The owner-operator-cook had the look of a recently retired All-Star wrestler: styled long hair and a brown VanDyke, his bull neck festooned in gold chains. Despite his powerful build, he always closed up and left the area before dark. There were no white people living around there then, unless you counted me, my roommates, and one other twentysomething boho I tried to follow home out of harmless curiosity the night I saw him get off at the same subway stop as me. He grew ill at ease, picked up his pace, and eventually climbed over a dumpster. I passed by without attempting any conversation.

The Diner guy was a shade of pale that probably originated in Bensonhurst. Or maybe, once upon a time, Williamsburg had been more like Bensonhurst. Back when a tree grew in Brooklyn. Indeed, the same indestructible acanthus trees that gave that novel its title were still omnipresent, seemingly nourishing themselves on root-crumbled cement. The Diner guy fried eggs and slopped coffee, waiting for the fog to clear and the planet he came from to reconstitute itself under his size-eleven feet.

So one day around dusk, I happen to be looking out the window and out comes the guy—he inserts his bulk into this hulking yacht of a beat-up seventies sedan, then presumably turns the key. Nothing. He gets out, pops his hood, and guess what?

The guy stands for a moment between his vehicle and his enterprise, staring down, ham fists cocked on his meaty hips. Then he shrugs, goes to the car that's parked behind him, steals *that* battery, and off he goes into the gathering night. I'll vouch for it.

I used the beautiful simplicity of this solution to improve on an idea I'd had earlier—I could probably have bought the batteries I'd lost back from the guys who stole them at half-price, probably more than they'd get from fencing them, anyway. But now I realized, this neighborhood didn't need all its batteries all the time anyway! Hell, it probably didn't need half of them. And we could have put the rest into a fund to support the arts, or maybe educate a few children...

PART IV

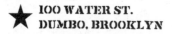

100 WATER ST.
DUMBO, BROOKLYN

EVAN'S RAMP
BY JOCKO WEYLAND

S now and cold are anathema to the skateboarder. The winter in New York can be a frustrating time to pursue an
activity best done wearing jeans and a T-shirt. Hard-core skaters
still hit the streets to skate Midtown's smooth plazas on frigid
nights, but that can be a slightly masochistic and uncomfortable
experience. One remedy is to move the action indoors.

Skaters have been taking their obsession inside to escape
inclement weather ever since someone broke the handle off of a
scooter and rode it as a board sometime in the 1950s. In cooler
climates, ramps and other skating environments have been built
in barns, houses, nightclubs, gyms, and apartments. In all shapes
and sizes, these ramps conform to and use interior architecture to
provide a place to skate even if a blizzard is raging outside. In
New York this can be difficult because of the compression of
multitudes into spaces that would be considered closets anywhere
else. Larger spaces are monetarily out of reach for most skaters,
and wooden structures the size of dump trucks just do not fit
into the average Lilliputian New York studio.

But New York does have lofts, and they afford the chance to
build on a fairly grand scale. If the tenant has the desire (along

with the collusion of a lax landlord) a mini-skatepark can be born. So under the Brooklyn and Manhattan Bridges, along the Brooklyn waterfront on cold nights, with the wind off the East River funneling between turn-of-the-century warehouse buildings, an unmistakable sound can be heard. Spinning wheels rolling on Masonite, a moment of silence, the slap of wood against metal, then the rolling sound again. A rhythmic, booming noise coming from high above.

A skater can roll down Jay Street with the Manhattan skyline in the distance, under the intersecting lines of trucks rumbling to the Brooklyn Bridge below D trains clanking ominously across the Manhattan Bridge; go up an elevator; and find himself at what is arguably the world's highest ramp—in the sense that it is situated ten floors above the ground. Down long gray hallways and past institutional sinks is a steel door that opens to Evan Becker's loft. In a raw studio with fifteen-foot ceilings and no bathroom, between the wall and a large supporting column, lies Evan's creation and playground: a ramp seven feet high that uses the concrete floor between its two curving walls as flat bottom.

Evan explains his motivation succinctly. "I wanted a place to skate and to work." The smell of paint and dust permeate the air. Evan's monumental cement and oil paintings lean up against the wall. The room is bare except for an old sofa, a green vintage bicycle, and a plastic trash can filled with old skate sneakers. When he isn't painting, Evan skates with a select group who are in on his secret spot. A Slayer or Melvins CD plays, the large windows are angled open to compensate for the building's uncompromising heating system, and a session commences.

Evan drops in from the top, riding over the metal where the ramp meets the floor with a loud slapping sound. His moves include grinds, ollies, fakie ollie disasters, 50-50s, and pivots to fakie. Riding to the top, he pops the tail of the board and launches four feet above the ramp before grabbing the board and floating vertically back down—his ollies to fakie grabs are the highest. He grinds frontside (the back truck of the board scraping the metal bar at the top of the ramp) and then quickly and smoothly reverses direction, sliding around and continuing his run backwards. He knows the ramp's kinks and bumps by heart. His mastery of the ramp translates into speed and self-assurance.

The moment Evan finishes a run or falls, the next skater drops in. There is an uninterrupted flow of skaters riding and doing tricks, either falling during their attempts or riding out of the ramp after a successful half-minute or so. The wall is barely missed, the column is narrowly avoided, boards fly off the ramp coming close to exiting out the window into the night air. Increasingly baroque maneuvers are tried, like Evan's kickflip to backside disasters, in which he ollies out of the ramp and spins the board three hundred and sixty degrees with his feet before landing half-in and half-out on the coping, instantaneously weighting the nose of the board, and riding back down the transition. Perspiration flows, the music plays, verbal utterances are reduced to yells of affirmation or groans when a trick is missed. Laughter and music intermingle with the hanger-deck decibel level of the ramp being skated.

The session over, Evan sits on the couch and enjoys a cigarette and a tall can of Budweiser. His cat, Joey, comes out from her hiding place among the rafters, nimbly jumps to the top of the ramp ("Her ollies are the highest," according to Evan), and slides down the Masonite on her paws before casually walking off. Evan looks away from Joey's antics and says, "This place might be a little crusty, but, it's me…I get a little nervous about bringing a girl here…but, whatever." The ramp and the paintings sum up two years of hard work, the fruit of Evan's impulse to create. Outside the wind blows. The ramp is quiet until the next session.

YEAR OF THE HORSE

BY KAEL GOODMAN

I went to XO on Walker Street last night. It's a small Chinese restaurant, far enough from Mott Street that little English is spoken there. It's the kind of restaurant where I like to go by myself—sit at the bar, suck down the rice noodles with shrimp and Chinese vegetables, and hide behind a paper, watching ancient eating rituals unfold. On this occassion, on the eve of Chinese New Year, I had the joy of watching the staff prepare for their own dinner. The waitresses pulled together a couple of tables, set down big bowls of salt-and-pepper shrimp and squid, a hacked-up chicken, braised string beans, and a bottle of Remy Martin. Then the men from the kitchen, skinny and dirty in their tired white kitchen outfits, streamed into the dining area one by one, each with a bowl of rice, chopsticks in the right hand and an empty glass in the left.

I very nearly pulled up to their table with my own set of sticks, if only to make them laugh, but then I thought it best left to my imagination and instead paid my bill, wished them a happy New Year, pulled on my overcoat and hat, and walked out into the quiet of Chinatown, New York City on New Year's Eve. Year of the Horse.

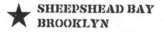
FINDING FRED:
DEATH AND ICE CREAM
BY ALLAN B. GOLDSTEIN

I was riding in our friend's red, rattling car. The car that had
been filled with balloons to celebrate my last birthday—the
time we traveled to visit Mom. Now my wife and I were going
to inform my forty-five-year-old brother of her death. To inform,
support, and console my kid brother—the brother who relied so
heavily on Mom for a connection to the world. The only connection that was organic, as opposed to those forged by people
paid to care for and teach him after sixteen years of neglect in the
Willowbrook State School for the Mentally Retarded. The
brother who would stroll on the boardwalk, holding her hand,
and consider it an exceptional day. The brother who would spend
an occasional Saturday night in "his" bed at her house, watching
television and looking at picture books or coloring with his horde
of crayons, freed, however fleetingly, from group living.

Listening to but not hearing my wife Lisbeth's words, I
looked at the passing concrete wall on the right, the moving traffic in front, the river browning in the dusk on our left.

I was going to tell Fred that Mom had died. He knew she was
sick, had visited her often at the hospice. Direct-care workers

455

had spent much time discussing death with him and his house-mates—what it meant, why it happened, how to acknowledge it. They knew to expect me. I felt Fred was prepared. But now that the event had finally occurred, I was afraid to tell him.

It hadn't yet settled in with me, even though my daily visits to the Bronx hospice over the past two months were officially finished. Before I could come to terms with my mother's death, I needed to recover from firing the first hospice doctor because he referred to my mother as one of "those kinds of patients"; I needed to recover from the always unavailable hospital surgeon who told my mother she was completely cured three weeks before the tumor returned; I needed to recover from hearing my mother's refrain of "I can't, I can't" when she was asked by a doc-tor and social worker in the cancer hospital to decide whether she wanted to undergo chemotherapy. "My hair will fall out! I'll feel sick!" And with tears spotting the hospital sheets, "I don't know…I don't know!" I needed to recover from speaking with psychiatrists called in to deal with my mother's hysteria, nasti-ness, and fear.

My mother was now dead; she was free. "I'm going to Irwin," she had often said with a smile when we knew her fate—her wish since my father died.

And I was free. I was free from the person who had so influ-enced my moods and choices that I fled to Denver and then Denmark for college, returning only because New York was the I was free. And I didn't now that I would soon miss her.

We arrived at my brother's Brooklyn Intermediate Care Facility (a group home for eight) in what seemed a momentary breath. I imagined myself wearing a long, black cloak, advanc-ing without feet, without effort, as we neared his first floor apartment. I opened the door and blaring light smacked into my eyes. I blinked as I sought out my brother's small frame among the scurrying blurs of counselors and residents. "Why don't you go into Fred's room?" someone said, and I followed my brother down the narrow hallway.

He sat at the head of his bed, pictures of him with Mom, Lisbeth with me, and Dad on the wall above. It was a neat room. He had asked the counselors to straighten it up. I sat at the foot of the bed, his stuffed animals, picture books, and music cassettes on the dresser behind me. Lisbeth sat on his roommate's bed, still wearing her coat.

I looked at him. His usually unruly hair was combed to the side, and I could tell by his smooth face that he had been assisted with his electric razor—there were no missed spots.

"How are you, Fred?" said Lisbeth.

Quiet. He looked at me.

"You know why we're here, right?" I said.

"Yeah," he said, allowing more words to roll from my stomach.

"You know Mommy has been very sick."

"Yeah." Composed, and unusually focused, his wide-lens eyeglasses lay cockeyed across his nose, balancing his droopy left eye.

"You saw her lots of times in the hospice."

"Yeah," he whispered.

"You saw she was getting very weak."

"Yeah."

"Mommy died." I studied my brother's face harder than I had ever studied it before. He looked like a stranger. "She's no longer in pain," I continued.

Pointing upward with his left arm, he said, "She's in heaven."

"Yes."

I was surprised at the immediacy of his response, and I was happy that I understood his incomplete sounds. The speech therapist assigned to his residence had stopped training him years earlier.

"She's with Daddy," he continued.

"Yes," I said, thinking how painful this process had been ten years before, when Mom and I needed the assistance of his counselor to tell him that Dad had died.

"I'm going to heaven," he said. "I'm next."

"What do you mean?"

"I'm going now."

"Not now," I said, suddenly realizing how he was connecting hospitals to doctors and doctors to death and thus to himself. His ability to create such a connection startled and haunted me.

"No?" he asked.

"No," Lisbeth and I chimed in at different decibels. "You're going to be here a long time."

Quiet.

"Mommy loved you very, very much. We love you too," said Lisbeth. "You're not alone. Allan is here, I'm here—everyone in the house is still here too."

Ideas never sank in with Fred immediately—he processed information about ten beats after hearing it—so we waited. But there was no aftershock. Fred seemed composed, maybe even happy to have visitors in his room.

"Would you like to go out?" Lisbeth said. "Maybe for some ice cream or McDonald's?"

"Ice cream," Fred said, and we began a new life.

No longer first and foremost sons, we were simply brothers. It was my turn to advocate for Fred, be there for him, listen to his constant, comic complaints about this body part hurting, that person bothering him, having a broken watch, and needing new clothes. His search for attention would no longer be met by the sighs and guilt of a mother, but by the skepticism and humor of a brother. A brother who, up until then, had never had to care for his sibling. A brother who knew nothing of the business of caring for the socially unwanted. A brother who was a hero by circumstance, not choice. A brother who rarely visited during the year. A brother who would again be in his sibling's life like when they were children, before every other Sunday became "Visiting Fred Day."

"Go get Fred with Dad," Mom would say in the parking lot, outside Building Six at Willowbrook, a campus built for 1,500 that housed 5,000.

It was the part of the visit she couldn't endure—entering the institutional halls that enveloped her son. Dad and I would walk along the concrete path that led to a metal door. The flat land around us green in summer, either brown or white in winter, and always eerily peaceful. It never warned of the activity within, of the stench of urine that didn't fit with the shiny floors and bright, pea-green wall tiles.

Inside the door, one of the child residents would spot us and all hell would break loose.

"Daddy," the stranger would bellow, such a huge sound from such a little person.

"Daddy," we would hear, and suddenly a cattle rush was on, only it was children three feet tall padding their feet against the ground, filling the eight-foot wide hallway with ferocious need. This tonnage of tiny humanity would pound its way toward my father and me, chanting, "Daddy, daddy, daddy," smiles bigger than the sun, eyes wider than the moon, little arms reaching out to be the first ones to touch us. "Daddy," I'd hear, the 3-D noise bouncing off unyielding walls. Then, zoom, phumpf, splat— grasping arms would be around my legs, trying to touch my face, hugging my waist, and the attached mouths would now be yelling, "Daddy, daddy, daddy!"

My father and I would shift our weight from one foot to the other, wading in the accumulating mass, peeling little hands away, fending off their intensity. "No, I'm not your Daddy," I'd say, smiling. "No, I'm not," I'd say, looking into misshapen faces. Over and over and over again I'd repeat my words of defense, while searching above their heads for my brother.

We'd catch the attention of the Resident Nurse who took such good care of Fred, maybe because she saw potential, maybe because she often saw his family. Nurses. Nobody was sick. But society labeled children with intellectual disabilities as nuisances, not people—menaces to society, without rights, to be treated with medication. Because imperfection was an embarrassment, they were to be isolated in self-sufficient institutions meant to "calm them." The nurse would wave hello, disappear, and then reappear holding the tiny hand of my little brother. Freddy's face would beam, a searchlight piercing the dark. Nearing us, he'd pick up speed, his little legs and poor balance never taking him quite as fast as he wished to go.

On the other side of the metal door, the peacefulness would slam into us as something out of a storybook. The change would be too sudden, too shocking, the outside smell too good. And we'd walk away, Freddy holding the hands of his father and big brother, pulling toward the parking lot where he knew his mother would be.

Now when Fred talks of his years at Willowbrook, he says, "I helped them get dressed," referring to his wardmates, as he moves his arms up and down as though pulling on a pair of pants. He doesn't mention the rows upon rows of cribs. The many side-by-side malfunctioning toilets. The overwhelmed staff spooning mashed dinner down gullets within three minutes, often causing pneumonia. The sickness induced by medical experiments conducted without informed consent. He doesn't mention the nudists, the hitters, or the simply defeated sitting on the floor in their own feces. Horrors our family didn't even know.

"Do you want a cone, Fred?" I asked, bright lights bouncing off the Carvel store's stainless steel counter.

"A cup," he said. I did not yet know of his difficulty with hand dexterity.

"Vanilla or chocolate?"

"Vanilla."

Waiting for our orders, we took a picture: Lisbeth's head is nuzzled between two stocking hat-topped smiling faces, a blue whale above us. It is winter. It is cold. It is dark outside. In that pastel-colored store, for a moment, we are a family.

KARAOKE FEVER
AT SPECTRUM
BY ANGELA CARDINALE BARTLETT

Auggie works in a nightclub called Spectrum in the Bay Ridge neighborhood of Brooklyn made famous in the film *Saturday Night Fever*. Since the days Tony Manero strode across the lit floor in his white suit the place has converted into a gay nightclub and has changed its original name. It's been Spectrum ever since.

Saturday nights at Spectrum are go-go boy dance parties. Feverish, tight-shirted gay men, mullet-clad lesbians, and some straight couples pack onto that famous floor. The flashing lights are distorted by their forms. Techno blares from body-sized speakers on all sides. The disco ball dangles over the center of the floor. Nothing escapes its smattering of flexible circles of light. The flashing surface of the crowd of heads forms a rhythmic, waving sea.

But Auggie works on Fridays, and things are different on Fridays.

Each Friday, Auggie gets to his day job at nine in the morning. He is a computer guy. He is also a professional singer. He leaves his day job at five, and heads over to Mambo's, an Italian restaurant in Brooklyn, where he sings for three hours, from six to nine. He then rushes from Mambo's to be at Spectrum by nine-thirty. He has done this every night for the past three years, without missing a day or even being late.

There is no need for Auggie to hurry, because the bar is empty at 9:30 p.m. The checkered wood bowls are overflowing with pretzels, and the bartender leans forward on his elbows to speak to two men who possess the easy quality of managers, or owners, during an off-peak time. Auggie and these men rarely speak. They call out a joke or two, and Auggie laughs, but mostly he's consumed with unwinding cords, flipping switches, inserting and ejecting tape cassettes and CDs. He says "testing" into the microphone.

Auggie's system cost him five thousand dollars. He refers to it as "phenomenal," and he does not appreciate when people do not respect it. His pet peeve is when customers cradle the very top of the microphone with their hands. This produces an echo chamber that results in a phenomenal amount of feedback, disabling the system. He also hates when people scream into the microphone. In his black pants, pointy black dress shoes, button-down shirt, and gold chain, Auggie eagerly awaits customers near the opening of the room, where it is brighter. The closer to the back wall of the bar, the darker things get.

Meanwhile, the dance floor is in the other room, popping colors at nobody. The DJ is slumped on a stool behind his equipment, fingering his CDs, eyes cast downward in concentration. Up the narrow hall, next to the door, the bouncer sits on a bench. The cuffs of his bloated, black jacket reveal hands patiently folded. With no crowd clamoring to get in, his largeness is ridiculous; his body overwhelms the room.

Auggie worries about the lack of customers. He used to think karaoke was a dying art form. "But in the past couple months," he says, "I've seen more places opening up for karaoke than I've ever seen in my whole life. Applebee's is doing karaoke. Can you believe that?" He glances almost imperceptibly at the bar, at the door. "I just don't know why they're not coming here."

By eleven, the crowd has grown, but there are still plenty of empty seats and space. People cluster around the bar, with mostly mixed drinks dotting the surface. The cranberry vodka seems most popular. The customers mainly consist of male couples, in their early thirties and forties, though there are two Hispanic women cuddling in the corner, flipping through one of the black-bound songbooks. Conversations are inaudible, private mumbles speckled with low laughter. A younger man leans against the wall, his expression detached, cool. With hands pressed behind his lower back, his eyes slowly scan the room. His dark hair is sleek and heavy with product; his shirt outlines his biceps and beginning potbelly.

On karaoke nights, Auggie thinks in white paper song slips. Stacks of slips can be found every third seat at the bar, along with a binder. One can also obtain a slip directly from Auggie. Each two-by-four-foot square provides blanks for names and song numbers. Auggie uses these to craft the mood of the entire evening. The biggest problem for Auggie arises when customers continue to choose depressing songs. He has to do some quick thinking: "If I have ten slips, and five are happy and five are sad, I mix them—happy, sad, happy, sad, or sad, sad, happy, sad, sad, sad." He also has music-video DVDs of cheerful, romantic songs accompanied by cheerful, romantic images, such as couples horseback riding or couples staring at the ocean, to break up the monotony. According to Auggie, this is one of the special services he supplies that other karaoke jockeys (KJs as they are referred to in the business) do not.

One of Auggie's regulars refuses to complete slips, disrupting Auggie's sense of order. This customer sits next to Auggie, and produces a chorus of "When am I up? When am I up?" Auggie forgets him, sometimes unintentionally, sometimes not, and the man gets angry. Auggie says he knows this man well enough now that he can command him to complete a slip. The man storms off, but minutes later, he obeys Auggie, and slinks back to his spot on the slouching burgundy couch up front.

LOST AND FOUND

The singers' choices are diverse; they include everything from Dean Martin to Christina Aguilera. But there is an undeniable predilection for show tunes and Streisand that even Auggie will admit to. When he has visited other karaoke clubs in Brooklyn, particularly within the notoriously working class Bay Ridge, he always felt limited, as a male singer, to Johnny Cash or Led Zeppelin. He would even dress differently at these places, switching to jeans and a T-shirt. He was not himself. Because Spectrum is a gay club, he says, men can sing women's songs and women can sing men's songs and nobody cares. Auggie feels free here. He dresses the way he wants to and sings what he pleases.

One of the regulars is Howie, a tiny man in his thirties who wears a red flannel shirt and jeans. Howie remains up front with Auggie. He does not complete slips. He is by himself. He says hello to the man at the bar, and to Auggie and to a few others who are clearly regulars. As others sing, he smiles serenely, watching.

When Auggie introduces Howie, his voice assumes the deep, professional quality of a television weatherman. He overpronounces his words. Upon hearing his name, Howie puts his hand to his mouth, feigns disbelief, then laughs good-naturedly. The people in the room clearly recognize him, and return his chuckle. The stage is a square of carpet illuminated in white light. Suspended above the bar, roughly fifteen feet from the stage, is the monitor, a television anchored to the wall with thick bolts. "Half-Breed" by Cher appears on the screen, in yellow block letters that disrupt the simple blue background. Howie closes his eyes and sways his head as he sings. He pushes invisible, Cher-length hair to the side, away from his face in a natural way, as if he's carried hair that long his entire life. His imitation is subtle, sincere. He does not sound like Cher, but he is trying very hard; he sings with authority, imitating every fluctuation of the original. When his song is over, he lingers on the stage and waits for the scattered clapping to cease before resuming his position next to Auggie.

There happens to be a drag queen show tonight, in the dance room, and at midnight, usually the peak time for Auggie, the room cleas, and Auggie resorts to one of his cheerful DVDs. The dance floor is only moderately congested, and the karaoke crowd is a negligible addition. Auggie sits on his couch in the other room with Howie. He waits for his people to return. Thirty minutes pass. An hour. Most of them never do.

When Auggie first introduced karaoke to Spectrum, he says that there were only two people in the bar. Within the first sixth months, he had the place packed. But then they dwindled away. Auggie thinks it is picking up again now, mostly because of his tremendous amount of energy. Aside from his system, his DVDs and his music (the best around, in his experience), Auggie will sometimes host free raffles, for T-shirts and CDs. He also keeps ten blank tapes close at hand, and will occasionally record a singer, and surprise them with the cassette when they are finished. Auggie doesn't profit; he mostly just breaks even. But he doesn't mind. His hobby gives him a chance to share his voice, to help others share theirs.

Auggie occasionally allows Howie to perform in special Cher-only karaoke nights. There is a photograph of Howie on Auggie's website. Howie does not look like the man he once was—his skin has been smoothed into porcelain. His eyes are made heavy with thick, dark lashes. His lipstick is rose-colored and perfectly applied. On Cher night, Howie will not need to wave invisible hair. He has a wig—black, shiny, and ample.

Though Auggie worries about the future popularity of his karaoke show, he is satisfied for right now. He believes in the release of karaoke, that it is an art form in itself: "There are artists out there who didn't do the right thing, meet the right people, who weren't in the right place at the right time." Auggie believes he is one of these artists. "Myself, I get it all the time. When I work at the restaurant, I hear the same thing every night. You could be on Broadway. What are you doing here?" Auggie pauses and leans forward slightly, as if he's telling a secret. "Well, I've found my own little corner of success. I have a day job. I'm enjoying myself. I'm better off."

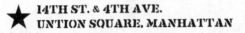

THE UNION SQUARE HORROR

BY IRIS SMYLES

I got all dressed up for the opening night of *Land of the Dead* at the United Artists Union Square multiplex. It was June and I wore a fine white picnic dress. My new boyfriend wore his usual tee with a funny message and ordinary jeans.

I have a tendency to scream. When I attended a scary movie with my last boyfriend, I accidentally ripped the collar off his shirt while crying out, causing his ears to ring for days. Three days later, the ringing implacable, he decided very loudly, "WE OUGHT TO BREAK UP." People are partial to different thrills, I guess. I like to scream at movies, on roller coasters, and in the beginnings of relationships.

I had been looking forward to the opening night of *Land of the Dead* for many weeks and had even prepped my boyfriend with at-home viewings of the Romero zombie film parade.

My boyfriend said he wasn't scared, why should he be? "They don't exist," he noted, while I looked around warily. Finding the coast clear, I shook my head. "That's how they get you!" I explained.

"A slow-moving ghoul might very well put the teeth on you—though you could easily outrun him—simply because you wouldn't expect for a zombie to appear and then bite you. You're caught off guard because you don't believe in zombies and THAT'S how they get you!" I poked him in the chest. We came upon the large red ticker listing the night's features. I breathed, steeling up, while he bought the tickets and we joined the crowd on the escalator up, ushered inexorably toward whatever fate.

The movie was bad. Not bad, really, just no good. I screamed nevertheless, being sure to get my boyfriend's money worth. There were some legitimately good scares here and there. It was the politically correct treatment regarding the predicament of the zombie population that I minded mostly. "They're just looking for a place to go," says one of the characters at the movie's end, while he holds back another from slaughtering a pack of them on their trek out of the city. Never mind that they eat people alive! These flesh-eating ghouls deserve our understanding apparently. Just 'cause YOU don't have a taste for human intestines, that doesn't mean eating them is wrong. It's just different, I guessed, was the moral.

We left the theater discussing the movie on a spirited walk south on Broadway. Breathing in the night, glad not to be undead, I felt I was falling in love and clutched my boyfriend's arm. I wondered if there was a place for us, too, a home like that for the zombies. Would we be left in peace?

He stopped in an all-night deli just a block down from the theater and I waited outside and watched the Friday traffic. Suddenly, a car stopped short. A man had staggered from the sidewalk into the middle of the street. The figure swayed, slammed his hands against the car's hood, and groaned. Jostled from my revelry, I watched the man stagger back onto the sidewalk.

My boyfriend emerged, and I pointed. Another pedestrian slowed in front of him. The figure stopped. His arms rose and he stumbled toward the passerby, who wrestled him off. The zombie fell to the ground. Getting up with difficulty, he began again undaunted.

The bodies of the living continued unsuspectingly down Broadway. He turned toward the locked doors of a furniture shop and pounded on it with his fists. People stopped at all corners of the street to witness the spectacle, including my boyfriend who was moving forward, too. I grabbed his arm trying to hold him back, but he broke away, curious. I stayed hidden behind a phone booth watching, frightened.

Finally, the shop owner opened the door and yelled something at the figure before the ghoulish arms rose again and the man was finally forced to clock him. The zombie stumbled back and fell once more. The man approached, concerned, as did others trying to help. But when he came again to his feet, he jumped out at them, snarling and gnashing his teeth.

I crept up carefully to tell my date we should go before the situation got the better of us, before THEY did. Fire trucks blared across the city. Three trucks stopped in front. Two police cars, an ambulance. A few cops tried to calm him while he bared his teeth demonically. The ambulance men worked to wrestle him into a gurney and strapped him down with some effort and then, "Look!" I pointed. "They've muzzled him." The attendants rolled him out of sight into the van.

"It's begun!" I noted as we walked away.

"Probably just some NYU kid on acid who saw the movie and thought he was undead," my date said calmly.

"There must have been a zombie in the theatre," I looked cautiously as I hurried him over to University Place. "He must have gotten bitten. It could have been us!"

"It's just some messed up kid," he repeated.

"That's what they all say, until it's too late."

"Very well," he acceded. "So would it be safer to hole up at your place or mine tonight?"

"Our first night together!" I screamed.

NEW YORK UNIVERSITY
GREENWICH VILLAGE, MANHATTAN

MY SEMESTER
WITH RALPH ELLISON
BY HAL SIROWITZ

In 1971, I took a class taught by Ralph Ellison, author of *Invisible Man*. It was my last year at the Washington Square Campus of New York University. In those days there was also a Bronx campus, but wannabe hippies like me went downtown. I was a little nervous about graduating, because most of the famous people who went to NYU, like Woody Allen and Stanley Kubrick, had dropped out. I was in no danger of doing that. The future looked dim. Years later when Spike Lee graduated from NYU Film School, I felt vindicated. It was cool again to graduate.

I had to hand in work to be accepted into the class. I dashed off several love poems. I got accepted. But I was expecting Ellison to praise my writing. He never mentioned it. On the first day of class he came with the secretary of his department, who attested that he was indeed Ralph Ellison. He was authentic, not bogus. I had heard of James Dean imitators, but I had never thought writers were able to draw that much devotion.

Ellison took out his lecture notes and read about the philosopher Kenneth Burke. Burke said the most important word in life is "No." Some students disagreed. They said the word "Yes" was more important. It was obvious from his response that he had never taught before. He told those students, "No. You're wrong," and continued reading his notes.

One student asked him to put down his notes and tell us what it was like being a writer and how he became one. Ellison grudgingly took time off from his notes to answer. He said earlier in the day he had seen a policeman giving a ticket to a woman whose dog had peed on the sidewalk. Ellison claimed the dog did nothing wrong. In fact, the urine would help the grass grow. That was what should have been there, not concrete. The dog was just doing what was natural. It was the sidewalk, not the dog or woman, that was at fault. But you can't give a ticket to a sidewalk. He said that was why he became a writer—to take the side of the dog, to represent those who have no voice. Then he went back to the importance of the word "No."

That was the way the class went for the rest of the semester. Students kept interrupting him during his lectures, asking for anecdotes. (I stayed out of the power struggle and didn't challenge him. I was trying to get on his good side. I was still waiting for him to make positive remarks about my poems.) He didn't like that. He said he had spent the whole summer writing those notes. Notes were difficult to publish. Therefore, if we didn't learn something from them, no one would. Then he'd force himself to tell another anecdote.

He told us he reads two books religiously the same time each year: *Huckleberry Finn* and *Moby-Dick*. I was amazed he could read the same books year after year. He read Mark Twain's book to appreciate the first attempt by an American author to write in the vernacular. He read Melville's book to remind himself that you can't exhaust a subject. He wished that book was even longer.

He'd also piss off the black students by telling them that no matter what they wore or what music they listened to, it'd be watered down and taken over by society. Culture is vulnerable to outside forces. Whites will be dressing like blacks and imitating their music. He thought of this idea long before it was proven true by the Beastie Boys. One black student claimed it was bio-

470

logically impossible for a white person to grow his style of Afro. Ellison said the stores would sell Afro wigs.

For the term paper, I wrote about the significance of the word "No." It was supposed to be ten pages. I ran out of original ideas after three. How much can you write about "No"? To make up for this discrepancy I included seven pages of love poems I wrote the night before. I made sure each poem revolved around the lover saying "No." A week later I got a call to see him. He said I didn't hand in my paper. I said I did.

"That didn't look like a term paper," he said. "There weren't any footnotes."

"It's all taken from personal experience," I said. "I wasn't able to footnote it because I don't want the woman to know the poems are about her."

"Is it okay if I give you a C?" he said. "That'll solve this problem."

"That's okay," I said. He still didn't comment about my poems. Yet, years later, I appreciated his silence. I realized he was being gracious. The poems were bad.

★ **4111 30TH AVE.**
ASTORIA, QUEENS

MONKEY BARS FOR A JAIL

BY HAL SIROWITZ

Whenever I took my second-grade special education class to the playground, they'd make a mad dash for the swings. The winners would seldom swing, though. They would spin in circles by twisting the chains. I'd warn them about becoming dizzy, but dizziness gave them an excuse, after their turns were over, to stumble into each other and see how many they could knock down. That gave them more satisfaction than ordinary swinging.

Another group would head for the slides. There was always one student who would climb to the top, then stay there, causing a traffic jam below. Eventually the ones behind him would shove him down. The perpetrator would get back on the slide and do his non-moving act again. If I caught him, I'd banish him from the slides. But there was always a risk he'd do his version of a sit-down strike, and not come with the class when it was time to go. Sometimes, it was easier to grab his legs and help the others push him down the slide. I wasn't taught how to do that in graduate school, but when the tough—my students—don't get going, intervention is required to get them going again.

Then there was always one overweight student who would sit on the seesaw and yell for someone to join him. It was usually the tiniest kid who would take up his offer. They'd sit there for the whole period, wondering why they couldn't get the seesaw to move. I'd push down the side the tiny student was on and explain the principles of weight distribution, but they'd never listen, preferring to be left in a wondering state.

A few would run to the sandbox, only to discover there was no sand. That wouldn't stop them. They'd mimic playing in the sand. But there's a limit to mimicking. After a while it stops being fun. Their solution was to go to the school's garden and import dirt. But dirt is different from sand. It may contain rocks. Being a teacher makes you an expert at spotting possible weapons. It's easier to remove the students than the weapons, so I'd banish them from the sandboxes.

The rest of the students were at the monkey bars. Instead of climbing them, they were used to play their favorite game—"Jail." It consists of placing certain students inside the bars and trying to prevent them from escaping. I don't know the derivation of the game, but with most of them having one parent or relative in jail, it became meaningful. The only problem was that the same students would always be the wardens and prisoners. I tried to change that, but once they took on a role, they wouldn't swap.

I was glad when the whistle blew and playground time was over. If only the equipment at the playground were used properly, it wouldn't have been so difficult. But my students used it for their own purposes. That took some creativity, which was what I was trying to teach. I didn't want to squash that.

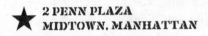

★ **2 PENN PLAZA**
MIDTOWN, MANHATTAN

THE GOLDEN
AGE OF LOSING

BY HAL SIROWITZ

The more games the New York Knicks won, the more they raised the ticket prices. I could only afford to see them at Madison Square Garden if they continued to have losing seasons. I'd buy a ticket from a scalper. Instead of charging more he'd sell it for a fraction of what it was worth, because no one wanted to see them.

Therefore, it was in my best interest to root for them to lose. I had to do it silently, so I wouldn't get beat up by a fanatic. I didn't mind if they won as long as they did it in moderation. I was afraid that winning could become addictive. I'd breathe a sigh of relief each time the other team ended the Knicks' winning streak.

In the early eighties, the Knicks had a center named Ken Bannister. He was nicknamed "The Animal." He had a strong set of teeth and liked to bite opposing players. He felt that since he was shorter than most centers he had a right to make up for his lack of height by creating fear. He'd usually try to bite the other player in the arm. But if he was knocked to the floor, he'd bite the leg.

He led the league every year at getting thrown out of games for biting.

He was a power forward, but because the Knicks didn't have a center, he was forced to play out of position. Since he wasn't playing his true position he had an excuse not to do well. The only times he had good nights were when the opposing players were tired of getting bitten and wouldn't guard him. But since the Knicks were doing so poorly they had the opportunity to get a center in the draft. Bannister was forced to play power forward again and no longer had any excuses. He was released.

The Knicks thought they could improve by hiring a new coach. They chose Hubie Brown, who loved to experiment by making a player play a different position from what he was used to. That way he could yell at them more. If the players played their natural positions he'd have nothing to teach them. But by making a shooting guard play point he had to teach him all the fundamentals.

Brown made Louis Orr, a small forward, into a power forward. Orr was as skinny as a string bean. Players at that position have to be strong. At first Orr did well, because when the power forward on the opposing team saw that Orr was guarding him he'd get overexcited and demand the ball. He'd usually commit a walking violation or miss an easy shot. But the more Orr played the more the opposing player would calm down. He'd get used to Orr and hit all his shots.

The Knicks would try to improve by getting the player they had wanted ten years ago. But by the time they got him he was either too old or too crippled by injuries to be his old self. They did this with Kiki Vanderwegh. He was once a great shooter, but when the Knicks finally got him he'd only shoot air balls. His shots were still beautiful to look at, falling in a perfect arc, but it was like his body was too tired to propel the ball the necessary distance. It kept falling an inch short.

The Knicks traded for a power forward named Truck Robinson. The year before he had led the league in rebounds, but as soon as he got to the Knicks, he said he was tired of doing all the dirty work and wanted to shoot. But since he had never shot the ball much, he wasn't good at it. He also didn't want to take easy shots, preferring to take them from far away. But when he took those shots he was no longer in position to grab the rebound. He was eventually traded.

At one point the Knicks were close to being good, because they got a superstar named Bernard King. But he soon became a victim of one of Brown's rules. Brown had many of them, because breaking one of them gave him another excuse to yell. You were not allowed to let the opposing player take an uncontested lay up. You had to foul him and make him earn the two points from the foul line. Brown thought if you were able to intimidate the other players they'd depart from their game and play scared.

One night, King stopped a player from making a layup, but by doing so he tore up his knee. The player didn't act intimidated. Instead he showed a lot of concern for King, even though the injury was not his fault.

King tried to rehabilitate his knee. He went swimming every day. He made great progress as a swimmer but none on his knee. He never played for the Knicks again.

The Knicks drafted Trent Tucker. He was a specialist at making the three-point shot. Calling someone a specialist meant he couldn't do other things well, like dribble the ball to free himself for a shot. Tucker would never miss, but in order for him to take the shot he had to be left undefended. The other teams knew that and made sure someone was covering him. Therefore, he had to take them from a longer distance to be left open. Instead of a thirty-foot shot he took a fifty-foot one. That was just too far for him.

The Knicks had this philosophy of hitting the open man. Instead of being selfish and forcing a shot, they were supposed to pass the ball to whoever was left unguarded. Since the other team knew about this strategy they'd purposely leave the worst Knicks shooter unguarded. As soon as he'd get the ball the opposing player would dare him to shoot. He'd miss most of the time.

The players would get frustrated watching the same players keep missing their shots. They accused each other of deliberately being a bad shooter so they'd get the ball more. It destroyed the team chemistry. I kept hoping for more team dissension. It meant there would continue to be cheap seats.

**THE 6 TRAIN, BROOKLYN BRIDGE/CITY HALL
LOWER MANHATTAN**

A SUBWAY GROPE

BY I. JENG

Having lived in the city my entire life, I should have had my guard up and my sixth sense alert for the criminally suspicious. But I had just come off an awkward date, and I was still reflecting upon its minute details, the shy looks and painful silences, and otherwise pondering the futility of finding love in this hard-worn city, so I was not in my most alert state of mind.

As I made my way down the long, dark passageway of the Brooklyn Bridge stop, (Idiot! Why did I choose to walk down an empty corridor? Hadn't I ever watched any of those scary teen flicks?) I suddenly noticed a man walking a little too close to me, invading my personal space. At this point, I was already halfway up the stairs leading out, with no one else in sight. I turned my head and noticed a tall white male professional, with light brown close-cropped hair and an average-looking face. He wore a long black wool buttoned winter coat, and otherwise looked like an innocuous professional, sort of a CPA type. I felt a huge sense of relief, until he said to me, a bit too loudly, "Hello. How are you?"

The occasional stranger's polite smile is already a shocking event to me, but that patently false greeting was alarming. I quickly chose to ignore it and hurried up the stairs. That was when I felt a large hand slide up my skirt and grab my. ass. I whirled around quickly. "What the fuck!" I shouted, and pushed him. My speedy turn jostled him, and he faltered slightly on the stairs. Unfortunately, my shove was not strong enough to tumble the asshole down the stairs. His eyes widened in surprise, but as he regained his balance, his face turned into a leer.

I knew this leer. I knew it well. I recognized it as that uniform expression of every sick motherfucker that has ever tried to exert some kind of power over a young girl or someone weaker. I was going to be damned if he thought he had any power over me.

"What the fuck is your problem?" I shouted. My adrenaline and anger had taken on a renewed surge, and I don't think I could have cared if he carried a gun or weapon. I lunged in front of him again, ready to strike. I must have shocked him by my readiness for confrontation, because his leer quickly faded. "Okay, okay," he said, trying to sound conciliatory, but his eyes shifted around us, assessing his next step, perhaps checking for witnesses. "Get the fuck away from me, you asshole. Don't you ever try that shit again!" My blood was boiling at this point, and I was about ready to push again, when he retreated and left. I'm not sure if it was because I really scared him all that much, or whether he thought any witnesses were going to appear. I prefer to think it's it was because my vehement anger shook him up a bit. With that anticlimax, I ranted and raved all the way home, wishing I had killed the bastard.

Afterward, I got all the typical responses from friends and family. "I can't believe you walked in that tunnel alone." "You should have pushed him harder." "I can't believe you were zoning out. You should have been paying more attention." "You should have taken a different exit." Strangely, people seemed to have a lot to say about what I should have done, but seemed to have forgotten that there just shouldn't be such incredible assholes in the world. I wondered, what did that man think was going to happen? That some girl would turn around and thank her lucky stars for getting groped and it would be happily ever after? Or perhaps he got off on the danger of how close he was to getting his balls kicked.

In the stark extremes of that night, from the awkward politeness of dating to the blatant coarseness of aggression, I once again pondered the futility of finding that rare seedling of love in our fair city. But for now, I'll be taking a different train stop.

57TH ST. BETWEEN 8TH & 9TH AVES.
MIDTOWN, MANHATTAN

I'LL GIVE NO TIP
TO CHAMPAGNE

BY RACHEL PINE

There's this place on Fifty-seventh between Eighth and Ninth called Dramatics for Hair. There are a few of them in the city. Dramatics has this thing going on where they give each of their employees a "dramatic" name, something like Flame, or Lightning, or Cognac. They are usually nouns, but once in a while you meet an adjective.

Naming the hairdressers is great for Dramatics, because if you develop a loyal relationship with your Dramatics hairdresser and that person leaves, you will never, ever find them again. Instead, you will have to find a new, perhaps even more dramatic Dramatics hairdresser. The alternative is to call every salon in New York City asking if Tornado works there. This is why you will eventually agree to have Angst cut your hair.

Sting is the name of my Dramatics stylist, and I think he is very good. When I needed to get highlights and a haircut, I called Dramatics and made an appointment two weeks in advance with Chaos, who is the receptionist at this Dramatics.

On the day of the appointment I arrived and waited for a while. I was the first appointment of the day and as the dramatic employees wandered in, I didn't see Sting among them. I asked Chaos for the second time when she thought Sting would be there, as it was already half an hour past my appointment. Chaos makes a call to "headquarters" and tells me that there's been a terrible mistake. Against Dramatics company policy, Sting was granted a three-week vacation, and he won't be back until next week. I tell her this won't work, as I am attending a wedding that night and must have my hair done. Chaos tells me that this is not her fault. I ask her whose fault it is and she tells me that she isn't sure. I tell her I'm not sure either, but I'm sure it's not mine. She tells me she will see if Champagne can squeeze me in. I start to yell.

"I don't *want* Champagne. I want *Sting*."

I am now leaning menacingly against Chaos's reception desk. A new Dramatics employee sidles up to me.

"My name is Shine, don't worry about anything," she says, trying to knead my shoulders.

"Worried? I'm not worried. *I'm fucking pissed off!*" I yell, and shrug her off.

Chaos tells me to calm down or else they won't be able to help me. I tell her that I'm not even warmed up yet. Then I start to cry. I am having a complete meltdown, right there in Dramatics, and they don't even appreciate it.

Shine tells me that Champagne is much better than Sting anyway, and that I'm actually lucky this is happening. I wonder if the fact that one employee has just said something unkind about another is meant to enhance the story arc, but I decide it's just nasty hairdresser sniping.

Everyone is looking at me. Chaos is rolling her eyes and trying to hide the fact that she's laughing at me behind her hand. Champagne, Shine, Glamour, and all of the other Dramatics employees are staring at me. I tell Chaos that if I let Champagne squeeze me in, I'm not paying full price. Chaos runs over to confer with Champagne and tells me that Champagne will color my hair for the Sting price, which she says is a terrific deal because

Champagne is a senior stylist and Sting is not. My roots are long and gray, and the wedding is that night.

"Well, it looks like I don't have a choice," I snarl at Chaos, before starting to cry again.

Shine leads me away gently and takes me to the dressing room so that I can put on a smock. I think for a moment that they would probably rather give me a straitjacket. I put on the smock and leave the dressing room.

I hold my head high as I stride across Dramatics. I sniffle and wipe my nose on my smock. I bask in the reflected glow of bright lights and mirrors.

★ **MUZE.COM HEADQUARTERS
SOHO, MANHATTAN**

ON NOT GETTING THE JOB

BY GREG PURCELL

Dear Muze.com: I was out on the front stoop today, where I have to smoke now that the super of my building has declared the fire escape off limits, on account of he found a few cigarette butts on the pavement underneath. There's a whole funny story about this, actually, considering my roommate begins tearing his hair out at the slightest hint of cigarette smoke wafting into the room, which I take to be a sign, along with some door banging and a general mannered shortness, that I'm beginning to get on my roommate's nerves, what with my having stayed on his couch for three months.

The superintendent of the building wears a ponytail and the slack, Giottofied Jesus Christ expression you find only on the faces of the terminally dumb and bullying. You can find him digging through the trash on any given day, making sure there are no recyclable bottles in there, since, according to him, any cop could happen to stroll by, poke his nightstick in among the banana peels, and give our super a whopping ticket.

This super, who hated me from day one, who in some sense considers me the milk bottle poking out of his perfect pile of trash, has made it his personal mission to regulate my every move, which

484

includes a rule about no smoking on the fire escape. So imagine me, Peter Krause (managing editor at Muze.com), scrunched in the windowframe as I have been for three months, trying to occupy some negative zone between outside and inside, between super and roommate, smoking furtively, lips expelling smoke as far into the night air as possible, a heavy, cold wind whipping in from off the ocean, knocking over the coffee can I use as an ashtray. Consider the consequences of this freak action, Muze. There I am, sore from scrunching up, panicking, trying to pick all those cigarette butts off the fire-escape grating like a child furtively gluing his mom's favorite vase back together, knowing that when the morning came, I'd see all the butts that fell through, like the bodies of little pets, on the inaccessible back porch below.

There I was today out on the front stoop, as per the new house rules, enjoying a cigarette, sort of contemplating why I didn't get the job at Muze, when one of the older ladies who lives in my building came up with one of those two-wheeled grocery carts. It felt awfully good to help her carry that cart up the stairs, though when I attempted to introduce myself, she began speaking in Polish and got a little nervous and she started pointing at all the apartment numbers, saying, "One, three, I don't know... I don't know," me saying, "No, no, my name is Greg, I just wanted to introduce myself..."

It was then that I came upstairs and decided to write this letter to you.

Muze, you provide content for online booksellers and informational retail kiosks. You needed an editor knowledgeable in Science Fiction and Mysteries, someone who had hands-on retail experience, an eye for detail, and a sharp, clear writing style. I was not that editor. But we had good times at that interview, didn't we? I mouthed on and on about the "really terrific" nineteenth-century sci-fi I'd been reading, and aced the test you gave me, the one where I cited Poppy Z. Brite as being an exemplar of the Splatterpunk genre. Remember when you said, "We sort of work in isolation here, and you'd pretty much be left alone to research books without a lot of interference"? Remember how my eyes lit up? There was something strange going on for me there, Muze. I was sort of thinking, I am unqualified to do anything but this job. But I was also thinking, *this* is why I moved to New York, to find just this sort of job. I walked out of that interview feeling happy and desperate, thinking, without a doubt, I had nailed this job. That feeling was compounded when I heard you had started calling my references.

Now Muze, I don't know what sort of super-intelligent beast you've put in my place, but let me assure you that the sum total of happiness in this world has been diminished because of the actions you have taken. Perhaps he or she is qualified enough for your position, even qualified to walk on water or do financial writing or become the lead editor at a prestigious magazine, fielding mind-boggling queries as to the beneficial nature of nepotism or how online dating is revolutionizing romance in the twenty-first century, on top of knowing everything there is to know about Science Fiction and Mysteries. Muze, your beast, this place-taker, will leave you soon, send you scurrying for some new person. All will be unhappiness in your world, and in mine, too. Perhaps even the place-taker will understand in time, hopping ever upward on his or her way to glory, what unhappiness is.

In the meantime, Muze, it's interesting to begin to feel that hackneyed emotion that all recent New Yorkers express after a few months in town, namely, that they feel invisible, friendless, and much less worthwhile than when they walked in. A new wind could soundlessly sweep me off the planet. My mother in Kalamazoo, a handful of friends in Chicago, would make calls at first, inquiring about my newfound invisibility. Then, after a short while, the silence would be absolute. I know this especially since my research in Science Fiction has taken me as close as Mars, as in the books of Edgar Rice Burroughs's Martian trilogy, and as far away as the outer edges of the cosmos, as in the case of Nebula-and-Hug-award-winning author Pohl Anderson, where the life of the Earth, not to mention, a single human being, can be measured in the proverbial blink of an eye.

Best,

Greg Purcell

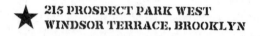

FARRELL'S

BY KEN NOLAN

There was McCawley's and the blinds that hadn't been cleaned in decades. One block over was Connie's Corner where Chris the German bartender would always announce, "I know your family, Nolan," cause we lived around the block and Chris served my parents, aunts, uncles and all. On the next was Val's, used to be Casey's, where my father went with my mom and his three sisters when he got off the subway after three and a half years in Africa and Europe fighting Hitler. One more over was Boops where young, somewhat tough guys hung out. All on Tenth Avenue.

On Ninth Avenue, there was McNulty's, which was across the street from The Shamrock, which was down the block from O'Neill's. Hilltop I don't remember but Langton's was on the circle (Bartel Prichard Square) and you have to count McFadden's Legion Post since everyone belonged. There were others, of course, Parkside, Frank's Prospect Avenue, Devaney's, Sullivan's, Fitzgerald's, Fogarty's, and many more. Rattigan's, which Pete Hamill always mentions. Most were small, somewhat dark and worn, just a place to sit and have a beer, maybe a shot, talk about sports or politics or local stuff with friends, on the way home from work, on weekends, after Mass on Sunday.

And then there was Farrell's. Gleaming brass, polished wood, clean plate-glass windows, bright, crowded with men in ties, some wearing hats, smoking, drinking cold Bud from stem glasses or shots of whiskey in one gulp. At the other saloons you could flash your brother's draft card and for fifteen cents they'd serve you a glass of beer. Not Farrell's. They knew you, your family, your father, mother, grandparents. After all, they were from here—Holy Name—played ball in the schoolyard, the park with your uncles, cousins. And if by chance Eddie Farrell, Hooley, Danny Mills, and the other bartenders didn't know you, one of your dad's friends would have one leg on the foot rail. So you waited till you were eighteen and then summoned sufficient courage to go in and plunk down your money. You were a man.

Growing up with a bar on nearly every corner didn't seem strange since we knew nothing else. Sure there were black neighborhoods, and Italian and Jewish, but except for CYO basketball and baseball games, we didn't go there. We stayed on the familiar streets where our parents were born, married, and died. In those innocent days, we passed these bars on the way to school, to church, bouncing our basketballs or our Spaldeens, peering in to see the Yankee score. After all, we were Irish and drink was what we did—at wakes and weddings and every county ball.

Of course as teenagers we snuck beers and at sixteen or seventeen would go to the Parkside or Connie's or some other dive with obviously phony proof and be served. But once we turned eighteen, and were legit, it was Farrell's. No one had the dough to go away to college so we attended Brooklyn or St. John's or St. Francis and lived at home. Friday and Saturday evenings we'd meet in Farrell's, have a few cold ones before heading to the Fillmore East, a frat party, or the park to smoke dope.

In the late sixties, early seventies, Farrell's was always crowded with iron workers, cops, Irish guys off the boat, and the many young with hair creeping toward shoulders and political views inconceivable. Vietnam split the neighborhood, with us college kids vehemently opposed and our parents and those who worked with their hands in support. It was Vietnam that drove all our families, who adored JFK, to Nixon in 1968, turned those born-and-bred Democrats into conservative Republicans. "The Democrats are for the masses, the Republicans for the classes," old Mr. Flynn would chant. I'm sure he went to his grave never voting Republican, but between the filthy anti-war protestors and liberal elitist Mayor Lindsay, the whole neighborhood changed from working-class Democrats to Nixon/Reagan Republicans. And never returned.

"I went to college," sneered the burly construction worker. "Red Hook." The blue-collar guys despised us. We had it all— education, a few bucks, wheels, unlimited potential—and we were burning the flag, cursing the President, hating America. We'd walk into Farrell's wearing our End the War buttons and guys our age but working full-time would chant, "Four More Years," in honor of Nixon. Soon the whole bar would join in, clapping and yelling "Four More Years," and Hooley would stop, a slight smile on his face, chuckling. It was Farrell's where we mixed, the scruffy college kids and the veterans, the union guys, those who spent years abroad fighting for freedom. "I don't get it," said Richie Van Pelt, who walked with a limp courtesy of the Viet Cong. "I lost a lot of good friends over there."

You shouted, cursed, but never fought. And as our hair got longer, our jeans rattier, we were met with bewilderment and disgust but still got kickbacks every fourth beer. We were stupid or nuts or brainwashed by those Commie professors, but we were neighborhood and essentially family. And when anti-war reformers like Joe Ferris ran for the Assembly, he was supported by most around the bar. Sure they disagreed on the issues, but he was a stand-up guy, one of them, and that's all that mattered.

The bar was clean, the beer cold, and when you walked through the doors, you knew nearly everyone. They'd get red in the face at our peace symbols, but then ask about your father or aunt or grandmother who they saw at church on Sunday. Men at the bar, women in the back only. When Joe Hajjar's Texan girlfriend innocently approached the bar, men booed. Legend has it that Shirley MacLaine, Pete Hamill's date, was the first woman served at the bar. Years later my mother was passing and my friends jokingly dragged her in the back, C'mon Mrs. Nolan have a beer. She said this was the first time in her sixty-odd years that she was ever in Farrell's despite living all her life within four blocks.

We didn't really know Eddie Farrell in those times. He worked days and we went at night with Jimmy Houlihan and the rest. But we knew how he would silently reach into his pocket if someone needed rent money or to pay a doctor. There was always a fundraiser for an ill infant, someone injured on the job, the nuns. Eddie had quiet dignity and class, in a white shirt and tie serving beer or whiskey with a shy smile. Eddie set the tone, not only with his pleasant demeanor but with his style and self-lessness. His bar was not just a place for a drink. Along with the church, it was the neighborhood center, not only where people met but where guys could come when in trouble or in need. Eddie would arrange a loan, a lawyer, a job. Come back on Thursday, talk to Tommy, he's a foreman, maybe he knows someone who could use you. And if Tommy couldn't help you, then he wrote a telephone number on a napkin and you called Jackie. If Eddie Farrell says you're OK, that's all I need to know. And as guys my age gravitated to law, medicine, or Wall Street, connections were made, and favors done, knowing that if you took care of your own, they'd someday take care of you.

But it was social too. Softball and football teams were sponsored, trips to Giants football games in Chicago or Philly or D.C. Busloads traveled to the Preakness or the Belmont. In Farrell's you learned the neighborhood news, who died, passed the fireman's test, bought a home in Jersey.

Eddie's acts of generosity were done without publicity. Yet on one occasion the guys threw him a racket at McFadden's Post. The huge hall was packed, seemed like the entire neighborhood was there. Eddie, Eddie, Eddie they shouted when he arrived, somewhat surprised, embarrassed, blushing. People just wanted to say thanks for helping so many, for being humble and just a nice guy.

For when I think about Farrell's now, forty years after my first beer, that's what I remember most. Nice guys. Eddie who I came to know quite well before his sudden death in 1995. I became a lawyer and he called me on occasion to assist. Jimmy Houlihan, whose goodness and generosity mirrors Eddie's. Timmy Horan, Danny Mills, and the late Vinny Brunton, FDNY, who moonlighted as a bartender and was killed on 9/11. Nice guys who do good. And this tradition continues, raising money for Holy Name or Bishop Ford in Vinny's name. Helping their own.

All the other bars are long gone and probably for the better. Farrell's remains, although it has changed over the years. When I stop in, I recognize a few faces but not most. The neighborhood of families living paycheck to paycheck has been replaced by writers, lawyers, doctors living in homes that cost a million or more. We used to joke that we had to do better than our parents, we had live in a better home than mine on Sherman Street—bigger, no bunk beds, a backyard where you could have a catch, a shower rather than a cold narrow bathtub. The piercing irony is that now most can't afford Windsor or Fuller Place or even the once smelly tenements on Fifteenth Street or Sixteenth Street. Had we foresight and a bank book, we could have bought half the block for what it costs to buy one home today. Only when we left did we realize what we'd had.

There are stools now and some of the beer is bottled, anathema to the purists. But Hooley, Timmy, and Danny are familiar faces, still raising money, throwing rackets. A few years ago, Farrell's ran a reunion at Bishop Ford and 1,200 people showed up, desperate to maintain the link to those same streets where they were raised amid sacrifice but with love and laughter. And one of the younger guys who lives in Michigan runs a blog called "Container Diaries," after the styrofoam cups that hold Budweiser. Photos and memories are published, all beginning with "Remember the time…" And we do.

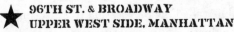

96TH ST. & BROADWAY
UPPER WEST SIDE, MANHATTAN

THE ATTEMPT

BY CATON CLARK

Just short of the Ninety-sixth Street station, the kid next to me started to get really agitated. He was digging around frantically in his pockets for a pen, and since I was sitting next to him he kept pushing and bumping me with his shifting. He finally found the pen in his pocket, but didn't have anything to write on. He started this craziness all over again, looking for a piece of paper. He even looked at me and my book as though he were going to ask me to rip out a page I'd already read so he could write on it. He finally pulled a receipt out of his wallet and starting trying to jot something down on it. I couldn't figure out what thought had gotten him so excited that he'd had to flail about get it down, before it flew right out of his head.

For a few seconds, I imagined he was one of those ecstatic writers who was so moved by his thoughts and ideas, he could-n't help but write day and night with the urgency of a meth addict. When I see these people on the subway they shame me, and I hate them. I never get very excited about my ideas. When I do finally get to writing down my ideas I always wonder if I'm wasting everyone's time.

I tried to read what the young man was writing so I could discover the ecstatic writer's thoughts—important enough to inspire manic episodes. His pen didn't work. It was out of ink. He looked up desperately at an attractive older woman across from him who was getting up and gathering her bags to get off the train at Ninety-sixth Street. She was about ten years older than he was and she looked tired. She didn't look like she had the energy to put up with any bullshit.

He begged me for a pen. I didn't have one. He looked at me for awhile to see if I would change my mind, but I went back to my book. A couple across from us was hunched over a crossword puzzle. The kid lunged at them for their pen. The boyfriend looked sternly up at him and told him that their pen didn't work either. The kid looked around hoping a pen would come from somewhere and rescue him before the ninety-sixth street stop. A woman to his left silently handed him a pen. She must have been admiring him as I was. He grabbed it without a word and began writing on his receipt.

He looked between the older woman now waiting at the doors and the paper. He was writing her a note. I wondered where the receipt was from. What if he gave her a receipt from some embarrassing purchase? Twelve dollars and nonety-five cents for a bottle of Lotrimin AF made specifically for curing jock itch? A crotch-fungus receipt? If I wrote a note to a woman on a train, I would pull a crotch-fungus receipt out of my wallet to write it on.

As we pulled into Ninety-sixth Street and stopped, the kid's hand frantically scribbled to get the note down. The doors opened and the woman stepped out. The kid shot up and shouted, "Wait! Excuse me." I don't know how the woman knew she was being addressed, maybe she'd noticed him staring at her before Ninety-sixth Street, but she turned around and faced him just after stepping out. The kid handed her the note through the door and she took it. She looked at it and then looked up at him confused as the doors closed. She asked him, "Did I drop this?"

LOST AND FOUND

He just stared at her as the doors separated them and the train pulled them apart.

When he turned to sit down again everyone in our section between the doors looked at him. When he looked back, we all looked away. He sat down next to me again and relaxed. A chubby black girl a few seats down and across from us giggled and snuck glances at him every few seconds. He noticed and looked back at her. He laughed with her. I doubt that woman ever called him. She was a lot older.

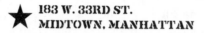

AT THE EDGE
OF THE FROZEN ZONE
BY CHRISTINE NIELAND

Take one large city already threatened into a constant low-level nervous breakdown with terrorism jitters and a rock pile of an economy. Scare away a large percentage of the population by placing a Republican National Convention in the city's center. Pour in five thousand delegates, half a million protesters, seven billion journalists, and a concentration of cops greater than the entire United States military force in Afghanistan—and voilá!—it's RNC Week in New York.

As part of the security plan, a Frozen Zone—no unauthorized vehicles or pedestrians—has been created around Madison Square Garden. The Zone itself is actually quite small, but the street closings and security checks create a major headache.

MONDAY, AUGUST 30

RNC Day One. The sun beats down and the air isn't moving. A demonstration travels up Seventh to the Garden. On Ninth from the Village to Midtown, cops stand posted at every corner, scanning the pedestrians, chatting, fanning themselves with their hats.

LOST AND FOUND

The closer you get to MSG, the more crowded, tense, confusing, and scary the whole thing gets. More cops mill around Thirty-first and Ninth; metal barriers line the curb. Pedestrians are stopped from crossing either north of Thirty-first or east of Ninth. One after another, they ask the cops questions; the cops point around the barrier and north. Inside the Zone itself, concrete barriers, TV satellite trucks, red-white-and-blue charter buses, orange plastic traffic cones, camera crews, the Garden itself, cops, cops, and more cops combine to form a picture of loosely controlled panic. It's a civic circus: the main attraction in a huge fenced-off ring, the spectators squashed together all around it.

The overstressed and overheated seek refuge in the Cheyenne Diner (featuring "Buffalo Burgers" and frescos of Indians astride steers) just outside the Zone at Thirty-third and Ninth. Manager Spiro Kasimas looks around at his two dozen or so customers—cops, firefighters, tourists, demonstrators, journalists, and locals. "Right now there are four people here I know. I asked around beforehand. Eight out of ten of my regulars said 'We're takin' our vacation this week.'"

Across the street, authoritative Officer Nesmith stands at the pedestrian bottleneck, answering question after question after question. He gives directions north, south, west, and all the way around.

With truck deliveries into the Frozen Zone prohibited, men pushing handcarts loaded with ice, soft drinks, and big square cartons of catered food line up in the baking heat. Eventually get to display their various forms of identification and get passed through. A low-flying helicopter buzzes the Garden. Again and again and again. A wilted-looking protester carries a sign: "Hermaphrodites are people too." He passes a woman with a sign of her own: "NYC Women to RNC: Get the Fuck Out."

TUESDAY, AUGUST 31

Today is the day designated for demonstrations involving, depending on which radio station you listen to, "non-violent protest and direct action" (NPR) or "Anarchists!" (1010 WINS).

But the weather has broken, the demonstrations are happening somewhere downtown, and life around the Frozen Zone has settled into its temporary routine. Seventh Avenue is now open, the sidewalks less congested.

The McDonald's is once again accessible. However, only a handful of customers sit inside.

Yesterday, Spiro had nailed the truth about business in and around the Frozen Zone. "I'm doing good, but there on the other side (east)—nothin."

Most notably, no Republicans. Mayor Bloomberg chirps about the $265 million benefit the Convention will lavish on the city. Nobody's seen it around here. The locals most imperiled and inconvenienced are taking a hard financial hit as well.

In the Thirty-third Street Galleria, past the Impressionist reproductions, New York posters, and A-Rod and Mike Piazza bobblehead dolls, manager Nasir Sharif sits all the way in back, all alone. "Last week was really busy," he says. "We hope we get a check in the mail next week from Mr. Bush. He wants to fix the economy, he can start here."

The bad times continue at the A&H Plaza deli. Cashier Cindy Bat sums up business: "Terrible! Look at me! I'm doing side work, there's no customers to serve!" Any problems getting deliveries? "Only two deliveries! Nobody's here!" A pair of actual Republicans, small people in conservative suits carrying slick Bush-Cheney folders, quietly purchase some lunch and slink away.

H&M security guard Shirley Grant would rather talk about the Sunday demonstration than the flagging business. "Did you see the coffins? That was great; that's something people need to see." Despite the massive police presence, she worries about Thursday. "He's coming, and you never know, it just takes one crazy person…"

LOST AND FOUND

Somewhere back there in the Frozen Zone, beyond the cops and the metal barriers and the satellite trucks and the concrete blocks, past the ID checks and metal detectors, Mayor Bloomberg quietly fantasizes about bringing the Olympics to New York City. And President George Bush, the man who promised to unite not divide America, will be staking his political future on the claim that he has made America safe.

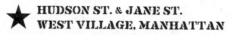

TWILIGHT IN THE TOY SHOP
BY CHRISTINE NIELAND

I'd dashed in about a half hour before closing time. This little toy store in the Village, whose shelves cheerfully overflow with cute wooden toys in primary colors, funny stuffed monkeys, and bright plastic puzzles. A friendly, crowded little place devoid of Game Boys and electronic pinging, the kind of place where you can reassure yourself you're in the company of rational, progressive Europeans and can therefore shop with ideological impunity.

I browsed my way to the back of the store, where I weighed the relative merits of the big plastic dinosaur versus the cinnamon bear hand puppet.

A teenage clerk sat behind the little counter, chewing gum as she read a children's book. Ballerina dolls and airplanes dangled overhead; toy jewelry and miniature books lined the countertop. The young clerk could have been part of the colorful display.

The doorbell buzzed.

The clerk didn't move.

The bell sounded again. Two, three, four times in a row.

I checked out the clerk. She only had to lean forward slightly to buzz the door open, but instead just sat there, rigidly hunched over the storybook, chewing assiduously.

"That book can't be that engrossing," I thought. "I wonder if she's hard of hearing."

The buzzing stopped, replaced by a polite tapping on the glass. "Hello?" a male voice sounded. "Can you open the door, please?"

On the sidewalk outside the door stood a handsome, impeccably groomed man in his late thirties, toting one of those rich-looking brown leather briefcases you see in the specialty stores, and wearing a trenchcoat that probably cost more than I make in a month.

"Hey—can you let me in?" he repeated.

Despite this guy's obviously stratospheric income bracket, I guessed that we did have one dilemma in common—an impending special occasion and no enthusiasm for noisy, battery-powered conventional toys. As the only customer in the store, I felt obliged to support my fellow deadline-beater. I looked at the clerk and started to say something, but the man at the door beat me to it.

"Aw, come on!" he complained. "You're not letting me in because I'm black!"

The girl hunched even harder over her book; I think she would have jumped in and closed it around herself if she could have.

Trying to approximate that expression that relief pitchers level at batters with two men out and a runner on third, I glared at the teenage clerk. She looked at me imploringly. "The last two times I let black guys in here, they robbed me!" she blurted.

I had no way of knowing whether or not that was true. I guessed it was an exaggeration—it's more likely that two guys robbed her once. But she was physically shaking, so I did believe that somebody had robbed her. Most likely not an investment banker.

I'm a writer. I spend a great deal of my time crossing out my first impulse, reworking every expression of thought before committing it to the public. It's a very enjoyable and reassuring process. Nothing reaches other people till I've satisfied myself that it's ready. But there is one drawback—I don't get enough practice thinking on my feet.

I felt terrible for the man outside. But I knew I had no authority whatsoever to tell the terrified clerk what to do. I couldn't think of anything to say. So I adopted an expression I hoped conveyed a plea for rationality, plus an assurance that in the event she let the man in and violent crime ensued, all one hundred and three pounds of me would leap to her defense.

She only ducked further into her book.

I exchanged looks with the man at the door, and shrugged sympathetically. He could have asked me to let him in, but he didn't. I could have gone to the front of the store and opened the door for him, but I didn't. I don't know why.

The man turned in disgust and walked away, taking his billion-buck briefcase with him. I reluctantly decided not to make my nephew suffer for someone else's racism with a late-arriving birthday present, so I paid for the cinnamon bear. The clerk's eyes never lifted above the cash register. I never bought anything in that store again.

This all happened several years ago, but the moment when the three of us stood paralyzed has always stuck in my mind. It is a grim, perfect image of some frustrating truths about the state of race relations in this country.

Behind the cash register, the terrified white person who can't tell a Crip from a Merrill Lynch employee if his skin color happens to be black. The wimpy liberal sickened by injustice, but too polite and unimaginative to do anything about it. And, banging on the window, the impeccably groomed guy in the thousand-dollar trenchcoat. Prosperous and successful, but on certain unforgivable occasions, still denied access to the beautiful toys.

YOUR TURTLE NEEDS A PLACE TO REST

BY AMY BRILL

I'm at the newsstand when the traffic light goes out. It has the same ominous, empty face a dark stoplight always has. Newsstand man looks up. His light went out too. We turn in tandem. The subway light is out. Now we look at each other. Not good. We shake our heads. Nothing like a little darkness to make you look each other in the eye.

Down Broadway, heading toward Times Square: the smokers huddled in doorways look smug instead of furtive, for a change. They have information. It's all up and down, they call out to passersby, who are looking up, who are looking down. Managers and cashier girls and the entire staff of Pluck U. are gathered in dark doorways. It's the whole block, I think, and then: the whole city?

That's what's starting to trickle in from the smokers-turned-newsboys, from the pedestrians-turned-reporters. Cell phones are busting from every pocket, digits punching, looking, listening. People are pouring out of the Paramount Building at Fiftieth Street and Broadway. The plaza is a universe of people on phones, an unchoreographed flashmob. Cosi is dark. Duane

Reade is dark. I find some people who, like me, might have been working on the thirty-second floor if we hadn't been kicking around doing chores. Now everyone wants to know what's happening, and the only people who know anything are those with parents in the hinterlands, parents who have TV and radio and light. Facts fly from group to group. Fire downtown. Fire at Con Ed. Fire in Jersey City. No power in the boroughs. No power in Connecticut. Ohio. Canada. Canada? Well, then, it's not terrorists, we joke.

But there's a whisper, a shiver. Fires. Many cities. It's a great way to get people outside, one practical producer muses. I want to leave, a younger girl says, meaning it. I see that one young woman is crying. Now I want to leave, too. The subway is dark. Rosie's Stardust Diner is dark. I decide to walk to my brother's place in midtown.

Broadway, Seventh Avenue, Avenue of the Americas: thousands of people teeming up and down sidewalks and whirling through revolving doors. Puffs of previously cool air exit with them. French Connection is dark. Apple Bank, dark. People line every step, bench, statue, fountain. They are waiting, it seems. Lots of people are trying to talk on the phone, but mostly they are just listening to their phones not work. The sound of the dark. My phone makes valiant efforts to call people. I don't know how I know this, but I feel like my phone works—it's other people's phones that aren't responding. This is weirdly comforting.

At every intersection, someone is directing traffic. Every intersection. Their personalities dictate their style. On Sixth Avenue, two boys with do-rags and NBA tank tops down to their knees are trying to hold up four lanes of traffic so that the cars on Fifty-third Street can crawl across. Put ya hand up, yo! one yells to the other, who looks more scared than official. But he does it, peeking in-between oncoming cabs and Mercedes and pickups, gearing up to jump in front of them as if he is about to get in on a round of double Dutch. I go on.

LOST AND FOUND

Il Gattopardo is dark. Manolo Blahnik is dark. Ladies stand outside, smoking. They don't look like they're sweating. I only have a few more steps to wonder how that's possible, and then I'm at my brother's place. He's out, the doorman says, but offers: Do you want me to let you into his place? I'm in jeans, sparkly flip-flops, a floaty fancy shirt. It's already obvious that I'll be walking to Brooklyn. Hell yeah. Before I go, I notice a beautiful unsweaty woman on the phone to her friend in Miami—I think it was Miami—dictating the news back to a very elderly couple who has walked carefully down the pitch-black stairs holding a candle in one hand and each other in the other.

The stairs are dark. Really dark. I count steps for no reason, just to know. At my brother's place I rummage through drawers, locate some running shorts and a tank top—though I'm stuck with the sparkly flip-flops—and then fail to find a battery with which to find out from the tiny bedside clock radio just what the hell is going on. And it's hot. Really really hot. The cat doesn't care that it's hot, or the turtles. Only I care. I can't stay here by myself. Nobody's phone works. Mine teases me: It seems to be connecting, it seems to be going, and then…nothing. Bitch phone. Fuck it.

I head west, to a friend's place in Hell's Kitchen. Now the streets are jammed. Most people in this part of town are going north. A woman on a curb rolls her eyes at a dramatic presentation by a citizen-traffic-director, and is chastised by her friend. My friend's neighbor lets me in and I light myself up five flights, finding her at home. She's cleaning out her closet. Humor me while I do this, she says, making me a gin-and-tonic, making one for herself. I have to do something or I'll go nuts. We wave to the kids in the apartment next door. They have a turtle, too, but theirs is swimming in a tank with no rock, no resting place. I make a sign: YOUR TURTLE NEEDS A PLACE TO REST—and press it to the window. Their mother reads it and calls, Yes, I know. Thank you. But my friend shakes her head. Then why is their turtle always swimming?

She is my shoe size and has a solid pair of running sneakers for me. Moving along Ninth Avenue, it's clear that half the people are rushing to get somewhere, and the other half are getting drunk. Uncle Nick's is dark. The Amish Market is dark. At the doorways of bodegas, enterprising owners are selling water out of coolers. In the doorways of buildings, neighbors are listening to radios. I'm offered water, beer. For once, nobody offers anything nasty.

I go west, hoping that maybe the DUMBO ferry will be running from somewhere. The sun is beginning to go down and the usual West Side collection of joggers, bikers, skaters, and guys cruising has been supplemented by what appears to be twenty thousand people trying to get to New Jersey. They line the waterside from the *Intrepid* to Chelsea Piers. They are crammed behind fences and resting on curbs. Lines of people five-deep stretch at least a mile. Some think they're going to Hoboken, others Weehawken. Where's Weehawken? I don't know, but I'm glad I don't live there.

As I go south, the sun sinks deeper, settling into a perfect summer sunset. The river glows orange, silhouetting the kayakers paddling north in formation. New Jersey is dark. Chelsea Piers is dark. But the pier is open, and the friend I'd planned to meet hours ago is there, and we drink beer and watch the sailboats ferry people with fifty dollars to spare across the water, trying to get them home. We on the pier drinking cheer whenever the boat slides gracefully into the slip, and cheer when it slips out again, loaded up with people. Fifty bucks for a sunset sail? They could do worse, we figure.

It gets dark, now, for real. Night and dark, black on black. My friend rides me on his crossbar to the West Village. The Duplex is dark. West Twelfth Street is dark. We call out all along the way: Coming through! Right behind you! and the streets are still thick with people and any windows that are not dark are the same ghostly yellow-orange, flickering and gentle. We sit on my friend's fire escape and watch his street. On every stoop small groups of faces lit by flashlight and candle kick back, drinking, laughing. The neon sign next to his window is dark. My neighbors, he sighs, half-joking, half-sad. Who are they?

Finally, I get on his extra bike, strap on his extra helmet, and, armed with water, tire pump, and Mag-Lite, start pedaling for Brooklyn. Bleecker Street is dark. Broadway is dark. As I'm heading south, a guy on a bike pulls up alongside me: "Are you riding to Brooklyn?" he wants to know. "Can I ride with you?"

Of course. We pedal on. Streets fly by, our tires somehow evading all the invisible potholes. Chambers Street, left turn, the cops wave us onto the bridge, we are on the inbound vehicle side of the Brooklyn Bridge and we are not alone. Out of the dark city at close to midnight we are joined by hundreds, thousands, people on foot, people with flashlights, lanterns, circus glow-sticks. People on phones, people with kids, people walking home to Brooklyn fill the bridge. We pedal on. The full moon lights the dark bridge. The East River is full of moonlight. People on the bridge are looking at the stars.

And then I'm home, I'm flying across Adams Street, pedaling up Court, and Cobble Court Cinema is dark but it's after midnight now so it's okay, and these streets in the dark are my streets, anyway. I stop at my friend's place around the corner, and in the backyard I find ten hardy souls drinking wine, eating a meal from the grill. Lamb, corn, pasta. I haven't eaten since noon and I dig in, so grateful. All the kids are crashed on a mattress in the middle of the yard, six small arms and legs flung in all directions. They're replete, because they're three, and five, and they are camping, and I wonder if this is a night they will remember for the low hum of grownup voices at a table, or the sticky way their skin will feel when they wake. If they'll remember that the light they quit fighting when their eyes got too heavy wasn't coming from the TV or the movie screen or the video game or the computer or even from the lanterns strung out along a wire all around the yard. I wonder if they'll remember that the last light they saw this night in Brooklyn was the sweet orange glow of a full August moon.

A DANCE WITH SPALDING GRAY

BY NEDA POURANG

When I was in college, I spent an entire night dancing at the Palladium in New York City with Spalding Gray. We danced and danced to every song—danceable or not. I didn't know who he was but my friends did and he was a very cool older man who seemed to still like the things I'd assumed you stopped liking when you turned gray. I had been in a fashion show at the Palladium that night and I still had on my long white Mary McFadden dress while bopping around to Madonna's "Express Yourself." My friends and I were new to the city, and looking back it seems perfect that Spalding Gray was one of the first ambassadors to guide us into the mysteries of New York. He treated me like a grown-up and was a perfect gentleman. More than anything, he reminded me of the shy art majors I was at NYU with. At the end of the night, my girlfriends and I walked him home before heading back to our apartment on Second Avenue—the first of many apartments during my time in New York.

That old apartment is gone—burned down. The Palladium is now an NYU dorm. All that thumping house and those lit staircases—razed to house the students who were babies or not even born when the dance hall was king. And this week I know for sure that Mr. Spalding Gray is gone too. Years later I saw and read his work and wished I'd asked him clever questions when we met, instead of just jumping up and down to George Michael.

I'm gone too. More than a decade of parties, boyfriends, school, and false career starts awaited me in New York after we left Mr. Gray at his brownstone. I am not anywhere close to being the unjaded newcomer that I was. I have left. I drive a green Honda in Los Angeles traffic and think about my own brief but unforgettable experience with depression. I didn't know what it was or how many pills there would be for it back when I was spinning around in my white gown with Mr. Gray. And I didn't know that not everyone could simply take up jogging, fall in love, and grow out of depression like I did. I didn't know that some people stayed trapped in the grief, no matter how good their lives got around them.

I always assumed I'd run into him again. New York is like that—you don't worry so much about exchanging information because you live by the city's serendipity. But I never did, and for a long time, I forgot all about it. Now I feel a loss I don't really have the right to feel because it is not sadness for the tragic death of a talented man—a good man. It is more about the loss of everything that changes and passes. From legendary clubs to my own unaccounted-for twenties. And then there is my feeling that I didn't so much leave New York as get spat out by it. All I know is that I danced one night in the nineties in New York City with Mr. Spalding Gray, and he never got tired or missed a beat.

TODAY'S PROPHET OF MISERY

BY KATIA MOSSIN

David is a sweet loser. David is a horny loner. David always complains about life. David is an artist who hates to draw. David likes women but is hurt by their coldness.

Till the late nineties, he would wear Miami-style printed shirts, his hair long and wavy. Back in those years, he had sharp-toed white Italian shoes and linen summer pants. It sounds fancy, but it did not look it. In the nineties, Russian men in Brooklyn favored the Italian look after Eurovision promoted Toto Kutunio. It lasted more than a decade, never switching to the simplicity of white shirts and jeans (like Eros Romasotti) or gracefulness the of wrinkled tweed jackets (Adriano Chelentano). It was a die-hard style. Finally, David trimmed his hair short.

One winter, he sported a long leather Dick Tracy coat and fake Rolex. Coming to parties he used to give doormen his name without hesitation: Bond, James Bond. Usually in this case he had a bottle of Napoleon cognac in hand and two blonds in tow. David is cool in his misery.

David lives with his *babushka* (grandma, not headscarf) and cat in Brooklyn and he collects used Jaguars. In the winter he brings boxes of auto parts and spreads them on the floor of his living room. Music plays softly at the dusty background: "I'm a loser, baby, so why don't you kill me!"

David is depressed. His therapist eventually gives up. She is a woman and David has too many problems with dames, enough not to trust them with his fragile psyche.

He hates America. He dislikes Russia. He is an anti-Semitic Jew. We, his friends, love David. His self-inflicted misery gives us a chance to see ourselves in better, brighter light—our pretty and smart spouses and cute children were results of adult decision-making and responsible behavior. And yes, we feel luckier. The rumor is that David has a big penis. One of his former girlfriends claimed that size was insignificant. But back then, she was disappointed with pretty much everything. Once, coming from an exhausting shopping trip, I overheard her whispering sadly "I am not satisfied, not satisfied…" She was in no condition to judge impartially.

Confronted with direct questioning at our usual loud drunken dinner in an Indian restaurant, David remains silent, smiling mysteriously. He has a big nose. You know what it means, don't ya? David's mom is a petite, attractive woman, covered with a thick cracked layer of makeup. She lives in Florida with her husband and occasionally visits David and *babushka* in New York. For his fortieth birthday she brought a photo album with her. We admired pictures of mother and cat in many shapes and colors. After thirty or so pages, we discovered a lonely picture of baby David.

David likes women and dates them sometimes out of habit, without much hope. He also surfs the web for dating purposes. A week ago, he forwarded me an e-mail with a personal ad from RussianNY.com from someone named Toma, who, in very specific and poetic detail, proclaimed her love for oral sex and desire to meet a suitor possessed of qualities described in her poem. David was obviously fascinated by her and thought we would be too. Aside from being dirty and unfunny, there were words in the ad that were unintentionally misspelled.

I wrote to him: "Dave—it is disgusting and makes me wish I never knew this beautiful language. Stop searching Russian NY.com and get a life. Or simply read a good book—or watch *Casablanca*. You are destroying your image of the lonely romantic."

He replied: "Unlike you, who gets whomever she wants, me horny very much." He left me no choice but to be direct and I opened my mouth (I have a big mouth on me): "My dear, jerk off and go to sleep. Nobody will caress and love you better then you."

I continued: "Lonely celibacy should be a conscious choice just for that reason. You do not need these loose women from RysskiNY—they have spotted skin and floppy underarms. They are used and screwed-up—they will not love you—and they are not there to give strangers oral pleasures—they are just hunting for their next victim of domestic verbal abuse, Kmart shopping, and Sunday brunch (nothing is wrong with that agenda, actually), but don't pretend you don't know it. There is no mystery in this ad—your fascination is not with the subject, but with the vulgar bravery of the offer. By the way, about me—at the moment I am proud to be asexual by choice in today's complicity of homo, hetero, and bi greed and despair. Besides, after a certain age people look ridiculous, cuddling, flirting, and fighting. Only very young teenage lovers, old couples, and animals still touch my heart in their truths. Good night."

At that he advised me to get a teenage lover, to explore the pleasures of a threesome with an old couple, and was more forgiving on the subject of animals (he loves his cat dearly) by suggesting that I adopt a pet.

A divorced friend of ours, mother of two, also placed a personal ad on match.com. Her picture did not show her face, only a quarter of profile and gracefully curved back. While on vacation in Italy, she checked her e-mail and found, among others, a message from a Russian artist. He lived in Brooklyn, admired her picture, and loved animals, children and music. How many Russian artists were there in Brooklyn? How many of them possessed the same unusual qualities? She wrote back: "It's me, David, Olga!"

He was not a bit surprised. "Sure, just my luck—from the bottomless ocean of web-dating opportunities I am picking an old friend. Misery, thy came a full circle…"

At the turn of the last century, when almost all of us crashed through divorces and separations, leaving shreds of skin on the thorns along the way, pathetically baring teeth in useless growls and moaning in pain, we become jealous of David's style of life— we thought his loneliness safeguarded him against betrayal and wrong moves. Bitter demons were eating most of us—we struggled, jumped, zigzagged, crawled, and ran. We languished in emotional comas, sank into financial pits, hid in the asylums of post-traumatic cynicism, and eventually emerged from ashes of former lives, beaten but not wise. David was consistent. After twenty-or-so years away from the motherland, he visited old acquaintances in Moscow and was surprised at the wealth of some and the pitiful existence of others. His first love had three sickly kids and lived in a tiny dusty flat on the outskirts of the city. His old schoolmate had three factories and a mansion on the Canary Islands. Some of the achievers and winners of childhood became losers and scapegoats of modern Russian reality. Some stayed put, but all of them kept balancing acts of their own.

The country itself was still quite uncomfortable for single living—people preferred to cling together in marriages or relationships to stay warmer during cold months, to form alliances of blood relatives against forces of nature, bureaucracy, and fate. They continued to take risks of remarriages; they conceived more children. People were stupid on both sides of the globe. David made his unhappiness stylish—it was without fail the subject of conversation at any dinner party or birthday, it was a good shtick for pick-ups. Anyone who had a tender spot for the lonely suffering artist in the cruel paws of capitalism was sympathetic.

Time passes. We are uncertainly moving along murky paths, fumbling blindly with our shabby fingertips, and feeling with tired unsteady feet bumpy roads, keeping eyes open as tired as we are, reading shapes and shadows in the half-light of another rising day.

David is smiling at us. I know he will surprise all of us one day with sudden change—today's prophet of misery, ambassador of rejects, master of his loneliness. He says that one day the chosen one will come and put her bony hands on his shoulder.

The cat purrs softly and jumps on David's lap. *Babushka* emerges from the kitchen, holding a steaming cup of tea. China is much valued by Russian immigrants in their seventies. The tea set is "Madonna," rich with gold and mother-of-pearl patterns and a picture of Holy Virgin and the Child. It represents wealth and good taste.

David is stoic and persistent. He came to this world to suffer and will make the most of it.

FROSTED FLAKES AND THE PRIMITIVE ANIMAL GOD: A NIGHT IN THE TOMBS

BY ANDY HILL

When the man in the bodega reached across the counter to hand me my cigarettes, I felt there was some hidden significance in the exchange. It was not until I left the store that I looked at the $3.25 I held and realized that it was all the money I had. The change felt heavy in my hand. It was my first night in the city and I had arrived with almost nothing. I used twenty-five cents to call an old friend from California, and two dollars to take the subway to his apartment in Bed-Stuy.

New York is notorious for being hungry, but I was surprised to find that it had eaten my friend whole, not even bothering to chew him up first. He lived on the top floor of a building that seemed to be falling in on itself. We sat in the apartment, drank Ballantine from the bodega downstairs, and smoked rollies while we were slowly digested by the living room.

I borrowed some money and took the train early the next morning to Union Square. It was a bright spring day and the park steps were crowded with young people. I entered the Whole Foods hoping to stock up on some food for the house as a way of saying thank you for their hospitality.

I have been told that I have "that type of face," meaning the kind that helps you get away with things. First I walked upstairs and had a snack. Then I began to fill one of the reusable "green" shopping bags, strolling through the aisle casually, pulling items off the shelves and checking their prices before putting them back or taking them with me. My bag was overflowing as I walked past the cash register. Automatic telling machines are often kept by the entrances to stores, and I fumbled in my wallet, pretending that I was looking for one as I approached the door.

A man in a white button-up shirt came up beside me and grabbed my arm firmly.

"May I speak to you for a moment, sir?" he asked, and before I could answer I was in his office, a small room close to the till. The security guard sits in there behind the video eyes of the store, fighting crime, like a vulture on the side of the road. I sat in the nest. He ruffled his feathers. He screamed. Bobbed his head up and down and poked me with his claw. The wall behind his desk was covered with Polaroids of other shoplifters, the "wall of shame." The value of the items that the perpatrator had attempted to steal was written below the photo.

"I know what you were trying to do," he said.

The manager came in. He heard my story, then the other man's. We both sounded like assholes.

"I think we all know what is going on here," he said.

He had better things to worry about, and left. I assumed I would be sent home and waited patiently while the security guard whistled along with the radio, "Why did you have to make everything so complicated?"

I have always paid larcenously close attention to detail. Cars approaching from miles off. The bobbing of a flashlight in the dark. The difference between the footsteps of a passerby and of someone who is searching. When I heard a radio chirping, leather belts creaking, and boots shuffling on the other side of the door, I knew immediately that the cops had arrived. This was confirmed by the smug look of contentment from the security guard. It said Justice was about to be served, and he had earned his pay. I smiled as he took my Polaroid to add to his collection.

For about five minutes I was the star of the grocery store as I was marched past women pushing strollers, businessmen, and NYU students. For a few seconds their eyes were fixed upon my glorious walk of shame. Petty theft had never felt so grand.

They serve Frosted Flakes in the catacombs below New York City. I poured milk into my small box of cereal and ate it, wondering if it was really five in the morning. That was the time the guards said they would serve breakfast but I had no way of telling—there were no clocks or windows. I was wondering if I was really twenty-four, or if I was sixteen. I had no way to tell; it felt just like high school, and there were no mirrors to see if I had grown younger. I suppose I could have asked someone else in the cell—there were over twenty other souls occupying the stainless steel benches and cement floor. But I felt as if I had slipped into a void where the only real question was if those crooked bastards on the other side of the bars would ever let us out.

Fifty people to a cell while the one nextdoor stands empty. Some are down there for thirty minutes, some for three days, sweating out alcohol and medication onto the floor. It's real slippery down there. Blood on clothes and the floor is new and still red. Blood on the wall is dried and black. All the corners are filled with filth of the invisible.

The men in the cell slept beside one another with a forced intimacy, curled up on the floor with their hands tucked between their legs or down their pants for warmth. But I couldn't sleep and a man, newly arrived, sat down beside me and started to talk.

516

"Came home last night, and there was another man in bed with my woman. So I went in the kitchen and I got the broom."

I looked over at him.

"This isn't my blood. Sent him to the hospital," he said proudly. Then he looked at me skeptically and asked, "What are you in here for?"

"Petty larceny," I said.

"Bet you'll run faster next time."

My name was on a piece of sacred paper held in the bestial hand of a primitive animal god, and called out aloud it meant I would go to wait for my trial. A few flights up and the air became much fresher. I felt like I was truly rising from a tomb! Fresh cellmates were sleeping on the floor in the morning sunlight coming through the windows.

Among them was a dopey man, shuffling from place to place on the benches. He was large, wearing old tennis shoes and sweat pants. All the others in the cell seemed to avoid him and when he saw me enter, he came up to me immediately and began to speak.

"What's a nice-looking kid like you doing here?" His voice was whiney and apologetic. It was like being the new kid at school. I wanted him to leave but he kept on talking.

"You go to college? Man, I'd kill to get a degree. I wouldn't be in here. I'm only in here because of a motorcycle wreck I was in a year ago. My leg is still fucked up. I was on painkillers but when they cut me off I started smoking crack, self-medicating." He reached over and grabbed a peanut-butter sandwich from the bench beside him. Someone screamed.

"You touch my sandwich again and you die you fat fuck!"

A man on the floor had pulled his shirt from off his face and was now sitting upright. The fat man threw his arms over his head and ran towards the door.

My cellmates had stolen their girlfriends' credit cards, beaten their childrens' mothers, robbed their sisters, hammered their wives' lovers with sticks, and held up donut shops for sixty dollars. The young kids bragged about the crimes they had committed and who they were going to beat the shit out of, and how. The older men were quieter. I overheard one say, "It is alright. I deserve to be here. What I did was wrong. I was selling counterfeit jeans. I knew it was wrong and I did it anyway. Now, I am paying the price."

When my name was called I took a seat in front of a small plastic window where I spoke to an attorney on the other side. I stared at his tie, it was horribly ugly, and I had a hard time concentrating. He said, "I'm a lawyer. I'm going to help you." It seemed like a funny thing to say. Soon afterwards, I lay down on the floor and fell asleep.

My first day of community service I swept seed pods and picked up cigarette butts in Tompkins Square Park. A young gutter punk approached me and introduced himself as "Pinner." While I worked, he bummed cigarettes off passersby, and we smoked below a large tree in the center of the park. I watched one kid sweep the same pile of leaves back and forth across the pavement the whole day.

On the second day, I met a man named "Q." He was a private security guard for politicians in D.C., and because of this he had only gotten one day of community service for assaulting a police officer. "Q" told me he worked for *Sex and the City* and said if I stuck close to him, I would get out early.

"Q" left early, but I was driven to Chinatown in a big van, where we had lunch in a small park beside tennis courts then drove down below the Brooklyn Bridge, close to the water. From the back of the van we were given trash bags, and a few people gloves, and instructed to weed the rose gardens beside the road. We started working slowly, keeping as much distance from one another as possible. I was determined to work hard and do my job well, even after the boss had stopped paying attention and only a handful of us kept weeding. With my face in the rose bushes, I felt like I was moving unconsciously down a hidden path, toward something. The boss leaned against his van, smoking a cigarette, looking at me, confused.

FEDORA

BY ALFRED H. LANE

Fedora is a few steps below street level. One steps down and pushes open the door into a red-hued room that feels like another world, or at least another time: warm, unpretentious, exciting, wonderful.

The other day I ran into Fedora (the proprietress) of Fedora's famous, popular-priced restaurant at 239 West Fourth Street, near West Tenth Street. We're neighbors but we hadn't seen each other for several months. Not only is she still charming, but she is a damn good cook. I first encountered Fedora at her restaurant in the early 1950s, shortly after the restaurant opened in 1952. That was even before Stonewall!

Fedora's had always been popular with those who didn't have a lot to spend, but mainly with the gay community, although the straight were also welcome. And what was important, the place didn't change: same pressed-metal ceiling, same small intimate tables, same great service by dedicated waiters, same welcome by Henry Dorato, Fedora's husband, who also bartended and cheerfully greeted all his regular customers by their first names. True, there were occasional paint jobs, but no basic changes except air conditioning.

LOST AND FOUND

I'm not sure how old he was when Henry died in 1997. There was great sadness among the regulars, but the restaurant continued on with their son, the dentist, filling in temporarily as bartender.

May it still continue as long as Fedora can continue to supervise the kitchen and put in her nightly appearances!

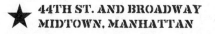
HOPE IN A JAR

BY SANDI SONNENFELD

I've become obsessed by wrinkles. Particularly the ones surrounding my eyes and across the map of my forehead that
extend like arid rivers across a fleshy terrain.

A year ago, I purchased my first wrinkle cream, Oil of Olay
Anti-Aging Eye Gel ($12.99) from the local Duane Reade. This
was followed by Olay's Regenerist Microdermabrasion Treatment and Peel Activator Serum with Lactic Acid ($26.99) which
I had to apply twice a week to my face and neck.

Next I turned to Lush's Sacred Truth, a green mud mask
made of kaolin, ginkgo biloba, linseed extract, talc, papaya,
yogurt and free range eggs, which required refrigeration, and at
$32.99, had a shelf life of just ten days. According to the sales-
woman, for maximum effectiveness Sacred Truth was to be used
in conjunction with Lush's Breath of Fresh Air Toner ($14.99)
and Skin Drink Rehydrating Moisturizer ($22.99) that smelled
slightly like whipped wet cement.

When the gingery freckles that playfully dotted my cheeks,
and my sunkissed arms and legs evolved into age spots (and you
can be sure that some Madison Avenue hack in the 1960s looking to score it big with Avon or Elizabeth Arden decided that

"age spots" would sell far more skin care products than "liver spots," "lentigos" or "hyperpigmentation"), I tried Missha's Illuminating XL 100 ($33.95), which involved my placing opaque latex-thin circles treated with a transparent gel directly on to the spots and letting the gel absorb into my skin for twenty minutes each evening before bed.

After one particularly hard day at the office, I made an appointment at the Antoinette Boudoir Spa in mid-town Manhattan for a rehydrating facial. For the privilege of one hundred dollars, a Russian cosmetologist berated me for ten minutes about how my decision to use face powder instead of a liquid foundation was responsible for my desert-like skin. I never returned to the Boudoir again, but nonetheless, and with more than a small amount of shame, I did switch to L'Oreal's Age Perfect Liquid Makeup.

Desperate, I finally consulted a Chinese herbalist on Grand Street who promised that with a specially prepared emollient at ninety-nine dollars per ounce, I would see immediate results, particularly as she said with those "bruised brown rings" underneath my eyes. Without hesitation, I plunked down my American Express card and reached for the magic potion. Only when I got home and read the label did I notice that this legendary elixir supposedly refined after three hundred years' knowledge of ancient Chinese medicine was actually made in Japan.

A few weeks ago, I was returning from a trip to one of our West Coast offices where I had been sent to see if we could generate some local positive press coverage. Compared to our headquarters in New York, this office was rather small and the attorneys there felt isolated and cut off. Though I had yet to make any recommendations or launch a proactive media campaign, the lawyers made me feel something of a hero just by showing up. They simply wanted to know that they mattered to management, were valued as part of the larger firm.

On the plane ride back home, I felt I had accomplished enough that I could eschew the work waiting for me on my laptop and take a break by reading a magazine. As I idly flipped through the pages of the publication, there was a brief story about which daily skin creams were the best. According to the reporter who tested ten of the latest anti-aging products, the most effective for "decreasing the look and appearance of wrinkles and fine lines" was Philosophy's Hope in a Jar available from the manufacturer's website for $38.00 for two ounces.

Though I live on email and do tons of Internet research, I rarely order products online, worried about hucksterism in the anonymous ether world where no one ever looks directly into a customer's eyes or has to show you their product beyond a one inch by one inch pixilated photo. But how could I resist? Particularly as the price seemed low in comparison to some of the other lotions and elixirs I had bought. After all, plenty of women, many much older than me, had plump, dewy complexions—I saw them walking on the streets of Manhattan every day, well-dressed, well-coiffed, and largely age spot and wrinkle free. Certainly they had a secret formula, some key to skin care—and maybe finally after all my searching and disappointments, this was it.

Hope in a Jar.

I tore out the story from the magazine and when I got home, ordered it immediately. Because we live in an apartment and have no mailbox, only a small slot by our front door into which the postman slides our bills and correspondence, I requested the package be sent to my office wrapped confidentially in plain brown paper.

It showed up six days later, a round no-nonsense white plastic container with "Hope in a Jar" printed in large black lettering on the front and directions for use on the back. I unscrewed the lid and looked inside. A thick, very white cream with a faint, clean smell. I scooped a small amount onto my right forefinger and daubed the cream over my forehead and cheeks. I drew a quick breath, put the jar back down my desk and returned to editing the press release one of my staff had sent me.

My assistant Bailey came in to my office. She is twenty-three, a year out of the Ivy League, model thin, ambitious, and set on a stellar career in public relations. When I hired her, I told her that while some of the tasks given to her would not be that exciting, I would nonetheless teach her everything that I had learned about strategic PR over the past fifteen years. She took me at my word, and was always asking questions about why I took a certain approach with a campaign or how come I chose the journalist at *Business Week* rather than the one at *Forbes* to pitch a specific topic or lawyer.

I watched Bailey and reconnected with my old self, the one I thought I no longer knew. She's hard-working, intelligent, eager to please and ridiculously self-confident.

I signed the paperwork she needed me to approve. She eyed the jar of cream on my desk and picked it up. Embarrassed at my weakness (oh vanity!), I began to explain that I had read an article saying the product was supposed to be very good.

"I don't normally buy products online," I said. "But I figured why not give it a try?"

Bailey nodded. "Yes. My mother uses it."

LYPSINKA SPEAKS!
BY JOHN EPPERSON

*J*ohn Epperson is Lypsinka, but Lypsinka—the performance
artist/drag superstar whose show, Lypsinka! The Boxed Set,
has been a smash hit off-Broadway—is not John Epperson. Or rather,
John is a lot of things in addition to being Lypsinka. He kept this diary
for Mr. Beller's Neighborhood in January of 2001.

JANUARY 10TH

There has been some reluctance on my part to have any of
my diary entries published because I believe I say too much and
am perceived wrongly. I have been in psychotherapy on and off
for ten years and have learned that it is okay to express my feelings. But when certain feelings are expressed I find that I am
perceived as "negative," whereas I may think of presenting
myself as a whole person. I have learned that it is okay to tell
someone I'm angry, but when I do tell them, they don't want to
hear it. And although I am still deeply confused sometimes when
I am having an argument with someone, I have learned that confrontation is not a bad thing. Nevertheless, when I initiate a
confrontation I am perceived as "the bad guy." I don't think of
myself as negative or downbeat. I see myself as a practical, whole

person with a slight tendency towards melancholy that I believe I keep in check.

I mention all of this, because today was a very frustrating day around the "lip-synching question." I am having a great success right now doing my first all-lip-synching show in New York in seven years and I am enjoying myself immensely. But what I foresaw has happened: once again, there are people in power in the entertainment business who have the ability to give me a job in another medium but they don't see how this particular theatrical event can translate into, for instance, television. And I'm not sure I disagree with them. I don't even want to pursue this avenue, but there are others who do, so the can of worms is opened, and it is painful.

On the positive side (and I CAN be positive) I had a great singing lesson yesterday. My teacher is amazed at the progress I have made in the past few weeks and so am I. Of course, I've been singing since I was in high school. And playing the piano and composing and acting and writing. I know I have all these abilities but the rest of the world doesn't know because I have made my name with the incredible gimmick of lip-synching. People will be so surprised when I have the showcase to present my other talents.

JANUARY 11TH

There was a frustrating, strained, confusing phone call with L.A. today. I'm afraid I raised my voice. My therapist has warned me about showing anger—when it's appropriate and when it's not. I'm afraid I don't control it as well as I would like. The conversation gave me what I call a "Helen Lawson Headache." And as it turns out, no one is offended. At American Ballet Theatre people used to have horrible screaming matches, and then an hour later the argument was forgotten. Maybe it's normal?

I returned the videotapes of *Querelle* (couldn't watch it; vaguely remember being bored with it when it came out) and *Heavy Traffic* (loved it; took me way back). Bought a videotape of Curtis Harrington's *Games* which made me very happy.

The audience for the show was great. The show was loads of fun to do tonight. Paddy Crofton and his mom were there; they invited me to South Africa. "If you don't mind the odd bomb," Paddy said.

Zora Rasmussen was there with Lisa Passero, Cassandra "Mrs. Greenthumbs" Danz, and her husband Walter. Also Peter Schlesinger and Eric Boman. Eric and I talked about the idea I want to do with Isabella.

We talk about *Valley of the Dolls* so much in the dressing room and Bradford has never seen it. So I brought him back here and showed it to him. The cycle continues: I had to sit Russ Clower down the same way over fifteen years ago and show it to him.

Bradford tells me that D. M., the leather-worker, said he wouldn't hold it against him for working with me. Wonder what that means? Apparently, he expected me to keep the costume that was made for the *Advocate* shoot eight years ago. I don't remember it being offered. In fact I remember being told I couldn't keep it. I also remember that we had to cut a hole in the back of it so I could get into it.

JANUARY 12TH

Slept late today, later than usual. 11:30 a.m. About an hour more than usual. Felt like Barbara Stanwyck in *The Night Walker*: "I can't wake uuuuup!!"

Therefore, the day was short. Phoning, phoning, phoning. And still didn't get it all done. Had to sit down and eat lunch so I can have energy for the show. Margaret Rutherford was doing the twist in *Murder at the Gallop*. Put in my new tape of *Can Heironymous Merkin Ever Forget Mercy Humppe And Find True Happiness?* Only had time to see the first few minutes as I finished my meal. Also plan to watch *The Unholy Wife,* which I taped yesterday.

It was the magic hour when I walked to the theater. Beautiful sky. The village was pleasant. Everything north of that was an obstacle course of arrogant yuppies pushing baby carriages, walking their dogs that take up the sidewalk with leashes, and the construction brought on by The New Economy. What New Economy? It sure has passed me by!

The sky was so beautiful I went down to the river near West-beth and looked at the river and the twinkling lights and the hideous buildings being built in New Jersey. Who will fill them?

The audience for the show was not as fun as the last two per-formances. Friday night. But still responsive. James Knopf was there. A friend of Bradford's, Michael, a rugby player from Vassar, was in the front row, so I tormented him. Bradford put my dance belt in the microwave to dry it and it melted into a puddle of black plastic ooze. Oh, brother.

JANUARY 13TH

Made my weekly Saturday trip to Chinatown for a vegetar-ian Chinese lunch. On the way to the video arcade after lunch, I bumped into Zora who was squiring around a group from Atlanta. Played one game of Pac-Man. The acupuncturist on Mott Street did some energy work on my foot that was painful. But as he said, "No pain, no gain." Beats having a needle full of cortisone stuck in it, I guess.

I walked to the theater from Chinatown and the sky was totally clear and the Empire State Building was a beautiful pink. Dazzling!

The show was sold out and loads of fun. Michael Kors came back afterwards as well as Deborah Eisenberg and Wally Shawn, Edward Hibbert, Gym DeMao and his friend John, and Deanie Albert and Anna Spellman, old friends from American Ballet Theatre. Kevin got Wally interested in doing *CAGED!* next month.

I'm going to miss doing the show. It's so much fun! Especially right now. Hopefully it won't be long until I'm doing it again.

Chal and Steve and I went to Moustache to eat and then I went alone to Bradford's Studio 42 party on the Lower East Side. I did-n't stay long because the cigarette smoke was thick. Subwayed home. *SNL* is on. Can't figure out if it's a new show or not.

JANUARY 14TH

Scott Peeper came over to cut my hair. I mentioned *Queer As Folk* and he went OFF—as well he should. The *New York Times* let the show have it today as well. I wonder if people are embarrassed that they bought into the hype?

Kevin and I went to see Mark Dendy's piece at the Joyce. Can't remember the name of it; it's a long title. We saw an early version of it at SummerStage about a year and half ago. I think I preferred that one; it was more of an event. Still, it was sexy and wonderful.

Watched the end of the new *Gatsby* on A&E. Fitzgerald's words, story, and vision are so moving. I was touched even though it smelled of TV movie. The *E! True Hollywood Story* of "The Last Days of Judy Garland" is on now. Another version of the waste of the American dream.

J—— was at the Dendy evening. I didn't get a chance to say hello. When I got home the porter had a Xmas gift from him for me. Hmm.

Also saw Flotilla on the other side of the theater. Jaime Bishton and Perry Souchuk were there. I've never been introduced to Bobby Pierce, but if I had known that was him when I was chatting with Mark before the show, I would have introduced myself. He did the costumes. Nice job. He's changed his hair color so I didn't recognize him.

JANUARY 15TH

Lazy, sleepy, foggy day. A holiday. Martin Luther King Day. Made phone calls. Spoke to Scott Wittman and Mart Crowley in LA. Watched the rest of the Judy *E! True Hollywood Story*. Of course, it was somewhat sensationalized, but there was lots of footage I had never seen before and I can never get enough Judy.

Read more of *Jane Eyre*. I must say, Bertha is fully revealed much sooner than I expected. I guess *Jane Eyre* is the mother of the Gothic romance. Why did I think the character's name would be spelled "Berthe"?

Peter Schlesinger and Eric Boman had a small dinner party for Don Bachardy at their large apartment on West Twentieth Street in the Flatiron District. They had also invited a nice couple—Jane and Robert Rosenblum. Rosenbloom? Peter and Eric made a delicious meal: pasta, turkey pie, and baked pears. Don is in town for a reading and a book-signing that happened tonight before dinner at A Different Light, which was, apparently, poorly promoted.

JANUARY 16TH

I had another good singing lesson today. I am able to hit notes and make sounds I have never made before. It's time to think about getting this out to the public. I need to make a recording— a simple recording with me accompanying myself.

I walked a few blocks through the park on the way to the lesson. The ice and snow are trying to melt. There are moments, even in the bleakness of January, when New York is beautiful, just as Jenifer Lewis and I agree that happiness comes in fleeting moments.

Made a few food stops on the Upper West Side and stood in the check-out line right behind Lauren Bacall. If she had acknowledged me I would have reintroduced myself and told her that I have met her at the one party I attended at Roddy McDowall's house in 1995. Nevertheless, I was content to take in the whole situation: the solicitousness of the manager; the "Ah, yes," when the cashier gave her the check to sign; the clothes; the physicality; the little ladies gawking and whispering nearby; the car waiting out front.

Went swimming and worked up the nerve to speak to a guy I've seen at the gym several times before.

JANUARY 17TH

Had a lunch meeting with Andy Cohen of USA Network at the Palm, which was covered in caricatures of celebrities à la Sardi's, but funkier. It seemed to go well.

The weather was pleasant so I walked through Times Square which was actually enjoyable. The tourists really must not be in town this month, and all the theatre-goers were inside since it was after two o'clock.

Went to the Virgin Megastore and poked around, then to Blowout Video across the street. Blowout is having a thirty-percent-off sale on widescreen movies, so I got *Lisa and The Devil* with Elke Sommer and *The Devil's Own* with Joan Fontaine. Went to the new video arcade on Forty-second Street and actually got to play Pac-Man there for the first time. Costs twenty-five cents more than the games in Chinatown, but the Forty-second Street games are a lot faster.

Walked home via Eighth Avenue and bumped into Flotilla at the corner of Twenty-eighth Street. She needed a script of *Legends!* so I brought her back here and loaned her mine.

Took a lovely nap, did my sit-ups and butt exercises, vocalizing, then went to see Chal's band the Chelsea Mountain Boys at Downtime nearby on Thirtieth Street. There were lots of people I knew there. The band was fun. I'm proud of Chal. I couldn't stay the whole time. Had to go to the gym to do my swim. Said hello to that guy again!

Ate dinner very late. Now one of my favorite Elvis movies is on—*Loving You* with Lizabeth Scott.

Lorna Luft called Kevin! She wants to be in *CAGED!*

JANUARY 18TH

Was inside all day making phone calls, getting phone calls, etc.

Walked to the theatre in the rain. Not unpleasant. The show was fun tonight. Good audience. Thierry Mugler was there, but didn't come back. Isaac Mizrahi, Lar Lubovitch, Mark Morris, and John Higgenbotham, one of Mark's dancers, did come back. I hadn't seen Mark in a long time and he's always fun. Lar seemed more serious. Would be fun to chat with him probably. They had a great time and it was a pleasure to see all of them and have a brief visit. They all seemed to enjoy the show and Lar said he had even seen me many years ago at The Pyramid Club!

Thurmond Smithgall was there with a couple friends, and he had brought me the brochure from the upcoming Salzburg Music Festival. It is filled with Francois Nars's photographs, including the dazzling picture of myself.

Joey Carman and Bob Sandla were also there. Joey and I have known one another for over twenty years. Hard to believe.

Bradford is such a funny guy. He's having a ball with the plastic cooked chicken that we keep hiding from each other.

Took the subway home and called Mart before eating dinner. Watched some of my favorite Barbara Stanwyck movie, Douglas Sirk's *All I Desire*. I still haven't converted Tom Beller to Sirkianism.

Thinking about taking a trip to L.A., Palm Springs and Vegas at the end of February. Wallace says I can stay with him in Los Angeles.

JANUARY 19TH

Started the day in tears as I watched the party scene in *All I Desire*. Seeing Richard Long and Barbara Stanwyck made the tears fly to my eyes. And it's a happy scene! Why does this happen to me when I see happy scenes in movies? Is it a longing for the past, for an idealism? When Debbie Reynolds starts dancing in the "He's My Friend" number in *The Unsinkable Molly Brown*, forget it; I'm a puddle. Same with Betty Hutton singing "I Got The Sun In The Morning" from *Annie Get Your Gun*. And there are so many others.

Rainy day again. It's a good thing. Washes away the old snow to get ready for the new they say is coming.

Went to Cotan on Third Street for the fried oysters and chicken don. Read the paper and some more pages of *Jane Eyre*.

Had a confusing meeting at Westbeth. My life is still in limbo—and I HATE that. I'm turning down other jobs; taking the gamble.

The audience was like so many other Friday nights—quiet. My cousins, the Caffreys, were there from Baton Rouge, also a man from Great Performances (Jack Venza?) and a fan, Robert Hogg, from Miami. He came back wanting an autograph.

Chal and Steve and I went to The Cowgirl Hall of Fame for dinner and I walked home. Late-night conversations with Kevin and Russell followed.

JANUARY 20TH

Slept till noon! My gosh! Frantic phone calls had to be made. When I woke up, had a message on my voice mail from Mike Nichols saying he wanted to come to the show and bring Tom Stoppard and Sinead Cusack. I made sure they were going to get in. Ate breakfast, putzed around, ate some lunch, then took the subway to the theater.

The theater was packed with a fun audience. All went smoothly until the sound guy played the wrong tape for post-show. Wouldn't you know?

Marcello and Gioia Guidi, looking as stylish as ever, and as friendly as ever, were there with the Italian ambassador and his Polish wife. They all came back. Michael Leeds was also there and he was very complimentary.

Mike N. had said he would not come back with his friends, but go to the restaurant with them and then send the car back for me. When I left the theatre the car wasn't there, so I wasn't sure if I should go to Bar Pitti to meet them. Nevertheless, I did, assuming there was a mix-up. I walked to Bar Pitti. There had been a mix-up: Mike forgot to tell the driver (just as Grady forgot to give me my wallet and ring before he left the theatre! Probably because he and I were so flummoxed that the sound guy made the incredible mistake at the end of the show).

So, Stoppard and Cusack were at the restaurant, along with Nicholas Hytner and Bob Crowley. They seem to be partners. Crowley was very friendly and chatty. Hytner a bit stand-off-ish, but then we weren't sitting next to one another. Stoppard was sitting next to me and I guess I held my own with him. Certainly he could out-word or out-vocabulary me in a second, but he was very easy to talk to.

I asked Cusack about her father's acting career in movies (Cyril Cusack, who had a small part in *Harold and Maude*) which launched her on a story about how TV's weren't allowed in the house when she was growing up.

Mike N. talked again (this was his second time to see the show, and our second dinner together) about Judy at Carnegie Hall being the greatest theatrical experience he ever had as a spectator. So thrilling! I told him some of my woes and he said something like, "Good work only happens in defiance of management."

The wet snow had finally started during dinner. I walked to the train station and took the subway home.

JANUARY 22

Yesterday was an Anne Welles day: fresh snow on the ground. Nevertheless, this Anne Welles stayed inside The Martha Washington Hotel for Women (code for my apartment) all day. Didn't go out once. (For those who don't know, Anne Welles is the main character in *Valley of the Dolls*.) The highlight of the day was watching Elizabeth Taylor (crash and burn; or totally manipulate the situation) on the Golden Globes. Well, if we can't have Suzanne Somers singing a Gershwin medley, we can have our Liz. All afternoon today was spent on boring business stuff. All afternoon! Russell wanted me to go to his show tonight so I did. Had dinner afterwards with him and Ken Page and David Drake. Ken is moving back to L.A. This week's Advertising Age chose the PETA ad I'm in as the "Image of the Week." Nice. Didn't get my swimming done yesterday or today and didn't do my vocalizing today. Have tomorrow off—so far.

JANUARY 23–25TH

Tuesday and Wednesday were really horrible. Helen Lawson days. I can't go into it here: too unpleasant. Thanks to the pool at the gym, I could knock myself out.

On Wednesday, I had to cancel my singing lesson, which I hated to do, but I was able to keep my meeting at Bob Avian and

Peter Pileski's apartment with David Drake, Stanley, and an actress named Passion. We worked on *Legends!* a bit, preparing for the read-through next Tuesday.

Today (Thursday) was a better day, although my sleep is not as good as I would like it to be. It was also quite a beautiful day for January in the city. Had an interview with a writer from the *Boston Globe*. Turns out she wanted to talk about "drag theater" in general, and not just about me. Me! Me! However, she did say the article I wrote for the *New York Times* was part of her impetus.

Bryan Batt called me to talk about the *Legends!* reading. Hope I can see him in *Seussical*.

Phyllis Newman and Adolph Green were at the show tonight and they loved it. It was wonderful to meet him. He seemed in good form.

Blaine and Robert Trump were also there with Billy Norwich. Hadn't seen him in a long time.

Johnny Meyer, one of Judy Garland's best friends in the sixties, was there with a friend of his. Chris Olivier from Houston was there and I had a nice visit with him. We're at the home stretch here with the show. Well, it's been a good run. Very exciting time for me. I will miss my camaraderie with Louis and Bradford and all the other people at the theater.

JANUARY 26TH–27TH

I did something on Friday that I don't usually allow myself: I went to see a movie in the afternoon. I had good reason. The Screening Room was showing the 1975 Diana Ross fiasco *Mahogany* and it was my first chance to see it on a big screen in twenty-six years. It didn't disappoint. Everything about that movie is heavenly! And since a lot of it is set in Chicago during the winter, when the movie was over and I walked out into our cold urbanity, I felt like I was still in the movie. So glamorous!

Went to Cotan to grab a bite to eat, then had the show to do. Fun audience. Afterwards I spoke to a group of twenty-two dramatic students from Vassar. They were all very intelligent and self-composed. Certainly a lot smarter and more mature than I was at that age.

Came home and crashed so I could rest up for doing the two shows on Saturday, something I have not had to do since September. Saturday afternoon I did my usual Chinese vegetarian lunch in Chinatown, a few games of Pac-Man at the arcade on Mott Street, acupuncture, and then the shows. Donald C. and Michael E. were at the first show, as well as my cousin Jim McKellar and his companion from Boston. Fatoyd was also hanging around, filming the show. We gave Flloyd a hard time for the shocking things he said in front of imperturbable Blaine Trump the other night.

Sam Harris was at the second show and he came back along with Alan Cumming and Alan's boyfriend, Nick. It was Alan's birthday.

Bradford, Chal and Steve were all nice enough to keep me company while I ate a sandwich after the show. I was so tired, there was like a cloud behind my eyes. Jumped in a cab after 12:30p.m., came home, and dropped out. Tomorrow night: the closing. Can we compete with the Super Bowl? Just kidding!

JANUARY 28–29TH

After two shows on Saturday, I was very tired and slept late today, resolving to rest as much as possible. Indeed, I only went out to get some fruit juice and soy milk. Managed to get a few phone calls done while I relaxed.

I walked to the theater. It was a beautiful afternoon and I enjoyed not feeling rushed. There was some concern at the theatre because the short film that Flloyd had made as a sort of "roast" wasn't transferring from his digital camera to VHS. Finally he got it to work and they held the show.

Then, when the show started, I did two numbers and had to stop the show. The sound was just awful. The substitute sound guy has not been doing a very good job in general, but tonight it was especially bad. And since tonight was the closing, I wanted it to be very good. So I stopped the show and announced, "The sound isn't good enough and, of all nights, I owe it to these people to give them a good show. Someone come talk to me backstage." The audience loved that!

Kevin and the sound guy came back, Kevin made an announcement, and we started over. The sound was better but not as good as it can be. Nevertheless, we got through it.

I needed some time after the show to go upstairs and take off my sweaty costume so I could sit in the cold theater and watch Flloyd's film comfortably. Flotilla did some stand-up, telling vulgar jokes, while I changed. The film was very embarrassing. I was going to go up and say a few words, but I felt the audience had had enough.

I did some stretching and then Chal, Steve, Stanley, Bradford, Flloyd and I all piled into Lily's car to go to Florent for a champagne toast and dinner. Bradford and Stanley and I sat with Lily (Tomlin) and Jane (Wagner) and their friends. They generously treated us to a meal. Lily may receive the Jean Hersholt Humanitarian Award some day. Mike Nichols says she's all good. That Emma Thompson is too.

Russell was there, Florent's friends, Grady, Kevin, Flotilla, et al. After Lily and Jane and their friends left, some of us hung out for a little while longer. It was an unsentimental closing which was the way I liked it.

It was after 12:30 a.m. by the time we left. I was exhausted. Right now, I feel glad that the run is over. It certainly was a good run. The audience demographics widened, which was one of the most important things to pull off. After a little rest, I'll be ready for the next assignment. Of course, there's still Mark Sendroff's fiftieth b-day party next weekend and then the *Caged!* reading on Feb. 19. And there's the other read-through tomorrow with David, Bryan, and Passion. I have plenty to do.

THE BREWBAR
BREAKUP

BY CHRISTOPHER HACKER

We had coffee the other day at the Brewbar with a man named Chistopher Hacker. Traffic careened silently up Eighth Avenue, past the Brewbar's red-painted window frames. The sky persisted with its threat of a Nor'easter, but in here Carmen Miranda was doing a tiki-version of "Fever," and it was cozy. The place is small (five café tables and a padded banquet) and in spite of the weather that day achieved an airy feel. There was a display case of breakfast pastries and a basket of H&H bagels, a sign announcing, "Ask about our Panini!" nearby.

Mr. Hacker had plenty to say on the changes he's seen over the years at the Brewbar.

"Where we're sitting right now," he said, tapping the marble table. "This place seems at first glance like just another one of the new, posh alternatives to Starbucks that've been cropping up in the past year, like the Chocolate Bar and that place down the street over there. But it's been around for a long time, I'd say almost fifteen years now? I used to work here. It was my first job after graduating college."

ON THE ACTOR WITH THE SCRUFFY DOG

We returned to our seats after ordering a slice of carrot zucchini bread, just as a woman entered with a wheezing pug. The young man behind the counter informed her that she would have to leave her pet outside before he could serve her. She did an about-face and called her order—tall hot chai—before ushering the dog out the door and securing it to a parking meter.

Mr. Hacker said, "They used to be dog-friendly in here. We even had a cookie jar up by the register there that had free dog biscuits. It would be a stop along the way for owners on their morning walks. Our boss, Stass, knew all the dogs' names. But not the names of the owners."

Was Stass incapable of remembering human names?

"He'd remember the names of people who didn't have dogs. Maybe he could only keep in his head one name per customer. 'Oh, here comes Champ,' Stass would say. And we'd have his latte and white-chocolate biscotti ready and bagged before the owner even got to the register."

Do you actually still remember the order?

"There are some things you can't forget," Mr. Hacker said. "So it was all going fine, according to Stass at least, until the incident with Kevin Spacey."

Mr. Hacker is a notorious name-dropper, and never hesitates to mention to all who will listen that he knew Vin Diesel growing up, when the superstar's name was Mark Vincent, and claims they were sparring partners at a Montessori karate class in the neighborhood. On the name-dropping front, today was no exception.

"Kevin was a short americano with half-and-half, and Stass, true to form, knew him only as 'that actor with the scruffy dog.' Pip was the dog's name, I think. Stass didn't like Kevin and was always very curt with him because Kevin let his dog do whatever it wanted in the store. Most owners were so grateful to have them allowed in at all that they'd treat the place with an almost church-like respect, heeling their dogs, and scolding them with a stern tug on the leash if they so much as whimpered. Not Pip.

LOST AND FOUND

Pip ran free. He jumped up onto the counter. He found his way back behind the food display, under occupied tables, and up customers' skirts. Stass wasn't the confrontational type, and had trouble asserting that Pip not do these things. He might say something like, 'You really need to keep that dog on a leash,' and Kevin would apologize and tell him next time he would, but next time he never did. One day Pip was particularly lewd to a customer, and the following week Stass found himself in possession of a health-code violation.

"And that was that for dogs in the Brewbar. The sign went up in the window, which seemed to give Stass the courage to confront Kevin about it the next time he came in. He just pointed to the sign and was like, 'Sorry, there's nothing I can do.' Kevin would afterwards try to sneak Pip in and I was forced, when Stass wasn't around, to tell him Pip wasn't welcome. He wasn't the only celebrity dog I kicked out. There was Ed Burns and his min-pin. Who else? I don't know what it is about actors and their dogs. I once saw Vincent D'Onofrio get into it with a Starbucks barista about his little Jack Russell terrier, and at another place I used to hang out at, Molly Ringwald would get all paranoid about leaving her little Pomeranian outside too long for fear of someone stealing it. Like anyone would want that little rat of a dog."

ON THE ORIGIN OF THE BREWBAR

Steve Austin is the money behind the Brewbar venture. He met Stass when they were both living in San Francisco in the seventies. Stass had just arrived from his native Greece, penniless and all of eighteen. They became a couple and moved to Seattle. Steve was involved in a real-estate deal there which proved very lucrative. Mr. Hacker had the following to say:

"This was way before the coffee revolution. Seattle was it. I don't think even Starbucks was there, or if it was, it was just another one of a thousand little places. This is all according to Steve who loves to brag about how he was the one to put coffee on the map in New York. It's true though. They came to the city in like eighty-eight, eighty-nine, I think? and opened this place. Steve bought the whole building. The storefront is the Brewbar, and they've converted the rest into a B and B. The Abingdon Bed and Breakfast.

"Steve's the behind-the-scenes guy. You don't see much of him. I'll point him out. He's tall, emaciated—for the longest time I thought he was sick, but that's just the way he is. Sunken, pock-marked cheeks. He stoops and wears these granny glasses on a chain around his neck, always talking into his cell, taking reservations for the B and B, and dealing with money stuff. Stass, on the other hand, was the face of the Brewbar. He was everywhere, compulsively tidying. He fluttered around with his gelled-out hair, neatening and straightening, rearranging the bagels in the basket, adjusting the pecan bars on their plates. Customers knew him. We all who worked there thought of him as a kind of mother hen. He'd nag us, get worried if we were late for a shift or didn't show up, be disappointed in us if we had a customer complaint. But often he would take our side in a dispute at the expense of the business, which was really nice."

We wondered whether they were open about being a couple.

"Steve and Stass were a neighborhood fixture. Everyone understood. Even though Steve was almost two decades older than Stass, even though they kept separate apartments, and even though Stass was a flirt, no one ever questioned it. They were a perfect fit. It was something about their temperaments. They were monogamous, no question. Married even. They'd bicker, Steve scolding Stass, or Steve trying to repair Stass's hurt feelings about something mean Steve had said. In addition to being a flirt, Stass was a gossip too, and most customers who cared to know would learn more than they wanted about the ups and downs of his marital life with Steve."

ON THE REGULARS

"Everyone was a regular. You could tell the ones who weren't. They'd be on a coffee break from a construction site, restoring some brownstone down the street, and they'd come in looking lost. 'You guys got cawfee? Gimme one light and sweet.' They'd look at the sip-top with suspicion, 'what's this?' and the plain white container. When you'd tell them it was a dollar twenty-five they'd be like, 'what are you, nuts?' and leave the coffee on the counter and go to the deli next door. But the regulars, they'd come in, get the same thing every day. Every single day. You'd get to put their face with their drink after a few times and have their order ready when you'd see them through the window coming up the street. They'd love that. They thought we were psychic. But it was the only way to handle the rush-hour rush. I worked the six to noon, so I'd set up, open the doors at seven, and until nine o'clock or so I'd have a constant stream of them. They snaked out the door here, and out onto the sidewalk. There was this constant panic during the rush, this blizzard of orders, like being under fire—bagels on the grill, espresso orders accumulating, tapping at the register keys like you were gunning for a high score. We had to keep the line moving so people wouldn't get fed up and leave, but for two solid hours it was a factory of cappuccinos and americanos. It was more impressive back then, in ninety-five, I think, because gourmet coffee wasn't part of the culture yet, part of its fabric, words like 'latte' and 'macchiato' hadn't entered the common lexicon. There was still something kind of mysterious about what we did, and almost, I don't know, glamorous?"

ON WHAT'S GOING ON THESE DAYS

We'd finished our coffees and got on our coats. Mr. Hacker gathered the empty cups and dropped them into the trash. It had remained empty for the whole of our stay. There was no sign of the crowds Mr. Hacker had mentioned, or Steve, or Stass. He was quick to point out, however, that this wasn't the time of day for them. A little bell above the door jingled as we left into the hard, dark December afternoon.

On our way up Eighth Avenue, Mr. Hacker said, "I ran into Stass not too long ago. I'm living in Brooklyn now, but my mom still lives here, and sometimes I come back to the neighborhood to visit. Like today. Stass seemed, I don't know, older. A lot's changed, and he told me about it." Mr. Hacker looked around and lowered his voice. "There was a certain regular who'd come in, a doctor I think it was. This doctor had his practice in the area, and he lived across the street. He was handsome, single, gay. He and Stass would flirt, nothing new for Stass. But this guy was persistent, and he wooed Stass into an affair.

"They managed to keep it a secret for a while I guess, but Stass, the incurable gossip that he is, couldn't keep it to himself anymore, and confided in someone, another regular, who in turn, no doubt, confided in someone else. There were rumors that Steve was being cuckolded. Stass tried to stop it from spreading, but eventually the thing got back to Steve, maybe some regular who didn't like the looks of what was going on. Stass thinks it was one of the dog owners getting revenge for not being allowed in with his scruffy pet. Who knows—it could have been Pip's owner himself.

"There was an ugly breakup. Steve barred the doctor from getting his chocolate-dipped biscotti at the Brewbar anymore but, amazingly, Stass continued working there. The employee turnover, though, which has always been extremely low—I myself had been there three years—suddenly began rotating weekly. There was a final fight, and Stass was fired. Steve said he never wanted to speak to Stass again. Stass looked exhausted talking about it. If they'd been married, no doubt Stass would have been entitled to some portion of the business, but Stass got nothing. He's unemployed now, or at least he was the last time I saw him. He's still with the doctor, and lives with him in that apartment right there across the street. He says he's always running into Steve and it's very awkward. They've taken to crossing to opposite sides of the avenue to avoid each other."

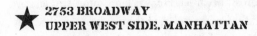

★ **2753 BROADWAY**
UPPER WEST SIDE, MANHATTAN

FOUND: TYRANNOSAURUS REX

BY PATRICK GALLAGHER

Earlier that afternoon I had come back from a trip to visit my dad in the Midwest. As always, I braced myself for the crush of people, but as I left the gate at LaGuardia, I immediately noticed that something felt different this time. First in the airport, then on the bus, and finally on Broadway, no one seemed to be in the same hurry as usual, and neither was I. As night fell I planned to have a leisurely single course of pizza at Koronet, but first I stopped at 113th and Broadway and looked through a green plastic kiosk for a fresh copy of a free weekly from the week when I had been away.

A streetlight pole beside the kiosk caught my eye as I bent down and rummaged. One of the flyers on the pole made me nervous. I couldn't put my finger on it, but I had the distinct feeling that it was not supposed to be there.

The flyer said, "FOUND: TYRANNOSAURUS REX." There was a picture—clip art—of a Tyrannosaurus Rex with its fearsome maw open toward the street. The paper had an appropriately fossilized look, wrinkled up and gray with hardened rain and obviously much older than all of the other flyers. I wondered

544

why no one had ever ripped it down or flyered over it when the streetlight served such a busy intersection.

Most alarmingly of all, the entire bottom third of the flyer was torn away. The information that supposedly stated the flyer's purpose was gone. That the Tyrannosaurus had consumed a portion of its own flyer was both as unprovable and as likely as any other explanation.

Minutes later, I sat two blocks down in Koronet chomping on my plain Jumbo Slice. No disrespect, but there is something gummy about the crust at Koronet which makes it a pizza that has to be chomped, not chewed, and especially not lamely suckled and swallowed whole like the pizza across the street at Famiglia. Try as they might, Famiglia will never drive Koronet out of business because Koronet hones the act of sitting on a stool and consuming a piece of pizza to its barest essentials. That is the only way to approach Koronet. The slices are too big to take on the street. There is something unsightly about being seen with such a vast, unwieldy portion of food covered in such sweaty-looking grease. You eat with your face down even if you aren't alone because Koronet is lit like a place you don't want to be. A hospital waiting room, a high school math class, the post office. The harsh overhead lights cast every nook and cranny of your physical being in the least flattering possible relief. Finally, Koronet's gummy crust sucks the herbivore straight off your teeth so that whole place fills with the sounds of lips smacking and furious, open-mouthed chomping.

I read Matt Taibbi's political column in a giggly mien while I chomped. Taibbi wrote, "Rove is not a genius at all. He is a pig, and the only thing that distinguishes him is the degree of his brazenness and cruelty." I thought to myself, *tee hee*. I was in the best possible mood until a voice from down the counter disturbed me.

"Hey, the way you eat that pizza…That's an interesting method you've got there," it said.

I looked up. It was a young man with a moustache and a goatee that looked scraggly, but still a little bit too full for his

Johnson & Johnson complexion. His thick head of dark hair, in a vaguely Einstein-esque fashion, made him look electrocuted, but at the same time pampered. If you looked closely enough, you could tell each fine, delicate strand apart from all of its neighbors. His round glasses filled out his weird pseudo-European aura, on top of which he wore a Hawaiian-style shirt that depicted images of the Manhattan skyline against a voluptuous tropical sunset. Over and over again, the shirt said "New York" in a hazy yellow font that seemed nostalgic for itself.

He tilted back his head and looked down his nose at me like a professor demanding that certain essential facts be repeated.

He asked, "Could you tell me if that is the way you always eat pizza, or are you deliberately trying to do something different?"

The gentleman was referring to the fact that I tend to eat the crust first. It's the eat-your-vegetables principle applied to pizza—get the crust over with and save the tastiest portion for last. I said, "I don't know." Then I returned to my article.

Taibbi wrote, "Karl Rove is a character of a type that reappears from time to time throughout history—an unscrupulous power-chaser of the highest order, who rises to the top by demonizing and defaming innocent people." I tried to get back into the groove.

"I'm just asking because I think that's very interesting what you're doing there."

I kept reading.

"Do you think I should start eating pizza like this?"

I looked up and saw him turning his own piece of pizza counter-clockwise in his hands, opening and closing his mouth to simulate chomping.

It was late at night. He was sitting only one stool away from me in a restaurant that I now realized was otherwise empty.

"Or, do you just want to get back to what you're reading?"

"Yes," I said. "I would like to get back to what I'm reading." I turned away from him accordingly. But then I turned back and added: "If you're really thinking about trying to eat pizza counter-clockwise, that would be cool." I mimicked the way he had turned his pizza, but without picking up my own slice, and continued, "Like, eating the pizza in a spiral, instead of in rows? That would be cool if that's what you're contemplating."

"No," he said, sounding serious. "That's not what I was talking about."

I said, "Okay." I went back to my article and at some point he left.

When there was nothing on my plate but a smear of grease, I stood up from my stool without lingering. I felt cool; I guess the low-key excitement that had struck me upon my return was persisting. When I stood at the trash, the single gesture with which the contents of my tray slid down into the open mouth of the receptacle felt masculine and decisive. I needed to walk downtown five blocks to return some DVDs that had been due before I had left on my trip. The thought that the fees incurred could be the final, single straw that cleared out my bank account and doomed me to constant, desperate foraging for crumbs throbbed away in the back of my mind, but the throbbing was quiet. To survive as a small-business owner you had to have real teeth, but despite that I truly believed that the owner of this rental outlet had the soul of an herbivore. Tonight, things just felt okay.

I had a spring in my step. I ambled under a corridor of scaffolding between Koronet and 110th singing "Cold Blooded" in my head. Uniform shadows loomed under the scaffolding that concealed pedestrians' faces, but not their iPods. I thought, *Is it not the loss of the inner iPod that is the true tragedy of the iPod?* I started trying to make up new lyrics for "Cold Blooded."

"Hey man. Do you want a cookie?"

I shuddered—he was back. He walked beside me, under the scaffolding all but invisible but for the silhouette of his absurd intellectual hair. I saw that he was a full head taller than me.

I heard the squeaky sound of the cookie pouch tearing open.

"I got 'em at Duane Reade's," he said.

I said, "No," as though he were homeless and I had never seen him before, sped up, and then crossed Broadway at 110th. From across Broadway I watched him ambling in front of the huge well-lit Gristedes, cookie pouch in hand. I knew that everything about his laid-back, surfer-Trotsky style was so over-the-top that it could only be explained as cover for a violent, irrationally aggressive personality, whether he knew it or not. Just after Gristedes, he disappeared from view. Either he was on an excursion, determined to buy at least one item from every single store on Broadway, or he was hiding. Or both? In any case, I knew the video store was on the east side of Broadway and that I would have to cross back over to his turf sooner or later.

My apartment was further uptown, on Riverside, and there were times when I would walk between there and the Columbia campus late at night and have to remind myself that it was not all one, single, continuous campus. The elegant stone facades of Grant's Tomb, Riverside Church, the Manhattan School of Music, and the stately faculty apartment buildings almost lent themselves to the fantasy, but at night an eerie silence reigned in Morningside Heights that compelled dread. On the very few occasions when I had experienced urban violence, the quality about it that stood out was its suddenness. One minute you're ambling, the next there's a knife in your face and whatever you had expected in the previous second now meant nothing.

How do you make it clear to a stranger that you don't want to know them? That is, how do you let someone know that you won't feel comfortable with them at least until they tell you their name? The fact that this idiot would offer me a cookie without even telling me his name was the ultimate proof that he was out of his mind. Crossing Broadway I envisioned him coming up behind me with a knife, a hammer, or just his elbow, a potentially life-changing act of retribution that I would lack even the privilege of having witnessed.

I slipped in and out of the movie store unnoticed. There had been no collection-agency flunkies lying in wait as I had feared. A group of drunk men of all different ages swayed from Broadway into a nearby bar. I hopped off the curb and into the street to get by as fast as possible. In this area, you know people are safe if you see them in groups. Elsewhere, the opposite may be true, but the point is that at moments like this, in which I was being stalked by a lunatic who was capable of literally anything, made me grateful that the language of social signs could at times be so precise. On this score, I began my trek through the gauntlet back uptown, regretting my earlier opprobrium for the iPod. Walking around carrying an iPod was a way of relinquishing any claim on society and embracing total atomization, right or wrong. The dead look in the iPod zombie's eyes said as much; it was impossible to imagine being robbed by such a mute, passive savant.

That was why the iPod looked the way it did, I decided. It was a white flag, a sign of peace in the urban war of all against all.

The streets grew emptier as one business after another locked its doors. Lights went out and I watched people get into cabs blocks ahead of me, only to have disappeared without a trace when I caught up to their point of takeoff. I walked backwards crossing 109th because it was a wide-open area, but there were a lot of trees below which he could have been hiding.

When suddenly I heard the squeak of the wrapper again I started, almost screaming until I looked around, found no one, and then realized that the sound had come from a cookie wrapper abandoned on the sidewalk that I had stepped on myself.

Could it have been the same cookie wrapper? I didn't have time to find out.

I didn't feel safe until I reached 113th, where I was in clear view of Columbia Public Safety. I found the flyer again and I studied it, "FOUND: TYRANNOSAURUS REX," and asked myself again what I thought it might mean. Irony—it was a joke of belonging. Anyone who understood it could breathe a sigh of knowing relief. The Tyrannosaurus Rex was the monster loose everywhere, the ever-present threat of violence that haunted the metropolis at even the best of times. It can never be lost because it is at home everywhere, and at the same time it can never be found…because it finds you. Like the counter-clockwise pizza-eating buffoon of my acquaintance, the monster wears New York like a Hawaiian shirt.

I took off into Columbia, behind its comforting black iron bars, to check my email at the twenty-four-hour computer lab. There, I would be safe until daybreak…

★ **59 CHELSEA PIERS**
CHELSEA, MANHATTAN

SIDDHARTHA OF CENTRAL BOOKING OR, JAIL WITH A FRESH COAT OF PAINT

BY PATRICK GALLAGHER

We were in a narrow space between barricades and a cement wall, on the far northern side of a vast concrete enclosure. Jason, our Arresting Officer, had divided us up into two parallel rows, one standing against the barricades, the other standing against the wall. Jason stood between the two rows talking about sports, TV, and how he was looking forward to his retirement. We were waiting in line to be processed, and listening to the details of Jason's life helped pass the time.

Jason was a twenty-three year old beat cop from Staten Island. Six-thousand NYPD officers had received special training in crowd control and civil liberties in anticipation of NYC's big event, the 2004 Republican National Convention. I doubted that Jason had ever worn riot gear prior to when he received the training, but the high of the costume seemed to have changed the way he thought about his body. Now that it was off it gave him an almost unnatural level of comfort and ease in the way that he carried himself. His bulgy stomach pumped up and down as he ambled between us, grinning. More than anything else, he acted like a rock star interacting with fans after a sweaty show.

He smiled and looked off into the distance. "We only want to get you outta here as soon as we can," he said.

A charter bus loaded with more prisoners rolled into the cavernous box while applause thundered from far away. I wondered whether the sounds were coming from protestors gathered outside or holding cells inside, in which case I wondered just how huge this place was. When the bus stopped, the prisoners stood up and walked to the front of the bus with their heads down and their hands behind their backs.

My girlfriend stood directly across from me in a parallel row. The rows weren't divided by gender; both were mixed up seemingly at random. Jason turned his back to her and she stuck her tongue out at him while he listened with an inscrutable, sage-like expression to the rumbling noise of the space. She dropped back into a toothy smile when he turned around. Our wrists were fastened behind our backs with cheap disposable handcuffs made out of white plastic strips, which the police could be seen sporting on their belts in thick stacks throughout the Republican National Convention. They pinched, but not like metal: the legality of the RNC mass arrests was questionable, so the NYPD had most likely decided to hedge its bets by cuffing all two thousand of us with cuffs designed not to leave a mark.

For the two of us, it had started with the mistaken idea that it was possible to be tourists in the middle of something like this. We went tooling around convention-packed Midtown together so that we could "just see what happens," and this is what happened: after they swept us up in a mass arrest, Jason and his fellow riot-gear-clad beat cops brought us to PASS (Post-Arrest Screening Site), new to the city since Spring 2004. Pier 57 on the Hudson River had originally found use launching cruise ships and, until 2003, for maintenance on city buses. Massive random arrests had been planned for the RNC, and New York's already crowded corrections system begged the question of where all of the arrestees were supposed to go. The NYPD assumed control of Pier 57 after the Department of Transportation had rejected an earlier proposal, in which the NYPD was to transform the Staten Island Ferry into a giant floating prison barge for RNC-related offenders.

After I got through processing, I was dumped in a narrow, rectangle-shaped chainlink fence enclosure full of my fellow men. I found it harder to sit still than most of the men, at least on the hard wooden benches that had been provided, so I spent the night pacing around. There was a lot of variety in the clothes: white dress shirts, colorful T-shirts, yachty polo shirts, and revealing wife beaters all covered with the same mysterious black stains. My shirt happened to be black itself, the result of which was that my appearance was unusually dapper in a chain link cage full of so many unsightly customers. Appearances can be deceiving, however, so I made sure to keep my hands away from my eyes at all times. I didn't know what kinds of chemicals went into performing city bus maintenance, and it was clear that neither the NYPD, the city, the GOP, nor the Chelsea Piers Commission had given a lot of thought to tidying up before our arrival.

There was a large group of women in a narrow, rectangular chainlink cage shaped just like ours, immediately adjacent. The space between them was just wide enough that we couldn't reach across and link warm fingers for moral support. As the night went on, the mind's ability to form complete sentences diminished, and even pacing around felt like breaking rocks. Sleep became the only real pastime in our cell, and I craved it badly. On the concrete floor, or on the benches leaning deep into the sagging chainlink backboard that we all shared, the men's sleeping faces were open-mouthed, dead from sheer exhaustion. I watched my girlfriend sleeping in the adjacent cell. She sat on a bench right up against the fence, her back leaned against it, so that I could see the back of her head slumping peacefully to one side. Since the moment Jason had gathered us up and stashed us both in the paddy wagon, there had been a quality about her that

I lacked the courage to imitate. The impression was that she was completely at peace with the present moment, showing no expectation of what would happen at any given time, how or when the present moment would turn over into the next one.

By contrast, the thought that kept me awake was that I could be released at any moment. I believed Jason when he told us, staring off into the distance, that we would be out as fast as possible. They had been doing it ever since we showed up—coming out every once in a while with a list of names and then spiriting the group of chosen men around some murky corner. The men often seemed legitimately happy when the police did this. I remember one man, possibly in his fifties, who prior to coming to Pier 57 had been very well dressed in a white dress shirt and elegant white slacks. Even with his blazing white get-up dappled with black PASS-stains he looked important, with a vaguely European air about him and gray hair swept back over his head like Donald Rumsfeld's. When the police called his name he pumped his fists just a little bit and grinned like a boy who had been exempted from taking out the garbage. I wondered how important he really was, whether there was a towncar pulled up to the shoulder of the West Side Highway waiting for him.

When morning came, all of the men were moved out of our cramped chainlink shoe box into a chainlink space about the size of a basketball court at the rear of the great bus-scouring facility. Through the links there was some kind of opening in the wall to the right. You could see the Hudson River through it, and it looked so vivid. A big line of guys went through an open door in the fence and lined up in front of a Port-A-Potty, but a cop came by and told us to go back inside because we weren't supposed to use that Port-A-Potty. Behind us he closed the door and the turning lock rang like a bell calling us to church. I went over and filled my cup with water, drank it, and then lay down in the sooty concrete and tried to sleep. But the big cell door up front was open and the police were calling names regularly so thoughts of being out by lunchtime preoccupied me.

As the names rolled on, hours passed and I had still not slept at all. I listened obsessively through each individual syllable of every name, unable to even try and make conversation with the others, until at last I became delirious. Two parallel lines of frowning cops wearing helmets and vests stretched like an equal sign from the opening of the cell to where the buses were parked and I approached them with all the speed in my step of any New Yorker on the street, walking to or from the subway and back to his job, his home, his life.

The armed parallaxis waited behind a cop holding the usual clipboard. He asked, "Where you goin'?"

I said, "Patrick Gallagher."

He looked at me as though he were still waiting for my answer.

"I-I thought I heard my name called. My name is--"

The cop shook his head. "Your name wasn't called." He didn't even have to look at the clipboard. He knew what he was doing.

Finally they did call my name and I thought, Fuck lunch, but at least I'll be out in time for happy hour. Before I went through the riot-gear gauntlet a cop approached me, removing another strip of ribbon-cuff from the big stack tied to his belt. With the movements of the cop's hip the stack of ribbons bobbed up and down and every one of them, with their two huge loops sized for the widest common denominator, became blurry in my exhausted eyes and looked like fat white bats flying out of a cave drawing. Then I was put on a bus to Central Booking.

I was in a holding cell facing some kind of reception desk. The cell had yellow cinderblocks like my dorm room freshman year of college. The cops milling around outside the bars almost danced through the station house, whether in uniform or in plainclothes. They had more swagger in their hips, emotion in their smiles, and boom in their voices than any group of people I had ever seen outside of some raucous club. The NYPD were ecstatically theatrical. I imagined that their constant proximity to incarceration had changed the way that they think about freedom itself. Rather than an abstract natural right, it became a rare and precious condition of the body that one relished and did not take for granted. I watched an overweight officer sit down at a table, somewhere behind the main reception desk, and lower a piece of cheese pizza vertically into his mouth. That he could be mocking us (which he clearly was), when Jason had gone to such trouble to make clear that they only wanted to get us through and out of there as fast as possible, was inconceivable to me.

Hours again passed, name after name was called and taken from the cell and, when I couldn't convince myself that I would be "back on the street" momentarily, I thought about the police and gritted my teeth. They made fine scapegoats. Meanwhile, a girthy young man in tie dye leaned back against the cinderblocks, hands clasping his knees, guffawing, his big chest pumping up and down. It was clear that everyone was beginning to get used to this and with that change came the physical signs. Stubble was gathering on faces where it looked foreign, sharing space with fancy-rimmed glasses and elite haircuts, as though the prisoners had been transformed into homeless men in disguise. The grease accumulating in everyone's hair reflected broad swaths of the harsh overhead light. I stewed while a crew of such young and middle-aged men with electric eyes gathered around the fat young man as he guffawed.

In my crippled mind I nicknamed him Siddhartha, the corpulent guru. He was what you would call a natural leader. He made the time pass. I couldn't so much as hear any of the other men's names besides mine, but whatever Siddhartha's name really was they called both of our names at the same time. They fastened me into a daisy chain behind him and three others, single metal cuffs all linked into a line as though they wanted us to help take care of some roadwork. Someone said, "I bet you could cut through this shit with a toenail clipper." Arching his back, a tall police officer with a laminated-looking bronzed face upturned and gleaming of tobacco boomed, "This way, gentlemen." We trudged at a uniform pace into a narrow cinderblock hallway. The cop continued, "One day, when you're older, you'll all be in the system just like us and you'll look back and say, 'In 2004, when the shit went down, I was there.'"

The problem was that many of us already *were* older, besides which the system in all its neediness may have wanted us back even more badly than we wanted to be rejoin it. Our jobs had to be done by someone. Rather than a routine case of youthful rebellion, this was a case of the system itself rebelling against…itself. The law had pre-empted the law, and the police, with all their hours of pre-RNC civil liberties training and now their babysitting of harmless middle-class would-be dissidents while real crime continued throughout their city, had essentially arrested themselves.

Four small holding cells, each with an aluminum-topped bench wrapped around its three walls, connected to a bright white room where a cop with bright red hair and a bright red moustache sat at a desk reading the *New York Post*. The cop looked like a cross between Thomas Friedman and Strawberry Shortcake; everyone in our cell made fun of him. Amazingly, the whole cellblock appeared to have just received a fresh coat of paint. Later I learned that opening up long-unused jail facilities in Central Booking had been part of the RNC preparations.

A ring of men accrued around Siddhartha while he laughed and exclaimed that there was no possibility, no possibility that we would be released before the end of the convention. The men in the cell nodded as Siddhartha said this. They all had the same shocked but grateful look, like they were only one step away from learning to master their own anger. A thin bearded man in a purple T-shirt who called himself John Doe talked to me about the discipline of comparative literature, very problematic, in which I was going to start graduate school in just a few days. Doe was a professor of philosophy somewhere in Georgia.

The cop turned the page of his *Post* loudly. People mocked the blazing streak of red across his upper lip until an old man yelled at them. "He is our only link to the outside world!" exclaimed the old man, who had also identified himself as John Doe. "It's not helping anything and it's just plain stupid."

Philosophy John Doe suggested that we have a meeting and Siddhartha intoned, "Yep, I think that's a really good idea." We all sat around, some of us on the aluminum bench and, since we had exceeded the bench's capacity, some of us on the floor. We worked out a plan to sleep in shifts, since there wasn't enough room for all of us to lie down.

It had been thirty-six hours since I had last slept, but the formalized procedure made me feel more comfortable than I had in the previous cells, where conversing had been a simple matter of holding other people's attention for the longest possible lengths of time. It re-energized me, so I volunteered to sleep in the second shift.

The six of us gathered around in the front of the cell, while the others slept in the back. I approached the bars and asked the mustachioed police officer if he could give us any of his *New York Post* to read, and he offered us the crossword puzzle. He tore it out of the paper and handed it to me through the bars and we huddled around it doing pretty well for twenty minutes or so, considering we didn't have anything to write with and needed to memorize our answers if we were going to play. With each clue we had more and more to memorize, and I was sure that we could have pulled it off had half of my cellmates not been lying asleep on the floor. We all laughed, me as much as I had since the incarceration had started.

At some point someone asked the red cop when we were going to be released and he said, "Well, I don't know. But if you want to know my opinion, they're gonna keep you until it's over. It makes sense, right?"

When I woke up the next morning on the floor of the cell, I felt crisp and polished. There were only two other prisoners. Siddhartha, the Does, even Friedman was gone, replaced by a black woman cop, and the whole *Post* was now scattered around the cell in sections, not just the crossword puzzle. When new prisoners came in I learned that a group of lawyers that had formed solely to address the RNC's massive-scale civil liberties violations had succeeded in getting a Federal court injunction on a writ of habeas corpus, which meant that we were getting out that day after all.

When they came for me, I stood with a single raised finger, having embarked upon a tirade, while two very young men sat on the bench on opposite sides of the cell nodding slowly. "This has been a lesson in corruption," I said. "The degradation of our police force and the privatization of our streets have proven only one thing once and for all, which is the dedication of the Republican Party to creating an America in which the principle of class survives but without the principle of liberty. And we could never imagine a more thorough demonstration of what that kind of America would be like than the microcosm which we are experiencing now," I said. "This version of jail, without violent criminals and without the poor business-class jail, hippie-class jail. Jail with a fresh coat of paint. If we lose this election, the same description will apply to our own homes. Scared to go outside, scared to walk the streets because of who you might piss off, all the creature comforts in the world won't be enough to disguise the fact that our whole lives are jail!"

"Patrick Gallagher."

"Okay." I gave the two boys a quick salute and hurried to the bars, lest the cops change their minds.

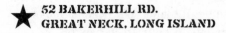

52 BAKERHILL RD.
GREAT NECK, LONG ISLAND

OLD NUNS

BY ANNE MEARA

I'm watching a documentary on the Sundance Channel, *Sex In a Cold Climate*—the source material for the fictional film, *The Magdalene Sisters*—and I'm having a flashback. It's 1936. I'm six years old in St. Joseph's boarding school in Monticello New York. My mother is ill and recovering from an operation for "lady problems." About fifty years later, I learned the specifics of "lady problems" were a hysterectomy and nervous breakdown. Which came first, I will never know.

In the documentary, these Irish girls are sent to the good sisters to atone for sins of the flesh, real or contemplated. The focus is on one of the girls who has had a baby out of wedlock. After giving birth, her infant son is taken from her and later placed in foster care. The girl is devastated. I watch the scene; I sip my chardonnay, smoke my cigarette, and weep. Black and white phantoms are doing aves in my head. Dead nuns still managing the store.

Of course, St. Joseph's in Monticello was just a boarding school, not a workhouse for wayward penitents. We didn't have to slave in a laundry like the Magdalenes; all we had to do was make our beds, clean our rooms, and on Saturday night polish our shoes for Mass the next day. Unfortunately, I had gotten shoe polish on the sleeve of my rose colored bathrobe, for which Sister quietly determined my punishment. I was to kneel with arms extended to each side and tell God I was sorry for being so thoughtless. I was in this position when my mother, who was staying at the St. Joseph's Guest House while recovering from the operation, walked into the dormitory and saw me kneeling.

"What are you doing?"

I told her.

"Get up," she said.

"But, Mommy. Sister said I had to kneel until she came back."

"Get up."

She pulled me to my feet. I was terrified of disobeying Sister. "I'll speak to Sister," my mother said. And she did. The following month I was sent to Ladycliff Academy on the Hudson for the rest of the school year. Mother heard the Franciscan nuns at Ladycliff were nicer than the Dominicans at St. Joseph's.

Before St. Joseph's and hysterectomies and nervous breakdowns, my parents and I were living in the first home I remember, at 52 Bakerhill Road in Great Neck, Long Island. I think of these first six years of my life as an idyllic time before everything crumpled into grayness. I began first grade at our parish school, St. Aloysius. Sister Mary Damien who was my first grade teacher, wanted me to learn to write with my right hand. My mother disagreed and said she didn't believe it was good to switch. I had a huge crush on Sister Mary Damien, I would have done anything for her. If she had asked me to go the island of Molokai, the land of her name-sake, and save all the Lepers, I would have done so. The fact that my mother insisted that I continue writing with my left hand, embarrassed me. My mother won the argument. Sister Mary Damien gave in and almost seventy years later I continue to be a lefty.

After my hiatus at St. Joseph's and later on at Ladycliff Academy, we returned to 52 Bakerhill Road and I got reacquainted with my third and fourth grade classmates in St. Aloysius. My mother was unhappy living in Great Neck, so in 1939 we moved to Bronxville in Westchester.

In those days, Bronxville was one square mile of Protestants. There was a smattering of Catholics and about three Jewish families living there at the time. African Americans were nonexistent, except as domestic daytrippers. There was no parochial school connected to our parish, so my parents were forced to enroll me in the public school, which happened to be one of the first progressive schools in the state. This was so exciting to me—no uniforms, no prayers, no "Yes, Sister. No Sister." I was gung-ho to start my non-sectarian fifth grade.

At Bronxville Public School, the arts were integrated with the courses being taught. Our history class studied Peter Stuyvesant and old New Amsterdam, so we were encouraged to experience the life-style of all things colonial. This was decades before reality shows in which modern families endured the hardships of more primitive eras in history. We learned how to dip candles, weave cloth and pewter spoons. I loved this stuff. Another godsend was an escape from math. If I found arithmetic overwhelming, I'd get permission to go to the art department to express myself. My father, upset with this curriculum, sent away to the New York Board of Education for the State Syllabus so he could coach me in the mysteries of fractions. During my year in Bronxville, I learned many things: how to make pewter spoons, dip candles, and that not all schools sang songs in Latin.

It's October 15, 1940 and I'm sitting on a milk box near the side door of a bungalow we rented far away from our old house on Bakerhill Road. We moved back to Great Neck and my mother was still unhappy. Family members would say, "Aunt Mae is just feeling blue." And she was. Many neighbors were milling about on the front lawn and an ambulance had pulled up to the curb. My father was in the house with paramedics who were trying to revive my mother who had turned on the gas and inhaled eternity.

For a brief period of time, my father tried to hold things together by having himself and me, his only child, move into his sister's home in Flatbush. My aunt was a loving, no-nonsense woman whose deeply lived Catholicism helped her endure the deaths of a husband and two children. Her remaining four sons and daughter, my father and me were in theory to live together in a family arrangement that would work for everyone. This did not happen right away. I had just turned eleven and was convinced that I was a changeling, the unacknowledged heir to the throne mistakenly left with a family of well-meaning aliens. My father, who must have been in deep despair, decided that my return to Ladycliff Academy would be best for all.

It's 1997 and Schindler's List is being re-played on TV. As I followed the little red dress weaving in and out of the gray mass of humanity, I thought of Anne Frank. Born in 1929, she would be my age today. We were adolescents together, she in her garret in Amsterdam, me in St. Agnes in Rockville Center.

That January, Jerry and I were on our way to Hamburg, Germany for the premiere of *After Play*, a play I had written that had been performed Off-Broadway in New York several years earlier. We decided to spend a few days in Amsterdam before the Hamburg opening. It was cold and damp and wonderful. Amsterdam, the land of Hans Brinker and legal marijuana. Our hotel was only a bridge away from the night club and coffee house area where a potpourri of herbal stimulants were available. For some reason we never took advantage of this largesse. Maybe we felt intimidated or too green to know what to ask for.

The day before we left for Hamburg, we visited Anne Frank's House. We went up the stairs and in and out of the hidden rooms behind the bookcase, searching for echoes of Anne and her family. Anne's room had movie stars' pictures on the wall, similar to my bedroom in Long Island.

LOST AND FOUND

The secret rooms were real but mainly a re-creation of the conditions under which the Franks lived during their enforced hibernation. Did Anne love James Mason and Van Johnson as passionately as I did?

I'm back at Ladycliff Academy. It's January 1941, three months after my mother's death. By now, I was an old pro at the boarding school game. After all, I'd been out in the world a bit. I'd experienced foreign cultures like Bronxville and had an incredible working knowledge of the life and times of Peter Stuyvesant.

A new girl arrived at Ladycliff and became my roommate. She was taller than me and more athletic looking. Her Aryan hair was cropped short in what was then called a "boyish bob". Her name was Helen Hauser. She was German and spoke English with a heavy accent. I don't think I liked Helen Hauser. She keept to herself and tacitly lett those nearby know she had boundaries. I realized this was not "best pal" material. She was at Ladycliff for about three months and then mysteriously left I say mysteriously because everything about her said *verboten*.

The drums of war were beating a tattoo across the Atlantic. London was already in the blitz and December 7th was not far away.

In my eleven year old imagination, I wove a sinister scenario for Helen Hauser. *She is the daughter of a Nazi General who has been sent to America for safe keeping.* No. Worse. *She is a Nazi spy masquerading as a twelve year old. Her mission is to steal war secrets from the military and send them back to her father via coded letters.*

This was not impossible. Ladycliff was in the town of Highland Falls, New York, home to the United States Military Academy at West Point.

So many years and so many wars ago, I'm still thinking about the enigma of Helen Hauser. Did she go back to Germany? Was her father tried for war crimes or did he escape to Long Island and start a new life under the friendly cover of neighborhood brewmeister? Is Helen Hauser even alive and if she is, does she ever think of our pre-teen contemporary Anne Frank?

On Sundays at Ladycliff, parents would sometimes visit their children. The Nun would come to the study hall or outside to the play area and tell you that you had company. I loved it when my father would make the trek up along the Hudson in his Studebaker and whisk me away from the usual parochial Sunday night supper. We would drive north of West Point to the city of Newburgh and have steak and baked potato and creamed spinach at the George Washington Hotel. Sometimes there would be a movie before this luxurious repast. I remember seeing Charlie Chaplin in *The Great Dictator* with Jack Oakie and Paulette Goddard. This wonderful reprieve would end too soon and we would drive back to Ladycliff, where the Studebaker would turn into a pumpkin and the wicked step-sisters awaited.

In my memory, I see him walking down the hill wearing a brown suit and fedora. I don't want him to go. The path down the hill is a short cut to the parking lot. The trail is worn bare from the footsteps of parents returning to the real world after huggy, kissy, guilty visits. My Dad shrinks in the distance. At one point he turns and waves to me. I wave back.

"As idle as a painted ship upon a painted ocean." That line alone would put Samuel Taylor Coleridge in the poetry hall of fame. I'm now in seventh grade in St. Agnes elementary school in Rockville Center, Long Island and my father I are living with my Aunt and cousins at 69 Hempstead Avenue, a big brown shingled, cream trim house purchased with a loan from the Federal Housing Authority.

At St. Agnes, Sister Miriam Virginia, a humorless pinched-faced nun, who years later I learned, relaxed her face and left the convent, assigned us *The Rhyme of the Ancient Mariner.* Samuel Coldridge, I discovered, had his own personal albatross, mainly a serious dope addiction. In those days, dope was an exotic thing that belonged to poets and Victorian ladies who assuaged their vapors with hefty swigs of laudanum.

LOST AND FOUND

It is 1949 and I am an apprentice in a summer stock company in Southold, Long Island. Being nineteen and actually getting to work in the theater was a recipe for a magical summer. We apprentices did everything—painted flats, worked on costumes, lights, and sound—everything necessary to get a new play mounted each week. Three or four hours sleep a night was the usual. Benzedrine tablets—Bennies—were available to keep us awake and invincible.

I didn't think of it at the time, but that was probably my first experience with dope. The next time, I was already married for about twelve years and in L.A. with Jerry and our kids. We were visiting with dear friends who also had two children. Avery was a wonderful actor, comedian, and improvisation artist, and his wife Shelly worked actively protesting against the war in Vietnam. They included "grass" in their lives as easily as we included vodka or beer. I was one of those straights who inhale a joint and announce to everyone around me that, "I don't think this is working...I don't feel anything." Then one of our friends would say something innocuous like, "Lets leave the kids with the sitter and eat dinner at Scandia." I would immediately burst into uncontrollable laughter: "My God, that is so hilarious, the wit, the insight!" Jerry would get very Hasidic and claim he was allergic to marijuana, that it infected his gums or something. Our brief sojourn into the land of pipe dreams didn't last long. We more or less went back to conventional drugs like wine or booze.

I wonder what my mother would think reading these words.
Before May Dempsey Meara married my Dad she used to teach third and fourth grade in a Brooklyn public school. She loved poetry and used to recite everything from "A Child's Garden Of Verses" to Wordsworth's "Daffodils", while cleaning our house. She would stand over the sink or stove and invent little poems. My father would take the scribbled rhymes to his office and have them typed up.

I used to know them all by heart. No more.

She loved movies and would take me with her whenever she could. I was thrilled. We would walk down Middleneck Road to the Squire theatre. The Squire Theatre was the Enchanted Wood of Great Neck circa 1935. We'd sit together in the expectant darkness.

Paul Muni and Henry Fonda, were May's favorites. My favorites too. Those silvery pretenders, they were the real deal. Then we'd emerge into the cruel sunlight that ruined everything.

I am seventy-nine as I write this. If May were alive now she would be over a hundred and something. My god, that is so surreal. One old lady wanting to talk to another old lady.

But I do.

I want to find one of those time portals and go back to 52 Bakerhill Road. I want to stand next to May as she composes poems at the sink or at the stove and tell her how much I loved Paul Muni and Henry Fonda.

[MOSES]
BY SEVERINE FEIST

I scrolled through last Saturday's call log on my cell phone to find his number. I hadn't saved it on purpose, never thought I'd be dialing it. I couldn't stop thinking about this guy. It wasn't a crush or anything (the thought of romance with anyone Y-chromosomed made my stomach turn), but I had to admit, his charisma had left an annoying residue in the back of my mind.

No answer. I left a message saying who I was and where we met, and to call me back whenever. He called right back.

"When are you leaving again?" I said.

"Well, tomorrow maybe, but I'm not in a big rush or anything," he said. "Maybe Friday? That way I can break out some new shit at the Bowery on Thursday."

"Yeah, cool, because I want to get together and talk. Why don't I take you to dinner before you go?"

He wouldn't say no to dinner. He was the type that was always hungry. Since his slam was at seven at the Poetry Club at Bowery and First, we made plans to meet for dinner at five. I looked up a place near the club that I thought would be safe for me and convenient for him.

I got to the restaurant fifteen minutes early to have a drink and collect my thoughts. I told the manager I was waiting for someone, and asked if we could have that booth in the back. At five sharp, Moses walked in, and I realized I halfway hadn't expected him to show up at all. We smiled at each other, and I got the manager to seat us.

"Do you wanna hear a monologue I'm gonna do tonight? I just wrote it today, it's just three minutes," he said. He looked around, eyes quickly resting on each body, counting his audience. We were few, but his eyes were sparkling anyway.

"I'd love to," I said. "Should we order first so they don't interrupt?"

"Nah, it's just three minutes, lemme just do it now so I don't get nervous."

He was more eager than nervous, but I told him to go for it.

His words were witty and smart, and intimidating. He seemed well-read, or at least very in touch with street-level politics and humanity. He had a knack for soaking up the atmosphere of the city.

"That was awesome," I said. "Good rhythm, nice flow, it builds up momentum; the whole thing is really clever and in-your-face at the same time. I wish I could go tonight. Maybe next time."

He smiled, looked down at his shirt, across the room, then began studying the stickers that said "Nobody Gives You Power, You Just Take It," "Ban Republican Marriage," and "Dreaming" on the little white suitcase that he brought with him everywhere. His ego was adequately fluffed, so we looked at the menu.

His grin faded. "Um, you know what, there's not too much I can afford," he said. "Do you think they'd give me, like, a side of mashed potatoes or something?"

"Listen, I invited you, and I'm buying dinner. I already told you that, anyway. Get whatever you want. What about the steak and fries?"

He said, "That sounds really good," and opened up his suitcase to reorganize his goods: the photocopied, hand-stapled booklets of poetry, various stickers, a strange assortment of post-cards, and other random items that people had given him or he had found with potential street value. He pulled out one of his self-publications.

"Hey, want me to sign it for you?" His smile was charming and he held out the signed copy as if it had "First Edition As New" value. "No charge, you know, since you're buying dinner and all."

I smiled, thanked him, and put it in my bag. I looked back at the menu realizing that I had just figured something out. His subtle manifestations of unassuming politeness were getting to me, in contrast with his confidence and obvious talent as a political writer and counterculture activist—a rare combination, especially in a young guy. He was reluctant to take charity, though that's why he came. The waiter came over, we ordered, and I asked Moses if he wanted a glass of wine to go with his steak. He looked at the waiter, then at the menu, then at me out of the corner of his eye, then back at the menu, saying nothing. I ordered another glass of what I was having.

I got out my steno pad and a pen, and his laugh teased and applauded me at the same time. He was a glutton for attention, so we got right into it, and started down the path my notes had laid out. We went over the basics, and he went on a few rambling tangents in between. In the end I didn't follow my list, despite my obsession with crossing things off, but we spoke too easily. I gave in.

After a half a glass of wine, his face was flushed. He leaned in and said, "I feel really comfortable talking to you." I had the feeling that mostly, he appreciated someone taking more than a sideways glance at him.

Just as our conversation was taking off, our dinner came, and his cell phone rang. He squirmed, trying to find it quickly, looking apologetic, irritated at how abrasive it was, though it was a cute little tone. I told him I understood, and to answer. Normally when I go out to eat with someone, I'd be infuriated and offended with them for answering their cell phone at the table. In this case, though it broke our rhythm, it was obvious that it was important, the one tenuous line between him and anyone else out there that wanted to find him. He needs this connection, needs people to care about him, to want to talk to him.

"I want more people to care about me than I could possibly ever give enough attention to," he told me later.

It was with a young woman he'd meet later that night. She asked what he was doing, and he said, "This thirty-five-year-old woman is buying me a twenty-two dollar steak and an eight dollar glass of wine."

I heard a mini-shriek come out of his phone, jealousy mixed with flirtation, then silence. His immediate, beaming grin told me she must have been whispering descriptions of where he'd be sleeping that night, and step-by-step what they'd be doing after the slam.

When they hook up later, she'll ask him all about me, if he doesn't tell her first. If he's the gentleman he's been to me so far, he'll focus on her before getting into his story. Maybe he won't tell any kind of story, or maybe he'll embellish. You don't really know with a salesman. Maybe he's not so much a salesman as adept at survival, though the two states are closely related, depending on luck and resources. Bottom line, she's interested, so he'll say what he needs to say to bridge the gap.

It's never one-sided. What you think is interesting and for your benefit always has another value all its own attached. I was talking to a young man of twenty-two who travels on charity, living place to place, showering and washing his pungent clothes when he can (not often enough for me to sit too close). He's attractive, and defies ethnic categorization. He's tall, thin, with dark shaggy hair, and a thin scraggly goatee. He's polite, well-spoken, mature for his age, and eccentric by choice. He wears layers of clothes, tucked into each other and artfully arranged. He easily passes for an NYU student.

By the end of dinner he had laid out a portrait of his history. "Moses" was born September 19th, 1982 in an indelibly red state to parents who never married and lived a fluid life. His mother took him to California when he was five, where they lived with friends for a while. Then to Minnesota for another while with other friends. When she felt the need to continue on without him, she left him with his grandparents in North Dakota until he was fifteen. His grandmother died almost immediately after she left, and since his grandfather couldn't be bothered with him, Moses decided to move back to Minnesota to find his father. He graduated high school at sixteen.

School was all too easy for him. He propelled through, raising the statistics in the school's favor. His dad gave him money to keep going to school, so he moved into a dorm at the University of Minnesota. He partied through his college money in about a year, and promptly dropped out. He spent the next year with friends, then sold his computer for a hundred bucks and hit the road.

He hitchhiked and bussed out to Portland, his backpack stuffed with a couple changes of clothes and two comp books full of poetry. He also brought what would become his trademark, a small, shopworn white suitcase he found on the "free" table at a garage sale with tapes inside on how to be a traveling salesman. The brilliant student that he was, he found it difficult to sell much in Portland, but he enjoyed meeting people and seeing what he saw.

But he's a salesman here in Manhattan, and survives on charm and the cash and other handouts it gets him. "Cash is where it's at," he said, and we agree it's important to be able to make some in order to spend it, and then make some more to spend some more.

He's still got a decent relationship with his family. His paternal grandmother (the only one who consistently lets him know she cares for and worries about him) continues to pay his cell phone bill. He can always go back to work for his dad to get cash for his next trip. After Pittsburgh, he says he'll go to Northern California to stay with friends. He'll end up somewhere in the hippy-dippiest part of Marin County living in a big empty crash pad with nine other "weird artist vagabond types" like himself.

They might make a movie, or some recordings, any of which would help his product supply, furthering his potential for income.

Moses isn't sure how long the "broke artist thing" will hold his attention, but he's confident he'll get by. He's willing to do odd jobs or carpentry when necessary. I have a feeling he'll be in California for a while, where it's easier to live outside. Why is it that he seems nobler to me in the streets of New York than he would in San Francisco? Maybe because I moved away from there after seeing too many kids on those streets who were completely apathetic and so junked up they couldn't write or speak.

Moses has always written, at least since he realized he could. Around fifteen he started taking his talent seriously after writing some poetry to impress a girl (and it did). His only fear is that his life won't be interesting enough to write about, an issue he's bent on getting around. He's had no problem thus far putting himself in interesting situations.

"I like to fuck up somebody's day," he says with a smile, and I take it to be an agreement with what I had been saying about my own desire to adjust people's perspectives for them, even if momentarily. I connected pretty strongly to his need to break through the numb consciousness some people walk through the world with, as if insulated from deeper thought.

He loves music, especially rap, which I cannot stand. I can understand why he likes it though, being a poet. He likes the lyrics and their clarity, and the way you're forced to listen.

Back at the dinner table, he began bouncing when some sort of rumba or bossa nova came on, took my hand, and put on a cute little show. He touched my arm shyly, then touched my back and asked, "Is this appropriate?" I had thanked him earlier for not touching me inappropriately before. I said, "So far."

I met him last weekend at my favorite all-night diner in the Meatpacking District. My friends and I were eating breakfast at 4 a.m. in an effort to detour an impending hangover. I had a cold that I was blatantly ignoring since my friends were in town and

I felt obliged to entertain. Moses somehow caught my attention. Maybe it was his salesman's intuition or my roaming, drunken eye, always in search of the alternative, the beauty in what's been judged as ugly by those before me. The details are hazy, but early in the conversation one of us had stricken up, he said, "I want to go home with you and smoke your pot." I figured this was a line he must use on many, because I have no recollection of mentioning that I had any weed at home. I laughed, my friends and I kept eating, and we eventually left.

He was outside waiting. As we hailed cabs, he shuffled up to me, kicking the sidewalk, glancing around and then up at the sky.

"Can I come home with you?" he asked, and I actually stopped to think about it. My friends read trouble in my expression. Janey grabbed my arm and dragged me down the block, trying to convince me I'd be crazy to bring home some stinky street kid. They couldn't figure out why I'd even considered it. My intention was not to get laid (I hadn't had sex with a man in three years, and was dating three women at the time). For a second, the night air had me doubting my sanity, but I snapped out of it. I looked at my friends and said, "I'll do what the fuck I want." They said goodnight and backed off.

I turned and nodded slightly in his direction. Without hesitation he came toward me, toward opportunity, having scrutinized the situation from twenty feet away. We got in a cab and went to my apartment. I told him to be very quiet since my roommate was asleep in her room just on the other side of a very thin wall. I had struggled with clarity again in the taxi, trying to reconcile why I was bringing him home. All I could think of was that I wanted him to feel comfortable, just for a night. I wanted to get him high, and to share my space. Something about him touched me, even in my drunken state. His behavior was hesitant, cautious, deferential, and respectful.

As soon as we walked in the door, I directed him to the shower and gave him some pajamas. We smoked, talked, and listened to music until 6 a.m. I pulled the twin bed out of my couch, and told him we'd have to share. I couldn't sleep; he hadn't quite washed off all the stink, and how could I possibly attempt sleep anyway, next to someone in a twin bed? The absurd logic of drunkenness had tricked me again. He asked if he could cuddle with me, and I said okay. He seemed to want some contact, and never touched me in a suggestive way. I don't know how or why, but I somehow trusted that he wouldn't, and I turned out to be right.

Three miserable hours later, no sleep and my cold getting worse, I woke him and said, "I just can't do it. I'm really sorry, but you have to leave." I felt bad about putting him back outside in an unfamiliar part of the city, but I was too tired and felt like such shit. I was in self-preservation mode.

He hopped right up and said, "It's no problem, thanks for letting me hang for a little while." He put back on his stinky clothes and folded up the pajamas.

I had stashed my purse earlier while he was in the shower to avoid any potential problems, but couldn't remember where. I asked him to call my cell phone from his so I could find my wallet and give him twenty dollars. So he did, and I did, and he left.

His real name is Leonard, which he doesn't mind the sound of, or if people call him Leo or Lenny, just as long as they're still talking. It's just that Moses attracts a lot more attention when he's introduced at open mics. He had been in New York for three weeks the night we met. He didn't say why he ended up staying longer, and I didn't ask, but my guess is he sensed my interest and gravitated toward it. Being an explorer and an opportunist, it was natural for him to answer even the slightest rapping of opportunity.

When I look inside the shadow of hindsight the present moment casts, all I can figure is I recognized something, thought I saw my reflection in him, and needed to figure out why. I read his disconnect from anyone's definition of society and felt an uncanny familiarity. I saw him paving a path that my feet struggle to remember themselves, one they swear they've kicked at. He was the unlikely brother of another only child.

LOST AND FOUND

Before we left each other after dinner, before his pending poetry slam at The Bowery, he tested a new line: "I want to see you again and smoke your pot and put my fingers inside you."

He laughed at his own forward wittiness. He was at ease with me, had a glass of wine, and he had not yet been inappropriate, which may be a hard thing for a young man. I have a feeling this character of his changes rapidly and often depending on what circumstance requires.

"I like ending on that note," he said, "with my hands inside you."

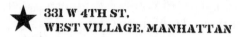

**331 W 4TH ST,
WEST VILLAGE, MANHATTAN**

CYCLES OF LOVE, SIN, AND REDEMPTION AT THE CORNER BISTRO

BY VINCE PASSARO

They were to be three for drinks: Ralph, a writer; his friend Alex, another writer; and the young woman from the magazine, Jessie, who was Ralph's connection. It was a modern kind of connection—Ralph had never seen her, had only dealt with her over the phone, by fax, by e-mail; but they were great friends now; and she had wanted to meet Alex (his old friend Alex was getting to be very well-known these days) and so Ralph had invited her.

He arrived early, by almost half an hour, because he could and because part of the treat of the evening was to sit alone by the window at the top end of the bar, in the brightness of a late summer afternoon, and watch the people pass outside, and have a couple of drinks.

And he proceeded to have his couple of drinks: Wild Turkey on the rocks, in fact; and he bummed a cigarette from a shy, nervous, acne-scarred, gay man near him and the cigarette was luxuriously good with the whiskey; and though he'd aged (he was forty-three and, what else, rising) and had gotten fat, he was still enough of a what—a mensch, perhaps?—that it was clear the brief conversation from the gay man's side had not been unwelcome; and so he felt beneficent.

The bar was pleasant but crowded, one of those old places in the West Village where the last remaining working-class men of the waterfront still felt comfortable enough to drink at the bar while the young and the prosperous and the profoundly under-employed came and went loudly all around them. It was called, with appropriate invisibility, the Corner Bistro.

These days Ralph and Alex saw each other only two or three times a year, usually at a literary gathering of one kind or another, when Ralph ducked away from his real life of demanding job and what he pleased himself to think of as wonderful children (because they were wonderful children, after all) and the endless stream of homework and housework and writing late into the night. On these rare occasions he ventured out to see the chang-ing but unchanging faces of the New York publishing community, as he had done tonight—only tonight was different. It was one of those weeks in summer when his family was out of town and he was at loose ends. He was near the end of a novel he had been working on (he hated to admit the number) for nine years, and normally should have stayed home doing it, but tonight was a travel night, to join the family for a long weekend, and he was merely lingering for a couple of extra hours for one of these parties, thrown by the magazine.

Alex traveled in this world much more than he; Alex ran a small magazine of his own and had published two books, one very recently, and had remained a bachelor, a figure of growing reputation and notorious good looks. Ralph and Alex had known each other for a decade or more and they retained that comfort between them of instant familiarity. Ralph was Irish Catholic and had been raised in the suburbs; Alex was Jewish and ten years younger and had grown up on the Upper West Side; but despite the differences in age and upbringing they seemed to have been issued at birth similar formulas for seeing the world, a highly sociable mixture of melancholy, sarcasm, and affection.

And of course Alex, who lived a few doors away, was late; and arrived with the self-conscious air of rumpled disregard for society and appearances that, despite its self-consciousness, actually had taken hold as an integral part of his beauty.

"Is it really seven twenty-five?" Alex said. He was looking with exaggerated shock at the clock over the bar. He was supposed to have been there at seven.

"I have twenty after," said one of the old men behind Ralph.

"And I have seven-sixteen," Ralph said, looking at the little four- dollar digital thing that he carried around. "Time moves backward at the Corner Bistro. I've been waiting here since 1934, actually, but I'm younger now than when I started. Go figure."

"How've you been?" Alex said, putting himself down on a stool.

"I've been fine."

"You look good."

"That's a lie," Ralph said. "What's keeping you so busy these days? Every time I e-mail you or leave you a message I keep thinking I'm reaching into the maelstrom."

"I keep as many fires burning as possible," Alex said. "It fends off having to think."

"Sounds expensive," Ralph said.

"Oh it is. Absolutely," Alex said. "In fact I was thinking, I should write a piece on how a hundred thousand a year not only isn't enough for a family in New York, it's not even enough for a bachelor. I'll be a pariah."

He was referring to a piece that Ralph had written a few years before, that landed him on television and made him the object of many denunciations. This led them to talk about money for a while, in the usual abstract ways, and about the financing for Alex's magazine; money was a subject you could rely on in New York, a real fencepost for leaning during long conversations, though from such discussions one never learned a thing.

They talked of money, they talked of recent books, and other writers, they talked of a friend who had died. Ralph sipped his drink more slowly; he would have to pace himself to make it through a long evening conscious. Alex was talking of the friend and his loss when Ralph saw out the window and down the walk across the small street a young woman, a Significant Blonde, young and athletic and rather glamorously dressed. He nodded out toward her and said, "I think this might be our woman."

"You mean you've never met her?" Alex said.

"Not in person," Ralph said. "I've talked with her on the phone. I've e-mailed her. We do a lot of e-mail." Jessie did all the research and copy editing of Ralph's monthly book pieces, and they had now had a long-running correspondence on a variety of topics, an exchange that of late had expanded (he knew but was not yet admitting that he knew) into realms of the dangerously personal. She had a modern-educated voice, which was to say he heard both culture and privilege in it—two attributes that when he'd been young had been merged seamlessly together in the voices of those who had been given them, but that now one almost always heard as distinct and competing influences. In the contest, privilege usually won, but it didn't sound to him necessarily as if it would in hers, which was part of what he'd grown to like and respect about her. She had self-confidence, he discovered over time, and she had good taste, and she showed a kind of enthusiasm for ideas that didn't go with the scenery of the New York publishing world. She had not yet picked up its expensive, super-scheduled world-weariness, its vulgarity, or, so far as he could tell, its distinctly off-center, flickering hungers; her ambitions seemed to be of a worthy kind. She presented a mind that yearned for knowledge; improbably, it might even have yearned for wisdom—counter to the times and certainly to the milieu.

And so in his way, vaguely but not altogether paternal, didactic, tentative but, he also knew, insinuating (like a Henry James character, an older American distant relation, the narrator) he had taken her up, and read her work, and given her things to read as well. She was grateful to him for his attention; it turned out that she was not a woman short of men's attention but she had been short of the right kind, or of this kind in any case, and the quality of his was what he had to offer, that and nothing else. It cost him nothing, it came easily to him, it blended with his passions and, unquestionably, it fed his vanity and his soft messianic tendencies; yet, for all that his paying of attention did for him, he also enjoyed believing it did something for others, that the men and women who had accepted it from him in his life had known a certain value. His wife had taken it and made good use of it for almost a quarter of a century, since they had been, he knew now, children. She was accustomed to it; and he wondered with the usual boring and mild resentment that builds in marriage whether she even recognized it as exceptional anymore, or noticed it at all.

The young lady had reached the door. Ralph leaned forward: "She's got a lot on her plate tonight," he said. "She's fitting us in."

"Kind of her," said Alex. Ralph looked at him with an arched eyebrow. "I mean it," Alex said.

She came inside then, and stood before them proud and nervous. He was shocked to discover that he could barely look at her: he had with ease been dealing with this woman for more than a year, writing her quite a bit in recent weeks on all sorts of topics, enjoying himself; he thought of himself as fearless and had earned the right to, it was one of his few strengths, real butt-hard nerve in the face of failure, humiliation, poverty, violence, or worse. But—he could barely look at this woman. And bare, alas, was one of the operative words. She was showing a lot of skin and it was very beautiful skin, arms and shoulders and collar and chest and muscled neck, and he hadn't been sleeping and he was very, very tired; too tired to brace himself into the relaxed pose of the accomplished and sexually mature older man; too tired to coolly withstand it. It was not arousal he had to contend with— he had contended with that every day since he'd been thirteen and it was as familiar to him now as his own belly and language and aching feet—no, it was the instant sense of fatigue he felt

upon looking at her, and the distant echoes of his predictable
early failures in courtship and in sex. All of her—no, of course
not all of her, but enough of her—the golden hair and skin, the
cell phone and lipstick and cigarette, the black tube top and tan
capri pants, the lovely shoes and the slight tremble around her,
like the shimmer of light viewed through rising heat—said trouble; trouble that had been cultivated with a knowing eye; trouble
as a kind of personal philosophy, half humorous and half lethal—
and she might, just might, grow out of it by the time she turned
seventy. Was he really so far beyond having the strength for such
things? He had married a woman like that; she rocked and she
rolled; she had no settings below "intense" and she had, he liked
to think, kept him alive and awake and at arm's length from the
world of gloom and death that would otherwise have been his
habitat. Suddenly he wasn't up to it anymore: that's what this
young woman made him feel. He tried to watch her eyes, which
were a backlit, peacock blue, but found that looking into them
was like staring through the windows of a burning house. "The
fire burns as the novel taught it how," was a line in a poem he'd
recently passed along to her and another editor at the magazine
at one point (they all shared a liking for Wallace Stevens, they
discovered one day), and now here it was again, art come back to
burn life onto itself, and onto him.

She knew them both by sight, presumably from their pictures,
which had been at one time or another in the magazine. "I
decided to be late," she said—she was quite late—"so you two
could bond."

"We don't need to bond," Ralph said. "We bonded fucking
years ago. They had to use a solvent to pry us apart. Jessie, this is
Alex Peterman, Alex, this is Jessica Traut." She took Alex's long
hand and held it before her momentarily and made a small move
with her body that hinted at a curtsy; he had to smile to see it.

"Alex barely just got here himself," Ralph said. "I was virtually stood up."

"The great thing about this whole arrangement was that you
knew at least one of us would show up," Alex said.

They were both facing him then. Her mouth had a slight curl that gave her face a look of permanent sardonic amusement, so that her smile, when it came, was a surprise, the delicate back of a tough-looking leaf. "Oh, no," she said. "He knew both of us would show up."

"Sure, sure," Ralph said. "What are you having?"

She wanted some damn complicated thing—Alex seemed to know what it was, one of the benefits of being a man about town—that the bartender not only didn't have, but clearly had never heard of; and then she asked for Guinness but they had only cans, which he thoroughly agreed with rejecting; so she settled for a vodka and soda.

"You have very precise drink ideas," Ralph said to her, handing the drink from the bar, over someone's shoulder, toward the window where she and Alex were standing. "That's good."

"Why is that good?" she said. "It's mostly a pain."

"It means you're a serious drinker," he said. "One likes to see that in a young lady today." They clinked glasses. He accidentally swished a little of his out and it spilled near her foot. He looked down to see if he'd hit her.

"Don't worry, it won't hurt my foot," she said.

"You know," Ralph said, looking up again, "I've been commuting by public conveyance all summer"—he worked at a university outside the city—"and because of the shoe fashions I'm seeing at minimum a thousand toes a day. It's the Summer of a Thousand Toes."

Alex swallowed his drink; he had a long neck and the Adam's apple slid up and down like the counterweight on a doctor's scale. He was looking off down the bar. "It has," he said with placid thoughtfulness, like a farmer talking weather. "It's been a very footy summer." This made Ralph laugh and he spilled a little of his drink again; again it was near Jessie's foot.

"You might think about getting some Totes," Alex said to her.

"Shut the fuck up," Ralph said.

She began telling Alex about people they knew in common, mostly, Ralph gathered, sensitive, unreliable body-pierced guys who on and off worked for Alex at the growing kingdom of his small magazine. (Ralph had an image, suddenly, of a gaunt, unwashed young man, walking into a body piercing shop—where? on the boardwalk in Wildwood, New Jersey?—and ordering up rusty spikes for his wrists and feet, and a lance for his side.) The young people and Alex were going to be launching a website very soon; Alex was outlining the basic premises.

Ralph half listened, drank his drink, stole one of her cigarettes, watched. And watching her, Ralph knew one thing . . . No, he knew two things, or three. Actually, it was a thousand. First (one always had to settle this question in one's mind with a good-looking woman), he was not and never had been the kind of man such a woman would be interested in; she was not interested in older men in any case; and even if he had been exactly her age, he would have been an older man, as it had always been in his nature to be forty. Her agenda of pleasure was clearly athletic and geographically wide and she was interested (he guessed) in quick rangy men who could keep up with her. If she had been one of those young women who openly pursued older men, women he invariably thought of as calculating, or at least misguidedly ambitious, he was not the right kind: he was very accomplished at this point in his life, a fact known to certain people in his field, like Alex; but had neither the money nor the standing to compensate for his age and his marital status.

More than that, he also knew something else: he himself was not interested. Or, he thought, to be more accurate, he was nothing more than interested. He'd had enough strife, and having tried once to "solve" the problem romantically, only to make it worse, he knew he wouldn't be trying it again. He and his wife were at this moment halfway across the river they'd been given to breach; they were up to their necks in hard current, in other words, with three children on their backs, and he understood, with an added, silvery light suddenly cast on the scene, that it was not a moment when it would be helpful to make any new fucking discoveries. Not when it meant—and invariably it would mean this—that the people he actually loved would be whisked off shrieking downstream.

Yet, that feeling he'd had when he saw her, it was like a little piece, of what? Masculine vanity? Something just slightly more precious than that? Whatever it was, it fell to the floor of the bar at that moment like a loose lens from an old man's cloudy eyeglasses and was crunched underfoot before anyone could retrieve it. Here it was in all its glory, the tragi-comic fucking midlife bullshit he'd always heard about . . .Well, it sucked was all he could say. It sucked inherently, like surgery sucked, and it sucked further than that: it sucked in its attendant meanings, it sucked that he, of all people, enlightened with hard-won self-knowledge, bloated with it in fact, a man who along with a few close friends stood—it was his great pleasure to think, especially after two drinks, or now he was just on to three—as a moral beacon in a corrupt world; it sucked to know suddenly, in an instant, that even were it only for an evening he would have to endure this, would have to be made foolish and ridiculous by it in his own eyes. He had a very high opinion of himself, and this was an insult.

But they talked; they had to talk, after all, they weren't all about to stand and stare at each other in glum silence. So Ralph told them of his walk down to the Village from Penn Station along Eighth Avenue, and of the assessing eyes of the gay men all along the way, and how amused he felt by it and how oddly confirmed, by frank sexual assessments that ranged from the mildly negative to the surprisingly positive with many stops in between; it made him feel, rare for him on the streets, as if he was being viewed as a living, breathing, sexually-active being. They talked then in comparison, about how men looked at women, about how women looked at women (the cruelest of all assessments, the two men believed, but she didn't think so), and then two children slipped past them at the bar, followed by their father, to sit in the corner, which was empty; it was that kind of place, open to all comers; he helped the little girl up onto a stool. "Ralph is very experienced with children," Alex said and she said quietly,

"I know." In this intensely crowded place, an absolutely grown-up place, with how many gallons of whiskey stained into the floor over the years, the two little children, a boy perhaps five and a girl no more than seven, showed that amazing courage that children display when they have no choice. Ralph was moved by it, and, as he made way for them and helped them up, he gestured to them by face and body and voice, in ways he knew they could take in, that this immense smoky crowd was actually safe and that their special status as children would be recognized and respected.

"So," Jessie said. "What about you? Did you like any of the men? Encourage any of them?"

"Not a one," Ralph said. Alex and she offered some cat calls on this. "Denial, denial, " she said.

"I don't like the whole Chelsea thing," Ralph said, "They all look like Michael Medved, except with too much drug use in their pasts."

"So what's your type, then?" she said.

Ralph thought about it. "Brad Pitt," he said. "Now there's a guy you could tolerate seeing lying around the house scratching his balls."

"Amen," she said.

"Maybe he brings Jennifer Aniston to the relationship," Alex said. "That could get interesting."

"She could be the houseboy," Ralph said. "She'd do the shopping and hang around scantily clad dealing with, like, all the recycling, you know, paper, plastics, metals."

Long married and parental, Ralph was the rabbi's wife in this trio; he had brought them together in an amusing little piece of matchmaking, to flirt; and they did flirt; but then, ominously, they kind of stopped, he noticed, or did so in ever more tentative little salvos. Being the matchmaker, he suddenly was able to see Alex as Jessie must see him; not merely good-looking but on certain nights (he assumed, from the woman's perspective), breathtaking: tall, warm, smart, funny, self-deprecating, and highly unattainable. He'd been with some very serious women in his time, as Jessie must sense, or even know, and he was with one currently. Still, Jess was good, she had some tools, Ralph thought; it certainly wasn't out of the question. Their slight, growing nervousness felt a little potent. And it occurred to him, with a jolt of surprise, that if these two actually hooked up his heart would give off a quick flame of jealousy—which was not the surprise; he was accustomed to that, he felt like that whenever anyone he knew got laid; the surprise was that he was uncertain suddenly which one he would be jealous of, or for, or about; he couldn't even nail down the damn preposition.

After Brad Pitt played himself out, Jessie went off to the ladies room, announcing that on her return they would have to go to this party because various people were actually waiting for her there. She turned and departed practically at a sprint; she did things quickly. Alex watched her until she disappeared. Then he looked at Ralph.

"So—you've never seen her before?"

"No. I had a feeling she'd be a knockout."

Alex made a face, pulled his head back.

"What?" Ralph said. "You don't think she's—"

"Oh, don't worry, she's a knockout, she's a lot more than a knockout," Alex said. They were staring out the window again. "All I can say is, you show admirable restraint."

Ralph wasn't certain he'd shown enough restraint at all; Alex could see only the restraint that was left. Restraint was the air he breathed. Restraint made life possible.

"That's like saying the people who don't use nuclear weapons every day show admirable restraint," he finally said.

"They do, they do," Alex said. "I admire them too." They finished their drinks, and stood, like two rumpled gentlemen, as she returned to them.

She and Ralph took a cab to the party; Alex was going as he did everywhere, on his bicycle. In the back seat, each at a far end, Ralph said to her, "So, are you recovering from your day?" She had juggled about three hundred things that day, she'd told them, finishing up at work in the largest sense of finishing up, since the magazine was closing, kaput—that's what this party was for, what gave the night it's feeling of apocalypse—so this had been her last day, plus she'd been doing all the arranging for a long weekend to Nantucket with four young men, a trip on which she planned to depart at one in the morning, with the four men, what, in tow? Or was she in tow? It was part of her appeal, he guessed, that he would never know which, although if it was she that was in tow, he had to give at least one of these guys credit because this one would take some real towing.

"Oh, I still have to go see this drug dealer tonight," she said quietly.

He looked at her. "You're the one who has to score the weed for the trip, tonight?" he said.

"It's not weed," she said, "it's . . ." but she was whispering now and he couldn't hear her.

"It's what?"

"Ecstasy," she whispered it again. She had the most remarkable look on her face, fear squelched by defiance, as if she thought someone—specifically Ralph, as he was the only one there—was going to scream at her or even hit her, and she was going to be ready to take it. It caused him to shift himself even farther away. Another gesture of safety.

"Ohhhh, ex-stacy," he said. "In Nantucket. Hmmm. Rave in the waves, you can call it." A song came back to him, some mighty guitar anthem, what? 'Nantucket Sleighride' . . . it was a heroin song, or a coke song, a celebration of some drug, he couldn't remember.

She was backed into the corner of the cab with that semi-frightened look still on; it was mixed, though, with the other look she'd had all night of amusement; she was pleased by disobedience, he thought; he wondered whom she was disobeying. Earlier that day he had glanced down at a picture that had turned up recently and that he'd left on his desk at work; it was of himself at five years old, and at the moment of seeing it—he had been reaching for the phone—he remembered the line of Flannery

O'Connor's, from "A Good Man Is Hard to Find," when the grandmother looks into the Misfit's face and says, "Why you're one of my babies . . .You're one of my own children," at which point, the Misfit, furious, shoots her. He saw himself at five that way because he did look in fact like his own children and because he'd been wounded then, deeply, and though he couldn't remember what he had thought then or how he had felt, in this picture that wound showed clearly in his face (he could see it there in the picture as directly and immediately as he could see his own children's pain), and right now, with Jessie looking at him that way—twenty-three going on twelve—the same feeling came over him and the same words, "one of my own children," unspoken but palpable, rose in his throat. His children often did what she'd just done, dashed into crime with defiance and fear and wonder, and, because they felt safe with him, with a deeper pleasure, pleasure with themselves and their daring. He wanted to tell her that the stakes were rising, she was a child no longer; or he just wanted to whisper, oh, be careful, but, quite properly, he said nothing. It occurred to him later (the thought gave away his age) that he should probably have offered to go with her, an amusing variation of chivalry: You never let a lady visit her drug dealer alone.

The party was at a forgettable restaurant in Tribeca, nicely expensive looking and fashionably Asian. It was all pleasant, unnecessary, and free. There was an editor there he'd worked with more than the others, a warm and funny man, it was nice to see him ("Stop hitting on my staff," he called out from the bar when Ralph walked in with Jessie; "Your ex-staff," Jessie said, and bolted for the corner) and Alex was around, which comforted him. Alex had not intended to go the party, Ralph knew, and so must have done so to follow either him or Jessie; but now they all avoided each other. Ralph holed up with the editor for a while, who, it turned out, said he had enough money stashed away to live "for three years," a numbing and, in some distant little hole of his resentment closet, infuriating concept to Ralph, who barely had enough money to get uptown. He met an older writer, much respected in the magazine trade, who had taken a highly commercial job and made some very internet IPO kind of money over the last three years, and looked like the boy who'd been forced to sit before the bowl of porridge from morning to afternoon—as if he were finally getting ready to have this arrangement of his life begin to appeal to him.

Other women he saw and spoke with that night struck him either as stupid, cynical or depraved—well there was one who was intelligently gracious and possibly nice but she wore a kind of high-fashion raincoat thing all evening, well cinched at the waist, over bare legs and high heels, and as it was a summer night and they were indoors, it had a feeling about it of Audrey-Hepburn-goes-flasher, and she was altogether too voluble and active for this late in the evening, at this late date in his life. By the time the party was well along he had joined the stupid. He would have preferred to be on the side of the depraved, but he never could get himself there. He drank too much for one thing, always a sign of sentimentality run amok... He was not capable of cynicism, though some people thought he very much was; nor was he in any way sufficiently the sybarite, though he heartily—too heartily—approved of being so: he had spent some fruitless hours of his life in a supplicant's relationship to depravity, kneeling before it, tossing offerings down into the swirl of lava and smoke and flames; he was davening at the rim of that hole again tonight. Afterward he always ended up back home, doing something ordinary, like making a pot of rice.

And so he would again. Jessie, on the other hand, now that the magazine was finished, would be traveling to South America shortly, where her sister, an anthropologist, was working on a project. She would be stopping at Machu Piccu in Peru, she was telling someone this—in the darkness Ralph didn't even take in who it was as he walked up to them, a small and somehow weary-looking woman being his only sense. Jessie was saying that Machu Piccu, with its soul-shattering views, had been a holy place, and he said, suddenly interrupting, "Well, maybe you'll have an experience like Eliot did. One of the Four Quartets is about him being at a place where prayer has been valid." It was a drunken thing to say.

"Exactly," she said. She was a little drunk too now, he realized. "The women who lived there were holy women, they spent their whole lives apart, meditating and making sacrifices on behalf of the people."

"May it not happen to you," he said.

"May something happen to me," she said quietly.

"Something will," he said. "It always does."

"Your friends are all going downstairs to smoke," she said.

"Ah," he said, and followed them out. Alex was outside with Francis, the editor, and another young editor named Lawrence, and off to the side some of the women. The men were warm to him and handed him the joint as he walked up. Alex was not unused to seeing him this way, passionate and lost. They stood on the sidewalk smoking the joint and joking; eventually more of them came down, Jessie among them. He checked his watch. Time was coming for him to go, to catch 'the last bus out' as he had taken to calling it; he wanted to be early, he wanted there to be no chance of missing it, none; no chance of opening a chasm of time and doubt in his life, a lost night, which this would become if he didn't get on that bus; so he went up for his bag and descended again and said goodbye to the men and was confused for a moment about which way was east and which west until they pointed him off in the right direction, and away he went, a rotund middle class Chaplin figure with his bag, toddling off drunk. He remembered her then, as he was walking away. He was going home. He was, with a great sense of relief, only thinking of that, of going home, and so had forgotten for a moment all the lovely turmoil of youth. He looked back, and there she was— under the silver streetlight, against the brick wall, her eyes still burning; she was literally surrounded, almost penned in by people and chatter and smoke; she stood at the center of them and either they were her audience or they were a group of hungry primates, wanting to pick her bones clean, but whichever it was, he thought with a bit of affection, she would handle it.

LOST AND FOUND

He got himself a cab on the avenue and felt the exhaustion begin to overwhelm him. He hadn't been able to sleep—for days, for weeks it seemed, always a problem when his family and its routines were removed, but now worse. Something was working on him these days, some slow enormous transformation. His accommodations of his age, his circumstances, his successes and failures, his marriage, all of it was occupying his mid section; he was like a snake in the first hours after swallowing a gopher. And this was when snakes slept, no?—but he could not, not until now, in the swaying taxi, when he began to fall under, aided by too much whiskey and a bit of weed. He was on his way out of town—get out of town!—to a little house in the Pennsylvania countryside, or what had been countryside until recently, when the boom time finally reached it. Something wrong with this gopher, he thought, it was a terrible fucking gopher—This gopher sucks! and he must have said it too, because the driver leaned back and said, "What sir? What did you say?" Ralph just waved his hand, "Nothing . . ." and put his head back onto the vinyl seat.

He would wake up in the morning with the arms of an eight-year-old boy around his neck and the lips of the boy on his cheek, the youngest of his children, one of the beautiful in the world. "I missed you, Daddy," his son would say in a cheerful, utterly-not-hungover tone of voice. "Do you want to say hi to doggy?" Doggy was a favorite stuffed animal . . . And through the quiet day with them, his family—or through most it, anyway, when no one was fighting or hungry or wounded in play—the time would be full of jokes and stories and little errands and walks, some good cd's from the library, and a couple of mighty embraces, including one in which his wife would turn to him with a sexy kiss, and as he leaned into it, would drop an ice cube down his shirt, making the children laugh. Through all this he would know the force that Hopkins said charged the world—god's grandeur—and know too a small piece of what that grandeur stood upon, the unimaginable, hard ground of love and mercy.

But that would be tomorrow; for now he slept.

**1359 AMSTERDAM AVE.
HARLEM, MANHATTAN**

TO THE WOMAN ON CRAIGSLIST WHO WANTED TO KNOW THE DIFFERENCE BETWEEN "BOOTY CALL" AND "FUCK BUDDY"

BY VINCE PASSARO

Dear Madame. Re: the difference between "booty call" and "fuck buddy," despite the alliterative pairing and their shared concern with fucking, these two phrases are ontologically different. The main distinction being that one is an incident or event, while the other is a type of modern relationship.

"Booty call" is a mid-eighties expression from a hip-hop, beeper-and-baggies, hat-and-colors world, or what we white media guys would call an "urban black community expression," meaning you hang all night getting fucked up with the your male friends, enjoying yourself, laughing, no stress (no women, in other words), comparing sneakers, Timbs, and huge jackets, and when bedtime rolls around, you call your girlfriend, or your occasional squeeze, or some chick who has the hots for you, or whatever, and head over there (or better yet, have her come to you) for flesh and moisture and warmth. (The "booty" is a female ass, but I assume you know that; I merely state it for the record.) It's an utterly male-oriented concept, in that the concept and the desirability both involve not having to spend *any* social/emotional/intellectual/spiritual time with the lady whatsoever, or even having to fake a willingness to do so. Paradise, no? Nowadays, you can use "booty call" in a context where there's a real relationship going on. You and the S.O. are out doing separate things, and decide when you're talking at 1 a.m. that one of you is going over to the other's place, because why not? This could, with ironic amusement, be categorized as a "booty call," though it isn't really, and you both know it isn't.

"Fuck buddy" is more a Clinton-era, Wesleyan-dorm sort of phrase. Picture young, semi-androgynous white professionals who were very early into mp3s and text messaging, and whose parents' marriages and subsequent relationships were so grotesquely bad that they, the kids, have no interest or ability whatsoever in having to have a romantic relationship. Sex being what it is (i.e., necessary—as is love, but they'll never use *that* word, even though they seek it in a leg-shackled sort of way), such folks have "friends" that they sleep with. Now, the phrase stands for any sorta-kinda-mostly uncommitted, laconically sexual, on-again, off-again relationship for which and in which, over the long run, if there's any real emotional engagement/attachment whatsoever (take my word for it), the woman pays the steeper price.

'Twas ever thus, as Mr. Bugs Bunny once said.

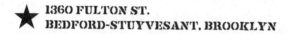
THE UPROOTING

BY DENISE V. CAMPBELL

I t's been one year since I moved to Bedford-Stuyvesant from Fort Greene, where I lived for about fifteen years. Like most change, uprooting myself was uncomfortable, but not nearly as painful as I thought it would be. I remember telling people that if I ever moved from Fort Greene, I'd be moving out of New York because there was no other neighborhood that I wanted to live in. I had laid down roots in Fort Greene, roots that grew long and deep. But the day came when I faced skyrocketing rents and the prospect of having to move.

I didn't move out of New York, as I had predicted. Instead, I moved to Bedford-Stuyvesant.

When I first came here, I thought I'd miss Fort Greene forever. But I found out that I didn't miss the screeching B54 bus coming to a halt at the bus stop across from my ground-floor apartment there. Nor did I miss the rumbling trucks and other colossal vehicles making their way to the Brooklyn-Queens Expressway via my block. More than anything, I did not miss the people next door who, laughing and talking, loudly congregated in front of my window at all hours of the day and night.

LOST AND FOUND

What I like most about my new dwelling, a garden apartment in a brownstone, is the unspoiled silence. One Sunday morning in early fall, the only sounds I heard were the wind rustling through the leaves of the mammoth trees right outside my window and the singsong of birds in the backyard.

My new block feels like a retirement community though. Many of the brownstone owners are senior citizens who have lived most of their lives in these homes. When I was deciding if I should take the apartment, I rationalized that perhaps the time had come for me to slow down. Living in Fort Greene was like living in the fast lane. The neighborhood was changing so quickly that to be in the midst of it all made you feel hip and on the cutting edge (of what, I really can't say).

One of my first observations about Bedford-Stuyvesant was the number of people I saw heading to church on Sunday mornings. The church definitely has a strong presence here, indicated by a preponderance of landmark church buildings. In contrast, most of the people out early on a Sunday morning in Fort Greene are on the way home after a night of partying. Recently, in a definite sign that I'm slowing down, I joined the go-to-church-on-Sunday crowd.

In moving to Bedford-Stuyvestant, I feared I wouldn't be as anonymous as I had been, living in a building in Fort Greene with neighbors whose names I didn't know, or even care to know. I hoped that people would not mind my business, and that I would be able to move about without feeling that all eyes were on me. In the beginning, all eyes were on me because I was a newcomer on the block.

Now, I seldom see my three neighbors in my brownstone, or even bump into them. I've learned their names from the mail dropped through the gate, which brings up another issue. At first, not having a mailbox seemed like a real invasion of privacy. Everyone can see everyone else's mail. But I finally concluded the only thing my neighbors could deduce about me from my mail is that I have a lot of bills.

For me the real selling point of my apartment, in addition to its lovely original details, is the backyard to which I have exclusive access. Having always lived in apartment buildings, being closer to the earth is a welcome change. There was some trepidation at first, since my relationship with nature had been limited to a few houseplants and store-bought flowers. Two or three annual visits to Brooklyn's Botanic Garden and excursions to Prospect Park and I have had my fill of nature.

But my affair with nature has been developing slowly. This past summer I had to learn how to coexist in the backyard with squirrels, bees, butterflies, birds, fireflies, mosquitos, and a black cat who would occasionally strut through as if it owned the place. (I won't say what I had to learn to coexist with inside the apartment.)

Through all of this, though, I don't feel quite like a brownstoner. Sometimes when I'm sitting out in my yard, I still have thoughts of living in a bright and polished apartment building, with squeaky-clean glass doors and a wall of mailboxes.

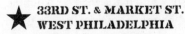

★ **33RD ST. & MARKET ST.**
WEST PHILADELPHIA

PHILADELPHIA: ITS OWN BOROUGH

BY DENISE V. CAMPBELL

"Philadelphia is nobody's sixth borough," proclaimed the heading of a column in one of Philly's daily newspapers. "Especially not New York's," the column went on to say. The writer was responding to a *New York Times* article chronicling the migration of New Yorkers to Philadelphia. It said that Philadelphians themselves occasionally refer to their city as New York's sixth borough. The columnist countered that Philadelphians do not even like New Yorkers. "New Yorkers are know-it-alls," he quoted a Philadelphian as saying.

I can understand the sentiment. Filled with my own sense of self-importance, I boasted "I'll be a big fish in a small pond" when telling people about my plans to move to Philadelphia. It was a rude awakening to learn that being from New York does not earn you brownie points. In fact, it can even be held against you.

My response to the *New York Times* article was one of angst. My fear was that it would now become common knowledge that Philadelphia was a city of "liberty and affordable rents for all," as the *Times* article quipped. The twenty-and thirtysomething artist types, described as being the first wave of New Yorkers who packed up U-Hauls and headed for the turnpike, caught on to this about four years ago. Having first been priced out of Manhattan, and then Brooklyn, they are credited with initiating the Brooklynization of Philadelphia. Following on their heels, as noted by real estate brokers, is an "influx of prospective buyers and renters from the city." Likely found within this group are empty nesters, couples raising children, and young professionals. They, along with real estate speculators and developers, are scurrying to partake of the spoils of gentrification. And thus, there go the affordable rents.

I believe I'm still ahead in the game, though. "Philadelphia is one of those best-kept secrets," I told those who pooh-poohed my city of choice. I had been priced out of Fort Greene and then Bedford-Stuyvesant, Brooklyn. But the decision to move to Philly involved more than its lower cost of living—which, according to the *Times* article, is thirty-seven percent lower than New York's. I fell in love with Philadelphia the very first time I visited with a college friend in the seventies. The neighborhood where my friend grew up, with its brick row houses and awninged wooden porches, reminded me of my southern roots. It brought to mind childhood memories of summers spent in South Carolina, when I would sit barefoot with my mosquito-bitten legs dangling off the edge of my grandparents' porch drinking a soda pop. Sometimes my grandmother joined me on the porch, and we would shell peas or snap string beans into a large basin seated on her lap. On that first visit and subsequent visits to Philadelphia, I found Philadelphians to be hospitable, friendly, and really easy-going.

Philly's slower pace is a further attraction for me. The chaotic ambiance of New York is absent. I read in a travel guide that Philadelphians think of their home as a "livable city"—not too hectic, not too crowded, manageable. The air itself seems to have a tranquilizing effect on me. This is probably what Philadelphia's founder William Penn was alluding to when he wrote back to England: "The soil is good, air serene and sweet from the cedar, pine and sassafras, with wild myrtle of great fragrance." Philadelphia is a quaint city with beautiful colonial architecture and a low population density. One day while walking through my new neighborhood of West Philadelphia, I realized that, for several blocks, I could be the only person on a block. *Wow, a whole block to myself,* I remember thinking. Philadelphia blocks are very long, equivalent to about two of New York City's.

And walking is what I did a lot of during the SEPTA transit strike. Philadelphians took the strike in stride, while I whined and complained for every single one of the eight days that it lasted. "New Yorkers would not tolerate this," I'd say to anyone lending me an ear. (New York's transit strike lasted three days.) Philadelphians walked, rode bikes, drove, carpooled, and went about their business seemingly unfazed. "What about the traffic?" I'd ask, trying to stir up resentment with drivers. One person responded that traffic flowed even better without the buses and trollies in the way.

All is not completely rosy in this City of Brotherly Love. In 2005, Philadelphia went down on record with the most homicide deaths in the city's history. There are blighted neighborhoods throughout Philadelphia where drug dealing and violence are wreaking havoc. The mayor, police commissioner and concerned citizens have joined forces in tackling the problem, but the task is a daunting one. The governor said he would provide state troopers and even the National Guard if asked to. The police commissioner turned down the offer, saying that more stringent gun laws are what is needed, not more manpower. Despite this blip on my beloved city, I feel safer here than I did in my old Bedford-Stuyvesant neighborhood, where I witnessed a shooting in the middle of the day just prior to my leaving New York.

With the passage of time, I have become even more enamored with Philadelphia. This past summer I beheld a beautiful sight while sitting on my porch. Children were playing outdoors without adult supervision. This was something I almost never saw in my Bedford-Stuyvesant neighborhood. What I saw instead were anxious parents who kept their children within their line of vision at all times. It was a joy to watch children lost in their own merriment as they ran around, jumped rope, rode bikes, or traipsed back and forth to the corner store. When fall came and school started, I was in for another pleasing sight. High school students were wearing school uniforms. Yes, the khaki pants were baggy, and the polo-shirts with the school emblem were oversized, but the teens seemed to be okay with the ensemble. You could sense their relief in not having the pressure of meeting fashion standards. And what can I say about my first winter in Philadelphia? I believe it snowed at most three times, and the public schools were closed each time. Even with a record twenty-seven inches of snow, New York City schools remained open. That alone should tell you that Philadelphia could not be New York's sixth borough, even if it wanted to.

INVASION OF
THE CAUCASIAN

BY DENISE V. CAMPBELL

Sitting in my first-floor apartment window, people watching, it hits me (hard) that three out of the last five people who just passed by were white. "When did this happen?" my daughter, who has been out of the country for over a year, asks in astonishment. It is her second day back in the States and in Brooklyn.

"It's the invasion of the Caucasian," I say to her, half in jest. I heard the term used recently on a radio talk show during a discussion about the gentrification taking place in Fort Greene/Clinton Hill, Brooklyn. The changing demographics in Fort Greene first caught my attention while riding the number 54 bus. The 54, or Myrtle Avenue bus, as it is called by some, starts out on Jay Street at the Metro Tech Center, loops around Tillary onto Flatbush Avenue and turns onto Myrtle Avenue. It stops at Prince Street, the second stop on its route, in front of a check-cashing establishment and across the street from Ingersoll Houses. As the 54 proceeds along Myrtle Avenue, it stops in front of several New York City housing projects——Whitman Houses, Tompkins Houses, and Marcy Houses. So one can understand why, until recently, white people were a rare sight on the 54 bus. As rare as they once were on the A train traveling from Rock-away Queens to Harlem. But Caucasian sightings are being reported in Bedford-Stuyvesant and Harlem. And the A train gets them there.

I recall my teen years growing up in Sheepshead Bay. I used to take the Flatbush Avenue train. I thought nothing of being among the few black people who stayed on past the Franklin Avenue stop. By the time the train arrived at Flatbush Avenue, the last stop, the passengers would be almost all white. This was an anomaly that was lost on my youthful naïvete and would only have meaning years later. Indeed, some years later as white flight transformed Flatbush, Brooklyn into a black neighborhood, I always found it amusing when some unknowing white person stayed on the Flatbush train beyond Atlantic Avenue. I always felt compelled to tell them that they should have gotten off at the stop where all the whites made their exodus, and that they were headed into black territory. I never said anything, though, assuming they would figure it out on their own. And if they did not panic and remained, clear thinking, they could get off at the next stop and reverse the course of their travels. Watching the whitening of Fort Greene, it is interesting to note that it is not black flight that is at the root of the changing demographics there.

White people are accounting for an ever larger number of the passengers on the 54 bus. I find myself making mental notes of the stops at they disembark. In so doing, I am able to pinpoint those enclaves in Fort Greene where the new homesteaders have settled in. Seeing them against the backdrop of graffiti-marred walls is arresting. So is standing beside them in the neighborhood bodegas. Trying to figure out who they are and where they hail from is intriguing as well. They're in the twenty- to thirtysome-thing age group. It's hard to pinpoint their socio-economic status. I think some of them take great pains to dress down. I've heard South Africans number largely among them. So now I'm won-dering whether they are newly arrived immigrants. Appearing comfortable in these environs, they don't seem half as curious about me as I am about them.

"I don't like it," my daughter whines. "This is where I grew up, and it doesn't feel the same." There is little I can say to soothe her. I have my own concerns. For the past six years I have sublet an apartment and was told by the owner that she wants to sell the apartment when my lease is up. Reality set in rather quickly. I know I will not be able to afford another apartment in Fort Greene, the neighborhood to which I have grown jealously attached. The willingness of the new homesteaders to pay exorbitant rents for closet-size apartments had pushed already rising rents even higher. It's over and out for me.

My world-travelled daughter has already sworn off Fort Greene and Brooklyn and even New York City. She talks excitedly about moving to New Jersey or Maryland. She informs me that quite frankly she has outgrown life in the hood. In the back of my mind, the thought of relocating to another state is starting to take hold. Too many times I've said there is no other neighborhood in New York City I would want to live if I were to move out of Fort Greene. Will I be forced to eat my words?

"Maybe white people are integrating into black neighborhoods because they want to relate to us," I say to my daughter.

"They're not trying to relate to me when they're paying $850 for a studio," she responds, alluding to an amount beyond her economic reach. We break up laughing trying to find the humor in a situation that makes us uncomfortable. We allow that there is very little relating going on. An invisible wall stands between the races. There is no eye contact, no words spoken, just quiet politeness. Beneath the silence, though, grumblings can be heard.

My daughter and I are walking to Sol, a stylish bar-restaurant on Dekalb Avenue. Two years ago, Sol used to be Claremont Lounge, a neighborhood bar. The conversation easily leads back to the changing neighborhood as we pass a newly constructed apartment building. A warehouse was turned into a forty-unit four-story structure. It's not clear whether these units are rentals or co-ops. But I don't even entertain the thought of getting an apartment in there, even though it's right around the corner from where I live now, and the specter of homelessness looms over me.

"They act like they were here first and we're the intruders," my daughter comments.

"And they don't have any humility," I chime in. "Not even when they walk by the projects."

"I'm even humble when I walk by the projects," my daughter says laughing.

The presence of white people in Fort Greene can only be a good thing, I'm beginning to tell myself. Neighborhood businesses are investing in making their property more visually appealing. The *New York Times* is more readily available. Well-stocked green grocers are replacing run-down fruit and vegetable stands. But best of all, I don't have to wait forever for the 54 bus anymore. There now appear to be more of them on that line.

LETTER FROM BEDFORD-STUYVESANT

BY DENISE V. CAMPBELL

An urgent tapping sent me scurrying to the front window of my brownstone garden-floor apartment in Bedford-Stuyvesant. I peeped through slats of the wooden shutters and saw two T-shirt clad white men with badges hanging around their necks.

"Yes?" I inquired.

"Police," they called out authoritatively.

"Someone upstairs must have called for you," I yelled through the slats.

"We want to talk to you."

"About what?"

"An incident that happened."

On my way to the front door, I deliberated whether I would talk to them through the gate. I decided to be courteous and opened it.

"We're investigating an incident that happened," one of the men said.

"An incident? When?" I asked with pretend alarm.

"About an hour ago."

"I just woke up from a nap. So I didn't hear or see anything," I responded earnestly. "What happened?"

"A guy was hit over the head two buildings down."

"Was it a robbery?" I asked with less-than-genuine concern.

"That's what we're investigating."

I came back into my apartment and looked at the clock on the wall. It was 9:45. After a quick calculation, I figured it had to have been around 8:30 that Sunday evening that someone was attacked on my lovely tree-lined block that is part of a designated historic district.

No way it could have been a random mugging, I thought. It had to be someone the victim knew. My mind went back several months to the time when I broke up with my boyfriend. He joked about how he was going to sit with a baseball bat in his SUV in front of my house and wait to see if a man left my apartment. I chuckled for even entertaining the thought. But my brownstone and several that adjoined it did look similar. Suppose my ex mistakenly... *Don't be ridiculous,* I chided myself.

The sound of muffled voices outside my window sent me back to peek out through the shutters. The two detectives stood in front of my window talking in low tones. When I ventured another peek, I saw a yellow tape had been wrapped around the balustrade of my stoop, pulled across the sidewalk to the curb, draped along the parked cars, pulled across the sidewalk again, and tied to the balustrade of the building two doors down, forming a perfect rectangle.

Real alarm then took hold. Wasn't a yellow tape only used when someone had been killed? I slipped into a hooded sweatshirt and went outside. A few people had gathered on their stoops. I searched their faces to determine the degree of gravity of what had taken place. But none of them had that "what a pity" look that onlookers wear when they've witnessed a tragic event. I stepped out and peered around the two detectives to get a view of the cordoned-off area. I half expected to see a puddle of blood, but all I saw were small pieces of paper strewn about. Refusing to stand around gawking like the rest of my neighbors, I went back inside my apartment. I figured whatever happened would fan through the neighborhood the following day. Or there would be something in the newspaper. Unbelievably, I heard nothing about the incident the next day. It was then I lamented that my former neighbor, a woman whom I had dubbed the nosiest woman on earth, had recently moved. Keeping her out of my business had become an arduous undertaking. Since she did not work a regular job, she was home most of the time. "You're home early today," she would stick her head over the railing and say if I arrived earlier than my usual time. I went out of my way to avoid her, and she went out of her way to engage me. My conversations with her were guarded and purposely kept short. She felt no embarrassment in coming straight out and asking about anything. She might say something like, "How's your daughter? I haven't seen her for a while." You had to think quickly on your feet with her. Or you could end up telling her how you and your daughter had had a big fight and were not on speaking terms. But then there were those times that she passed on information I was well off knowing about. Like when she told me that the apartment of the lady on our block who drives the pink Cadillac was robbed, or that the UPS delivery man had been ripped off. One morning when I was returning from the grocery store, she told me about a mugging that had taken place in the middle of the night.

"A white guy was mugged last night," she said to me as I was unlocking the entrance to my apartment.

"Oh, that's where those bloodstains on the sidewalk came from," I responded.

"I haven't been feeling so safe around here lately," she said.

"Neither have I," I said as I stepped inside and closed the gate.

"The only thing that's going to stop gentrification is crime," a friend said to me as we strolled leisurely through Fort Greene on our way home from dinner one night. Both casualties of Fort Greene's spiraling rents, my friend ended up moving to Atlanta, and I moved to Bedford-Stuyvesant. In moving to Bedford-Stuyvesant, I felt I was just a step ahead of gentrification. But after four years, it's apparent that the turnover is not going to be an easy one. This was echoed in an article in *Time Out* magazine entitled, "The Battle for Bedford-Stuyvesant." It seems that some people living in Bedford-Stuyvesant are going to make a last stand to stay here. Among them are the knots of young men I push by to enter a bodega or the Chinese takeout restaurant. Where would they go to ride out a sluggish economy, or survive a fifty-percent unemployment rate? The moniker "Bed-Stuy Do Or Die" has most significance for them.

From my front window, I am able to see the comings and goings of the neighborhood residents. A person interviewed in the *Time Out* article said in a radio interview that gentrification in Bedford-Stuyvesant wasn't so much evident in a changing complexion, but in rising rental costs. But the slow complexion change can also be attributed to the fact that people are moving in and turning around and moving out. I soon will be among those who are moving out. My cute efficiency apartment with its sunny backyard that I pay just under a thousand dollars to rent is not enough for me make a last stand. Then again, I'm not the "do or die" person I used to be.

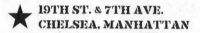

19TH ST. & 7TH AVE.
CHELSEA, MANHATTAN

THE SILENT BEAUTIES
OF WEST 19TH STREET

BY CAROLYN MURNICK

Entering the Rootstein Mannequin Showroom on West Nineteenth Street is just like entering a typical gallery opening, only there's no art on the walls. Very slender people wearing fabulous clothes stand in groups of twos, threes, and fours engaging in hushed, exclusive discussions. You're offered a drink and the stereo plays some kind of untraceable world music. No one turns to look at you as you approach them and you're not sure what to do with your hands.

Only after a moment do you realize that everyone in the room is a mannequin.

Junita, for example, will not meet my gaze. I stare at her from across the room and no matter which way I turn, her cold gray eyes continue to evade mine and she maintains an expression of practiced indifference.

"What's she like?" I ask Michael Steward, executive vice president of Rootstein America.

"Junita?" He pauses, considering the question for a moment. "Junita is just the most fabulous, gorgeous creature you could ever set eyes on. I mean, look at the body, the legs, the breasts, the face…" He trails off admiringly.

He passes me a glass of white wine and we continue to ogle her. Junita, like every woman in this room, with the exception of me, is made out of fiberglass.

It's a Tuesday evening and I'm at the New York showroom of Rootstein Mannequins in Chelsea.

Rootstein is a British company, started in 1956 in London by Adel Rootstein, a former window dresser and prop stylist for department stores. The brand was the first to sculpt mannequins from contemporary models and celebrities of the time: Jill Kennington and Maggie London represented the sixties, and faces like Pat Cleveland and Joan Collins followed in collections released twice annually.

"Adel believed in realism," Michael tells me. "Fashion in the sixties was becoming more and more provocative, culminating in Rudy Geinrich's topless dresses, and some of the Saint Laurent see-through dresses. Realism as far as breasts were concerned was very important. A mannequin had to have breasts, nipple shape, and also with the see-through, you had to color it, it had to be painted, as part of the makeup."

So, um, does the realism extend below the belt?

"No," he says shortly. "No it doesn't." We are silent for a moment.

"But it would if it were on the catwalk," Michael adds. "Whatever is going on in couture, we reflect here. I'm sure it will come one day. Unfortunately, or fortunately." He laughs self-consciously.

Michael himself is British. Formerly a buyer from Rootstein for twenty-two years while at Burberry, he's been on this end of things for two years. He's attractive and dressed in black pants and a jacket, his face showing a few days of calculated blond stubble.

As he walks me around the gallery, pausing intermittently to point out particular attributes of particular mannequins, it's clear that Michael has quite an affection for his "girls," as he's taken to calling them.

"She's what we called a tweenie mannequin," Michael says, gesturing toward Bubbles, a mannequin with very close-cropped hair and long, silver false eyelashes. "She's not a teenager and she's not a junior, she's like a Britney Spears fan. She can look very sexy, but she can also look very innocent. She's a very sweet girl."

Next we come to a group of three women and one man.

"One of the most important things you can do when you make a presentation is make them relate to each other," Michael explains. "Grouping is very important. There's a tension behind them, a point and counterpoint thing going on. There has to be a story, that's what attracts people. It's subliminal."

I ask what he thinks about the tension in the group in front of us.

"Alex and Axelle? I think they're just getting to know each other."

"I think Alex looks a little upset though," I attempt.

"He's just a little pissed off about the way she's been acting lately. And she over there..." he says, pointing at Junita, "she probably had an affair with him a number of years ago."

We sit down on a large banquette at the front of the room, silently staring out at the forty-five figures in front of us. Reedy, vaguely Asian-sounding music with wind chimes is playing in the distance, and the scene feels like some sort of sci-fi super-model wax museum.

It's as if we're seeing beauty in stop-time, caught under a strobe light.

"I really don't get the chance to sit here and look around like this too often," Michael says. "Like most creative things, you tend to become inured to it, and then something will stop you and you'll go, 'Oh my God, this is so incredible.' It's like life, really."

MAY–DECEMBER IN AUGUST

BY CAROLYN MURNICK

I'm trying to peg their relationship as they approach the bar. She's in her mid-twenties, dressed sexy, with full make-up and carefully cantilevered hair. He's something different. Older, probably near sixty, over-tanned skin and shirt unbuttoned low, I predict a necklace or a flashy watch before I can even see it— condo in Boca type of guy, or else a recent divorce. But the two of them are not together, I don't think. Definitely not married. Relatives perhaps? But what kind?

She's clutching her purse tightly and he's a step behind, his right hand reaching around her waist as he inches between tables.

He pulls out her bar stool and waits for her to sit down before turning to me.

"I'll have a gin and tonic, miss, and," turning to the woman, "do you know what you'd like?" She stares off into the mirror behind the bar.

"I don't really know," she says, more uninterested than unde- cided.

He looks at me with slight discomfort.

"How about Campari? Do you like Campari? She'll have a Campari and soda."

"Fine, whatever," she says, finally turning to make eye contact with me.

"Can I talk to you for a minute?" she asks me.

"Sure," I say, a little confused but trying to go with it. She directs me to the far end of the bar with a motion of her head.

We huddle over the service area, waiters periodically interrupting our space to peer into the dessert refrigerator behind us.

"I'm pretending that I'm just asking you for a tampon," she says, sotto voce, "But really I'm on the worst blind date of my life and I need you to help me get out of it. I could just kill the friend who got me into this."

"Of course," I say, amused and strangely excited by the idea of a role play.

"I'm going to ask you for a piece of paper, and then I'm going to write my cell phone number on it without him seeing. I need you to call me if you can, and then I'll say that I have a prior engagement and have to go."

"Okay," I say, "I'll do it."

"One more thing. Do you actually have a tampon?"

She heads to the bathroom and I head back to the guy who's now fiddling with his coaster self-consciously. I pour his drink slightly stronger than usual and proceed to attend to a young couple on the opposite side of the bar.

The woman flags me over a few minutes later. Game on.

"Would you happen to have a piece of paper and a pen?" she questions, on cue, but, to my slight disappointment, without even a hint of a knowing glance. She's done this before, clearly.

As I turn to rummage through the drawer for a waiter's carbon pad and a pen, I overhear the man's struggling attempt to engage her.

"So these two guys were standing outside a hospital when an ambulance pulls up…" he says. She's staring over his shoulder and draining her drink fast.

"…and these guys watch the EMTs get out of the ambulance and open the back to wheel out a cat. And the cat is strapped to a gurney, motionless, and he gets wheeled into the emergency room. 'What happened?' one guy says, and the other one answers, 'Curiosity.'"

He leans back on his stool with a self-satisfied smile, and I giggle under my breath. She continues to stare straight ahead.

"I don't understand," she says.

"Curiosity," the man replies.

"But curiosity is important."

"But curiosity killed the cat."

"Curiosity is important in life," she says, now noticeably annoyed. He pauses, glancing at his drink and then again at her. I interrupt to ask if they'd like another round.

"Not for me, but here's your paper and pen, thank you again."

Now comes the knowing glance, and this time it's a double.

"I'll have another," he says brightly.

I hold her gaze and smile slightly but suddenly I don't really want to play anymore.

Suddenly my perception of the two—and my allegiance—has flipped. What I first read as cocky and lecherous on his part I now see as simply tired, and what I first saw in her as trapped boredom, I now see as juvenile.

I pour his drink and deposit the pad back into the drawer and busy myself restocking glasses on the shelves from the dishwashing trays that have been brought from the kitchen. I'm trying not to catch the woman's eye as I reach up on my toes to straighten the rows of brandy snifters and champagne flutes.

When I finally turn to face her, this time to make change for a waiter, her eyes are questioning and pissed. I look right through her and smile calmly. Here comes my role play after all.

He continues to talk and she continues to choke out responses through clenched teeth and I'm pouring a cognac for a man at the other end and I'm stacking some more glasses and I'm brewing fresh coffee and the next time I look up she is gone.

THE GRAMERCY PARK LITMUS TEST

BY ELIZABETH BELLER

I moved into Gramercy Park through sheer dumb luck. I did-
n't discover Eden with my own bumpkin nose; I had help in
the form a lanky, soft-spoken boy who was returning home after
living as a piste-addicted ex-pat. I met him after some of my own
colossally unproductive post-college years in Colorado. We had in
common a faux-elitist notion that productivity was only useful in
a culture that made use of it, a convenient theory for people who
spend their days sitting on large rocks drinking Moose Buttock
Brown Ale. So under the guise of transitions more meaningful
than switching from beer on a mountain to dainty thimbles of
syruped vodka on barstools, we moved to Manhattan.

It was the nice boy who had insisted on downtown. Everything
we liked soared past our means. Dejected, we walked north. The
boy said, "There's this other great neighborhood I want to show
you, but just to see. Even if there was a place available, which there
surely isn't, we could never afford it".

It was heavenly. A wrought-iron fence announced a hush, an
elegiac enclave we circled in awe. Orderly hypericum cradled a
bounty of peonies. The gravel of the landscaped paths shushed

like a lullaby whenever a fortunate inhabitant strolled by. The grass was green as emerald; lush trees glimmered in the boundless sun.

Besides being the most beautiful sanctuary in the city, Gramercy Park validated my decision to return east. It was the epitome of a Jamesian quest for reason amid humane spirit and beauty, the antithesis of the towering menace of the Rocky Mountains, which always seemed to suggest the puny temporality of humans, even a kind of cruelty. One summer some friends and I had taken a lift to some ungodly peak and walked down, a sort of downhill sightseeing tour. It was perfectly safe, warm enough and with plenty of daylight. But I had to fight against tears of terror the whole five hours down. This was most likely because I am a ninny, but I felt there was something to my wish for a kinder earth.

I found it between Twentieth and Twenty-first Street. Strolling Gramercy Park's perimeter, we gazed through the fence. Smitten couples sat flirting on benches beside the dogwoods. Children darted about, engrossed in games independent of large plastic vehicles requiring Buzz Aldrin headgear. Gawking at a stately, Gothic building boasting hordes of cherubim, waterspout gargoyles and two silver knights, I spied a quietly lovely Tudor building on the corner. On it was sign: "Apartments Available Inquire to L&M Management."

"Look!"

"No, no, they leave those signs up at all times. I doubt there's been an vacant place there in decades," said the boy.

"That sign is not decades old. Let's call."

"There's no number."

We went down the block and into Pete's Tavern, past the afternoon old guard weighing down the bar with their whiskeys, and snaked over to the pay phone. The operator gave me a number for L&M Management that was not in service. Minutes later I was back at the Tudor building, ringing the superintendent's buzzer. The boy hopped about the sidewalk like Mozart's bird man Papageno, apoplectic at the padlock on his mouth.

LOST AND FOUND

The super answered the buzzer, and I asked him if there were any available apartments. Yeah, he said. He sounded tired and angry. After a long pause, I asked if we could see it, thereby establishing a pattern of dependence and resentment that would ballast a decade-long relationship. He said he'd have to get the key. Another pause. Okay, I said.

It was hard for me to beg Mr. DeBattista to call the owner for a price while I was expecting feathers to pop out of my boyfriend's mouth, but I did anyway. We were led up to 2C. It was everything I hadn't dared hope for. It had an actual bedroom. But what really got me were the tall French windows—they spanned ten feet of wall and opened onto a lovely English Plane tree where the boy could perch for hours during any recurrent episodes.

Somehow the owner, an extremely nice, retired NYPD investigator who had bought the apartment when he was based at the Thirteenth Precinct, was only asking $900 a month. I tried to imagine exactly what Sam Spade-ish debacle he was in when he sustained the head injury that caused him to rent this gem at such a steal. Turns out it wasn't a head injury, but it's closest equivalent: a daughter. His little girl was now twenty-eight, living in London, a big new city where he feared she would get emotionally, financially or physically screwed, and he hoped by behaving paternal toward some strange young woman from God Knows Where, that he might, through karmic intervention, ensure the same treatment for his own child.

The boy and I soon settled in. Unfortunately we settled heavily. I'd imagined his culinary aspirations as a sign of a creative, innovative thinker, but when he came home smelling of pungent fish—even though he worked in a fancy hamburger joint—he wanted to spend every moment immobile and mute in front of the television. Fancying yourself as Isabel Archer was hard while spending your evenings with *Everybody Loves Raymond*. He had also insisted that to gain a coveted key one had to live directly on the park, that our building wouldn't have access. I took his word for it, but every time I walked by those enticing gates, my yearning rivaled that of the junkies lined outside the methadone clinic a few blocks south. Like the junkies, I tried a substitute, Madison Square Park. But it too was full of swaying addicts and I wanted to be able to sit on a bench without the jingle "Weebles Wobble But They Don't Fall Down" playing incessantly in my mind.

One day, walking by the gates, trying not to lick the wrought iron for a quick fix, I saw our neighbor Susan exiting the park. She told me that our building had two keys we could check out from Mr. DeBattista, just like library books. I ran home and rang his buzzer.

"Hi Louis! It's 2C. Is there a key to the park available?"

"Yeah."

"May I check it out?"

"You'll have to sign it out on the sheet."

"Okay," I said.

He disappeared for a while. I rang his buzzer again. Is his buzzer louder than every one elses? I wondered.

"Yeah?" came his voice.

"May I check it out today?"

"Yeah."

Another very long silence. I rang again. His buzzer was louder.

"May I check it out now?"

The manna of the key was the end of me and the boy and the beginning of me and the park. Some less admiring family members implied that I'd used him just to get my footing in New York but I felt that his insistence on keeping life small barred me from a nebulous fantasy that involved great books, artists and thinkers, who, had I ever met them, would've asked me to spit out my gum and corrected my pronunciation of words like *cacophony*, which I had only read in books and never heard spoken aloud. The mental and emotional leaps I sought weren't satisfied by contemplating the socio-cultural differences, although admittedly vast, between Lucy Ricardo and Mary Richards. Getting the key had been so simple, and somehow the boy complicated everything, or maybe diluted is a better word.

LOST AND FOUND

Soon after, he moved out. It was a surprisingly simple transition except for when he drunkenly returned a week later and, convinced I wasn't alone, kicked in the door. Once I realized he wasn't going to kill me, I had the tiniest tinge of regret that I'd missed out on a hidden passion. But it was just a tinge compared with the splendor of park.

I reveled in the glorious green. I would go as often as the key was available, and earned yet more of Louis' somnambulant vitriol by failing to return it until harassed. If it was already checked out, I gave the hairy eyeball to whoever I imagined had usurped my playground. It was a holiday every time I entered. I soon learned that I could procure my own key with a letter to the park's board. Once I had the key, I would sometimes walk through the park pretending it was the grounds of my own palatial home. The other residents were an army of groundskeepers keeping the tulips a perfect hue of yellow. Flight of fancy became a turbo-jet tour de force.

I immersed myself in fantasies of turn-of-the century gentility. If I could've found whale bone corseting I would've worn it. I made do reading Anthony Trollope novels and imagining myself in 1850s haute couture pagoda sleeves, which had I actually worn them, would've only terrified the squirrels.

In retrospect, I see that my fantasy was armor against the mating wars of the city. After all, my appeal as a non-Ivy educated, non-wealthy, non-properly compensated drone at an auction house didn't reach everyone. I was also beginning to take on the mannerisms of Emma Thompson. Since the appeal of the park had jettisoned one mate, I developed a syllogistic theory to test a replacement by his response to it as well.

The Gramercy Park Litmus Test started innocently enough. If a date went well enough and I wasn't sobbing to my cat by 9:30, I'd invite him downtown for a nightcap. Not in my apartment, mind you. Margaret Schlegel would never have a man she didn't know up to her rooms. I'd take him to what I considered my extended living room, the Gramercy Park Hotel Bar. This was before Ian Schrager got hold of it, when it was a lovely dive that served stomach-burning whiskey with peanuts and still had stains on the mottled carpet from the Eisenhower administration. If we lasted until they closed, we would stroll out of the bar and into the park, a kind of holding pattern before seeing if it was safe to land. Getting blotto and carousing outside at 2 a.m. wasn't particularly Jamesian, but here's where I let my Lucy Honeychurch sensibilities come into play.

One date, a real estate developer, wasn't sufficiently impressed with the opulence of the park. He walked in casually, sat on the nearest bench, and tried to neck. I suddenly remembered I had to go sell ashtrays from Camelot in the morning.

The art dealer genuflected too strenuously. He sprinted in and exclaimed about the zinnias so loudly I worried the that knights guarding the cherubs to our east would come to life and spear us. I couldn't help but suspect him of using me for the chance to bask in weekend sunshine and greenery, or being a Judy Garland fetishist, or both.

The investment banker just wanted to go into my apartment. He told me he had a Hampton house with grounds four times this size minus the rodents. I said goodbye to him at the bar, and watched his cab lurch toward the Upper East Side.

The politically charged artist raged about the bourgeois pigs who would cordon off a section of the city green for private use. It was criminal, and how could I willingly partake in such an elitist affront? He wanted to set up a protest in the park. I showed him to the gate.

Yet another investment banker decided to jump the gate when I realized I'd left my key at home. I tried to dissuade him, saying I could be back with the key in minutes. He struggled for a good five minutes, and eventually toppled over. I felt assaulted and ran home. He then discovered that one needed a key to get out as well as in.

There were more dates, more failed take-offs. There were a few who happily acknowledged the worth of the park, and sometimes, me. But most of the attempts to land in the apartment were averted. Wind sheers I'll call them, like the man I quite liked but who had mysteriously taken months to call after getting my phone number. When he finally called, he felt compelled to share with me the information that the delay was due to a horsy heiress he tried to land before bothering with the chick in the imaginary plumed hats. Or the hapless preppy who would vanish every time he got an invitation to a ball, fundraiser, gallery opening, club opening, drum circle, knitting class or dog show where he might meet someone else. Which was often.

Then there was the mid-air collision with the gallery owner. He adored the park and me, he said, which I believed until I learned six months in that he had a gardening-mad wife who would adore the park as well.

I was walking around the park one day, shaken after crawling out of the incinerated wreckage of this affair, when I saw the Old Crazy Lady. She was always stationed outside painting beautiful but incoherent images that resembled what might have happened if Bonnard had gone through a Cubist phase. I'd offered to let her in the park so she could render the likeness close up, but she always refused. She never spoke to anyone. Until that day, when she smiled.

"Hi. How are you today?"

"Horrific," I said, thinking I didn't need to stand on Austen manners with a fellow loon.

"What's your name?"

"Elizabeth," I replied.

"Saint Elizabeth. She was mistreated by her husband, but accepted her lot and is now a celebrated martyr."

I'm doing something very wrong, I thought.

Although I had made some friends there, the neighborhood began to change as well. The revamp of the Gramercy Park Hotel turned my holy dive into a lounge indistinguishable from any other cosmo-spewing establishment below Twenty-third Street. I don't like my alcohol to come in colors louder than my underpants. Around the corner, Park Avenue South suddenly became a daytime conglomerate mecca and nighttime tourist trap, and it was hard to pretend it's 1850 when drunks walked around the park bellowing "Bootylicious" at the top of their lungs. Along with these changes, traffic increased. Sometime after 2002, cars inexplicably kept plowing into the park's North Gate as if the enormous display of orange lights flashing in their face didn't signify the end of Lexington Avenue.

Although I still loved Gramercy, I gave it up the second my husband asked me to move in with him. He had attachments of own: his neighborhood, the West Village, and the idea of himself as a flaneur whose unspoken duty it was to observe this particular epoque of the city. I didn't put him through the Gramercy Litmus Test. I was too busy reveling in my reaction to him, and especially his reaction to me. Someone found parasols amusing, rather than reminiscent of Miss Havisham and dusty old houses smelling of cat urine! It turns out my husband and I share, if not the same neuroses, then complementary ones. Our mutual delusions are part of a bonding elixir. The first morning we spent in the park, he simply strolled in and sat imperially, as if he were a baron surveying his domain.

Reality has, however, pulled us into the modern world. Some delusions shatter after the arrival of a child—niggling little things like jobs and space for a family have propelled us out of both the West Village and Gramercy Park. It's impossible to be in the nineteenth century when your two-year-old daughter tries to swing her hips like Beyoncé whenever she hears even the crudest of beats. My husband can't fancy himself a flaneur when faced with the unprincess-like contents of a pink Princess Potty.

Thankfully the boundless love for an adored child is more than enough compensation for one lost suit of armor. We assume an air of pragmatic adulthood for our daughter, so she can hopefully build imaginary tenets of her own, strong enough, improbable enough to buffer, and just able to be sewn into the real world. Because a little bit of denial is what it takes in life. Of course my husband and I build other delusions together because, frankly, we're good at it, and it's a prerequisite to loving as we do our current neighborhood in New Orleans, a city that sits somewhere between six to eight feet below sea level.

But sometimes when we go visit our friends on Gramercy, I'll peek across the street into the huge French windows and picture myself in crinoline, my husband in a cravat, and our pinafore-clad daughter heaving tea and scones before an afternoon spent strolling those hallowed grounds.

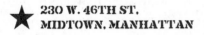

★ **230 W. 46TH ST.**
  MIDTOWN, MANHATTAN

JFK ON BROADWAY
BY PATRICIA BOSWORTH

Eventually everything is history—even one's own life. I once caught a glimpse of President John F. Kennedy in the flesh, and that image, so radiant and energizing, has stayed with me for over forty years. I saw him when I was an actress in a comedy called *Mary, Mary* on Broadway. Next door to my theater (the Helen Hayes) was the Forty-sixth Street Theater, where the great musical *How to Succeed in Business Without Really Trying* was running. It starred Robert Morse.

One afternoon in mid-November 1963, I ran into Bobby in Times Square and he told me excitedly that the President was coming to see his show that night and maybe—since my show ended before his—I could sneak backstage and watch the finale from the wings.

I did just that. As soon as my play finished, I raced through curtain calls, threw a coat over my costume, and sprinted next door. I could hear the music from the finale swelling up from the orchestra as I slipped into the wings and watched Bobby strutting around center stage as he joined the chorus in the rousing number "The Brotherhood of Man." Sweat streamed from his face; he was singing his heart out, directly to the President.

Suddenly it was over. The house lights went up and I recognized the President sitting amidst a sea of pink faces in the center of the house. He looked tanned and incredibly handsome and then he jumped to his feet and was applauding Bobby, who was bowing and applauding back. Kennedy seemed enveloped by an absolute roar of love and yearning as the entire audience rose up and applauded him. The emotional intensity in that theater was palpable.

A week later I was having coffee in a Greek diner on West Forty-fourth Stret when I heard the news that President John F. Kennedy had been assassinated in Dallas.

Every actor on Broadway assumed he or she wouldn't play that night—we were sure our shows would be dark in tribute to our fallen leader. But as dusk fell over Times Square we were all ordered to "go on." The shows were going to stay open in spite of the nation's huge grief. And so we performed, but we all wore black arm bands, some more defiantly than others since there were certain producers who didn't want us to wear them.

As soon as my play ended, I ran next door to watch Bobby— the great trooper. I reached the wings just as he finished belting out "The Brotherhood of Man." He was giving it his all but he had tears streaming down his cheeks.

PART V

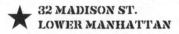

KNICKERBOCKER VILLAGE

BY PHILLIP LOPATE

block or so north of the Brooklyn Bridge, just behind the
old New York Post Building, between Catherine and Market Streets, squats Knickerbocker Village. This unassuming
enclave of bare-brick apartment towers, privately managed,
which might easily be mistaken for one of the nearby government
projects, made history as the first major housing development
even partially supported by public funds. Though currently in
scale with everything around it, it seemed huge when it opened in
1934, "a blockbuster," according to the *AIA Guide to New York
City*, which added that "It maintains its reasonably well-kept
lower-middle-class air today." The other historical significance of
Knickerbocker Village is that it stands on the same site as the
notorious Lung Block, which it obliterated.

Ernest Poole, the journalist and novelist of *The Harbor*, wrote
journalistic exposés about the Lung Block, which had the highest tuberculosis incidence of any street in the city. Poole was part
of a circle of idealistic young reformers (including Isaac N.
Phelps-Stokes, who later wrote the monumental study *The
Iconography of Manhattan Island*) trying to raise a moral outcry

about housing conditions in the Lower East Side. In *The Bridge*, Poole's 1940 memoir, he describes how he went down to the Lower East Side in 1902:

"The Lung Block, as I named it then, was far down on the East Side near the river. In early years, when that quarter was a center of fashion in our town, many of the buildings had been great handsome private homes, but long ago they had been turned into grimy rookeries, the spacious rooms divided into little cell-like chambers, many only stifling closets with no outer light or air. I can still smell the odors there. In what had been large yards behind, cheap rear tenements had been built, leaving between front and rear buildings only deep dank filthy courts. Nearly four thousand people lived on the block and, in rooms, halls, on stairways, in courts and out on fire escapes, were scattered some four hundred babies. Homes and people, good and bad, had only thin partitions between them. A thousand families struggled on, while many sank and polluted the others. The Lung Block had eight thriving barrooms and five houses of ill fame. And with drunkenness, foul air, darkness and filth to feed upon, the living germs of the Great White Plague [tuberculosis], coughed up and spat on floors and walls, had done a thriving business for years."

Poole vividly describes a young, tubercular Jew, near death, crying out for more air. The paradoxical proximity of the Lung Block to the expansive, world-connecting river is also noted: "There was a huge Danish woman too, on the Lung Block, who became my friend. Sailors came and stayed with her, 'deep-water' sailors, by which I mean that they shipped on voyages around the Horn to Singapore and Shanghai and other fascinating ports. As gifts or loans when they sailed away, they had left a lively marmoset, a scarlet parrot, heathen idols, painted shells and other things that pulled my thoughts out of the stinking rooms near by and sent them careering far off over the Seven Seas. I sometimes felt the Wanderlust and, in those lovely days of spring, wandered along the East River piers where lay the last of the ships with sails, listening for 'chanteys' of their crews as they heaved on the ropes and slowly, slowly the big ships moved out on the river, bound by the sea. But from such whiffs of the ocean world back I would dive into the Lung Block, all the more bitter that human beings should be choked to death in such foul holes, when there was so much fresh air and health and sunlight so close by."

Poole went to work, writing up the horrors in strong muckraking fashion. A radical friend, scoffing at the notion that the pen was mightier than the sword, told him: "What the Lung Block needs is the ax." (Later, Robert Moses would similarly remark: "When you operate in an overbuilt metropolis, you have to hack your way with a meat ax.") Undaunted, Poole shouldered on: "My report was featured in the press. Reporters came to write up the block. I took them around, with photographers. Hearings were held up at Albany. I gave my testimony there. So we raised hell with the politicians, and at twenty-three I thought that our campaign would succeed. I was wrong. For the landlords on the Lung Block had many influential friends. So came delays, delays, delays, until in the papers the story grew cold. It took thirty-two years to bring the ax. It came at last, under the New Deal. The rotten old block was razed to the ground and in its place you may see today the airy sunny apartment houses of Knickerbocker Village."

Fred C. French, the same developer who had built Tudor City a few years earlier (1925-31), put together Knickerbocker Village, which, completed in 1933, housed four thousand persons on five acres in twelve-story blocks around inner courts. During the Depression, the federal government had made available a small pot of funds for private developers nationwide to clear slums and construct housing developments in their stead, based on a set of guidelines regarding building standards and occupational density. French had to travel to Washington over fifty times, hat in hand, to get an eight-million-dollar loan from the federal government's Reconstruction Finance Corporation for the housing development. The sticking point was the government's objection that the complex had a density at least double that recommended by federal guidelines, but which the developer argued was needed for a satisfactory investment. In the end, the government agreed. French, who was both public-spirited and profit-minded, told some impressed Princeton students in 1934: "Our company, strangely enough, was the first business organization to recognize that profits could be earned negatively as well as positively in New York real estate—not only by constructing new buildings but by destroying, at the same time, whole areas of disgraceful and disgusting sores." French helped offset the costs for buying the land and developing Knickerbocker Village in two ways: first, by raising the density of land use through taller apartment towers, and second, by replacing low-income tenants with middle-income households. (This same strategy would be followed later by the Metropolitan Life Insurance Company, which tore down another chunk of the Lower East Side along the river to build Stuyvesant Town and Peter Cooper Village.)

There was certainly an argument to be made for the state's helping middle-class, white-collar workers in urban areas defray housing costs. Less valid was the argument that by subsidizing new housing for the middle class, you would then free up thousands of units for rental by low-income tenants. The trickle-down theory, applied to housing, proved as faulty as elsewhere, since rents in the vacated apartments were still beyond the reach of the poor. The effect of slum clearance on its inhabitants was thus to push them into new slums, as Anthony Jackson show in his study of Manhattan low-cost housing, *A Place Called Home:* "When 386, mostly Italian, families had been forced to leave the old 'Lung Block'...to make way for Knickerbocker Village, four-fifths of them moved into other nearby tenements. At Stuyvesant Town, a survey showed that roughly three-quarters of the three thousand displaced families would move into other slums."

Not everyone saw the slums on the Lower East Side as blight. Jimmy Durante, the entertainer, who grew up in the Lung Block ward, reminisced to Joseph Mitchell about a time "'when the East Side amounted to something'...Sitting there in the dark theater, nursing his hangover, the big-nosed comedian began to talk about his childhood, the days when he used to run wild on Catherine Street, raising hell with the other kids, the days when he liked to go barefooted and they had to run him down and catch him every winter to put shoes on him..." Like most children who were reared in slums, he had a slightly different perspective than the housing reformers: "'We kids used to have a good time,' he said. 'They tore down where my home was and where my pop had his [barber] shop. They tore it down to put up this high-class tenement house, this Knickerbocker Village. Most of the old-timers moved out long ago.'"

There was, it seems, in the insular poverty of the Lower East Side, a yeasty substance breeding ambition along with despair. You have only to read the charged memoirs of Anzia Yezierska (*Red Ribbon on a White Horse*) or Mike Gold (*Jews Without Money*), to sense their pride in the ghetto they were so desperate to escape. The emotional glue that bound the tenement-dwellers to the Old Country dissolved when the rickety buildings were demolished and replaced by anonymous, modern high-rises. As Alfred Kazin wrote about a similar urban renewal, "despite my pleasure in all the space and light in Brownsville...I miss her old, sly and withered face. I miss all those ratty little wooden tenements, born with the smell of damp in which there grew up so many school teachers, city accountants, rabbis, cancer specialists, functionaries of the revolution, and strong-arm men for Murder, Inc."

Some of the nostalgia of Kazin and Durante for slum-bred ambitions seems in retrospect a disguised ethnic boasting. The ghetto may have proven a launching-pad for Jews and Italians to reach the middle class by the second generation, but it was not having the same catapult effect for the Hispanics and African-Americans who had taken their place. The new, non-white poor were in no position to organize protests at the razing of tenements, nor were they necessarily as attached to them as previous groups had been.

Thus Robert Moses had a point in scoffing at the notion that "since the slums have bred so many remarkable people, and even geniuses, there must be something very stimulating in being brought up in them." But the more debatable point was Moses's leap from asserting that the "slum is still the chief cause of urban disease and decay" to contending that its "irredeemable rookeries" had to be eradicated. It takes a certain literalism to go from deploring the disease and crime in a poor neighborhood to indicting the very buildings themselves as criminals. After all, the hovels that comprised the Lung Block had begun their existence in the early nineteenth century as respectable houses for well-off families; only later were they were subdivided and rented to the poor at unspeakable densities. Current medical science suggests that even the Lung Block buildings might have been spared— given a good disinfectant cleaning and spruced up, their rear tenements removed for better light and ventilation—and restored to salubrious respectability. But that is not how it appeared to most social reformers of the day (including those far more committed to helping the poor than Moses): they hated the suffering they witnessed in the tenements so much that they came to blame the very mortar, bricks, staircases, walls. Having invoked so often the metaphors of pathology (slums were described as "cancerous," "pestilential," "abscessed," "a tumor," "puss-filled"), it seemed the most sensible course to call for their surgical removal.

Among the lower-middle-class strivers attracted to Knickerbocker Village were Julius and Ethel Rosenberg, who moved into a three-room apartment in the spring of 1942. They paid $45.75 a month for their river-view, eleventh-floor accommodations, and made use of the project's nursery school and playground after they had children; and it was there, the bulk of evidence now suggests, that Julius conspired with Ethel's brother, David Greenglass, to spy for the Soviet Union.

Knickerbocker Village had one of the strongest and most insurgent tenant unions in the city, the Knickerbocker Village Tenants Association (KVTA). In 1947, when the landlord, French, tried to raise the rent twelve percent and evict tenants who exceeded income limits, KVTA waged a campaign against him in the press and the courts, vowing a rent strike as well. I like to picture Julius going to these meetings and putting in his two cents' worth, though he probably regarded such local efforts as trivial, compared to stealing atomic secrets.

If you grew up in a Jewish ghetto in the 1950s, as I did, you could not escape the Rosenberg case. Newspaper photographs of Ethel in her mouton coat and upswept coif looked strikingly like my mother. In fact every other woman in our neighborhood looked like Ethel: dark-eyed, pudgy, scared, self-righteous, and exalted with ideals of social justice. We felt personally imperiled by the Rosenbergs' persecution, removed as we were by less than a few degrees of separation. When my mother joined a fight to have a traffic light installed in front of our nursery school, many of her fellow protestors were Communists. She became friends with these Party members, up to a point, but then they bored her by turning every conversation into a political harangue. Never mind the millions of kulaks slain by Stalin, or the Moscow Show Trials; my mother didn't like Communists because they violated the rules of conversation. No one in my family, to my recollection, ever maintained the Rosenbergs' innocence; if anything we assumed they were guilty, but thought they shouldn't be executed because the secrets they stole were probably small potatoes, and because capital punishment was wrong.

My Aunt Minna was a Communist: when my brother and I stayed one summer with her in California, she would get apoplectic as soon as anyone appeared on television who had named names. Lloyd Bridges in *Sea Hunt*? "He sang. Change the channel!" I thought of Communists as a slightly cracked set of familiars, character actors left over from the Yiddish theater, admirably wanting to make the world a better place but rigid in their refusal to consider opposing facts. Who knows whether I might have joined the Party had I grown up in the thirties instead of the fifties? By the time I started college, in 1960, JFK was off to the White House; Arthur Schlesinger, Jr. was advising him; and the Communist Party no longer counted, except as a joke. My mother told me: "If you're ever on unemployment insurance and they send you to interview for a job you don't want, just bring along a copy of *The Daily Worker*."

In one of the best New York waterfront movies, Samuel Fuller's *Pickup on South Street* (1953), a number of key scenes were set a stone's throw away from the Rosenbergs' apartment, on a South Street pier. Coincidentally, it revolved around a plot by Communist spies to steal government secrets. "If you don't cooperate," the FBI agent tells the cynical hero, "you'll be as guilty as those traitors who gave Stalin the A-bomb."

Our hero, or anti-hero (played by Richard Widmark) is a pickpocket who hides out in an abandoned bait shack, perched on pilings in the East River and reached only by a flimsy catwalk. The atmospheric night scenes prove again that the waterfront and film noir make an irresistible combination. Through the shack window we glimpse the Manhattan Bridge and a dependably passing tugboat or barge (courtesy of rear view projection, since the film was really shot, for the most part, in California).

The great supporting actress Thelma Ritter gives the film's most memorable performance as Moe, an aging necktie-peddler and stool pigeon in a tired flower-print dress, who is saving up for a fancy funeral. She tells the threatening Communist agent, Joey, in her weary Brooklyn accent: "Look, mister, I'm so tired, you'd be doing me a big favor, blowing my head off." Moe and the Rosenbergs: both from the same New York working-class milieu, striving to reach the lower middle class; both doomed to a premature, unnatural death by the Cold War.

Apparently Julius and Ethel felt cramped in their small apartment in Knickerbocker Village, after their two children were born. I stare up at the nondescript brick towers and wonder what they would have thought about the transformation of the Lower East Side in our day. They did not live to see the particular horror of 1960s "urban renewal," with its wholesale destruction of neighborhoods deemed slums and its displacement of the working poor. Gentrification, which began later, in the 1980s, probably displaced as many poor tenants in the long run as did urban renewal, but it had a gentler effect on the streetscape—indeed, it preserved what might otherwise have crumbled into dust. Those surviving parts of the Lower East Side's old tenement environment have seen their housing stock slowly improved and renovated through gentrification for the past twenty years, while playing host to bohemian cultural activities and chic little boutiques: not so bad a fate for the old ghetto, all things considered.

The esplanade gives out and becomes an inhospitable parking area and repair shed for city sanitation and fire department trucks. So I cross over to the inland side. One public housing complex after another: the Rutgers Houses, Laguardia Houses, Two Bridges, Vladeck Houses, Corlear's Hook Houses. The one architectural standout is Gouverneur Court, which used to be the old Gouverneur Hospital. It has those magnificent red-brick rounded bays with black wrought-iron balconies that I've often admired in a car from the FDR Drive. Now I'm seeing it at street level and it's quite impressive. A plaque informs me it was built in 1898, and is now on the National Register of Historic Places. Its red sandstone has wonderful carved ornamental detail. Surprisingly, it was not turned into expensive condos but preserved, under a deal brokered by then-Mayor David Dinkins, for lower-income occupants (the management sign says "Affordable Housing for NYC").

An affable, proprietary tenant in blue shorts, with incredibly thick glasses, who looks like he hangs out often in front, tells me, "It's all single-room apartments. Section 8." Section 8 is a Federal program that provides subsidies for impoverished, often elderly people, or people on disability.

"It's beautiful."

"You should see the courtyard."

"I'd like to," I say. "Can you take me in for a moment?"

"Nah. You can't go into Gouverneur House without photo ID. They're very strict about it."

Just then another tenant, a middle-aged woman in shorts and curlers, comes out of the building. "Hey Denny, want some coffee?"

"Nah. I never had a taste for it. I get all my caffeine from Coca-Cola."

"It's getting cold."

"September, it's all over. You won't be able to wear shorts no more."

"I went to the doctor, they say it's a heat rash. I was afraid it's diabetes. Everyone I know got diabetes."

"You'll be okay."

"You're a saint, Denny," she waves at him, and walks away. He nods: Saint Denis. He continues to guard the steps, looking out across at the stern Vladeck Houses, angled all different ways. I head back towards the East River, to try to pick up a navigable walking trail along the waterfront.

**38 WHITE ST.
TRIBECA, MANHATTAN**

SAD SONG SCENARIOS

EDITED BY JEFF JOHNSON
AND HUNTER KENNEDY

There are some songs that if heard in the right situation might push you to the brink of something horrid. Some of these situations are real, some are fiction.

"Rain" by Blind Melon, through the ceiling of a Married Student Housing apartment while you're bidding for seventies-era cereal boxes on eBay against a guy whose screen name is Ratbrain.
—*D.C. Berman*

"Mandy" by Barry Manilow, going over the Rip Van Winkle Bridge into the Catskills after Pilates.

—*Mike Fellows*

The Home Depot Trifecta: "Dancing on the Ceiling" by Lionel Richie, "If Ever You're in My Arms Again" by Peabo Bryson and "Caribbean Queen" by Billy Ocean, heard from roughly 2:20 a.m. to about 2:34 a.m. on a Sunday morning while waiting for my new gas grill to get put together.   —*Trent Buckroyd*

639

LOST AND FOUND

Billy Joel's "Vienna" piped into an examination room while a doctor you found on an HMO list and called randomly gently kneads your balls because you've convinced yourself you have testicular cancer but the doctor says, "I'm sorry, I don't feel anything."

—*Sam Lipsyte*

"Every Rose Has Its Thorn" by Poison, as performed by Green Bay Packers' QB Don Majkowski in a profile of him on TV before a game against the Chicago Bears.

"The Rose" by Bette Midler, as heard while getting your four hundreth perm in the last twenty years at a Des Moines, Iowa, hair salon.

—*Blaire Bundy*

"Wayward Son" by Kansas, on the last day of tennis camp at Gustavus Adolphus College in 1987.

—*Craig Finn*

"Hey, Mickey" by Toni Basil, anytime you have a hangover.

"Hot Hot Hot" by Buster Poindexter, first thing on Monday morning when you haven't had coffee yet.

—*Erin Flaherty*

"Broken Wings" by Mister Mister, while buying a rolling suitcase at Kohl's Discount Department Store, Eagan, Minnesota.

—*Colleen Werthmann*

The Muzak version of El DeBarge's "Who is Johnny?" from the movie *Short Circuit,* at a thrift store in Austin, Texas.

"The Sound of Silence" by Simon & Garfunkel, on a rainy afternoon in a yarn store in Portland, Oregon.

—*Gigi Guerra*

"Everybody Wants to Rule the World" by Tears for Fears, after you've just been laid off as a dishwasher at Shoney's, on any weekday morning.

"Shout," by Tears for Fears, while waiting to talk to your junior high guidance counselor about someone picking on you too much.

The theme song from *Taxi* at Pizza Hut, while listening to the only other people in the restaurant, a married couple, fight about the bill.

—*Jeff Johnson*

"Ventura Highway" by America, in an empty Food Lion grocery store.

ELO's "Strange Magic" while in line to buy caulk at Lowe's in order to patch the hole you punched in the wall.

—*Hunter Kennedy*

Muzak versions of "Walking on Sunshine" by Katrina & The Waves, and "Dancing On The Ceiling" by Lionel Richie, as heard in the lobby of the Times Square hotel I was checking into following evacuation from my home on September 11th.

—*Steve Martin*

The opening organ notes of Smashmouth's "Walking on the Sun" as played during the start of a TV profile of an Olympic athlete.

LOST AND FOUND

"Love and Marriage" by Frank Sinatra, in the opening credits of the *Married with Children* reruns.

—*Brant Louck*

"Words Get in the Way" by Gloria Estefan, at the Key Food on Avenue A.

"Mr. Bojangles" (Muzak version) at a Kentucky Fried Chicken.

"Thanks for Christmas" by XTC at the Toys R' Us in Buffalo, New York.

"These Dreams" by Heart, as I get stoned (for the second time ever) and watch two friends break up.

—*Joshua Lyon*

"Lady in Red" by Chris deBurgh, regardless of the circumstances.

—*Austin McKenna*

"Radar Love" by Golden Earring, while getting spanked by either lover or parent.

"Africa" by Toto, overheard from someone's headphones while taking a timed math test.

"Bennie & The Jets" by Elton John, while ordering popcorn shrimp at T.G.I. Fridays, with co-workers and the boss.

—*Tony Mogelson*

"Takin' Care of Business," by BTO. On the car stereo, accompanied by the operatic karaoke stylings of my mother, who articulates every single syllable ("tay-kingg care of bus-i-ness...") while tapping her hands slightly off-tempo on her brown leather briefcase.

"Smooth" by Santana & Rob Thomas. A car stuck at a red light outside my apartment in the summer has the windows down and the volume cranked. I hear a voice singing along and am chagrined to discover that it is my own.

—*Jenny Eliscu*

"Don't Forget Me When I'm Gone," by Glass Tiger, while waiting in a thirty-minute line at the bank.

—*Tiffany St. Vincent*

"Where It's At" by Beck. Hearing it in a coffee shop or a mall food court fills me with despair.　　　—*Matt Sweeney*

"Uncle Albert" by Wings, when, having just hitched a ride to Brattleboro, you slam the door shut and realize the woman who picked you up is in fact a man and not wearing pants.

—*Thomas Beller*

"Nights in White Satin" by the Moody Blues. When I found out the title was not actually "Knights in White Satin." Different meaning entirely.

"Whiter Shade of Pale" by Procol Harum, seeing a wedding party dance to it.

—*Mary Timony*

"One Toke Over the Line" by Brewer & Shipley, while driving home from the night shift at Poppin' Fresh Pies.

"Wildfire" by Michael Martin Murphy, anytime.

"Afternoon Delight" by the Starland Vocal Band, while sitting in the Squirrel Cage, a Lisle, Illinois, bar on Route 53, at one in the morning.

LOST AND FOUND

"Jack and Diane" by John Cougar Mellencamp. Hearing every customer at Ray's Pizza on Eleventh Street in New York at a 1 a.m. sing-along.

—*Mike Topp*

"Whoop There It Is" by Tag Team, as rapped over by a Chicago wedding DJ with a cordless mic as the dance floor was heating up at my cousin's wedding.

"Summer Wind" by Frank Sinatra, as sung by the same DJ as he paced the empty dance floor about an hour later.

—*Tim Rutili*

"Gimme Three Steps" by Lynyrd Skynrd, as played by my bar band for the 3,000th time while watching a drunk woman dancing barefoot through the vomit her boyfriend was geysering up.

—*Joe Leatherwood*

Every song on Gary Puckett and the Union Gap's Greatest Hits as played on an 8-track tape on an endless loop while hitchhiking between New York and Boston in 1970.

—*Rob Vaughan*

Hearing a Cantonese "country" rendition of "I Saw Mommy Kissing Santa Claus" in a Guangzhou, China mall's food court in March.

—*Manny Silva*

Hearing a girl at a Boston College football game tailgate in 1991 sing "way down south" every time the chorus to Eric Clapton's "Lay Down Sally" kicked in.

—*Kevin Fahey*

"Paradise by the Dashboard Light" by Meatloaf, as sung by the bridal party—verses perfectly split along gender lines on the dance floor at my cousin's wedding.

—*David O'Neill*

"Waterloo" by Abba, in Kmart, mid-morning, in the cosmetics department while looking for cheap lipstick.

—*Gigi Capetola*

"Like a Virgin," by Madonna, as the first dance at our wedding reception. It was not the mellow Marley song we had agreed upon, and the older guests were not amused.

—*Steve Pollock*

"Elvira" by the Oak Ridge Boys, at 4 a.m. while sitting in a jail cell with twelve other people in Lafayette, LA.

—*Joe Bement*

"The Greatest Love of All" by Whitney Houston, at an elementary school assembly in fourth grade. The speaker was a female athlete from Little Rock, Arkansas, who had won the bronze medal in tae kwon do.

—*Martha Brantley*

"Things We Said Today" by the Beatles, on the hospital speakers immediately after delivering twins.

—*Kelly Ehlinger*

"Nobody's Gonna Break-a My Stride" by Matthew Wilder, heard at the abandoned shopping center in Levittown, Pennsylvania, from a passing car, while looking at the quarter-operated helicopter ride I used to love when I was five.

—*Jesse Pearson*

"Lady" by Kenny Rogers, at 2:30 p.m. on a Tuesday in the plus-size section of Fashion Bug on Atlantic Avenue in Ozone Park, Queens.

—*Jane Farrell*

"Sad Songs Say So Much" by Elton John, sung (off-key) by my hygienically challenged lab partner in eighth grade science class.

—*Amy Sterk*

"Buffalo Stance" by Neneh Cherry, in an abortion clinic waiting room.

"Rich Girl" by Hall and Oates, on a snack stand radio in Gaza during a street riot.

—*Gideon Yago*

"Cry, Cry, Cry" as performed by Third Eye Blind on a PBS documentary about Sun Studios. Sad Sad Sad.

"It Wasn't Me" by Shaggy, as three or four ten-year-old girls dance and sing along, completely oblivious to the song's meaning.

—*Wells Thiede*

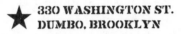

**330 WASHINGTON ST.
DUMBO, BROOKLYN**

THE CONDIMENT WAR
BY DANIEL MAURER

Anyone who passed by the intersection of Adams and Plymouth on the summer evening of August 9th must have been confused—violent splashes of every color imaginable had turned a dull concrete lot under the Manhattan Bridge into a gargantuan Jackson Pollock painting. Not that shocking in artsy DUMBO, but closer inspection revealed that this was no street painting. In fact, the mess was entirely edible: the street was littered with chunks of hot dog, lettuce, dough, mushrooms, and coated with ketchup, mustard, vinegar, and slime of unidentifiable origin. The sort of wreckage that can only be sowed by a Condiment War.

Earlier that week, the Madagascar Institute had put out a call to duty promising "havoc, folly, and mayhem, featuring the pride, pomp, and circumstance of glorious war, without any of the, you know, killing." There was to be "fierce fighting, crushing condiment cannons, and nasty weapons of mass disgusting on bikes, in carts, and mano a mano." It could be really fun or really dorky, except that the Madagascar Institute has a history of delivering: the last time they had invaded DUMBO—the

"Drive-By Arting"—was to blast syncopated fireballs off the back of their truck.

Emerging six or so years ago from the Burning Man festival in the Nevada desert (which at least one member has subsequently disavowed as the "annual naked hippie on acid festival"), the Madagascar Institute has grown to become one of the city's most subversive art/event collectives. Their first street event was "flaming soccer," when a bunch of folks in soccer and cheerleader uniforms spontaneously took over Ludlow Street to kick a flaming ball around. Their Halloween event on the Lower East Side entailed the mass beating of a seal-shaped piñata equipped with 100 pounds of candy and an exploding head. Their "Running of the Bulls" event in Gowanus, near their shop on Butler Street simulated the Spanish tradition—with the crowd running from a flamethrowing bull, bicycle and motorcycle bulls with giant horns attached to their handlebars, remote control bulls, and a hipster-hungry "art bull." Recently, the Institute kicked off summer by holding a five-minute satirical dance routine on the steps of the New York Public Library. Dancers dressed as giant rats, doughnut-eating cops, fat Midwestern tourists, and Williamsburg hipsters did a synchronized ditty culminating in an illegal fireworks display. The invite promised it would be "the most fan-fucking-tastic three minutes and nineteen seconds of your life so far, guaranteed, or double your money back, or our gayest event ever."

The Condiment War was similarly a gamble. My nineteen-year-old cousin was in town from Chile and I wasn't sure whether it was the best way to "show him New York," as my parents had instructed. But he seemed into it—when I told him the event would require white clothing and a yellow arm band, he eagerly stole some "Caution" tape from a construction site. We combed my refrigerator for condiments, coming up only with some rancid mayo and some jelly that had congealed into a gooey blob while sitting in my fridge for over a year. The cabinets yielded vinegar, which was discouraged, but the six-thirty sharp meeting time was upon us and we were desperate. Finally we broke down and bought four squeeze bottles of ketchup from a bewildered store clerk. On this humid Sunday afternoon, I was dressed in a pair of white pants two sizes too big and an oversized white dress shirt that reeked from having been stuffed in a suitcase too long. My cousin was similarly outfitted. In the subway, the smell of leaking vinegar raised still more eyebrows.

We had just a few minutes to get to the rendezvous on Jay and York, and it was becoming obvious that the G train wasn't going to cut the mustard. I suggested we call a car service and we bolted from the subway with our condiment canisters clinking in their plastic bags. A straight shot down Flushing Avenue and we'd be there in no time. Except that halfway through the ride, the driver's salsa music was interrupted by the crunch of metal on metal as a car slammed into our side. I looked back to see an angry punk girl with facial piercings and dyed hair emerging from her battered car. The cabbie and the woman exchanged some words. Even as my ears rang, all I could think was, "How am I going to get to the condiment war on time?" I wished the two luck, secretly grateful for a free ride, and my cousin and I bolted for the staging area.

We arrived late. No one was around. Suddenly we heard a chorus of cheers and we raced down the street just in time to see the tail-end of the hot-dog-eating contest. Perhaps a couple hundred people milled around, all of them in white. And then the opening salvos. From atop a coffee cart procured especially for the occasion, the Madagascar Institute, uniformed in shirts that declared "We rule, You suck," catapulted lettuce onto one of their rivals, the Toy Shop Collective—a Brooklyn-based group of fifteen to twenty artists who, like Madagascar, often mount their unconventional displays in the city streets.

There were supposed to be four armies: Madagascar Institute, the Toy Shop Collective, the Greenpoint-based art collective WAMP, and "the bloodthirsty public, banded together in an Irregular Militia." (Several civilians also posed as pacifists, meditating in the lotus position even as they were pelted.) The teams were demarked by the color of their armbands (civvies in yellow) and were stationed in opposite corners, but as soon as the schnitzel hit the fan, all was chaos. Noisemakers and air-horns filled the air, as did a dizzying plethora of condiments. Suddenly I felt like I was in *Saving Private Ryan*. Men and women in plastic coveralls ran around spraying each other, or throwing chunks of hot dog, dough, pretty much anything edible. A woman wheeled an ice cream cart into the center of the staging area and pulled a hose out of it, spraying everyone around her. Another combatant hid her condiments in a baby carriage disguised as an elephant. Someone with a Super Soaker pumped vinegar into my eye. From the rooftop of an adjacent ten-story building, people threw balloons full of god-knows-what onto the street below. At one point I looked up to see an operative rappelling off the side of the building. The figure stopped halfway down to drop a cluster of condiment bombs. All the while I ran around squeezing my wimpy squirt bottle of ketchup, feeding off the thrill of soiling total strangers while trying not to slip on a lava bed of spent ammo. I looked over to see my cousin soiled from head to toe.

Meanwhile, a friend of mine, who had been wearing a George Bush mask upside-down, had fashioned quite the weapon—he was using a mop to lap up puddles of slime and whipping it at people indiscriminately. I was amused by this, until he decided to turn the weapon on me and I was forced to wrench it from his hands and give him a taste of his own mop juice. At some point there was a ceasefire and a winner was declared. I couldn't tell who it was and I have no idea how it was decided since everyone (save the hundred or so bystanders) was layered in slop. It may have been Toyshop, since they started chanting, "Whose shop? Toyshop!" Madagascar started loading their weapons into their pick-up. Someone called out, "Let's go, move it, we're not here to wait around and see what happens," and sure enough a couple of police cars finally pulled up.

An officer yelled into his loudspeaker, "What are you doing here today, people? Who's in charge here?" I shouted to my cousin, who was across the way getting hosed off, that we had better go. Fire trucks were racing to the scene with sirens blaring, presumably because Madagascar had crowned the event with one of their homegrown fireworks displays—or maybe to hose off the parked cars that had suffered collateral damage. The Institute was eventually stopped for questioning (with the coffee cart hitched to the back of their truck, they were the obvious suspects), but they managed to get back to their shop in time for the after-party. My friend the mop-slinger was stopped as he was about to drive away. A police officer asked him whether he was involved in the fight.

"You're the detective," he said, dressed only in his underwear. "You figure it out."

My cousin and I used an alley to change into clean clothes. We went into Pedro's to get a beer and wash up in the bathroom. By the time we got on the train, we looked perfectly normal. Strangely enough, we were sharing a subway car with a group of eighteen-year-old girls in bikini tops, caked head to toe in dirt. One of them caught my eye and said proudly, "I bet you don't know where we came from!" Turns out they had been mud wrestling. I turned to my cousin and smiled. This was summer in New York.

THE JOB OF THE FORCIBLE ENTRY TEAM

BY THOMAS R. ZIEGLER

Autumn has arrived, and the cooler air has dampened but not ended the fires of this year's summer offensive. Somewhere the trees are changing color, but here in Hunts Point it has been one of those days.

We've already caught more work on this day tour than any company outside the ghetto will see in six months, and the smoke we're now smelling ain't from chestnuts roasting on an open fire.

Engine 94's boss comes up on the radio, Engine 94 to the Bronx, 10-75!

Turning into the block we see 94 stretching its line into a five-story tenement. As we stop in front of the building I unass the rig to size up the fire; there are no flames showing but we got smoke pushing out from four closed windows on the fourth floor. The Lieutenant, Big John, and I are Ladder 48's forcible entry team and we run past the engine guys as they climb the stairs beneath the burden of their hose line.

We reach the fire floor well before the engine and go right to work forcing the door.

The job of the forcible entry team is to get the door open, crawl in and search for the location of the fire and any trapped victims. The public hallway instantly fills with smoke as we pop the door, drop to our bellies, and crawl into hell. Searching in this apartment is accomplished by feel because sight is nonexistent, nothing, and I do mean nothing is visible. With all the windows closed, the fire has smoldered a long time, producing an extremely heavy smoke condition right down to the floor.

To put it another way, you couldn't see shit! And the heat is extraordinary, to stand upright here is an instant trip to the burn center. Our team splits into three to cover the flat faster and my search leads to a crib in a back bedroom.

Getting to my knees I reach over the railing and sweep the mattress with my gloved hand, discovering what I did not want to find, a limp silent baby.

Hollering "I got a kid!" I drop again to the floor and backtrack to the door where the engine guys have started to advance their line into the apartment.

They stop and allow me to crawl across their backs and into the public hallway where I get to my feet and race down the stairs heading for the ambulance that's hopefully there. It's a tiny baby.

I hold the head in my left palm, torso on my forearm. His arms and legs flap wildly with each step I take as I perform one-man CPR on the run.

Word has reached the street, and as we exit the building a cop grabs my arm and points to an ambulance waiting at the intersection.

Cover the mouth and nose, don't blow too hard, two fingers compressing the chest, oh fuck live, please live. Reaching the ambulance the baby is taken from me and for the first time since exiting the building, I am aware of the huge crowd that is watching these events unfold. The clutch to my brain is slipping: I can't get it into gear. Immobilized, all I can do is stare back into the crowd and then I lock eyes with a girl of about ten.

Today I can still see the little hairclips attached to her cornrows.

She's terrified: her eyes stretched open to the size of silver dollars.

She begins slowly backing away then suddenly turns and runs into the crowd. I want to run after her and tell her, BUT I DIDN'T DO IT! Instead, I head back to the fire, there's still work to do there. As I pass, a cop hands me the helmet that I didn't even know had fallen from my head and asks with great tenderness, "Are you okay buddy?"

"Yeah, I'm okay."

Re-entering the building, I hear the word come over someone's radio, the kid didn't make it.

I sit alone in a corner where no one can see me as the tears start.

Yeah, I'm okay.

★ **462 1ST AVE.**
KIPS BAY, MANHATTAN

THE LIQUID
STRAIGHTJACKET

BY THOMAS R. ZIEGLER

It's 1983. I'm on the job ten years and have received my first promotion.

Yesterday as a firefighter I carried an axe and fought fires; today as a Fire Marshal I carry a gun and fight crime. In most departments around our country, the title Fire Marshal denotes a person who performs inspectional duties. In New York City, that title identifies an arson investigator with full police powers. The task of the Bureau of Fire Investigation is to inquire into any fire declared suspicious by the firefighters who extinguished it. A team of marshals is dispatched to figure out the cause and origin of these fires and if it is determined to be arson, a criminal investigation is initiated. It was during my tenure as a marshal that the most subtle yet horrible act of violence I have ever witnessed took place.

It wasn't a multiple murder in some rundown shithole of a tenement, rather it was a medical procedure in a municipal hospital emergency room. Earlier that summer Saturday evening, two marshals arrested a suspect for arson. Immediately upon being handcuffed, the suspect started complaining of difficulty breathing so his next stop became a well-known city hospital for medical evaluation and treatment. The triage nurse took one look at the prisoner and knew he was full of shit, which put him at the bottom of the list to be seen by a doctor.

This was exactly what the perp wanted; he'd rather spend this Saturday night sitting on a chair in an air-conditioned emergency room people-watching instead of watching his back while sitting on the floor of a sultry cage in Central Booking.

For a dedicated watcher of exotic people there is no place that can compete with a city hospital ER on a summer weekend night, but after six hours of waiting the two marshals had had enough of people-watching and just wanted to get out of there for a while and get a bite to eat.

Enter my partner and me. We are the meal relief.

It's our turn to people-watch now.

Circulating around the room is one seemingly normal individual completely garbed in hospital-issued patient attire, slippers, pajamas and bathrobe.

He's smiling, shaking hands, and chatting with anyone who will listen; it appears to me that he's campaigning to become mayor of the emergency room.

Spotting us, he approaches.

Hello police.

Hello patient.

Looking at our prisoner he asks, what did he do?

Before I can answer, a nurse is standing beside him and she says, time for your injection. Instantly he turns pale and begs… no, oh please no, I'll sit down, I'll be quiet, I won't move, please, please no.

With a barely discernible nod of her head, she summons two large orderlies who take hold of the mayor, one on each arm and then lead him towards a an unmarked room. She follows.

Looking back over his shoulder at us, I see his soft begging is now accompanied by tears as the door closes behind him. Moments later the door opens, the orderlies reappear and depart the room, the nurse emerges next and she holds the door open for the mayor to exit. However, what comes out of the room isn't what went in.

Moments earlier the mayor was a human being, he was smiling and talking, then he was terrified and begging, but he was alive. What came out was a walking corpse. The nurse guides him to a chair, seats him and walks back into the treatment area.

Curiosity has gotten the better of me so I go over to the mayor and ask him what happened; he just stares straight ahead as if I wasn't there.

Now I had to know; tracking down the nurse I ask what had just taken place. She replies, "He does not like the police and he was about to give you trouble, I will not tolerate trouble in my ER, so I stopped it before it began."

How did you do that?

I shot him full of Thorazine.

What's that?

With a big smile on her face she says, We call it liquid straightjacket and it works every time!

How can you get away with that?

Have you ever heard of medication over objection?

No.

Well, once admitted to a psychiatric institution and a doctor proves to a judge that a patient is incompetent to make a decision I get to make his decisions for him, and I decided it was time for this guy to sit down and shut up!

Holy fucking shit!

In the Soviet Union, this type of treatment was called psychiatric imprisonment (*psikhushka*), and was used to segregate political prisoners and then break their wills.

Shortly thereafter, the arresting marshals return and my partner and I bolt for the exit.

Taking a last look back over my shoulder I see the perp grinning at the world; he has played the system and beaten it. I also see the mayor, who, staring intently at nothing, has become the latest victim of the same system. As the door pivots closed behind us, I realize that the movie *One Flew over the Cuckoo's Nest* isn't just a movie, it's a documentary!

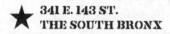

★ **341 E. 143 ST.**
THE SOUTH BRONX

WE'RE DOING IT
FOR THEM

BY THOMAS R. ZIEGLER

L ooking around for the lieutenant, I find him standing alongside the firehouse, staring down into a neat row of freshly
clipped hedges. I hurry to his side and he tersely commands, "Get
to work." Right then and there, my life changes forever.

For firemen, there is nothing more startling than a Verbal
Alarm—the riotous banging of fists on the firehouse door. It can
sound as loud as a stampede of buffalo trying to crash their way in,
and it has only one meaning—something dreadful is occurring
just outside of quarters.

It's early summer 1973, and we are having roasted chicken for
dinner. As a newly assigned Probationary Fireman, I am expected
to eat faster than everyone else, and then get to the sink to do the
dirty work. It is there, while scrubbing baked-on chicken skin
from a roasting pan, that I hear my first verbal alarm.

The instant the banging begins, dinner is forgotten and the
kitchen empties. Not knowing what's occurring (because they
don't teach you this in Proby school) I simply follow along as
everybody hurries to the apparatus floor, where they put on their
gear and climb aboard the rigs.

My lieutenant runs outside and then returns in a flash. "Proby, get the first aid kit and follow me," he orders before disappearing outside again. Grabbing the kit from the rig and rushing outside, I encounter a mob. I know intuitively that something horrible has taken place.

Where the bush ends and the child begins is impossible to tell, but the rapidly expanding pool of blood in which she lays, face first, cannot be ignored. Holy shit, how did this happen and what in God's name can I do about it? *Think, Tom, think,* a little voice inside my head speaks. Nothing can be done with her tangled up in this bush. Get her out.

I grasp her legs and attempt to pull her free of the bush and onto the lawn. She doesn't budge. Now what? I pull harder and still she doesn't move. It's almost as if she is nailed to the ground. I force my head among the branches to get a closer look, and the realization hits me like a knee in the nuts—she is nailed to the ground. A branch the diameter of my thumb has penetrated her cheek. I slide out of the bush and kneel next to her. *Okay Tom, just lift her face a bit and she'll be free,* the voice inside my head says. I try, but to no avail—her face isn't moving. I exert a little more force. Still nothing. At this point, the voice shouts *Stop fucking around and get this kid loose!* I stand and reach down, placing one hand on each side of her impaled head. Finally, I yank her free of the branch, which, after going through her cheek, had pierced the roof of her mouth and then buried itself somewhere deep inside her skull.

As gently as possible, I turn her over, realizing as I do that every bone in her body feels broken. I am prepared to start CPR, but when I open her mouth I discover that it is filled with leaves. In addition to her broken body, she is bleeding slowly, weakly, from ears, nose and mouth. She isn't breathing. Even a Proby could tell this kid was dead.

In the four or five minutes that have passed since I was scrubbing pans, the crowd has grown enormous and angry. Something bizarre is going on. Kneeling beside the lifeless body, I look up at the lieutenant.

"She's dead."

"Don't move," he replies, and then walks over to where the Chief is located. After several seconds of discussion, they both return to where I am kneeling and the chief orders me to begin CPR.

"But Chief, she's dead."

The chief is an old-timer. He knows the mob wants to make someone pay for this atrocity, and he's going to make sure that we aren't the ones to pick up the tab. Covertly pointing at the agitated mob behind him he tells me, "We're not doing it for her, we're doing it for them."

Suddenly I understand. We aren't saving a life; we are simply maintaining an uneasy peace. I am just another actor, performing his role in this theater of the street. Pressing my mouth over hers, I give a breath and in return get a close up view of blood and leaves as they spew out through the gaping hole in her face. Thank God, an ambulance arrives and I do not have to continue the charade.

I join the other firemen who are standing in a cluster several yards away just as a cop begins filling them in on the particulars of what has transpired. Two eleven-year-old boys had taken the girl, who was eight years old, to the roof of the twenty-story project building adjacent to the firehouse. Once there, they attempted to rape her. The girl tried to fight back, threatening to tell their mothers. They all lived in the same building. She knew both of them and their families. They threw her off the roof.

Just then, flanked by cops, the two little killers exit the project building in handcuffs. They are both laughing. I am not. I return to the firehouse and strip off my clothes, which are encrusted with mud, sand, and blood. A long, hot, soapy shower cleans my body but I don't have a clue as to how to cleanse my mind.

It's not until years later, after I become a lieutenant myself, that I figured out why the boss chose me, the least experienced man, to work alone on this child. It's simple: he was friends with all the other firemen. I was just a newly arrived Proby. Ask yourself the question, who gets the nightmares? A friend or a stranger?

JUST ANOTHER PART OF THE JOB

BY THOMAS R. ZIEGLER

I nside the firehouse, sweeping floors, cooking meals and main-taining equipment are routine parts of the job. However, when the doors go up and the rigs go out you have to be as flexible as Gumby, because you do not know what you are going to be faced with next.

While responding to alarms, we always scan the sky for smoke and the streets for crowds because different combinations of these factors can be early indications of what is awaiting us. Arriving at this box, there is no smoke in the air but a crowd has gathered so my brain shifts from thoughts of firefighting to assisting a civilian.

It is 1978 and we are on Edgewater Road, the street made famous in the HBO documentary about the hookers of Hunts Point, one of whom I am about to become very intimate with.

Lying atop the garbage that has been dumped in this vacant lot, she is staring directly at the summer sun. If ever there was a crime scene this is it, so I am thinking bullet hole and not heart attack when I start examining her. In cases that have no obvious wounds, SOP is to start at the head and work your way down. As my fingers probe through her hair it slips from her head and I nearly shit my drawers.

She's been scalped!

That was my first thought but in reality it was just her wig that slipped off. Let me tell you something, if it is possible to feel relief while kneeling in a pile of stinking garbage, examining an unconscious hooker for bullet wounds, well then I felt relief! It doesn't take long to find those wounds either. There are two of 'em just above her right ear, from the size of the holes my guess is a .22. Twenty minutes ago this was a person, now it's just another DOA to be bagged and toe tagged.

While I am wiping her blood from my hands, one of her co-workers walks over to me and says, hey FIREMANS, those mother fuckers by that van did it.

Let me ask you something, if you just murdered someone in front of witnesses no less, would you be hanging around the scene of the crime?

Getting on my radio I call the boss.

Ladder 48 roof man to Ladder 48.

Go ahead Tom.

Hey Lou, one of the girls just told me those guys by the van are the perps.

10-4

The Boss relays this info to the PD who is already on the scene.

As the cops approach the van, the assholes realize somebody has fingered them and it is time to leave. Hopping into the van they take off with the cops right on their tail, the chase is on. The sound of the police siren fading in the distance starts to get louder again when suddenly; from around the corner here comes the van. Can you believe this, they are driving around in circles! Apparently, the same amount of planning that went into the crime has gone into the escape. Before reaching the end of the street their way is blocked by another cop car and they are arrested. Just then an ambulance arrives and we take up.

A few hours later, the cops who made the collar stop by the firehouse for a cup of coffee and to fill us in on the details. The six occupants of the van picked up the hooker and, after agreeing on a price of ten dollars each for blowjobs, had a fuckfest. After finishing them off she asked for her money and they refused to pay.

Big mistake!

For those of you who don't know, Hunts Point hookers are the great white sharks of prostitution. You do not fuck over a Hunts Point girl without paying a price. She made a fist and punched the closest one of them right in the snotlocker. That is when he produced a gun and she started running away across the lot. She was tougher but he was faster and when he caught up to her…two slugs in the head.

Anyway, in those days the idea of universal precautions was unknown to us. I have been squirted by arterial bleeds, delt with traumatic amputations, even had people puke into my mouth during CPR, hooker blood was just more of the same. At least it was until finding out that I was Hepatitis C positive.

So, am I saying I got this virus from a Hunts Point hooker? No. What I am saying is, just liking sweeping the firehouse floor, getting Hepatitis C was just a routine part of the job.

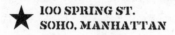

**100 SPRING ST.
SOHO, MANHATTAN**

THE POLITICS
OF HAIR REMOVAL

BY ALICIA ERIAN

L ast August, when the Russian woman who waxes my legs in Brooklyn went on vacation, I made an appointment at a spa in SoHo. I'd actually been meaning to switch for some time. It wasn't that I didn't like Vicki—I did. She was dirt cheap, and we shared an interest in politics. Even though her accent was kind of thick, I was happy enough to nod and say, "Uh-huh," when I didn't understand her. It was actually very freeing, especially when I suspected she was probably saying something like, "I think George Bush is doing a great job."

The only problem with Vicki was her wax. I knew gentler stuff existed for one's face and bikini line, and that I should probably be searching it out, cost be damned. Still, I was jittery about my first appointment in SoHo. If you wear pretty much the same clothes every day—and no makeup—downtown tends to be a little intimidating. It's no place for the style-less. The posh waiting area only made matters worse, not to mention the clients loafing around in their waffle-weave robes and slippers. Who were these people? How were they able to turn a public place into their own personal bedroom?

664

Soon Wanda, my waxer, came out to meet me. She was small, pretty and of Eastern European descent. Like me, she wore no makeup, though her skin was dewy and clear from some kind of suitable cream. As I followed her back into her workroom, I began to panic at the thought of the Mediterranean overgrowth coating my body. Should I apologize to Wanda for the state of myself, I wondered? Was I an animal?

The first thing I noticed when Wanda opened the door to her room was the size. It was an actual room, as opposed to the walk-in closet at the back of the hair salon where Vicki worked. Soothing music came through the speakers, and the walls were cobalt blue. Most importantly, there was more than one type of wax heating on the counter. Balled up on the sheet-covered table was a pair of paper panties, which Wanda told me to put on before stepping out of the room to allow me some privacy. With Vicki, I was forever going home to find wax on my own cloth underwear.

Wanda returned a few moments later and got busy with my legs. We didn't really talk, which made me nervous at first, but slowly I began to resign myself to what I assumed were the ways of SoHo. About halfway through our session, Wanda looked at me, smiled, and said, "Everything okay, Alicia?" I nodded, and soon we were engaged in some light conversation. I learned that Wanda had two kids, lived in New Jersey, and was concerned about my many ingrown hairs. She suggested I purchase an exfoliating cream sold by the spa, but when I learned at the checkout counter that it was ninety dollars, I took a pass. I did, however, leave Wanda a generous tip. It wasn't the conversation that mattered anymore, I now decided. It was that my bikini wax had been unbelievably bearable, and that for once, I was leaving my appointment without a red burn mark in place of my mustache.

The next visit was different. Maybe I was in a better frame of mind—less intimidated—or maybe Wanda was. Or maybe we both were. For whatever reason, though, we started talking immediately. It was my first visit after September 11th, and somehow we got onto the subject of politics. I probably brought it up, my old standby. Laid out on all those vinyl tables over the years, I'd come to learn that no one followed world events like an Eastern European. Perhaps this was because they so often were world events. In any case, Wanda's face seemed to brighten at the opportunity to share an opinion.

"You know," she began, "I grew up in Poland, and—"

"You're Polish?" I interrupted.

"Uh-huh," she said.

"I'm Polish."

She looked at me, surprised. I'm a little dark for a Pole.

"And Egyptian," I added quickly, filling in the missing piece for her.

She laughed. "Really? My husband is Egyptian!"

"You're kidding!" I said, immediately remembering her two kids. I couldn't believe it. As far as I'd ever known, my brother and I were the only two Polish-Egyptians on Earth.

When I mentioned this to Wanda, however, she shook her head. "No," she said. "My children are from a previous marriage."

"Oh." I tried not to sound disappointed.

She smiled at me then and said, "But I'm pregnant."

"You are?" I looked at the small stomach under her loose smock. I hadn't really noticed it before, but now I thought I saw it, the baby she was carrying.

Wanda nodded. "It's a girl."

We went on to talk about her husband, how his software job required him to travel, how upsetting it was for him to be stared at on airplanes. Before I left that day, Wanda said, "Looking at you, I have a very nice idea of my daughter in thirty-four years." I wanted to kiss her. Actually, I think I did.

A few months later, Wanda had her baby and went on to maternity leave. Once again, I was in need of a new waxer. I made an appointment with a woman named Dina at the same spa.

Dina was the opposite of Wanda in many ways: chubbier, chattier, smilier. Her workroom was downstairs, not up, and the walls were some nondescript, pale color. Still, she used all the same wax, and clearly hailed from some Eastern part of the world.

After I put my paper panties on and laid myself out on the table, Dina came in and got busy on my lip and chin. "You have beautiful hair," she said, and even though her accent was thicker than Vicki's, I understood the compliment. We settled into conversation easily, and soon I was telling Dina all about Wanda, her husband, and their new international baby. Suddenly, Dina stopped what she was doing, her waxy little Popsicle stick applicator held aloft. "Wanda's husband is Egyptian?" she asked me.

I didn't know how to respond. The look of alarm on her face made me think that she'd missed the point entirely. This was meant to be a charming story. "Yes," I said finally, "he is."

"Interesting," Dina murmured. She then asked, "Is Wanda's husband nice to her?"

I couldn't believe it. Wanda herself had told me that sometimes, when she mentioned to people that she was married to an Arab—and this was pre-September 11th—they'd tell her, "I feel sorry for you." It had seemed like a preposterous story, but now I understood that, while it remained preposterous, it was also true.

"Of course he's nice to her!" I blurted out, though I'd never met the man. All I knew of his effect on Wanda was what I perceived to be her general good health and happiness.

"Hmm," Dina said, apparently not buying it. "Tell me," she went on, "do you know what Wanda's husband does?"

"He's in computers," I said, which suddenly sounded terribly suspicious.

"Interesting," Dina said again.

She went on to tell me that she was an Uzbeki Jew. "You know Uzbekistan?" she asked, and I nodded. She wanted to know if I was a Muslim. I said no, I was an Arab Christian. She said she'd never heard of such a thing. She told me again that my hair was beautiful—a gift from both of my parents.

LOST AND FOUND

After a while, we stopped talking. She put gloves on to wax my bikini line, then took them off when she was finished. Interesting, I kept hearing her say, over and over in my mind. And I wanted to tell her no, that it wasn't interesting at all about Wanda's husband. It was only interesting that there were now at least three Polish-Egyptians on the planet, that we were a small but growing minority, and that none of us would grow up to hurt another living soul.

THE CAPTAIN
BY BILL SCHELL

The Captain sensed an uneasiness in the room. The two men in front of him were looking off to their right. They had strange expressions on their faces. Was it disgust? Was it fear? Was it an expression of embarrassment or shame? None of these emotions had been noticed by this Captain during several years of physical fitness training.

He was testing the new firefighters on the stairmaster. Every new firefighter goes through a physical fitness program. This also involves testing the probies in the number of push-ups, sit-ups, pull-ups, and timing a mile-and-a-half run. As an aside, all have their body fat recorded by a simple measuring of the size of the waist. This measurement is compared to a chart and the body fat is determined by this. It is a ball park figure. There is no body fat requirement for firefighting, and people of all body compositions have been excellent firefighters. In this makeshift gym, there were seventeen probies being tested. These seventeen represented one squad of two platoons of three squads each. Also in the room was one Lieutenant and three firefighter instructors.

LOST AND FOUND

The Captain turned around to see what these men were looking at and was shocked at what he saw. A big man, probie, standing at stiff attention at the front of the room with his pants and underpants pulled down to his ankles. His fully exposed genitalia dangled in the faces of ten probies sitting on chairs five feet away.

The dangling man had his eyes focused forward, not looking at anything, but with an expression of what I would describe as bewilderment, embarrassment, humiliation, disbelief that he was in this position. That he was going through this.

I noticed that the other men sitting in front of this naked man were squirming in their seats. Trying to look away. They were embarrassed. They knew that this was some kind of perversion and that they soon would be put on display like this. This was surreal. Could this really be happening? How did this happen?

A little confused and shocked at what was happening, the Captain asked the Lieutenant, who was responsible for this activity, "What are you doing?"

"I am measuring their body fat," the Lieutenant replied.

"You can't do this," said the Captian.

"Fire Commissioner Tom Von Essen. He said I can do whatever I want."

The Captain was unprepared for such a remark. This activity forced upon subordinates, or anyone else, was wrong. It was immoral. It was abusive and humiliating. It was also very uncomfortable for the other instructors in the room.

The Captain was stuck. No one should allow such activity. The Captain would have, under normal circumstances, stopped this activity, but the Fire Commissioner and Mayor Giuliani were involved. The Captain knew that Giuliani had created a cult of personality about himself. Giuliani selected his Commissioners based upon personal loyalty to Giuliani, and not the oath to obey the laws and rules of New York City and the State of New York. All civil servants take an oath to uphold the laws of the land when they are hired.

Commissioner Von Essen would eventually fire a Fire Marshal with sixteen years of duty as a cop and firefighter. The firing offense would be that this Fire Marshal, John O'Brien, did not have his tie wrapped around his neck properly. The Giuliani circle of friends imposed cruel punishment to those who would use their freedom of speech to voice their opinions. Freedom of speech does not protect NYC employees.

The Captain did not follow what he knew to be right. He did not stop this activity. He was afraid of losing his job after nineteen years as a firefighter. He told the other instructors not to take part in this activity. In a low voice he apologized to the probies for this activity and said that this activity is "not right."

The Lieutenant went back to what he wanted to do. Each man would come up to the front of the room. He was ordered to pull his pants and underpants all the way down to the floor. Half measures were not allowed.

The Lieutenant would get down to his knees in front of or to the side of these men. He would take a tape measure in one hand and put the tape around the naked buttocks. He would grab the tape with his other hand. He would adjust the tape tightly around their thighs, buttocks and pubic hair. He wanted a good measurement so he would pull the tape tight, crushing the man's pubic hair. And with his face at the same height, the same proximity of the man's genitalia, he would look at the tape and read the measurement. If he dropped the tape or the man was large, he would have to lean against the man. His face sometimes on the naked thigh, sometimes leaning against the penis. This the Captain did not see but others told him this happened.

These men would have to go through this at least one more time.

In December of 1996, this Captain overheard one probie say to another probie when talking about a second measurement "He wants to look at my penis again. What is wrong with that man?" And of course it did not matter what was wrong with that man. He was in the protected circle of Giuliani. He could do whatever he wanted.

ORIGINS

BY BROOKE SHAFFNER

On Broadway between Eighty-fourth and Eighty-fifth streets, next door to Häagen-Dazs and Godiva, is the Origins cosmetics store. Outside the store sits the Origins gumball machine. Someone has scratched off the "e" in "Peace of Mind," so that the gumball machine now reads, "Pace of Mind."

The pace of the gumball is slow. Intended to evoke the purity of unspoiled origins, it is white and winds leisurely down a long, transparent, spiral tunnel like an egg descending through the fallopian tubes.

At 9 a.m. on a Tuesday morning, the pace of people passing the Origins gumball machine is quick—swish of pleated slacks and briefcases, rustle of the business section, rhythmic click of heels over concrete. But if one steps outside the sidewalk rhythm and reads the faces, the pace shifts.

The spinning slows, tunnels into a slow-rolling space of private association. That man isn't really reading the business section. Notice the sly smile parting his lips, the pleased raise of his eyebrows, quick lick of his lips and then the smile again; he is remembering last night, rewinding, replaying, rewinding. And the twentysomething girl in the cashmere turtleneck and A-line skirt—watch how she tilts her head from side to side, her lips moving slightly, the gruff, furrowed brow to one side, the poised, confident smile on the other. She is a legal assistant, enacting the witty dialogue she will not have with the daunting attorney she works for. In actuality, he will call her into his office to point out the errors in the e-mail she sent to fifty employees; her cashmere turtleneck will feel itchy, constrictive, her face will turn tomato-red. But for now, she has the perfect insightful, humorous observation, her ill-tempered boss irresistibly lured into laughter, into looking at her as more than the origin of irritating mistakes.

Once the egg is released, it travels down the fallopian tubes for a period of about seven days. Sometimes, in the midst of this slow, winding journey, fertilization occurs. A middle-aged woman with black running tights and Nikes sticking out of her overcoat walks briskly, shivering and guzzling Starbucks coffee. Suddenly, her blank look bends into a crooked smile and she laughs out loud, remembering something funny someone said this morning at the gym, a quick, unconscious laugh that surprises her. And at her laugh, the man smiling slyly at the business section looks up from his paper, opens his eyes wide, and smiles at this woman, chuckling at the fact that they are walking side by side in two separate reveries. For a moment, inside and outside have merged, winking at one another as if to say choosing is not necessary, not now, before separating again, descending into the subway, sinking from the bodies pressed side-upon-side in the crowded car.

The tug between inside and out, the inner world relieving the chaos of the outer world, the outer world relieving the turmoil of the inner, the missing letters we hardly notice are missing anymore.

THE SEED

BY BROOKE SHAFFNER

At 7:30 on a Monday evening, my apartment on 122nd Street and Broadway filled with the voices of young Mormons singing hymns. For the past half an hour, around forty clean-cut, fair-haired, smiling twentysomethings, some bearing baked goods, had been arriving in a continuous stream. They bustled down my bowling alley of a hallway to the living room, where they proceeded to comment on their surroundings. "What's all this weird stuff on the walls?" (Just my MOMA posters.) "Don't tell me you read *The Village Voice* now, Nat."

I was twenty-three and in my second year in Columbia's graduate writing program. Since I lived in student housing, my roommates were randomly assigned by the Housing Department. That year I was assigned two roommates from the School of Social Work—Amanda, a twenty-four-year-old Jewish girl from Tucson, and Natalie, a twenty-four-year-old Mormon girl from Salt Lake City. Amanda was pretty uptight about cleanliness. First semester, she'd pinned an abrasive note on the fridge chastising Natalie and me for occasionally leaving dishes in the sink or letting the garbage pile up. And she was unpredictably moody, chatty one minute and sullen the next.

Natalie, on the other hand, was friendly and laid back and easy to talk to. We'd chat in the kitchen about nothing out of the ordinary—work, classes, dating. Natalie was always going out on dates with guys she said she'd met through her church. She had the same complaints that I did and we could pretty much finish each other's sentences until she started talking about marriage, which was where I stopped relating. But there was plenty that Natalie and I saw eye-to-eye on—enough to make small talk while my pasta boiled anyway.

So I didn't think much of the Mormon thing until there were forty of them singing hymns in my living room. Natalie frequently had groups of people over for dinner unannounced. Granted, these dinner parties were sometimes loud, and it was a little strange how her guests made themselves at home in our mini-kitchen, seemingly oblivious to Amanda's and my attempts to squeeze through their casserole commotion for a bowl of cereal. But Natalie was so accommodating in other ways that I was willing to overlook these inconveniences. Until she ushered in a full-on worship service.

The surprise Mormon congregation in my living room that spring of 2002 was unnervingly similar to a gathering my father had dragged my sister and me to Christmas Eve of 2000. My parents had divorced when I was nine, my sister three, and we'd since divided our holidays and summers between them. My father, though not without charm, is a difficult man—simultaneously uncommunicative and prone to hypercritical bloviation, domineering, temperamental, emotionally predatory, and womanizing. These characteristics only worsened when a parasailing accident a year after the divorce left him a quadriplegic. Even the womanizing.

His mystery woman of the moment, Susan, was apparently the reason he'd taken us to The Seed's Christmas banquet. Susan had somehow been involved in The Seed, though the nature of her involvement—whether she'd been through the program, herself, or was a staff member or volunteer of some sort—was unclear. The nature of her involvement with my father—whether she was his nurse or girlfriend or both—was also unclear.

Though Susan would accompany him to bed that night, open gifts and come to the Shaffner Christmas brunch with us the next morning, Dad would only introduce her—if he introduced her at all—as his *friend*. This was paternity as my sister and I knew it.

So imagine our surprise when, upon entering a banquet room at the rear of the Marriot Harbor Beach Fort Lauderdale Resort and Spa, our undemonstrative father was swarmed by an adoring crowd of middle-aged white people wearing red and green sweatshirts with fuzzy reindeer, blinking Christmas bulbs, or jingle bells on the front. They squeezed his shoulders, laughing, jingling— mere foreplay before *The Embrace*. One by one, men and women alike leaned over and wrapped both arms around my father, held him for several long seconds, slapping his back then easing into a snug clasp before pulling back, gripping his shoulders, locking eyes, and loudly, firmly enunciating: *I love you, Jeff*.

We sat down to eat with the Andersons, a group of eerily eager siblings, who introduced themselves as Snowie, Rosie, Sunshine, Stringbean, and Hotpants, explaining that the founder of The Seed, Art Barker, had given them these nicknames *to make them feel special*. Susan said that Art had Parkinson's Disease and had recently contracted shingles in the brain that led to meningitis. "He's just been released from the hospital and has no business being out of bed, but he wouldn't miss this for the world," she said. The Andersons grinned and shook their heads in mock-consternation. After we'd eaten, the Anderson sisters got up to sing Christmas carols with around twenty other banquet attendees. Some of the songs, such as the "Seed Song," sung to the tune of "Greensleeves," had lyrics altered to reflect the group's philosophy:

> *The Seed, indeed, is all you need,*
> *to stay off the junk and pills and weed!*
> *You come each day from ten to ten,*
> *And if you screw up, then you start again!*
> *They lock you up away from the world;*
> *If you want to get clean, you've got to go by the rules!*
> *Faith, love, and honesty will prevail,*
> *and if you can't dig it, you'll go to jail!*

Every head in that cavernous banquet hall turned to watch a bent man with a rotund middle and a white fringe of hair around the base of his head shuffle up to the microphone on a walking IV, and I knew that this could be none other than Art Barker, hallowed Father of The Seed. "Who wants to tell me why we sing 'Jingle Bells' at The Seed?" he asked, and without skipping a beat, everyone, including my father, responded in grade school sing-song unison: *We sing "Jingle Bells" because at The Seed, every day is like Christmas!* Then we all sang "Jingle Bells," at the end of which, everyone put their arms around each other and sang in slow motion while swaying back and forth, *Oh what fun* (right)... *it is to ride* (left)...*in a one* (right)...*horse* (left)...*o-* (right)...*pen* (left)... *sleigh!* (right). At "sleigh," everyone rubbed his or her neighbor's back. Susan rubbed Dad's, and Snowie sidled over between my sister and me and rubbed ours, so we wouldn't feel left out.

Art then gave a speech in which he said it was the final year for The Seed, that the state was shutting it down because he and the rest of the staff weren't licensed counselors. "It's a bunch of *bullshit!*" he cried, pitching forward, almost losing his balance. "We all know it doesn't take a license to save lives! Over the last thirty years, The Seed has taken *thousands* of druggies, alcoholics, losers, and lost souls into its care and turned them into honest, successful, decent men and women! I want you to know that I look at each and every one of you as one of my own *children*. I'm really going to miss all you people! I'm really going to miss *this*..." Art stopped and shook his head at the floor. When he looked up, tears were rolling down his face, rivulets awash through the gullies of his wrinkles. Susan began to sniffle, and soon all of the Andersons were crying, too. Even my father cried. Slow, heavy tears rolled down his cheeks and he did not blink; he did not lift his curled hand to wipe them away.

"Everyone give the person next to you a hug," Art said. "That's what we're here for, to be family to each other! And while you're at it, everybody give Jeff Shaffner a big hug! We couldn't have done any of this without him. Now there's an amazing guy for you! *We love you, buddy!*" Cries of *WE LOVE YOU, JEFF!* ricocheted through the room and again my father was encircled by Seedlings.

Susan was with us for the rest of our visit. We talked about the weather and Dad's dog and other inconsequential things, but never once about The Seed. The first time I was alone with my father was when he drove me to the airport. I confronted him about The Seed; his *friend* Susan; his failure to communicate the most fundamental things, to spend so much as one second alone with us; all the years he'd demanded we drop everything in our lives to visit him for the forty-two summer days specified by the divorce decree so that he could ignore us, the long litany of his paternal failings. He dodged and averted and shifted the blame; called me a selfish, insensitive, ungrateful bitch; and when that didn't silence me, he hit me. "Shut up! Shut up!" he yelled through my words, and the knuckles of his curled hand flew against my mouth.

My father was paralyzed, essentially, from his elbows down, though he has enough mobility in his hands to drive. In order to hit me, he had to hold his torso steady, to swing from his shoulder. When I called my mother from the airport in tears, she asked if he'd hit me *hard*. I told her there wasn't a bruise. That was what she wanted to know, whether this transgression was visible to the public eye. She said I should apologize to my father.

There wasn't a bruise. But seeing my quadriplegic father use his last muscle to hit me was a life-altering revelation, one that ultimately destroyed any sentimental notions I had about family. The wobbly arc of his loose fist was unspeakably ugly and empty and sad—not unlike the mechanics of a cult. I could not take it in whole. I shut up and sat there motionless, my vision blurring at the edges.

A series of badgering calls and e-mails from my father, in which he demanded I spend forty-two days of my summer with him, ensued. Though he repeatedly insisted that the problem was mine, not ours, that I lacked *real-world tools* and *people skills* and needed an *attitude adjustment*, he claimed at one point that we would go through joint counseling. My mother and stepfather said, again and again, that God gives our parents to us for a reason, that my relationship with my father would always be a huge part of my happiness, and that if I cut him out of my life, I would never be whole. They said I needed to do everything in my power to repair our relationship. I fought and fought, but in the end I agreed to spend the six weeks with him. He was my father.

When I arrived in Fort Lauderdale that summer, my father revealed his intentions to have me attend group meetings at The Seed. He would say only that it was not a drug rehab program, but a program to teach me *basic life skills*, to *equip me with the tools I needed to survive in the real world*. He said I was *severely fucked up* and that I was *going to fall on my ass when I got out in the real world* if he didn't do everything in his power to save me. He arranged for me to attend two-hour group meetings called *raps* three days a week, and volunteer at the Habitat for Humanity hardware store, where I sorted screws and paint cans, in between these meetings.

Raps were supposedly based on *The Three Persons: The Person I Was, the Person I Am, and The Person I Want to Be*; *The Seven Steps*, a simplification of the Twelve Steps; and *The Three Signs: 1) Think, think, think! 2) First things first!* and *3) Easy does it!*; but the fifteen or so kooky fortysomethings who attended would ramble indiscriminately about things like the snakeskin bellbottoms they'd worn in high school, mild acts of self-mutilation, smoking pot in their parents' basement, and blasting *The White Album*. It seemed they could say anything as long as long as they emphasized that they were *miserable and full of shit before they came into The Seed*, and on *a fast track to insanity, suicide, or the slammer*. When each speaker finished, the group responded with a sing-song *I love you!* I was expected to get up and speak, and I did. I spoke about my father, who was not there. (He attended only two raps.) I cried about my father in front of that group of very strange strangers. Afterwards, I was reprimanded for defending myself, which was not done at The Seed because it was *a fast track to insanity, suicide, or the slammer*.

At the end of the six weeks, I house-sat for my aunt and was able to do some Internet research on The Seed. I discovered that it was far more than a strange little group of smiley head-bobbers in Fort Lauderdale, that my sense of the malevolence underlying its philosophy and practices was more than justified. At its height of operation in the seventies, The Seed has been a controversial youth drug-rehabilitation program with four locations in South Florida and thousands of clients. It utilized coercive techniques such as aggressive confrontation, intimidation, verbal and physical abuse, sleep deprivation, and restricted access to the bathroom to tear down a teen's sense of self and replace it with the ready-made identity of a Seedling. In 1974, the U.S. Senate published a study that accused The Seed of using methods similar to North Korean communist brainwashing techniques. The bad press, in conjunction with legal pressure from NIDA and the drying up of federal funds, forced The Seed to scale back its operations and admit only voluntary clients. 2001, the year that I attended raps, was its final year.

I went through my father's program mainly because I needed to know, once and for all, who he was—whether he was wholly delusional or narcissistic or both, whether his mirror neurons—responsible for triggering an empathic response when a loved one expresses vulnerability—were at all functional. Once I understood the way in which he'd employed The Seed to fortify and extend an assault upon my identity, I knew that a relationship with my father was impossible.

That, too, is a truth you absorb in stages, over the course of years. I desperately needed New York—the unflinching grit of its streets, people like me who'd fled the stifling values of small-town America, graffiti taggers who crawled through rat nests and cesspools, pressed flesh against death, to let their names breathe in the subway's underworld. I needed to plumb that pain from a distance, from the sanctuary of liberal erudition I expected Columbia to provide. I needed space and silence to listen for my voice, but the sound that filled my ears that spring night in my university-subsidized apartment was the upwelling of Mormon hymns.

Unable to work, I found myself cowering in Amanda's room, which was adjacent to the living room. It was the first time I'd been in her room. We sat on her bed, amidst a lot of lacy throw pillows, one of which said *Princess*.

"Natalie knows I have to get up at six to go work in the Bronx tomorrow morning," she said. "Jeez, with all the Jews in New York, you'd think I'd wind up with at least one of them for a roommate. Instead, I get a Mormon. What are the chances?"

To the extent that Amanda felt this was an invasion, I felt it tenfold. But I didn't talk about The Seed. I told Amanda that early on, I'd made the mistake of mentioning to Natalie that I was a lapsed Presbyterian, and afterwards, she never failed to invite me to join her gatherings.

Later that night, Natalie popped into the kitchen, commented on my "interesting" scramble of spinach and Morning Star soy meat, and invited me to play Trivial Pursuit. I saw that it would be necessary to state the obvious: "Natalie, there are about forty people in our living room. It's a little loud." Her sweet moon look vanished. She frowned and said it wouldn't happen again. I almost ran after her and said, "Okay, just one quick round of Trivial Pursuit!" But I didn't.

Instead I read disturbing posts on the Web forum for Seed survivors, such as the one about the Spanking Machine. Originally, uncooperative Seed clients were beaten in the back offices, but later, concerned about liability, Art devised the Spanking Machine, wherein fathers were called in to beat their children in front of staff and old-comers

Then I researched the Mormon Church. I discovered that like The Seed, the Mormon Church also enforces withdrawal from society, strict sexual divisions, and the suppression of homosexuality. The reason that most of Natalie's social life took place at church and inside our apartment was that Mormonism prohibits the consumption of coffee, tea, and alcohol and warns members against exposing themselves to "the gross evils that are so prevalent in societies today" (from Elder Alexander B. Morrison's *No More Strangers*). Beyond bars and coffeehouses, dance clubs also present a danger: "When dancing, avoid full body contact with your partner. Do not use positions or moves suggestive of sexual behavior. Plan and attend dances where dress, grooming, lighting, lyrics, and music contribute to a wholesome atmosphere where the Spirit of the Lord may be present." Strict Mormons wear Kevlar underwear to protect their nether regions. Survivors of the 1970s Seed describe a similar environment, in which romantic relationships, sex, and even sexual thoughts were forbidden, and sexual confession raps were used not only to enforce celibacy and induce guilt, but to further humiliate clients. Traditional sex roles were rigidly enforced, the "idea that women should sew and cook while men should pursue carpentry or mechanical work," and parents enrolled their children in The Seed not only to get them off of drugs, but to make them heterosexual.

I discovered that the Mormon Church has a frightening amount of political pull—that in 1976, it launched a five-year campaign against the equal rights amendment and is now conducting a similar campaign against same-sex marriages. *Time* calculated the Church's net worth in 1997 at a minimum of thirty billion dollars and its annual income at about six billion dollars, which, if it were a corporation, would place it in the middle of the *Fortune 500* list.

The Seed and its offshoot programs also have considerable political pull. Melvin and Betty Sembler, Seed parents who founded Straight, Inc.—a treatment program modeled upon The Seed's *intensive encounter* tactics and repeatedly charged with physical and mental abuse and violations of civil rights—were well connected to the Bush administration. Melvin Sembler was the national finance chairman for the GOP when George W. Bush ran for president, and was later appointed ambassador to Italy; Betty Sembler was Jeb Bush's finance cochairman. The Sembler family and company were substantial contributors to the Bush administration and the Republican party, and heavily involved in determining national and international drug policy. Charles Crist, Florida's first Republican governor and formerly the state Attorney General, graduated from the St. Petersburg Seed and is a tireless advocate of both The Seed and Straight, Inc.

Later that semester, Amanda moved to a studio on the Upper East Side, and it was just Natalie and me in the apartment. That summer, Natalie would move into an apartment with friends from church. Not long before she moved, she invited me to one of her dinner parties. She and her friends had somehow managed to cook a pot roast and green bean casserole in our tiny kitchen. My mother always made green bean casserole at Thanksgiving—southern comfort food. I loved it.

Natalie, a girlfriend, and two boys were gathered around the table when I walked past the dining room. "Come eat with us," Natalie said. "Really, there's more than enough food."

Believe me, I was hungry. More lonely than I'd ever been in my life. But I thanked her and said I had work. I did. I had a lot of work.

As I headed to my room, I saw them clasp hands, close their eyes, and bow their golden heads. I remembered how at the end of raps, we'd always clasped hands and said the Lord's Prayer; how when Art Barker was there, the Seedlings would grin adoringly at him as they said, "Our Father who *Art* in Heaven."

I sat down in front of my computer. My writing had become increasingly surreal since the Christmas my father dragged my sister and me to The Seed banquet. My professor recommended Donald Barthelme's *The Dead Father*, and I read it the way that literalists read the Bible. The story of the immense carcass of a half-dead, half-alive, part mechanical father being dragged through the countryside by a cable was one I knew by heart, by weight.

Do you really want to find this father? What if, when you find him, he speaks to you in the same tone he used before he lost himself? Will he again place nails in your mother, in her elbow and back of the knee? Remember the javelin. Have you any reason to believe it will not, once again, flash through the seven-o'clock-in-the-evening air? What we are attempting to determine is simple: Under what conditions do you wish to live?...Ignore that empty chair at the head of the table. Give thanks.

I gave thanks for the hunger and loneliness, and the chance to fill them with something real.

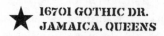

★ 16701 GOTHIC DR.
JAMAICA, QUEENS

LOADED HALLWAYS
BY JB McGEEVER

The campus of my public school building in New York City is a fortress these days. Gazing through the mesh caging of any stairway window, I can spot faculty deans, campus security (a branch of the NYPD with arresting powers), as well as regular NYPD uniformed officers patrolling the grounds like medieval sentries. As I move through the halls of this majestic, seventy-year-old building, I'm forced to sidestep a quartet of firefighters in full regalia, escorted from the building by two police officers, nine millimeter Glock handguns bouncing off their hips. The students are unfazed, just part of life in the big city, but imagine, New York's Finest, Bravest, and Brightest, all right here in one high school—and no one's quite sure why. Was there a fire in the building today? That's really none of your business. Information will be doled out on a need-to-know basis. Oh, and welcome back to a brand new school year.

Lunchtime. I find my way into one of the faculty men's rooms, a police officer's cap resting on a windowsill, its owner inside one of the stalls, making and taking phone calls like the commissioner himself. In the library, where I go to grade papers, yet another officer. I ignore him, he ignores me, two separate entities here for completely different reasons. I grade my quizzes. He makes his phone calls. Apparently that big sign on the door with the red slash across a cell phone no longer applies. I leave a bit early to beat the rush, an officer on the second floor sees me and bows into a wall, as if in prayer, only he calls the wall "Sweetie" so I assume he's not speaking to his respective deity.

It's not so much the constant cell phone use, the squinting, dirty looks as I enter a corridor, or the fact that no one notified the faculty of a police presence in the building. It's those Glocks in their holsters, the "hand cannons" at their hips. It simply looks obscene in the halls outside my classroom. This is supposed to be a sanctuary. Any literature teacher in the city will tell you, a few well placed props change the entire setting of a location. I wouldn't dream of teaching a lesson on *Macbeth* from the backseat of a squad car. What in the world are these people doing with loaded weapons in our halls? It's just no way for a kid to go to school.

Last semester I had an opportunity to experience what the students go through. While snapping photos of the building to display in the school's literary magazine, I inadvertently stepped off campus. An NYPD van immediately rolled up and demanded identification. I didn't have any. Then who was I? Terms like "pedophile" and "terrorist" were used as casually as one might order up, say, a box of doughnuts. Terms like "overkill" and "police state" were hurled back at them. The conversation went downhill from there.

Yet this is the way that many of the city's teenagers attend high school each day. Instead of using the auditorium for assemblies and school plays, it's been turned into a weigh station for students to adjust their backpacks and redo their belts after removing them for the metal detectors twice a week. Maybe this type of indignity is worth the trouble at the airport, or on your way to vacation in the islands, but to gym class? My first year in the building the assistant principal of security would prove to the students how effective the scanners were by pressing one against the fillings in his teeth. Definitely a yearbook moment, boys and girls.

You see, once a building has been labeled an "Impact School," the police arrive. Once the police arrive, negative publicity ensues. Negative publicity results in a failure to attract good students, and low test scores are right around the corner. Low test scores simply mean that your school building is doomed. In order to avoid this nightmare, many schools fail to report the petty crimes in their buildings. My building, however, was recently praised for a policy of "zero tolerance," everything from cell phone theft to verbal harassment was reported in good faith. Nothing was swept under the proverbial rug, and now the place is surrounded. Catch-22, anyone? At the end of the day, my girlfriend, who also teaches in the building, likes to give me the day's news. Since the matter has never been addressed by administration, all the faculty has to go on is hearsay, nothing more than ridiculous trench-coat meetings in hallways outside of classrooms. She tells me that police guns were pulled on two students today. " 'If I tell you to do something, you better do it,' " she says was the cop's explanation before bragging how, in a separate incident, a Muslim student attempted to enter the building using another student's ID and the terrorist unit was called in. Then the officer asked my girlfriend out to dinner. "Well, did you feel a whole lot safer afterwards?" is all I have to say.

This fall, to pound the student body's collective esteem further into the ground, a *Daily News* sports reporter covered one of our home football games. The article made its way throughout the school, passed from hand to student hand until a tattered copy reached my desk. For some reason, the reporter's article got personal. He ridiculed our field, mocked the students who showed up to watch, even jeered the parents who cooked the hot dogs. He questioned our school's heart, never bothering to wonder if other factors for a lackluster season might be at play. Though, in the reporter's quest to deride the school, he got our nickname incorrect. For the record, we are the Beavers, Sir. The Fightin' Beavers, and don't you forget it.

All it takes is for one student to have a bad morning, to carry that burden to school with him, and then to act out on it, something that occurs in countless variations throughout schools nationwide. Instead of a routine suspension and a call to Mom, Dad, or even Grandmama, with the NYPD presence inside a school the end result could be a world of hurt that no one ever imagined.

On our way out of the building, we pass one of the flyers some of the students have taped to the walls in an effort to win back their school. It shows a graphic with a pair of young hands gripping steel bars. This is not a penitentiary, it says. We are students, not inmates. If tales of danger are truly what you seek, dear reader, I'm writing this essay during the first semester of my tenure year. Now that is truly frightening.

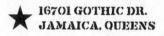

**16701 GOTHIC DR.
JAMAICA, QUEENS**

A FAN'S STATISTICS

BY JB McGEEVER

Twice a year, the New York State English Regents Exam visits the high schools of our fair city, four comprehensive essays over a period of two days, and this January's results are in. In my building, preparation for the exam begins in the ninth grade and continues right until the students enter class to take the exam.

"Hey, Mister—" a voice will call down the hallway just minutes before the test. "Who wrote about those mice and men? George Steinbrenner, right?"

Due to the No Child Left Behind rule, everyone takes the exam during junior year regardless of their proficiency in English. The student who's been in the system since kindergarten takes it, as well as the child who recently arrived to America and whose second, third, or fourth language might be English. Whether they have designs on going to college after graduation or going on to become mechanics and electricians, they are going to sit for that exam.

The more students a school gets to pass, the better the school looks. As a result, many schools have pushed up the date for students to take the test. Rather than taking it for the first time in

June, why not usher them in five months early and see what happens? If they pass, great, if not, get ready for round two. Better still, let's start grading the teachers on the results.

The Department of Education has been conducting a secret pilot program where 2,500 teachers at 140 city public schools are being measured without their knowledge on student performance on standardized tests. Sadly, the local media has weighed in with typical comments and clichés regarding the teaching profession. "Imagine teachers treated like other professionals—having their performance monitored and quantified," writes Adam Brodsky in an op-ed piece for the *Post*. In his late January article, Mr. Brodsky even cites Tom Brady of the New England Patriots as a good lesson to all of us regarding the power of impressive statistics. But the city recently discovered, in the most stunning way imaginable, that gaudy, blown-up stats aren't everything.

Despite his condescending attitude toward teachers, Brodsky still raises a good point. So let's "monitor" and "quantify" some of my students on their recent performance on the English Regents exam, then determine my net worth once we're through. Out of five classes taught this past semester, I had one class of juniors, three groups of sophomores, and one senior elective. The juniors were an interesting bunch, bright, friendly, and respectful, one of the most enjoyable classes I've ever taught.

But before we can examine their performance on the test, as well as my accountability, we need to establish setting. My building was falsely labeled as an Impact School last year, which means it is now regarded as one of the most dangerous schools in the city. Coincidentally, before the DOE can get its hands on a building and chop it up into "smaller learning communities," it must first get it labeled as dangerous.

Once a school is branded as Impact, a script is then followed to shut the place down. Security is intensified. Letters are sent home to parents, notifying them that their child may transfer out of a "dangerous" building if he or she chooses, and incoming freshman opt to go elsewhere when it's time to select a school.

The faculty is left to shrug and wonder where all these dangerous kids are hiding, but come away with nothing. The school's hallways then begin to shrink, teachers are excessed, and the budget is cut. The atmosphere becomes bleak, like something out of an old Western. It's time to shoot the horses and circle the wagons because rations are low and the enemy's closing in.

Yet the DOE machine keeps rolling. During Regents week, my school was notified that a "new" school will exist inside of our eighty-year-old building next year. It will be the same building, the same amount of kids, just with an imaginary border put into place, a brilliant new version of divide and conquer.

One of my colleagues recently began her graduate-school semester. When she introduced herself and her school, the DOE official moonlighting as an instructor explained that she was familiar with the building and that the school's fate had already been decided. "Jamaica High School is a warehouse," she said. She then advised the teacher to stop battling the DOE, to comply with the inevitable, or transfer out.

A warehouse. Any adult who's witnessed children passing through metal detectors each morning then frisked with scanning wands, not because they're dangerous, but for political reasons, knows what an absolutely disgraceful remark this is.

Let's return now to my classroom of juniors and Mr. Brodsky's pomposity: "Why not make teachers prove their worth?" Very well, but shouldn't instructors be given an equal playing field before they're forced to compete? Do Stuyvesant High School, Brooklyn Tech, or Bronx Science, three of the finest specialized schools in the city, have Jamaica's problems to contend with? They have waiting lists to get in, while Jamaica struggles with a two-year-long DOE chokehold. Whose test scores do you think will be more impressive?

As I scan the list of results I find that my class ran the gamut, lots of highs and lows. Some overslept and missed the exam, while others arrived early and pulled off stunning victories. Jamal got his ninety-seven, but Forrest received a fifty-one.

As much as I would like to take credit for Jamal's grade, the truth is that he's a self-starter who sits up front, takes notes, and never misses class. Forrest, however, disappeared into the West Indies around holiday time: "Going to my country, bye." He was gone for nearly six weeks, missing all of his Regents preparation. I'm sure he was visiting family he hadn't seen in a while, but should his extended vacation have any bearing on my teaching career? Of course not.

There's also no need to congratulate myself when Clarissa scores an eighty-six. She's quiet, attentive, and likes to read. I did my job each day and she did hers. Or Victor, who managed to get himself suspended for three weeks then recorded a forty-seven. All four of these kids were in the same class and all four of them are responsible for their test scores. Not their teacher.

When it comes time to give Jamal's family a call to congratulate them on their son's success, I find out that he lives in a group home. I'm taken aback on the phone. I expected to speak to the man Jamal identified as his father on parent/teacher night, but he was really just the counselor on duty.

There's no way to explain Jamal. He defies DOE logic and statistics. He left his group home each morning, reported to his "persistently dangerous high school," where he was scanned, frisked and instructed to readjust his belt in the auditorium, then sat down to record one of the highest scores in the state. The kid's a winner, a true New York Giant, and I would love to bask in his glory or dance in his victory parade, but I'm nothing more than a fan.

THE DIFFERENCE BETWEEN CHICKENS AND GOATS

BY DANIEL NESTER

A Goat walks in with a camera, wants to document me, the Best Administrative Assistant in the World, diligently at work. I turn off the Atari emulator on my computer, open up a word processing document, and get to my Work, processing, retrieving, shrugging off calls in triplicate. Each call and customer needs to feel like they are wanted, even as I dissuade them. And they are indeed dissuaded, most of them, like these little Space Invaders that come in at me with only a single gun turret to defend myself.

For much of my tenure at a film department at a well known "University" with "New York" in its name, I labored as an administrative assistant—pay grade seven—behind a north-facing desk in what is known as the Inventory Insult Booth. It was a meeting place where the film students—which, with the help of the search-and-replace feature on my word processing software are referred to henceforth as "Goats"—are first greeted with the news that they had slept in a marijuana cloud through their phone registration slots, and so therefore cannot receive their degree, cannot attend classes, or both. Goats were invariably disappointed at the news, and usually declaimed their ignorance as the brand of their innocence.

Goats have spit on me, flipped middle fingers, and threatened legal action. Goats have called me "The Man." Goats have farted, cropduster plane–style, across the front of my desk; they have accused me of embezzling, mental retardation, and laziness; they have called me "faggot," "dumbass honky," and "jackass." Nipping at the Goats' heels in the Inventory Insult Booth are the "Chickens." This is the name I give to non-film majors who stop at nothing to take a film class, save switching majors and actually being polite. From mid-1996, when I completed my graduate poetry studies, until mid-2000, I decided, in the face of all this adversity, to keep my chin up and become the Best Administrative Assistant in the World! I recently found this notebook on a 3.5-inch floppy disk, in which I had set out to chronicle my efforts.

A small woman walks straight up to my desk, the ding of the elevator still ringing in the air. She's a Chicken, but wants to be a Goat. I say that it's impossible, that there must be some confusion here, for I can only help with Goat classes, and you are not a Goat. She says No, she is indeed a Chicken, but wants to become a Goat to take Goat classes. I say Goat classes are only for Goats, and, as a Chicken, you are therefore ineligible to take part in the Goats' curriculum. I tell her that, furthermore, there are no forms or appeals available to her to become a Temporary Goat, other than The Big Form, which would wait until the autumn, when all Big Forms are processed. She is an able opponent, this ornery Chicken. It is at this moment that I realize that my dreams of being the Best Administrative Assistant in the

World have already begun to come true, right here, before my eyes!

But I who aspire to be The Best Administrative Assistant in the World, have taken on the full brunt of her thrusts and parries. I am talking Chicken to her, dissuading her from the ways of the Goat. This small Chicken shrugs, says she'll be back, with more documentation for her to become a Temporary Goat.

Several Philosopher-Goats have asked me questions in math. Pure math, no stuttering. They are numbering requests to me, directly across my desk's counter space, they are yammering on in zeroes and ones. It takes me a while to decipher what is going on, but as their administrative assistant, I give them the necessary papers, or I file something, and they go on with lives that are much more nourished than mine. I applaud them, these Philosopher-Goats, those who question each word others say, but applaud themselves after their words find articulation in the mouths of others, no matter the originality or even the verity. It is an unconditional language, like math, except with a sort of acknowledgment before each utterance, as if each sentence were footnoted with the same exact sentence printed in smaller font.

Several Goats have crank-called me—this is funny, since they are artists. Most times, I go along with it, since as Goats they need a supportive audience, and I know this. Most of the time, they will reveal who they are—Dude, it's me, Joshua the Goat!—but sometimes they don't. Those that don't go on to become administrators here after graduation. Usually they are short and have a background in student government. It's okay, though; I'm not jealous. This is part of the job that I have chosen. Or did the job choose me?

You can ask anyone who the toughest customers are. Old ladies with coupons at a busy grocery checkout? Good guess. Haggling young mothers in Egyptian street shops? Another good one. Trust fund kids on a budget, reading their section of a diner tab? Again, close. Goats pumped up that they are the next generation of cinema, faced with the crush of doing their own quotidian paperwork? Bingo. Those are the toughest customers, and it is they whom I, the Best Administrative Assistant in the World, aspire to serve.

A group of Goats walk up to me and ask me a question: if there are twenty-four cameras in a classroom, and twenty-four desks, then why can we not join the class as guests, who can, on occasion, sit in a desk or get behind a camera, under the scenario, say, of a suicide or extended absence. They are indeed able opponents, these Goats, and I respect them. But only to a point. To serve film student Goats, there has to be a certain amount of antipathy involved, a certain hatred. They will approach you, challenge you, ask to be a Goat when they are a Chicken, ask to take dead peoples' cameras, and you must hold your ground. All the while I know this: the Chicken never wins. The Goat has hooves.

According to legend, Goats are so awful at figuring out how to graduate, and—after being told they were the heir apparent to such alumni as Spike Lee, Martin Scorsese, and Jim Jarmusch—are so rude to the folks in the Central Inventory Insult Booth that the Department had to set up its own Inventory Insult Booth, in-house. And I work there.

The Best Administrative Assistant in the World walks into a bar. He sees other Administrative Assistants there, ones who have assisted the same Goats and Philosopher-Goats. We share a pitcher, gossip, jibe each other. When one of us sneezes, we all say God Bless You. We talk about Goat Forms, Chicken Forms, Temporary Goat Forms, The Big Form. We let off some AA steam. But as the Best, they wait and give space for my stories, for I am the best and my stories are the best. I am deeper in the trenches than my comrades, I have met all of the Goats, all of the Philosopher-Goats, at their most vulnerable moments. All of my comrades have certain defining characteristics. Facial tics. They wait for me to speak more. I finish my beer. I tell them I have an appointment. One of them hugs me.

I kept track of how many times a Goat asked the question, "Do you know who I am?" The number: twenty-seven. That's about 6.75 times a year in my four-year tenure. The only time I really "knew" who a Goat was when a Goat, in turn, actually told me. In his case, he was a son of a major producer in Hollywood who had forgotten to pay his son's tuition and was now de-enrolled from all his classes. I took pity on this Goat, and sent him to my supervisor's Insult Booth.

My speech would have gone something like this: "Friends, Hallelujah! Those who have been in New York this long, and who have midwifed the future Goats of cinema as long as I, we have a task. Hallelujah! A dirty task, one in which the entire world waits for these gods' visions to come to the fore. Hallelujah! We cannot stop these visions. Hallelujah! They are holy, they are purely and simply youthful. Hallelujah! Sure, they haven't written a single script. Hallelujah! Sure, they are Goats, Temporary Goats, even Chickens. Hallelujah! But we must help them, control their anger, their deprecation, assist in their baptism. Hallelujah!" I knew my fellow Administrative Assistants would have many questions if I had given that speech, and I really did have an appointment, of sorts. So I'm glad I held back; there'd be other times. Hallelujah!

Today the Best Administrative Assistant in the World had no air conditioning.

He played electric guitar in his cubicle while a business student asked questions. To him, I was the Facilitator of Goats. I felt this as I hit an open E chord, finishing off with a blues-based run that felt as comfortable as an old pair of sneakers. How can I, a lowly business student, learn to approach your greatness? he asked. I responded, "Don't try to be like me. When your emotions are pure, you will see what you have to be. If you are a Chicken, be a Chicken. If you are a Goat, be a Goat. If you are a business student majoring in entertainment management at the Stern School of Business, then be that. Don't be a Chicken trying to be a Goat, as you are today. That's too messy, and no one will know who you are. Just do it, as they say around here. Strive for greatness." The phone rings. The business student shakes my hand, give me his card, takes the next elevator down to the street, filled, no doubt, with thoughts of greatness, not Chicken-Goat thoughts.

A continuation on that Chicken girl. While all of this has transpired, she has come by, every morning, to ask me if the situation has changed. Am I a Temporary Goat yet? I look something up on the computer. I look at her. No, I say. You are still a Chicken. She says that she has filled out The Big Form, and it will only be a matter of days before her Chicken status will change—poof!—into that of a Temporary Goat. I tell her I have no documentation or proof, and neither does she, and so we stand there, eye-to-eye, waiting for the Chicken air conditioning to change to Temporary Goat air conditioning. The phone rings. An e-mail arrives. I look forward to the tasks ahead of me.

I also want to be famous. I have to admit it: I also want to be the Most Famous Administrative Assistant in the World. No, wait, I just want to the Best. How I will do both, I have yet to know. But I know that when it happens, it will be a fluid moment, there will be no epiphany in the third-act sense. Somewhere, where things are less prosaic than where we are now, such methodologies are actually sought after at a high price, but I know that my wisdom in the small world I live in has afforded me much patience. I am ambitious, yes, and I can wait until something as great and as inevitable as my crowning will happen. And I will be the Best, and maybe no one will know that. I have

to face that. I may not be Famous. I may not be Famous. I may
not be Famous. And it will be nothing like the movies.

One big secret I've learned: Many people in this great city,
New York City, do not have to work to survive. They have either
attained a level of wealth that facilitates a life of leisure, or the
wealth of their forebears have given them luxury, a bequeathed
greatness. I see this in Williamsburg, SoHo, or the East Village,
when I, the Soon to Be The Most Famous and Best Administrative Assistant in the World, call out sick for mental health
holidays. For being the Best takes Rest. I make $27,573 a year, in
the mid-range of pay grade seven, and a lot of those funds have
to go to what I call "upkeep," as I call it, care for my physical
being. Hot-temperature aerobic classes. Body sculpting. Tae-bo.
Jazzercise. Russian-Turkish baths. All of the pressures of helping
Goats sometimes catch up to me, and sometimes even I have to
spend time in crowded cafes, drinking iced coffee and eating a
pastry. And in these cafes, I see these people of luxury. And they
are so relaxed! The way they sip their beverages, the way they
talk to each other! It reminds me sometimes of the Goats I serve,
but I shan't think any more along these lines, for I know most
Goats cannot be this rich and lazy. Surely not. They are not waiting for the visions to meet them here—they are out there getting
them, seizing them. And I help them do this. That is my job.

The fame has not yet arrived. Nightfall during the winter
precedes my release from my desk, and so I walk home in the
dark. My soul, filled as it is with feathers and hoofprints, slowly
freezes over, thankfully, and I thank all of the gods that have put
me in the place where I can midwife the stories of Goats for the
next twenty years. The stories they will tell! And all of these full-
fledged Goats, walking strong, never falling, four-legged,
whinnying to me via phone, fax, e-mail, and in person, the din it
creates! By the time I get to Houston Street, the music returns
full-blast. The Famousness will arrive soon. So, too, will the Best-

ness, I tell myself. And the Goat's music resumes like buskers in the shadows of tall buildings.

Goat music has a tinge of sadness in it. It is like Schubert or Schoenberg in parts, or, if I dare compare it to cinema, mid-period Ron Howard. All of this is in vain, since I cannot describe the Goat music to those who have yet to create cinema. But it is my job to stop them, these Goats, and ask them questions about their music; to put into words what no one else has done. After all, I will face the world for them, I will negotiate on their behalf. Their movies will have sadness, joy, and poor people they've never met. And I must protect them.

Goat music is indeed distant, but when I speak to other Administrative Assistants, they say they cannot even hear it. I play them other music to make sure the other AAs aren't deaf. Hear that music? I ask. It's the lost saxophone solo from the Beach Boys' "God Only Knows" from the Pet Sounds Sessions box set. Blank stares all around. It is at these moments when I am reassured of my Bestness. The words I speak are other-worldly. Sometimes I go up to one of my colleagues or so-called superiors, and speak to them as I have been speaking to you now. They look at me half-askew, confused but in some way in awe of my candor. It is at these moments I am reassured my greatness, my Bestness.

A team of Philosopher-Goats walk up to me. They are asking about Goats and Chickens. No, scratch that. It is I who brings up the subject. Philosopher-Goats speak in math, but they listen patiently, and I tell them about the Chicken Forms, the Goat Forms, the Temporary Goat Forms, and The Big Form. They reply in ones and zeroes. These logicians high-five each other and walk away.

The Chickens come in today. This is the day they get to be Temporary Goats and even full-fledged Goats. They are so happy! And I am happy for them, basically, because it distracts me from some of the very real pain of being the Best AA in the world. As I type this, two Chickens are looking at me, thinking that I am entering in their passwords into the world of Goats. Wrong. Oh, they are so wrong, as Chickens usually are. But I need to get down and transcribe some of my thoughts. They will be Goats soon enough, I say. My pain will subside. Give me just a little more time.

Sometimes I see a Goat, or a former Goat, out on the street. It is usually in Williamsburg or the East Village. This may happen in a cafe on my mental health holidays, or it may happen in passing on weekday evenings, when I am on my way to an appointment. They usually insult me, call me a ball-buster, but I know these are merely cries for help, or perhaps they are thanking me for my years of "tough love." Invariably, they are former Chickens who have endured my explanations of the difference between Chickens and Goats. And it will be a while before their Goat-Chicken status catches up with their inner spirits, the kudzu crawling in their inner Goat-child. I usually wave, and pass along a nugget of wisdom down to them. I think they enjoy seeing their Best AA out in what they call the "real world," and sometimes, if they are really special, I'll help them with their bills.

I do pray, you know. It's just that it's highly esoteric. There's one that I save for the deep summer, because it is in the summer that the distinctions between Goat and Chicken evaporate. And yes, on a summer day like today, when the girl Chicken-Goats wear little or no clothing, you may think that the difference between being the Best AA and the Most Famous AA is little or naught. Who cares? People aren't wearing any clothes, male or female. Just the opposite: it is these days, when I am forced to wear shorts and reveal myself, show myself, that I feel most vulnerable. The Famousness has got to come soon. I am so lonely.

The Goats of whom I speak: they must be taught by someone. And they come in the form of a semi-professional lot, the Philosopher-Goats, the ones who have gone out to the farms and met other Goats and even Chickens and told their stories. I respect them and what they do. And the way they speak to the little Goats! Such a blessing they give them! It is the foreign-speaking Philosopher-Goats of which I speak most fondly, for as I write this, one is flirting with a Goat-Chicken (or is it Temporary Chicken-Goat?) and she is laughing heartily, hoping to be signed into a class that Goats usually get. It is such respect the Philosopher-Goats give back, the kind that Goats need in order to survive.

Anyone who has seen a Goat being born will understand what I am about to say better than those who haven't. But the general thrust is this: All Goats, when they are born, land on only three feet. Not all four. The newborns, wet, soaking in the waters of their mother, struggle, and, gradually, like all good prose, they will land on four feet, struggling with the first shaky steps. But to these Goats who land on three legs, whom I assist as the Best Administrative Assistant in the World, I am that fourth leg. It is I who prop them up, giving them advice on how to keep orderly. They may insult me, yes, but this is because they do not understand the wisdom. And when they go back to Westchester or Connecticut or Southern California and eat their festive winter feasts, they will think back to my desk, where I have eaten my own feasts in front of them, where their fourth leg waits for them, even in their absence.

REVISING THE FOOTLICKER STORY
BY DANIEL NESTER

1. *Saturday, January 27, 1996. Last Wednesday night, Anna (name changed here and hereafter) told me the story of how she made ten dollars letting the night security guard that she worked with lick her feet. From what she tells me, he was really into it—licking her toes, the in-between areas, the heel. She said she even "threw in the other foot for free." I told her this was clearly an act of fetishism, and insofar as the night guard derived sexual pleasure from doing this, she was in effect prostituting her feet to this man. Anna didn't agree. She said it was like some "summer camp dare."*

a. That's an entry from the journal I kept while in my single dating years. I have long pointed to the Footlicker Story as a cautionary tale for freaky women. Looking again at this immediate account, however, I feel as if I may have pushed the narrative into caricature. What follows is an attempt to, among other things, parse out any details I may have forgotten or gotten wrong.

b. The Anna in question was a newcomer to New York City. And like many newcomers, Anna worked several jobs. At least three jobs that I can still remember: the first selling expensive art markers in SoHo; a second as a housesitter/subletter for a rent-controlled lesbian couple's apartment on the Bowery who lived in rural Connecticut; and a third as a data entry clerk at a fairly well known international investment concern that rhymes with "Stare Burns."

2. It was at that third Stare Burns job where the nightguard footlicking story took place. Anna worked the second shift from 4 p.m. to midnight as a word processor, and I suppose things got slow one night.

3. Anna and I were on our third date when I heard this story. This is a major dating event. The first date often counts as meeting at a bar or on the subway; a one-night stand even. The second might be more formal: drinks at an appointed hour or a dinner party. The third is invariably a one-on-one affair, a summit. The third date is also often a chess game, a comparison of career, pedigree, future goals. As the defunct reality TV show *Third Date* calls it, it's the "make-or-break date with love in the air."

4. There was love in the air for Anna and I before our third date on Wednesday, January 24, 1996. We had first met on the L train, that hipster singles bar on wheels. Anna was attractive, blonde, tall, with tomboy freckles and no makeup. She was also a painter. I was always a sucker for female painters. They always seem so tactile, with paint spots on overalls that bare their toned, usually tattooed, arms. They are unusually detached in their demeanor. Most seem stoned, mellow.

     a. Female painters never paid attention to me. I have always been a jumpy, approval-seeking comic, who used wit to compensate for a schlubby appearance. Put those two types together—the comic schlub and the effete, foxy painter—and you have an assload of bad date stories.

5. Anna, however, was a painter who paid attention to me, even laughed at my jokes, and so I was smitten. But that night, I couldn't wrap my head around this Footlicker Story. The detached painter tone I could understand; but "summer camp dare"?

6. Something didn't feel right. That's all I knew back then.

7. Anna had been in New York City for two months. Perhaps, as in the case of Joe Buck in John Schlesinger's 1969 classic *Midnight Cowboy*, Anna was being sucked into the footlicking scene for want of making the big time, getting in a good group show, or to pay the rent.

8. I should have mentioned this first, but Anna is from Utah. She wasn't a Mormon, but being from Utah, to my mind, makes her more naïve about matters footlicking. I suspect there are not too many other self-identified footlicking enthusiasts in Utah, on the giving or receiving end.

9. Google results of search term variants of "Utah AND footlick AND footlicker" yield bupkis. There just doesn't seem to be any verifiable Utah-footlicking connection.

    a. There is a "mature busty fitness model" named Utah Sweet. You can book Ms. Sweet for, among other things, "Cuddling/Hugging Sessions."

    b. There are a couple of bi-curious men in Salt Lake City who express an interest in licking feet on the relevant discussion boards.

    c. And then there is the public policy tome *Truth and Consequences: How Colleges and Universities Meet Public Crises*, which uses as one of its case studies "the integrity of cold fusion research results at the University of Utah."

    d. The author of the above-mentioned book is the unfortunately named Jerrold K. Footlick.

e. When I switch gears into some real research into more scholarly databases, many of the articles that turn up address folklore's connections with fetishes and other dark sides of human nature. The first versions of Cinderella's wide-eyed innocence, for instance, are cast against the relief of a very real, dangerous element of dark sexuality. It's not just the foot that goes into that missing slipper. The stepsisters chop off their toes to fit into the slipper to meet the prince. The first Little Red Riding Hoods are portrayed as overtaken by the Big Bad Wolf when she goes outside to take a shit, the moral being a little girl should not take a shit outside by herself in the woods. These and other tales are rendered uniform and respectful as they are disseminated in print. It is often the typesetter or publisher who sees these dirty details, which offend their bourgeoisie sensibility. The fetishes and scatological details are in turn expurgated.

10. Perhaps I expurgated the only other detail I can remember from the Footlicker Story. The night guard in question was an older African-American male.

a. By ignoring or withholding this detail, am I too over-cautious? What I mean is: Am I too polite, like those middle-class printers? Or am I casting the guard as a black buck, the stereotype described by Donald Bogle in *Toms, Coons, Mulattoes, Mammies & Bucks: An Interpretive History of Blacks in American Films* as "oversexed, savage, violent and frenzied"? Or am I exhibiting an ageism in the very mention that he was older?

b. I know I am doomed to error in the night guard's portrayal. In casting him as almost neutral in this story, in withholding these two details I knew about him, I am taking him out of the picture entirely.

c. Another attempt: The guard was an older black guy. That's all I know.

11. I also did not consider the guard's proclivities for footlicking not one, but two feet of his co-worker in the middle of a cold

winter night, behind his guard desk at a midtown building. The guard's motives may have been some gesture of love, a mark of tenderness, a crush.

      a. Or hers.

12. I interviewed my wife recently. She had heard the story before, but I wanted to know what she thought, on the record. She is a reluctant interviewee.

Me: So what do you think?

My wife: Two things. One, ten dollars is pretty cheap. And two, I'd prefer you not tell it so many times.

Me: Would you lick somebody's feet?

MW: I wouldn't lick anybody's feet. Not even yours.

Me: What about summer camp? Anna described it as a "summer camp dare." You went to summer camp, right?

MW: Maybe I'd lick someone's feet at summer camp. Okay, if I'm eight, I can see that. There's some conceivability.

Me: But how about when you were a counselor as a teenager, like those trust games they have?

MW: Trust games? I went to Camp Walden. [Name changed here and hereafter. There's a really well-known Camp Walden, but this is the other one. This is the one that closed because they ran out of food one summer gradually. Everyone had really bad lice and we ate oatmeal at every meal.]

Me: So you wouldn't lick anybody's feet by the campfire at Camp Walden?

MW: No.

13. What do I really remember? That winter night more than ten years ago, I didn't freak out. I also didn't laugh.

      a. More than anything, more than repulsion, more than shock, more than the desire to look at her feet to see what the guard saw in them, I felt jealous. Very jealous.

b. Anna laughed about the incident; she was giddy; she sounded like she had met the perfect man. It was, actually, the first thing she told me that night as we ordered a round of beers on our third date.

c. Her naïveté about the footlicker's intentions must have bothered me, sure. But what really I wanted was her to feel just as giddy about me.

14. I now remember I was also pedantic with Anna that night; I lectured, point by point, the way insecure men in their twenties do, that footlicking is a fetish, that is to say it's quite possible that this is the only way the night guard can be sexually aroused. I remember she kept smiling through all of this.

15. We did have a fourth date and fifth date. The fourth was the night after two of my wisdom teeth were taken out. The sutures were still in my mouth. I pleasured her—I think in high school we called it "third base"—and she wanted to go to sleep when I was done. Before she did, she told me her younger brothers sleep in igloos in Utah. They burn a candle in the middle of it and it keeps them warm all night. I didn't believe her. "Weren't you ever in the Boy Scouts?" she asked me.

a. On the fifth date, she bit me on the shoulder. We weren't even doing it. She just bit me.

16. That was our last date. I never spoke to Anna again after that night. The night guard and Anna may have dated after that. I don't know. They might be married by now, living in Queens somewhere. Salt Lake City, Westchester.

a. In the middle of winter, when my wife and I are sharing the couch at either ends, wrapped in blankets to keep us warm, I sometimes lick my wife's toes to get on her nerves. One night I held onto one of her legs for dear life as I licked away. She kicked back like a horse and gave me a bloody nose.

b. In the marginalia in my journal's account of the Footlicking Story, I've written down the following language. I am fairly sure it's by contemporary philosopher John R. Searle. It's called "How To Promise: A Complicated Way": *Given that a speaker S utters a sentence T in the presence of a hearer H, then, in the literal utterance of T, S sincerely and non-defectively promises that p to H.*

c. I think at some point I thought I could figure out The Footlicker Story using math. Or something. I don't know what "p" represents in the above point. The truth is, none of this makes sense, especially in the winter in the mid-nineties, in New York City, on a second shift in midtown, on the L train, or on the Bowery in an illegal sublet, even with the folklore studies and the philosophy of language thrown in, even now as I write this in my office at a historically Catholic college in Albany. Licking someone else's feet for ten bucks probably makes just as much sense as anything else.

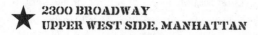

★ **2300 BROADWAY**
   UPPER WEST SIDE, MANHATTAN

THE SAWED-OFF PAST
BY ABIGAIL THOMAS

I'm sitting in the essay aisle at Barnes & Noble trying to change my socks. I don't have an apartment anymore so this is my pit-stop, Broadway and Eighty-third Street. On one side of me is Vivian Gornick's *At Eye Level,* and on the other the complete essays of Montaigne. I'm planning to take a look at both, but first things first. I bought new shoes on my way to the city and wore them out of the store, and the shoes are green with pink dots and my socks don't match. Normally this wouldn't bother me but these really don't match, it offends the eyes to look at my feet. A young couple appears and settles down at the tail end of fiction which is four feet away. They are making a sound, which if they were older would be called chuckling, and he wants her to buy a book called Sex Something-Something but she doesn't want that one. He won't let go of her or stop doing to her whatever it is he's doing until she agrees to buy the book with sex in the title, but she continues to resist.

If I weren't busy, I'd be eavesdropping properly but instead I'm struggling to remove the black sock with red peppers from my left foot. I had hoped for privacy. It's hard to sit on the floor and change your socks without looking as though you're sitting on the floor changing your socks, especially when you're sixty-three. I finally manage to yank them both off and slip on the new pink anklets, then slide back into my shoes. My feet are now a vision of loveliness. The young couple is whispering, perhaps discussing the likelihood that I am insane, but I don't glance in their direction. I open the Montaigne at random. "Of Drunkeness." Ah yes. You can do most anything in this friendly Barnes & Noble; it was at this branch that a man once sat undisturbed in a chair in the travel section, all day and all night, only to have it turn out, at closing, that he was dead.

Hours later I'm sitting on a bench in front of the bagel store on Sixth Avenue and Thirteenth Street eating an everything bagel with cream cheese and trying not to spill any of it on my student's story when a gentleman with reddish-gray stubble on his face sits down next to me. This is a small bench. He smells of unwashed hair, old sweat, and he is talking. At first I think he has a cell phone because he speaks and pauses, speaks again, asking someone if he'd like to come home. I check quickly, no cell phone. He asks again, politely giving himself time to think about his answer. From the corner of my eye I see him pull a pack of cigarettes out of his breast pocket and then he searches for a light in the pocket of his jacket which is right next to the pocket of my jacket. "Some other time," he is saying. I am still carefully eating my bagel but the everythings are falling on the title page. Finally he stands up to retrieve the matches, lights his cigarette and sits down. Two drags later he gets up again. "Well," he says to himself, "see you tomorrow," and then he takes off.

Bagel eaten, I rummage through my bag, which is stuffed to overflowing with twenty or thirty single-spaced typed pages held together with a bobby pin and many creased soiled manila envelopes, a camisole (I can explain everything), a pair of dirty socks, three lipsticks, one mascara wand, a paper bag stuffed with tissue paper, napkins, two empty plastic bags, one poetry anthology (paid for), three diaries full of scribblings and shopping lists, various other pieces of balled-up paper, a pen from a realtor in a different state and another from a hotel in South Carolina, and some cutlery just in case. I have a friend who always carries a copy of the United States Constitution in her bag in case she gets a chance to read it someday. It isn't lost on me that to the casual observer I might appear for the second time today to be a person whose eye it is advisable to avoid, but I want to see if there are poppy seeds stuck in my teeth and I'm looking for my mirror. Pawing through this rubbish I'm about one plastic spoon shy of starting to shriek or mutter, but here comes my student. Well, I just won't smile at him, that's all. Thank god I changed my socks.

Class is over, it's ten-forty-five and I take the subway to 111th where I parked under a construction scaffolding this morning thinking *que sera sera*, and after I buy my big black coffee I am happy to find the car unscathed. This is my old neighborhood. One block from here, a painting that used to hang in my apartment went for sale on a card table in front of Academy Hardware. I know because the painter herself found it on the street and bought it back and then she called me up. I had not meant to throw it out, I told her, but in truth, I had.

I've got more past than future, why drag it around? I threw out everything when I moved. Thirty years of diaries. I even tossed the one that began "Today I married my darling" (but not before sitting down on the floor to read it through). It was terribly personal and terribly boring, not even useful as Cliff Notes on a life. How liberating! The minute I threw it into the trash I remembered how the judge had been late and the party in full swing. I'd been afraid he wasn't coming, that he'd forgotten, or lost the address, or the phone number, that he was sick or stuck, that he was going to be a no-show. Rich put his arms around me. "Never mind," he said, "we'll go on our honeymoon and get married when we come back." Was I comforted? I must have thought, that's sweet but where's the judge Now I think, oh my god, what a nice man I married.

I drive back to Woodstock drinking coffee and blasting Leon Russell and I get home at twelve-thirty to three excited dogs. There is a varmint in the yard and they'd like to get busy. Forget about it, I say, this is bear season. I breathe the night, go to bed with the rest of my pack, and wake up in the morning with a sawed-off past and a future I can't imagine.

In the morning I decide to go through the rubbish in my bag, most of it easy to toss. I gave up the keys to my old apartment, but there are still four keys left on my key ring; I have no idea what they used to unlock, but I'm going to hang on to them. One of them might have opened my parents' house, which was sold years ago. My sister has dreams that our parents appear at her door, asking why they can't go home.

"What do you tell them?" I ask, horrified.

"I skirt the issue," she says and we both laugh. "But there was this one dream, I think they were younger. They were in the driveway and so was I. They wanted to go in the house and I told them they'd been gone a long time and somebody else lived there now."

"Then what?" I ask.

"I don't remember," my sister says.

"How did they look? What did they say?"

"It was a dream. I woke up."

"But…"

"It was a dream," my sister says again.

There was a very old magnolia in their yard, and I remember standing under it with my father one day when the thick petals were mostly on the ground, making a lush slippery carpet underfoot. "This is an example of nature's profligacy," my father said rather proudly, as if he had been somehow responsible. My memory has filed this together with something else he said another time—how nature wastes nothing, everything is used again and again, nothing vanishes, it is only forms that change. Did he say the next thing outright or did I make it up? Why go to all that trouble just to waste a soul?

SURVIVING THE FIVE BORO BIKE TOUR

BY BRYAN CHARLES

That winter, I spent two months in Michigan working on a book. Halfway through, my girlfriend called and said her parents were visiting New York soon, coming from California to ride in the annual Five Boro Bike Tour. She said they wanted us to do it with them. I said I'd think about it, which really meant no. A couple days later she brought it up again, this time saying she thought it'd be a cool thing—we'd see the city as we'd never seen it before, ride in places typically closed to bicyclists. She said her parents were so eager for us to accompany them they'd spring for the entry fee and rent us some gear.

"When is it?" I said.

"I'll have to double check," said Karla, "but it's sometime in May."

In the end I said yes. I had other things on my mind and May seemed far away.

Around the first of April I rolled back to the city. Shortly after my return Karla and I had lunch with my friends Saïd and Karen. We went to Patsy's, on University Place. Saïd and Karen

713

are the quintessential urban bike-riding couple—they ride pretty much everywhere and own sturdy bikes with baskets on the handlebars for parcels—and as we sat there eating pizza I mentioned this thing, this race or whatever, that Karla and I would be doing, the details of which were vague in my mind.

"The Five Boro Bike Tour?" said Saïd.

"Yeah. Have you done it?"

"I've done it a couple times."

"How is it?"

"Well it's interesting but it's—"

He looked at me with a measure of concern. I've known Saïd a long time—he knows I'm not Mr. Fitness. I don't belong to a gym or own a bike or go running or anything like that.

"When it was over I definitely felt it," he said.

"How long is this thing?"

"It's probably a good...forty, fifty miles."

"Forty or fifty miles."

I suppose on some level I should've known this—I mean it's all five boroughs of one of the world's largest cities. But the whole thing had come together quickly and I hadn't given it much thought.

"Fuck that," I said, "I can't do that."

Karla reminded me I'd already been entered. A number had been assigned to me, a bike rented in my name. Everyone assured me I'd get through it—it wouldn't be that bad. All right, I thought. I still had some time. I could start training somehow, get myself in some kind of shape. I reached for another slice of pizza, shoved it into my face.

The days passed. I thought of nothing but finishing my book. I spent long hours working on it, moving only from the desk to the bathroom to the kitchen and back, breaking the monotony with sets of push-ups, which I'd read in the *Times* were an excellent barometer of physical fitness. At the end of the day, I'd watch three of four episodes of *The Wire*. Finally the draft of my novel was complete.

A week before the tour, Karla and I went to Provincetown, the beautiful resort community at the tip of Cape Cod. Many of the businesses were just opening up for the season. Saturday afternoon we stopped at a place on Commercial Street and rented some bikes. I asked the kid who worked there where we should go. He gave me a map and pointed out some trails. We set off for them. It was leisurely at first—we rode along on a residential street, crossed a highway, and went up a small hill. At the top of the hill, we crossed over and entered the trail, which was mellow for a time, then became more challenging. Soon it was clear neither of us was prepared for this. We were out in the middle of some dunes, climbing steep hills in the blazing sun with no water. My chest burned and I was panting and my legs had gone rubbery. Occasionally other bikers would pass us, real bike people with helmets and biker shorts and water bottles in holders attached to their bike frames. I thought of the Five Boro Bike Tour as sweat poured down my face. We came to a particularly grueling incline and Karla and I stopped and walked our bikes.

"I can't do this thing next week. You're gonna have to tell your parents."

"Let's talk about that later," she said. "For now let's just get to the visitor's center and get some water."

But the visitor's center was closed, it wouldn't be open for another week, and the water fountain was turned off. Karla and I sat there catching our breath. I felt like I'd just completed a triathlon, though we'd only ridden about four miles.

"I'm serious," I said. "I can't do that fucking race."

She didn't respond.

The following weekend her parents arrived. The night before the tour we all stayed in Manhattan, at the Maritime Hotel. We ate a huge meal at La Bottega, the Italian restaurant in the Maritime, then retired for the night. Karla and I read for a while, then got ready for bed. Around eleven o'clock I lay my head on the pillow, feeling full and sleepy. I closed my eyes, began to drift. Seconds later the noise began. I had trouble placing it at first—I thought it was a TV or a video game in one of the neighboring rooms. It was loud and low, bass-heavy—not only heard but felt.

"What is that?" said Karla.

"I don't know."

"Is it coming from outside?"

I went to the window and pulled back the curtain. Across the way were dark windows and the figures of people moving behind them. Occasionally what appeared to be a camera flash would go off. The noise—the music—was coming from there.

It was a fucking nightclub.

Inside the hotel.

I lay back down and tried to ignore it. We tried to sleep but we couldn't. We called the front desk to complain and a young man with a laid-back demeanor came to the room moments later holding a large circular pad resembling a hot tub cover, which he fitted snugly into the room's window.

"There you go," he said, "that oughta do it."

But it did not do it. The music continued through the night and in fact only got crazier and more bass-heavy the later it got. I'd never experienced anything quite like it—it was as if our room was inside the club's bathroom, is how fucking loud it was. We called the front desk another few times, explaining that we had to be up quite early and that this noise was outrageous. Finally we asked to be moved the next day.

I'd abandoned the idea of getting any sleep. I went on the Internet and read Frank Rich, whose column had been posted on the *Times*' homepage at midnight, then scanned some travel websites to see if I could find anything about this crazy scene at the Maritime. I learned the club was called Hiro—the name appeared in several negative user reviews of the hotel.

"SHOCKING LOUDNESS!" read the most emphatic. "Don't stay here unless you plan on staying up till 4 a.m. every night."

Sure enough, a little after four the music from Hiro cut out. A while after that, for the first time that night, I fell asleep.

Three hours later I was on a rented bike, unsteadily navigating the wet empty streets of Sunday morning Manhattan. I wore jeans and a helmet and a hoodie. I rode to the starting point in lower Manhattan. I joined a gathering of thirty thousand other cyclists waiting for the event to begin.

The early stages had a hallucinatory feel—did I really just see a giant pro-Obama sign in the window of Gray's Papaya? I rode up Sixth Avenue unaware of what my body was doing. It was an overcast morning, cool and damp. The wind numbed my fingers. A few blocks south of Fifty-seventh Street came the first of several delays. I found myself stopped on Sixth Avenue, between Fifty-fourth and Fifty-fifth, staring at the office building I'd worked in the previous year—it was the job I'd quit right before I went to Michigan. The building seemed to mock me somehow. A moment later I was in Central Park, cruising along, breathing in the smell of wet trees and grass, checking out the early morning joggers and dog walkers as I passed. Already it seemed like I'd been on the bike a long time.

After the park we rode through Harlem, were briefly in the Bronx, then shot down the FDR Drive. There were rest stops every few miles that supplied water and bananas and energy bars and, inexplicably, those little packages of bright orange peanut butter crackers. I ate pack after pack of those crackers throughout the day.

We rode over the bridge into Queens. Around this time the clouds moved on and the sun came out. I had to hand it to Karla's folks—they're in excellent shape. They rode along as if it were nothing. I myself passed through many phases: exhilaration, exhaustion, delirium, boredom, wonderment, anger, exhaustion, exhilaration. At one of the rest areas I saw a sign that said "15 miles to Festival Site."

"Fifteen miles," I said to Karla, "that's not too bad."

Then I said, "Wait, what the fuck am I saying?"

We crossed the Pulaski Bridge into Greenpoint, went down through Williamsburg. I got my second and third and tenth winds. At last we reached the Verrazano Bridge, on the other side of which was Staten Island and the Festival Site—in theory at least the end of the line.

I entered the ramp to the bridge, clicked into the lowest gear. Here, after everything, was the most punishing part of the day, ascending that long, deceptive incline. I kept thinking I'd reached the summit, kept realizing I was wrong. I vowed not to walk, or stop and admire the view, as others were doing. Riding across the Verrazano Bridge became a metaphor for every hard or impossible thing I'd ever done or dreamed of doing: moving to New York City, writing and selling my first novel, finally finishing the second one, surviving job after shitty fucking office job with my head still intact. As I pedaled I realized I could end the pain by getting off my bike, walking a few steps and jumping over the side of the bridge. The cool blue water below called out to me. It was a strange feeling but I got through it. I reached the top of the grade. The downhill began.

Back at the Maritime, I carried my bike up the stairs and went into the lobby. I was the first to arrive. I went immediately into the bar and ordered a beer. My body felt like a used-up thing. But it was all right. It felt good. I took the first sip of cold beer and it was wonderful.

"What's with that club?" I said to the bartender. "It kept me awake all night."

"Hiro?" she said.

"Yeah. Who would put a nightclub inside a functioning hotel?"

"You can talk to the front desk and see if maybe they can move you."

It had already happened. Our things had been moved to a different room on a higher floor while we were out on our fifty-mile odyssey. That night sleep came instantly, as if I'd dropped from a great height into a permanent void.

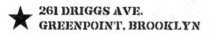

★ **261 DRIGGS AVE.**
  GREENPOINT, BROOKLYN

BEING STEVE MALKMUS

BY BRYAN CHARLES

Sometime in, I think, the summer of 1993, I was walking with a friend of mine down Westnedge Avenue, in Kalamazoo, MI. We were talking about rock music, and my friend, who's about as brainy as they come, got onto the subject of the band Pavement. More specifically, he began deconstructing what he perceived to be the average Pavement fan. "College student," he said. "Sensitive, liberal politics, probably with an interest in literature or some other academic pursuit. Someone just like me, in other words."

I didn't understand or really care what he was getting at until many years later, when, standing in a crowd at a Pavement show, waiting for the band to come on, I took a good long look around from my usual position near the front of the stage, left side, and saw in the crowd my own face reflected a thousand times. That is, the room was filled largely with young white gentlemen, many of them bespectacled, with vaguely unkempt brown hair, faces either blank or fixed in portraits of smirking cool, seemingly unaware that a band they enjoyed enough to spend twenty dollars to see was at any moment going to take the stage. This was at Irving Plaza in June of 1999, the first show of a three-night stand. Pavement was touring in support of *Terror Twilight*, their most highly polished album. It was also rumored, even then, even that night, to be their last, but I was not prepared to accept that. I was having difficulty enough accepting the mere fact of my fandom.

It's always a bit of a crusher to realize one is not unique—or should I say, when I realize, as I often do, that I am not unique?—but it hit me particularly hard that night, as I stood ensconced in all those me's. And it hit me the next night, too, at the second show, when I looked around and saw all the same faces. Well, different but the same.

Recently, Stephen Malkmus's new band, the Jicks, played at the Warsaw, a relatively new venue only about five blocks from my apartment. Despite the novelty of having one of my favorite musical artists play so near me—Greenpoint, I've been told by every friend who's visited me here, is a pain in the ass to get to—I was fully prepared not to go. I had anticipated the crowd's sameness and was willing to forego the probability of pleasure in order to escape its diminishing effects. But a friend offered me a free ticket and then another friend signed on to the deal and the next thing I knew we were sitting in my living room, waiting to go to the Warsaw.

I explained my theory—is it worthy of even being called a theory?—on the homogeneity of the average indie rock crowd. And my friend Al said, "It can be tough to take, but it's especially hard at a Steve Malkmus show when you realize that not only are you like everyone else there, you're also not Steve Malkmus."

It is often said of a certain kind of male figure: "Women want to be with him, and men want to be him." This statement could not be truer of Stephen Malkmus. I saw Pavement four times and I've seen the Jicks twice now, and if there is a factor that unifies the crowds at these shows even more than whiteness, it's the outpouring of love and envy Malkmus is able to evoke with the slightest grin or flip of his skater bangs. Although perhaps I am projecting; perhaps I sense that love and envy most strongly in my own head.

In *Side Effects*, Woody Allen wrote that "his one regret in life is that he is not someone else." I understand this completely, and have regretted more than once, more than a dozen times, that I am not Stephen Malkmus. Malkmus envy, for me, began on a very basic, fundamental level: with the songs.

The first of his songs that I wished I'd written was "Here," from *Slanted and Enchanted*. It had that quality—simplicity—that causes would-be songwriters to go, "Fuck, why didn't I think of that?" ("Smells Like Teen Spirit," if you'll recall, was a thunderingly simple riff, with the same four notes repeated throughout the verses and the chorus.) Most of "Here" (at least the way I learned it) is just A, E and D. But that's only half of it. There's the melody, which pretty much makes the song, and the lyrics—particularly that famous first line ("I was dressed for success/But success, it never comes")—which still have the power, under the right circumstances, to cause to me to doubt every decision I've ever made.

In 2001, "Here" was described in the *New York Times* as Malkmus's "crowning sad-sack song," but I think that's doing it a disservice. (The article, in fact, was tinged with condescension, devoting columns of unnecessary ink to the tired concept of Malkmus as an "ironic" "slacker" and ending with the line, "The longing for the genuine, musically or otherwise, calls for brighter corners.") True, the song is a downer, but it's also about as exhilarating as recorded music gets in terms of sheer evocative power. The passing decade may have dulled the memories of certain rock critics now busy praising the White Stripes, but it's all still there, the power and beauty and energy of Pavement. Pick up the *Slanted and Enchanted* reissue if you don't believe me. Put on disc one and pretend that you haven't read a thousand articles about how the Strokes are saving rock and you'll see what I mean. I like the Strokes well enough, but a dude in a leather jacket with greasy hair singing about fun in the sun will never have the same resonance as the wordless chorus of "In the Mouth a Desert."

I could go on all day praising my favorite Malkmus tunes and quoting my favorite lines from, say, *Brighten the Corners*; I could relate at least two memorable anecdotes from my life that had "Grounded," my all-time favorite Pavement song, as the soundtrack; I could tell you about riding the Lexington Avenue subway with the Jicks' first record playing in my headphones, on my way to end a weird emotional stand-off I had going with an ex-girlfriend.

Then there's the period, approximately one month in duration, where I played "Vague Space" every morning as I walked from the subway to my job in the World Trade Center. (The song lasted exactly as long as the walk from the Cortland Street subway platform to the elevator banks.) And then there's this morning, when I stood alone in my kitchen, guitar strapped on, and played a cover of "Jenny and the Ess-Dog" for no one.

But Malkmus envy is about more than music. It's about attitude.

For the purposes of writing this, I've tried to trace the origins of my fixation on Stephen Malkmus as something other than a songwriting entity, and believe it struck first in late 1997, at a club in Grand Rapids, MI, called the Intersection. It was the first time I'd seen Pavement and also, because I was largely oblivious to much of the band's press over the years, my first encounter with the Stephen Malkmus persona. It happened like this: the band took the stage to great fanfare before a crowd of mostly young white males. Malkmus, after rubbing his nose and acknowledging his allergies, said something like, "It's great to be here in central Michigan." Some kid to my left, distraught by the geographic inaccuracy of the statement, yelled, "It's Western! Western Michigan!" Malkmus looked the kid in the eye, with apparent disdain, and said casually: "Whatever."

Yes, I thought, and felt the vague first stirrings of infatuation.

Flash forward to the Irving Plaza shows. There's a guy in the front row shouting intermittent requests for "Harness Your Hopes." (This is a B-side from the U.K. "Carrot Rope" single, and presumably a cooler song to request than "Cut Your Hair,"

Pavement's one and only near-hit.) Finally, about mid-set, after maybe the fifth or sixth exhortation, Malkmus stares the guy down, flashes the old index-and-thumb okay sign, and says, "Yeah, that's one of our songs. Congratulations."

I'm fairly high-strung and tend to envy people whose inner monologues I perceive to be smoother than my own (whether they actually are or not), and those kinds of breezily dismissive comments from a person so talented and handsome, so seemingly self-assured, were something I felt irrational glee at having witnessed.

I also noticed during that show Malkmus's tendency to alter slightly his delivery of certain lyrics, as if to squash potential sing-alongs on purpose. The chorus of "Shady Lane," for instance, became a staccato "Ev-ry-body. Wants. One." And the "Range Life" diss of the Smashing Pumpkins which supposedly kept Pavement out of Lollapalooza '94 became something else entirely: "Out on tour with the Smashing Shitheads / Nature kids, they don't have no shit in their heads."

Critics of Pavement—and later, Malkmus's solo work and even the man himself—claimed this alleged detachment was exactly the thing they disliked about the band. But I never quite saw it as detachment, just as I never bought into the myth of Pavement as a group of self-consciously ironic slackers (no band makes it to *The Tonight Show* by virtue of a half-hearted try). My own interpretation of Malkmus's sarcasm is that it's a form of resistance or confrontation: fuck you if you get it, fuck you if you don't. Sort of like Kurt Cobain flipping off the world on the inside of the *Nevermind* album, only more subtle, possibly even more interesting.

Speaking of Kurt Cobain, there's a bit in *Heavier Than Heaven,* the biography by Charles R. Cross, where Kurt's walking through the MoMA—this is at the height of his fame and drug addiction—and is approached by a young black fan. "Kurt had been asked for his autograph a hundred times that day," Cross writes, "but this was the only time he responded with a smile. Kurt told (Amy) Finnerty, 'No one black has ever said they liked my record before.'"

It seems that Kurt, in addition to numerous other troubles, was plagued by at least a touch of white guilt. (Think also of the *Incesticide* liner notes and his somewhat misguided attack on white corporate America.) So what is it about punk and indie rock that prevents large-scale acceptance across the color lines? Hip-hop, though still largely the domain of black artists, has crossed over so thoroughly that the majority of rap records are now purchased by white suburban teenagers. I'm not suggesting the reverse could ever be true for indie rock, but aren't there at least a few black people out there who get turned on by songs about Yul Brynner with lyrics that go, "I'll tie you to a chair/the house music will blare/and turn your ears into a medicinal jelly"? If so, they were not in attendance at the Warsaw on the night of the Jicks show. Instead it was the typical assemblage of unemployed, hopelessly-aspiring-writer grad students, teetering on the edge of spectacular personal failure. But I suppose I shouldn't speak for everyone.

The Warsaw, which looks from the outside like just another dingy Greenpoint bar, is actually a terrific place to see a show. Bands play in an adjoining space resembling a large high school gym with a stage at the end, similar to the Bowery Ballroom, only larger. I arrived with friends but the group splintered after the opening band and I wandered through the crowd until I was standing a few feet from the stage. Again I glanced casually around and took stock, but the sameness of the crowd didn't trouble me as it had in years past, though I admit I briefly tried to force the issue. I was heartened to see some younger faces. Indie rock has evolved considerably since Pavement's heyday, and I was unsure if the kids had pledged allegiance entirely to Bright Eyes or any of a host of newer bands competing for time on their iPods.

I'd like to report that the intervening years helped put my Malkmus infatuation into perspective as well, but that's just not the case. The moment he took the stage and began tuning his guitars—what, no more guitar techs?—the old feelings of inadequacy came rushing to the fore. I'll never have a sound or vision that recognizably my own, I thought, and my hair could never look that cool.

The band was in fine form, far tighter and more confident than the first time I'd seen them, shortly after the first record came out. And while the band was tighter, Stephen Malkmus himself seemed far looser and less icy than at three of the four Pavement shows I saw. (The last was the Matador tenth-anniversary show—the band's final appearance in New York—in September of 1999, and he seemed happier to be up there, maybe because he knew the end was near. Or here.)

Listen to all five Pavement records and the Jicks records back to back and you can trace Malkmus's prodigious growth, not only as a songwriter, but also a guitar player. The turning point, I think, from indie guy with a penchant for writing beautiful drop-D-tuned melodies, to potential guitar hero, is the solo in "Rattled by the Rush," which I've never bothered trying to figure out because I don't want to deconstruct, and therefore diminish, its greatness. The flurry of guitar brilliance at the Warsaw reached an obvious zenith during the show's closing number, "1% of One." I swear it lasted twenty minutes, and though I usually hate a monster jam (I once walked out of a Built to Spill show in a near-rage), the sheer fine guitar playing was enough to carry the day.

Not only that, but my crush on Malkmus was eclipsed suddenly by a crush I developed on Joanna Bolme, the Jicks' bass player. The indie rock trail is littered with foxy female bassists, but Bolme has something that elevates her above, say, Kim Deal or D'arcy Wretsky, and it could either be the way she looks when exhaling cigarette smoke or the bass line from "Church on White."

The show that night was a holiday benefit, complete with a raffle, and between the end of the set and the encore, Malkmus came out with a piece of paper and announced he was going to read the winning numbers. It seemed perfectly reasonable at first, but as the process wore on—there was an unusually long list of prizes, from T-shirts to DVDs—and he dutifully recited row after row of digits, I had an odd perception, confirmed moments later by Malkmus himself. "I feel like I revealed myself more just now," he said, "than any time during the whole show." Then he threw down the paper and picked up his guitar.

200 W. 34TH ST.
MIDTOWN, MANHATTAN

A WAITRESS ON THE CONVENTION FLOOR

BY MARTHA BURZYNSKI

I expected to lose some dignity, I just didn't expect to lose it on the convention floor.

During the month of August, the New York party business is in a coma—waitstaff and chefs either decamp to the Hamptons where there is plenty of work or to vacation themselves. But last summer there were so many parties in town that the waitstaff could pick and choose. I was broke and the only one I turned down was the "W" Stands For Women party.

The night I cried on the convention floor, I had seen tears of joy from excited delegates—Dick Cheney was about to speak. Our kitchen was on Radio Row and every time I trundled another tray of cheeseburgers to the biggest contributors to the RNC—one million dollars plus—I'd hear the voices from my nightmares asking for another. They ate so much their stares didn't linger on my cleavage until the tray was empty. But for every innocuous comment about the food ("good for New York") there was the author of *It's My Country, Too* who had never worked in his life but wanted to speak for everyone his age (my age) who

726

had to, and the red-state blogger who asked where his dessert was after he grabbed my ass.

The chefs just joked that he was just doing what they all wanted to do. I went back out with two trays precariously balanced and heavy. Pausing at the end of the row, waiting for the area to clear, I listened as a delegate gave a radio interview. He wasn't a local politician, he wasn't anyone's boss but he was representing his home and spoke for his people when he said that the issue that deserved the most attention was the greed of the gays. They wanted special privileges, he said, more than they needed, and they wanted everyone else to pay for them. I dropped the trays on the dirty grey carpet and just cried. A service napkin, a coarse polyester rag, was the only thing I had to hide my tears, but it was full of hamburger grease and only irritated my eyes. The delegate didn't notice, nor did anyone but my boss, because they only saw the free food gone and the trays empty.

Breaking down the kitchen at the end of the night, I was approached by a couple of print reporters asking how many of the staff were Democrats and what we got out of this. I said that I had no problem taking their money. That Friday, two dear friends of mine were getting married, and it was the RNC that was paying my way to go to their same-sex wedding.

PAUL NEWMAN ON SIXTH AVENUE

BY MADGE McKEITHEN

He kneels on the gray-black slate in front of the Jefferson Market, rendering blue eyes in pastels on the sidewalk, the magazine cover of Paul Newman under his left knee—only the eyes done after several hours.

I had passed by the artist at ten in the morning. He was just starting, no eyes yet, only the box of pastels dumped onto the sidewalk, a few marks bringing to mind the elaborate pastel Virgin Mary often underfoot a block east.

Since then, I'd read papers, marked them, read Ian Frazier and Jason Shinder and Virginia Woolf and a bit of a Coltrane biography trying to find inspiration to pass along to my students. I'd eaten pesto chicken at Lenny's chopped with a cleaver in a stainless steel bowl. I'd read what I wanted to more than what I should. I had scribbled the beginning of a poem once the edge was off my hunger.

Earlier, on the elliptical at the Y, I'd had what seemed a bit of an epiphany about love and the story I'm working on, not long after I saw donnybrook in Maureen Dowd's column that put Paul Krugman in his place though he'd done that himself the day before. And I'd updated my will, wondered why I had said yes to another date with a man, booked a Halloween flight to North Carolina to hear what the doctor had to say about my father's aging brain. I'd felt relieved because the day before, Crystal, who cuts my hair, had asked me what I was going to be for Halloween and I'd planned nothing, already feeling enough like a loser what with my "wusband" announcing he'll remarry in 2009, proving himself a grand optimist in our age of pessimism. I was the one who'd encouraged him to go to the power of positive thinking counselor. Where would I stand now?

At two o'clock, I pass by again and the crouching artist has completed the eyes—only the eyes. Did he erase them several times? Would the hair, the forehead be harder? Would it end up looking like Paul Newman? For only a second, he looks up at me and then he's back to work. For only a second the broad man sitting in the sun at French Roast in the brown corduroy blazer spread open to show a white shirt spread open to show white chest hair grins broadly from behind black glasses. The sky is blue and the day clear and the poet I've just read, who died in April, wrote: *to be in love is like going outside / to see what kind of day it is.*

I knew Paul Newman could not really have been eighty-three. Since *Butch Cassidy*, I had known Paul Newman was my age and belonged to me. My son, Nick, long familiar with Newman's Own salad dressings, knew him to be perpetually sixty-one. A few days after his death, I saw a *USA Today* on the counter at the Holiday Inn Express in the small North Carolina town where my parents live. In the upper margin of the front page boxed in red was: "Paul Newman: 'Nothing ever came easy to me.'"

My father is eighty-three. We have few sustained conversations now. I think of him pulling up a soft coverlet of dementia. Usually gently, sometimes not, he is nestling down beneath it. He says to me, "Not everything is to be set right in this world." Emphasis on *this*. It's always been that way with him; the afterlife as matter of fact to him as summer corn and spring honey. Many days now he marvels aloud at how good people were to him when he was seventeen and eighteen and a private in the army. He said to me on the phone not long ago, "I'm just now figuring out how to love you."

I'm new to the doorman feature of life in New York. I watch others in my building and try to imitate them—friendly but formal. I try to respect the doormen's need for space and privacy. Yet on some days the kindness and respect they show as I pass form the richest of moments. *The tenderness / that comes from those / I don't know / has become a fire / that burns / even after the fire / is out*. Edwin, with the most beautiful brown eyes I've bothered to notice in a long time, opens the door. "The mail is already here," he says and smiles and calls me by my name.

I #&($*! NY

BY BONNY FINBERG

6:30 a.m. I've only been able to sleep about six hours because there are three bars downstairs which close at around 3 a.m. It's just getting light. I'm in a corner apartment on the sixth floor overlooking Orchard and Stanton Streets facing south and east. The morning sky is streaked with indigo, pink and brown. I close my eyes hoping to sleep another hour. I lie in bed as long as possible listening to the radio because it helps me wake up thinking about something other than the job I don't want to go to.

With my eyes closed, I listen to: war in Iraq; a black man killed by cops on the morning of his wedding day; mental exercises to keep you from losing your memory.

But what if you lose your mind first, or get killed by a terrorist, or rogue cops, or die from a lack of water, air, or a planet to live on?

8 a.m. I get up from the air mattress, which is covered with navy blue bedding except for a red pillowcase—I only mention this because I'm renting a room, so they're not my sheets, and I'm enjoying the exoticism of someone else's color sense.

8: 30 a.m. I usually get up because I want time make coffee, but it doesn't matter today because I ran out about ten days ago.

LOST AND FOUND

I've been buying my morning coffee at the deli on the corner on my way to the bus stop.

Everyone speaks to each other in Arabic, except when they ask how you want your coffee. I wish I could understand what they're saying. There's a young guy at the cash register whose name is Ahmed. His eyelids are always half-closed. I ask for a cup of coffee, and he says before I do, "coffee—no sugar, milk." He smiles because he knows what I want.

8:45 a.m. Today I'm working in the West Village and can walk there across Houston Street, which I don't enjoy because one part of the street looks like Dresden after the war, and another part looks like a big night in Cincinnati. But I can walk along Allen Street past the Chinese pastry shop and get a red bean bun to go with my coffee, breakfast on foot, even though I would rather eat it sitting down.

Houston Street is a broad boulevard that runs east/west from river to river. I come to the first big intersection, which is Lafayette Street. Kate Moss and Kate Moss loom overhead, with four breasts as big as cars and four eyes as big as windows. The two of her peer down at the chaos below, silky clean, threatening to step off the side of the building onto Houston Street like Kate-zilla.

9 a.m. I turn up Sullivan Street, late for work, where I spend a few hours and get it over with. It sounds like prostitution, and that's pretty much what it feels like.

2 p.m. I leave work hungry, so I walk east and stop at Yonah Schimmel's Knishes. The place smells like fried onions mixed with mashed potatoes—the homiest smell I can think of because after school my grandmother used to give me warm potatoes mashed with fried onions and chicken fat, spread on matzoh.

I'm eating my knish in mindless bliss, walking past the Indian guy who sells fruit on First Street and First Avenue. He jumps into my path and asks, "What are you eating?" I tell him and he asks if he can have a taste. I break off a lump. "That's good!" he says, and asks where I got it. I point across the street. "Can you get me one?" he says. "I can't leave my fruit stand."

"I'm in a hurry," I say. "Want some of mine?"

"Sure."

3:00 p.m. I drop in on my friend Shalom's Fusion Arts Museum on Stanton Street. He bought the building about twenty years ago from a man named Mr. Human, who kept it full of garbage and dogs and who never went outside.

Shalom cleaned out the building and opened his gallery, which features art that is "multi-sensory." ("Why submit to a canvas?" he says.) We talk about the current exhibit, "Heavy Water," honoring the work of Italian artist Enrico Baj. This is a fitting show for the Lower East Side, where neighborhood artists are threatened with extinction in the wake of rising real estate prices and more bars per capita than Dublin.

9 p.m. After a nap, I take a bus down to the Seaport area where some fashionistas are having a party. A couple with a baby bought this historic building near the old Fulton Fish Market. They occupy the top three floors. I try to find the right buzzer and see a sign for the party, which says: "If we don't answer, call somebody you know." Someone coming out of the building lets me in.

The crowd is young and well-groomed. Happily, I see two friends. The wine flows, we talk about nothing I can remember, dance like idiots and soon it's time to go. As I'm leaving, I look out the front windows at the parking lot below and the glass-and-steel monoliths a few blocks west. Why would anyone want to spend so much money to live here?

1:30 a.m. I get off the bus and decide to buy a candy bar. I go into Ahmed's deli where he's still behind the counter, his eyes, half-closed. "You're still here?" I ask.

He smiles. "Yeah."

2 a.m. Lights out. In a few hours it will be another early morning that comes too soon.

★ MANHATTAN AVE.
GREENPOINT, BROOKLYN

NEIGHBORS
BY GRAHAM T. BECK

I first went to the northernmost point in Brooklyn after reading an article in *The New Yorker* about the oil spill there—seventeen million gallons, half again as big as the *Exxon Valdez*—which at a geologic pace, made its way from a long gone Standard Oil holding tank in the eastern part of Greenpoint, to the aquifer beneath the neighborhood, to the creek that marks Brooklyn's northern boundary with Queens. The article said there was only one public access point to the water, "a rickety assemblage of wooden boards at the end of Manhattan Avenue," and one Saturday morning I ended up standing there with my friend Dan. We spied the shining water, the Pepsi distributor in Long Island City, the Pulaski Bridge in its muted red, scraps of fishing line, a metal ruler screwed down to the dock and marked at eight and ten inches to measure fresh catch.

Two years later, I moved to the end of Manhattan Avenue—two blocks from the Newtown Creek, caddy-corner from a notorious S.R.O. called the Greenpoint Hotel—into a one-bedroom apartment with crooked wooden floors, a pressed-tin ceiling, and my girlfriend, Erin. We talk about leaving New York like farmers talk about rain, but we're happy where we are for now, cozied into our little place at Brooklyn's end, well past the Polish storefronts, two stories above the final bus stop, diagonal from the hotel, and down the road from the creek.

Long before I read of the Greenpoint Hotel's troubles—the drug dealing, the violence, the hard-up boarders called "a mix of addicts, AIDS sufferers, the recently homeless, and those who are all three," by the *New York Times*—I was spying on it like a nosy neighbor. Almost every day, I'd stare at its crumbling face, pock-marked with buckling tiles. I'd wait for the bus in its messy shadow and sneak past the browning curtains and the spider-cracked glass to the front office, where black and white monitors cut between high-angle hallway shots, and mop buckets and milk crates rest on one another like neatly stacked eggshells.

The sign above it says, "HOTEL," but from the outside it looks like four homes draped in a quilt of siding. The building farthest to the north, the one on the corner of Clay Street and Manhattan Avenue, has a laundromat downstairs and five almost arrow-slit windows splattered along its northern wall. Their slap-dash pattern gives no clue as to how many floors or rooms there might be inside, but offers the impression of a low, narrow, dark interior filled with an improbable number of perpendicular junctions.

Around dinnertime, I'll usually see some of its residents in front of the P&A Deli and nod to the guys I know by sight. There is the young skinny kid with oily ribbons of hair in his face and bad legs who sits folded outside of the expensive grocery store hustling for change at Christmas time. And there's Eddie with the tremors who everyone calls Elvis on account of his matted pompadour. He has the sunken cheeks and the slow stutter of a long-broke drunk and always feeds Rachel's dog; feeds her big bull terrier right out of his shaking hands. Sometimes I talk with Charles—a skinny black guy who wears a mesh-backed union cap and drinks coffee after coffee with my downstairs neighbor Segundo and always nods and waves when I pass him. We'll mostly talk about the weather or the headlines. Sometimes we talk about Flatbush—where he used to live—or his son, or girls. No matter what their age, they're girls. Whenever something happens on the block, we'll talk about the changes and the city. We talk a lot about the city and what it's doing.

LOST AND FOUND

On the Fourth of July that followed my first trip to the northernmost point in Brooklyn, I found myself standing again on the creek's lone dock. We had been riding bikes and drinking beer, looking for a place to watch the coming fireworks. There was a chubby little boy, maybe ten or twelve, out there as well. His hair was wet and his shorts were too; his body goose-pimpled by the breeze. He insisted the water was fine for swimming, cannonballing to prove it. As his head bobbed on treading legs, he called, "it's great," and sprayed a jet of water from his mouth to our feet.

The city replaced the dock at the end of Manhattan Avenue with a vest-pocket park last year. It's still under construction, but the wooden planks are gone, swapped for plantings and benches and mosaic stonework that came in sheets and shows its seams. There is still plenty of oil in the water, along with green and brown films, truck tires, pocket trash, and a few crab pots made from five-gallon buckets and chicken wire. The view, save for some residential skyscrapers now off in the distance, is just about the same.

The city is working on the hotel too. Federal prosecutors filed a motion of foreclosure for it a few years back. In the supporting documents, they allege that since 1998, twenty people have died there, at least one of which was a drug-related murder. 194 rooms, that's how many the brief says are in there; 194 neighbors who might step out to buy milk and bread and twenty-five-cent cakes and return through a labyrinth of halls to find a body.

When there are police cars, fire trucks, or ambulances out front, the shop keepers, coffee-shop girls, and Pentecostal church kids who play touch football on the sidewalk across the street keep on with their business. Deli-front chatter opens from its circle to an observant U.

You can still get down to the water by walking under an industrial building's back stairs. And the Department of Environmental Protection opened a new waterfront park a few blocks south and east of the Avenue. The path there snakes around a bit—through a water treatment plant, past a sand and salt storage yard—but once you're out there you're right on the bank of the Newtown Creek. The city's grasses flap with the gusts of wind that move from Midtown across the East River up the inlet. The water laps at the cement-lined shore with heavy, brackish indifference.

THE FATE OF THE PEAR TREES AT GROUND ZERO

BY BRAM GUNTHER

Two weeks after the shock of September 11th, I was sent to ground zero by the Parks Department Commissioner to make a quick evaluation of the damage to the plant life in the area. The Commissioner wanted to know what had survived, what plants would need to be replaced and how much it would all cost. He was eager to help rejuvenate the area with trees.

I was deputy director of Central Forestry, the unit of the Parks Department that oversees all the city's street trees. If a Park Ranger in Yellowstone is responsible for the preservation and safety of that landscape, Central Forestry is no less responsible for the preservation and safety of New York City's street-tree forest. For my job, and my pleasure, I think about New York City's plants.

I pictured the flora in lower Manhattan covered in a film of ash. After a fire in the forest, the trees and shrubs and wildflowers are all coated in a dust of embers. I assumed that the trees immediately adjacent to the towers, like trees in the direct path of a storm, would be destroyed completely. But nature is unpredictable. Small skinny trees whacked from all sides by powerful winds are left standing

737

and big strong oaks on the periphery of the squall are felled. When I made it to ground zero, I was surprised to see that there were three pear trees no less than two hundred feet away from the carnage which had survived with just a few blemishes.

Pear trees figure often in my professional thoughts. There are about 500,000 street trees citywide. Each year, Central Forestry adds to this number (it's not a straight increase—many dead trees must be removed) by money received from the Mayor, Council members, and Borough Presidents. Since 1997, we have planted approximately 12,000 a year. Thirteen percent of this number are Callery pears (*pyrus calleryana*), the tree most requested by New York City citizens and the fifth most populous tree on our sidewalks. It is particularly widespread in Manhattan, where residents favor its blast of white flowers in the early spring.

In the 1950s, urban landscapers discovered and fell in love with the Callery pear tree from Asia. Shipped home, it was genetically tinkered with here in American plant nurseries, and then turned into a splendid street tree. It didn't drop messy sticky pears on the sidewalk and cars. It flowered richly. And it was unflagging, thriving despite the pollution, the salt used to melt ice, the shit and piss of dogs, and the general ripe debris of the metropolis. For decades, tens of thousands of these trees sprung up along the roads of New York City.

They are not, however, without their weaknesses. They tend to be short-lived and weak-limbed. They have "poor structure," the branches fragile at the juncture with the trunk, which can make them burst open or fall off during bad frosts and storms. And they have a dark furrowed bark that gets stained and ugly.

But they have, in the long run, proven to be a staple of street tree planting, their virtues outweighing their drawbacks. City residents don't seem to tire of the tree's glamorous cloak of white flowers; and when one household suddenly has a specimen on the sidewalk in front of their home, all the neighbors rush to have one too.

On September 25th, I went to ground zero with two colleagues, Gail and Doug. Gail is the chief landscape designer for the unit and Doug an excellent urban forester. As we traveled from our office in Queens, life, viewed from inside our jeep, seemed regular. At Canal Street, however, the police presence surged, and we were only able to get through the checkpoints because of my badge. As we approached the towers, the smell in the air changed from standard car exhaust sootiness to a fire-laden decay. There was a layer of sparkling gray soot on the leaves, on the soil in the tree pits, on the surface of the buildings, on people's clothes, flaking the streets.

Gail was pregnant, and her husband had banned her from getting out of the car and inhaling the impurities in the air. He had even restricted her from having the windows opened in the car. Being banned from something is antithetical to Gail, and she was near bristling. She is assiduously independent. She tends to trust that her strength and purity of spirit and enterprise will prevail over the world's rottenness. To have to seriously consider being caged in the car while Doug and I got to venture into the "war zone" was like breaking the legs of a world-class runner. ("I feel like a dog," she said.) Self-pityingly, however, she accepted her husband's logic and stayed in the car as Doug and I set out.

After showing my badge and snaking around a line of large trucks, we were told by an officer to go to the second floor of the Burger King to get hard hats and respirators. On the side of the building was spray painted with the word MORGUE and an arrow facing south.

If I had been able to ignore or block out what I knew had happened on the 11th I could have looked out at the devastation and come to the conclusion that lower Manhattan had experienced perhaps an earthquake or volcano blast. It could have been a sad, but sinless site. The rescue workers talked about sports and took bets on the next mayor, and looked fatigued and ponderous. In their midst, Doug and I felt awkward, like trespassers. I averted my eyes downward as I passed the sweaty men and women who had obviously been toiling day after and day since September 11th.

But we wanted our look, we had come all this way. We moved closer to the toppled towers, which looked like an angry frozen dragon. The folded and twisted metal all but snarled.

Then we noticed, on the plaza, perhaps just about two hundred feet away from the towers, three pear trees still standing, alive and unscathed. If you were to have hugged one of these trees during the attack, all the falling wreckage would have missed you. It was amazing, really, and I was bit stunned. We took a few more moments to register what we were seeing, and then turned around and left.

The next day, the three of us came up with an estimation of the injury done to the street trees. It was an educated guess. The real damage to the plants in the near radius of the former Towers won't be revealed until the spring. Most, we gather, will sprout their buds and then their flowers and leaves. Plants have been long adapted to swirls of heavy dust, to eruptions, to fires, to great disturbances. A good rain and a sunny day can usually bring them back to life. By all accounts, if not removed because of the clean-up effort, the pear trees on the plaza of the World Trade Center on some sunny day next April will flower their brilliant white again.

During the week of November 5th, before World Trade Center Number 5 was demolished, the three pear trees were lifted out of their tree pits and taken to a new home. First, a Bobcat removed the decorative wrought iron grating that surrounds each tree. For the most part, the grating was undamaged and was recycled in street-tree pits in other locations. Then a tree spade, which is a bulldozer with a circular claw attachment, sank its teeth into the small hollow and lifted the tree out. The entire specimen, its roots now hanging and loose like disheveled hair and the root ball a giant head of soil (this root ball will be wrapped in burlap), was put on a flat-bed truck and taken to a gardened spot across from City Hall, adjacent to the approach to the Brooklyn Bridge. There, the tree spade dug a large hole and then the pear trees were fit snugly into the ground—quiet green reminders of September 11th.

I LEFT MY YOUTH AT FRED & RUDY'S CANDY STORE

BY PETER CHERCHES

In the sixties, in Brooklyn, a candy store was not the kind of place you went to for chocolate truffles, or even a Whitman sampler. In New York, for many years, the candy store meant the local luncheonette/newsstand. When the Shangri-Las, three girls from Queens, sang "I met him at the candy store," this was the kind of place they were talking about. Old New York candy stores had a similar function to the barber shop in small towns and working-class black neighborhoods. They were places where generations mixed and local gossip was shared.

There were three candy stores in my immediate neighborhood, but our favorite was Fred and Rudy's. Up front were the newsstand, the candy counter and the ice cream case, where they stored the tubs of Breyer's for our cones. Then, as you moved further into the shop, there was the lunch counter, with revolving stools, of course, and booths. As kids we preferred the counter. It was our bar. We'd sit on stools and drink malteds, or egg creams, or cherry-lime Rickeys, or Rock 'n' Root root beer in frosted mugs, or Cokes, large or small, in official Coke glasses. I remember when the price of a small Coke went up from six cents to seven. We often munched on long two-cent stick pretzels while drinking and shooting the bull.

Fred and Rudy were like night and day, good cop and bad cop. Fred Leibowitz was a slight, bald guy with a mustache, a good-humored sweetheart. He reminded me a bit of Groucho Marx. Rudy Schiffman was a big bastard, mean and humorless. We spent less time in the store during Rudy's shifts, especially since he often kicked us out when we got rowdy. There was even a little ditty, well known in the neighborhood, that summed up the two men. It was sung to the tune of "Camptown Races," but all I can remember now is:

Fred's okay but Rudy stinks,

Doo-dah, doo-dah!

I was a wise-guy, even as a little kid, and I was always rousing the ire of Rudy. When I was ten or eleven years old, I had been learning about largely defunct diseases, a favorite subject of sixth grade social studies in the New York City public schools. Mr. Malachowsky had taught us about scurvy, and rickets, and berri berri, as well as a rare tropical disease called yaws. Well, in Brooklyn we pronounce "yours" and "yaws" the same way. Rudy, when he would take our order, would often say, "What's yours?" So one day I responded, "A rare tropical disease," and my friends on the adjoining stools started cracking up. "Out of the store," Rudy yelled. "All of you!"

When Fred and Rudy weren't looking, we'd often stand by the magazine rack and peek at the *Playboy* centerfold. If Rudy caught us he'd make us stop. Fred usually turned a blind eye, though sometimes he'd say, "What do you think this is kid? A library?"

A couple of celebrities grew up in the immediate neighborhood. One was a minor stand-up comic named Morty Gunty. The bigger star was Lainie Kazan, whose real last name was Levine. Lainie, who got her big break as Barbra Streisand's understudy in *Funny Girl*, was extremely well endowed, and in 1970 she did a photo spread for *Playboy*.

Lainie was long-gone from the neighborhood by this time, but her mother still lived in the old apartment. Lainie's mother had to give Fred and Rudy a wide berth for a while after one of the neighborhood wise-guys (not me this time) said to her, "Hey Mrs. Levine, I saw your daughter's big tits in *Playboy*! Hubba-hubba!"

Fred and Rudy's closed some time in the seventies, a few years before I left the old neighborhood, and for the most part the candy store is just a memory of a bygone New York, and of my bygone youth. I always think of Fred and Rudy's whenever I hear the song "Leader of the Pack," but unlike that girl from the Shangri-Las, I never met anyone at the candy store I didn't already know. By the way, I did sneak a peek at Lainie's tits in *Playboy*—during one of Fred's shifts, of course.

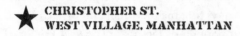

AROMA-DEO
BY SUZANNE COMEAU MARS

The women lined up early for a chance at the best gift bags. Some had spent the past twenty hours miserable and sleepless on a Greyhound from Iowa, such was the desire to inhale some combination of cupcake accord, sumac leaf note, or diet brambleberry liqueur that was reputed to possess magical and potentially aphrodisiac qualities unknown to the women's experience and previously unavailable in the United States, despite their already owning several hundred bottles of perfume each.

Some complained that their bag did not contain a sample of the latest absinthe scent, the one with a sprig of lavender spiked clear through the heart. Who cared if it smelled masculine, or like gin dregs at last call? The point was to say that you had smelled it—been there, sniffed that—before anyone else.

"Aren't you going to have a lookie in your bag?" the organizer asked. She was petite, I was Amazon-ish, she was a brunette, and I had black roots. She made me wonder why petite women—brunettes especially—are never at a loss for gumption and drive and do quite well for themselves in public relations and marketing. Exactly the opposite of what I do, categorically speaking. She took the bag from my hands, breaking the paper handle, and spilled the bag's contents out onto the counter at Bar-ney's, chiding me for not realizing that I had somehow miraculously come across a sample of La Mer skin foundation, lotion-style, color "Deathwatch." "The others didn't get that, I don't think. Hmmm. Paula, do you have a sample of the La Mer lotion foundation? Renée? May I have a show of hands for those who have a sample of La Mer lotion foundation in their gift bags?"

There is a simple premise behind this cosmetic rodeo: We are assembled one and all to partake of special olfactory events (personal appearances, bottle signings, atomizer huffings, and secretive, closed-door shopping hours that must aggravate the hell out of the shopkeepers, who endure it with forced good cheer and tight grimaces) offered through various Web forums dedicated to the discussion of things scented and potentially repellent. There are candles, eau de toilette, sachets, incense, and silky panty powders. Not a Glade Plug-In air freshener in sight. We are vain, middle-aged, overweight, flat-footed, and largely secretarial by occupation. We are invisible, but we stink good.

The only life we have is the one we can smell. The redhead with the panty-powder purchase lumbers over and asks if I'm married. "No," I say. "Good," she chirps. "We have some common ground." She spends five minutes outlining the many benefits of the panty powder, not the least of which is to cover up funk in case of a lack of shower facilities after a blistering date.

She shadows me on the way to the West Village, where we are going to crowd into the small Aedes shop on Christopher Street. Many of the women call this shop "Eeds" and are politely corrected. The men who run the shop are German and very, very kind, although with a thin brutality that would surface like a fin if the waters were too grandly disturbed. These men are elegant and sleek; the perfume fanatics are dressed in polyester and sweat. Several break out copies of *Perfumes of the World*, the most recently released edition, and gush about the conjunction of wine and scent that has led to the shared official descriptions of rubber, tar, wet wool, wet dog, and cat urine. The perfume book even has a little descriptive color wheel developed by the vinology program at the University of California at Davis. Neat. The shopkeepers are accommodating about the subsequent interrogations and even have

745

wine on hand in little plastic flutes. You can learn about grace here, even when your arse threatens to overturn a delicate display.

My red shadow asks if I have purchased a bottle of the scent that perfumes the rooms at the Hôtel Costes in Paris, and whether I know if there are matching soaps available. "I'm having a soapy incense month," she confides. Personally, I am in a strange vanilla month in which I insist on smelling like a patisserie, and a cheap one at that—a common bakery, or perhaps even a plastic brioche. Someone had pointed that out earlier. It's not the first time I've had something pointed out to me: You smell like burnt leaves and grade-C maple syrup. Do you want to smell like that?

"If you buy that Costes, I want a decant of it," the shadow whispers. I quickly toss up some rough figures in my head: If I purchase a 1.7 ounce bottle of this perfume I am reconnoitering out of the desire to appear involved and nasally stimulated, I will spend somewhere in the vicinity of seventy dollars and probably not get any free samples, because I am loath to ask for them. I've worked a perfume counter in my day and was fired for giving away too many samples without immediate mega-purchase. Both the customers and the management hated me. I stank. I cannot sell three thousand dollars' worth of perfume on a weekend. I will have to share at least ten milliliters of the bottle with my newly acquired companion, who has smartly brought along some empty atomizer bottles for this exact purpose. And then her friend from the makeup forum will want some, and twenty minutes later I'll end up with twenty milliliters for myself—less than half the bottle—and a sample vial of Paris Hilton's perfume, which is not hot at all.

We have lunch at a Swedish restaurant where everyone takes out all of their purchases and participates in a round-robin distribution and an informative presentation by the maker of what I will forever after refer to as Dung Ho perfume (chocolate, jasmine, gym sock and dreadful animalic) and I am forced to give up my sample of the La Mer lotion foundation to the organizer, and when we disperse I realize I have purchased nothing, want nothing, and can't afford anything to begin with. It has been a very productive day, and I reek magnificently of day-old bread and the sweet toxin of wanting what you aren't stamped out to buy.

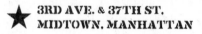
THE SPOILS
BY SUZANNE COMEAU MARS

I took the subway uptown to stop by my old boss's townhouse. Drop by any time, she'd said. Just ring the bell. We were on good terms. I had quit that job to take something downtown. The new job paid a little bit more, but it hadn't worked out. Now I was back working as a waitress. My old boss would need to give me a reference for something else. The waitress job made my feet ache.

I learned a lot from that old boss. The old boss spent a lot of her time getting her roots dyed golden blonde. She said that if you were going to color your hair blonde, you couldn't have roots. It was against the rules. You wouldn't get waited on in shops if you had black roots. You wouldn't get any service. You had to go once a week to have those roots dyed the same color as the rest of the hair. It had to look expensive or people would think you were cheap. The boss said it wouldn't do and that I should see Andre. Everyone saw Andre for blonding. Those were the correct terms to use.

She said that when she started out, it was very competitive. Like now, but with more taste. Now she was almost seventy. She liked to talk while I arranged her shoe closet. I had to keep track

of which shoes she had worn with which dress and when this
had taken place. I had to remember handbags and bracelets. She
had a diary and I wrote in it the next day. Getting dressed was an
exhausting competition and it had to be just right, every time.
You couldn't slip up. It was competitive. It was in the papers.
The boss's husband had been a philanthropist, but he had died.
The boss had been disorganized until I started cataloguing everything. I didn't know what to call that on my resume. I couldn't
just say "organized things."

I poked at the bell and waited until someone came to the door.
The boss usually had a lot of people running around. There were
three types of staff there. If you didn't know any better, it seemed
like the boss was running a real tight ship. The people who
worked there always looked busy, but this was because Cleopa-
tra never left her barge of a bed. You'd think it would work the
other way around. You'd think people would be reading magazines in the living room, putting their feet on the upholstery.
Instead, the boss kept them scooting around, looking for a hair
clip or a receipt from Bergdorf's that had been thrown out two
weeks before.

When the boss did get out of bed, it was like an opening
night. She had parties there. The lights came on. This had to be
planned a month in advance. That was another part of my job. I
had to schedule things. I had to get just the right lavender roses
flown in. The flowers had to match the walls. This is what I like
about you, the boss had said. You know about things. I don't have
to explain like I do with Nancy or Carmelita. It makes my life
easier not to have to explain the difference between a good rose
and a bad one. You know.

Yes I do, I said.

I went right into the living room and sat down like I owned
the place. Someone should arrange the magazines and water the
plants. Someone should take care of the details. It's not that hard.
It's not my job anymore, but I pinched off a dead bloom and
stuck it in my pocket. Attention to detail is important when you
have this kind of job. It's what keeps people coming back with

smiles on their faces. The boss's house was like a hotel or an ocean liner. It was exhausting to keep it looking fresh. It was plain old hard work. Someone had to do it or it wouldn't get done. This room was the lobby for the rest of the house and another part of my job had been to keep the curtains drawn relative to the amount of sunlight coming in. The sun would bleach the carpet if you let it. You had to keep the curtains drawn in the morning and then open them little by little during the day. Whoever was doing it now had gone too far and half of the carpet had faded. I shut them partway and sat back down with one of the magazines. I read an article about how not to overcook fish and then looked at some pictures of a vacation home out in the Hamptons. This home was unusual in that it only used organic materials inside. It sounded as if it might go up in flames and as if it might be irksome to spend the weekend there.

After twenty minutes I got up and took the elevator up to the third floor where the boss's bedroom was. Walked right in and said hello. Even though the boss lived like Mrs. Astor's pet horse, she herself was pretty casual. Informal. She said she the simpler things were, the better. She said most people didn't understand that idea and paid the price later. I probably shouldn't have quit this job. When I walked in, the boss was getting her hair styled. There was a dress form in the corner that had been modeled after the boss's exact measurements and the dress form was wearing a bright red suit. It was headless, this torso, so someone had put a black straw hat on top of the neck.

What a surprise! she said. Would you bring me a hand mirror? I need to see the back. The back is never right.

I didn't want to waste her time, so I spilled it. I need a job reference, if you don't mind, I said. That's why I'm here. I don't want to disturb you, but you said to drop by any time.

Of course, Sally! Don't you worry about that. I handed her the mirror. She clucked and picked at a curl. The hairdresser fussed with the hair near the ears, saying that the hair had gotten thinner since last time. This was a new hairdresser. Andre had died and this new one was called Franco. Franco had on black slacks and a pink shirt and he patted the old boss on the top of head like you'd pat a small dog.

I am always happy to help, Sally, she said. Now, tell me, what did you do here? It is Sally, isn't it? She motioned for me to sit down next to her.

Guess, I said.

She thought this over a bit, and then sat back and smiled. Yes, it's Sally. You worked with Isabelle in the kitchen. Yes, I remember now. You are the girl who brought in that wonderful recipe for trout. You made an appetizer that everyone said was superb. I remember that party. That was your trout, wasn't it?

No.

Now don't fib, Sally. It was delicious. You're not in catering any longer? Oh, dear. What are you doing now?

I was a waitress at a steakhouse, but I wanted something better this time around. It was better forked over plain. The boss would appreciate my asking for a reference directly. You couldn't be mistaken for weak that way. That was another thing I learned on that job. I reached over and took one of the boss's cigarettes and fired it up. I wasn't used to smoking in anyone's bedroom.

Sally, you were very good help. That steakhouse will be sorry to lose you, I can just tell. I always know when a waitress is good or not. It's all about eye contact. Always look people right in the eye, Sally. I do understand, though, that you probably feel more at home in the kitchen. I think you have some real talent there.

We got a lot of Japanese tourists at the restaurant. They liked to drink and they liked to tell you that you reminded them of some mermaid painted on a sushi platter. They didn't speak enough English to say "mermaid," so instead they made the shape of a mermaid with their hands and then they laughed. When they paid the bill, they left a key to their hotel room. The wrong person could get one of those keys and rob those businessmen blind, so at the end of my shift I'd put the keys into an envelope and mail them to the hotel. I didn't put a return address on the envelope.

I was used to addressing envelopes. I used to sit at this table every morning, listening to the boss dictate invitations and thank you notes. These all had to be done by hand—my hand—because I had won a penmanship award in the sixth grade. I did this well, better than most. You don't realize how difficult it is to get it just right. It can be slow going. It has to do with geometry above all and then you worry about the thickness of the letters and how hard you have to bear down on the paper to get the right effect. Fat or thin, it made all the difference in the world.

The boss motioned at the dress form and asked what anyone thought about that red suit. Exquisite, Franco said. What can I say? Just exquisite. He asked the boss to shut her eyes while he shellacked her with a can of hairspray. He waved the fumes away by flipping his hands like he was going after a fly.

Where are you wearing that? I asked. It looked like one of her uptown suits. The red was too bright.

I am going home, she said. It was too hot in the city. The haze gave her a headache. She hated sitting in her town car while the heat throbbed off the asphalt. The city was a sweat-soaked mirror. You couldn't bear to see your own reflection. Everyone went out of town in August anyway. People would think something about her if she didn't go herself. They'd think she had money problems and they'd yammer it raw. Franco agreed with this. He had clients at Sag Harbor already and they'd be talking. The boss didn't like Sag Harbor but had gone there anyway. Her husband had said it was expected. When the boss saw her picture in the papers, she'd use the word "dreadful." There I am with that dreadful neighbor. And look at this, the dreadful Miller beach house. What a dreadful chore it all is. I am dreading this summer already, and it hasn't even started.

I am very tired, she said.

She was going upstate. Her family had a summer house on the St. Lawrence River. She inherited the house and she despised it. It nagged her like a bad tooth, but she wouldn't sell it. It just sat there waiting and nagging. The house was built of stone and it sat on a bank overlooking the river. It had thirty rooms all paneled in wood. There was a circular turret at the top of three flights of stairs. This turret had a view all the way into Canada. You could sit up there like a sentinel, alone as can be, and watch autumn creep over the border. The shadows would take a long time to fall, but when they did it was as if they'd never left in the first place. You'd find yourself back in the city, waiting out winter.

So why go? Franco asked. I would go in a heartbeat, he said. I'd take Dennis and stay the whole month. Some people, he said, and he rolled his eyes. Some people don't know when they have it good.

The stone house had been shut up like a mausoleum for the past thirty years. The boss said it cost a fortune to run, that's why it was easier to lock it up and forget about it. There were no children. There was no one to take on the responsibility. Who'd want that anyway? There was more that came with it. She said the house reminded her of what it was like to be twenty and pretty. She'd been twenty and pretty in a straw hat and then she was not. She said what was the point of remembering something like that? When she was twenty, she had run off in the woods and had lost her hat and had not come home for two days. There was something out there she wanted to see.

She had heard about a girl who had drowned in the river. If she ran as fast as she could, she could almost pace the currents and imagine where the girl had flushed out into the sea. Even though she couldn't see that far, she knew the girl had gone as far as the mouth and probably much farther.

She knew that the water was cool. She knew that much.

And they looked for that girl for weeks that summer. They thought she'd gotten lost and maybe was hurt, maybe had fallen and broken her ankle on a rock. She might sit out there in the woods until deer season. She might not know the way home.

And with everyone looking, the boss said, they forgot about the dancing. They forgot about the rowboats and the picnics and the fireflies. The girl's mother thought the girl had been snatched away in the night. There had been a search party and then a mob. No one thought the girl had gone out on the tide.

The boss said that it had taken a while to see where the girl had gone into the water, but that she knew when she had found the exact spot. She had followed the shore for half a day when she came upon it. It was a little sandy dent that the river had lapped out of the bank. The water was clear there and very shallow, but there were some rocks that poked out of deeper water. Some of these rocks were quite smooth and others were larger and sharp. The boss sat on one of the rocks for a while and listened to the river nudge the bank. She trailed her fingers through the water and touched them to her lips. It was a place where you could watch the boats go by. She said she thought the girl had tripped and fallen, but you couldn't be sure. It would have been easy to step out onto one of the rocks and slip. Or it might have been just as easy to step on one of those rocks and let yourself slip away like an otter. You could float on your back for a while, just star-ing at sky or nothing in particular, and then you could roll over onto your belly, flip your tail and be gone.

The boss said that she had taken her straw hat and had placed it where the water met the bank. At first the hat had dipped back towards the shore, but then it moved away. It stalled for a minute and then decided on its course. The boss watched it sail and then went home through the woods.

I wanted to know how the boss knew this was a pivotal moment in her life. What we were looking at here. The idea excited me. How you could tell those moments and when not to go back the way you came in. What it felt like to disappear from the shore like you never existed, like you had no weight in the world. How a boat couldn't rescue that girl even though there were plenty of boats on the water that afternoon. How there was some delicacy to this, even though it was plenty appalling.

The water is very cold there, even in summer, was what the boss had to say. There's a current. She put on her red jacket and frowned at herself in the mirror.

I don't think I like this, Franco, she said. Her hair was rigid as aluminum. She touched it and pushed the sides towards her ears. I don't think I'm going to tip you today. In fact, I think I'm

753

going to wash it out. She hurried into her bathroom and turned on the taps. She bent over the sink while Franco watched. He stood there staring at her in her red jacket. It was how she had always had her hair done. It was or it wasn't his fault. Water ran down her shirt and dripped on the floor at her feet.

That's enough, Franco. That's all. You can go.

He paused. Her checkbook was on the desk.

I said you can go now, Franco.

The boss sat on the edge of her bed and asked me if I didn't think some of this stuff was ridiculous. Like what? I asked. Blowouts?

Oh, most of it. All of it, she said, motioning around the room. The spoils. She pointed. The chaise longue. A Chinese screen with herons against a white background. A bloated gilt clock and most particularly the contents of a cedar closet that had its own thermostat.

Isn't it silly? she said. A wine cellar for coats.

She said that I should take it all down to the street and leave it there. Someone would take it away. Someone always did. There'd be jackals before sunrise, after she'd left. You could count on that no matter where you were. It was maybe the one thing in life that was dependable. If there was anything remaining in the morning I was to put it into the dumpster and not leave it for people to trip over. We had to avoid attractive nuisance. And the birds? The boss had a cage of society finches, maybe twenty of them on little wooden perches. She told me to ask Hans to let the birds fly out the front door. Those finches were going to sing regardless, that was their job, even if it was only the males that made any music. The hens were tuneless. Hans would probably be smoking a cigarette in the pantry, his back turned towards the door, and I'd ask him to let those finches free. The boss said that Hans could take a coat for his wife if he wanted to. The black one was probably the best. His wife could wear it to bingo night and tie a scarf over her curlers.

You could auction it at Sotheby's instead, I suggested. I could call them for you. I could call them and let them take the stuff off her hands. It was more dignified and ladylike. She ran her hand up my arm and stopped at the elbow. When she stopped, she clutched, and I could feel her in my muscle.

She said that was what she was trying to avoid. Dignity. Dignity drowned in the river. Her hair was soaking wet and she mashed her straw hat down on top of it and stood up. She draped her red jacket across her shoulders and said it was time to go. I had come on that day. I didn't want to bother about that reference. I was the one with good penmanship. That always impressed people. They thought you paid good money for something with that much class. There were engraved note cards with her name inked across the top. I had practiced her signature until it was perfect. I could say that I had worked for her for two years, smoked in bedrooms, and that I was most often honest and reliable. Most of the time. I asked if she didn't want me to drive with her, ride with her, just a little bit of the way. Not all the way there, but far enough.

ALTERED STATES

BY SUSAN CONNELL-METTAUER

When I first met Lance I was in an altered state. I was six-teen, back in 1963, when you could still buy a Benadryl inhaler, break it open and find a cotton wedge soaked with amphetamine. I'm not sure who first noticed this, but it might have been Jack Kerouac. I hope not, but it probably was.

It was late spring in Cambridge, Massachusetts, and warm breezes stirred up dust on Franklin Street, one side of which was a no-man's-land of trampled grass sloping up to the back ends of stores on Mass. Avenue; on the other, low clapboard houses with clinking wind chimes and bright Marimekko curtains had a pleasant trashy feel. The heat felt good on my skin and the dust felt good sticking to my face and hair and, if I had been a dog, I would have rolled in the dirt for joy.

I was hurrying along with my friend Naomi who was a year younger than me and six feet tall with haystack hair that she frizzed by braiding it wet and letting it dry and then taking out the braids. Naomi was telling me about this party and a guy she met who was so gorgeous she almost fell over when she saw him, a potter or an artist or something. I calculated days, arriving at the fact that the party was on a school night, and this both thrilled

756

and unsettled me. Her boyfriend had also been at the party and the two of them had fucked among the jackets piled in the bedroom—an act Naomi described in agonizing detail, each stroke punctuated with high-pitched hoots and cackles razoring my speed-brain. Then she grabbed my arm and said, "That's him. What did I tell you?"

She was right: he was gorgeous. He had large wide-set eyes, haggard cheekbones, a sensuous mouth like Antonin Artaud, only an Artaud who lifted weights. He was a few yards in front of us reciting, "Oh as I was young and easy in the mercy of his means…" to his friend, George—who was almost crying from laughing so hard—and he was under the influence, I believe, because there was great pathos in his voice, the kind that often has a chemical base. I had my mouth gaping—like, holy shit where have you been all my life?—and he sauntered up and put his arm around me as if I were a dear, long-lost cousin.

That's how I met Lance.

Later that afternoon Lance and I ended up in bed at his wife's apartment lunging at each other like professional wrestlers on a dismal clot of sheets. I described it to Naomi as being "athletic" when she demanded details a few weeks afterwards. Perhaps I was too immature for sex, or my hormones were as fried as the rest of me from all the amphetamine I took. Either way it was hump-hump-and-slammin'-the-mat.

By this time George had gone home and Naomi was sitting alone outside the bedroom, listening. It was a tangible, sticky listening and, even though I kept telling myself that she was out there and I was in here, that he chose me and not to worry, I was half expecting it when Naomi sidled in all simpering smiles. Then silently plopping herself between us, she moon-eyed Lance and stuck her lips out at me; she stroked his face as if sculpting the bones; and then the two of them had a go at it.

I was stunned. Snatching my gear I retreated to the room where Naomi had been a few minutes earlier. The floor was splintery and bare, with toys and books and clothing scattered about in untidy snarls. I wanted a delicious treat, like cake, but there was no food in the kitchen cabinets. Then, crouched before the open refrigerator and gazing at a half-stick of margarine perched on a metal rack among crumbs and yellowed celery leaves, my heart started to race and I knew I had to get out of there. To get out the front door, I had to pass the bedroom which now emitted the creak of bed slats and rustling noises each one of which provoked a minor swell of nausea in me. My heart was pounding so loud it echoed in my ears. I should have foamed at the mouth, but I didn't. I climbed on the kitchen counter, squeezed out a dwarf-sized window, fell in a bramble patch, and lurched off leaving my shoes behind in the sink.

Over the next few days I played the episode back to myself to figure out what had gone wrong, why I felt so incriminated and puny, so undignified. This was a tough question. Really, how can anyone know why she or anyone else did something after it's already happened and they've all done what they were going to anyway? Unless a person is set on inventing some rule to follow so it will not happen again, whatever it was. I didn't have rules and it was not clear to me that I wanted to avoid everything that had happened, only the painful parts.

So I thought about rules as I visited Lance and George at the Cambridge Potters, their shop and studio on Mass. Avenue; even as I examined the oozing clay pots wet on the wheel or massive pots ready for firing with woolly mammoths and dancing minotaurs drawn on. I contemplated my rules while hiking over to the slums of the South End where Lance and George were rebuilding a house, unremarkable outside; but inside, whitewashed and shaped like a church—a molded church as if growing spiraled similar to the inside walls of the Guggenheim Museum. I considered my rules while listening to him and George in the studio and at the construction site as they belted out "Mr. Tambourine Man" along with a scratchy recording of Bob Dylan. And rules were in the back of my mind when Lance did wine-powered encores of "Fern Hill" while George leered and I watched spellbound and delighted and wounded all at the same time.

After following Lance around trying to figure a way to be close without feeling too humiliated, I decided that some men are good for boyfriends, some for friends, some for teachers—a simple matter of who was good for what. After all, Lance was a genius. He had secrets, special tricks that only geniuses know, things I could not get from school or from ordinary people. I could absorb it all by osmosis, take Lance-lessons, append him to myself. Considering this, it was best to ignore the painful incident with Naomi. Anyway a new genius-friend was a prize catch. I proposed this friendship and he accepted. Then there were the prints, a series of five large crazy lithographs on brown wrapping paper. He had drawn them in a metal plate, whipped off one of each, and I wanted one. As he was now my friend, I decided to ask Lance if I could have one.

So on a sultry night, across the street from the house in the South End, while we sat on stone steps surrounded by tall weeds, Lance expounded on his own rules: how no one could take anything from him he wouldn't willingly give. No one. Somehow the force of his will made giving and receiving less a rip-off; as if willful consent shaped both these acts recasting them as aspects of Lance himself. Considering his drift, it was not that easy to bring up the lithographs, but I asked anyway. He said, "Yes, I'll give you one because I know you will take care of it."

Later he chose a print that was not my favorite. It was an abstract-looking guy waving hands around at another guy, only there were large penises instead of fingers and big butt cracks shaped into the hand meats on the bottom—not the kind of thing to show your mother or try to impress strangers with. It was called *Two Men Arguing Over Coffee*, measured three and a half feet square, and was rolled up in a cardboard cylinder.

When I last saw Lance in New York on St. Marks Place— outside the Electric Circus (a hulking structure, which is now painted black and boarded up, and will soon be condos)—I was twenty-two. It was 1969 and I asked him why he had fucked Naomi that time, and didn't he know how much I liked him back then. He said, "Why didn't you just tell me to stop?" I

759

remembered the logy feeling I had traipsing back and forth across that kitchen before I pitched out the window. I remembered telling myself to rise above what was happening. I remembered rage and fear canceling each other out—the sense of powerlessness, not knowing what I wanted or how to fight for it or even if I wanted to fight, period.

"Really, you would have stopped?" I said.

"Yuh," he said.

Lance went to Hollywood and got into movies. He was in *Aliens* and recently landed his own TV series, an *X-Files* knock-off about serial killers. *Two Men Arguing Over Coffee* survived framings, peelings off pressboard, cleanings of corrosive glue. My husbands have all been fond of the penis hands although I never told them the exact nature of my friendship with their creator. I wasn't lying; I'm not sure I know myself.

EDITOR'S NOTE

Not long after this piece ran I got a call from an editor inquiring about Susan Connell-Mettauer. He had discovered her writing on the site. His taste is literary and eclectic. One of his pet subjects, as an editor and writer, is the sixties. It made sense that her writing had caught his eye. He wanted to know if she was working on a book, and thought her pieces could be the start of one.

I passed this news on. I didn't expect effusion, exactly, but I felt this would be happy-making.

"Interesting," was her response. Just that one word. She sounded not so much excited as amused, somehow, as though there was some irony to the timing. But there is always an odd aura of irony around intense news, good or bad. "Why now?" one always asks. Maybe I had just read into her tone of voice, I thought, and decided not to press the matter.

As it turns out there was something going on. Last year I got the news that Susan Connell-Metauer had passed away. I didn't know her very well, but she was a regular contributor to this publication early on, and helped establish its tone and style. Her pieces often looked back to intense episodes of her life when she was living on the Lower East Side. They were wild, almost asphyxiating experiences involving drugs and sex and grasping towards love. Reading them one was both nervous somehow for the fragility of the protagonist, Susan, back then, and impressed with the calm, impassive, clear eyed take on it from her current vantage point.

It's always gratifying to see someone hit their stride doing pieces for this site. But as I said, we were not close and I didn't know her life beyond what was in these pieces. We spoke on the phone several times over the years. Once, there was a reading in Boston scheduled for the Before and After: Stories from New York *book but instead I went out to San Francisco to attend the Webby awards, where Mr. Beller's Neighborhood was nominated in the print and zine catagory. She filled in as MC in Boston. This was 2002. The Webby awards—could there be a goofier name?—were held at the the California Palace of the Legion of Honor in San Francisco, a grand, beautiful, slightly fascist-looking campus overlooking the water. We didn't win (Salon.com did), though I did get to see the two Google guys dressed (pre-IPO) in matching tracksuits, a kind of geek Run-D.M.C. look.*

After our category came and went, I went outside to peer at the view and call Susan. I was three hours behind, the Boston reading had already happened. She said it went well. I found her temperament, like her writing, to be ideally suited to this enterprise— whimsical, respectful of the fates, but caring about it, too—that edge of unrealistic commitment that you see in writers. She said that an old high school friend of mine came and seemed put out I was not there. We laughed about this. Her cool delivery on the phone matched up well with sight of the San Francisco landscape rolling down to the dusk-lit water. That is the image I associate with her now.

—T.B

WAR AND DUANE READE
BY SAÏD SAYRAFIEZADEH

Day Fourteen. United States troops four miles from Baghdad. It was 9 p.m. and I was out of Breathe Right strips. If I don't have Breathe Right strips I can't sleep soundly because I have a deviated septum. So I put on my brown coat and my orange button that has a photograph of a very sweet little Iraqi girl and the words "Stop the War on Iraq," and I rode my bicycle to Duane Reade, located on Sixth Avenue between Twelfth and Thirteenth Streets.

All Duane Reades are unhappy stores and this one is no exception. It is filled with unhappy employees moving around in a kind of pudding atmosphere, commingling with cute, well-heeled West Village customers and illuminated by the brightest fluorescent lights. On the hottest day of the year last summer the store's air conditioning happened to be broken, and a young black man, who was stocking shelves and dripping with sweat, said to me, "They've gone and put me back on the plantation."

I selected two boxes of Breathe Right strips and took my place in line behind one other customer. Almost immediately a man approached. He was looking at me intently, muttering under his breath, and shaking his head with displeasure. He was a light-skinned black man, somewhere in his early forties, and dressed in a security-guard uniform. In his hand was a packet of cookies. As he rapidly walked towards me I realized this: just a moment ago he had seen that there was no line at the register and so had decided to take the opportunity to punch out for his break, rush as fast as he could to the cookie aisle for his cookies, then rush back to the cashier who would be able to ring him up instantly, thus allowing him to utilize every minute of his fifteen-minute break.

But now here were two people waiting in line.

I had bagged groceries in a supermarket for two years when I was in high school and so I knew all about those totalitarian rules requiring you to punch out before purchasing your snack, and the rules requiring you to wait patiently in line like a regular customer, and so on and so forth. On one occasion my boss had apprehended me arriving from my break three minutes late and put me to work cleaning behind the garbage compactor. So I understood the nature of this man's dilemma. And feeling magnanimous and in touch with my past, I was prepared to let him cut in front of me if he were to ask. "Sure," I would say. "Go ahead, man."

As he neared me, however, I saw that his security-guard uniform was not, in fact, a security-guard uniform at all, and that he did not appear to be associated with Duane Reade in any official capacity whatsoever. He was a regular customer like me. And furthermore, rather than ask if he could cut in front, he stood in line behind me and said in a loud voice, as if he were resolving a discussion with someone sitting in another room, "Fuck Saddam! And fuck Osama!" And then to clarify who exactly his conversation partner was, he said, in that same loud voice, "Yeah, I see that bullshit on your button."

It was my turn to be rung up. The cashier, who was very short and looked like she might be Caribbean, scanned my Breathe Right strips with exhaustion.

"We're going to kill that motherfucker tonight," the man continued behind me. "Hell yeah!"

I could tell he was just getting started and that he was preparing to gleefully egg me on for the remainder of my time in the store. My emasculation was unfolding before me. I was on the verge of becoming the flushed white man that you sometimes see in a subway car being cursed by a person of color, a faraway gaze in the white man's eyes, a reconciliatory smile playing at his lips. "I am friend to all," the smile seems to say, "even you who now attack me."

I resolved not to be a victim. Especially since I'm not just a white man but also a half-Iranian man with a stake in what happens in the Middle East. And so I decided to answer the man's charges as put forth. "Just because I'm against the war doesn't mean I support Saddam," I considered saying. But this had a defiantless tone and reeked of reasoning and goodwill and inclusiveness, and therefore defeatism. My goal was to win not a political argument but a physical one. I decided to choose a different approach.

"You like that shit, huh?" I said to him contemptuously. "You like the fact that America's running all around the world killing people? And you're here celebrating." I looked him in the eye and punctuated my words. I wanted to make it clear I wasn't cowed. He stared back at me with a crazed incredulity. Looking at him closely I realized that there was a very good chance the man wasn't in his right mind. There was also a possibility that his irritation with my button stemmed from the fact that he had family in the armed services. I suddenly feared that I had antagonized a man who was unstable and whose very thin emotional line had just been crossed.

The cashier said, "That's twenty-seven dollars and twenty-six cents."

My hand trembled as I swiped my debit card. "May I have cash back?" I asked.

"Hell, yeah I like it!" the man rejoined. "It's going to be just like when Qaddafi was talking all that shit."

I was impressed that he had brought up Qaddafi. It seemed politically astute. I wasn't quite sure what his point was but my mind raced to find a comeback. I thought briefly about the fact that Qaddafi's daughter had been killed in a United States bombing raid and that perhaps I could somehow equate her murder with the overall oppression of black men in the United States. I wanted to make it personal. But I wasn't entirely certain this man was black. Maybe he was Puerto Rican. If he was Puerto Rican I could talk about the bombing of Vieques. But if he wasn't Puerto Rican I might enrage him by presuming that he was. He would accuse me of making racist, uninformed assumptions. And he'd be right. And then I'd be stuck and everyone in the store would hate me. Including the Caribbean cashier…who might not be Caribbean.

The cashier said, "We don't give cash back."

"And then Ronald Reagan put a shotgun to Qaddafi's head," the man continued, "and you don't hear no more shit out of him, do you?"

That was my in. It wasn't a great in but it was most likely the only one I was going to get.

"You like Reagan, huh?" I asked. I snickered and glanced at the cashier with a look that said, "Can you believe a black man is actually defending Ronald Reagan?" She stared back as if she had no idea what the conversation was about and didn't care enough to find out.

I pushed further. "Reagan did right by you, huh? He took care of you?" I said it loud enough so that the tough black man would have to admit to the entire Duane Reade store that he was indeed a supporter of Ronald Reagan.

His response was sudden and unequivocal: "Fuck Reagan! And fuck Bush!"

I had nowhere to go now. We were in agreement. The cashier put my Breathe Rights in a plastic bag.

"I don't need a bag," I said.

"I voted," the man said. "My mother asked me what I was doing. I tore that piece of paper up. Fuck all them motherfuckers."

LOST AND FOUND

There was conviction there and I respected it. But conviction about what? If someone were to enter the store right now there was a chance that I might appear to be the one being chastised for being right wing and pro-war and a supporter of Ronald Reagan. I wanted to say something back to the man but I no longer knew what the argument was.

And now my transaction was over.

I thanked the cashier, who looked at me like I was a fool who had disrupted the peaceful equilibrium of the store. "It wasn't my fault," I wanted to say.

I put the two boxes of Breathe Right strips in my coat pocket and walked out the door. On the street I could still hear the man talking. Was he mocking me? I took a long time unlocking my bicycle because I was resolved that I would have the last word. When I looked up again the man was standing in the doorway chatting with the Pakistani security guard—maybe he wasn't Pakistani. The two of them chuckled. At my expense, no doubt. Then the man started walking up the street, unwrapping his packet of cookies. I got on my bicycle and slowly rode past him on the sidewalk, ready to taunt him, but not knowing quite where to begin.

"They all suck," he said to me as I passed.

"Yeah, man, they all suck," I thought to respond. But I didn't want to agree.

THE AFFLICTED
BY SAÏD SAYRAFIEZADEH

It is winter, it is night, it is cold—Christmas is coming—and
I can feel deep down inside of me an infectious bug of some
sort beginning to develop. It is far away in my feet, making them
ache, but soon I know that, as always, it will creep up my legs,
through my pelvis, into my torso and that will be the end of me.
My body, in the meantime, in its gallant effort to ward off the
invader, has left me hungry and exhausted.

"I need to go home, eat something, and go right to sleep," I
think to myself, "and tomorrow I will wake anew." But as I enter
my apartment my girlfriend is holding her index finger in agony.
Just a moment before I opened the door she had been happily
cutting wrapping paper for a gift with a brand new pair of scissors and then...

"Let me see! Let me see!" I say. And with great reluctance
she unclenches her hand and reveals the injured finger: a thin
line running along her fingerprint from which deep, rich blood
courses. It is by no means a severe incision, but I know from a
previous career as a fairly incompetent short-order cook that cuts
like this can be painful and distressing and will require a few

stitches. My girlfriend covers her poor wounded finger again, leans her head against my chest, and begins to sob.

Having grown up without a father, I am often at a loss as how to behave in situations that call for a paternal response. At these times I am forced to compensate by piecing together various moments of behavior I have witnessed in males older than myself. For instance, there is my third-grade teacher who would horse-play with us at the end of the school day; or Muhammad Ali; or the guy who taught me how to stock shelves at the grocery store; or my friend's older brother, who rushed over the time I stumbled and fell hard while playing basketball, and picked me up lovingly by my waist.

"It's going to be OK," I say to my girlfriend, imitating some-one's voice I have plucked from the database of my mind. I put my arms around her and hold her tightly and soon her tears subside.

Mount Sinai is only four blocks from where we live, and after a brief parsimonious internal debate (which I am embarrassed to admit) as to whether to ask my girlfriend if she feels up to just walking to the hospital, I hail a cab.

"Mount Sinai," I say to the cabdriver, whose name is Kruszewski, and who wears the kind of cap and jacket you see in films from the fifties where everything is gray and rainy.

He makes a left instead of a right on Fourteenth Street and heads toward the FDR Drive.

"Mount Sinai," I repeat nervously.

"That's what you said," he says.

"I would like the one on Sixteenth and First," I say politely.

"Mount Sinai is on One-hundredth Street," he says.

"That's not the one I want," I say. "I want the one on Six-teenth and First."

"That's Beth Israel," he says.

"That's the one I want then."

"If you want Beth Israel you have to ask for Beth Israel."

"I'm sorry," I say. "I want Beth Israel."

He chuckles derisively and says under his breath, "They ask for Mount Sinai." He makes an aggressive U-turn in the middle of Fourteenth Street that tosses us in the backseat. I feel emasculated in front of my girlfriend.

Two minutes later he pulls up in front of the entrance to Beth Israel. The fare is $2.40. I'm suddenly stumped as to whether such a fast trip demands a large tip or a small one. I err on the side of generosity and tip him three dollars thinking that under such grave circumstances he has done us a great service for which I am indebted. We are travelers who have been borne across the Klondike. I feel that this public display of over-compensation vindicates me for my earlier private stinginess. I'm not such a cheap-ass after all, I think to myself.

Instead of thanking me for the tip, he says, "Mount Sinai," and snickers again.

"Look, man," I say, "don't be a pain in the ass." I expect him to be shocked and even frightened by my bravado, but instead he laughs harder.

The David B. Kriser Division of Emergency Medical Services at Beth Israel is located on Sixteenth Street between First Avenue and Stuyvesant Square. Its emergency room is dirty white and contains, on this night, about thirty or so patients lolling about on chairs as if they are midway through a cross-country bus trip. A television set is playing the local news with the sound turned low. The top story concerns Alonzo Mourning, who is about to undergo a kidney transplant operation. There is stock footage of him fiercely dunking a basketball against the Knicks, followed by him sitting meekly at a press conference, dressed in a bulky suit and surrounded by concerned doctors. It seems to be a parable of sorts. Two Coke machines stand against the back wall and across from them is an ominous blue door that says, "Do Not Enter." There are three windows—numbered one, two, and three— where the sick are summoned to process their forms by a needlessly loud and garbled loudspeaker that sounds like the subway PA. On the wall above the windows is a clock whose hands read 9:05.

A very friendly nurse greets us as we enter the emergency room and briefly examines my girlfriend's bleeding finger. "Oh, that's a shame, honey," she says, like a loving elementary school nurse. "You're going to need sutures." She gives my girlfriend some gauze and instructs her to keep the finger above her heart. "Make sure you fill out the form, honey." And then she exits through the blue door that says "Do Not Enter."

"What are sutures?" my girlfriend asks. "Are they the same as stitches?"

"It's a simpler procedure," I say paternally, but the truth is I don't really know.

My girlfriend can't fill out the form, so I do it for her. It takes her half a minute to get her precious insurance card out of her pocket, and another half a minute to sign her name, which she does in wonderfully precise cursive, leaving beside it a small dramatic drop of blood.

We hand the form to the woman behind window number three.

"Take a seat and we'll call you," the woman says.

We take a seat. "They'll call us soon," I say confidently.

Ten minutes later no one has called us.

"When will they call us?" my girlfriend asks.

The clock reads 9:21. Sixteen minutes have passed.

One can't help but notice that the emergency room on this particular winter evening is filled completely with black, Hispanic, and Asian patients. Of the thirty or so patients, there are only three exceptions to this rule: the first being my white girlfriend; the second being a white man with an enormous, Three-Stooges lump on his baldhead; and the third being myself—a bizarre amalgam of Iranian and Jewish parentage that leaves me somewhere between white and non-white. A number of the patients are holding small dozing children on their laps who wake from time to time from their restless slumbers to produce prolonged adult-like coughs which indicate that it is they, and not their parents, who are the patients. A piece of paper taped to the wall exclaims, "Stop the Germs!" And it asks all coughing and sneezing patients to cover their noses and mouths. The children viciously hack away, taking no note of these instructions. Nor do their parents. After one little four-year-old girl has finished emitting a cough worthy of the Black Plague, a woman next to me in a large floral dress shifts aggressively in her uncomfortable chair, sighs obviously and says under her breath, "Cover your mouth, bitch!"

There is no ventilation in the waiting room. I remember that I have not eaten dinner yet and I worry that the illness percolating in my feet will commence its northward journey. I feel hot and sweaty and slightly nauseous. It is now 10:03 p.m. and it occurs to me that we have been waiting patiently for nearly an hour. A short Hispanic man enters holding his small feverish daughter in his arms, followed by an apologetic-looking mother. I watch with trepidation as they choose seats dangerously close to us.

When I was sick as a little boy my mother would leave me home alone while she went off to her secretarial job, so frightened was she of missing a day of work and falling out of the good graces of her boss.

"Call if you need anything," she'd say before shutting the door. It was a meaningless offer, because what I needed was her companionship. I would lie in bed and imagine that my illness was a hurricane making its way through my body and for some odd reason I found this soothing. When lunchtime arrived I would rise, eat my brown bag lunch that had been packed as if I were going off to school, and watch *Magilla Gorilla*, followed by *The Price is Right*, followed by hours and hours of soap operas that both bored and frightened me. All day long, interspersed throughout the commercial breaks was the peppy station identification jingle that sang out: "Channel 53, come in from the cold."

It's 10:33 p.m.

"I'm so hungry," I say, thinking aloud.

"Why don't you go get something to eat," my girlfriend says, now apparently fully composed and acclimated to her surroundings.

It's a tempting offer and I contemplate it until the image appears of me happily stuffing my face in a diner while she sits here alone, staring straight ahead, finger above heart.

"I would never do that," I say.

At 10:43 an obscenely loud voice calls over the loudspeaker, "Sanchez. Window Three. Sanchez. Window Three." An old Asian man—could this actually be Sanchez?—attempts to bring himself to a standing position with the help of an empty shopping cart.

"Too slow, he's missed his chance," I think shamelessly. "Call the next name, Window Three! Call the next name!" The old man slowly shuffles past me using his cart as a walker.

At 10:51 the blue door opens and a doctor sticks his head out and calls a name. A mother and father rise with their flu-ridden son and disappear behind the door. I envy them and their access to that blue door.

Meanwhile a very muscular older black man with a cane has taken it upon himself to surf the channels on the television set and now the faint sound of the opening theme for *Sanford & Son* can be heard wafting through the emergency room. Soon the man with the cane is laughing loudly at something Fred has said. I can hear nothing of the dialogue, but I watch along. One can learn a lot by viewing television programs without the benefit of sound. I notice that when Lamont walks he exaggerates his strut by swinging his arms wide in the style of seventies blaxploitation. Furthermore, I commend myself at how easily I am able to discern the arc of the story simply by my familiarity with the characters. It is a model of commedia dell'arte. I begin to explain this discovery to my girlfriend who interrupts me by saying as gently as she can, "I really don't know what you're talking about."

Fred stakes his claim, Lamont throws his hands up in frustration, Aunt Esther counters Fred defiantly, Grady is confused. And then the crescendo: Fred suddenly withdraws a baseball bat from beneath his jacket and waves it threateningly at Aunt Esther. Across the waiting room, the muscular man with the cane guffaws. Whatever Fred has said must be very funny. I laugh too.

At 11:03—two hours after we first arrived—the blue door opens and a patient enters the waiting room, purchases a can of Coke, and attempts to return back through the blue door, but finds that the blue door is locked from the outside. He knocks on the blue door. No one answers. The patient knocks louder. No one answers. The patient pulls hard on the doorknob. The blue door does not budge. The patient looks around to see if there is another means of egress—there is none. He looks to us, the audience, as if we might be in a position to help. We are not. With great desperation the patient pounds on the blue door and miraculously it is swung open. He slips back in having learned a lesson.

At 11:13 my girlfriend makes an empirical observation: flu victims have priority over everyone else. That's bullshit, I think selfishly. We could be here until midnight. I do not say this to my girlfriend. Instead I say, "It shouldn't be too much longer." I congratulate myself on my ability to provide comfort.

A tall teenager with acne enters, now the third white person in the emergency room. He is dressed in baggy jeans and a New York Giants jacket, and is pressing a bloody rag to his forehead. I look for the blue door to swing wide and for him to be whisked inside. Instead, the elementary school nurse hands him gauze and tells him to fill out the form, honey. He takes his seat beside us. I'm sure we've been bumped lower on the list now.

"I think they should take him before us," I say to my girlfriend magnanimously. But a moment later, as if to test such moral resolve, the loudspeaker summons us to Window Three and I shoot out of my seat. My girlfriend fills out the forms in triplicate, signs her name all over the place without reading what she's signing, and then presents her insurance card. I'm proud of that insurance card. I assume that once Window Three sees that we are armed with an insurance card Window Three will usher us promptly through the blue door with an apology for having wasted our time. Window Three takes the insurance card, photocopies it, hands it back to my girlfriend, and then instructs us to return to our seats and wait until the blue door calls us.

"But don't you understand that the insurance card means we have jobs?" I want to say to Window Three. It's an impulsive thought and I am shocked to realize I am in possession of it. I am further unnerved by the awareness that just the other day I heard Rush Limbaugh saying something similar and I had derided him for it, priding myself on my thoughts of equality and justice and brotherhood. Now, however, I am thinking: "We work. We pay taxes. We went to college. We were born in this country. We speak English. Shouldn't that add up to something?" A sign above our heads reads, "No patient without insurance will be refused service. That's the law." I find the egalitarian nature of that sign remarkably unfair.

We return to our seats. I am not like Rush Limbaugh, I reason with myself, I want the poor to have access to good, affordable healthcare—I just want to have access first.

The bald man with the Three Stooges lump on his head is loudly and drunkenly pestering the bleeding teenager for how exactly he got his head wound. The teenager looks down at the floor and says something mocking under his breath.

The man presses on with advice as if he has found a soul mate. "Well, you go and tell them that—"

"Shut the fuck up, man!" the muscular man with the cane in charge of the television says suddenly and all ill heads turn.

"You shut the fuck up," the man with the lump says.

At this the man with the cane stands, revealing a paunch and a bad leg that causes him to bend slightly to one side. Despite this he has retained the physique of someone who might have played high school football some thirty years ago—aggressive muscle lurks beneath the surface of fat. "I'm not trying to sleep out in that cold tonight, motherfucker."

It is then that it becomes apparent to me that half the patients in the waiting room are, in fact, not patients after all. The man with the lump looks up at him contemptuously and chuckles.

The muscular man cocks his cane as if preparing to swing at a fastball. "Say one more word, motherfucker. Go ahead and say one more word." He speaks with the utter confidence of someone who is prepared to make good on their promise. A moment passes. Then another. And then the man with the lump slouches in his seat, mutters something that only he himself can hear—a private act of defiance—and closes his eyes.

My girlfriend, who is usually frightened by such antisocial behavior, has seemed to thoroughly enjoy this spectacle. It has helped to make two and a half minutes pass and for this she is thankful to the man with the cane. It had also made me forget about my gnawing hunger and the fact that I had gone home this evening with the intention of being in bed by 9:30. The man with the cane now settles back peacefully to watch the television.

The disembodied voice calls for Smith to come to Window Three. A family of five rises and shuffles over obediently. It is now 12:13 a.m. and three hours have elapsed since we first stepped foot in the emergency room.

Sitting in front of me are two Hispanic women in their early twenties with a small boy of about five, and they are causing me consternation. One of the women is pretty and slim and wears jeans that reveal an ass so enormous you would think she weighed two hundred pounds. The other woman, possibly her sister, has curly hair and bug-eyes and a bandage that runs the width of her throat. How does one manage to come by a wound like that?

But it is the little boy who is most disquieting. Dressed in a snazzy velour sweat suit, the type worn by hip-hop artists, there is something about the way he moves and holds himself that is incongruous for a little boy. He seems to be both big and small at once. He speaks in unintelligible baby talk, indecipherable to all but his guardians, but he stands and holds himself like a grown man. There is an adult-like violence in him that manifests itself in little boy ways, like boldly standing on tops of chairs, or sticking his hand up the slot of the Coke machine, or knocking on the glass window of Window Three, or pulling hard on the door knob of the forbidden blue door. He appears far too comfortable and familiar with being in the emergency waiting room. The more I watch him the more his body seems to shrink, a five-year-old in the body of a three-year-old, a five-year-old in the body of a two-year-old. Or is he twelve years old?

The woman with the large ass—let us assume she is his mother—says, "You better stop that, Manny." There is a friendliness in her tone that I distrust, a permissiveness that belies a deep violence. Manny continues to climb from chair to chair.

"See, that's how you got the bump on your head in the first place, Manny," his mother says. (There is no visible bump.) "Come here and give me a kiss." And when he declines her invitation, she rolls her eyes as if to say, "just like a man."

When I was little boy about Manny's age I also got a bump on my head. I had fallen off my tricycle in the playground and was knocked unconscious. My father had left home long ago, but my nine-year-old sister was still living with us and when I came to she was sitting beside me.

"It's going to be OK," she said lovingly. Then she carefully picked me up in one arm and my tricycle in the other and proceeded to carry me home.

At the entrance to our building a kind man saw the situation and offered to help. "Let me carry your brother," he said.

"No, I'll carry my brother," my sister said. "And you can carry the tricycle."

Sometime after that episode, months maybe, my sister went to see my father for a weekend visit and on her return my mother, without provocation, flew into a hysterical, jealous rage. "Decide tonight which one of us you want to live with, you little bitch!"

My sister stared back at her wide-eyed, silent. And my mother, to emphasize her displeasure, picked up a dozen of my sister's markers and flung them across the bedroom. Then she began screaming again.

To occupy myself I went about retrieving the markers. When I had gathered them all up, I handed them back to my sister. Even in the midst of my mother's rampage my sister had the presence of mind to turn and thank me softly.

Later that night I watched from the bedroom doorway as she packed a small bag of her things. "Will you be coming back?" I asked shyly.

"No," she said. And she never did.

It is 1:03 a.m. and the television is showing images of Guantanamo Bay. Emaciated Middle Eastern men in orange jumpsuits are slowly being led around by armed U.S. soldiers. The prisoners' faces are covered with blacked-out goggles and surgical masks and their arms and legs are shackled. Others sit cross-legged in steel-mesh cages with their heads bowed low. Then an extreme close-up of a grainy photograph of a prisoner fills the screen, his face expressionless, his bushy beard unkempt, his eyes like cold-steel. I understand that the viewer is not supposed to feel sympathy for these men, but should instead find them frightening, and feel relief that they are safely encaged. But our faces and names are too similar for me to feel threatened. The news cuts to a white, female newscaster with an expression of worry and the features of a Playboy bunny. I imagine the prisoners (and me) having their way with her. Then it's back to Alonzo Mourning.

It is 1:12 a.m. and the teenager with the bleeding head wound is arguing heatedly with Window Three. "Fuck that, man! Fuck that!" The glass in the window prohibits us from hearing Window Three's response. The teenager returns to his seat and proceeds to put his Giants jacket back on, judiciously avoiding getting blood on it.

"What did they say to you?" I ask him.

"They said they're not going to be able to see me until six in the morning. Fuck that shit. I'm going home." He leaves, still pressing the gauze to his head.

There is a stunned silence in the waiting room as this news settles in. Could it be? My girlfriend and I look at each other. Six in the morning? I look for the kindly nurse, but the kindly nurse is long gone. I go to Window Three, but no one is behind Window Three except for a gaunt orderly who is tiredly filing and refiling manila folders. I tap the window to get his attention. "Excuse me," I say. "Do you have any idea—"

"It's going to be six in the morning before they get to you and that's all I can say. I've got nothing else to say." He says it like a man who has been ordered around for most of his life and has decided that it is simply more expedient to alienate the patient before the patient can alienate him.

"I'm just asking you a simple question, man," I say, forgetting that I have not even asked him a question, and picturing myself taking him by the collar and shaking him roughly like they do in Westerns. He looks at me with the startled expression of an indoor cat unsure if the glass will really be able to keep out the barking dog. I imagine that the orderly still lives with his mother and I'm sorry for having raised my voice.

"It's going to be six in the morning," he says sadly. Then he collects his folders and turns away with a world-weary expression that says, "I told you that's how they are, Ma."

It is 1:22 a.m.

The poor are used to waiting and are quite comfortable with it. That is what it means to be poor. The poor wait for the mailman to deliver the check, they wait for the slow, broken elevator to arrive on their floor, they wait for their friend or family member to get out of prison, they wait in long lines at crappy supermarkets to purchase bad food. The poor are rich with time to kill. When I was a poor child living with my poor mother in our poor apartments, we would spend our time waiting for buses that took a long time to arrive, especially in winter. But it was better for us that they did not arrive right away—we had nowhere important to go.

My girlfriend is still holding her finger above her heart. The man in charge of the television set has fallen asleep, his hands folded over his cane, his chin in his chest. His nemesis is sleeping, too. A couple of febrile children have arrived and then been ushered away for treatment. My body has achieved a transcendental state, and my hunger and fatigue have receded.

The woman with the bandage across her throat is speaking softly about a relationship gone bad. Manny is climbing happily from chair to chair. I envy him, his aggression, his determination to make the best out of a bad situation. Whereas the circumstances of my miserable childhood made me shy and turn inward, his have made him turn outward. "It is OK that you make me wait," he says, "but it will cost you. That is our contract." I, on the other hand, sit submissively.

The *Andy Griffith Show* is on television now. When I was a child it came on right before suppertime and I would watch it imagining that I was Opie, and that Andy was my dad, and that we lived in Mayberry and we went fishing together. And then my real-life mother would break this reverie by calling me to dinner, and I would sit down with her at our fatherless table and eat a pathetic meal of frozen peas and carrots and Uncle Ben's rice. I would spread the concoction evenly over my plate and pretend that it was a pie. Then I would eat a slice of it and reshape it again, filling in the missing wedge.

My mother was a latter-day Bolshevik, and in addition to leaving me during the day when she went to work, she would leave me alone at night while she went out to plot the revolution with other socialists. Sometimes I would wake in the middle of the night and pad into the living room where she slept and see that she was still not home. On these occasions I'd turn on all the lights in the apartment and pull out my toys. Brothers Grimm thoughts of her never returning would dance around my mind as I played. I'd listen intently to the sounds of the apartment building, doors opening and closing, footsteps coming and going. I have an early snapshot in my mind from shortly after my sister left, sitting on the floor in the living room, my sticker book clutched in my hand, tears streaming down my face and then the front door, like a miracle, opening and my mother coming to the rescue.

And in the midst of this memory, the blue door swings open and we are summoned. It is 2:17 a.m.

A combination of hunger, fatigue, and five hours of quiet contemplation had produced trance-like, fantastical visions of what lay beyond the blue door. A quiet, clean room, food, a doctor waiting just for my girlfriend, a bed for me. I would be able to eat and rest as my girlfriend's finger was being sutured. A car service home. Once past the blue doors, I had imagined, it would only be a few minutes before we were done.

Instead, I find a corridor filled with unfamiliar patients and their loved ones, all lounging uncomfortably in uncomfortable chairs as if their flight has been canceled and they are waiting for the first one in the morning. Hospital beds line the hall containing the more unfortunate patients in various states of undress. At the end of the hall are makeshift little rooms, no more than six feet wide, divided by curtains, like a triage set up near a battlefield. A constant, low hum of voices and footsteps can be heard, punctuated now and again by an exceptionally loud loudspeaker directing doctors here and there. The extreme fluorescent lighting and lack of windows gives the space a feeling of Anytime. The clock above my head reads 2:18, but perhaps it is the afternoon.

My girlfriend and I take a seat facing a door that reads, "X-ray. Do not enter." Beside us are two men who I had not seen in the waiting room. One is a thin black man in work boots, with a fine white powder covering his jacket, pants, hands and hair. The other man is Hispanic, with a wide friendly face, who holds a pizza delivery bag on his lap. On a hospital bed directly in front of us lies an elderly white man, sound asleep. In the bed in front of him, lying on her stomach, is a very sexy young Hispanic woman sporting a white undershirt and a foul mouth. Standing next to her, with a shaved head and a lazy eye, is her boyfriend or husband, his hands resting lightly, respectfully, on the edge of the mattress.

"Fucking bullshit," she says, regarding something or other. Her husband giggles.

Paramedics enter suddenly, swiftly, pushing a young man in a stretcher. His neck is in a brace and his shirt is covered in blood. He vanishes through a door. Several police officers and a distraught young woman follow them in. The chatter in the hallway falls silent for a moment. A young black orderly walks by unperturbed, pushing a cart.

"Can you rub my back?" the sexy woman asks her husband, who obliges while looking down at her with affection and concern. I suddenly feel insecure about the amount of care and attention that I have been showing my girlfriend.

"Are you OK?" I ask, putting my hand on her knee.

"I'm tired," she says matter-of-factly.

A young white man, dressed in khakis and looking like he has just come from law class at NYU, passes us; he is doubled over, grimacing, clutching his groin as if his penis has been sliced lengthwise. With short mincing steps he takes his place in line for the bathroom. Everyone eyeballs him anxiously, concerned that at any moment he may defecate on the floor.

The orderly pushes his cart past us. "My mom said that I'd grow up to be something," he says good-naturedly to no one in particular, "but all I do is push stuff around."

When I was about twelve years old I sliced my middle finger trying to unclog the brushes of the vacuum cleaner while they were still whirling around. I had mistakenly thought that if the bristles were soft at rest they would be soft in motion. It felt as if my finger had been torn off and I ran screaming into the kitchen where my mother was cooking dinner. We fled outside into the night prepared to walk the mile to the emergency room. A man was opening the door to his car and my mother screamed out to him, "Mister! Mister!" We had all the trappings of a mother and son lost in the Bavarian Forest. I remember the man's startled look as my mother pleaded with him to drive us to the hospital. Even in my distress I felt embarrassed and ashamed for us having to rely on the kindness of this stranger in the middle of the night and I was convinced that if I were him I would not be so generous. Beneath my embarrassment and shame my missing father lurked, watching from afar.

"Ooh, yeah, that's where it hurts," the woman receiving the massage says. Then she calls out loudly, "I need to see a fucking doctor." Her husband giggles the way you do in school when a friend says something obnoxious to the teacher.

The orderly passes by again. "Excuse me," I say to him, summoning courage, "do you have any idea how long it's going to take until we're seen?"

He stops and examines my girlfriend's forms. Then hands them back. "It shouldn't be much longer now," he says with a friendly smile.

"Thank you," I say triumphantly, "thank you very much."

Then he presses on with his cart.

"He's really helpful," I say to my girlfriend.

"He hasn't done anything for us."

"Well, here comes our doctor now," I say, as a short doctor with a large Adam's apple approaches us. He passes by without stopping and goes into the X-ray room where he wheels out a man in a stretcher. The delivery guy beside me stands with his pizza bag and goes to them. The elderly white man passed out in the hospital bed in front of us has not stirred. "Do you think that man might be dead?" I ask my girlfriend. The door to the bathroom opens and the two people waiting in line display that rare quality of goodwill and humanity by letting the NYU student with the injured penis cut in front of them. Even gripped by pain, he turns to thank them politely.

"Can you tell me if there's a bruise on my back?" the massaged woman says, pulling her shirt up, revealing a sexy black bra.

Her husband flushes. "Oh, I don't know if I should be looking there," he says, giggling, trying to avert his eyes from her bra. In deference to my girlfriend I look away, too.

"Oh, come on," the woman says. "I need to know."

"I've been to Fordham Road. I've seen your brothers," he says.

I realize that the man is neither her boyfriend nor her husband, and that what I have been witnessing is something of a first date.

It is 4:12 a.m and seven hours have now passed since we arrived. I am reminded again how hungry I am. I wonder if I was foolish in deciding to stay with my girlfriend this entire time. Should I have taken up her suggestion to get some food? Of course, I should have! Perhaps the offer still stands. I sneak a peek at her. Again the image of the diner materializes, but this time it is not me, but rather my father who is contentedly stuffing his face, enquiring of the waiter if they serve wine. My life is one continual struggle against the impulse for flight. I put my arm around my girlfriend's shoulders and say nothing.

"I'm so tired," she says and leans into me. I am struck by the realization that in spite of often feeling like a frightened little boy, I am in fact a grown man and that my girlfriend expects me to behave the way a grown man would. Yet here we are in this hospital, begging for care, and I am powerless to do anything about it. I think about Manny's bravado and how if he can survive to adulthood he will be fearless.

The NYU student emerges from the bathroom, but strangely his condition has not changed; he is still bent at the waist and wincing. Slowly he makes his painful way to a folding chair, step by step, like a man with severe osteoporosis, and with the greatest of difficulty, he sits.

"The leg is broken in two places," the doctor is saying to the pizza deliveryman, who in turn translates this into Spanish for the man with the leg broken in two places.

"I'm going to give you a sedative that's going to make you sleepy," the doctor says. And he demonstrates "sleepy" by briefly closing his eyes and wobbling his head.

The man with the twice-broken leg is wheeled away and his friend the translator sits back down with his pizza bag.

"What's wrong with your friend?" I ask him.

He tells me that the man in the stretcher is not his friend but his brother, and that he was delivering a pizza when he was knocked off his bicycle by a BMW making a U-turn. Apparently, the driver had been talking on a cell phone. I picture his brother pedaling furiously through the cold to deliver the pizza in under thirty minutes: an updated version of a Dickens story.

"The doctor says it's going to be three months before he can go back to work."

The orderly passes by again. "Excuse me," I say.

"They still haven't seen you?" he says as if he's never seen anything like this before.

"No," my girlfriend responds.

"Any minute now," he says cheerfully.

"Thank you," I say. "Thank you." I am happy to be lied to and he is happy to lie. Together we construct our make-believe.

A nurse with a nametag that says "Violet," appears and stops abruptly in front of the injured NYU student. With her nurse's uniform snug around her thick body and her gray-brown hair pulled back in a bun, she resembles a high school gym teacher. "Who said you could sit here?"

"It was empty," the student says meekly, looking up at her from his waist.

"But who said you could sit here?"

"I just needed a seat."

"Well, you can't sit here."

I want to say something to defend him, but I don't. Violet watches impassively as the young man slowly rights himself as best he can, and hobbles off like a refugee in search of a place to rest for the night. Then she proudly folds the chair and removes it from the hallway.

Another doctor approaches. "I bet this is our doctor," I say.

The doctor stops before the elderly white man on the hospital bed. "Mr. Sizemore," the doctor says loudly, tapping the man sharply on the chest. The man does not stir. "Mr. Sizemore. Mr. Sizemore." The doctor shakes him by the shoulders, then aggressively pulls up the man's eyelids. The man snorts awake. "What were you drinking tonight, Mr. Sizemore?" he asks. He goes about examining the vital organs as if he were a veterinarian examining a cow.

"Vodka," the man mutters.

"What do you want us to do for you, Mr. Sizemore?"

No response.

"Do you want to sleep it off?"

The man grunts in the affirmative and then passes out. Perhaps he will sleep there forever, I think, and the rest of us—he deserving—will wait here forever.

"Fuck these motherfucking doctors," the sexy woman in the black bra yells out to no one in particular. She sits up and puts her jacket on slowly. "I've been here eight fucking hours." Her date looks down at the linoleum floor like a little boy witnessing his mother in dispute with a store clerk. "I don't have eight fucking hours to wait, you heard?" She painfully climbs down from the hospital bed, her date holding her elbow lightly, as if helping her out of a car, and the two depart.

The man in the fine white dust and work boots wastes no time going to the now-vacated bed. It reminds me of stories I have heard of soldiers in war removing the boots of fallen comrades to wear for themselves. This is a world where only the assertive survive. The man lies down in the bed. Then he gets back out. Then he gets back in. Then he gets back out. He plays with the various knobs, trying to adjust the angle, but can't seem to figure it out. In an act of brotherhood, the pizza delivery man joins him and the two together position the curve of the bed just so. The man lies back down. First on his stomach and then on his back and then on his stomach. Then he attempts to take off his boots. For some physiological reason he can barely bend to reach his feet so the removing of his boots is a long and confusing ordeal. His legs bend and his back bends, but somewhere between the two there is something dreadfully wrong. Perhaps his ass is broken. It is an interminable process and there seems to be some danger that at any moment something deep inside him could snap. He manages finally to pull off one boot and then the other. And then he takes his socks off and then he puts his socks back on and then he puts his boots back on. Then he falls asleep.

It is 5:01 a.m.

At that moment a doctor appears before us, much to the jealousy of those who wait. Any ill will I had immediately vanishes and is replaced by an all-is-forgiven attitude that reminds me of an ex-girlfriend I eagerly took back after she had broken up with me to sleep with other guys. The kindly, absentee doctor lovingly unwraps the gauze from my girlfriend's finger, which by now has congealed and has stopped bleeding altogether. Did we even need to be here? He examines the wound, cleans it briefly, and says it'll need suturing—which he explains is the same as stitching. He produces a needle from his pocket that, without so much as a warning, he plunges deep into her finger. The bystanders in the hallway look in horror and then look away. Blood drips down her hand and onto the waiting room floor. When will that be cleaned? My girlfriend clutches my arm in agony. I move my legs quickly so that her blood does not drip onto my pants, realizing shamefully that the well being of my clothes should not be foremost on my mind.

After that we are ushered like Hollywood celebrities into one of the makeshift rooms where my girlfriend can lie down comfortably. We wait for the Novocain to take effect, the chemical reaction being the only thing between us and freedom.

In the cubicle on our left is an elderly black woman sitting beside an even more elderly black woman, impossibly thin, dozing in her bed. There are wires and tubes connecting her to various machines and bottles. The woman in the chair is watching her intently. "Keep your arm up, Ma," she says. And the old woman tiredly raises her arm.

In the cubicle on our right lies the NYU student who had been bent in two. He is fast asleep now. A young woman with bed head sits beside him, staring off, a look of fatigue on her face.

Two young white doctors arrive, and the old woman in the chair pushes herself to stand.

"OK, Ma. They're here." There's admonition in the daughter's voice. It's that tone poor people take in the presence of authority, to let the authority know that even if their partner is unable of achieving it, they at least are aware that they should be on their best behavior. I had often found myself as a child standing beside my mother as she spoke with a person in power, the landlord maybe. "Yes, yes," my mother would say with utmost formality, "I will most certainly be sure that will not occur again in the future."

"Hello, Mrs. Sampson," one of the doctors says, as if he's speaking to a child. "How are you feeling tonight?"

"They want to know how you're feeling tonight, Ma."

Mrs. Sampson nods. The doctors look over her chart and confer with one another. Then they tell the mother the various elements of her treatment and what she'll need to do. The doctors depart.

"Did you understand that, Ma?"

But Ma has drifted off to sleep.

A few years ago—before I had found my girlfriend and fallen in love—I had a horrible allergic reaction to an antibiotic called erythromycin. I had taken six capsules as prescribed, but when I boarded the Four Train at Eighty-sixth Street, the muscles in my chest and stomach had begun to clench involuntarily, causing intense pain in my abdomen.

The pharmacist made a mistake, I thought as the train hurtled southward, they gave me the wrong prescription. My breathing became short and labored and it was all I could do to keep myself from collapsing on the subway floor. I knew I would not be able to make it all the way to Fourteenth Street without vomiting, so as the doors opened at Fifty-ninth Street I exited the train swiftly. A phalanx of disinterested rush hour commuters surged around me, jostling me from side to side. I felt suddenly, acutely, what it would be like to be old and frail in New York City. I pushed through the crowd and mounted the stairs, and another wave of people came toward me like soldiers at Normandy. I was convulsed in pain as I began the long march up the steps, flight after flight, until I reached a platform and made my way toward the exit sign, only to be greeted with more flights of stairs.

I'm going to die, I thought. I'm going to die because of a pharmacist's error. Here, face down in the subway station. I'll be a bizarre article in tomorrow's *Daily News*. And I haven't done a goddamn thing in my life!

When I finally arrived outside it was like emerging after days in a cave. I was surprised that it was sunny and warm and that there was still buoyant life. A cop was directing traffic on Lexington Avenue and I asked her where the nearest hospital was. "Two blocks away," she said. And as she pointed me in the direction my torso folded in two and I collapsed on the sidewalk.

A crowd gathered around me. I wondered what I looked like to them. I wondered if they would say to their friends later, "You'll never believe it, but I saw some guy die today." I wondered if my jacket was getting dirty. I could hear the cop radioing for an ambulance and I feared that I would die waiting for an apathetic EMT to make his way through rush-hour traffic.

More cops surrounded me and an elderly woman asked, "What happened to him?" In the distance I could hear the sound of a siren approaching.

At the hospital they hooked me up to an IV and put me in a bed in the hallway because all the rooms were filled. Eventually a doctor came by and told me that it would take several hours for the antibiotic to move through my system, but once it did I'd be fine. I promptly vomited all over the floor. A black orderly came by to clean it up. The loudspeaker was over my head, barking its orders directly into my face. A group of medical students listened intently to someone explaining my condition. Then they moved on. A little boy lay in a bed nearby, staring up at the ceiling, unmoving. An older man in a suit sat beside him. I watched them for a while. And then a doctor and a nurse arrived, and the older man introduced himself as the boy's father, and the three of them talked for a while between themselves. It was hushed conversation. And then the doctor and nurse left and the man put his hand on the boy's forehead and stroked it gently.

My girlfriend's Novocain has taken effect. On cue the doctor arrives with the needle and thread for the five sutures. The stitching kit terrifies her.

"Will this hurt?" She says it like a little girl.

The old woman in the room beside us is trying to keep her eyes on her mother without falling asleep. She looks as if she's been in the hospital for a long time and that she knows she still has a long time still to go, but she has resigned herself to it. She shakes her head from side to side to stay awake. For a moment we look at each other and smile.

I take my girlfriend's good hand as the doctor prepares to sew. One day maybe, sometime in the future, if all works out OK, I will ask my girlfriend to marry me, and I will one day find myself sitting beside her in a hospital room, holding her hand as she prepares to deliver our baby. I will surmount the misery of my childhood and become the father I never had. I will invent it out of thin air.

The doctor begins sewing the wound. The procedure will take all of ten minutes.

It is 5:50 a.m.

LOST AND FOUND

BY THOMAS BELLER

It began when I was walking down the street in all innocence and several people called out at once, "You dropped your glove!" And just like that I was swept up in one of the unseen subterranean currents of the city, the current of lost and found. It holds you longer than you expect. It holds you and spins you around and around. I looked down behind me and there was my glove on the sidewalk.

I picked up the glove and thanked each of the three people who had intervened on my behalf.

An hour or so later I walked into a Starbucks and saw, on the floor, a wad of cash. I picked it up. It was a ten and a five. Not a fortune, but no insubstantial sum either.

"Is this yours?" I asked the man who was standing at the cream and sugar counter, near where the cash had lay. He said it wasn't.

Another said he thought it belonged to a woman who had left.

"Which way did she go?" I asked.

"To the right."

"Describe her."

"She was with a kid."

Out the door, to the right—I moved quickly and soon I saw a woman with a kid. They turned into a Barnes and Noble and I followed.

Just as I came up behind her, the kid dropped her pink hat. It fell to the floor like a weightless little cloud. This seemed proof enough. Between the two of them, they couldn't hold onto anything.

"Excuse me!" I practically shouted. They stopped and turned. I pointed to the girl's hat and then, seized with feelings of chivalry at my immanent gesture of altruism, I bent down and picked it up for her. The woman said thank you. She was a bit breathless, for some reason.

"Is this yours?" I said to the woman. I held out the crumpled bills. She looked confused, glanced down into her purse, then again at the bills. "Fifteen dollars?" she said.

"Yes."

"I think it is," she said. I gave it back. She smiled. The little girl in the pink hat hardly took notice. Perhaps this happened all the time, I thought. People run up to her mother and return things she has dropped.

It all would have been a bit of random city choreography were it not for the fact that a couple of days later I came home and realized my wallet was not in my pocket. Deep panic. A lost glove is annoying, but a lost wallet is a statement. You have misplaced your identity, your money, your credit, and various gift certificates accumulated over the holidays and birthdays given to you by your mother. What does it mean to be so careless with love and money?

I tore through the apartment and then emptied every pocket in my coat. Two of the pockets in my coat had holes. They had long had holes. Therefore I never put anything in these pockets. But I had hastily stepped out of the deli just before coming home, my wallet and loose dollars still in my hand. Maybe, in my moment of haste, I had put the wallet in one of the pockets with holes and it fallen to the street.

I pictured it lying on the street. I wanted to rush outside to look for it. But then I thought, "No, don't do that, it's crazy to think it's lying in the street. Keep looking in here."

But barely a minute went by before I stood before the open refrigerator. There comes a time in all searches for objects lost at home when one capitulates to the irrational urge to check the refrigerator. You realize that rationally, there is no way whatever you are looking for is in the refrigerator. But it isn't anywhere else and what's the harm in looking?

No sooner had I seen the fridge light blink on, I slammed it shut and raced outside. What is more irrational, looking for your wallet in the fridge, or on a city street?

I trotted back to the deli, eyes on the ground. I know there are worse tragedies than losing your wallet, but are there worse feelings than walking down a city block in New York looking at the ground with the deluded idea that your wallet, with eighty bucks and credit cards and license and gift certificates from your mother, will be simply lying on the street untouched?

In front of the deli, right in the middle of the street, wet, flattened by many tires, lay my wallet.

But it wasn't over. The next day I sat in a restaurant with big picture windows facing Prince Street, and watched placidly as a tall, handsome man strode confidently down the street while his wallet plopped out like a horse dropping from his back pocket.

A woman walking in the opposite direction picked it up. I leapt to my feet, not sure which of them to address. I went after the guy. "Hey!" I called. He didn't hear me, or ignored me. He was wearing a big black puffy down jacket. I slapped him on the back, quite hard. Why was I so annoyed? The man was making the same mistake I had made, and in some irrational way I could express my annoyance with myself by being annoyed with him.

"Hey!" I said again, and it was all I could do to refrain from adding, "Idiot!" He turned to face me, wide-eyed, but before he said a word I said, "You dropped your wallet. That lady down the block has it."

I went back to my seat in the restaurant and watched as the man hurried after her and tapped her on the shoulder. He explained himself to the woman and she handed him his wallet, smiles all around. My role in this seemed to bring me full circle to the dropped glove; a cycle was complete.

For a while after that, I didn't lose anything.

PURSUITS

BY THOMAS BELLER

I wouldn't have noticed her at all if she hadn't stepped on my foot. Her hair was in a tight braid that bounced against her exposed shoulders as she rushed past. She wore a skimpy red top, extremely tight white pants and high heels.

I glanced after her with a tiny bit of indignation—Hey! You stepped on my foot—but before the thought could form, a man came through in her wake. He had broad shoulders and wore a black button-down shirt, untucked over jeans. Something in his posture was seething with intent.

"You saying I'm done?" he said, calling after her. The phrase hung in the air.

It was eleven at night, and the cobblestone streets of the Meatpacking District were swarming as if it were Mardi Gras—a turbulence of lipstick, credit cards, alcohol, the percussive rhythms of taxi doors slamming shut and the clatter of tiny shoes on pavement. It had rained earlier, a torrent, and it was as if the evening's late start, and the soft, close air had sent everyone into a delirium. I was waiting for a friend from Washington, D.C. He was a guy I associated with the chaos of foreign markets and improvised travel arrangements. I thought he would like this place.

The girl arrived at the corner and paused, looking this way and that. It seemed clear she was upset, though I saw her only from behind. The man caught up to her and stood in front of her even as she tried to turn away.

The man was twenty-four or twenty-five years old, thick in his chest, and wore his brown hair in a bit of a shag. His body registered a restrained violence, but his face was more vulnerable, as though struggling to assimilate an unassimilatable insult. He seemed to be asking her a question, perhaps repeating the one he had already said: "You saying I'm done?"

The girl kept scampering a few steps away from him. He kept putting himself in front of her and talking to her. Something was slipping away from him that he did not want to slip away, and he was now being drawn toward violence against what he wanted to keep. It was like watching a glass fall off a table in slow motion.

Then, as she turned away again and he again stepped in front of her, she slapped him. Not in his face. She slapped his chest. But it was a slap.

"Oh boy," said the guy standing next to me. Skinny and smoking and watching the passing scene, he had a pleasantly detached manner, as if he were waiting for someone, too.

The girl was still moving this way and that with small nervous steps while the man hovered. She slapped him again, in the shoulder. All around us, as far as I could see, were swarms of men and women darting about as efficiently as schools of fish, but here was a dissonant movement, a break in the choreography. The scene seemed poised to explode into something ugly.

Finally she crossed the street. He strode after her, gesturing emphatically as she moved ahead with purpose, hugging herself and looking down. They faded into the darkness outside the bright rim of the Meatpacking District. I never saw her face, but I felt sure she had been crying the whole time.

"That didn't look good," I said, to no one in particular.

"After that second slap I though he might hit her back," said the guy beside me.

"Did you hear that line, the thing he said?" I asked. He had.

" 'You saying I'm done?' Wow."

"It was like a bomb," he said.

"So much information in that one line, I mean, the way he said it."

"But no factual information. No back story."

"What do you think happened?"

"Hard to say," he said. "They could have just met tonight, they could have been together for a while."

"If you had to guess, what do you think was going on?"

"I don't think they met tonight," he said.

"Me neither."

"I think they had been dating a bit."

"I'd say a month."

"Do you think they slept together?"

He thought about it. "Yeah."

"I agree. That intensity on his face."

At this point a couple of Italian men stopped in front of my new friend and offered him a just-opened pack of Marlboro Lights. "I am quitting, please take these," the Italian guy said.

My new friend said thanks. The Italians walked away.

"Most people start smoking when they get drunk," he said.

"This guy got drunk and decided to quit!"

"You want one?"

I didn't.

"Yeah, they kill you." He lit up. "So, what set it off?" he said.

"My guess is she had been fading on him for a while, and they went out and had some drinks, and he did some tiny little thing, totally insignificant but it annoyed her, and that was the pretext for this thing going off in her head. She hadn't even really known she felt this way, felt it that forcefully, but then suddenly she's just grossed out by him, and it goes downhill fast from there."

"Or maybe she had some drinks, and she starts flirting with another guy, and he gets really upset, and she's like, 'Who do you think you are? Get away from me.' "

"You think he'll get her back?"

"Nah."

"Me neither."

"Hope not," he said. "I thought he was going to hit her."

Cabs arrived and departed. None of the people spilling out of them was my friend from Washington. The guy and I chatted a bit. It turns out he was from Los Angeles.

"I live across the street from this hotel," he said, "I see all kinds of things. I have these binoculars and if something good happens, I turn off the lights and settle in."

"People leave their curtains open with a building across the street?"

"All the time! But the thing is, the sexual exhibitionists are never young people. It's always these older guys in their fifties, sixties, with these young girls, probably hookers, and they've got the lights on and the curtains wide open."

"That's amazing. Do you ever get too much of it? Like one night you just want to hang out and read a book and you look out the window and are like, "oh no, not this again?"

"Nah, it doesn't happen that often. But I really wish I could have some sort of *Rear Window* experience, you know? See some crime and then get into Jimmy Stewart mode, and solve the murder."

My friend showed up at the same time his friends—four women—did. Suddenly we were a large, awkward group, and my new friend and I tried to convey the scene we had witnessed. No one really responded, and then my friend Chris said, "I've been that guy about seven times," and I looked at him and I could tell from his expression that we hadn't really conveyed the flavor of that moment, the way the guy in the black shirt was clenching his fists towards the end. If we had, I don't think Chris would have volunteered that information even if it were true.

We all said goodbye. Chris and I went into Pastis and had a good dinner, though as I looked around I was struck by what seemed like the villainous nature of all the men in there; they wore velvet slippers, or blue blazers with white polo shirts with the collars popped, grown men dressed in distortions of little-boy prep. They were middle-aged, surrounded by young women, and glowing with petty cash. It was like a casting call for James Bond villains. I thought of the men in the hotel with the lights on and the curtains open, surely the same guys surrounding me in Pastis at midnight. Compared to them, that young guy in the black shirt, with his youthful, wounded pride, almost seemed sweet. Almost.

iPOD ON THE TRACKS

BY THOMAS BELLER

I was bounding down the stairs into the subway, three steps at a time, hoping to make the train. The stairs were wet. The air was cold. It was a day of harsh weather, a gusting snowstorm, but I was listening to my iPod and was experiencing everything dreamily.

To say it was a new iPod was only half of it. I had sent it in for repairs. It had stopped working just before the warranty ran out, a very modern kind of good luck, given that some iPods seem to stop working just after. It had been delayed in its return. Weeks turned into months. By the time it arrived, it felt like a reunion. This was only its second day in action.

The subway doors were still open. I was listening to a Chopin prelude and I was moving fast. I took the last few steps in a giant jump, sidestepping a man in a wheelchair who was shaking a cup of change. The sounds of piano filled my head. I was going to make the train.

Then I felt a brief tug on my ears, and silence. The iPod had fallen through a hole in my coat pocket and skidded across the platform like a bright white hockey puck. There was a sharp thwack as it slammed into the side of the subway car and fell into the crack between platform and subway, down to the tracks. The whole moment had the brisk finality of a goal in air hockey.

Everyone facing the open subway door, and a number of people standing behind them, watched the iPod drop to oblivion. Then they looked up at me.

The man in the wheelchair sprang to his feet. A miracle?

"What you drop?" he demanded. "I get it for you. No problem."

I turned my back. I couldn't let them see my despair. I waited for the doors to close. But the doors did not close.

"I go down there for you?" the man said. One of his eyes was gray and cloudy.

"It's all right," I said. "I can get it."

"I go for you!"

The train was still there. It was being held in the station. I turned to face the people in the car.

"I can see it," one of the men on the train said. "It's safe."

I went over and peered down through the crack. There it was on the black, grimy floor.

"If you go and tell them, they'll get it for you," someone else said. It was a sympathetic crowd.

The guy in the wheelchair had returned to his wheelchair. His body language suggested that it was a seller's market. I would come around. Or not. It was all the same to him. I took out my wallet, hoping to see a ten. Five would seem too cheap, and a twenty would be profligate. But no. I could not pay a man in a wheelchair to do my dirty work, even if his actual need for the wheelchair was now dubious.

I waited until the train and the two that followed it were finally gone. The iPod lay there on the floor of the tracks. The tunnel was dark and quiet. My knees were a little loose, like those of someone about to jump off a diving board.

New York is a vertical town. The emphasis is on things that rise. But the New Yorker's panic-stricken need for accomplishment—the need to go up—is matched by a kind of vertigo that comes with being constantly aware of the distance below.

I took a breath and hopped down. I grabbed the iPod, its whiteness streaked with dirty water. I stood there a moment rubbing it dry, petting it, really, as if it were a small animal that had gotten itself into trouble. Then I dropped it into my pocket, planted my hands on the filthy platform, and hoisted myself up.

I didn't make it. I bonked my shin, and fell back down. On the next try, no problem. But in the few seconds between the two tries, I felt a pang of awareness. I was on the tracks. I'd stared down at the tracks all my life. It had always been rats, the third rail and garbage that provided that space with its faint air of horror, but it turns out that the most powerful feeling while I was down there was simply being lower, almost beneath, everyone else. I looked up and saw a lot of knees. I wanted only to rise.

Back on the platform I brushed myself off. An older woman, well dressed, looked at me as though I were the Loch Ness monster.

"You get it?" yelled the man in the wheelchair, still shaking his change cup.

"Yes!" I yelled back. And I thanked him profusely for some reason and pushed ten dollars into his cup. Perhaps for giving me courage, even if it arrived via shame.

The iPod, though now scuffed, worked fine. I washed my hands several times before I sat down to lunch half an hour later. I kept rinsing and soaping and rinsing and soaping long after my hands seemed perfectly clean.

The whole episode should have been a fleeting moment, something barely remembered, but that evening, my fiancée said, "What happened to your leg?"

I looked at my shin. There was a small cut, no more than a tiny red line, and a bump.

I explained about the iPod. She was amused as I described it skidding across the platform, and the fellow in the wheelchair jumping up to help. Then her face darkened a little. There were three months to the wedding.

"You didn't go down there, did you?"

"I couldn't bring myself to hire the guy in the wheelchair," I said.

"You went down on the tracks?"

When I said I had, she got worked up. It really bothered her.

"You're not alone anymore!" she said. She asked me to promise that I would not jump down onto the subway tracks in the future. I promised. She shook her head.

"I ought to put some of your sperm in the freezer," she said.

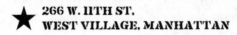
THE LADY WITH THE CUPCAKE

BY THOMAS BELLER

I looked out the window and saw a woman come walking up the street eating a cupcake. She was blonde, in sneakers, alone. The cupcake's icing was white. The woman's timing was perfect—I had begun reading on the computer at dusk; by the time it ran out of power, and the screen went suddenly black, the sky had become dark and the streetlamp outside my window, which shines bright as a full moon, had switched on. There were no lights on in the room. I sat in darkness and looked out the window hoping for something, some gift. I saw the woman with the cupcake come up the street. I looked out the window hoping for something, some gift to bring me back into the world of the living. The lady with the cupcake appeared at just the right time.

There is a famous cupcake store on the corner. Once upon a time in this town people lined up to get into nightclubs with names like "The World." Now the world comes to New York and lines up to buy cupcakes.

I watched this lady walk with her cupcake, preparing to take a bite. She had a box in one hand, with a couple more cupcakes in it, and the cupcake in the other. She pushed the edge of the cupcake to her mouth, took a bite, but it was an indelicate maneuver even from four flights up. I wondered if she had traveled a long way to get to New York and was now achieving one of her goals, to eat these cupcakes, or if she was local, and was giving herself a Sunday treat on the way home. I also wondered if she was going to eat the cupcake by mashing it into her mouth while she walked.

She seemed to have the exact same thought about the indelicacy of eating a cupcake while walking and carrying a little box. She paused in front of the stoop across the street. She gave it a once-over and then looked around, as though she were about to sit on someone's car hood, and wanted to make sure no one was around to yell at her.

No one was around. She sat down. She crossed her legs. She ate her cupcake in small hungry bites.

Just behind her, in the window over her shoulder, I saw some movement. It was the guy with two poodles. The guy with two poodles lives across the hall from the large woman with the pit bull who walks other people's dogs for a living. I thought the movement was the man with the poodles, but it wasn't. The movement was a poodle. There is a brown one and an off-white one, and this was the off-white one, which seemed to be standing on the back of the couch, where I had never seen it before. Behind the poodle, the man seemed to be hovering, as though trying to coax the poodle down off the back of the couch. I was sure that he was talking to the poodle. He held out his arms and seemed to be pleading with the poodle to get down from the ledge. The poodle ignored him and watched the lady eat her cupcake

Now we had the solitary, Hopper-like figure of the Lady with the Cupcake, and unknown to her, just over her shoulder, a poodle and its owner, talking. Next to her was the entrance to the stairs that lead down to the basement apartment, where the building's superintendent lives. He is from Ecuador, has a wife and baby, and maintains, I have heard, a carefully organized collection of DVDs and videotapes featuring live performances of

Jimi Hendrix and Bob Dylan. There was a spot on the building's
sandstone surface, just below where the poodle now stood, that
was a lighter shade of brown; the word "shadi," written in white
spray paint, had been emblazoned there a decade and change ago;
I knew it must have been at least fifteen years because its author,
Dave Scilken, who I had known a little bit (he played guitar in a
band called The Young and the Useless with Adam Horowitz)
had been dead that long.

The Lady had the stoop, and the street, all to herself, and
seemed to be enjoying this quiet cupcake moment. Meanwhile,
I could see all this life crowding in around her, the gesturing poodle owner over one shoulder, the flickering TV of the pit-bull
owner over the other, the poodle dancing hungrily on the window ledge, and just below her feet, perhaps, a family of
Equadorians watching a video of Jimi Hendrix kneeling before
his burning guitar at Monterey. The world and its mysteries were
available to me, visible. I was elated, and ran to get my camera to
capture the tableau.

But the camera malfunctioned when I turned it on. A memory card error, it said. I turned it off and back on, and now it
worked. But the lady had finished her cupcake and the poodle
and come down from the couch. The scene was over. The stoop
was empty. But I was very glad to have seen it. I was so grateful.
I was thinking, "You can leave New York. You can leave it and
it is all right, because you can always come back. It will always be
here! Everything is going to be all right!"

I calmed myself by taking a picture of the empty stoop.

THE STUFF OF LIFE

BY THOMAS BELLER

I only wanted it to be over, even as I dreaded its arrival. For weeks I walked around in a clenched state of anticipation, unaware of how tense I had become.

"An adventure or an exile?" I asked myself. I couldn't decide.

A few days before the big move—from Manhattan to Roanoke, Virginia for one year—I was sitting in front of Rice, a restaurant on Mott Street with delicious food, watching a couple of guys carry someone's possessions into a truck. The underwear paraded by, then the sheets, the lamp, the chair, papers, etc. I thought of that Raymond Carver story in which the guy recreates his living room in the front yard, but it's for sale.

It occurred to me that high on the list of my concerns about moving was who might be around to see our own possessions paraded out the front door and into the truck. Totally unimportant, yet there it was, floating around amidst the more pressing concerns.

On one end of the spectrum was the slightly blind billionaire who lives next door. Having a billionaire as a neighbor brings many peculiarities with it, but these are greatly compounded when he is about your age, and, as I have been told, legally blind.

LOST AND FOUND

The only manifestation of this blindness I ever saw was when I would now and then venture a hello as we passed on the street. My hello was invariably met with serene and total indifference.

"It's because he's legally blind!" I would tell myself, but I would always feel a bit slighted. A year would go by, I would try again, with the same result.

On the extreme opposite end of the spectrum, though geographically just across the street, was Shienbaum. Shienbaum always wanted to talk. I avoided conversation with him for years. Perhaps I was for him what my billionaire was for me. I was worried he would be there on his stoop when we moved, watching.

THE STOOP

Shienbaum had been occupying his tiny studio apartment—rent controlled, bathroom in the hall—for forty years. He spent a lot of time on the stoop. He had a salt-and-pepper beard, and walked with a defiant, bearish strut, as though at all times ready for a fight, even when simply going around the corner to get a coffee, practically the only act in which I had ever seen him engaged.

Once, back when I had first moved to the block, I saw Shienbaum out in the world, dressed up, on a date. We were in a restaurant, and he leaned toward the woman across from him with tenderness, his neck bulging in a dress shirt. But later, when he went to get his coat, he marched over as though he were going to attack the coat stand, as though he had been fuming with rage at this coat stand for years and had finally had enough. That was the only time I saw him with a woman.

After I finally gave in and made small talk with Shienbaum, he hectored me with remarks for years, which he yelled from across the street, such as, "Hey Doctor! What happened to your Knicks?"

It was such an old-school kind of annoyance, I endured it. Plus it's nice to be called doctor. But then the day after the 2004 election, Shienbaum, a communist, had glanced at my Kerry button and said, "Too late for that," and I exploded, and he exploded, and we cursed each other on the street. It ended with his remark, "I never liked you anyway!" I found this oddly touching for some reason. But I didn't want him to see me moving.

THE MOVE

"You leaving here for some redneck town where you don't know anybody?" said Udi, the mover, as he picked up another astonishingly heavy box as though it were a tissue. "Why do you do this?" He turned toward the door and then gestured with his bald head at the window overlooking my block in the West Village. "Now this," he said. "This is living!"

Udi was a tough, polite, somewhat chatty Israeli.

It turned out that Udi had left New York five years ago and now lives in Florida. "In a redneck town, no one to talk to," he said. "My wife wants to move back to Brooklyn. But we have a kid."

"So what's all this about a redneck town! You're projecting."

"Maybe," he said. "Maybe not."

We stopped our fraternizing when Udi announced that we had much more stuff than we had contracted for and that their fee would double. I had a meltdown; he called his office; we worked it out.

Downstairs, the other mover, Carl, was loading the boxes from the sidewalk into the truck on the corner with the same remarkable grace with which Udi had carried them down four flights. With Carl, the exchange was less fraught. He saw my T-shirt, which read, "Vassar Basketball," and asked if I played there. When I said I had, he told me he had grown up in Pough-keepsie, and as a senior in high school had gone with his best friend to the Vassar campus bar every night.

Carl was a good-looking black guy, well spoken and in excel-lent shape, and he communicated with a minimal amount of inflection—just a flicker of tone—the lascivious feast this high-school adventure among the college kids had been.

He looked around at my corner, West Eleventh and West Fourth streets; noted the crowd at Tartine, where I usually have breakfast; and let his eyes graze the patina of the old brownstone on the corner and then the newly renovated one across the street. He nodded with the connoisseur's gaze of a man who has seen a lot of places. Carl lived in Atlanta, but he hadn't been there in weeks.

It turns out the moving business is a bit like the Merchant Marines. Crews get on their trucks and set off for weeks. They sleep in motels, or on the truck, or not at all, and never see home as they travel the high seas of the interstate highways, moving people's stuff.

Finally everything was packed. "Take care of my stuff!" I called out.

They got into the cab of the truck and looked out the window at me and laughed in a not-entirely-encouraging manner, but they were joking. We were buddies now, in a way. I had admired the economical force of their movements. We had talked about life. They had sized up the way I was living—and me—and seemed to judge it all as interesting, if overpriced.

Also, when they had arrived on Eleventh Street, they had parked beneath the deliciously lush, low-hanging tree on the corner with the one branch that had time and again been threatened by these huge, boxy moving trucks. I had been so worried that the truck that finally broke the branch would be mine. But Udi and Carl had been careful. The branch had not broken.

Later that evening, my wife and I set off for a stay with friends in the country, where we would wait out the interval of several days before the movers arrived in Virginia.

DARK HORSES

We had been at our new place, at the edge of the Hollins University campus in Roanoke for two days before the pink truck showed up, bright and early, with Udi and Carl in it, looking sleepy.

"Nice place you got here," said Udi, and I confess his approval pleased me enormously. They unpacked everything into our neat little bungalow, and then Udi marched down to the corral to look at the horses.

We live next to a horse corral. With horses in it.

I repeat this fact to myself, and corroborate it by looking out the kitchen window, frequently. It helps me adjust to the new reality.

In truth I know nothing about where I am. Hollins itself is still a mystery, though it echoes my own alma mater somewhat, a plush little jewel box enclosed within a slightly depressed city. But then that could describe many, many academic institutions.

The other night I took a walk by myself at midnight. The school sits on a ridge. Above loom gorgeous mountains, and in the hollow below runs the interstate, which in the daytime is an invisible whoosh. At night, though, the mountains vanish, and there above the interstate are all the bright signs of corporate hospitality that generically dot interstates all over the country, and which unfailingly freak me out. The addictive comfort of being inside the fort, inside the city walls, was totally gone.

To my right, down a hill, was the white fence of the horse corral, and within it, the shadowy movement of three horses.

I veered down into the darkness, a half-eaten apple in hand, clucking and making little whistle sounds. The horses moved toward me, but stopped ten feet away. After a lot more clucking and whistling, the white one came forward, sniffed the apple, and then, with a great flapping of lips, snorted it out of my hand.

My terrible fear of leaving the city ended that night, in the dark, with a sliver of moon above and three shadowy horses standing beside a fence next to their trough. Two drank and grazed, and one stood by while I stroked its long muscular face, its huge nostrils dilating hypnotically as soft, warm breaths pulsed onto my hand. Its inquisitive eye stared at me for a whole minute before it gave a snort and pulled away into the dark.

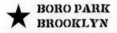

LOOSE TILES

BY JONATHAN AMES

I n the late 1960s, when I was a little boy, I used to go to Boro
Park to visit my grandparents. I was six when they moved
from there, so I don't remember too much of the neighborhood
or their apartment, and to make things worse my real memories
are tangled with memories of photos which I haven't seen for
some time.

But there are two things that I recall which don't come from
pictures: to get to their apartment, which was on the third floor
of a brownstone, I had to climb a long, dark, narrow staircase
and about halfway to the top my grandmother, a redhead who
usually wore an apron, would come out of her door and appear
on the landing, smiling at me, ready to hug me, ready to love me;
the second genuine memory is of a small loose tile in the bathroom. The tile was a white rectangle, about two inches long and
an inch wide, and it was right next to the toilet and I could nudge
and displace it with the toe of my shoe, and then put it back with
the toe of my shoe. I liked to do this every time I visited. I liked
to see the gap beneath the tile; it was dug out, kind of like a small
grave.

What was most remarkable about this piece of tile, which was rather thick and probably ancient, was that in our bathroom back home in New Jersey there was also a loose tile right next to the toilet. No one else in my family (mother, father, older sister) seemed to be aware of this coincidence, and I thought, with the logic of a child, that it must be some shared trait between my mother and her parents, that the two houses were meant to have loose tiles for me to play with. I do remember being very sad when my father changed the tiling in our bathroom and I asked for the loose tile to be returned and my father thought I was joking, or he ignored me; it was some combination of those two responses.

My grandmother was a very good cook and very neat and very unhappy. She collected little antique things made of glass and china. I think they gave her some pleasure. In the mid-1980s, she was diagnosed as having Alzheimer's. She ended up in a nursing home for about a dozen years, sitting in a wheelchair, not thinking, as far as I can tell, and definitely not speaking, though the first year or two, she did say one word, over and over, "What? What? What? What?"

She was fed by attendants, a spoon pushed against her lips until she opened her mouth, and she was lifted in and out of bed once or twice a day and put in her wheelchair. I don't know how often they'd bathe her.

On her floor of the nursing home were many other living-dead sitting in wheelchairs. There seemed to be no care or thought as to how they were placed—behind a door, facing a wall. My grandmother, luckily, was always placed near a window, though she never looked out.

I'd look at the people in the chairs, about forty or fifty of them, and I'd imagine how they were young once—had jobs, love affairs, concerns. I thought they would be disgusted to know what had become of them. And I wondered every time I visited—and I still wonder—if I will be one of those people in a chair some day.

LOST AND FOUND

My mother visited my grandmother every month, sometimes less often—the nursing home was in Pennsylvania. I would go once or twice a year and I would watch my mother brush my grandmother's hair, which, with only a few streaks of orange-white, somehow stayed red up until she finally died in 1999 at the age of eighty-nine.

My grandfather was a little heavy and bald and had blue eyes. He was a very sweet, quiet man, but I guess at one time he had a terrible temper. He was about five-ten, not very tall, but there was the implication of a former great strength—he supposedly had carried a small piano on his back into our home in New Jersey, and for many years he was the foreman of a shipping yard, which he ruled with a baseball bat kept under his desk. By the time I knew him, when he was in his late fifties and early sixties, his head had a permanent wobble to it and he was supposedly a reformed drinker. He had shown up once at our house in New Jersey late at night, quite drunk—I was just a baby, this was around 1965—and my mother told him he had to quit drinking or he would never see me or my sister again. After that night, no one ever did see him take another drink. But when he died of a rotted gut in 1981, at the age of seventy-two, we found many vodka bottles hidden beneath his work table.

In 1971, my grandparents, whom I called Nanny and Poppy, moved from Brooklyn to Williamsport, PA, because my uncle, my mother's brother, lived there, and because Brooklyn was changing. They got a cute little house on a corner, and I guess there was the hope that they would be happy.

My grandmother for years had wanted a house, longing for her childhood in Saratoga Springs, NY, and the big house she had grown up in. That house in Saratoga was on Lincoln Street, and this new house in Pennsylvania was also on Lincoln Street. This was supposed to be a good sign. But I guess it wasn't. It must have been too late to go back to her childhood, or there was no going back, anyway. Or maybe she did. If she had recalled correctly, she would have realized her childhood had been tragic and difficult—her mother died when she was eleven and she had to drop out of school and raise her brothers. So my grandmother was consistent—a miserable childhood, a miserable old age.

In 1972, my grandfather left her in the car with the engine running, he was doing a quick errand, but something went wrong—the car wasn't in park, perhaps; this mystery was never solved—and she and the car slid through a plate glass window of a store. Her back was wrenched, she was in pain for years—maybe until the Alzheimer's robbed her of all sensation—and she never forgave my grandfather for this.

She had never forgiven him for anything, though, so this was nothing new, but I guess this car accident was the final blow. Whereas once they had fought, now they hardly spoke to one another; she gave him a sort of silent treatment up until he died in 1981.

So in that new house, they slept in separate bedrooms, and she made him build a shower and toilet in the basement; she didn't want her beautiful new bathroom soiled (she had hated, it turns out, the old rotting tiles in Brooklyn). She could use the upstairs bathroom and shower—she must have scrubbed it down immediately afterwards—but he was not allowed. The Alzheimer's may have kicked in earlier than we realized—I've read that one of the first symptoms of Alzheimer's is an obsession with cleanliness, and she had always had that, but it got worse and worse.

My grandfather, who, like my grandmother, never went to high school, was secretly smart, I think. He'd write my mother and me and my sister two-page letters in beautiful cursive writing, always ending with the phrase—"And on we go." To bring in some money in his retirement, he worked flea markets, selling old coins and pocket-watches that he had repaired at his work bench. He would write in his letters tragi-comically, "I'm nothing but a peddler."

Sometimes, I'd stay with them in Williamsport. My grandfather bought me a bicycle. It was orange with a black seat. It was a pretty good bike, not great. The front tire would rub in a funny way and that was never fixed, but I liked riding it on the uneven sidewalks of Lincoln Street.

Now, when I visit my uncle in Williamsport, I walk past their little house, empty of them for a long time now, but I'd like to go in there and find them and talk to them. I always want the dead to come back to life, but they never do. I have often thought of going to Boro Park and finding the old brownstone, maybe I could conjure them up there, but I never go. The result would be the same. No ghosts, no living people, no one to love that I had once loved.

I can see it, though: a sidewalk, a brownstone, a concrete front staircase, and a closed front door. And behind the door, a narrow staircase that probably wouldn't seem very steep to me now as I climbed it and there would be no one coming onto the landing to greet me, unless it was to ask what I was doing in their home.

THE JEWISH HOLLY GOLIGHTLY

BY JONATHAN AMES

I try to call my Great Aunt Doris every day. She's ninety years old and lives alone. I love her desperately, and as she gets older, especially of late as she becomes more feeble, my love seems to be picking up velocity, overwhelming me almost, tinged as it is with panic—I'm so afraid of losing her.

I usually call her around six o'clock and when she picks up the phone, she always says, "Hellooooo," drawing out the o's to sound like a society lady, but when she's not feeling well the o's aren't so drawn out, so I like it when her affectation is present. Daily, we have just about the same conversation.

"Did you need any money?" she says. "Don't be ashamed to tell me. Aunt Doris is here to help you." Sometimes she speaks of herself in the third person, like a professional athlete.

"I don't need any money," I say, "but thank you."

"Have you had your dinner yet?"

"No, I'm going out."

"Treat yourself to a steak. You're not a vegetarian any more, are you?"

"No, not a vegetarian."

"That's smart. A steak is good for you. Wear a hat when you go out."

My period of vegetarianism about fourteen years ago still haunts her, and she's been telling me to wear a hat for over thirty years.

"Well, I'll talk to you tomorrow," I say. "I love you."

"I love you more than that," she says.

My great aunt was raised in Saratoga Springs, New York, one of six children, including my Grandmother Nancy, who died several years ago. When my great aunt was ten her mother died and she and Nancy had to take care of their father, the house and the boys (three brothers), as well as the infant son of their sister Anna, who had died in childbirth.

When she was fifteen, my great aunt started working as a manicurist in a beauty shop, Fresham's, where she attended to the wealthy ladies who came to Saratoga for the racing season, and this was to be her lifelong profession.

In the thirties, she'd follow the wealthy set—working at different Fresham's—by the seasons: Saratoga in August, New York City in the fall, Miami Beach in the winter, and resorts along the Eastern seaboard in the spring. By the forties, she was in New York full-time, working in the salon at Saks Fifth Avenue. She had a brief marriage during the war years, followed by a ten-year marriage in the fifties, and then in the sixties she was single again and worked for many years in the barbershop at the Harmonie, a private men's club off of Fifth Avenue. In my family, she was legendary for being a wild, great beauty: a tiny, stunning, voluptuous redhead, who had many lovers. A sort of Jewish Holly Golightly.

She wasn't able to have children and so my mother, her sister's daughter, was like a child to her and I, later, was like a grandchild, and clearly her favorite. All throughout my childhood, she'd come to New Jersey to visit us for weekends. I loved to meet her with my mother at the little station—she'd descend out of the bus in her colorful dresses and heels, and kiss me a thousand times, but I didn't mind.

When she was in her mid-seventies, my great aunt lost a breast to cancer, and for the last twenty years she has lived in Queens in her tiny studio apartment. Her couch is her bed, the place is cluttered with antiques, but kept neat, and there are many paintings on the wall. My favorites are these small water-colors done by a French lover of hers, whom she met in Paris in 1947. All of them feature a tiny redheaded woman with an hour-glass figure—you see her sitting in a cafe, standing on a bridge over the Seine, kissing a lover on a park bench under a night sky.

Two weeks ago, I went to see my great aunt on a Sunday, as is our habit. I make it out there about twice a month. When I can't make it, she always says to me, "If I can't see you, we still have our telephone romance."

Right in her subway stop is a little florist and I picked up some irises. Aunt Doris smiled so happily when she saw me. I hugged her to my chest—she's very small—and stroked her hair, which is no longer flame-red but has faded to a pretty strawberry blonde.

Our routine is to have lunch and then play gin-rummy, but before playing cards I told her I wanted to talk to her about her life, that I was going to write an article. We sat on her couch.

"You already know everything," she said.

"I want to make sure I've got the stories right."

"What should I tell you then?"

"Just some memories. What do you remember from Saratoga?"

"From Saratoga…I remember when mother died. I was ten years old and Nancy was eleven. I knew that a person wore black. So we went to the dime store and bought black dye and put our kerchiefs and gloves in the dye, and when I finished my hands were black, couldn't get that off. Washed. Scoured. For two weeks I walked around with black hands."

Eighty years later, my great aunt sometimes still cries about this—her mother's early death took away her childhood and shaped her whole life.

"What do you remember from working in Saratoga?" I asked.

"Let me get my thoughts . . . How old was I? Sixteen. Working at the Grand Union Hotel. A woman came in for a manicure. She was looking for prostitutes, but I didn't know that. This was in the thirties. She says, 'When you come to New York call me.' I was supposed to go to New York until the season started in Miami Beach. There—"

"In Miami?"

"Don't say Miami. Miami Beach. There I had the experience of manicuring the wife of the writer Damon Runyon. She was a bitch. After I put four coats of polish on her, she rubbed it off. Said she wanted to see if redheads had a temper. Can you imagine? I also took care of Mrs. Jimmy Walker there, the wife of the mayor of New York."

"What happened to the woman who was looking for the prostitutes?"

"The madame? I called her when I got to New York."

"What happened? You didn't work for her did you?" This would have been new information. The family didn't know about this!

"She told me she wanted me to be a prostitute, and that was the end of that, naturally. I said, 'You've got the wrong girl.'"

"Really?"

"Of course."

"In the thirties is when you had the abortion?" I asked. It may sound like I was being rude, but my great aunt and I have talked about everything for years.

"Yes, that was the thirties. When I had that I went to the drugstore. 'Al,' I said to him. 'My best girlfriend is pregnant. I have to help her.' So he gave me the name of a doctor, also in Brooklyn. I got an appointment, a private house. This wasn't legit. Got me on a table, not even an aspirin. Spread my legs. Not even an aspirin! Took an instrument, hurt like hell. Wonder I didn't die from the pain. Lasted ten minutes. He says, 'You stay here until I tell you to go home.' He comes back a few minutes later, I'm still bleeding, says I should go home. I go home and I tell Nancy it's my period. It was my secret. I didn't tell anyone. Two days later I stopped bleeding. And then it became a memory."

"Did that keep you from having children?"

"More or less, I think so...Let me get my papers, there are things in there that'll be good for an article."

She went to a drawer and removed an envelope stuffed with letters and clippings—obituaries of her Harmonie Club clients, who were well-to-do businessmen.

She began reading the obituaries, and she came across one, a yellowed piece of newspaper, and kissed it. "This one I loved," she said. "Had a real crush on him. We had an affair. He was so sweet. He cared for me. What people I had in my life. Good people."

"When did you have an affair with him?"

"I don't know. Before he died! I can't remember everything."

She found another obit. "This one was crazy about me. Those were good days. I had my apartment on Fifteenth Street. I had my little dog. He didn't like the dog."

"Did you have an affair?"

"Not really. He just liked to be near me. He wasn't interested in sex. Neither was I. His car would drop him off at my house. He'd just sit on the couch. Liked to be near me."

"How many lovers do you think you had in your life?"

"What's your idea of a lover?"

"Someone you had sex with."

"I don't know. I can't figure that out. I was very active in sex. I was sexy."

"Make a guess."

"Six."

"That's it? Your whole life?"

"You want to add two, add two. I didn't screw around with everybody. These were men who stayed. But I didn't play it right. I screwed my life up."

"How so?"

"I had offers to live on Fifth Ave. I had wonderful chances. I was too…not pious…too righteous. I always knew the difference between good and bad and I always chose good. I should have relaxed and done a little bad. I should have stuck with one good man and not cared if he had a wife. Now look at me."

"Are you saying a man would have taken care of you?"

"Sure. Why would I be a mistress to him if he didn't give me a car, an apartment? I wouldn't have to live like this on a couch. These were wealthy men. Not salesmen. The mistress sometimes gets more than the wife. Don't you know that?"

We looked at the clippings for a while longer. "I wish I knew some of the people I used to know," she said, and then she put everything back in the envelope.

We were quiet, and then she said, "What's happening with you lover-boy? You pop out girlfriends like pizza pies."

"I'm still hung up on this one girl," I said. "She doesn't want to be with me. Did you ever have that, where you think about someone all the time?"

"Worse. The people are dead. They never come back. But time heals and in that time you just run away from it, and running away means you get involved with someone else quick…Where is this girl?"

"Out of the country. Has a new boyfriend."

"So let him enjoy her. It's past tense. It's gone. If you don't want to get over it, it will stay with you, that's for sure."

"Should I try to get her back?"

"A lot of fish in the ocean, brother. Lots of fish."

"But how come I can't stop thinking about her?"

"Like me with all the people in here"—she squeezed the envelope—"but you have to go on without thinking. If you can't work up a veneer around your heart you'll wind up going to a psychiatrist and throwing your money away…Know what makes a person strong? You have to take failure. Another person had to experience what I had to experience, they'd go on the booze and stay on the booze until they dropped dead. You don't see me doing that. If I had to take my life serious, I'd be up shit's creek."

"I wish I could get over this girl."

"You pine for her. Bullshit. I wouldn't give her a minute of my time. She doesn't think of you. It's a one-sided affair. What's good is that you don't need her. You're intelligent, respectable home, good-looking, you're not out of prison—you don't need her. Choose a good woman. Not a cold tomato. Forget her."

"Of course I haven't been to prison!"

"That's because you're from a good family."

"Anyway, didn't you ever pine for someone?"

"No, not me. I want respect. If I don't get respect, they can go fly a kite…Where'd you get this haircut?"

"My neighborhood, why?"

"I don't like it. It's not tapered in the back. Looks like a wig."

That cracked me up, so we stopped talking about love and went and played cards. As usual, she won. Then she walked me out to the elevator. I hugged her while we waited for it. "I worry about you," I said.

"Don't worry about Aunt Doris. I'm a survivor. It's my job to worry about you."

"All right," I said, consoled. The elevator came. I got in and held the door. "I love you," I said.

"I love you more than you know," she said, and she leaned in and kissed me goodbye.

SNOWFALL

BY JONATHAN AMES

This recent snow made me think of my friend Glen Seator, who is dead. In January or February of 1996, there was a bad snowfall— Glen and I were very good friends then.

I was living in Clinton Hill, Brooklyn, next to the BQE, and Glen was about two miles south of me, right next to the Manhattan Bridge. He lived on this weird little street—Duffield Street—of old houses, which somehow had survived both the building of the BQE and the Manhattan Bridge. Glen owned one of these old Duffield Street houses. He lived on the first floor and rented out the other two floors. It was a house he had bought with his longtime boyfriend back in the 1980s, but that relationship ended and Glen was left as the sole owner. He loved his building, but it was also, I think, a constant reminder of his heartbreak, of something lost.

So there was a blizzard this one day in January or February, and Glen called me up late in the afternoon as it was getting dark, as the storm came to an end, and asked if I could come over and help him shovel off his roof. The roof was going to collapse or leak, something like that.

I walked under the BQE to Glen's. Nothing had been plowed. I felt like an adventurer.

We went up to his roof. Glen was in his late thirties, tall, red-headed, handsome, and a little arrogant. But the kind of arrogant that is charming—it made people crave his approval, which is probably why I was on that roof. He was also terribly funny, a WASP from the Midwest who could do the best imitation of a yenta I have ever come across, and I should know, having grown up with yentas. Once this talent of his was revealed, we spent most of our time together talking in what we called "yenta," which meant that we harassed and insulted one another in our best yenta-Yiddish accents:

"You're horrible! You're selfish!"

"You're the one who's self-centered! I come to your home and you don't even think of offering me something to eat! I could starve to death and you wouldn't even notice!"

"I know better than to give you something to eat! You're a *shnorrer*! A pig! If I gave you a cracker you'd eat my whole freezer!"

So we were up there shoveling. The snow was wet and heavy. The sun went down. I was terribly cold. The roof was slippery and slanted. It seemed an impossible task. I kept hoping Glen would say we should quit, but with light coming off the Manhattan Bridge, just enough to see by, we somehow cleared that roof in about two hours—the white snow giving way to black tar. Then Glen made me dinner. He was a wonderful cook. We spoke, as always, in yenta, which gave me great pleasure; I've rarely laughed with anyone as much as I laughed with Glen. After dinner, I walked back home under the cover of the BQE.

Over the next year or so we drifted apart. We talked less and less. He was often out of the country for weeks and months at a time. He was a genius artist: museums all over the world solicited him for the architectural installations he would build. It's not easy to describe his work, but if I was to simplify things, I'd say that he took apart the museums and galleries that hired him in order to expose these institutions, or, conversely, he rebuilt their structures within their structures. I think his idea was to displace, as well as to reveal. And once he said to me, describing his work, "I like to make a mess. It's a way to be bad."

This seemed fitting, because Glen's arrogance made him careless, distracted; he didn't like to be bothered with the annoying things one has to do, and so his affairs were always a mess—bills went unpaid, documents were lost, his building was always falling apart—and yet he managed to make breathtaking work that required precision and discipline, even as it disrupted. His art was a rebellion: I'll play by the rules to show that I can't stand the rules. So the results were displacing, revealing, and mess-making, but also beautiful.

These last few years, I didn't see him at all, except once by chance in a restaurant about two years ago. Seeing him I immediately missed him, and we said we'd get together, but we didn't.

Then a mutual friend, Ava, called me this winter, a few days after Christmas. She said, "I have something to tell you."

"Okay," I said, and I knew from her voice to gird myself for something terrible.

"I'm sorry to be the one with bad news, but I'm just going to say it…Glen Seator died. He fell off his roof. He was up there fixing something and fell off. They found him the next day. Can you believe it?"

I couldn't believe it and I still can't. I never fully believe that people die. Don't want to believe.

I told Ava—because I'm self-centered, horrible—that one time I had been on that roof with him and I found it slanted and dangerous. I told her this, I think, to show that I had once been good enough friends with him to have been up there shoveling in the freezing cold, and that I had intimate knowledge, in a way, of how and why he died. It was my ego asserting itself: I was there, we were good friends.

My ego did this to compensate for the fact that I hadn't really seen or spoken to him in years, that actually he had died for me while he still had been alive. Our friendship had died.

I don't have any photographs of Glen and I haven't cried over him, but if I had a picture I probably would cry—it would drive home to me that I'll never see him again; that there's no second chance of running into him at a restaurant and this time making a call. I've had other friends who've died and it's when I look at their photos that I want to scratch at the picture and bring them back, bring them back as alive as they were in the moment the picture was taken.

Ever since Ava gave me the news about Glen, I often morbidly wonder what he thought as he plummeted. I think he must not have believed that it was happening, he must not have thought he would die—he always seemed so sure of everything, so certain. Or maybe there was terror and horrible fear, the realization that he had made a grotesque mistake.

I'd like if it was the former, that he felt momentarily annoyed and inconvenienced, that he figured he'd just be bruised, but all right. What I'd really like, though, is to go by his house and see him, to knock on his door like I used to seven years ago and have him be there. He couldn't possibly have fallen.

ACKNOWLEDGEMENTS

I owe thanks to many people for helping produce Mr. Beller's Neighborhood and for making this book. Bryan Charles, Patrick Gallagher, and now Jean Paul Cativiela have all done stellar work as managing editors of the Web site, reading and editing submissions and sending out the Story of the Week mailing. Sabin Streeter has been a guiding and calming influence since the site's inception in 2000. Elizabeth Grove worked as a senior editor for the first four years of the site's existence and continues to make valuable contributions behind the scenes. Rowland Miller has provided valuable help with our summer reading series, Park-Lit, a collaboration with the New York City Parks Department. James Thoms has been the back-end wizard on the Web site. Nick Stone has done fantastic design work on both books the site has produced. Joanna Yas, my brilliant colleague at *Open City*, has always regarded the site as my own private thing and has mostly kept her distance from its goings-on, unless things start to get extremely hectic and out-of-control, which they did fairy quickly with this book. She took pity and intervened with all sorts of assistance, advice, and support, and in the end put in a lot of work for which

LOST AND FOUND

I am deeply grateful. Leni Zumas and Matthew Rossi also provided valuable edits in the manuscript's late stages.

I thank my mother for her wisdom and support, and my daughter for her totality of feeling (she's two) and for existing. My beautiful wife Elizabeth has been a reader and collaborator, a constant guiding presence, an inspiration, and a gift.

Finally, the amazing Michelle Legro assisted me enormously in the production of the book, which bears the influence of her editorial sensibility, her organizational capacity, her patience, and her zeal. I am privileged to have worked with her. She has my deepest gratitude and respect.

BIOGRAPHIES

ROBERTA ALLEN is the author of eight books, including two story collections, a travel memoir, a novella-in-shorts, and a novel. She is also a visual artist in the collection of the Metropolitan Museum. She is working on a memoir called *Forbidden Territory*, and has recently completed a manuscript of stories. She teaches at The New School and in private workshops. Her Web site is robertaallen.com

MINDY ALOFF has written extensively about the arts and cultural subjects for periodicals in the United States and abroad. Her third book, *Hippo in a Tutu: Dancing in Disney Animation*, was published early in 2009 by Disney Editions. She teaches dance criticism and writing at Barnard College and works as a telefundraiser for the New York Philharmonic.

JONATHAN AMES is the author of the books *I Pass Like Night*, *The Extra Man*, *What's Not to Love?*, *My Less Than Secret Life*, *Wake Up, Sir!*, *I Love You More Than You Know*, and *The Alcoholic* (a graphic novel illustrated by Dean Haspiel). He is the editor of *Sexual Metamorphosis: An Anthology of Transsexual Memoirs*. His next book, a collection of fiction and nonfiction, *The Double Life is Twice As Good*, will be published by Scribner in July 2009. He is the winner of a Guggenheim Fellowship and is a former columnist for *New York Press*. Mr. Ames has also written *Bored to Death*, a TV series for the HBO network starring

Jason Schwartzman as "Jonathan Ames." "Snowfall," "Loose Tiles," and "The Jewish Holly Golightly" were published in *I Love You More Than You Know*.

KATE ANGUS's poetry has appeared or is forthcoming in *Barrow Street*, *Subtropics*, *Gulf Coast*, *Mid-American Review*, and *The Saint Ann's Review*, among other places. Her fiction can be found in *North American Review* and *Barrelhouse*.

TONY ANTONIADIS's fiction and nonfiction has appeared in *Open City*, *The Brooklyn Rail*, *The Village Voice*, *The New York Times*, and elsewhere. He co-curates the Littoral Reading Series for Issue Project Room, and collaborates with Freebird Books and the Continuous Mammal of East Village Radio.

ADAM BAER is a New York–born writer currently living in Los Angeles. His work has appeared in *The New York Times Book Review*, *The New Yorker*, *GQ*, *The New Republic*, and many other publications and anthologies.

HADARA BAR-NADAV's book of poetry *A Glass of Milk to Kiss Goodnight* (Margie/Intuit House, 2007) won the Margie Book Prize. Recent publications appear or are forthcoming in *Beloit Poetry Journal*, *Colorado Review*, *Denver Quarterly*, *The Iowa Review*, *The Kenyon Review*, *Ploughshares*, *Prairie Schooner*, *TriQuarterly*, *Verse*, and other journals. She is an assistant professor of English at the University of Missouri-Kansas City. Of Israeli and Czechoslovakian descent, she currently lives in Kansas City with her husband Scott George Beattie, a furniture maker and visual artist.

JILL BAUERLE is a journalist and writer who lives in Brooklyn. After the soul-searching incident of waiting on her agent, she turned in her leather pouch and went to journalism school. She has received fellowships for her fiction from the Mac-Dowell Colony, the Millay Colony for the Arts and the Ludwig

Vogelstein Foundation. Her novel-in-progress is titled *Liechtensteining*.

GRAHAM T. BECK is a writer, editor and critic based in Greenpoint, Brooklyn. He rides a bike to work.

MADISON SMARTT BELL was born and raised in Tennessee. He has lived in New York and London and now lives in Baltimore, where he teaches at Goucher College. He is the author of twelve novels, including *The Washington Square Ensemble*, *Waiting for the End of the World*, *Ten Indians*, and *Soldier's Joy*. His eighth novel, *All Soul's Rising*, was a finalist for the 1995 National Book Award.

THOMAS BELLER's short stories have appeared in *The New Yorker*, *The Southwest Review*, *Ploughshares*, *Harper's Bazaar*, *Elle*, *Mademoiselle*, *Best American Short Stories*, and *The Saint Ann's Review*. He is the author of three books, *Seduction Theory* (stories), *The Sleep-Over* (a novel), and *How to Be Man* (essays), all from W.W. Norton. *The Sleep-Over Artist* was a *New York Times* Notable Book and a *Los Angeles Times* Best Book of 2000. He is a founder and co-editor of *Open City* magazine, and creator of Mr. Beller's Neighborhood. He has edited three previous anthologies of original writing: *Personals*, *With Love and Squalor* (with Kip Kotzen), and *Before and After: Stories from New York*. He divides his time between New York and New Orleans, where he teaches at Tulane University.

ELIZABETH BELLER is a writer who has worked at Sotheby's auction house and as a reader for Miramax films. She lives in New Orleans and New York with her husband and daughter.

BETSY BERNE is the author of the novel *Bad Timing* and the co-author of *Narciso Rodriguez*. She is working on a book called *Single White Mother*.

PATRICIA BOSWORTH is the author of four books, including biographies of Diane Arbus and Marlon Brando. She is a contributing editor at *Vanity Fair* and is completing a biography of Jane Fonda for Houghton Mifflin.

MICHELE BOWMAN lives in Brooklyn with her two dogs, Doxy and Rico. Rico is an adopted Welsh Corgi who also loves the park. Her poetry has appeared in literary journals, and she is currently trying to find a home for her first book of poems. Living in New York inspired her to begin writing essays; "Off-Leash" was one of her first. She has an MFA in creative writing from the University of North Carolina–Greensboro and a JD from the University of Texas School of Law.

JAMES BRALY is the writer and performer of the Off-Broadway monologue, *Life in a Marital Institution*, a *New York Times* Critics' Pick optioned for film and television by Meredith Vieira Production. His memoir of the same title is forthcoming from St. Martin's Press. The only two-time winner of The Moth GrandSlam storytelling competition, James's work has been featured on NPR's *Marketplace*, and in the new anthology, *Afterbirth*. His Web site is JamesBraly.com.

AMY BRILL is a writer and producer. Her articles, essays, and short stories have appeared in *Salon*, *Time Out New York*, *Ballyhoo Stories*, *Guernica*, and the first Mr. Beller's Neighborhood anthology *Before and After: Stories from New York*, among others. She has been awarded fellowships in fiction by the Edward Albee Foundation, the Millay Colony, the Constance Saltonstall Foundation, Jentel, and others, and has been nominated for a Pushcart Prize in fiction. She lives in Brooklyn with her husband and daughter, and is working on her first novel.

ANDREA BRUNHOLZL still carries New York City around in her heart, though she has since migrated to other parts. She writes fiction and essays, and lives with her family in Austin, Texas.

MARTHA BURZYNSKI is a writer and photographer living in Brooklyn. Her work has appeared in *The Village Voice*, *Publisher's News* (UK) and online for *Gawker*, *Gothamist*, *The Black Table,* and others. She has photographed rock stars, abandoned and forgotten New York, mermaids, weddings and politicians. She still waits tables.

CHRISTINE CALIFRA-SCHIFF is the author of numerous essays and short stories. She was raised in Greenwich Village and lived in Brooklyn for many years. She was a member of the Writers Room in New York City. She currently lives in Cincinnati, Ohio, with her husband and two sons. She is a member of Woman Writing for A Change, where she is working on a novel.

DENISE V. CAMPBELL began writing for Mr. Beller's Neighborhood after taking a creative writing course with Thomas Beller at Columbia University, where she graduated with a BA in literature and writing. She wrote for, and was the associate editor of, *Fort Greene News*, covering community news and local politics. She is currently a doctoral student in African American studies at Temple University.

ANGELA CARDINALE BARTLETT received an MFA in creative writing from Columbia University. Her writing has most recently been published in the *Chaffey Review* and *Sand Canyon Review*. She lives in Southern California with her husband and two sons and teaches composition and creative writing at Chaffey College.

MICHELE CARLO has lived in four of the five boroughs of New York City and remembers when a slice of pizza cost fifty cents. She is a frequent contributor to NYC's storytelling community, and has been a two-time Grandslammer at The Moth. She has been published in the anthology *Chicken Soup For The Latino Soul,* online at Mr. Beller's Neighborhood, and is the winner of *SMITH* magazine's *Next Door Neighbor* contest. The stories "Kill Whitey Day" and "After Dark" are part of Michele's memoir, forthcoming from Citadel Press in 2010.

JEAN PAUL CATIVIELA is the current managing editor of Mr. Beller's Neighborhood. A graduate of the writing program at New York University, he has also studied at The Second City training center in Los Angeles, and has received a grant from the New York Foundation for the Arts. He is currently at work on a novel.

SAMANTHA V. CHANG is a writer, yogini, and mother of twins on the Upper West Side. She is writing her first novel and has written for *The New York Times Magazine*. She currently blogs about a variety of funny things and everyday occurrences on mascararivers.blogspot.com.

BRYAN CHARLES is the author of the novel *Grab On to Me Tightly as if I Knew the Way*.

PETER CHERCHES is the author of the short prose collections *Condensed Book* and *Between a Dream and a Cup of Coffee*. His fiction has appeared in numerous magazines since 1977, including *Harper's*, *Semiotext(e)*, *North American Review*, and *Fiction International*. In the eighties, he was active in New York's downtown performance scene as a singer and monologist. He currently blogs about food, travel, and the writing life on Word of Mouth: petercherches.blogspot.com.

ANDY CHRISTIE is a partner in Slim Films, an NYC-based illustration and video effects studio. His writing has appeared in the *The New York Times*, in snooty literary journals and online. His humor book, *I Wasn't Kidding*, was published by Random House here and in the United Kingdom. He is creator and host of *The Liar Show* (TheLiarShow.com). But this story is true.

CATON CLARK is a New York–based television editor, aspiring screenwriter, and occasional writer of short nonfiction.

RACHEL CLINE has published two novels with Random House, *What to Keep* (2004) and *My Liar* (2008). She lives in Brooklyn, not far from the apartment she grew up in. In a conversation prompted by the initial publication of "The God of High School" on Mr. Beller's Neighborhood, she learned that Eli's life was saved. He has since thanked her for remembering him so well.

GABRIEL COHEN's latest novel is *Neptune Avenue*. He is also the author of *The Graving Dock*, *Boombox*, the nonfiction book *Storms Can't Hurt the Sky: A Buddhist Path Through Divorce*, and *Red Hook*, which was nominated for the Edgar® Award for Best First Novel. He has written for *The New York Times*, *Poets & Writers*, *Shambhala Sun*, *Page Six Magazine*, and *Time Out New York*. He has taught writing at New York University and lectured extensively. He lives in Brooklyn, where he runs the Sundays at Sunny's reading series.

SUZANNE COMEAU MARS left the East Coast for Ruralia, a mythological city located just south of the Georgia/Florida border, where she lives with her two Pug dogs and a bad case of culture shock. Suzanne has a degree in Russian language and currently works as a freelance fundraiser for local arts programs. She writes the blog Le Style Sauvage, (stylesnatcher.com) a slumgullion of political cartoons, cultural commentary, style editorials, and movie reviews. Content from the blog has been syndicated to *Reuters*, *The Palm Beach Post*, *Dayton Daily News,* and *The Chicago Sun-Times*.

SUSAN CONNELL-METTAUER was a regular contributor to Mr. Beller's Neighborhood. Her story, "Speed Freaks," appeared in the anthology *Before and After: Stories from New York*.

JEROME ERIC COPULSKY is an assistant professor of philosophy and religion and the director of Judaic studies at Goucher College. His stories, essays, and reviews have appeared in such places as *The New York Times, The Christian Science Monitor, Salon, Nextbook, Zeek,* and *Azure*.

COURTNEY COVENEY used to want to be a career Miltonist, but now she writes for the Internet. She has an MA in British literature from Georgetown University and lives and works on Long Island.

CHARLES D'AMBROSIO is the author of *The Point and Other Stories*; *Orphans*, a collection of essays; and *The Dead Fish Museum*, which was a finalist for the PEN/Faulkner Award. He is a 2009–2010 Lannan Fellow.

JILL SAND D'ANGELO is the author of *A Real Dog, Dear Clara,* and *Stories of Men*. Her work has been published in *The New Yorker*. She resides on the Upper East Side of Manhattan and is currently completing a new collection of stories. Her Web site is jillsand.com.

DAPHNE lives in Brooklyn with her eighteen-year-old cat, a lot of books, a small garden, and the thoughts jumbling round her head. She is pursuing an MFA in poetry, while contemplating the juxtaposition of flesh versus disassociation.

MEGHAN DAUM is an opinion columnist for the *Los Angeles Times* and the author of the essay collection *My Misspent Youth* and the novel *The Quality of Life Report*. Her articles and essays have appeared in *The New Yorker, Harper's, GQ, Vogue,* and *The New York Times*, among other publications. Her third book, a work of nonfiction about real estate and identity, is due out in 2010.

STACIA J. N. DECKER's work has appeared in *Nerve*, *The Missouri Review*, and *Post Road*, among other publications. A former editor at Harcourt, she lives in Manhattan, where she works as a literary agent.

COLIN P. DELANEY is a playwright whose work has appeared in New York City and Philadelphia. Productions include *Sunday in the Shower with Seymour*, *Scratch's Last Lament*, *A Hat for You*, *Mask & Cape*, and *The War, the Horse, the Woman Done Wrong*. Colin's play *The Red Mollies*, first produced at the Producers' Club in 2005, was adapted for the screen by Ward Picture Company and was released in 2008.

TOM DIRIWACHTER is a graduate of Rutgers University, with an MA in Cinema Studies from CUNY. He has been doing theater in NYC for over a decade. It is his tradition to meet friends every New Year's Eve for dinner at "69."

MELISSA DUNN is an editor and writer living in Brooklyn. She is formerly an editor at Flash Art International as well as Phaidon Press, and has taught American literature at the Pratt Institute.

Originally from Canada, **OPHIRA EISENBERG** is a stand-up comedian and writer who has appeared on Comedy Central, VH-1, the E! Channel, and has also starred in her own half-hour comedy special for CTV's *Comedy Now!* She regularly hosts and tours with The Moth, and is a core performer in the hit shows *Nice Jewish Girls Gone Bad* and *The Liar Show*. Her writing has been featured in the anthologies, *I Killed: True Stories of the Road from America's Top Comics*, *Rejected: Tales of the Failed, Dumped, and Canceled*, also the upcoming *Heeb Magazine*'s "Love, Sex and Gelfite Fish." She is also a regular contributor for *US Weekly*'s Fashion Police, *The Alcoholmaniac,* and *The Comedians Magazine.*

ERICH EISENEGGER is an attorney and writer living in Brooklyn. His short story "A Ticket For Kat," appeared in *Open City* #16.

JOHN EPPERSON was born in Hazlehurst, Mississippi. Film actor: *Witch Hunt* with Dennis Hopper, *Wigstock: The Movie*, *Angels in America*, *Kinsey*, *Another Gay Movie* and *Another Gay Sequel*. Theatre actor: *I Could Go On Lip-Synching!*, *Now It Can Be Lip-Synched*, *Lypsinka! A Day In The Life* (two Drama Desk nominations), *As I Lay Lip-Synching*, *Lypsinka Must Be Destroyed!*, *Lypsinka IS Harriet Craig!*, *Lypsinka! The Boxed Set* (2001 Drama Desk nomination, Washington, D.C. Helen Hayes Award Outstanding Non-Resident Production, L.A. Weekly Theatre Award Best Solo Performance), the Stepmother in NYCO production of Rodgers and Hammerstein's *Cinderella* at Lincoln Center's New York State Theater, and *The Passion of the Crawford*, a fantasia on the personality of Joan Crawford.

ALICIA ERIAN is the author of a short story collection, *The Brutal Language of Love*, and a novel, *Towelhead*.

DAVID EVANIER is the author of the recent novel, *The Great Kisser*, as well as *The One-Star Jew*, *Red Love*, *Roman Candle: The Life of Bobby Darin*, *Making the Wisguys Weep: The Jimmy Roselli Story*, *The Swinging Headhunter*, and with Joe Pantoliano, *Who's Sorry Now*. He is a former senior editor of *The Paris Review* and a recipient of the Aga Khan Fiction Prize.

SEVERINE FEIST is an erotica and creative nonfiction writer and experiential therapist. She has been a guest lecturer at The Lorimer Series in Brooklyn, has been a repeatedly offensive reader at Forbidden Kiss: The Erotica Series in Manhattan, and blogs regularly on Whether You Like It Or Not (SeverineFeist.blogspot.com). With the help of her tireless devotion to deviancy and a perverse sense of humor, Ms. Feist hopes one day to stick a well-lubed crowbar into the minds of the general public.

PAUL FELTEN is a screenwriter who lives and works in Brooklyn. He co-wrote the film *Bomb* with director Ian Olds.

BONNY FINBERG's chapbook, *How the Discovery of Sugar Produced the Romantic Era*, was published in 2006 by Sisyphus Press and was documented in the feature-length video *5 Guys Read Finberg*. Her fiction is included in four *Unbearables* anthologies, *Best American Erotica of 1996,* and *Van Gogh's Ear #6: The Love Issue.* She is also included in *The Outlaw Bible of American Poetry.* She is a frequent contributor to *A Gathering of Tribes* and *Le Purple Journal.* She recently finished her first novel *Kali's Day.* She lives in Paris and New York City.

ELIZABETH FRANKENBERGER is a copy chief at St. Martin's Press. She recently had an essay published in the anthology *Believer, Beware: First-Person Dispatches from the Margins of Faith.* She lives in New York City with her husband, Noah Wildman.

ABIGAIL FRANKFURT is a freelance writer. Her work has been published in *The New York Times*, *The Minneapolis Observer,* Mr. Beller's Neighborhood, and she has read on NPR's *Savvy Traveler.* She currently lives in Astoria, Queens.

PATRICK GALLAGHER is from Ann Arbor, Michigan. His essays and fiction have appeared in *The New York Times*, *PopMatters*, *Wheelhouse*, *Smyles and Fish*, *Anamesa*, and elsewhere in addition to Mr. Beller's Neighborhood, of which he is also a former managing editor. Patrick currently runs the monthly Mr. Beller's Neighborhood Reading Series at Happy Ending and is writing his PhD thesis in the comparative literature department at NYU.

DAVID GERLACH has written for a variety of publications including *Newsweek* and the *New York Post*. Currently, he is a writer for *Good Morning America* on ABC.

FRAN GIUFFRE is a frequent contributor to Mr. Beller's Neighborhood. Her work has also appeared in *The New York Times* and *Newsday*. A "Brooklyn Girl" since her emigration from Rockaway Park, Queens, in 1981, she is currently working on a collection of personal essays.

ALLAN B. GOLDSTEIN is an essayist, memoir writer, and English as a second language writing instructor at the Polytechnic Institute of NYU. "Death and Ice Cream" is the first chapter of *Finding Fred*, his memoir-in-progress about two brothers, one having intellectual disabilities (findingfred.blogspot.com). His essay, "The Hidden Brother," appears in *Thicker Than Water: Essays By Adult Siblings of People With Disabilities* edited by Don Meyer and published by Woodbine House (Summer 2009). Fred now lives in Manhattan's Financial District. At his Neighborhood Day program, he loves doing industrial piecework to earn money, using the computer to learn letters and numbers, and volunteering to deliver meals to the elderly. Fred misses his Mommy and Daddy.

KAEL GOODMAN writes a blog (blog.blankslate.com) where he writes mostly about tech, startups, and these days, finance. He lives in DUMBO, Brooklyn with his wife and son.

ELIZABETH GROVE is a writer and teacher currently working for The Man in New Jersey. She was, for a time, the senior editor of Mr. Beller's Neighborhood. She has no residual fear of small cars or fire hydrants.

BRAM GUNTHER is the deputy chief of forestry, horticulture, and natural resources for the New York City Parks Department.

CHRISTOPHER HACKER teaches writing at Northern Virginia Community College and is working on a novel. He lives in the District of Columbia with his wife Joanna and their cat Homer.

V. L. HARTMANN's work has appeared in *The New York Times* and on Mr. Beller's Neighborhood. She lives in Brooklyn and is currently working on her first book of nonfiction.

ANDY HILL was born in 1981 and grew up in Covelo, California. He has traveled throughout the United States and Mexico for seven years by freight train and the kindness of strangers. Andy is currently living in Brooklyn and studies English and writing at Columbia University's School of General Studies.

GERALD HOWARD is a book editor in New York. His reviews and essays have appeared in *Bookforum*, *The New York Times Book Review*, *Slate*, *n+1*, *The Nation* and other publications.

I. JENG is a single, thirtysomething professional who has an MBA and works as a marketer. She lives in a studio in the Financial District and dreams about owning a washer/dryer. When she isn't writing, she is looking for love and eating copious amounts of chocolate.

JEFF JOHNSON lives in lower Manhattan with his wife and kids. He has written for Mr. Beller's Neighborhood, and also *Open City*, *The New York Times*, the *New York Post*, *Jane*, *The Minus Times*, ESPN, *Vice*, and *McSweeney's*. A barely-read, barely-literate compendium of his complaints and irritations can be found at fittedsweats.blogspot.com.

MAURA KELLY's personal essays have appeared in *The New York Times*, *The Washington Post*, *The New York Observer*, *New York Press*, *Salon*, *Marie Claire*, *Glamour*, *Penthouse*, *Before and After: Stories from New York*, and *Going Hungry*. She writes a dating blog for *Marie Claire* and recently finished her first novel.

LOST AND FOUND

HUNTER KENNEDY lives in Charleston, South Carolina, where he edits the underground literary almanac known as *The Minus Times*. Occasional updates and other intrigue can be found at minustimes.com. His writing has also appeared in *Open City*, *The New York Times Magazine*, *Vice*, and *Garden & Gun*.

SAKI KNAFO writes for *The New York Times*. He lives in Brooklyn.

JOSH LEFKOWITZ is the writer and performer of two full-length autobiographical monologues, *Help Wanted: A Personal Search for Meaningful Employment at the Start of the 21st Century*, and *Now What?* His stories and poems have been published in several journals online and in print, and he has recorded personal essays for NPR's *All Things Considered*. As an actor he has worked Off-Broadway and in Boston, Chicago, Washington, D.C., Baltimore, and Louisville, KY. Josh received the Avery Hopwood Award for Poetry at the University of Michigan, and was recently selected as one of New York's Best Emerging Jewish Performers.

SAM LIPSYTE is the author of *Venus Drive*, *The Subject Steve*, and *Home Land*, a New York Times Notable Book of 2005 and winner of *The Believer* Book Award. His writing has appeared in *Bookforum*, *n+1*, *McSweeney's*, *Open City*, *Tin House*, *NOON*, *The Quarterly*, *Esquire*, *GQ*, and *Playboy*, among other places. A 2008 Guggenheim Fellow, he teaches at Columbia University's School of the Arts.

PHILLIP LOPATE was born in Brooklyn, New York in 1943. He is a professor at Columbia University, and also teaches at Hofstra, The New School and Bennington. His latest books are *Two Marriages* (novellas) and *Notes on Sontag*. "Knickerbocker Village" was included in *Waterfront,* published by Crown in 2003.

ELIZABETH MANUS was born in Manhattan, where she currently lives. She has written about literature, buildings, and land. She can be reached at elizabeth.manus@gmail.com.

DANIEL MAURER is a staff writer at *New York*, and won a James Beard Foundation Award as an editor of the magazine's Grub Street blog. He is the author of *Brocabulary: The New Man-i-festo of Dude Talk*, and his humor and nonfiction has appeared in *The New York Times*, *Nerve*, *McSweeney's*, and others. "The Condiment War" was his second published story.

ANNA McDONALD teaches in the expository writing program at New York University. Her poetry has appeared in *The Paris Review*.

JB McGEEVER's stories have appeared in *Hampton Shorts*, *Confrontation*, *$pread Magazine*, *The Southampton Review*, and *The East Hampton Star*, with nonfiction in *Newsday, The New York Times, Family Circle, The Long Island Press, City Limits Weekly*, and The ACLU's Racial Justice Report. He's received consecutive IPPIE awards for Best Editorial from The Independent Press Association, as well as a full scholarship to attend The Southampton Writers Conference.

VESTAL McINTYRE is the author of the story collection *You Are Not the One*, which won a 2006 Lambda Literary Award and was named a *New York Times Book Review* Editors' Choice. He is the recipient of fiction fellowships from the National Endowment for the Arts and the New York Foundation for the Arts. His first novel, *Lake Overturn*, was published by HarperCollins in April 2009.

MADGE McKEITHEN writes and teaches at The New School. Her first book *Blue Peninsula* was published by Farrar, Straus & Giroux in 2006. The lines of poetry in "Paul Newman on Sixth Avenue" are excerpted from "Morning" and "Invisible

Groom" by Jason Shinder from *Among Women*, published by Graywolf Press in 2001.

Born in Brooklyn, **ANNE MEARA** is an actress and comedian who has appeared in numerous theater, film, and television roles. She is also the author of the plays *After-Play* and *Down the Garden Path*. For many years, she and her husband Jerry Stiller worked as the comedy team Stiller and Meara. In 2007, they were honored on the Hollywood Walk of Fame, only one of four married couples ever to be given their own star. They are the parents of actor/comedian/director Ben Stiller and actress Amy Stiller.

SARAH MILLER-DAVENPORT is a writer and graduate student living in Chicago.

KATIA MOSSIN was born in Moscow and lived in New York for seventeen years, running an architectural and development practice in Williamsburg. For last five years she had lived and worked abroad, traveling extensively in India, Nepal, Tibet, Thailand, and Russia. She is currently working on a book about kriya yoga lineage and traditions.

CAROLYN MURNICK is a senior editor at *New York* magazine online. Her work has also appeared in *Interview*, *Food & Wine*, *The Daily*, and *Before and After*. She lives in Brooklyn.

MR. MURPHY is a doorman on the Upper East Side.

DEBBIE NATHAN grew up in Houston and first visited New York in 1959, when she stayed in her uncle's fourth-floor walk-up in Williamsburg and encountered more horses on the street (property of rag pickers screaming in Yiddish) than she'd ever seen at home. Later, as a teenager skulking around Guy's Newsstand in Houston, she devoured *The East Village Other*, with its news about Charlotte Moorman in SaranWrap, and vowed to someday emigrate. She's been in New York off and on since the 1970s and is still trying to figure out if this place is really so different from Texas.

DANIEL NESTER is the author of *How to Be Inappropriate* (Soft Skull Press), as well as *God Save My Queen: A Tribute* and *God Save My Queen II: The Show Must Go On*, experimental essay collections that center around his obsession with Queen, and *The History of My World Tonight* (poems). His work appears in places like *The Morning News*, *Open City*, *The Daily Beast*, *Time Out New York*, *Nerve*, and *Bookslut*, and has been anthologized in places like *The Best American Poetry*, *The Best Creative Nonfiction*, and *Third Rail: The Poetry of Rock and Roll*. He teaches writing at the College of Saint Rose in Albany. His Web site is danielnester.com.

A native of Chicago, **CHRISTINE NIELAND** graduated from Northwestern University. She worked as a staff writer for the late *Chicago Daily News*, and her work has appeared in *The Chicago Sun-Times, The San Diego Union-Tribune*, National Public Radio's *All Things Considered*, *Esquire* and other publications. She currently works as a writer, researcher, and story analyst for RHI Entertainment, and in her spare time she's a figure skater.

KENNETH P. NOLAN is a lawyer who, like his parents, has always lived in Brooklyn.

WILLIE PERDOMO is the author of *Where a Nickel Costs a Dime and Smoking Lovely*, which received a PEN/Beyond Margins Award. He has also been published in *The New York Times Magazine* and *Bomb* and his children's book, *Visiting Langston*, received a Coretta Scott King Honor. He is co-founder/publisher of Cypher Books. His Web site is willieperdomo.com.

STACY PERSHALL's first book, *Loud in the House of Myself: Of Tattoos, Jesus, and Madness* is forthcoming from W.W. Norton. When she's not sitting in front of her computer slugging coffee and trying to write something brilliant, usually at 3 a.m., she can be found obsessing over one or more of the following: belly dance, knitting, Super 8 film, and her impending marriage to Jon Stewart. (He just doesn't know about it yet.)

RACHEL PINE is a media marketing executive and author, who has published a novel (*The Twins of Tribeca*, Miramax, 2005), as well as several short stories and essays that have appeared in anthologies. Her monologue, "Hummus, Halvah, and Hearts" was performed as part of the show *Love and Israel* at several theater festivals. A native New Yorker, she lives on the Upper West Side with her husband and daughter.

NEDA POURANG is of Iranian heritage but grew up in England and the United States. She studied art at NYU, has been a costumer and designer for film, television and theater in New York and Los Angeles, most recently designing John Patrick Shanley's *13 Plays* for Theater 68. She has also been a radio producer and reporter for WNYC's *Studio 360, The Leonard Lopate Show* and *Radio Lab*. She's editing her novel, living in L.A., and missing New York.

THOMAS PRYOR's work has appeared in *The New York Times*, Mr. Beller's Neighborhood, *A Prairie Home Companion, Underground Voices Magazine,* and *Ducts*. *The New York Times* City Room section picked up his story blog, "Yorkville: Stoops to Nuts." It can be found under their People & Neighborhoods category. His column appears in the Upper East Side newspaper the *NYC Informer*.

GREG PURCELL is now more or less happily employed, still lives in New York, and runs the St. Mark's Bookshop Reading Series. You'll find his poetry in issues of *Fence* and *Open City*.

KURT RADEMACHER grew up in rural Michigan. He is now a lawyer in New York City, where he lives. His work has also appeared in McSweeney's Internet Tendency.

JANE RATCLIFFE is the author of *The Free Fall* (Henry Holt), picked by the New York Public Library as one of the most notable books of 2002. She recieved her MFA from Columbia

University. Her work has appeared in *Carve, Vogue, Tricycle, Interview,* among others. She's also collaborated on many books, most recently, *One Can Make A Difference: How Simple Actions Can Change the World*, with Ingrid Newkirk. She teaches creative writing in Ann Arbor, Michigan, and is working on her new novel, *Outside the Lunatic's Asylum*, about London during WWII.

MATTHEW ROBERTS has worked as a photographer in five countries over fifteen years. He was the original photo editor (and a part owner) of *The Cambodia Daily* newspaper in Phnom Penh. He was the national photo editor for Citysearch-Ticketmaster during the internet boom years, and, more recently, he worked for six years as a photographer for the *New York Daily News*. He now lives with his family in Northern California and is the VP of Sales and Marketing at the finest small-scale biodiesel equipment manufacturer in the country: Springboard Biodiesel.

SUHAEY ROSARIO lives in New York City. She received her BA from Columbia University's School of General Studies in 2006. Miss Rosario is a literature writing expert.

PATRICK J. SAUER is a contributing editor at *Inc.* and a senior editor at TheDailyTube.com. He has also written for *Fast Company, City, Details, Popular Science, Portfolio,* Huffington Post 23/6, and ESPN.com. He is the author of *The Complete Idiot's Guide to the American Presidents* and is featured in both of *SMITH* magazine's anthologies of six-word memoirs. A native of Billings, Montana ("The Magic City"), Sauer now lives in the greater Union Square area of New York. His Web site is patrickjsauer.com.

SAÏD SAYRAFIEZADEH is the author, most recently, of *When Skateboards Will Be Free: A Memoir of a Political Childhood*, about his experiences growing up communist in the United States. His essays and stories have appeared in *Granta, The Paris Review, Open City,* and elsewhere.

Born and raised in Brooklyn, New York, **JOSEPH E. SCALIA** taught junior and senior high school English and creative writing on Long Island. He started his writing career in elementary school scribbling "terrible rhyming poems on bathroom walls" and later made the move to paper. Over the years he has published *FREAKs*, a young adult novel about being different set in a suburban junior high school, *Pearl*, a novel inspired by John Steinbeck's *The Pearl*, as well as *No Strings Attached*, a collection of his short stories. "The Shave" and "Oasis" were published as a part of *Brooklyn Family Scenes*, a volume of family stories, essays and original poems. *Scalia vs. the Universe or: My Life and Hard Times*, a collection of his humor, will be published in 2009.

BILL SCHELL was born in the Bronx in 1952. He was an NYC firefighter Lieutenant-Captain between 1978 and 2000. He had a great time working as a plumber on the WTC in 1972 and 1973. He attended Manhattan College, Lehman College, and Hunter College. He is completing his Master's degree in history at Lehman College and is currently practicing physical therapy.

REBECCA SCHIFF's fiction has appeared in *n+1* and *Guernica*. She is a graduate of Columbia University's MFA program and is working on a collection of short stories. She lives in Brooklyn.

CANDY SCHULMAN's essays have appeared in Mr. Beller's Neighborhood, *The New York Times, New York* magazine, *Newsweek, The Washington Post, The Chicago Tribune, Travel & Leisure, Glamour, Family Circle, Parents,* and *Parenting*, among others. She has written a memoir and is currently working on a novel. A member of the writing faculty at The New School for over twenty years, she teaches creative nonfiction writing workshops.

BETH SCHWARTZAPFEL is a freelance journalist whose work has appeared in *The New York Times*, *The American Prospect, the Nation,* and *Ms.*, among other places. She studied creative writing at Brown University and the New School, and is an adjunct lecturer in English at Brooklyn College, and a fact checker at *Esquire* magazine. Her dog, Tucker, is the cutest mutt in Brooklyn. Learn more about her work at blackapple.org.

JENNIFER SEARS has received fiction awards from the Money for Women Fund, Mid-Atlantic Center for the Arts, George Mason University, Summer Literary Seminars, Millay Colony for the Arts, and Columbia University School of the Arts. Her writing has appeared in *So to Speak, Fence, Ninth Letter*, *The Boston Globe*, and the *Gilded Serpent Journal for Middle Eastern Music and Dance*. She teaches English and belly dance in New York City.

BROOKE SHAFFNER received her MFA from Columbia, where she was a Dean's Fellow. The opening of her memoir, *Proximity*, appeared in *The Hudson Review*. She is currently completing a novel, *Fight/Flight*, for which she received fellowships from The MacDowell Colony, the Edward F. Albee Foundation, Jentel, the VCCA, Byrdcliffe, and Summer Literary Seminars. She lives in Brooklyn, where she curates a monthly reading and artist talk series at Park Slope's 440 Gallery.

RACHEL SHERMAN is the author of the *The First Hurt* (Open City Books), a book of short stories, which was a finalist for the Frank O'Connor International Short Story Award, shortlisted for the Story Award, and was chosen as one of the Twenty-five Books to Remember from 2006 by the New York Public Library. Her fiction has appeared in *McSweeney's, Nerve, Post Road, Conjunctions, n+1*, and *StoryQuarterly*, and in the book *Dirty Words: The Unabridged Encyclopedia of Sex,* among other publications. She holds an MFA from Columbia University and teaches creative writing at Rutgers and Columbia. Her forthcoming novel, *Living Room*, will be published in October 2009 by Open City Books.

SAID SHIRAZI lived in New York for eight years before decamping for the suburbs. His stories have recently appeared in *Ninth Letter, Fifth Wednesday* and *Open City*. He also writes essays and criticism for the online journal *Printculture*.

HAL SIROWITZ is the former Poet Laureate of Queens, New York. He's the author of four books of poetry: *Mother Said, My Therapist Said, Before, During & After,* and *Father Said*. They were published by Crown and Soft Skull Press. *Mother Said* was translated into nine languages. Garrison Keillor has read many of Sirowitz's poems on NPR's *The Writer's Almanac*.

PETER NOLAN SMITH left New England for New York in a stolen car in 1976. He spent many years as a nightclub owner and doorman in New York, Los Angeles, Paris, London, and Hamburg. After a career in the international diamond trade, he traveled extensively throughout the Far East before residing for most of the twenty-first century in Pattaya, Thailand, with his wives and children. Most recently he summered in Palm Beach writing *Bet On Crazy*, a semi-fictional book detailing his career as a diamond salesman. Presently a diamantaire on West Forty-seventh Street, his future travel plans remain fluid.

ENNIS SMITH is an MFA graduate of The New School. His work there won him a National Arts Club Literary Scholarship in Nonfiction. A theater major at the University of Cincinnati, he earned his BA at Empire State College, where he was a Richard Porter Leach Fellow. His essay *The Rapunzel Effect* was recognized as an outstanding work of nonfiction by *In Our Own Write*. Other published work has appeared in the literary journal *Ganymede,* and *Attitude: The Dancer's Magazine*, where he is a resident critic. For his volunteer work with Lifebeat's Hearts and Voices (Musicians Against AIDS) in 2000, Ennis was the featured subject on PBS's *In the Life*. His blog is smokinroom.typepad.com.

IRIS SMYLES's stories and essays have appeared in *Nerve, BOMB, New York Press, The New Review of Literature,* and the anthology *Heads and Tales,* edited by Heide Hatry (Charta 2008) among other publications. She writes a bimonthly column for *Splice Today* and is currently finishing a collection of humorous personal essays titled *Iris Has Free Time.*

SANDI SONNENFELD is the author of the memoir *This Is How I Speak* (2002: Impassio Press), for which she was named a 2002 Celebration Author by the Pacific Northwest Booksellers Association. Her short stories, personal essays and journalism pieces have appeared in numerous literary magazines including *Sojourner, Voices West, Hayden's Ferry Review, ACM: Another Chicago Magazine, Raven Chronicles* and others. A graduate of Mount Holyoke College, Sandi holds an MFA in fiction writing from the University of Washington, where she studied under National Book Award Winner Charles Johnson. She currently lives in Brooklyn and works in Manhattan as Director of Public Relations for a leading national law firm.

DOROTHY SPEARS is a writer and arts journalist whose work appears frequently in *The New York Times* and *Art in America*. Her anthology, *Flight Patterns: A Century of Stories About Flying*, will be published this June by Open City Books. She lives in the West Village with her boyfriend and two sons.

LAREN STOVER's published works include the cult-classic novel, *Pluto Animal Lover*, a finalist for the Barnes & Noble Discover Great New Writers Award; *Bohemian Manifesto*: *A Field Guide to Living on the Edge;* and *The Bombshell Manual of Style*, pivotal in exploding Bombshell conscious into a popular genre. Laren is a fellow of Yaddo and Hawthornden Castle and has received the Ludwig Vogelstein Foundation grant for fiction and the Dana Award. Her libretto, *Appalachian Liebesleider*, premiered at Carnegie Hall to a standing ovation.

JEAN STRONG writes songs and stories in Hell's Kitchen. She is also the co-founder of Bay Bridge Productions, a theatre, film and new media production company.

ABIGAIL THOMAS has written three memoirs: *Safekeeping, A Three Dog Life,* and *Thinking About Memoir.* "A Sawed-off Past" was included in *A Three Dog Life*, published in 2006.

JASMINE DREAME WAGNER's writing has previously appeared in *American Letters & Commentary, Verse, Colorado Review, Indiana Review, North American Review,* and *32 Poems.* She is the author of a poetry chapbook, *Charcoal* (For Arbors, 2008), and was a writer-in-residence at the Hall Farm Center for Arts & Education. Wagner also performs folk and experimental music as Cabinet of Natural Curiosities.

MIKE WALLACE is co-author of the Pulitzer–Prize winning *Gotham: A History of New York City to 1898*, and author of *A New Deal for New York*, which examines the future of post-September 11 Gotham in the light of its past. He is a distinguished professor of history at John Jay College of Criminal Justice. He is also founder of the Gotham Center for New York City History at the CUNY Graduate School, devoted to the study and popular promotion of the history of New York City. He is now working on the second volume of *Gotham: A History of New York City*.

KATE WALTER is a freelance writer based in the West Village. Her essays have appeared in *The New York Times, Newsday, The Daily News* and many other places. She teaches personal essay writing at NYU/SCPS. "Filing Away" was later published in *Newsday* and "Downtown Dyke in a Midtown Sports Bar" was later published in *The Villager.*

JOCKO WEYLAND is the author of *The Answer is Never: A Skateboarder's History of the World* (Grove Press, 2002) and has written for *Thrasher*, *The New York Times*, *Vice*, *Cabinet,* and other publications. He is the creator of *Elk* and a contributing editor for *Open City* magazine.

MARK YARM is a former senior editor at *Blender* magazine. He is currently writing an oral history of grunge for Crown. He lives in Carroll Gardens with his wife, Bonnie.

Born and raised in Astoria, **MICKEY Z**. is probably the only person on the planet to have appeared in both a karate flick with Billy Blanks and a political book with Noam Chomsky. He can be found on the Web at mickeyz.net.

THOMAS R. ZIEGLER was born in 1950. He is a veteran of the United States Army and the Vietnam War, serving from 1967–70. He was firefighter, Fire Marshal, and Lieutenant for New York City Fire Department from 1973-2000. He is now a flight attendant with JetBlue Airways and having the time of his life! He is married, the father of three, grandfather of four, and a lifelong resident of the Bronx. "Thank you Linda Morel, without you my pen would never have met my paper."